MUSEUMS, U.S.A.

MUSEUMS, U.S.A.

A History and Guide

HERBERT & MARJORIE KATZ

Garden City, New York
DOUBLEDAY & COMPANY, INC.

1965

For MAY *and* CHARLIE
who we hope
already know our love
and understand our gratitude

CONTENTS

ILLUSTRATIONS

(following page 132)

1. Detail from *Exhuming the First American Mastodon,* by Charles Willson Peale.

2. The Peale Museum, Baltimore, as it looks today.

3. The Alms House after it became the New York Institution in 1816.

4. P. T. Barnum's American Museum in 1851.

5. Opening day at the American Museum of Natural History.

6. Professor Bickmore at the American Museum of Natural History.

7. Birds at the American Museum as they once were exhibited.

8. American Egret Group in the American Museum's new Hall of North American Birds.

9. Architect's rendering of the Philadelphia Museum of Art.

10. Louis XVI reception room in the Philadelphia Museum of Art.

11. An art gallery at the New-York Historical Society, about 1860.

12. 17th century Dutch and Flemish works of art at the Toledo Museum of Art, today.

13. and 14. Two galleries in the Museum of Modern Art, New York.

(following page 252)

15. Classical Gallery, New Wing, Cleveland Museum of Art.

16. A typical exhibit in the main gallery at the Cranbrook Academy of Art.

17. The Panoroll, at the Fossil Mammal Hall, Carnegie Museum, Pittsburgh.

18. School children confront the prehistoric past at the Chicago Natural History Museum.

19. The Orrery at the Cranbrook Institute of Science.

MUSEUMS, U.S.A.

BACKGROUND

THE history of the museum in America is a uniquely American story. Even while the colonials were groping toward independence and a revolutionary declaration that all men are created equal, an American museum was demonstrating democracy's way. The treasures of Europe were still in the private possession of princes and kings; but a group of American patriots had already begun to collect and put on view, for the enjoyment of all of the people, objects illustrative of their country's brief past. Two years before Paul Revere's midnight ride, this group, known as the Charleston Library Society, established the first museum in His Majesty's American Colonies.

When the Library Society itself had been formed, many years earlier, not much thought was given to the establishment of a museum. In 1748 "some gentlemen, by contribution among themselves, imported a few books and pamphlets, chiefly for amusement. From this small beginning they soon perceived the great advantages their scheme might be if prosecuted with spirit and enlarged in its plan. . . . They were soon joined by many lovers and encouragers of science." But by 1773, a committee was appointed to collect materials "for promoting a Natural History of" South Carolina; and a museum was imminent. The co-operation of the public was requested in a newspaper advertisement of the Society's intention, four curators were appointed, and donations soon began to arrive. The first recorded acquisition was "a drawing of the head of a bird."

The Revolutionary War and then a fire that destroyed most of the Society's books as well as the museum were only temporary interferences. In 1792 a new home was found on the third floor of the Court House. And there the fledgling institution remained for more than twenty years. During this period the items in its possession included a cassava basket from Dutch Guiana and an Hawaiian helmet. The Library Society's interests had broadened to include ethnology.

The vitality with which the new nation's social and political life were charged characterized our cultural development as well. An inspired citizen of a mind to turn a private passion into a public interest would work at his self-appointed task until he succeeded. Such a man was Charles Willson Peale of Philadelphia. An artist by profession and a naturalist by inclination, Peale was determined to do something about the fact that there was no place where Philadelphians could come either to see his fine portraits of contemporaries or to view his growing natural history collection. Hitting upon what must have seemed to him at the time an ideal solution, he turned a wing of his home into an exhibition hall. And so Philadelphians were invited to enjoy, amidst a sprawling display of animal and mineral specimens, a group of paintings that would eventually number close to three hundred. Most of them were by Peale himself; but there were a few by his sons, a niece, and one or two unrelated colleagues. In addition to three portraits of Washington, Peale had painted John Adams, John Paul Jones, Zebulon Pike, Robert Fulton, John Hancock, Jefferson, Monroe, Hamilton, and Martha Washington. His subjects also included lesser-known friends and, of course, relations. Well known to Philadelphians was his life-size portrait of two of his sons. The painting, called *The Staircase*, was described this way in a catalogue when the collection was eventually put up for sale: "All who have visited Peale's Museum recollect this remarkable painting; its perfect truth to nature is such, that many people have been deceived into the belief that it was a real staircase, with persons ascending it, and place one foot on the first step, which was a real one, and dogs have been known to run against it, in the attempt to ascend."

The same catalogue says of Peale's early efforts: "Having gradually been forming a Gallery of Portraits of distinguished Americans, he commenced in 1785, the collection of a Museum of specimens in Natural History and the Arts, to embrace every subject in nature or art which might be curious or instructive,—some of the bones of the Mammoth which he purchased, and a Paddle Fish presented by Robert Patterson, being the first articles."

Peale's love of nature was so closely bound up with the deistic philosophy then prevalent among American intellectuals that a ticket of admission would in a few years exhort: "The Birds and Beasts will teach thee! Admit the Bearer to Peale's Museum, containing the wonderful works of NATURE and the curious works of ART."

He was so zealous a naturalist that he dreamed of acquiring live and mounted specimens illustrating every category of animal life in Linnaeus' classification. Hoping to interest his townsmen in a subject obviously more dear to his own heart than to theirs, he pointed out, in *A Scientific and Descriptive Catalogue,* some practical, spiritual, and moral reasons for studying natural history. And in a statement of his aims and purposes he reassured visitors that, "directed by the precepts of Linnaeus, the first of naturalists, in whose steps we are ambitious to tread, we will not fail to correct our errors as soon as they are discovered."

A list of his exhibits at this time included "skeletons of an Indian man and woman of the Wabash Nation . . . skin of the thigh, and part of the leg, of an Indian, dressed in the Indian manner; this piece of skin belonged to a warrior, who was wounded in general Sullivan's expedition into the Genesee country, and who, not being able to defend himself, would not yield," and "a piece of human skin, tanned with bark in the common way." He also had an "Ant-eater," a "nine-zoned armadillo," the "Grinder and tail of an Elephant . . . several teeth of an unknown animal, called the mamoth [sic] . . . Skulls of tygers . . . an Ichneumon or Mongooz," and a "Jackall Dog" of which he wrote: "One could scarcely believe that so small an animal as this, could have produced cries so strong and sharp as those with which it frequently alarmed the whole neighborhood."

By 1794 this accumulation finally outgrew the Peale household. The American Philosophical Society, in which Peale was an active member, invited him to move his family and museum to the new Philosophical Hall, where he was granted both gallery space and living quarters in return for his services as librarian and curator for the Society. The Society reserved two spacious second-floor rooms to itself. But within eight years Peale's acquisitions again outgrew their home, and permission from local authorities was granted for a move to the State House (now Independence Hall) where the exhibits would remain for more than two decades.

Upon the return of the Lewis and Clark expedition to the Pacific coast, Peale, as proprietor of "the nearest thing to a National Museum then in existence" was given Indian artifacts and many of the natural history specimens brought back by the explorers. Doubtless his friend and fellow naturalist, President Jefferson, was influential in assigning to Peale's care such items as Indian costumes, tobacco pouches, ornamental belts, Lewis' famous mantle fringed with one hundred and forty ermine skins and studded with iridescent shells, and small mammals and birds, many of which had been unknown to zoology. In 1807, the year after the travelers' return, a study of Lewis by Peale was added to the Gallery of Portraits.

Peale received a diversity of objects from all over the world. Exchanges with individuals and museums in Europe, items gathered by his sons as they made the Grand Tour, and objects donated by American travelers, sea captains, and merchants enabled him to list in his meticulously kept Accession Book such wonders as "a wooden pillow, a piece of sandalwood, cloth and thread from the Fiji Islands, a handsomely ornamental kreese or dagger from the East Indies, a wooden spear from islands in the South-Seas, feathers of the Red-tail Tropic Bird from the island of Tongataboo, and a paddle of wood, beautifully carved from New Zealand." Minerals from France, rock salt from Germany, and a vase from Herculaneum were also on view.

Peale's institution was flourishing and would continue to flourish for a while even after his death. But, as Philadelphia's intellectual community grew in sophistication and two new academies emerged as centers of the city's scientific and cultural life, the demise of Peale's museum became inevitable. A melancholy postscript is provided in the last pages of the catalogue of sale.

"After the death of Peale, a fine building was erected for the reception of the Museum, with funds borrowed from the United States Bank, the failure of which Institution, with the Museum, involved the ruin of this magnificent monument of American Science and Art, which was sold to pay the claim of the Bank, separated into several parcels, and scattered to enrich the Museums of several other cities."

In 1782, another Philadelphian, Pierre Eugène du Simitière, opened his home to the public. During the two years before his death, he displayed records and historical materials that he had accumulated while the Revolutionary War was going on. He was the first in this country to advocate documentation of historic events as they occurred, and he was a crusader for the use of primary sources in the writing of history. After he died, everything he had was sold.

While America was creating a museum of the people, France, in the wake of its own revolution, opened the Palace of the Louvre as the Museum of the Republic. Although other European collections had been put on public view earlier, the scope and fine quality of what was in the Louvre, coupled with the new social and political philosophy of which it became an expression, made this an event that was to have repercussions—although not immediate ones—all over Europe. In the 1790s an American traveling abroad was still not likely to complain of walking his feet off in museums. The masterpieces of Renaissance art familiar to today's tourists were then almost entirely hidden from public view in private residences. And the antiquities had, for the most part, yet to be excavated.

The word "museum" itself had been used first by the Greeks to designate the home of the Muses, those deities who presided over the arts and sciences. Subsequently the word was applied to the area of the Palace at Alexandria which contained the Alexandrian Library and was given over to scientific study. The word and the institution it was coming to describe both disappeared during the Dark Ages; but with the coming of the Renaissance those who could afford to amassed collections, sometimes known as "cabinets," of artistic, scientific, and merely curious objects. During the age of exploration, Europe in general and England in particular began to receive samples of the natural wild flora and fauna of the New World and the newly accessible East in addition to articles of native manufacture. Such collections were the foundation of the Ashmolean and British Museums. Of the Old World countries England had the largest number of museums; and in the Ashmolean of Oxford University, established in 1683, England boasted the oldest. The great British Museum of London was opened in 1753; Spain's National Museum of Natural Sciences was begun in 1776, the Vatican Museum dates from the 1740s, and in the 1760s a Roman villa was donated by Cardinal Albani as a home for the classical sculpture collection of the German art historian, Johann Joachim Winckelmann.

But none of these were public museums in the American sense. The British Museum received daily only thirty visitors, each of whom had to apply for a permit well in advance. As art critic and historian Walter Pach has pointed out, there was "nothing in all Europe to suggest the way in which the museums of America, in a democratic response to a general demand, [would] spread from coast to coast. In the Old World they [represented] the gathering together of material already on hand; in America, everything save collections of local relics had to be built up from nothing. Most significant of all is that the institution is ours as the gift of private citizens and not as a gathering of things forfeited to governments."

Perhaps even more significant is the fact that, in the vast majority of cases, those private citizens, starting from scratch, built up collections not only of exceptional quality and good taste, but also of lasting interest to their descendants. The members of the Charleston Library Society, Peale, and his sons after him were only the first of a multitude dedicated to providing a place where ordinary people could come to be informed of the meaning of history, instructed in the workings of science, and exalted by the presence of art.

The first museum to grace the streets of New York was made possible by an organization still very much with us but no longer remembered for its original cultural ideals—the Society of St. Tammany. To extend the cultural benefits both to its members and other New Yorkers at large that part of its program was designed to offer, the Society petitioned the City Council in 1790 for a room in City Hall. There it would house Indian relics already on hand and await the enlarged collection to which it aspired. Since the national capital was just then in the process of being removed to Philadelphia, one of the rooms that had been occupied by Congress during its brief sojourn in New York was made available, rent free. John Pintard, a leading citizen and Grand Sachem of Tammany, and the energetic Gardiner Baker, a founder, were the leaders in the new enterprise. Pintard hoped to acquire "all that could be found of Indian literature in war-songs, hieroglyphic writings on stone, bark, skins, etc." Baker became keeper of the museum, and his enthusiasm soon produced all manner of curiosities, as well as a substantial menagerie. Admission was two shillings a visit, or a yearly ticket could be purchased for one dollar. Tammany members and their families were, of course, admitted free. Visitors and donations of articles were welcomed every Friday and Saturday.

After a few years, the Tammany Society began to turn in the direction for which it would ultimately become famous. Politics came to take precedence over cultural affairs, and John Pintard, a Hamiltonian, withdrew from active participation in the Jeffersonian-oriented society. His disappointment was undoubtedly compounded by the fact that the museum for which he had had such high hopes was already degenerating into a mere collection of curios. In 1795 Tammany assigned all rights in the museum to Baker. There was some conjecture, at the time, that this was done in settlement of Baker's wages, although the records of the Society describe its motivation as a desire to recognize his services.

A variety of financial reverses, plus his own eclectic interests, made Baker attempt all kinds of promotions: pseudo-scientific demonstrations, freak animals, and a much touted balloon ascent that never came off. It wasn't long before the public lost interest. And shortly thereafter, troubled equally by a failing business and an unfaithful wife, Baker died. His widow managed Baker's American Museum for a brief period until it became necessary to sell the exhibits in order to settle the estate. After being accommodated for a short while on the premises of one William I. Waldron, a grocer, Baker's enterprise came into the possession of Edward Savage, a sometime artist who had visited the museums of Europe as well as Peale's establishment in Philadelphia. Arriving in New York in 1801, Savage had set up the Columbian Gallery, "containing a large collection of Ancient and Modern Painting, Prints and Sculpture." He purchased the Baker objects with a view to expanding his gallery after the example set by Peale, and he hired naturalist John Scudder to put the zoological materials into shape. Scudder was able to buy Savage out some years later and announce, in March of 1810, the opening of The New American Museum with "true-to-life displays of hawk, hummingbird, rattlesnake . . . polar bear . . . [and] waxwork figures. . . ."

By 1816 larger quarters located on the second floor of the Alms House in City Hall Park were granted by the City Council for a token rental of one peppercorn per annum. There was now space for a lecture hall and demonstrations of a more or less scientific nature. In the center of a large room containing a forest scene in which eighty mammals, snakes, and birds were realistically displayed, there was an exhibit case with over six hundred natural history specimens. Nearby, a gallery displayed minerals, ancient coins, and thousands of shells and butterflies. Crowds flocking in to the tune of "Yankee Doodle" played by a brass band paid twenty-five cents for the privilege of viewing the wonders.

By the time Scudder died in 1821, three more large rooms had been added to accommodate all of his acquisitions. In the two decades following his death, however, despite the growth of the collection to more than one hundred and fifty thousand "natural and foreign curiousities, Antiquities, and Productions of the Fine Arts," the side-show aspect of the museum became its predominant feature. The "curiousities" included kangaroos, an anteater, hundreds of East Indian birds, "and the first giraffe in this country." But it was the waxworks, automatons, chemical and electrical experiments, primitive implements, mummies, magicians, minstrels, and ventriloquists that brought in an average of $150 per week. Since the curator's salary of $11 per week, an annual rental of $2250 (the museum now occupied four stories of a five-story building), and an annual advertising budget of $317 were the major expenses, a tidy profit was left for Scudder's heirs. Eventually John Scudder, Jr. (who headed the museum until he was discharged for drunkenness) and his four sisters sold out to P. T. Barnum for $12,000. And from that time on it became even more frankly a side show. It was, in fact, the foundation stone of Barnum's entertainment empire, which ten years later would absorb much of Peale's natural history collection when it was sold in Philadelphia.

In the meantime, the hopes of John Pintard—who had started the enterprise that was to pass by stages from Baker to Barnum—were by no means crushed. In 1804, with DeWitt Clinton and ten other politically and socially prominent colleagues, he founded an institution of permanent value, the New-York Historical Society. It had its first home in the City Hall, adjoining the office where Pintard worked both as clerk to the Corporation of New York and as city inspector. Pintard's prominent friends and influential acquaintances helped provide pictures, manuscripts, medals, coins, books, and antiquities relevant to the Society's purpose. Pintard himself was a generous contributor. It was he who donated Bradford's early map of the city and a copy, in perfect condition, of Eliot's Indian Bible. (John Eliot, a "teacher" at a church in Roxbury, Massachusetts, had taught himself the language of one of the neighboring groups of Algonkian-speaking Indians, and after devising a scheme for writing it down, translated both the Old and New Testaments into Algonkian. He then taught the Indians—for whom the first Bible printed in America was expressly made in 1663—how to read their own language.)

New York's was among the first of those societies that developed museums of history, science, or the arts still active today. One of the earliest was in Massachusetts: the East India Marine Society, established in 1797 and destined to become the Peabody Museum of Salem. Massachusetts also gave birth to the Pilgrim Society at Plymouth in 1820, and the Essex Historical Society of Salem (now the Essex Institute) in 1821. Elsewhere in New England the historical societies of Portland, Maine; Providence, Rhode Island; and Concord, New Hampshire, were born in 1822 and 1823. In the Middle Atlantic States there could be found the Maryland Academy of Sciences of 1797 at Baltimore and the Albany Institute of History and Art, which had been founded in 1791 as a "Society for the Promotion of Agriculture, Arts and Manufactures" and then reincorporated in 1804 as the "Society for the Promotion of Useful Arts." The Albany Institute did not really get into the museum business until its 1824 merger with the Albany Lyceaum, founded the year before to acquire "respectable collections in the various branches, especially mineralogy, geology" and paleontology. The expanding Institute began immediately to add to its store. One month after the merger took place, its log noted that "the following donations were received: From Henry W. Snyder, 14 silver and 67 copper coins; from Simeon De Witt, Chinese coins . . . a dried specimen of the pulmonarie virginica and a betel nut; from Samuel M. Lockwood, alabaster from Sandusky, Ohio. . . ." And several weeks later it was recorded that from James Eights there came "61 species of insects" and that "Lewis C. Beck deposited the right valve of the unio crassus." Similar items poured in at every meeting. Although the present-day museum has paid little attention to the *Unio crassus,* its displays of all periods of American art provide compensation for the loss.

The cultural center of the nation and the birthplace of two of the earliest museums that are as prominent today as at the time they first took an active part in the intellectual life of their city, was Philadelphia. The founding of one of them, the Pennsylvania Academy of Fine Arts, had been anticipated by an unsuccessful attempt of the ubiquitous Charles Willson Peale to provide a showcase for artists. In those early years there were neither galleries for artists to exhibit in nor places where they could view the production of their colleagues. The short-lived institution Peale established was called the Columbianum or The American Academy of Painting, Sculpture, Architecture Etc. (sic) and in 1795 it had the distinction of housing the first sizable exhibition of American work. Unfortunately, political dissension forced the termination of this project within the year.

A decade later Peale was among the seventy-one founders, almost all of them non-artists, of the Pennsylvania Academy. Hoping to inject European influence into the training of native artists, the directors imported a large number of casts of classical sculpture. In describing these tastemakers of early America, critic James Flexner noted that they acquired "pictures attributed to the great names of the past; or (to prove themselves up-to-date) of living artists with great European reputations. To show a picture that might just possibly have been touched by Raphael or that was the work of Sir Thomas Lawrence (a knight!) was a greater badge of culture than to buy the picture of some poor devil who walked the streets of your own city and did not dress like a gentleman."

Not surprisingly, this expression of middle-class snobbery was an irritant to the local talent. One hundred strong, the painters of Philadelphia banded together in 1810 into the Society of Artists of the United States. The Pennsylvania Academy of Fine Arts, although aware that it was regarded by the new Society as "intended merely for a museum, and consequently not likely to become of much importance either in the improvement of artists or the correction of public taste," housed the Society's first exhibit nevertheless. As a result, under circumstances not unlike the happy ending to a fanciful operetta, the two organizations merged; tastemakers and artists joining to strengthen the Academy so that it endures to the present.

The other Philadelphia museum whose vitality would last was the Academy of Natural Sciences of 1812. At this time there were in the entire country "very few persons devoted to the investigation of natural objects. . . . The Natural Sciences attracted very little attention from the public; and the very few persons who cultivated them contended with many difficulties. There were neither cabinets . . . nor libraries. . . . There were in the city two or three collections of minerals in the possession of gentlemen who had brought them from Europe; but they were not accessible to the public. There was no book on mineralogy for sale in this country. . . ." Peale's Museum, while a place of "daily resort" for amusement, was "unavailable" for the purposes of serious and co-ordinated study.

"There were some young persons, however, disposed to study the laws of the creation . . . [who] were prone to fall into discussions upon natural phenomena. . . . In the evening they met without appointment at such places of common resort as the city afforded for those of their social position. Comparison of ideas, soon forced upon them a conviction that they were ignorant of even the rudiments of those branches of knowledge which had attracted their attention. . . . [One of them was] Mr. John Speakman . . . an apothecary . . . [and Quaker who] earnestly sought to improve the condition of mankind by seeking knowledge himself, and imparting what he did to others. Yet he did not devote himself methodically to study, but sought information in conversation with friends and acquaintances. . . . His shop . . . became a center of the literary and scientific gossip of the day. . . . Among his social companions was Mr. Jacob Gilliams . . . a leading dentist . . . [who was] an intimate associate of Mr. Thomas

Say," a prominent zoologist. Gilliams' love of nature reportedly began when, as a boy, he persevered at gathering minerals and catching caterpillars despite being frequently "censured" by his mother for soiling his clothes.

One day "Mr. Speakman suggested that they and their acquaintances could . . . meet together at stated times, where they would be secure from interruption, to communicate to each other what they might learn about the phenomena of nature." Accordingly, one January evening, "Dr. Gerard Troost, Dr. Camillus Macmahon Mann, Messrs. Jacob Gilliams, John Shin, Jr., Nicholas S. Parmantier, and John Speakman, assembled at the residence of the gentleman last named. . . . At this first meeting various plans of a society . . . were discussed. It was agreed that the exclusive object of the society would be the cultivation of natural science."

After several more organizational meetings, "the gentlemen were reluctant to be continuously indebted to the hospitality of Mr. Speakman"; so two or three sessions were held at Mercer's Cake Shop, known as "the first public establishment at which ice-cream was sold in Philadelphia." But this proved unsatisfactory. The Philadelphia gentlemen were "under an impression that all visiters [sic] to such houses must in courtesy become customers," and because they "feared that the infant society might degenerate into a club of *bon-vivants* . . . more private accommodation was sought."

Although within a few years the membership and activities would expand beyond anyone's original expectations, these early meetings were so limited in attendance that the first new member to be admitted had to sit alone for the duration of his initial meeting while the board of directors—i.e., the founding members—retired to another room for their private deliberations. A decision that religion and politics were never to be allowed to distract the members from the business at hand caused the young organization's reputation as "atheistic." But it survived these and other vicissitudes, and consistently attracted the nation's budding natural scientists. Publication of research done by members followed its founding by only a few years.

The museum of the society was first contained in a small room on the second floor of a private dwelling, but by 1815 a building was erected for the Academy's activities and museum on property donated by Jacob Gilliams and at his expense. By 1826 the society again had outgrown its quarters, and purchased and altered the New Jerusalem Church. The museum was open to members of the Academy at all times; in 1828 it was opened on Tuesday and Friday afternoons "for the gratuitous admission of visitors" who were not members. By its fiftieth year a member could announce to the general public that the museum was "acknowledged to be the finest on this continent." And by the end of 1851 it contained nearly 150,000 items, including a library of over 13,000 volumes. Its eighteen departments ranged from mammalogy, ornithology, ichthyology and herpetology through conchology, entomology and botany to mineralogy, geology, and paleontology.

One member expressed his "hope that the Academy will be cheered on in its course, till the Museum shall become an epitome of all created things; so fully displayed, that the student may resort to it with a certainty of learning what has been ascertained in the world of nature; just as inventors now seek the Patent Office to learn whether they have been preceded in mechanical discovery. . . . The Museum of the Academy should be, indeed, an office filled with Nature's patents, in which all may behold the wonders it has pleased an all-wise Creator to devise for the benefit and instruction of man."

By now the nation's capital had been permanently established in Washington. The War of 1812 was fought and ended. And soon Washingtonians were busy launching the Columbian Institute for the Promotion of Arts and Sciences. It proposed "to collect, cultivate and distribute the various vegetable productions of this and other countries . . . to collect and examine the various mineral productions and natural curiosities of the United States . . . to invite communications on agricultural subjects, on the management of stock, their diseases and the remedies . . . to form a topographical and statistical history of the different districts of the United States. . . ." A Congressional charter was received in 1818. However, activity was slight and by 1820 some reorganization was in order. Five "classes" were established; in mathematical sciences, physical sciences, moral and political sciences, general literature, and the fine arts. And each would have its own study committee according to the interests of the members. At this time too, five acres of land were granted by the Congress for the botanic garden. Additional land was added later. Eventually, the Columbian—its books, land, collections, and so forth—was absorbed by the Smithsonian Institution.

Not all of the early attempts were to have lasting results. New York's American Museum fiasco was a case in point. Baltimore, where two sons of Charles Willson Peale carried on an ambitious scheme for sixteen years, was the scene of another. But the enthusiasm Rembrandt and Rubens Peale showed for their project, their knowledge and ability, and their several innovations made Peale's Baltimore Museum a worthy effort. It was, moreover, the first structure built in this country specifically to house a museum.

In August of 1814, Rembrandt Peale had the highest hopes for his "elegant *Rendezvous* for taste, curiousity and leisure." He had planned it as "an institution devoted to the improvement of public taste" in the fine arts "and the diffusion of science." In his Gallery of Heroes he hung about fifty portraits of contemporary leaders, and in among his natural history exhibits was the "Stupendous Skeleton of the Mammoth," one of two skeletons that the Peale family had unearthed in New Jersey. (The other so-called "mammoth"—they were actually mastodons—was in Peale *père*'s Philadelphia establishment. These were the earliest skeletons of prehistoric mammals to be reassembled and exhibited anywhere.) The natural history display consisted primarily of stuffed and mounted animals. In addition, Rubens Peale, an expert taxidermist, presided over a sizable menagerie. As soon as a fatality occurred, his skills in preserving and mounting were put to use. These specimens, shown whenever possible against painted habitat backgrounds, were all meticulously labeled according to the Linnaean classification in which both brothers, trained by their father, were expert. The live menagerie included wolves, a fox, elk, a baboon, an eagle, turtles, alligators, and more. One time Rubens advertised a "LIVING TIGER (young) which may be seen with perfect security by the most timorous." There came a time, however, when "the Eagle broke his chain and in passing the Tiger Cat was caught by him and was instantly killed." And Rubens, the taxidermist, went immediately to work.

The collection ultimately acquired such irresistible attractions as the "Head of a NEW ZEALAND CHIEF, very richly tattooed," an Egyptian mummy with a sarcophagus and a mummified cat, a knife with ninety-eight blades, Indian headdresses, and an opium pipe and chopsticks from China. But it was the illustrated physical science lectures that drew the largest audiences. When Rembrandt held a demonstration of the use of coal gas for lighting purposes, he so impressed the public that four local merchants joined him in organizing the Gas Light Company of Baltimore to brighten the homes and streets of the city. Financial reverses finally caused his withdrawal from this enterprise, and to improve his economic situation he shortly withdrew from the museum as well, leaving it entirely in Rubens' hands.

As knowledgeable about art as the world of nature, Rubens began, in 1822, to hold annual exhibitions. It took him less than a month, with the aid of his family connections in Philadelphia, to round up nearly three hundred examples of "Ancient Painting, Modern, Architectural Drawing, Engraving, Drawing in Crayon, and in Water Colours, Sculpture, Etc." Despite his strong start, only five not-so-annual exhibitions were held altogether.

Toward the close of the decade, Peale's Baltimore Museum began to lose its audience. After several attempts to revive it, it was forced to close its doors. The building itself was reopened, though, and during the century that followed served a variety of civic purposes. Today it houses the Baltimore Municipal Museum, known as the Peale Museum. And here, Rembrandt and Rubens were ultimately vindicated. One hundred and forty-two years after Rembrandt first advertised his "Rendezvous," a commemorative exhibition was held, re-creating the original atmosphere and bringing together whatever could be located of the original contents. Among the displays were some of the Peales' scientific models, more than a hundred of the paintings, and the mastodon skeleton which was on loan from the American Museum of Natural History in New York. The new museum's printed tribute to the old stated that "the key to the idea behind Peale's Museum lies in the new spirit of inquiry about the natural order of the universe." It was, in short, one of the American expressions of the Enlightenment which had been pervading European intellectual thought.

Rubens attempted to recoup his fortunes by opening Peale's New York Museum on Broadway, across from and in obvious competition with Scudder's American Museum. In the crash of 1837 he failed, and speculators took over his scanty collections.

Boston, not to be outdone by the efforts of other cities, also tried its hand. A local guidebook of 1829 tells the story:

"The first movement towards a Museum in Boston, commenced by exhibiting a few wax figures at the American Coffee House, in State-street, about the year 1791. Mr. Daniel Bowen was the proprietor, who moved his curiousities to a hall over a school house, in Broomfield-st till 1795, when it took the appellation of Columbian Museum. January 15, 1803, just as it had become nearly profitable to the proprietor, the whole was destroyed by fire." There followed a new building, another fire, and yet another building, before the collection was sold to the New England Museum in 1825 "for about $5000, and this closes the history of the first museum in Boston."

The New England Museum had been opened in 1818 under a legislative charter and was "owned in shares." This corporate ownership enabled it to begin by buying some materials from Scudder's New York collection, and then to make other large, quite heterogeneous purchases. In the center of its Lower Hall stood "the great elephant, Horatio" and the "Vampyre of the ocean, a very wonderful nondescript, which weighed 5 tons." There were portraits and wax figures "representing the Incas of Peru and their wives," and a visitor could view "the musical Androides, the mechanical Panorama, musical Clock, stone Sarcophagus (and) curious Mirrors." A Marine Room displayed a "great variety of fishes, monsters, and curiosities from the sea," while the Lobby offered "40 cases of birds, some heathen gods, Indian implements, antiquities, etc." Elsewhere in the "spacious halls and apartments" were a mermaid, a Monkey Room, birds from France, domestic fowls, wild ducks, and "Chinese Punishments." A Shakespeare Room contained prints from the plays, other historical prints, and a large painting "in an elegant frame" by "Rembrandt Peale, Esq. of Philadelphia."

But times were changing, and this conglomerate approach was unsatisfactory to those who aspired to a scientific knowledge of the world around them. Early in 1830 a group of Bostonians founded the Society of Natural History. It began modestly. In a rented hall over a savings bank, a lecture series was offered to the public. For several years there was a prevalence of topics such as the "relation of natural science to revealed religion." In 1837, the Society helped initiate the State Survey. And not long after that a bequest from merchant Ambrose S. Courtis helped it broaden its activities. Its primary interest was research until 1860, when a grant of land from the state made possible a building that could adequately display the specimens native to the New England area that members had been collecting and studying for years.

Meanwhile, those who wanted small doses of general information along with massive servings of entertainment could patronize the Boston Museum, which had opened in 1841. Its proprietors boasted of "two magnificent, well-lighted, airy and spacious halls" and an auditorium in the Picture Gallery in which "upwards of 1000 persons" listened every evening to "concerts and other entertainments, free of extra charge." For twenty-five cents one could see a "great Egyptian giraffe" as well as a "recumbent statue of Venus at the seashore" and "Sully's splendid painting of Washington, crossing the Delaware, of immense size, said to be the finest picture ever painted in America." Glass cases contained "rich and beautiful specimens of the beast, bird, fish and reptile tribes" along with Indian implements and "utensils excavated from Herculaneum and Pompeii." This private enterprise became well known for its stock company dramatic productions which could be safely attended, it was said, by those whose scruples did not permit them to view the other theatricals offered in the city.

Another acceptable twenty-five-cent diversion for this same scrupulous group was the two-month-long annual art exhibition offered by the Boston Athenaeum. Having functioned primarily as a library from the time of its founding, the Athenaeum decided that because these annuals were so successful, a permanent picture gallery would be incorporated into its building of 1845. Despite continuous patronage, however, the Athenaeum stopped being an active art exhibitor, and its paintings were given to the Boston Museum of Fine Arts as a permanent loan.

During the formative period in the American museum movement, colleges and universities were only passive participants, despite the early example of Oxford's Ashmolean. As centers of the intellectual life of the growing United States, the colleges naturally became recipients of material bearing on scientific and philosophical studies. Harvard and Princeton received mineralogy collections in the 1790s; and Harvard, which had been acquiring "curiosities" since the 1750s, eventually set aside a Musaeum Room in a move that would lead to a complex of mineralogy, botany, geology, and comparative zoology exhibits. Princeton scored a coup in 1817 by acquiring the minerals accumulated in London by David Hosack, the first American to study the subject intensively. But it was not until the middle of the nineteenth century that science collections began to be displayed coherently for educational purposes. It was at about that time that natural history societies on several campuses became active in helping museums get started, and state-sponsored geological surveys began providing universities with botanical, zoological, and geological specimens. Then, in the 1860s, a major event occurred when large bequests of money were left to both Yale and Harvard by George Peabody, inaugurating the practice of museum endowment.

Collections of paintings were given by James Bowdoin to the college that bears his name as early as 1811, but the museum to house them did not appear for many years. In 1831 Yale purchased Colonel John Trumbull's Revolutionary War paintings, to be hung a year later in the first college art museum, the Trumbull Gallery. In the 1850s the University of Michigan purchased casts of classical sculpture, and at about the same time Harvard received the Gray collection of engravings. By 1871 a gift enabled Yale to purchase the James Jackson Jarves collection of 119 Italian paintings from the thirteenth to the seventeenth centuries, up to that time very likely the most comprehensive group in the New World. In the seventies art history was introduced into the curriculum at Harvard, where it was taught by Charles Eliot Norton, and in 1895 the university received the bequest in memory of William Hayes Fogg with which the Fogg Museum was started. By the 1880s Princeton, Smith and Wellesley had built art centers of their own and educational interest from that time on would grow and grow.

By the time the nation was ready to celebrate its hundredth birthday the potential of museums was just coming to be recognized. The Centennial Exposition of Philadelphia, held in Fairmount Park from May to November of 1876, spurred both academies of that city to construct new buildings. In addition, Memorial Hall, which had been built specifically for the arts exhibits of the Exposition, lingered on afterward as the home of the new Pennsylvania Museum of Art. Although the Pennsylvania Museum of Art ultimately renamed itself the Philadelphia Museum of Art and moved to other quarters, it maintained Memorial Hall as the home of its extensive industrial arts collection, making it the oldest public art museum building standing in the country today.

The United States National Museum, a branch of the Smithsonian Institution, took shape shortly after the Centennial. The Smithsonian itself had been launched by an act of Congress in 1846, after eight years of debate on whether the Government ought to accept the bequest of James Smithson, an Englishman who left his entire estate to the United States "to found at Washington . . . an establishment for the increase and diffusion of knowledge among men." While the debate was still raging, a National Institute was founded as a sort of rudimentary national museum, under the directorship of the Honorable Joel R. Poinsett, who happened also to be Secretary of War. Poinsett was the only American museum director ever to hold cabinet rank. His cherished hope to disseminate "a taste for the fine arts" by distributing copies of all Congressionally commissioned "pictures, statues, and medals" to the "populous plains and fertile valleys of the land" was, fortunately for our cultural welfare, never put into effect.

It was not until after the War between the States that the Smithsonian was on a solid enough footing to create the National Museum. In addition to its heritage from Poinsett and the earlier Columbian Institute, the new enterprise would contain "collections which had been kept in the Patent Office, the private collections of Smithson . . . the results of the great exploring expedition of Captain [Charles] Wilkes [in 1838–42 to Antarctica, the South Pacific, and the Oregon Territory] . . . the gifts of private individuals, and . . . the valuable objects presented to the United States Government by foreign nations at the close of the Centennial at Philadelphia." Other museums were to come under the wing of the Smithsonian Institution as well. The National Collection of Fine Arts, the Freer Gallery of Art, and the National Zoological Park are among its branches, and the National Gallery of Art is a related but independently organized bureau.

The year of the Centennial also saw the construction of the first wings of what were to become three of the largest, most important, and most influential museums in the country: New York's Metropolitan Museum of Art and American Museum of Natural History, and Boston's Museum of Fine Arts. With them came an innovation in museum organization. Earlier institutions had been initiated by individuals, societies, and academies. The new plan that was evolved provided for a corporation governed by a board of trustees and aided, in New York, by city tax funds; in Boston, by public subscription. In return for this fiscal benefit the American and Metropolitan Museums were urged by their city to repay their debt by being "as important and beneficial an agent in the instruction of the people as any of the schools or colleges." And Boston's newest adornment to its cultural life helped boost civic pride. The red brick edifice with buff and red terra-cotta trim, built around two open courts which let natural light into the picture galleries, was erected upon city-owned land and financed initially by a public subscription of $250,000.

Meanwhile, the new awareness of the museum movement's importance was resulting in active support all across the country. Congress increased its appropriation to the National Museum. Four state museums, functioning with state-provided funds, were established. Smaller communities were supporting their own local museums in increasing numbers. There were by now about two dozen state historical societies, and more than thirty local ones. The first historic house museum had been established in Newburgh, New York: George Washington's Headquarters, redecorated with furnishings from the Revolutionary War period owned by families living in the area. By 1876 six more buildings in different states were permanently preserved in the fashion of their periods, and more than a dozen cities possessed natural history societies with museums. On its one hundredth birthday, the nation boasted more than two hundred museums, most of which would last well into the next century. The movement was spreading westward—to Cincinnati, Grand Rapids, Milwaukee, Chicago, Davenport, and as far west as San Diego. And from Washington to Sacramento, from Baltimore to Boston, rich men were amassing art collections that would, in a few generations, be available to the public.

Luman Reed of New York is generally credited with being the first American collector of art. Having purchased a good number of paintings from the studios of contemporary artists, many of whom were personal friends, he established a gallery on the top floor of his home for their display. His collection finally went to the New-York Historical Society.

A more influential patron of the arts was William Wilson Corcoran of Washington, D.C., whose purchases were intended to fill a building he had begun in 1859. His activities were interrupted, however, by the Civil War, during which time the Union Army turned his building into quartermaster's headquarters. The Corcoran Gallery was officially opened in 1871 with the arrival of President and Mrs. Grant at a Gala Ball for the benefit of the Washington Monument Building Fund.

William T. Walters of Baltimore, who was to be a trustee of the Corcoran, had been purchasing the work of Maryland artists since before the Civil War. During the war he resided in Paris, where he acquired many pieces of Oriental art and a multitude of porcelains. Taking his son Henry with him on viewing and buying excursions, he trained the taste of the younger Walters, equipping him to carry on with the collecting of beautiful objects. In the seventies the Walters house and some of its treasures were put on public view for a fifty-cent donation to charity; and more than fifty years later, a new home that Henry Walters had built for all these purchases was given by him to the city.

The Walker Art Center of Minneapolis has a similar history. T. B. Walker, a wealthy lumber merchant who had been collecting paintings and *objets d'art,* opened his residence to the public in 1879. But he did not build the present Center and establish a foundation to support it until 1926, when he was eighty-seven years old.

In nearly every big city and in many smaller ones, the privileged would provide for the unprivileged according to the former's unyielding preference and predilection. For the most part—despite motivations that often had nothing to do with magnanimity, and despite frequent absences of real sensibility—they would provide remarkably well. They were, after all, men who built their enterprises upon an instinct for the right decision. Why should that instinct fail them when it came to valuable objects that money could buy?

The end of the nineteenth century saw a reappraisal of the museum's functions. The scientific community, having been electrified by Darwin's insight into the origin of species and having seen the methodology of scientific inquiry applied to archaeology, was now obliged to examine its work in a new light. The research that had been carried on had been restricted to classification and description. And the interested amateurs who had been collecting had been doing it haphazardly. Now it was time for professionalism, for the systematic acquisition of specimens, and for the museum as teacher to exhibit its specimens in a way that would relate them to the new understanding of the laws of nature. It would never again be enough merely to display. The museum's new job would be that of interpreter to the lay viewer. The natural history institutions in Buffalo, New York, and Davenport, Iowa, were pioneers in this method of presentation. New York's American Museum was carrying its researches into the field, with expeditions of specialists going to the far corners of the earth to study specimens in their natural habitats and then to bring them home. Museum work became a profession, attracting trained scientists. In the field of art, the development of criticism and art history as valid disciplines spurred the educational function of the art museum. Europe led here: Paris' Musée de Cluny initiated the arrangement of art according to period; and six rooms arranged by period were opened in Nuremberg in 1888.

But it would take time for these developments to come to their ultimate fruition. These were the tentative beginnings. It would be many years before our older museum collections were weeded and pruned to eliminate the trivial, the tasteless, the extraneous; many years before personal inclination tempered by education would adequately instruct both the staff member and the beneficent donor; many years before architecture, exhibit techniques, and new synthetic materials would work together at their most effective; many years before education, mobility, and leisure would provide a receptive audience.

A prime force in the improvement of quality and services has been the American Association of Museums. Shortly after the turn of the century, nine dedicated directors held a meeting at the National Museum in Washington preparatory to calling a gathering of museum personnel from all over the country to join their ranks. When the first session was held at the American Museum in New York on May 15, 1906, over seventy prospective members showed up. Letters from more than fifty others unable to attend announced their intention to affiliate. The group got down to business at once; an organization committee was formed, and while it deliberated upon the first draft of a constitution, scientific papers were read and discussed. At the second session, held at the New York Botanical Garden, the constitution was adopted and officers were elected; and resolutions were passed to co-operate with the National Education Association, to lobby for more advantageous postal rates for museum publications, and to get out a bulletin. The group's constitution stated: "The object of this organization shall be to promote the welfare of Museums, to increase and diffuse knowledge of all matters relating to them, and to encourage helpful relations among Museums and those interested in them." The work of the Association has had a direct effect on the quality and training of personnel and on the diversity of the museums' subject matter. In addition, its research on aspects of administration has been of inestimable value to countless new and small institutions.

New subjects for museum concern had begun to appear in the last half of the nineteenth century. In Europe several museums of industry had been founded following the London Crystal Palace Exposition of 1851. The need to explain the new industrial procedures to the layman, to provide research centers for engineers and other specialists, to preserve, display, and encourage traditional design even in the industrial age, and to encourage the study and emulation of the best examples of new design were all factors in the development of institutions in London, Munich, Vienna, and Paris. In this country the Philadelphia Museum of Art was the first to include industrial art in its program. And by 1880 the National Museum in Washington had its Arts and Industries Building, whose leadership would soon inspire others to get started in this field.

The museum designed specifically for youngsters originated in

Brooklyn in 1899. Prior to that time, however, other cities had been pioneering in developing closer ties between the museum and the school. Special visits had been organized, and the lending of materials to schools and libraries for display or use as teaching aids had been begun. But the Brooklyn Children's Museum was the first to conceive of an after-school "please touch" program, a program that has not only now spread throughout the country, but has become a model which observers from other lands have come here to study.

The twentieth century put the nation on wheels. This alone would largely account for both the astounding proliferation of historic houses, and the development of trailside museums. Local and state historical societies had been assiduously preserving the structures that illustrate the cultural and political history of the nation, furnishing them appropriately, and putting them on public view as tangible illustrations of the past. But the movement was given such great impetus by the new audience brought along by the automobile, that this category of museum today outnumbers all the rest.

Trailsides, exhibits of limited scope related to their location, usually in national or state parks, and illustrating the geological, botanical, zoological, and anthropological history of the area, are another distinctively American contribution. The first of them, in a log cabin in Yosemite National Park, was opened to the public by naturalist Ansel Hall in 1921. Soon a grant from the Laura Spelman Rockefeller Memorial enabled the Committee on Outdoor Education of the American Association of Museums to transform this beginning effort into a model trailside, to erect another one in Yellowstone, and to investigate the possibilities of developing similar ones in other national parks. Eventually eight trailsides resulted from this project. In the same year John D. Rockefeller, Jr., became personally interested in the movement when, with three of his sons, he visited several of the parks. A few days were spent at Mesa Verde, where he observed the archaeological ruins and questioned Jesse Nusbaum, the park superintendent, about the Indian civilization that had dwelt there centuries before. Rockefeller deplored the fact that there were no facilities to provide the ordinary tourist with the kind of informed guidance that had deepened his own appreciation of this unique spot. Learning that private funds were being solicited for a museum (federal appropriations having been completely spent on the development of the park site itself) he gladly contributed.

These early programs were soon co-ordinated under the National

Park Service. Additional trailsides in state and national parks would be financed by both the federal government and the Rockefeller Foundation. And natural history museums in large cities would try to bring the spirit of trailsides to their own public by establishing branches in local parks.

Other new categories of twentieth-century interest were the company museum and the planetarium. The first of the former was established by the United Shoe Machinery Company of Boston in 1901, to tell the story behind its industry. Company museums have since been sponsored in virtually every field, from drugs and dinnerware through furs and furnishings to trains and telephones.

The modern planetarium originated in Jena, Germany. The first in this country was the Adler Planetarium and Astronomical Museum which opened in Chicago in 1930. There are now more than a hundred of them in America.

Since the Philadelphia Centennial, scarcely an exposition or fair has come and gone without leaving a permanent museum in its wake. In addition to two new buildings in Philadelphia, the 1876 Exposition was responsible for the development of at least one other institution elsewhere in the country. Three women from Providence, comparing the Rhode Island display with those of other states, found their own state wanting and decided, upon their return home, that local improvement was in order. They agitated for and succeeded in getting an appropriation to start the Rhode Island School of Design and its now well-known museum.

Chicago's Columbian Exposition of 1893 announced that city's intention of matching its growing industrial prowess with cultural achievements. The Art Institute, which had been founded more than a dozen years earlier, at this time acquired the first section of its present building. The Chicago Natural History Museum dates from the Exposition, and the Museum of Science and Industry, founded many years later, occupies one of the buildings erected for the fair.

The St. Louis World's Fair of 1904, and those of San Diego in 1915 and Dallas in 1936, also left behind them buildings that would come to house museums.

When Chicago had its second fair, the Century of Progress Exposition of 1933–34, the Art Institute became the official exhibition hall for the paintings and other works that were shown. Two years later the Cleveland Museum of Art served a similar function, housing an outstanding exhibit of American art for the Great Lakes Exposition. And curators of San Francisco museums were on the planning staff of the Golden Gate International Exposition of 1939.

Seattle's "Century 21" World's Fair of 1962 left a permanent civic center, set in a 74-acre park, just a mile by monorail from the downtown heart of the city. Here are theaters, restaurants, convention facilities, the Seattle Art Museum Pavilion (providing space for annual exhibitions and the overflow of contemporary sculpture from the museum's main building), and the Pacific Science Center (a five-building complex of classrooms, laboratories, and demonstration galleries made over from the $9,900,000 federal government exhibit).

The New York World's Fair of 1964–65 at long last launched the city's new science education center. The multimillion-dollar Hall of Science, located on city-owned land at Flushing Meadows, will revel in the largest parking facilities of any museum in New York.

The most effective force in removing what a critic once referred to as "the gloom of the museum" has been modern architecture. Until well into the twentieth century, museums were built only in revival styles, modeled after Greek temples, Gothic churches, and Italian Renaissance palaces. There was virtually no attempt in their design to provide for the special activities carried on in their halls. Although the new Boston Fine Arts building of 1909 had pioneered in the use of natural illumination, and two or three other buildings of the twenties and the decade before had incorporated practical ideas, functionalism in museum design did not become a vital factor until the thirties. From then until the Second World War brought about a halt in construction, modern, functional design was the rule and neoclassicism the exception. It was during this time that the museum became one of the chief exponents of modern architecture. Outstanding among the structures with this new look were New York's Museum of Modern Art of 1939, with its sleek exterior and flexible, partitioned interior, designed by Philip L. Goodwin and Edward D. Stone; the Dallas Museum of Fine Arts of 1936; the Colorado Springs Fine Arts Center of 1935; and Eliel Saarinen's twins at Cranbrook, Michigan—the Academy of Art and the Institute of Science of 1938 and 1942.

It was not until the postwar wave of construction got under way, however, that the new approach to design was adopted throughout the country. It could be seen at the Des Moines Art Center in 1948, and culminated in New York in 1959 at Frank Lloyd Wright's Solomon R.

Guggenheim Museum building, whose circular descending ramp has proved a greater challenge to curators arranging exhibits than any century-old neoclassic temple.

Traditional styles, nevertheless, are being used today with a new effectiveness. History museums tend to be located in buildings that architecturally recall the early settlers of the area. In the East these are Georgian; in the West, Mission. The Door County Historical Society building of Sturgeon Bay, Wisconsin, is adorned with a decorative Scandinavian motif; a French Provincial structure houses the museum of Ste. Genevieve, Missouri; the Landis Valley Museum of Lancaster reflects its Pennsylvania Dutch provenance. And trailsides are likely to be in log cabins or other rustic structures.

The internal architecture—the typical plan of organization—of the museum has also undergone changes. In most museums today, policy is controlled by an independent board of trustees; the chief financial support coming from endowments, gifts, and membership dues. Additional aid is likely to be provided by state or municipal governments, possibly in the form of land, buildings, or maintenance.

The chief executive is the director, responsible only to the board of trustees. The original source of policy, he supervises an administrative staff consisting of a public relations expert, a publications editor, a registrar to keep all records of accessions, and an assortment of secretaries and bookkeepers. Scientists, historians, and art experts find places on the curatorial staff. They are responsible for the expansion and care of collections, designing and cataloguing, and publishing their research results. In an art museum, expertising—the authenticating of works of art for the public—may also be a curatorial function. Such diverse skills as those possessed by photographers, restorers, ceramists, taxidermists, lighting and sound engineers, artists, and even interior designers may be needed in the preparatorial or technical department, which does the actual work of mounting exhibits—preparing specimens, creating special settings and background effects, and using both the written and recorded word to convey information. The education department might have an extension director in charge of bringing museum knowledge to the community via radio, television, and actual extension classes; an education director to organize classes and film and lecture series within the museum; and docents or guide-lecturers to explain the collections to visitors.

Volunteer workers are sometimes welcomed and, for a bright student, such work could lead to a promising career. The American Association of Museums aids universities in developing training programs for future museologists and operates the only national placement service in the country, hoping to alleviate the shortage of trained personnel and raise the standards of operation and programing, particularly in the smaller institutions.

Donations to museums have, over the years, often been as much of a burden as a boon. Until museums learned to determine upon definite accessions policies they were frequently troubled by gifts to which some very definite strings were attached; most often the directive that an entire group of paintings or objects be kept intact, placed on permanent display, and remain in the museum's possession indefinitely as a monument to the donor. Few if any museums today will accept gifts under these conditions. Their needs, as well as the times, have changed. An item that might be of benefit to a study or loan exhibit might also be a white elephant in the permanent exhibit halls.

In 1962, after one hundred and eighty-nine years of service, the museum in America was, at last, defined. Pressured by the desire to obtain for donors the same tax deduction that contributors to schools, libraries, and hospitals could claim, the American Association of Museums drafted this definition:

"The word 'museum' means and shall be deemed to mean a non-profit, permanent establishment (not existing primarily for the purpose of conducting temporary exhibitions) exempt from Federal and state income taxes, open to the public and administered in the public interest, for the purpose of conserving and preserving, studying, interpreting, enhancing and, in particular, organizing and exhibiting to the public for its instruction and enjoyment objects and specimens of educational and cultural value, including artistic, scientific (whether animate or inanimate), historical and technological materials.

"Museums thus defined shall include botanical gardens, zoological parks, aquariums, planetariums, historical societies, historical houses and sites which meet the requirements set forth in the preceding sentence."

Although a definition is always a comfort, this one leaves something more to be said. In an acquisitive society in which knowledge and "culture" have become commodities, and where glitter and gold are set side by side in the market place, one very often indistinguishable at first glance from the other, the museum remains a stronghold of the permanent values. The fact that the vitality of its activities as tastemaker, researcher, and interpreter has increased and is still increasing is one of the best indications we have that the intellectual aspiration of the American community, attested to in dozens of superficial ways, is also very real and very wonderful.

Chapter II

ART

I F there was ever any doubt about how continually surprising and marvelously paradoxical a country the United States truly is, a study of our cultural development as reflected in our art museums would quickly make the point. First, one has to reconcile the lingering vestiges of a cultural inferiority complex with the astonishing wealth of our public institutions—both large and small, in small towns as well as big cities—in works of art. Then, it has to be realized that our inclination towards "culture" is neither new nor sudden. From the beginning, we stridently "sought refinement," subscribing at once to the claptrap and the genuine. Although museum attendance seems to us now to be increasing dramatically, our museums have always been enthusiastically supported; the proportion of attendance being highest where populations have been smallest. Although recent purchases are among the most highly publicized of our acquisitions, many of our greatest treasures have been quietly residing here for a reasonably long while. And whether the wealthy individuals who brought them over from Europe were collecting solely for themselves, motivated by nothing more elevated than ostentation, or were collecting out of a sincere desire to bring back a sense of beauty to the people whose physical environment had been made bleak by their factories and industrial sites, they sooner or later contributed to the democratization of our museums; their purchases were either put immediately on public view in buildings they themselves helped endow, or into private collections that would ultimately be made available to the public. But the most striking aspect of the surprise is that the great art America owns is scattered, literally, all over the country. How this came about is not one, but many interesting stories. A good story to begin with is that of the city of Baltimore where a continuous history of art collecting, beginning with Colonial times, culminated in two museums.

When Cecil Calvert, the second Lord Baltimore, and his country-men settled on the shores of Maryland, they brought with them family portraits that were to be treasured for generations, and a way of life modeled as nearly as possible on that of the landed English aristocracy. Tobacco soon provided a basis of exchange for the luxuries of the Old World, and Baltimore's fine natural harbor, from which its clipper ships sailed, became a point of continual contact with Europe. English silver and French china adorned the houses of the successful merchants. And soon there were portraits by Gustavus and John Hesselius, Charles Willson Peale, Stuart, and Sully on their walls.

Robert Gilmor, Jr., who enjoyed the advantages of his father's success at business, became one of the first collectors of art in America. Comfortably wealthy, he nevertheless feared that the compulsions of a collector might push him beyond "the bounds of prudence and reason." But, he wrote in his diary, "as long as I can restrain it . . . I am convinced . . . [it] will prove one of the greatest sources of pleasure, amusement and relaxation from the serious concerns of life." A New York dealer, a Mr. Flandis, was one of his sources of supply. On a June morning in 1826, shortly after Colonel Trumbull had paid Gilmor a visit for the specific purpose of seeing his pictures, Flandis arrived in Baltimore. In his diary for that day Gilmor wrote: "Devoted the whole morning to shewing Flandis my pictures. Many of them I had bought of him, and he wished to exchange some he had in New York which I had seen for some of mine, but we could not agree, as he overrated his own, and underrated mine. Discovering his views, I was on my guard and foiled all his adroit attempts to take me in."

Gilmor made purchases from other dealers both at home and abroad. But the difficulties of being so early a collector were compounded by the fact that it was impossible to tell an original Ostade or Jan Steen from a dirt-darkened copy. Even the American artists whose work he closely followed often made copies. At least when Gilmor and his wife sat for their portraits in Sir Thomas Lawrence's London studio they were able to return home with canvases that were undeniably authentic.

The local families who commissioned their own portraits were by no means collectors. Their chief concern was immortality, and many of them succeeded in achieving it. The Calvert family members were among those who, thanks to Hesselius, lived on. Among the paintings now hanging in the Maryland wing of the BALTIMORE MUSEUM OF ART is John Hesselius' *Portrait of Charles Calvert* with his Negro slave.

As descendants became ancestors, however, a tradition of collecting did begin to grow in the city, although it was not until the late nine-

teenth and early twentieth centuries that the most important private
collections were formed. One of these collections would be opened to
the public as the Walters Art Gallery; others would be donated to the
Baltimore Museum of Art. Two of them, the Jacob Epstein and the
Cone sisters', would make the Baltimore Museum internationally famous.

Mr. Epstein, who came to Maryland's biggest city from Lithuania
and slowly developed a major business out of a wholesale notions store,
started collecting in 1888. The paintings, as an aspect of the decoration of his home, were intended to be admired along with the china, the
silver, and the furniture. In 1927 he upset a group of British art lovers
who had hoped to raise money to save Van Dyck's *Rinaldo and Armida*
for London's National Gallery, by buying the famous romantic masterpiece for himself. The picture, which takes its subject from Tasso's
Jerusalem Delivered and shows Rinaldo asleep under the spell of the
enchantress Armida, was commissioned by Charles I through his
agent Endymion Porter. It passed in a direct line from Charles to the
collections of the Dukes of Newcastle to Mr. Epstein, by way of a London dealer; the route of its journey being authenticated in a letter by
M. Knoedler & Co. In the same year as his purchase, the collector's
portrait was painted by Augustus John, while his bust was brought into
the world by a sculptor named, quite coincidentally, Jacob Epstein.

The Epstein bequest included examples of the work of the Flemish
painter Justus Sustermans, Titian, Raphael, Tintoretto, Goya, Hals,
Rembrandt, and the English school; the Hals being his portrait of
Dorothea Berck and the English school being represented by Reyn-
olds' *Lady St. Asaph and Her Child* and Gainsborough's *Mrs. Charles
Tudway*.

At a time when the Baltimore Museum of Art would not dream of
daring to exhibit any one of the paintings from the Cone collection that
it now cherishes and recognizes as its major attraction, Dr. Claribel
Cone and Miss Etta Cone, two spinster sisters whose home had become
a cultural refuge for local intellectuals, were traveling abroad acquiring Matisses and Picassos. Encouraged by Gertrude, Michael, and
Sarah Stein, they met Matisse and Picasso in 1905 and began buying
their work. While they browsed through Picasso's studio, picking up
sketches for a few dollars each, they would entertain him with a collection of comic strips from American newspapers which they regularly
saved for him and which he loved to look at. By buying what they
liked, Dr. Claribel, who was a medical researcher, and Miss Etta, an

accomplished musician, managed to acquire over a period of many years one of the most important collections of Matisse paintings and bronzes in the world. Shortly before Claribel died in 1929, they bought the *Blue Nude* which had passed from the hands of Gertrude and Leo Stein to the collector John Quinn. Etta, who lived on for another twenty years, kept buying one Matisse a year as well as some earlier French art, such as Delacroix and Courbet. Previously, the sisters had bought Renoir, Van Gogh, Cézanne, Manet, Corot, and Gauguin, not to mention a remarkable collection of Near Eastern and European textiles, laces, Spanish and French eighteenth-century jewelry, and furniture.

Renoir's canvas of *The Washerwomen,* Cézanne's *The Bathers* (one of many canvases on the subject), Gauguin's *Woman with a Mango,* and Picasso's *Woman with Bangs,* painted in 1902, are among favorites of travelers to Baltimore. When the collection was bequeathed to the museum after Etta died in 1949, it was valued at $3,000,000.

Mrs. Saidie A. May was another collector with vision. Aware of what the Cones had done, she hoped by her own efforts to supplement it. Concentrating on more advanced twentieth-century paintings and sculpture, she added Léger, Mondrian, and Pollock. Going back in time, she added ancient, medieval, and Renaissance sculpture and *objets d'art,* and textiles of the fifteenth to seventeenth centuries. Recent American paintings, among them Mark Tobey's *Five A.M.,* were added later as the Edward J. Gallagher Memorial.

In 1936 a group of mosaics, ranging from the second to the sixth century A.D., excavated in or near Antioch, Syria, was presented to the museum. This group, a collection of Maryland silver, a display of eighteenth-century Maryland furniture, and a new sculpture garden are other noteworthy aspects of the Baltimore Museum of Art.

All of the noteworthy aspects of the WALTERS ART GALLERY are the results of the avocation of a father and the consuming passion of his son. William Walters, a rich Baltimore merchant before the Civil War, became richer at the war's end by establishing the railway system known as the Atlantic Coast Line. And during this transition, his collector's eye wandered from the works of Maryland painters to Oriental art to French sculpture. His son Henry continued his work with both the railroad and the collection.

Writing of the younger Walters' eclectic taste, Francis Henry Taylor said, a "man who has it and the means to satisfy his desires, more often develops independent judgment and courage of convictions than a collector traveling a clearly marked path. . . . So great was the variety of his interests, that once acquired and thus made part of the treasure house of his mind, the object ceased to have further significance save as a piece of property to be stored away. . . . It is axiomatic that the quality of the Walters Collection could not have been achieved without the quantity; for not only did he rush in where angels feared to tread, but he refused to be led by the hand. . . ."

Hanging his paintings and piling his objects of art literally one on top of the other, he showed no apparent concern for the disconcerting effect this arrangement would have on the visitor. When the Florentine palazzo built to contain this clutter of treasures was given to the city in 1931, unopened crates were found in the basement. Even after modernization, the Gallery lacked space to adequately display at one time more than twenty per cent of what it owned.

The journey from William Walters' rare Chinese porcelains and potteries to Henry's outstanding collection of illuminated manuscripts from the ninth to the fourteenth century was a marvelous one. (The illuminated manuscripts are second in importance in the country only to those of New York's Morgan Library.) En route were amassed, in no particular order, Sèvres porcelain and Renaissance jewelry, Byzantine and medieval objects, the arts of the Egyptians, Etruscans, Romans, Greeks, and Persians, Barye sculpture, early Italian and nineteenth-century French paintings, and—the word is truly etcetera. The periods have of course been arranged and sorted, and order has been made from the beautiful chaos, despite the continued crowding.

The story of how a Walters acquisition was exchanged, in 1953, with the authorization of the mayor and City Council, for a gift from the Metropolitan Museum of Art illustrates one of the ways in which scholarship motivates co-operation. James Rorimer, then curator of medieval art at the Metropolitan and director of The Cloisters, discovered that a late fifteenth-century panel from a Brussels tapestry belonging to the Walters Gallery made up most of the central section of a work of which the Metropolitan owned the right panel and a dealer the left. Even though a lower portion of the Walters panel was missing, the Metropolitan offered the Gallery the finest tapestry it could find in exchange for it in order to reunite the three parts. The Gallery agreed to trade and its reward was a Brussels tapestry dating from about 1490, illustrating the parable of the Prodigal Son, considered one of the finest of its kind anywhere.

To find the center of early America's intellectual life, one had to go north of Baltimore, to Philadelphia, where the PENNSYLVANIA ACADEMY OF THE FINE ARTS, the country's oldest public art museum, was organized in 1805 to serve as both art school and exhibition gallery. The first museum art exhibit in America was held at the Academy in April of 1807. The featured paintings were Shakespearean scenes by Benjamin West; the *pièce de résistance* was a group of plaster casts made from statues in the Louvre with the permission, carefully obtained, of the Emperor Napoleon. Since several of these represented nude figures, Mondays were reserved for exclusive viewing by ladies, in order to spare them the embarrassment of having to look in the company of men.

The Academy has the longest record of annual exhibitions of painting and sculpture in the United States. The first of them, held in cooperation with the Society of Artists in 1811, included portraits by Stuart and Sully. In later years awards for painting would go to Whistler, Sargent, Cassatt, Bellows, Hopper, Kuniyoshi, and Burchfield; for sculpture, to Malvina Hoffman, José de Creeft, and Jacques Lipchitz. (There would also be an autumn annual for water colors, miniatures, etchings, and drawings from which purchases would be made for the large graphics collection.) In the Academy's permanent collection are portraits by and of early Americans. George Washington can be seen as a subject for Gilbert Stuart, Charles Willson Peale, and Rembrandt Peale. Benjamin Franklin is of course on view, and so are Francis Scott Key and Henry Clay.

The elder Peale, a founder and member of the board of directors, was the first teacher in the Academy's art school; Sully was added to the faculty soon afterward. Eakins came on as an instructor somewhat later and was forced to leave in disgrace. Eakins held that artists should study anatomy. But when dissected cadavers were one day discovered in his studio, he was summarily dismissed. The Academy's school managed to survive the contretemps; and the museum itself continued to flourish. When it came time to celebrate its 150th anniversary, instead of waiting to receive a gift, the Academy sent abroad an exhibition of American paintings from its own and other collections.

By the middle of the 1950s, when this celebration took place, America was not only rich in domestic art, but very rich in the imported product as well. And so the PHILADELPHIA MUSEUM OF ART, having added nine American works to the Academy's Europe-bound gala,

now loaned to the Louvre—at the personal request of the artist—its
Picasso *Self-Portrait* for a retrospective showing in honor of his
seventy-fifth birthday. Two of the Philadelphia Museum's Cézannes,
The Bathers and *Mont St. Victoire*, and Daumier's *Print Collector* had
already left for a different Paris exhibition, one made up entirely of
nineteenth-century French masterpieces from American collections.
And an important Juan Gris was en route from Philadelphia to Swit-
zerland.

The museum that could spare these masterpieces in order to en-
hance American prestige abroad had been systematically building
its collections only for three decades, under the sometimes erratic,
frequently controversial, and always brilliant direction of one of the
most exuberant personalities ever to appear on the museum scene.
Fiske Kimball, an earnest, burly student of architecture and head of
the art department at New York University, came with his wife and
some misgivings to Philadelphia in 1924 to take over a fifty-year-old
institution about to move to a new building. The old building, and
what it contained, had been left over from the Centennial, and had
changed little since then. Still in the basement of Memorial Hall was a
series of lighted three-dimensional dioramas to be looked at through
peepholes: the "Views of Pompeii." Still in the dust-clogged halls were
the plaster casts and pictures that Kimball dismissed as "stuffy clutter."

The new building was slow in going up. Its prime supporter was
Eli K. Price, who never faltered in his resolution, made more than a
decade earlier, that an art museum would stand at the entrance to
Fairmount Park. At the time Price made his vow, the Benjamin Franklin Parkway, which runs diagonally through town from City Hall to
the park, was being planned at the instigation of Mayor John E. Reyburn. Reyburn, indicating the park entrance, had said succinctly, "That
is where the art museum will be." But when Price heard someone re-
mark that the project would never become a reality, he somehow felt
forewarned; and he dedicated himself to seeing the job accomplished.
Actually, he was doing nothing more than adhering to family tradition.
The grandfather whose namesake he was had been instrumental in
1867 in creating the park itself, along with its governing body, the
Fairmount Park Commission. The grandson had served on the Commission for many years and was, as befitted a Main Line Philadelphian,
on the board of practically every civic institution. The art museum was
to be his crowning achievement.

When Fiske Kimball met Eli Price, work on the new museum had been in progress for four years. The foundation and steps leading up the terraced hill were in place. At lunch, Price showed Kimball the architect's plans and told him of the huge amount of money required to carry them out. When Kimball asked, "Can you get more money to finish it?" he was told that another million dollars was available. When he asked whether Price would use that money to build the central section of the building, he was told, "No, if I did that, they would never finish it." Price then explained that he planned to put up the two end pavilions before completing the mid-section that would join them into a whole structure. Later, Kimball asked, "Mr. Price, if you are run over by a taxicab today as we come out of this club, how many of these plans will be carried out?"

"All of them," said Price, delightedly revealing the method to his apparent madness. "The city will never be able to leave a building with ends and no center."

And that was exactly what happened. Although a part of the central section was opened the next year, the first main gallery was not completed until four years later, and additional galleries were being opened at intervals for the next twenty years.

While waiting for the first floor to be in readiness for exhibit purposes, Fiske Kimball and his wife Marie were given a trip abroad to study museum achievements in Europe. That trip was to change the course that had been set for Philadelphia. After seeing how antique architectural fragments had been incorporated into the new halls of the Berlin museum, not yet opened to the public, Kimball envisioned the use of old rooms in their entirety as settings for paintings and decorative objects. Museums were then just beginning to display "period rooms," usually reconstructed versions in the style of whatever era they were supposed to represent. The transplantation of real rooms was rare; and then the rooms served only as architectural exhibits. The use of real period rooms as actual exhibition halls was brand new.

Fired with enthusiasm for what he wanted his galleries to look like, Kimball wrote a message to the membership: "Philadelphia . . . is rich in works of American Art, and will never neglect its duty to preserve and show them. To make a great museum, it must have also, in rich measure, the works of other countries and civilizations, not only paintings and sculptures, but tapestries, textiles, porcelain, crystal— everything beautiful, everything inspiring to the public, the artist, and the craftsman. . . ."

And he set about making his vision a reality. In his first year as director, in a half-finished shell of a building, he installed four English rooms filled with works of Gainsborough, Romney, Lawrence, Turner, Hogarth, and Reynolds, and three American rooms, including one elegant Philadelphia drawing room of 1760 and its country counterpart, a Pennsylvania Dutch setting. Later on he added a Dutch room from Haarlem; several French rooms featuring eighteenth- and nineteenth-century paintings, Beauvais tapestries, and Sèvres; an Italian room dominated by a Luca della Robbia medallion; a German Renaissance room dominated by an immense tile stove; a Romanesque cloister complete with Gothic chapel, halls, and bedrooms from the Abbey of Saint-Genis des Fontaines near the northeast border of Spain; the pillared hall of an Indian temple; two rooms from the summer palace of Persian Shah Abbas the Great (1586–1628); and a Chinese palace hall (1621–27) from near Peiping. At the time of his death a Japanese temple, tea house, and garden, and a Chinese temple and scholar's study, were being assembled.

A tribute to this vital man appeared in the museum's annual report: "Perhaps his greatest contribution . . . was his concept that a museum should express the world's artistic culture in all mediums, merging architecture, painting, sculpture and the decorative arts. . . . Each year seemed to stimulate Mr. Kimball to greater effort. . . . Our thirty-year history of acquisition by purchase does not reveal a single erroneous step."

The grandest coup of Kimball's administration was undoubtedly the acquisition of the Louise and Walter Arensberg Collection of modern paintings and sculpture, hailed by the museum as "the most important assemblage" of the 1911–14 turning point in modern art. It includes Marcel Duchamp's *Nude Descending a Staircase,* the painting that dramatized the arrival of Cubism in America at the 1913 Armory Show.

Also in the museum is the John G. Johnson Collection of more than one thousand works ranging over the entire history of Western art from the twelfth through the nineteenth century, and particularly attentive to Flemish, Italian, and German primitive painting. A corporation lawyer who could not aspire to the flamboyant art purchases of his clients J. P. Morgan, Sr., and P. A. B. Widener (a fellow Philadelphian whose collections ultimately went to the National Gallery in Washington, D.C., despite Kimball's efforts to retain them), Johnson was interested more in the quality of the painting than in the greatness of the name at the bottom of it. He planned his purchases systematically and willed them to his city, to remain in the house he had provided "unless some extraordinary situation shall arise making it extremely injudicious." Johnson died in 1917, leaving Chardins in the boot closet and French Impressionists on the servants' staircase of a building that was too small for more than a handful of visitors and was, furthermore, an obvious firetrap. The city decided that the situation was already "extraordinary" and that it would be "extremely injudicious" *not* to transfer the Botticellis, Cranachs, Brueghels, Rubenses, Rembrandts, El Grecos, and the rest to the new museum. All these were canvases which, for one reason or another, were not "blue chip" when Johnson bought them; they merely pleased him esthetically, and therefore measured up to his only criterion.

Supplementing the Johnson is the Wilstach Collection, the foundation of which was bequeathed to the museum in 1893, along with a substantial fund whose income has been used to make some very distinguished purchases, such as a version of Cézanne's *The Bathers*. Three of the nineteenth-century French and American painters in this group are Degas, Whistler, and Mary Cassatt, who left her native Philadelphia and its Academy to study in Europe and join the Impressionists. Another party of bathers, this one by Renoir, arrived with the fine Tyson Collection. And the recent Louis E. Stern bequest included Rouaults, Rousseaus, and Soutines.

A set of seventeenth-century tapestries, depicting incidents in the life of Constantine the Great and designed by Peter Paul Rubens and Pietro da Cortona for the Barberini Palace in Rome, are a gift of the Kress Foundation.

Outstanding among the sculptures is the *Prometheus* of Jacques Lipchitz, winner of the Widener Prize at the Academy's annual in 1952 and purchased that same year; it stands on a pedestal at the foot of the entrance steps. There are works by William Rush, a Philadelphian who was the earliest American sculptor and, in the opinion of art critic Walter Pach, both the "founder of art appreciation in the city" and "a man of delightful talent." There is a *Diana* by Augustus Saint-Gaudens. (*Diana* topped New York's first Madison Square Garden in the late 1800s and caused a bit of a stir as a result of the prominence this location managed to give to her nudity.) And from the Stern bequest, there are pieces by Picasso, Renoir, Maillol, Epstein, Moore, and Giacometti.

The most complete collection of Rodin's work outside of Paris is in the nearby RODIN MUSEUM, which is under the direction of the

Philadelphia Museum of Art. Businessman Jules E. Mastbaum, visiting Paris with his wife and daughters in 1924, persuaded the curator of the Hôtel Biron (later the Musée Rodin) to let him purchase a bronze small enough to take back to Philadelphia in his pocket. Until that time Mastbaum had been a collector of first editions. But his increasing regard for the sculptor soon pre-empted this former interest. By the time the family sailed for home later that year he had several more Rodins in his baggage. Once home he persuaded both the Fairmount Park Commission and the French Art Commission to cooperate with him in establishing a public museum containing bronzes, plaster casts, and drawings illustrating every phase of the master's work. A formal garden outside the building contains *The Thinker* and *The Gates of Hell,* which the artist worked on for years and which, as a result of Mastbaum's efforts, was posthumously cast in bronze in 1926.

On the outskirts of Philadelphia, in Merion, is the least accessible art museum in the country; and ironically, it has the country's largest collection of Impressionist and Postimpressionist works. The late Albert Barnes, who made his fortune from the invention of the patent medicine Argyrol, hand-picked not only his works of art but also the visitors who would be privileged to view them. Under the terms of his will, the BARNES FOUNDATION was to be opened only two hours a day, four days a week, to a limited number of people, all of whom had to apply in writing well in advance for permission to enter the holy of holies. The legality of these provisions was questioned, and visiting hours were extended. Recent visitors have commented on the numerous Pinkertons and the fact that one cannot wear a coat or carry a handbag. Ladies are advised to have dimes handy to check their purses. The dime is returned, however, with the purse.

If Baltimore and Philadelphia do not sufficiently contradict any narrow notions that the enjoyment of art in the United States is a new phenomenon, Toledo, Ohio, will contradict them further. Since 1906 the TOLEDO MUSEUM OF ART, a community responsibility that began in the dreams of Edward D. Libbey, has been a source of education and pleasure for the city's adults and children. By 1938 *Fortune* magazine was able to report that the museum was drawing "2500 children every Saturday and 104 per cent of the population of Toledo in a year."

Edward Drummond Libbey was a New England glassmaker at-

tracted by the idea of using Toledo's natural gas as fuel for his factory.
Eager, in addition, to escape labor problems at home, he moved west
in 1888. Libbey Glass, which he brought with him, was his father's.
On his own, he built up Toledo Glass; and with the help of Mike
Owens who invented a bottle-blowing machine, he organized both
the Owens Bottle and the Libbey-Owens Sheet Glass companies.

To Libbey, art was neither a whim nor a status symbol. He loved it
and saw in it, as he said once in a speech, the means of awakening the
people to the value of "the things of the spirit." But he wanted the people to work for their education. He wanted their museum to be, from
the beginning, a community project. He was willing to help the city
help itself. In 1901 he rented rooms in downtown Toledo and founded
an institution.

At a time when the museum owned absolutely nothing, Libbey managed to solicit, in addition to a board of fifteen trustees, 120 members
each willing to pay annual dues of ten dollars. Within the next two
years, anticipating the paintings yet to come, the new organization
acquired lights for them. Anticipating visitors, it moved to larger quarters and acquired a carpet. And anticipating work to be done, it acquired a desk. Its one collection item at this time was a mummified
Egyptian cat. But in one month seven visitors came to see it and Libbey
took heart. It was then that the originator of the Toledo Museum met
George Washington Stevens, the man who became its director and is
credited with its actual creation.

A former circus rider, actor, publicity man, and newspaper colum-
nist, Mr. Stevens had both the imagination and polite disrespect for
tradition that was sorely needed. Before the museum could educate
its community, it had to find the way to stimulate it, and this became
Stevens' job. He started a campaign. He stopped people on the street;
he planted publicity wherever he could; he wrote letters. He shared
Libbey's feeling about the importance of attracting children and, after
deciding to admit them free and unaccompanied by an adult, he asked
his wife to help him conduct drawing classes for them. Attendance
picked up and in 1904, through a sympathetic appeal to a friend to
buy and donate a painting that had just won a bronze medal at the St.
Louis exposition, Libbey helped the museum acquire its first picture.
In the same year, a collection of Russian paintings en route home from
the exposition were for some reason refused clearance by U. S. customs
and were put up for sale. With $2000 that had been raised during a
lightning-fast door-to-door drive and a vision of walls filled at last with

a featured attraction, Stevens raced to New York and the museum acquired, in a swoop, its first gallery-full of pictures. An appraisal of their quality is unimportant; it was a beginning.

From that time on, while attendance increased, paintings were regularly added to the collection. Libbey himself, whose trips to Europe were bringing him into contact with the Dutch and Flemish schools, contributed most of them. Meanwhile, the museum's appeal to children became so strong that by 1908 crowds of them had to be kept waiting in the street while the first shift went in.

When the time came to raise money for a new building, Libbey put up half, the other half being subscribed in a short time by the people of Toledo in sums ranging from ten cents to thousands of dollars. And when it became necessary to expand again, he donated twice what he asked the public. When he died he left the museum his entire personal collection, trust funds of over $4,000,000, and an estate of over $13,-000,000. The next expansion, which completed the neoclassical building, was inspired by Mrs. Libbey during the Depression and created jobs for three thousand of Toledo's unemployed.

Among the great paintings enjoyed by visitors are Velasquez' *Man with a Wine Glass* and Holbein the Younger's portrait of *Catherine Howard,* both of which delighted Libbey personally. Piero di Cosimo's *Adoration of The Child* and Rubens' *Child Jesus Crowning St. Catherine* are two other important acquisitions. Bellini, Zurbarán, El Greco, Dürer, Goya, Poussin, Boucher, and the Dutch school are all impressively represented. There is a good selection of Impressionist and Postimpressionist works. The American names include Blakelock, Copley, Stuart, Inness, Ryder, Marsh, Mark Tobey, and Andrew Wyeth. The father of the Hudson River school, Thomas Cole, is represented by *The Architect's Dream.* And to provide a change of pace, there is a substantial group of contemporary English paintings.

Not surprisingly, the museum has one of the world's best collections of glass, ranging from ancient Egyptian to modern. Its treasures are highlighted by a Roman cameo vase of the first century A.D., and a richly enameled Arabic flagon from about 1300. A first-century Syrian chalice inscribed in Greek with the phrase "Wherefore art thou come; rejoice" caused a near-riot in 1926. First, an English historian, in an enthusiastic display of bad judgment, pronounced the resemblance of another cup—one he himself had found—to those used at the Last Supper. Then a London newspaper printed a story in which it mentioned the existence of six similar cups. One of them, it reported, was in Toledo. By the time the local press rewrote the story, it was firmly believed throughout the city that the Holy Grail itself was inside the museum. And not even the strongest denial could either hold back or disabuse the crowds now aroused by the very same quest that had once stirred the Knights of King Arthur.

The Stevens Gallery, illustrating the history of man learning to write, and the museum's concert hall in the form of a peristyle are also noteworthy.

"No city is great," George Washington Stevens said, "unless it rests the eyes, feeds the intellect, and leads its people out of the bondage of the commonplace."

Of course, Ohio's largest art museum—and certainly one of the most important in the country—is the CLEVELAND MUSEUM OF ART. It is also one of the most magnificent; a handsome classical building surrounding a garden court and situated near a lake in scenic Wade Park. Outstanding collections of Egyptian, classical, Near Eastern, Indian, Japanese, and Chinese art are to be seen here. There is a choice group of fifteenth-century Italian to twentieth-century American drawings, paralleled by an extensive print collection—some highlights of which are the Tiepolo and Piranesi etchings, a comprehensive series of Dürer prints, a number of color lithographs by Toulouse-Lautrec, a group of Whistler etchings and lithographs, and an almost complete collection (193 of 196) of Bellows' lithographs. In what is known as the Treasure Room, Coptic, Early Christian, Byzantine and Gothic silver and gold, textiles, jewelry, ivories, and enameled pieces are on view. From the famous Guelph Treasure there are the jewel-encrusted Gertrudis portable altar, two matching crosses, and six other objects. (Most of the remaining pieces of the Guelph Treasure were acquired by Hitler for the Third Reich.) And further enriching the decorative arts department is an extraordinary display of Spanish, Hispano-Islamic, and Italian textiles and ceramics. The Severance Collection of arms and armor is displayed handsomely in the Armor Court. The arts of pre-Columbian Middle and South America, and of pre-colonial Africa are well represented: a Mochica gold mask, a Mayan stone head with stylized features, and the bronze head of a Benin princess being three unusually beautiful examples.

The extensive painting collection begins with the Italian school, which is thoroughly covered. Elsewhere, an early El Greco, the *Holy Family,* can be compared with a late *Crucifixion.* The opulence and grace of Van Dyck's *Genoese Lady and Child* can be contrasted with the stern elegance of his portrait of the Englishman *Sir Thomas Hanmer*. And one can see a lovely portrait by Rubens of his first wife, *Isabella Brant,* as well as three portraits by Rembrandt. A distinctive group of portrait miniatures is headed by a rondel of *Sir Thomas More* by Hans Holbein the Younger (a full-sized version is in New York's Frick Collection). The English are represented by Reynolds, Gainsborough, Raeburn, and Lawrence; Turner's *Burning of the House of Parliament* is very well known. The French paintings, from Poussin and Claude Lorrain to Matisse and Rouault, are highlighted by Watteau's *La Danse dans un Pavillon* (which was sold by the artist to Frederick the Great, and in 1918 by his ultimate successor Kaiser Wilhelm II to Commodore Louis D. Beaumont, who presented it to the museum twenty years later), and Picasso's *La Vie* (blue period). A comprehensive and exceptional group of American paintings are displayed in four galleries. Among the earliest are portraits by Robert Feke and John Smibert; slightly later, there are two by Copley and five by Stuart. Among the best known are one of the several *Peaceable Kingdoms* by the untrained nineteenth-century Quaker Edward Hicks, *Turning the Stake Boat* by Thomas Eakins, *Death on a Pale Horse* by Albert P. Ryder, and *Stag at Sharkey's* by George Bellows. An excellent handbook is available to guide the visitor to these and other works.

Three other important institutions in Ohio are the CINCINNATI ART MUSEUM, the DAYTON ART INSTITUTE, and the COLUMBUS GALLERY OF FINE ARTS.

Cincinnati's museum describes itself as a huge picture book of human history. Beginning with the ancient world, the displays move through time to the present, telling their story in terms of sculpture, paintings, objects, furniture and musical instruments. Among the famous paintings here are Andrea Mantegna's *Esther and Mordecai,* Botticelli's *Judith with the Head of Holofernes,* Titian's portrait of *Philip II of Spain,* El Greco's *Crucifixion with View of Toledo,* Zurbarán's extraordinarily fine *Legend of the Bell* and Grant Wood's *Daughters of Revolution.* Artists of every period and school are well represented. American artists and Cincinnatians in particular have, since before the turn of the century, been given the kind of special attention that results in an excellent collection. Highlighting the American section is the work of Frank Duveneck who in 1913 was dean of the museum's art academy.

In addition to its fine Oriental galleries and its European, Ameri-

can, and pre-Columbian art, Dayton's Institute owns a portrait of Elias
Jonathan Dayton, the man who founded the city, by Thomas Sully.
Another feature of this museum is its circulating gallery of paintings.
The rental library system of borrowing museum art was initiated here
in the 1920s. Much more recently, Dayton made a significant con-
tribution to the body of Baroque art in America when it acquired
Claude Vignon's *The Adoration of the Magi,* painted in 1619. Vignon
was French, and a student of Caravaggio.

The Columbus Gallery of Fine Arts, thanks to Ferdinand Howald,
an unassuming collector who lived alone and bought what he liked,
boasts excellent contemporary American and modern French paintings. Howald bought early works of Peter Blume, Max Weber, and
Kuniyoshi. And he bought Picasso, Rousseau, Matisse, and many
Pascins. Of the Americans, he assembled outstanding groups of Pren-
dergasts, Demuths, and Marins. The gifts of other benefactors rounded
out the museum's collections, adding Renaissance, baroque, and nine-
teenth- and twentieth-century examples. But the joy of Columbus is
what it owns of the work of George Bellows, whose realistic pictures
of drunks, prize fighters, and lovers at night in city parks began to
shock the public just five years after he left Columbus and headed for
New York in 1904. Although his most famous canvas, *Stag at Sharkey's,* is in Cleveland, some of his best are here in his home town.

In the bracing air of the north woods, which a traveler is likely to
inhale either as a result of a visit to the University of Minnesota or the
Tyrone Guthrie Theater, culture in the form of art appreciation began
to thrive well before the turn of the century. In the WALKER ART CEN-
TER and the MINNEAPOLIS INSTITUTE OF ART, the land of the Paul
Bunyan prototype years ago acquired two museums destined for excellence.

While the railroads were still pushing westward from Minneapolis,
Thomas Barlow Walker was getting rich on lumber and discovering
how much he enjoyed buying a portrait of George Washington by
Rembrandt Peale or hanging a copy of a Raphael Madonna on his
wall. In 1879, having acquired about twenty paintings in addition to
some lithographs, he added a wing to his house and built the first gallery in the Midwest that was open to the public—a skylighted room
measuring sixteen by thirty feet. By 1892, having become both an
omnivorous and eclectic collector for the community, he found it necessary to add three rooms to his gallery in order to display bronzes,

objects of art of every description, and still more paintings. Thirty-four years later, when he reached the age of eighty-seven, he built the Walker Art Center and established a foundation.

Between then and now the emphasis at the Walker has shifted to contemporary art. However, after viewing the Lipchitz sculpture of *Prometheus and the Vulture* and Franz Marc's painting *Blue Horses,* one can still find a reminder of the Center's founder in the antiques that are shown, the few old paintings, and the sampling of a fine collection of seventeenth-, eighteenth-, and nineteenth-century jades.

Another collector of jade objects, whose specialty, however, was Chinese bronzes, left his collection to the Minneapolis Institute of Arts while his family's name—Pillsbury—was growing famous in the American kitchen. The bronzes are among the highlights of a museum that can trace itself back to 1883 when the Minneapolis Society of Fine Arts was incorporated for the purpose of promoting a knowledge and love of art in the community. But it was 1915 when the Society opened its building (designed by the New York architects McKim, Mead and White) to the public. Rich in European paintings of the seventeenth through nineteenth centuries, the Institute also boasts possession of one of the two casts made of Ernst Barlach's remarkable eighteen-foot, German-commissioned, Nazi-denounced statue called *The Fighter of the Spirit.* El Greco's *Christ Driving the Money-Changers from the Temple,* and Matisse's *White Plumes* are two famous favorites. A recently acquired Fra Angelico is a rarity not only for Minnesota but for the country. And for those who love a Pollock, there is Pollock in the company of selected contemporaries.

Among the many extraordinary aspects of America's cultural wealth is the number of Flemish paintings we have, over the years, managed to acquire. Thomas Jefferson is credited with being the first American collector to buy a work of the Flemish Renaissance. In 1784, when he was our minister to France, he bought a Jan Gossaert *Ecce Homo.* (The painting, now owned by the New-York Historical Society, is on permanent loan to Jefferson's home, Monticello.) From then on our interest in and liking for Flemish art grew steadily. The most important collection of Flemish primitive paintings in America is in New York at the Metropolitan Museum of Art and The Cloisters. Washington and Chicago have their share and so have Boston and Philadelphia. And there is a beautiful collection of Flemish art in Detroit.

In 1960, E. P. Richardson, then curator of the DETROIT INSTITUTE

OF ARTS, initiated an exhibit organized co-operatively with the Belgian city of Bruges called "Flanders in the Fifteenth Century." The exhibition was given additional support by the Centre National de Recherches Primitifs Flamands of Brussels, which prepared the highly informative catalogue. The Centre had several years before begun to analyze the body of Flemish work in the United States as part of a world-wide plan of research. The exhibition, which was concerned with giving a sense through its art of fifteenth-century Flanders as a civilization, was consistent both with the philosophy of the Detroit Institute and with its history of enjoying an effective relationship with its public.

The home of many European immigrants, Detroit had been founded by French settlers and remained for many years French in tempo and spirit. Even after the original town was destroyed by fire in 1805, the French influence was felt in the new city that began to grow. But early in the twentieth century it disappeared forever, its mood incompatible with the exigencies of automobile manufacture. Detroit's cultural development ever since has been the result of an interaction between the city and its industrialists. In the case of the Detroit Institute of Arts, interaction between the city which maintains the museum, wealthy individuals (Fords, Dodges, and Firestones among them) who endow it, and community-oriented citizens who enjoy it has resulted in a uniquely satisfactory arrangement.

In 1932, when Diego Rivera was invited by the Detroit Arts Council, an arm of the city government, to execute murals for the Institute's Garden Court, the money was donated by Edsel Ford and the city itself was stipulated as Rivera's subject. The resultant frescoes showing the industries and assembly-line workers have attracted large numbers of the workers themselves each year. And no one ever seemed to notice—or, if they did notice, become upset by—Rivera's socialist irony which expressed itself in what he must have regarded as a satisfying private joke played upon his patrons. One of the workers immortalized in his mural had worn a funny hat that said "We want beer." Placing the worker's head in such a position that a full view of his hat was impossible, Rivera managed to turn the simple phrase into a subtle exhortation: "We want."

In an introduction to one of the museum's many publications, Mr. Richardson wrote: "The aim of the Detroit Institute . . . is to represent within one building, in a single, clear, organic sequence, the whole story of the arts in human society. The collection begins with the first appearance of the instinct of design in the flints of prehistoric man and traces its development through every important stage of art down to the present day. Each stage is represented by a gallery which aims to illustrate, by carefully chosen examples, the culture of a single age as it was expressed by the arts. In consequence all the different media of art are shown together—painting, sculpture, furniture, metal work, glass, enamels, whatever else may be an important form of art in that age being grouped together as the organic expression of a period of life. The arts of the more distant past are installed in architectural settings which, though modern, endeavor to suggest the original setting in scale, color, and decoration." Also to Detroit's credit is its pioneering in the display of the creative works of all the Americas' Indians as art rather than artifacts.

The scope of its acquisitions is so vast that in addition to outstanding showings of Italian, Dutch, Flemish, French, and American art, the museum boasts important Oriental and classical collections. From the beginning, standards were high. Between 1884 and 1888 James E. Scripps, publisher of the *Evening News,* put together a group of European paintings that got the museum going on its quest after excellence.

Jan Van Eyck's *St. Jerome in His Study,* Rogier van der Weyden's *St. Jerome in the Desert,* Pieter Brueghel the Elder's *The Wedding Dance,* major works of Rubens, Van Dyck, Hals, de Hooch, and Steen, Ruisdael's *The Cemetery,* and Rembrandt's *The Visitation* are just the beginning of a list of highlights.

Among the French masters, Degas' *Dancers in the Green Room* has been a favorite with visitors. The Italian masterpieces are too numerous to mention, but visitors have singled out Titian's *Man with a Flute* and three Sassettas. A favorite sculpture is Andrea Pisano's *Madonna and Child.* And a six-by-five-foot altarpiece by Giovanni Battista Tiepolo, originally designed for a Venetian baroque church, has been greatly admired. The Spanish masterpieces include El Greco's *St. Francis in Ecstasy* and *The Flight into Egypt* of Murillo.

The American section, considered one of the best in the country, is one of the country's most complete. Matthew Pratt, Lucy Bradley, Ralph Earl, Copley (one version of his *Brook Watson and the Shark* is here), Trumbull, Charles Willson Peale, Rembrandt Peale, Sully, Mount, Kensett, Inness, Winslow Homer, Eakins, Mary Cassatt, Ryder, Bellows, O'Keeffe, Burchfield, Feininger, and Kuniyoshi are all on the roster. A Whistler *Self-Portrait* and his famous *Nocturne in*

Black and Gold: The Falling Rocket are also here. So is the popular *McSorley's Bar* of John Sloan.

Out of its interest in American art, the Detroit Institute has established the Archives of American Art for the purpose of bringing together, on a national scale, original documents (letters, diaries, notebooks, etc.) relating to all of our artists and craftsmen (not only painters, sculptors, and engravers, but silversmiths, cabinetmakers, clockmakers, glassmakers, print makers, ceramists, etc.) as well as collectors, critics, dealers, historians, and museums and other institutions. Original documents that have already found a safe home in a library or other institution will be put on microfilm to complete the Archives' files. The plan of the Archives is to become a central source for the researcher and student.

The Institute was the recipient of Elizabeth Parke Firestone's collection of eighteenth-century French silver and William Randolph Hearst's collection of arms and armor. It is the home of the Detroit Puppet Theater. And it is, in addition, the publisher of the *Art Quarterly*.

That it is dedicated "to the knowledge and enjoyment of art" is made known immediately at the entrance door over which these words are carved. But it is not necessary to read the dedication to know that this is so.

Just a few years before James E. Scripps presented the Detroit Institute with its first important gift, another newspaperman, William Rockhill Nelson, formed some first impressions of Kansas City, Missouri, that would ultimately result in local improvement on a nearly wholesale scale and a splendid gallery of art. "When I came to Kansas City," he said years later, "it was incredibly commonplace and ugly. I decided if I were to remain here the town must be made over."

He was thirty-nine years old and already imperious when he left Indiana, where he had been in real estate, a cotton grower, a contractor, and a small-town editor. In 1880 he founded the Kansas City *Star* and began building it into a great newspaper. To his good taste, which came naturally, he added his notion that the public had broader interests than most papers were then willing to give it credit for. In addition to reporting the news, the *Star* published a variety of features from home decorating to child rearing. And in the meantime, the stormy, independent, dominating Nelson badgered the citizens around him into better architecture, sidewalks, parks, and boulevards.

In the 1890s, during a trip to Europe, his instinctive enjoyment of paintings led him to galleries where he began to buy modestly for himself, and to museums where the thought kept occurring to him that there ought to be a way of sharing his exhilaration with the people back home. He then went to Florence where he met the Pisani family, proprietors of a gallery of copies of European masterpieces, with whom he made an appropriate deal. The Pisani group, along with others that included copies of Dutch paintings the Netherlands Government had exhibited at the Philadelphia Centennial, were sent to Kansas City where they helped establish the Western Gallery of Art which paved the way for the WILLIAM ROCKHILL NELSON GALLERY OF ART AND MARY ATKINS MUSEUM OF FINE ARTS.

By the time of his death, Nelson had made sure that not only his widow, but his daughter and son-in-law (the Kirkwoods), and the family lawyer (Frank Rozelle) were all proselytes to his cause and would add to the money he left some of their own for the establishment of a new museum. In addition, the Nelson residence with its twenty acres was given to the city as a perfect museum site. According to Nelson's wishes, a board of trustees charged with the responsibility of forming a new collection was appointed by the presidents of the state universities of Missouri, Kansas, and Oklahoma.

With more than a million dollars to spend, the board and its advisers went shopping in 1930 both in Europe and the Orient. Meanwhile, the museum building itself was becoming a reality; the Nelson funds having been combined with a trust fund left by Mary Atkins, another local lover of art who dreamed of endowing a museum. The plans called for a single structure, of which the eastern section would be the Atkins Museum.

The building, classical in design, was opened in 1933. The central sculpture hall with its columns of black marble from the Pyrenees took its name from the Kirkwoods, and a court was named after Frank Rozelle.

The galleries themselves are comprehensive not only in exhibits of paintings and sculpture but in the decorative arts as well. Exciting period rooms range from the fourteenth to the nineteenth centuries. On a limestone capital in a Gothic cloister a rare example of twelfth-century French Romanesque sculpture depicts a circle of dancing children. The English pottery collection of Mr. and Mrs. Frank Burnap of Kansas City is a famous one. From ceramics that date back earlier than the sixteenth century, through Lambeth delft and slipware, through eighteenth-century Ralph Wood figurines and Wedgwood, these pieces are more than important; many are unique. Also famous are the galleries of Oriental art which include a seventeenth-century mahogany-walled Hindu Temple Room with a carved ceiling, and one of the most important groups of Indian bronzes in the country. In addition there are Chinese figures made of stone, pottery of the Han Dynasty, and Chinese jade, bronzes, and paintings.

The museum's share of classical, medieval, and Renaissance sculpture is of high quality. Its paintings survey all the important schools from the thirteenth century onward. Exquisite interpretations of the *Madonna and Child* by Hans Memling and Petrus Christus are among the Flemish. Among those representing the Italian are works of Lorenzo di Credi and Veronese, and portraits by Tintoretto, Titian, Bronzino, and Strozzi. El Greco's portrait of *The Penitent Magdalene,* works of Velasquez and Murillo, and Goya's well-known *Portrait of Don Ignazio Omulryan y Rourera* are some that represent the Spanish. Poussin's *The Triumph of Bacchus* (one of several bacchanals commissioned by Cardinal Richelieu, considered one of the best Poussins in America), Chardin's wonderful study of children, *The Bubble Blowers,* a portrait by Ingres of the sculptor Paul Lemoyne, and Gauguin's *Rêverie* are just a few of the French. One of the best known of the American paintings is Raphael Peale's surprisingly modern still life, *After the Bath,* painted in 1823. Two Americans represented thoroughly here are George Inness and George Caleb Bingham. Bingham's *Canvassing for a Vote* shows the mid-century artist functioning at his best as a reporter of the American scene.

Not too far away from the Missouri home of William Rockhill Nelson, American art has been further explored as the result of the love and money of one of Nelson's contemporaries, Mrs. Roland P. Murdock. Kansas' WICHITA ART MUSEUM is a place where John Steuart Curry's *Kansas Cornfield* looks right at home with paintings of Marin, Hopper, Kuhn, and Kuniyoshi. Back again in Missouri, St. Louis' art museum has been dynamically pursuing its policy of representing developments in all the fields of art since 1879.

At the time of the Louisiana Purchase Exposition in 1904, the previously established St. Louis Museum of Fine Arts had already applied to the city for permission to build in Forest Park. When the Exposition management realized that the educational influence of their work could be perpetuated by leaving the museum a permanent building, they co-operated with the city and designed their Palace of Art to be a lasting structure. In 1912, the Museum of Fine Arts was succeeded by the CITY ART MUSEUM OF ST. LOUIS, supported then as now by public funds derived from a special property tax of one fifth of a mill on the dollar.

Sculpture has always had an important place here and whether the visitor's taste is for the Egyptian, Etruscan, classical, Oriental, Renaissance, or contemporary, he is more than likely to find something that suits him. From an early head of Buddha to Rodin's *Despair* to Lipchitz' *The Bathers* to a Moore *Reclining Figure,* the choice is wide.

The period rooms are unusually fine and concentrate on the taste of England, France, and America. The Chinese ceramics and bronzes are of exceptional quality. The medieval decorative arts are beautifully represented by a Gothic court and oak stairway from a house in Morlaix, a paneled oak door that is either French or Flemish, tapestries, stained glass, and metalwork. The decorative arts of the Renaissance are given their due, and the sixteenth-century arms and armor make an outstanding exhibit. The James F. Ballard Oriental rugs are of the fifteenth to nineteenth centuries. The painting collections pay respectful attention to the old masters, include a fine Holbein portrait and a Titian *Ecce Homo,* and trace developments in Europe and America right up to the present. In addition the museum has a regional section that pays tribute, through art, to Mississippi Valley history.

Not too long ago, the City Art Museum made headlines as the result of a stolen Cézanne canvas that was first recovered, then found to contain an extra painting on its reverse side. *The Artist's Sister,* painted between 1867 and 1869, had been loaned to a Cézanne exhibition in France where together with several other works it was abducted by thieves. About eight months later it was found in an abandoned car in Marseilles, out of its frame and slightly damaged. St. Louis' museum director Charles Nagel took it to the laboratory of James Roth, an art conservator, at the William Rockhill Nelson Gallery. Mr. Roth began the job of replacing the torn liner on the back of the canvas and soon discovered beneath a thick layer of glue a portrait of a peasant woman. It was decided that the painting on the front could not be separated from the painting on the back without doing damage to both. And so for a while, until the peasant woman would have to be covered over once again to assure proper care of *The Artist's Sister,* both paintings were exhibited on a special easel that swung from one side to the other. The newly discovered portrait was judged more important historically than artistically, having been painted most likely when Cézanne was in his mid-twenties and just beginning to develop his portrait technique. Nevertheless, it added an estimated $75,000 to the value of the canvas. *The Artist's Sister* itself had been bought by the museum in 1934 for $7500. Including the woman on the back, its estimated value now was $225,000. All in all, its return to St. Louis was cause for a celebration.

A celebration of a very different kind was in order in the neighboring state of Illinois in 1904 when, on the occasion of its twenty-fifth anniversary, the ART INSTITUTE OF CHICAGO noted proudly that it ranked "among the first three or four in the country." Chicago's interest in the arts dated from the founding, shortly after the Civil War, of a school which, according to an early catalogue, featured "work from the human figure" as opposed to the more prevalent and stultifying practice of using only casts as models. These activities, although temporarily interrupted, survived even the great fire of 1871 and a decade later were absorbed by the Art Institute. During its first years, according to the same catalogue, the Institute acquired "a very few good pictures, marbles, and casts." However, by the time of the next major local event, the World's Columbian Exposition of 1893, "the Institute had not only become possessed of valuable collections of casts of sculpture, pictures, metals, antique vases, etc., but had gained the favor of the community. It was prepared, therefore, to take advantage of the opportunity offered by the Columbian Exposition to obtain a footing upon the Lake Front." Funds provided by the Exposition, public subscription and the sale of a previous site made available $648,000 to put up a handsome building to which additions were subsequently made no less than thirty-three times.

While the lake-front structure was rising, two Chicago millionaire businessmen—Charles L. Hutchinson (banking and grain), president of the Institute from the time of its founding, and Martin A. Ryerson (lumber), a most generous patron and donor—went to Italy. Entering the major leagues at a sprint, they spent $200,000 on thirteen old master Dutch paintings (including works of Rembrandt, Rubens, Hals, Holbein, and Van Dyck) from the collection of Prince Demidoff. Ryerson subsequently purchased El Greco's *Assumption of the Virgin* for Chicago and, jumping across the centuries, went on to collect Renoirs and other Impressionists.

Another contributor to the Institute's exceptional Impressionist col-

lection was Mrs. Potter Palmer, who had started buying the works of
Degas, Pissarro, Renoir, and Monet as early as 1889. Berthe Honoré
Palmer, whose husband owned the Palmer House Hotel and a fortune
in real estate, was beautiful, energetic, and intelligent. In preparation
for the Columbian Exposition, of which she was chairman of the Board
of Lady Managers and undisputed queen, she had added an ornate
picture gallery to the already elaborate, turreted "gingerbread castle"
in which the Palmer family dwelt amid velvet, marble, gilt, leather, and
mother-of-pearl. It was expatriate artist Mary Cassatt who led Mrs.
Palmer (and other affluent Americans of her acquaintance) to contemporary French art, and who was therefore indirectly responsible
for providing the Art Institute with many of its most popular works,
among them Renoir's *Two Little Circus Girls* and the *Rower's Lunch*.

One official visitor to the Exposition was the Swedish painter Anders
Zorn, who quickly became accepted into Chicago society. His portrait
of Mrs. Palmer, in the gown and jewels she wore for the opening of the
Exposition, is in the museum; so is an important group of Zorn prints,
collected by industrialist Charles Deering, another friend he made at
this time.

These prints are only a fraction of a huge collection of graphic work
that includes old master drawings of the fifteenth and sixteenth centuries, close to two hundred impressions from plates etched by Rembrandt, a complete set of Van Dyck portrait etchings, an outstanding
group of Whistler etchings and lithographs, and an unusual number
and variety of twentieth-century American prints.

Noteworthy in the decorative arts department is a large selection of
English pottery and porcelain, including Wedgwood, a remarkable
collection of eighteenth-century Toby jugs, and lusterware. A medieval
gallery is furnished with the very fine Lucy Maud Buckingham collection of sculpture, goldsmith work, enamel, miniature painting, textiles, and pottery from this period.

The department of Oriental art presides over a distinguished group
of early (third to fifth century) Chinese ceramics and a large number
of bronzes and fine sculpture, Korean pottery, Cambodian and Indian
sculpture, and important acquisitions of Japanese painting, sculpture,
and minor arts, including illustrations of the entire course of wood-
block printing.

But of all the works in a museum that is still proud to be ranked
among the best in the country, it is the paintings for which the Art Institute of Chicago is most famous. Among them: a roomful of Renoirs,

unique in both number and excellence; substantial numbers of canvases by Monet, Modigliani, and Picasso; a room of works by the American George Inness; Seurat's monumental pointillist masterwork, *Sunday Afternoon on the Island of La Grande Jatte;* and Grant Wood's astringent comment on the farm folk of his native Iowa, *American Gothic.*

Among the socialites from the East who journeyed to Chicago for the opening of the Columbian Exposition in 1893 were Mr. and Mrs. John Lowell (Jack) Gardner of Boston. Mr. Gardner was both a Lowell *and* a Peabody; his wife, née Isabella Stewart, daughter of a wealthy New York family, more capriciously claimed descent from the royal Stuarts, and all the noble Isabellas of Spain and Italy. It was never difficult to shock Boston society. Nonetheless the petite and vivacious Mrs. Gardner worked hard at it, scrubbing the steps of the Church of the Advent during Lent, frolicking at the Boston Zoo with a lion named Rex, flirting openly with all the most desirable men, and (so rumor had it) dallying more privately with several.

In Chicago the Gardners saw *Omnibus,* a painting by Anders Zorn. They inquired for the artist, met him, and purchased his painting for $1600. They patronizingly allowed the *nouveau riche* Mrs. Potter Palmer to entertain them in her new mansion. The next year, during their regular trip abroad, the Gardners met Zorn again, in Venice, where the artist painted "Mrs. Jack."

That year, too, began her association with Bernard Berenson. With the young expert-to-be as her adviser and preceptor, in less than a decade she created a fabulous and unique museum crammed with thousands of beautiful things: paintings, sculptures, furniture, textiles, rare books, vases, and "sundry other objects." When the incredible Venetian palazzo began rising, hidden by high walls, on a one-time marsh known as The Fenway, curious Bostonians could only crane their necks and speculate about what was going on.

Both Berenson and the ISABELLA STEWART GARDNER MUSEUM are primarily associated with the Italian Renaissance. One of the scholar's early acquisitions for his patroness was *The Rape of Europa* by Titian, among the most celebrated Italian works in this country and at the time of its arrival undoubtedly the greatest. (Painted for Philip II of Spain when the prolific master was eighty-five, it became one of the most copied pictures of all time: it was incorporated into the background of a painting by Velasquez, copied by Rubens, and inspired

Watteau's treatment of the same episode. Van Dyck copied the Rubens copy, and a preliminary sketch can be seen on a table near the Titian. Nearby is a bronze plaque, *The Rape of Europa,* which the artist Paul Manship gave to Mrs. Gardner.) In the Titian Room are other distinguished works: a bronze bust of *Bindo Altoviti* by Cellini, and a portrait of Philip IV by Velasquez.

The Raphael Room features that master's portrait of *Count Tommaso Inghirami* and an early *Pietà,* along with Botticelli's *Tragedy of Lucretia* and some of the most opulent fifteenth- and sixteenth-century furnishings ever to depart their native land.

Other noted works to be seen in Fenway Court include a *Madonna and Child* of Zurbarán, Masaccio's *Young Man in a Scarlet Turban,* a Piero della Francesca fresco of *Hercules,* the *Madonna and Child of the Eucharist* by Botticelli, *The Concert* by Vermeer, and several Rembrandts, including two subjects unusual for him, *Landscape with Obelisk* and *Storm on the Sea of Galilee.* Among the later artists represented are Turner, Corot, Degas, Manet, Matisse, and Sargent. These and her many other treasures were placed by Mrs. Gardner in a highly personal arrangement, with little regard to their chronological or national relationships. (The museum's handbook gives guidance through the maze.)

Her work virtually completed in 1902, she lived on in her Boston palazzo until her death in 1924. In her will she provided that "no works of art shall be placed therein for exhibition other than such as I, or the Isabella Stewart Gardner Museum in The Fenway, Incorporated, own or have contracted for at my death." Mrs. Jack thought of everything, and the visitor to her home today still sees it exactly as it was during the last years of her life, when she was a beautiful and alert invalid, living parsimoniously in the splendid setting she had created.

In her will, flowers and music, which she considered indispensable, were ensured a permanent place in her museum. In vases throughout the palazzo and in planned profusion in a tiled, glass-roofed interior courtyard are plants and floral arrangements provided throughout the year by the museum's greenhouse, two head gardeners and four assistants. Music can be heard every afternoon in the concert hall on the second floor where the acoustics are enhanced by ten sixteenth-century Flemish tapestries that line the walls.

Sargent painted two portraits of Mrs. Gardner, one when the subject was eighty-two. The other, done many years earlier, of the seductive-looking young Isabella with her beautiful pearl necklace worn around her narrow waist, caused such a scandal that Mr. Gardner forbade its display. His obedient wife complied, but with becoming vanity saw to its exhibition after her death. It hangs in the Gothic Room, near the chapel in which an Anglican high mass is celebrated every year on April 14, the birthday of the irrepressible provider of all this bounty.

By the time the death of its creator froze the Isabella Stewart Gardner Museum for posterity, Bostonians had been flocking to the MUSEUM OF FINE ARTS for nearly five decades. World-renowned for its classical and Oriental collections, the Fine Arts pioneered in the appointment of scholar-specialists as curators and in providing docents for the visiting public. The first building, at Copley Square, was opened to the public on the centennial anniversary of the signing of the Declaration of Independence. By 1899, however, the directors had the foresight to realize that more extensive facilities would be needed to ensure the institution's future growth, and a twelve-acre site was purchased. Ten years later, at a total cost of close to $3,000,000, the most carefully planned museum building in the country was completed. In the interval the architects and directors had spent months touring over one hundred museums and galleries in thirty European cities. A temporary building had been erected in which experiments with gallery lighting were carried on for two years. Even wall colors and textures were tested. The art world held its collective breath, waiting to see the result of all this planning. It was not disappointed. A visiting critic, expressing the general reaction, hailed the new structure as "one more monumental edifice [added] to the lengthening list of the world's great art museums." He went on to describe the "Boston Plan" in which the museum "is divided in segments to accommodate departments which are structurally separate, each forming a museum complete in itself. The upper or main exhibition floor contains the cream of each collection, and the lower floor holds the research or study collections, more comprehensive and more compactly installed. More attention has been given to the lighting than to any [other] single detail . . . and each room is supplied with an amount and kind of light, falling in a direction appropriate to the objects displayed."

Highest praise was given to "the Chinese and Japanese art collection . . . unequalled elsewhere." Arranged in galleries opening off a charming Japanese garden court, the Oriental display provided "a most satisfying atmosphere of harmony and complete reposefulness. It is not often that one feels that a given museum room is just right, that there is nothing left to be done in the way of improvement, that it is complete, final, a perfect expression of the spirit of the art of a nation or of a period; but . . . this may be said of the Oriental wing as a whole. The working out of the 'Boston Plan,' so far as the Oriental department is concerned, is already a triumphant success."

Almost as remarkable as the building itself is the fact that, of the nation's three most important art museums, the Fine Arts alone was financed without the help of municipal funds or the largesse of a small group of millionaires. Its first gift of money appeared while it was being chartered, when someone discovered that a fund for a statue of the orator Edward Everett had been oversubscribed to the extent of $7500. The sum was turned over to the museum's trustees; and subscriptions, gifts, and endowments have carried on from there. At one time, after the death of a local schoolmaster, the museum was surprised to learn that he had quietly willed to it a gift of $93,000.

Many great works of art gravitated to it in similar fortuitous fashion. A number of paintings that were borrowed from the Boston Athenaeum (including Gilbert Stuart's twin oval portraits of George and Martha Washington) for the Fine Arts' first exhibit, are now on permanent loan. Other portraits of the Revolutionary period are on indefinite loan from the city. When Boston merchants and scholars traveling to Japan in the 1880s brought back a wealth of Oriental art (it was a time when the Japanese, anxious to become a "modern" nation, were more than willing to sell the artistic treasures of their past), their vast purchases of sculpture, lacquer work, arms, ceramics, prints and paintings were put on view. Subscriptions made it possible for the museum to buy some of these items, but many of them were placed on permanent loan and subsequently became gifts. With the addition of excellent examples of the arts of China, Korea, and Central Asia, Boston could glory in an Oriental department that would be just as highly regarded in the years to come as when its acquisitions were first shown.

The renowned Egyptian collection consists primarily of objects assigned to the museum by the Egyptian government as its share of artifacts dug up during Boston-financed excavations at the Great Pyramids of Giza. This venture yielded such important finds that the collection in Boston is second only to that in Cairo.

The Fine Arts' classical collection, which shares American honors with that of the Metropolitan Museum of Art, was built up largely during one decade (1895 through 1904) of systematic buying. Many of the marbles are original Greek works of art, as opposed to Roman copies which are more frequently seen. The bronzes, engraved gems, and coins are also from the hands of Greek artists. Virtually every style of Greek ceramic ware from the prehistoric Minoan age on can be seen in the pottery collection, including an exceptional group of red-figured vases from fifth-century Athens. Also from the Golden Age of Greece is a large rectangular piece, decorated on three sides with carvings. This so-called Boston Relief is invariably compared to the similarly shaped Ludovisi Throne in the National Museum in Rome. Both were found in the same area, and it is believed that they were the decorative ends of a long narrow altar.

Boston also has what is generally considered to be the finest representation of the arts of India in the United States, and its Indian paintings, covering five millennia from 3000 B.C. to the nineteenth century, have been termed the most important anywhere. The museum's excavations in the Indus Valley in 1935 uncovered the remains of a culture that was previously unknown and provided it with the only examples outside of India of the art of this prehistoric civilization.

In the decorative arts wing a room (1694) from Britain's Hamilton Palace and a Louis XVI salon of about 1760 can be contrasted with a group of American rooms spanning the same period. The entire framework of an Ipswich house, and a room from the West Boxford home of a well-to-do family, show the earliest architecture of Massachusetts and now rare seventeenth-century American furnishings. And the work of Paul Revere, who was a master silversmith before he became a legend, is an important part of an American silverware collection that dates from 1640.

Boston's museum continues to be enriched by generous Bostonians. Two of them, Maxim and Martha Codman Karolik, have spent more than thirty years systematically acquiring examples of American furniture of the Colonial and early Federal periods, and paintings, drawings, and water colors of 1800 to 1875. The result is the most complete representation of the work of American artists and artisans from this time to be seen anywhere. Their aim has been "to make a collection not of 'Americana' for the antiquarian, but of American art for the nation."

Of exceptional importance also are the Near Eastern collections, the textiles and fashions, and the prints. The painting collection is rich in Early American portraits, Venetian and Siennese works, eighteenth-century British works, and nineteenth-century French Barbizon and Impressionist canvases. From Spain there are a series of Catalan chapel frescoes of the thirteenth century, and works by Zurbarán, El Greco, and Velasquez. A brief list of famous paintings here would include: Rogier van der Weyden's *St. Luke Painting the Virgin,* Velasquez' *Don Baltazar Carlos and His Dwarf,* Millet's *The Sower,* Renoir's *La Bal à Bougival,* Gauguin's monumental *Where do we come from? What are we? Whither are we going?,* and a fairly recent acquisition by the Norwegian artist Edvard Munch, *The Voice.*

Near the center of Massachusetts is the WORCESTER ART MUSEUM which in 1948 celebrated its fiftieth birthday with the publication of *Art through Fifty Centuries,* a guide to its enviable collections. Yet this museum had spent the first ten years of its existence with scarcely an acquisition to its name. The Worcester story begins back in the Gay Nineties when the museum was only a gleam in the eye of Mr. Stephen Salisbury III, whose family had prospered here since colonial days. Inviting some prominent fellow townsmen to his home, he promised to donate land and $100,000 to be divided equally between building and maintenance funds, if they would carry it from there. The proposition was accepted and a museum corporation was formed. Mr. Salisbury had taken the initiative, and the people of Worcester were not far behind. In sums ranging from five cents to $3000, they succeeded in nearly doubling the building fund. And in May 1898, a handsome Italian Renaissance structure was opened for the display of a loan exhibition.

When the town faced the problem of filling what one visitor referred to as "a treasure house without treasures," the citizens were roused once again. It was then fashionable to display casts of statues and copies of paintings. (Only a few years earlier, Congress had seriously considered a scheme to bring to America the art wonders of the ages by reconstructing in Washington, on a 62-acre site, full-sized replicas of famous monuments and buildings from every part of the world, and to fill their interior halls and walls with reproductions of celebrated works. Grandiosely disregarding anything that even vaguely made sense, "the United States was to be represented by an elaborate Acropolis in true Greek style, with a model of the Parthenon, which, in characteristic American fashion, was to be much larger than the original.") And so, thinking *à la mode,* Worcester's lawyers gave their museum a cast of a statue of Socrates; the Quinsigamond Boat Club presented *The Warrior* in facsimile; a woman's club offered a replica of the *Victory of Samothrace;* some factory workers chipped in to provide a version of Mercury; and the Foresters contributed a likeness of the tomb of Lorenzo di Medici.

But the museum's board had bigger and better things in view. Taking advantage of its location near a resort area, and of the fact that good paintings were easier to borrow from galleries during the summer (a slow season for art in big cities), exhibitions were arranged for every July and August. In 1908 it was decided to purchase one work or more from each exhibition instead of awarding the customary prizes. The first two seasons saw the acquisition of nine works, including a *Mother and Child* by Mary Cassatt. In the meantime Salisbury died a bachelor, having named the museum his heir to nearly $4,000,000. And from then on buying was done on a substantial scale.

The Worcester Museum has been particularly fortunate in its directors. Francis Henry Taylor spent nine busy years here before going on to head the Metropolitan in New York in 1940, and returned briefly for the two years preceding his death in 1957. His successor, Daniel Catton Rich, was formerly director of the Art Institute of Chicago.

It was during Taylor's first incumbency that Worcester's holdings outgrew their quarters. In 1933 a major addition to the building provided for the chronological display of the collection in twenty galleries surrounding a large courtyard. The anniversary handbook follows this orderly sequence in describing works which range from Mesopotamian and Egyptian examples of the third millennium through classical, medieval, Italian, and Northern Renaissance art, to European paintings of the seventeenth through the twentieth centuries, Early American through contemporary American paintings, and Asiatic, Islamic, and pre-Columbian objects.

Universally admired are the Antioch mosaics set in the floor of the central courtyard; an entire chapter house from a French Benedictine monastery; early Italian Renaissance frescoes; a group of Persian textiles, miniatures and illuminated manuscripts; *The Discovery of Honey* by Piero di Cosimo and *The Rest on the Flight into Egypt* by Flemish painter Quentin Massys; portraits by Hogarth (of country squire William James and his wife) and Gainsborough (of his two daughters); and the collection of original graphic work by Picasso, Braque, Demuth, and others commissioned by the *Dial*, the "little magazine" that gave voice to the literary and artistic ferment of the twenties.

In direct contrast to the Worcester Museum, which took years to reach its maturity, is the STERLING AND FRANCINE CLARK ART INSTITUTE of Williamstown, which was given, ready-made, to this college community in the northwest corner of Massachusetts in 1955. Mr. Clark, whose collecting spanned the half-century preceding his death in 1956, was an avid purchaser of works of nineteenth-century French artists—Academic, Barbizon, and Impressionist—and American artists, of whom Homer and Sargent were particular favorites. There are over thirty Renoirs, eleven Corots, nine bronzes of Degas as well as many of his paintings, prints and drawings, and several Lautrecs. Earlier European painting is not neglected: an *Enthroned Madonna with Angels* attributed to Piero della Francesca and a *Portrait of a Man* by Hans Memling are two highlights. There is also a fine collection of eighteenth- and nineteenth-century furniture and sculpture, and some English, French, Dutch, and American silverware that would be exciting anywhere. And to commemorate Mr. Clark's interest in horses, there are equine subjects immortalized both on canvas and in bronze by Degas and Remington, and on canvas by Winslow Homer.

New England's oldest public museum began when Daniel Wadsworth included a Gallery of Fine Arts in the library building he erected not far from the State Capitol in Hartford. The WADSWORTH ATHENEUM opened in the summer of 1844 to display five Revolutionary scenes by the recently deceased Colonel John Trumbull and some works purchased from the recently defunct New York Academy of Fine Arts. Four years later Wadsworth himself died, and to the Atheneum went his collection of American paintings which included six more Trumbulls and five works by contemporary Hudson River artist Thomas Cole. The second half of the century saw little activity at the Atheneum, but beginning in 1893 things began to hum; and they haven't quieted down yet.

Fortunately for Hartford, John Pierpont Morgan was born there. One of Morgan's cousins who remained in the Connecticut town while J.P. built his legend was the Reverend Dr. Francis Goodwin. When Goodwin was president of the Atheneum's board of trustees in 1893, Morgan provided half the financing for an addition to the building. (The next addition was built to contain Elizabeth Hart Jarvis Colt's bequest of decorative arts, paintings, and firearms in memory of her husband, revolver inventor Samuel Colt.)

The Morgan Memorial Wing, erected by J.P. in memory of his father, was the next addition after that. Then, four years after J.P. died in 1913, J.P., Jr., presented a multitude of objects from J.P., Sr.'s famous collection—seventeenth-century silver-gilt, eighteenth-century porcelain, Italian Renaissance *objets d'art,* and eighty-six classical bronzes. Less than a decade later J.P., Jr., followed this munificent gift with another—the American furniture and household objects systematically assembled by Wallace Nutting, a retired minister whose pioneer collecting made him an authority in this field.

The arrival of the Morgan treasures marked a turning point for the Atheneum. Almost a century old, it suddenly found itself the envy of the art world. And it began living up to its new reputation, under the leadership of its flamboyant new director, A. Everett ("Chick") Austin, Jr. He arrived the same year (1927) as the Sumner Fund for the purchase of paintings, which enabled him to go on a shopping spree that lasted until he left for Sarasota in 1944.

But Austin was a frugal shopper. Because many of the baroque works were not yet fashionable in the late twenties and thirties, and were consequently still moderately priced, he set his sights on those more readily available masters of the sixteenth and seventeenth centuries—Caravaggio and Juan de Valdés Leal (both rarely seen in this country), Rubens, Poussin, Murillo, and Panini—ultimately building up the first, and one of the best, such collections we have. At the same time, still frugally, he was buying the moderns—Miró, Gabo, Arp, Calder, Hopper, Pevsner. In 1931 he held the first comprehensive exhibit of Surrealist art in America, and three Dalis were affixed to the Atheneum's walls before the decade was out. In the mid-thirties, when Piet Mondrian's *Composition in Blue and White* joined the growing company in Hartford, Austin wrote to his friend, the art critic James Thrall Soby:

"I went to Mondrian's Paris studio and there were all those arrangements of rectangular and square forms in primary colors. They had always seemed limited in scope and meaning. But the longer I stayed, the more convinced I became that Mondrian was a true artist, intense, dedicated and on the track of enduring discoveries. I bought this picture from him. It cost almost $400."

While the Atheneum's accessions catalogue expanded, its halls expanded too, thanks to the Samuel Putnam Avery fund. In 1934 the Avery Wing (its discreet exterior, designed to blend with the diverse earlier segments of the Atheneum, concealed a striking inner courtyard, a fully equipped theater, and the most modern galleries in the country at that time) was opened with the first Picasso retrospective in America and the world première of the Gertrude Stein–Virgil Thomson opera, *Four Saints in Three Acts*. A quarter of a century later, the art dealer Julien Levy recalled the première:

"I remember the tiring train ride to Hartford, wondering what to expect . . . men changing from traveling clothes to white tie and tails in the lavatory of the Heublein, and the late Francis Henry Taylor, Austin's young rival in the museum world, in grey flannel underwear dourly commenting on the 'unfeasability of Chick.' "

The New York *Herald Tribune's* Lucius Beebe wrote, at the time, of "bedlam . . . as . . . Julien Levy [and a friend] burst into unabashed tears because they 'didn't know anything so beautiful could be done in America,' " and that at least one member of the audience "smashed his opera hat and howled for Mr. Thomson . . . tore open his collar and shouted for Mr. Austin."

While the cognoscenti applauded Austin's ventures into the *avant-garde* and the performing arts, there was no such approval from the citizens of Hartford. Their disapproval, in fact, terminated one of his most exciting projects before it even began. Austin had conceived the idea of importing George Balanchine, the last ballet master of Serge Diaghilev, and establishing a resident ballet company and school at the Atheneum. As Lincoln Kirstein, now general director of the New York City Ballet, recently pointed out, Austin "was the first person to think he could find institutional support for an endowed ballet company which would give, in a museum, performances equalling in intrinsic interest and excellence the important objects of a museum's permanent historic collection."

So Balanchine came to Hartford in 1933 and, as Kirstein recollected, "flatly refused to have anything to do with a plan which involved non-profits. America was a rich country. This Museum bore the Morgan name. Was it not proper that an artist be allowed more than a mere pittance?" Balanchine was concerned less with personal remuneration than with his conviction, gained from experience, that the "prestige and potential of the provinces" could be measured only in monetary terms. But the *coup de grâce* came "from quite another direction. Two charming sisters of a certain age appeared in an Italian operatic rage. They had been teaching dancing for years in Hartford. Mr. Austin, who should [have been] supporting the local dance teacher, was attempting to put them out of business by hiring a Russian (presumably a Bolshevik, as well). The authorities would not hear of this; indeed, the newspapers promptly published the story. That did it. One train ride back to New York was longer than that from Moscow to Vladivostock. . . . The whole notion . . . was mad . . . [but] who can say whether or not Balanchine would ever have come to New York rather than pursuing a logical European career" had it not been for this?

And so Austin set in motion the series of events that would culminate in America's possessing a classical dance company equal to the best in the world. By the end of 1934 the Atheneum's auditorium saw what Kirstein calls the "relatively modest but not entirely inauspicious debut" of Balanchine's new New York company. And it purchased, through the Sumner Fund, the collection of ballet designs that had been bequeathed by Diaghilev to his leading male dancer, Serge Lifar, at his death. Most of the more than 150 drawings, water colors, and oils—by Braque, Léger, Max Ernst, Léon Bakst, Derain, di Chirico, Gris and others—were set and costume designs for Diaghilev's Ballet Russe productions.

Even after Austin's departure exciting things kept happening in Hartford. And impressive displays of Impressionist and Postimpressionist paintings, American glass, American painting of the nineteenth and twentieth centuries, pre-Columbian figures, pottery and silver, and modern sculpture help keep the Atheneum a lively place.

Much more staid than the Wadsworth is Manchester, New Hampshire's, fine CURRIER GALLERY OF ART. The paintings range from Perugino to Picasso, and with pardonable chauvinism include Charles Sheeler's tribute to the *Amoskeag Canal* that runs alongside the city's textile mills. The small but select decorative arts displays also have chauvinistic leanings; New England silverware and New Hampshire furniture are emphasized.

Further south in New England, where the diversified industries include jewelry making, there is a famous school of design. The constitution of the Rhode Island School of Design, opened in Providence in 1877, makes clear that, from the outset, high on its list of aims was the exhibition of works of art. The founders fully realized that an institution giving instruction in the fine and industrial arts but lacking a museum where good examples of these arts could be studied would be as much handicapped as a university without a library. Three years later, therefore, the RHODE ISLAND SCHOOL OF DESIGN MUSEUM OF ART was established.

It was the idea of a gentleman of taste, Charles L. Pendleton, to buy furniture and decorative objects that a local gentleman of equal taste might have chosen for his own home in the late eighteenth century. This collection, given to the school in 1904, decorates the interior of a Georgian house that epitomizes Rhode Island Colonial architecture. Adding a larger building to this house in 1926, the school was better able to accommodate its growing museum.

Classical, medieval, and Renaissance objects—jewelry, marbles, bronzes, paintings—can be counted upon to inspire visitors as well as the school's student body. So can the nineteenth-century French paintings and drawings—Van Gogh, Cézanne, Degas, Lautrec among them. And a changing display from the Abby Aldrich Rockefeller gift of Japanese prints is just one of the rewarding aspects of the Oriental galleries. This museum owns much, from various fields. Its acquisitions, rich and beautiful, are also beautifully displayed.

New England has an exceptional concentration of college museums. The Yale University Art Gallery, the oldest university art museum in the country, was started in 1832 as the Trumbull Gallery featuring paintings by the Revolutionary War colonel. When it acquired a modern building in 1953, it at last gained adequate display space for its Early American paintings, furniture, and silver; its Near and Far Eastern art and textiles; its Société Anonyme Collection of modern art; its Linton Collection of African sculpture; its Stoddard Collection of Greek and Roman vases; its medieval sculpture; its prints; and the Jarves Collection of Italian Renaissance paintings which came to Yale in the 1870s after Boston's Fine Arts and New York's Metropolitan turned it down.

Harvard University presides over a complex of museums. Best known is the Fogg, whose acquisitions include drawings (Blake, Dürer, Watteau, Degas), Far Eastern art, Egyptian and Greek antiquities, and collections illustrating the history of Western art. Harvard's Busch-Reisinger Museum of Germanic Culture, founded in 1902, covers the art of Germany from medieval days on, and owns a striking group of modern works by Nolde, Barlach, Arp, and others. In the Peabody Museum of Archaeology and Ethnology, Harvard has a repository for the display and study of a multitude of artifacts from Africa, the Pacific, prehistoric Europe and pre-Columbian America.

One of the most remarkable school museums, belonging not to a college but to a preparatory school, is the Addison Gallery of Phillips Academy at Andover, Massachusetts, which has been in the vanguard of American art since it opened in 1931. Among the artists represented are Eakins, Hopper, Bellows, Prendergast, Shahn, and Hans Hofmann. And there is Winslow Homer's *West Wind,* generally considered his masterpiece.

The Smith College Museum of Art has been called by Walter Pach a "superbly developed college museum, containing examples of Egyptian, Greek, Gothic and Renaissance art [and] European and American painting." It is the oldest and largest such institution maintained by a woman's school.

The Lawrence Art Museum of Williams College at Williamstown has important groups of Spanish painting in addition to Spanish and Italian furniture, Oriental art, medieval and Renaissance painting, Roman glass, and Egyptian, Greek, Etruscan, Peruvian, and Mayan pottery.

Amherst, Mount Holyoke, Dartmouth, and Wellesley also add to the treasures owned by the colleges of New England.

Official cognizance of the relationship between the American people and the art of Europe was taken in 1941, just nine months before entry into the Second World War committed America irrevocably to an international outlook. The occasion was the opening in Washington of the NATIONAL GALLERY OF ART.

Four years earlier, Andrew W. Mellon sent a letter to President Franklin D. Roosevelt that said: "My dear Mr. President: Over a period of many years I have been acquiring important and rare paintings and sculpture with the idea that ultimately they would become the property of the people of the United States and be made available to them in a national gallery to be maintained in the city of Washington. . . ."

This letter was not entirely unexpected. Two years before it was written, the government had confronted the reticent and enormously rich Mr. Mellon with a $3,089,000 claim for outstanding taxes. It was then revealed, in his defense, that more than that amount had been put—in the form of paintings—into the A. W. Mellon Educational and Charitable Trust, a tax-exempt foundation set up for a variety of purposes that included the facilitating of his eventual gift. Neglecting to inform the Bureau of Internal Revenue of his magnanimous maneuver must have seemed expedient, since these large expenditures for art were made while Mellon was officially coping, as Secretary of the Treasury under President Hoover, with the worst depression in the nation's history. The claim against him was dropped, but his intention was hardly a secret after that.

(This was not the first time the Treasury Department had had a run-in with the owner of a collection that would one day benefit the public. In the early years of the century Isabella Stewart Gardner found it necessary to restrict her purchasing after having been compelled to pay an import duty of $150,000 for a group of objects valued at $82,000. Other collectors resorted to smuggling in order to escape these crippling duties. An extra exhaust pipe attached to an early automobile became a successful hiding place for some Van Dycks purchased in Europe by the Philadelphia trolley-car magnate P. A. B. Widener. Ironically, or justly, these paintings are now in the National Gallery.)

According to S. N. Behrman, the true originator of the idea for the National Gallery was Joseph Duveen, the fabulous art dealer, who "sold Mellon art on a grander and grander scale," and whose efforts culminated in "the largest transaction ever consummated in the world of art." He sold Mellon forty-two paintings for $21,000,000 at one fell swoop. It had not been an easy deal to consummate. The imaginative Duveen had rented the apartment below Mellon's in Washington and, after hanging his paintings, departed for New York leaving Mellon the key. Visiting the apartment with increasing frequency, Mellon grew accustomed to its face, and Duveen made his sale.

In this history-making purchase Mellon broke his own record set a few years earlier when he spent close to $7,000,000 for twenty-one paintings sold by the Hermitage in Soviet Russia. Mellon was far from an easy mark. But he recognized quality and was willing to pay well for it. And quality he certainly got from the Hermitage—Raphael's *Alba Madonna* and *Saint George and the Dragon,* Botticelli's *The Adoration of the Magi,* Jan van Eyck's *The Annunciation,* and Titian's *Venus with a Mirror* were all in the lot, and are among the favorite paintings of visitors to the National Gallery.

Mellon's gift of about 150 works ranges from the thirteenth through the mid-nineteenth centuries. John Walker, director of the National Gallery, describes them as "supreme achievements of painting and sculpture." He adds that "Mellon set himself the task of acquiring nothing but masterpieces [and] he succeeded. If the Gallery had only the one collection it would rank high among museums in America." In *The Proud Possessors,* Aline Saarinen points out that the building, the endowment, the paintings, and the sculpture constituted the largest gift ever given to a government by an individual. This beneficence cost approximately $50,000,000.

Behrman credits Duveen with selecting John Russell Pope to design the National Gallery building; with talking Mellon into using marble instead of the ubiquitous limestone; and, after the Gallery was well on its way toward becoming a *fait accompli,* with persuading the five-and-ten-cent-store tycoon, Samuel H. Kress, to give up the scheme of building his own museum in New York in favor of adding his collection to Mellon's in the nation's capital.

Kress had begun his chain of popular stores in Memphis in 1896. Recognition of a commercial need had not only brought its profits but made possible his decision, while traveling through Europe on business, to emulate an Italian count who owned a substantial art collection. A few years later he met Bernard Berenson in Florence, made a lifelong friend, and decided to specialize in Italian painting and sculpture. Concentrating first on the Italian Renaissance, he later broadened his interests to include Flemish, Dutch, German, Spanish, and French masterpieces as well. Just when his expanded collection was about to burst out of the confines of his New York house, he was offered the marble halls of the new National Gallery. But even before the Gallery could open its doors, one of its Kress acquisitions was shown to the public. Perhaps to honor the approaching Christmas season, perhaps to inspire generosity on the part of prospective customers—whatever the reason, a window of the merchant's largest New York emporium, on Thirty-ninth Street and Fifth Avenue, was temporarily emptied of its display of baubles in order to receive Giorgione's *Adoration of the Shepherds.*

Kress continued to expand his collection, and by the time the National Gallery was fifteen years old his gifts occupied close to a third of the available display space. The collection was further increased by the Samuel H. Kress Foundation headed by Rush H. Kress, a younger brother. And it soon became necessary for the Gallery to refine this magnificent assemblage. "Only the examples of painting and sculpture most needed there" were to be retained, according to director John Walker. Those not needed were given back to the Foundation, where they became available for a new and unique project: donation to museums throughout the country.

The choice of museums receiving these gifts, John Walker has stated, "was determined by the very simple and human desire to make some return to certain cities for all they have done for the Kress Company." The eighteen cities so favored were Allentown, Pennsylvania; Atlanta, Georgia; Birmingham, Alabama; Columbia, South Carolina; Denver, Colorado; El Paso, Texas; Honolulu, Hawaii; Houston, Texas; Kansas City, Missouri; Memphis, Tennessee; Miami, Florida; New Orleans, Louisiana; Portland, Oregon; Raleigh, North Carolina; San Francisco, California; Seattle, Washington; Tucson, Arizona; and Tulsa, Oklahoma. The recipients had to promise only that the entire collection would be on permanent exhibition, well lighted and effectively displayed, in fireproof, air-conditioned, and humidity-controlled galleries. The importance of the gift made it necessary for many of them to build a new wing and made it possible for some of them to raise enough money for an entire new building.

The director and staff of each museum worked with the Foundation's art experts in choosing works that would go into their collections. Everything was planned for. The Foundation provided all necessary cleaning and restoring of the paintings; restoration was performed on hundreds of Italian Renaissance frames; each regional collection was unveiled with formal ceremony; and each was provided with its own catalogue. In addition, preparation of a seven-volume catalogue of the combined Kress Collection was begun. The first published volume is *Art Treasures for America: An Anthology of Paintings and Sculpture in the Samuel H. Kress Collection.*

When all of this was done, there were still excess treasures. These were grouped together into small study collections and distributed among our colleges and universities.

In the meantime, the National Gallery had acquired three more major collections, those of P. A. B. Widener, Chester Dale, and Lessing J. Rosenwald.

The Widener group, assembled by P. A. B. and Joseph E., his son, contain some of the best-known works in the Gallery. The Wideners were among the earliest Americans to take an interest in the Impressionists. Their acquisitiveness extended, however, to Chinese porcelain, medieval tapestry, ceramics and jewelry of the Italian Renaissance, and eighteeth-century French furniture. And they were not immune to the appeal the great masters had held for their fellow millionaires. Their collection was described by David E. Finley, Mellon's long-time art adviser and the first director of the National Gallery, as being "notable not only for the variety and beauty of the works of art which it contains but for the faultless discrimination shown in the choice of each object." The more than one hundred paintings include Vermeer's *A Woman Weighing Gold,* Bellini's *Feast of the Gods* (with a background later repainted by Titian), a good number of Rembrandts (*The Mill* among them), El Greco's *The Virgin with Saint Inés,* Manet's *Dead Toreador,* and Degas' *The Races.*

Chester Dale was a collector of post-1800 French painting, whose gift brought important canvases by Corot, Cézanne, Renoir, Monet, Gauguin, Van Gogh, and others to Washington. Most of the twentieth-century artists Dale invested in, however, came to Washington not as part of this gift but "on indefinite loan"; the Gallery trustees having ruled that work by men living, or dead less than twenty years, may not be admitted as permanent acquisitions.

The National Gallery's graphic arts collection, one of the most important in the world, was built around Lessing Rosenwald's accumulation over the years of more than 20,000 prints, etchings, drawings, water colors, and illuminated manuscript pages, a substantial nucleus for a department that would before too long acquire twice that number of items.

As the dwindling supply of master paintings available for purchase and tighter European export restrictions began to make it virtually impossible for later American collectors to duplicate the achievements of the great earlier ones, attention was slowly turned to the work of America's primitive artists, which within the last few decades has become the focus of several major collections. The most ardent enthusiasts of American primitive painting are Edgar William and Bernice Chrysler Garbisch whose collection of over two thousand items is the largest in existence and is still growing. In 1953 they selected a group of these works by untrained, exuberant eighteenth- and nineteenth-century artists and artisans and gave it to the National Gallery. Following the example set by Kress, Colonel and Mrs. Garbisch made plans to give gifts to other museums throughout the country as well.

Of the American master paintings in the National Gallery, a partial list would include Winslow Homer's *Breezing Up,* Bellows' *Both Members of This Club,* Eakins' *The Biglen Brothers Racing,* and works by Whistler, Cassatt, Sargent, Ryder, Luks, and Henri. An early canvas by George Inness, *The Lackawanna Valley,* had been commissioned by the Delaware, Lackawanna and Western Railroad for use in an advertisement. Although at the time only one track entered the new roundhouse of which the road was so proud, Inness was asked to depict several more that the directors were hoping to add. The painting would have been lost if the artist and his wife had not, quite accidentally, discovered it about thirty years later in a used-furniture shop in Mexico City. After buying it back Inness asked his wife: "Do you remember, Lizzie, how mad I was because they made me paint the name on the engine?"

Copley, West, and Sully are some earlier American masters represented in the National Gallery. And there are more than forty works by Gilbert Stuart, including *The Skater,* a full-length portrait that is credited with having made his reputation in London. He had been commissioned to do a likeness of one William Grant of Scotland, but because the day of the first sitting was quite cold, Mr. Grant suggested they go skating instead. And Stuart was inspired with a new approach to his subject. When Stuart's colleagues first saw the graceful figure cut by Grant on canvas, they could hardly contain their surprise. "Before that time," a contemporary London critic reported them as saying, Stuart "made a tolerable likeness of a face but as to the figure he could not get below the fifth button."

There is much, much more in the huge marble building that boasts five and a half air-conditioned acres of exhibition space, and the Gallery does much more than merely exhibit. It has its own orchestra, which gives late afternoon concerts every Sunday from September through June, and its spring Festival of American Music frequently premières works by contemporary composers.

The National Gallery of Art is a bureau of the Smithsonian Institution, but it is administered autonomously by its own board of trustees. There are three other art museums under the wing of the Smithsonian. Two of them, the NATIONAL PORTRAIT GALLERY and the NATIONAL COLLECTION OF FINE ARTS, have for many years been inadequately housed in the Natural History Building of the Smithsonian's National Museum. Both are moving to the 120-year-old Patent Office Building where a $7,000,000 renovation is making the interior as practical as the exterior is picturesque.

The Portrait Gallery, which was chartered by Congress in 1962, moves with a nucleus of 250 works to which it expects to add, from the National Gallery, about fifty paintings whose interest is more chauvinistic than artistic. Gifts and purchases will provide for the expansion of a collection of portraits "of men and women who have made significant contributions to the history, development and culture of the people of the United States."

The National Collection, which has held stepchild status for many years, is looking forward to expanding its activities and more effectively displaying its inventory of over six thousand objects. In its new galleries it will survey American art, display recent art from around the world, and build a collection of contemporary American work including decorative arts and crafts. Although the National Collection's existence was provided for in the act of 1846 that established the Smithsonian, its acquisitions arrived haphazardly. It was not until 1906 that the first sizable gift of paintings was received, following the death of Harriet Lane Johnston, who had been official hostess during the administration of her uncle and guardian, President James Buchanan. The belle of her uncle's inaugural ball had spent her formative years with him in London when he was ambassador there, and this evidently determined her taste, for the finest of her small group of paintings are the English portraits by Reynolds, Romney, Hoppner, Lawrence, and others.

The most substantial gift to come the Collection's way arrived in 1929 from John Gellatly, an eccentric millionaire whose fortune allegedly began with the sale of some property owned by his first wife. At the age of seventy-six he gave sixteen hundred items of decorative arts, including about 150 paintings, to the Smithsonian. His gift was valued at $5,000,000. For himself he left only a spartan annuity of $3000, as his thirty-three-year-old second wife discovered soon after their marriage a few months later. Despite her attempts, both before and after her husband's death in 1931, to recover what she considered rightfully her own, the Gellatly Collection remained government property and the highlight of this museum. Works by American painters contemporary with the donor are here in wholesale lots—twelve Twachtmans, fifteen Hassams, fifteen Ryders, seventeen Dewings, and twenty-three Thayers. Gellatly was equally fond of ancient Egyptian and Italian Renaissance jewelry; antique glass from Egypt, Syria, Greece, and Rome; and sculpture and stained leaded glass of the twelfth through fifteenth centuries.

The fourth art collection under the Smithsonian's wing is the FREER GALLERY OF ART. It was the first important offer of art the Regents of the Smithsonian received. And it took them from December 1904 to January 1906 to decide, urged by President Theodore Roosevelt, to accept it. The Regents were offered a collection of over two thousand objects of Oriental art—primarily Chinese and Japanese painting and pottery—and paintings by donor Charles Lang Freer's American contemporaries, with particular emphasis on James MacNeill Whistler. Freer proposed to expand the collection and pay for a building that the government would maintain. By the time the Gallery was opened to a mostly mystified public in 1923, the frail man of refinement who was its author had died, leaving a $7,000,000 collection and a building worth $1,000,000.

The public would have been less mystified had it known more about the life and interests of the retiring millionaire bachelor. Freer's income derived from the highly profitable manufacture of railroad cars by immigrant labor in Detroit. After the proceeds from the sale of his shares of the American Car and Foundry Company enabled him to devote himself to the cultivation of an esthetic life, to which he had already introduced himself by purchasing a large quantity of etchings and becoming friendly with some of the artists then working in New York, he set forth to meet Whistler during a trip to Paris in 1894. The close friendship that quickly developed between them was uniquely memorialized after Whistler's death nine years later.

It was the expatriate painter who had opened the tourist's eyes to the fragile beauty of Oriental art. Under this expert tutelage, and then on his own, the apt pupil, Freer, became a connoisseur. He visited the interior of China and tactfully persuaded usually suspicious men to part with centuries-old treasures; he searched out ancient stone sculpture, bronze work, pottery, and jade in Japan and China, bringing back things never seen by Westerners before; and he encouraged others to learn and collect by spreading his enthusiasm, sharing his knowledge, and even parting with many of his treasures.

The Freer Gallery is as important to those interested in Whistler as to those interested in the Orient. More than half of the artist's total life work is contained here—oils, water colors, etchings, and the Peacock Room, the only example we have of Whistler's ideas applied to interior decorating. The spacious galleries form a rectangle surrounding a garden court. In accord with Freer's belief that beautiful objects can be appreciated only in an uncluttered setting (he would display his treasures to his chosen guests one by one), only about a tenth of the exquisite collection is on display at any one time. The remainder is readily available for study, as is the excellent library.

The Whistlers are at the end of the rectangle opposite the entrance. To reach them one must go either left through the Chinese collections or right through the Japanese. Either way the visitor cannot escape Freer's method of accomplishing his "great desire . . . to unite modern works with masterpieces of certain periods of high civilization, harmonious in spiritual and physical suggestion, having the power to broaden esthetic culture and the grace to elevate the mind."

An earlier successful venture into broadening the esthetic appreciation of Washingtonians was made by the nineteenth-century banker William Wilson Corcoran with his gift of a building, an endowment fund, and the nucleus of a collection that concentrates on American painting and sculpture. The CORCORAN GALLERY OF ART was chartered by Congress in 1870, and before the century was out a larger building became necessary to contain its growing number of acquisitions. The Gallery has continued to grow ever since, aided by an important Biennial Exhibition of Contemporary American Oil Painting. A group of John Marins and a group of Stuart Davises are part of a recent gift from Edith Gregor Halpert of New York. The chronologically arranged display, from which scarcely a recognized American artist is absent, moves through the successive "schools" from Hudson River to Ashcan to the modern, and ranges from Colonial portraiture to abstract expressionism. An impressive number of Presidents and statesmen are portrayed, beginning with two Stuart studies of Washington and including interpretations of Clay, Calhoun, "Stonewall" Jackson, and R. E. Lee. Also here are all eighty-six members of the 1822 House of Representatives, ambitiously depicted on one piece of canvas by the versatile Samuel F. B. Morse.

The small sculpture collection contains works by Hiram Powers, Remington, Augustus Saint-Gaudens, Paul Manship, and others. A *Bronze Turkey* by Sargent is one of the few works of sculpture done by that artist. But the most important part of the collection is the group of bronze animals by the Frenchman Antoine Barye, purchased in 1873 at the instigation of William T. Walters of Baltimore, a Corcoran trustee who had met Barye in Paris.

In 1926 the Corcoran had grafted onto it a gift of highly heterogeneous items that had been accumulated by the late Senator William A. Clark of Montana. The senator, who had loaned some of his paintings to the Gallery years earlier, was the contributor of the prize fund for the Biennials and, during the last eleven years of his life, an active member of the board of trustees. His bequest is contained in a separate wing provided by his widow and daughters. Despite the family's generosity, however, the collection seemed an anomaly to art critic Frank

Jewett Mather, Jr., who returned from its opening in 1928 "with mixed feelings."

He was able to praise the ceramics that included a "superb group of majolica, Palissy ware and Delft"; a "panel of late thirteenth century stained glass from a church at Chartres"; and the antique lace. The Gobelins and Beauvais tapestries he pronounced "first class"; the classical group of small vases and terra cotta figurines were "amusing but almost negligible"; while the Louis XVI salon with its original ceiling and furniture represented "an exceptional moment of pause and pedantry in the creative spirit of France."

Of the paintings in the Clark Collection, Mather commended to his readers in *The Arts* the large canvases by Joos van Cleve, one of the two Rembrandts, and a Lawrence. Otherwise he advised them to "ignore all apparently important pictures and to scrutinize most carefully all pictures that are small." Among these latter could be found "three of the earliest Corots . . . three first-class Daumiers . . . half a dozen tiny ballet scenes by Degas . . . a magnificent Rousseau; and finally a consummately fine nude by Corot, The Bacchante. Add to these half a dozen Millet crayons, and twice as many old master drawings [and you have] the heart of the collector and the collection."

After a pungently conducted tour of everything on display, the critic made an attempt to give the collector his due: "It is clear that an amateur of Senator Clark's idiosyncrasy could not possibly form a collection most of which would be desirable for any public museum whatever. It is equally clear that he left many objects and groups of objects that any museum must covet. . . . The fact of the gift greatly increases the artistic resources of Washington. The form and contents of the gift will recall in perpetuity the confusion of taste in which we are now living."

There was no confusion of taste apparent ten years earlier, however, when a young collector and art patron founded what he called a "museum of modern art and its sources" in his family's Washington home. The PHILLIPS COLLECTION reflects its creator and his wife as surely as Fenway Court reflects Isabella Stewart Gardner—and the contrast is marked. Duncan and Marjorie Phillips have been active enthusiasts for the art produced by their contemporary countrymen, and the main criterion for inclusion has been the Phillips' personal predilection. The display changes frequently, as acquisitions are welcomed, old favorites sent to loan exhibitions, and ideas for new and perceptive juxtapositions occur to Mr. Phillips. The house that the

Phillips family first called home in 1897 has recently acquired a new gallery wing; but the atmosphere of a private home is still maintained as visitors sit, smoke, wander from room to room, view the collection, and very likely listen to one of the frequent concerts.

Three moderns generously patronized by the Phillips' over the years are Arthur G. Dove, Marin, and Karl Knaths. Other contemporaries and earlier Americans are also well represented. The "sources"—artists of earlier periods who in some way anticipated the concerns of the present—go back to the fifteenth century, from which there is a wooden panel by Giorgione, and include *The Repentant Peter* as interpreted in the seventeenth century by El Greco and in the nineteenth by Goya. (Many an American who has traveled in Spain and looked at a copy of *The Repentant Peter* on an easel in El Greco's Toledo home has returned completely unaware of the naturalized citizenship of the original.) Daumier's *The Uprising*, and—probably the best known Impressionist canvas in this country—Renoir's *The Luncheon of the Boating Party* (*Le Déjeuner des Canotiers*) are here. The largest group of Bonnards in America, a roomful of Klees, and significant works by Picasso, Matisse, Rousseau, Gris, Braque, Rouault, Soutine, and Kokoschka are among those representing the twentieth century on the continent. This is one of the few museums in the country where works by the British moderns can be found.

It might be thought that Washington needs more museums as much as it needs more lobbyists. Undaunted by the competition, however, three hundred and fifty citizens banded together in 1962 and generously contributed $100 or more each to become "originating members" of the new WASHINGTON GALLERY OF MODERN ART, a museum dedicated to the *avant-garde* and contemporary American work. It opened with a Franz Kline retrospective; and in its first year produced exhibitions of WPA art, pop art, and "Sculptors of Our Time."

Still another, but very different organization concerned with art is the TEXTILE MUSEUM, begun in 1925 to house the collection of Mr. George Hewitt Myers. There are about four hundred old and rare rugs and rug fragments and some six thousand textile examples here. Activities are centered on cataloguing, conservation, research, and exhibits which are changed annually. Egyptian rugs from the tenth century, an old Roman tapestry, and pre-Columbian Peruvian textiles are among the museum's possessions.

Washington is also the home of the DUMBARTON OAKS RESEARCH LIBRARY AND COLLECTION of Byzantine art, presented to Harvard

University in 1940 by Mr. and Mrs. Robert Woods Bliss. The 1801 mansion contains sculpture, ivory, enamels, ceramics, mosaics, paintings, coins, textiles, and other arts of Constantinople and nearby eastern Mediterranean lands, and is primarily a center for advanced study in Byzantine civilization. The Blisses were also collectors of pre-Columbian art, and in 1963 a new wing was added to contain about two hundred pieces from Mexico, Peru, and the lands in between. Through the glass walls of this modern addition can be seen the beautifully landscaped grounds and terraced formal gardens that are as much of an attraction at Dumbarton Oaks as what is inside.

Those who are interested in the work of George Catlin and are aware that the most important body of it is owned by the Smithsonian, should also realize that it will be found not in any of the Smithsonian's art galleries, but in the Natural History Building of the National Museum. "The collection," for which the artist himself wrote the catalogue, "contains near 600 paintings, 350 of which are Portraits of distinguished men and women of the different tribes, and 250 Other Paintings, descriptive of Indian Countries, their Villages, Games, and Customs. . . ." He hoped that, as "every painting has been made from nature, BY MY OWN HAND—and that, too, when I have been paddling my canoe or leading my pack-horse over and through trackless wilds, at the hazard of my life—the world will surely be kind and indulgent enough to receive and estimate them, as they have been intended, as true and fac-simile traces of individual life and historical facts, and forgive me for their present unfinished and unstudied condition as works of art."

The art-minded visitor to the District of Columbia has only one problem; that of choice.

Those who live in or travel to the Rocky Mountain states of Colorado, Wyoming, Montana, Idaho, Utah, and New Mexico need only stand still out of doors to experience beauty or be overwhelmed by wonder. To provide a sense of the area's past, there are museums that deal with the history of each of these states. And if, after a while, one should wish to turn from the physical beauty of the land itself and survey the history of art from the classical to the contemporary, there is an exciting museum in Denver.

The DENVER ART MUSEUM is exciting not only because of the special significance its collections have long had to the people of the Rocky Mountain area and the millions of tourists who flock there each year, but because of what it has been accomplishing in its own more immediate community ever since the day in 1949 when a joint decision was made by Director Otto Karl Bach and the board of trustees to transform a one-story garage and factory into the first unit of a modern structure. Until then, Denver had for years been talking and dreaming about a new building. But the talk and the dreams had been so grandiose that a $350,000 bequest left to the city for its museum went untouched because it just wasn't enough money to pay for what everyone seemed to want. When at last a handsome, functional gallery was made from the former factory it was named the Schleier Memorial after the lady who had given the $350,000. The lady would have liked it. One of its unique features is a series of display windows along the front façade that allows the museum to spotlight its exhibitions and at the same time lure the window shopper inside.

The museum now consists of five units. In addition to the Schleier gallery, where special exhibitions are held, there are: Chappell House, where American Indian art predominates; the Oriental Museum; the South Wing, for Mediterranean and European art; and the Living Arts Center.

Among the old paintings, portraits of course abound. In the German and Austrian section there is a pair of them, dated 1549, by Lucas Cranach the Younger. The subjects are the recently married *Augustus, Grand Duke of Saxony* and his duchess, Anne. In other sections there are one of Rubens by his pupil Van Dyck, one by Corot (known primarily as a landscape painter, he exhibited only two of his portraits during his lifetime) called *La Femme à La Pensée,* and Renoir's *Portrait of Coco,* his youngest son whom he painted many times from infancy to boyhood. The period from the early to the high Renaissance is covered in paintings and sculpture by a characteristically magnificent gift from the Kress Foundation. From the sixteenth century and a different donor (W. Averell Harriman) there is *December,* a wool tapestry by Lucas van Leyden. Woven in Brussels, it is one of twelve *Months of Lucas.* From the eighteenth century and later there is a collection of Spanish art dealing with the bullfight (Goya etchings are, of course, included). Three period installations the museum is particularly proud of are its French Gothic oak-paneled room, its English Tudor Room and its Spanish Baroque Study which is a composite room assembled from several seventeenth-century sources. The Oriental acquisitions have been culled from the arts of China, Japan, Korea, India, Tibet, Persia, Sumatra, and Bali. And a recently established

fashion, costume, and textile institute will do research and issue publications as well as plan exhibits. Among the first items it could call
its own were 146 exemplary American dresses covering the period
1800 to 1950.

Through its Living Arts Center, the museum works co-operatively
with the public schools. "Color," "Structure," "Shape and Form,"
"Space," and "Light" were exhibits designed to analyze aspects of our
visual environment and to supplement the studies of the city's school
children. The Junior League has had a hand in these activities as a
co-sponsor. It was intended that all of the exhibits in this series—the
plan called for twelve of them—would become permanent installations.

North American Indian art is of major significance not only because of the high quality of its many objects but because it was from
here that the rest of the country was made aware of the importance
of these pieces—as art. Particularly unappreciated, except where it
had been displayed as ethnological specimens by a few museums in
the East, was the work of the Northwest Coast Indians, until Frederic
H. Douglas, then Denver's curator, organized a show at San Francisco's Golden Gate International Exposition in 1939. Dr. Douglas
had worked closely with René d'Harnoncourt and when the Exposition
was closed in 1941, they moved the exhibit to the Museum of Modern
Art in New York. Soon after that they collaborated on a book called
Indian Art in the United States.

From the American Southwest, the museum has assembled work of
quite a different sort; a small but very fine group of *santos*. Santos are
a form of Spanish Colonial ecclesiastical folk art indigenous to Colorado and New Mexico. Santos means saints, the subject of many of
these pieces. Christ, the Madonna, and Death are other subjects. The
santos are of two kinds. Some are sculptures carved of wood. These
are called *bultos*. The paintings done on wooden panels are called
retablos. The artists—Spaniards and Indians taught by the Franciscan
fathers at the time of the missions—were called *santeros*. The greatest
period of activity of the santeros was the hundred years between 1750
and 1850. The santeros were both amateurs whose art was intended
only for themselves and professionals who sold their work. Much of
what they created is sweet and gentle. But the Penitentes, a sect that
practiced flagellation, often concentrated their efforts on depicting
Death, standing terrifyingly in a cart (*La Carreta de la Muerte*), holding a threatening bow and arrow.

A very good publication on santos, with many illustrations, was issued by the Taylor Museum of the COLORADO SPRINGS FINE ARTS CENTER, which owns many excellent examples. Alice Bemis Taylor who built and endowed the Center was interested in American Indian as well as Spanish Colonial art. For this reason, the John Frederick Huckel collection of copies of sacred Navaho sand paintings was placed here in 1946. (Huckel was by marriage a member of the family of Fred Harvey, proprietor of the celebrated hotel and restaurant chain.)

Sand painting is an integral part of Navaho religious practice. These paintings—symbolic pictures made by trickling colored sand on the floor of the hogan—are made for a variety of rites having to do with purification or healing. Each painting, completed just before the ceremony begins, is created specifically for that one occasion, after which it is destroyed. The total number of different designs the Navaho use is not known and no written or graphic records have been kept. The rituals have been handed down orally from generation to generation. Despite the traditional Navaho unwillingness to admit observers, water-color and crayon copies of these dry paintings have been made. Huckel managed to acquire 111 of them. Each was well documented and a good number were done by the Navahos themselves. An excellent explanatory catalogue, written by Leland C. Wyman, goes into detail about the ceremonies.

In the remaining galleries of the Fine Arts Center, Walt Kuhn's series of twenty-nine paintings that make up his *Imaginary History of the West* is joined by the work of Georgia O'Keeffe and other contemporary American and European canvases. In addition the Center has a professionally equipped theater and a view of Pike's Peak.

The largest museum collection of Navaho sand paintings is in Santa Fe, New Mexico, at the MUSEUM OF NAVAHO CEREMONIAL ART. The most important museum complex in this part of the Southwest dealing with the history and ethnology of the area in terms of its art and artifacts is the MUSEUM OF NEW MEXICO, also in Santa Fe.

What might be described as its main building is the Palace of the Governors, erected by the Spaniards in 1610. The museum is made up of five basic units. And art, in some form, is to be found in every one of them. The Laboratory of Anthropology, for example, contains Pueblo pottery and Pueblo and Navaho textiles of the post-Spanish period; the Hall of Ethnology has Navaho sand paintings as well as models of prehistoric villages and contemporary Indian utensils and handicrafts. It is one of those places where art and science are happily inseparable. There are separate art galleries, however. In one of them, contemporary work by Santa Fe and Taos artists can be seen. Elsewhere there are rare sacred paintings done on buffalo hide by the Franciscan fathers about two and a half centuries ago, fine pieces of Spanish Colonial religious art and furniture, and a separate MUSEUM OF INTERNATIONAL FOLK ART (one of the five units) which goes beyond the work of the area into the sculpture, ceramics, textiles, jewelry, dolls, and costumes of more than fifty countries, from Mexico to Japan. The catalogues and publications of the Museum of New Mexico are exceptionally good.

Southeast of Santa Fe, the ROSWELL MUSEUM AND ART CENTER has both an art and a science division. The emphasis in the former is on paintings, prints, sculpture and crafts by artists who have worked in or are originally from this region—John Marin, Marsden Hartley, Georgia O'Keeffe, Peter Moran, Henriette Wyeth and many others. A major part of the work of Peter Hurd is here. And the Zuni, Hopi, Acoma, and San Ildefonso Indians are represented by their pottery.

And in Arizona, the PHOENIX ART MUSEUM is quickly expanding to include Renaissance and baroque works, Oriental art, and good contemporary European and American examples.

The importance of the artist as a recorder of regional history is perhaps nowhere better recognized than in the Northern Plains city of Omaha, Nebraska where the JOSLYN ART MUSEUM has become the nation's outstanding center of documentary art on the early West. The museum houses all the illustrations and records of the Maximilian-Bodmer expedition of 1833 and paintings by the Baltimore artist, Alfred Jacob Miller, who went West in 1837.

Karl Bodmer was a member of the Pennsylvania Academy of Fine Arts and a very successful portrait painter regularly commissioned by the wealthy. Eager to interpret Indian life, he began traveling. When the German naturalist, Prince Maximilian of Wied-Neuwied, started to plan his North American journey and inquired for an artist who could illustrate his observations, Bodmer's name was given. One of the results of this collaboration was the book *Travels in the Interior of North America,* with a scholarly text by the prince and eighty-one plates made from Bodmer's sketches. Although the book became well known in several languages, Maximilian's papers and diaries, his library of reference books, and more than four hundred of Bodmer's sketches were locked up, apparently forgotten after the prince's death, in a room of his German estate. They were rediscovered only recently. In 1962 the Northern Natural Gas Company of Omaha bought them and made the Joslyn Art Museum custodian. The sketches record flora and fauna as well as the faces, ceremonies, and customs of the Plains Indians. There are also some water colors painted by the Indians themselves, who had been prompted by the white artist to work in his medium.

Rounding out Joslyn's regional collections are paintings by George Catlin and Seth Eastman, maps, artifacts, and art in a variety of forms; everything here reflecting an aspect of the history of the Northwest Territory, life on the prairie, the Lewis and Clark Expedition, or the life of the Plains Indians.

The rest of this museum, presented to the public by Sarah H. Joslyn in memory of her husband, is given over to paintings that are displayed in terms of their relationship to furniture, architecture, and other media of design from the same period. And the relationship of art to music can be satisfactorily explored, in accordance with Mrs. Joslyn's wishes, in a sizable auditorium. Among the prized acquisitions to be found in the various galleries are Lorenzo di Credi's *Madonna and Child with Two Angels* and Titian's *Man with Falcon*. Copley's *Portrait of Lord Cornwallis,* Constable's *The Lock,* Lipchitz' *Hagar* in bronze and Pollock's *Galaxy* are more than notable. Also represented are El Greco, Rembrandt, Goya, Renoir, and Prendergast.

The affinity between the art museum and the region of the country that surrounds it continues to be strongly expressed, although in different ways, in Oklahoma and Texas. In Oklahoma the collections are largely indigenous; in Texas the galleries reflect the exuberant aspirations of the people who live there.

As a result of years of searching by Clark Field, a Tulsa businessman, and the help given him in identifying and authenticating by the Laboratory of Anthropology in Santa Fe, many rare specimens of Indian pottery and baskets were painstakingly gathered. In 1942 they were given by Mr. Field to the PHILBROOK ART CENTER of Tulsa, Oklahoma. Examples of nearly every type of pottery made by the Pueblos of New Mexico and the desert people of Arizona can be found here. Since most of these pieces were made by the Indians for their own use and not for the tourist trade (which began about 1870), 75 per cent of them are not now obtainable. The baskets represent nearly every basket-making tribe of the United States and some from Mexico and Central and South America. Of these 85 per cent are no longer obtainable.

The Philbrook has several other displays—of costumes, artifacts, and paintings—that depict American Indian life, in addition to an impressive research library.

Jumping abruptly to the Renaissance, there is a Kress group; and from the eighteenth and nineteenth centuries there is a group of paintings, both European and American, that includes a Thomas Moran view of the *Grand Canyon*. Moran is the landscape painter who first went West, into the Yellowstone area, in 1871 as a guest artist accompanying Dr. F. V. Hayden's Geological Survey of the Territories. He fell in love with what he saw, kept returning, and portrayed the wonders of what were to become national parks—Yellowstone, Yosemite, Zion, Grand Canyon, and Grand Teton—in pictures that became familiar all over the country. Mountains and promontories have been named after him and, perhaps even more impressive, Congress twice appropriated $10,000—in 1872 and 1874—for his oils, *Grand Canyon of the Yellowstone* and *Chasm of the Colorado*, which were hung in the Capitol.

Moran's paintings and sketches number high in the hundreds. Some of them can be seen in national park museums in juxtaposition with their subjects. And a very large group of them is in Tulsa's THOMAS GILCREASE INSTITUTE OF AMERICAN HISTORY AND ART. Established as a private museum, then acquired by the city, the Gilcrease has within its walls a huge multimillion dollar agglomeration of art and artifacts related to the history and prehistory of America. The emphasis is on the Southwest; the focus, the American Indian. Pictures by Catlin, Miller, Charles M. Russell, and Frederic Remington are here together with some of Remington's best-known bronzes, the bucking broncos of William R. Leigh (which have only recently found a home here), and contemporary Indian painting and sculpture. Not far from the "Westerns" hang canvases by John Smibert, Robert Feke, Edward Hicks, Audubon (*The Wild Turkey*), Whistler, Eakins, W. M. Chase, Sargent, and Robert Henri. The artifacts cover a period of two thousand years and represent most of the culture areas of North and Middle America. And there is a library of more than 65,000 rare books and documents that contains among its many essential sources for historians the 10,000 original Cortez papers relating to the conquest of Mexico.

Gilcrease built his collection out of love, money that came from oil, and, finally, out of his own archaeological diggings. A contemporary of Gilcrease who shared his enthusiasm for Remington and Russell and devotedly acquired the work of both of them was Amon Carter, a larger-than-life Texan and publisher of the Fort Worth *Star Telegram*. He bought one group of Russells right off the walls of The Mint, a saloon in Great Falls, Montana, that is regarded as a kind of shrine to the cowpoke painter who was the best-loved man in that state's history. The brand new AMON CARTER MEMORIAL MUSEUM of Fort Worth is full of scenes of cowboy life, in painting and sculpture. Not far from Remington's *The Old Stage Coach of the Plains* there is a picture by Russell of an Indian pursuing a buffalo. He called it *Wild Meat for Wild Men*.

Another gallery in the same city is the FORT WORTH ART CENTER, which features American painting of the nineteenth and twentieth centuries and a very good print collection that goes from the sixteenth century in Europe to the present. Eakins, Inness, and Feininger are in the former group; Dürer in the latter.

But the big state's biggest art museums are in Houston and Dallas. The MUSEUM OF FINE ARTS OF HOUSTON has a history that can be traced back to the beginning of the century, a large collection of Remingtons, a new wing designed by Ludwig Mies van der Rohe, and a taste for the lively and controversial that it began to indulge in 1961 when James Johnson Sweeney became its director.

Mr. Sweeney's policy has been to avoid specialization in any one area, to avoid an historical or documentary approach to art, and to broaden the collection with a variety of works of quality. Besides acquiring objects that range from the classical to Rodin and from Calder to the primitive, he has kept Houston aware of all the latest trends in the world of art, including its fads. But it was Mr. Sweeney's love of the permanent that took him, a few years ago, on a well-publicized, triumphant adventure. Supported by letters from President Kennedy and Vice-President Johnson, he asked Mexico to lend him an enormous ancient stone head that he had heard about, for a pre-Columbian exhibit he was planning. Mexico agreed; the only catch being that the head lay half buried in the jungle and no one knew for sure where to find it. But Sweeney found it. And the Mexican Government built a road just to get the sixteen-ton, nine-foot-high sculpture out of its remote hiding place. It came from the Olmec culture of 500 to 100 B.C. It went—on loan—to Houston.

Over the years, bequests of several intact collections plus a gift of the Kress Foundation have brought the museum examples of Egyptian, Greek, Roman, and Byzantine art, and some fine pieces of Italian Renaissance sculpture, in addition to Fra Angelico's *Temptation of St. Anthony, Abbot,* a Sebastiano del Piombo portrait, a market-place scene by Bernardo Bellotto, two panels by Giovanni di Paolo, portraits by Frans Hals and Goya, Cézanne's portrait of *Madame Cézanne in Blue,* and Renoir's *Still Life with Bouquet.*

Contemporary works are of course among the Museum of Fine Arts' interests. But since 1948 another Houston organization has been exploring this field exclusively. The CONTEMPORARY ARTS ASSOCIATION features modern painting, sculpture, and constructions. Its aim is to translate ideas; whether they are the ideas of Surrealism, neo-Dada, the art of the machine, or the art of the African primitive.

At the DALLAS MUSEUM OF FINE ARTS a strong belief in American painting and sculpture and a special commitment to the artists of Texas have for many years been an important part of the over-all policy. The scope of its American holdings is broad. The work of a good eighteenth-century limner is as much appreciated as a Gilbert Stuart, an Inness, or a Jackson Pollock. The collections survey figure and portrait painting, landscape painting from the Hudson River school to the impressionistic work of Childe Hassam, and contemporary art. Wyant, Ryder, Blakelock, Duveneck, Bellows, Thomas Hart Benton, Edward Hopper, and Andrew Wyeth indicate the range of painters. William Zorach and Calder are among the sculptors. One of the many Texans who have been chauvinistically supported here is the one-time cowboy H. O. Kelly, who upon becoming too old to ranch, began to paint scenes such as *Hog Killing Time.* Another, and equally late starter, is Clara Williamson, who resembled Grandma Moses in her fondness for painting memories of her childhood. In *Get Along Little Dogies* a little girl—herself—watches a cattle drive.

The Dallas Museum of Fine Arts has not neglected the schools of Europe, but when it comes to the American product its vitality is limitless. A few years ago, having already purchased Andrew Wyeth's *Becky King* and having been exposed to his portrait of *That Gentleman* during a loan exhibition, the museum's officials, its Art Association, and the public joined forces to buy the latter canvas. The $58,000 that was solicited came not only from members who could afford to give a substantial gift, but from a little box under the painting which visitors filled each day with small bills and their change. When Wyeth heard how the money had been raised he wrote to the museum's director, Jerry Bywaters, expressing delight and adding: "For an American museum to be convinced enough of American painting to work at such lengths to acquire what they feel is a top example . . . is to me one of the most refreshing and stimulating pieces of news I have received in a long time."

Elsewhere in town there is the DALLAS MUSEUM FOR CONTEMPORARY ARTS which, defining its policy not too long ago, made clear its intention to bring several quality exhibitions to town each year, whether they "came from Europe, Asia, Milwaukee or Texas." Its first exhibit, "Abstract by Choice," was a success; and all has gone well ever since.

Two more Texas repositories worth noting are the MARION KOOGLER McNAY ART INSTITUTE in San Antonio and the EL PASO MUSEUM OF ART. In the first there are more than two hundred Pascin water colors and drawings, together with works of Pissaro, Gauguin, Cassatt, Bonnard, Klee, Dufy, and Vuillard. In the second there are a Kress gift from the fourteenth through the seventeenth centuries and representative European, American, and pre-Columbian collections.

Of all the famous residents in the state of California, there is only one who has never entertained a moment's speculation about the condition of his immortality. And he is inanimate. How *The Blue Boy,* one of the best-known portraits in the world, came to San Marino, is a marvelous story that will not be diluted here. Anyone who wants to know should read Chapter 5 of Behrman's *Duveen.* It was Duveen, by the way, who had the canvas scrubbed clean enough to make it clear to the painting's purchaser, Henry E. Huntington, and the angered British press, that age and not Gainsborough had rendered the boy green. Duveen rendered it blue again.

The HENRY E. HUNTINGTON LIBRARY AND ART GALLERY was opened to the public in 1928 offering, in addition to *The Blue Boy,* Gainsborough's *The Cottage Door,* Lawrence's *Pinkie,* and Reynolds' portrait of *Sarah Siddons as the Tragic Muse* among the highlights of a specialized collection.

Henry E. Huntington was one of Collis P. Huntington's heirs. Collis, the Central Pacific Railroad man, was Henry's uncle. One of the concomitants of Henry's inheritance was Collis' wife, Arabella, whom Henry proceeded to marry. She fancied Van der Weyden, Bellini, Velasquez, Hals, Rembrandt, Renaissance bronzes, French sculpture (including Houdon), and eighteenth-century French furniture. Her new husband fancied British painters of the latter period, and rare books and manuscripts. To help them indulge their expensive tastes there was, of course, Duveen. The collections they ultimately left behind them were expanded. The gallery, which offers one of the best surveys of Georgian art available anywhere, also features *The Noble Pastoral*, a set of Beauvais tapestries with which the Huntingtons enjoyed living. They were woven in 1755 and 1756 from designs painted by Boucher, whose superb work was then dominating the medium.

Arabella Huntington's fondness for French furniture and decorative objects was developed during the lifetime of Collis P. and much of her collecting in this field was done for their Fifth Avenue house in New York. When Collis died, the house was inherited by their son Archer. And Archer, who lived in California, donated a good part of its contents, in memory of his father, to the CALIFORNIA PALACE OF THE LEGION OF HONOR in San Francisco. There Arabella's items contributed significantly to one of the best collections of eighteenth-century French furniture, *objets d'art*, painting, and sculpture in the country.

Architecturally based upon the Palace of the Legion of Honor in Paris, the building was given to the city in 1924 by Mr. and Mrs. Adolph B. Spreckels as a memorial to the soldiers who died in World War I. One of the many gifts of Mrs. Spreckels, who loved French art, was a large and important selection of Rodin bronzes and marbles. (These were later supplemented by a group of original plasters; a gift of Mrs. Spreckels' son.) *The Burghers of Calais* and *St. John the Baptist* can be found here, while out of doors sits *The Thinker*.

Other contributors broadened the Palace's scope to include Renaissance masters, and Dutch, Flemish, English, and American works. But the art of France remains the famous specialty of the house; paintings by Largillière, Nattier, Greuze, Fragonard, Corot, Manet, and Renoir; sculpture by Houdon; and tapestries and porcelains by a variety of master craftsmen.

The San Franciscans were at the turn of the century, as now, a vigorous lot. One of them, Michael Henry de Young, publisher of the San Francisco *Chronicle,* having been impressed by Chicago's Columbian Exposition, helped to bring about the California Midwinter Exposition of 1893–94, and then to establish a fine arts museum in one of its pavilions. From these efforts there eventually grew the M. H. DE YOUNG MEMORIAL MUSEUM.

De Young once explained the development of his motivation this way: "Most intelligent men and women go through life with fads, some for literature, some for art, some for gathering things. When I was a young man, and my business as a newspaperman took me to many places and many stores, I acquired a fad for antiquities and I passed along. I do not know how I got the fad. I began by collecting stuffed birds. I had more than 300 of them. Then, in the course of time, I went to an auction and bought a large collection of Chinese carvings. I had to take the birds out to make room for the carvings, and I thought I would give them to the city. I told the Park Commissioner about it, and they laughed. They would not take them, and at last, for there was no room in my home for them, I had to put them up at auction. The auctioneer returned me $56 for a collection that cost me $600. Never to this day have I forgotten that $56. It burned a hole in my brain. I did not want to dispose of them. I wanted to keep them. That is where I got the museum bug."

Much has happened at the De Young Museum since its founding. Today it houses painting, sculpture, period rooms, and examples of the decorative arts of the Western world from ancient times to the present. From the Eastern world, it has recently received a multimillion dollar gift from Avery Brundage of Chicago. San Francisco voters authorized a $2,725,000 bond issue to cover the cost of a new wing to house the Brundage collection.

When the museum was approached by the Kress Foundation to state its request, it boldly asked for a "miniature National Gallery," and was given a selection of thirty-nine works covering the entire field of European painting from Bernardo Daddi's *St. Catherine* of the Middle Ages, to a Goya portrait of 1801. These, plus donations from other sources, have made for a rich harvest of art.

Major Rembrandts, Rubenses, Van Dycks, and El Grecos are here with masterpieces of Fra Angelico, Bellini, Titian, Bronzino, Joos van Cleve, Pieter de Hooch, Poussin, and Boucher. Among the sculptures are a Verrocchio figure and a Cellini bust of Cosimo de Medici. There are enormous Brussels tapestries that came from the William Randolph Hearst Foundation. There is a gallery of musical instruments. The history of California can be viewed in terms of prints, furnishings, costumes, and so forth. And the contemporary art of California is given a helping hand.

Contemporary art is emphasized in a big way at the SAN FRANCISCO MUSEUM OF ART which William W. Crocker helped found. (William's grandfather, Charles Crocker, with Collis Huntington, Leland Stanford, and Mark Hopkins made up the Big Four of western railroading.) Across a courtyard from the Opera House, the museum is involved both in the social activities of local high society (from which it directly benefits) and the experimental activities of the nearby artists. The Bay Area Annuals are held here. The museum's permanent collection concentrates on the painting, sculpture, and graphics of the period between 1900 and the present.

The most expensive cultural expansion program in California has just taken place in Los Angeles, where the biggest art museum to be built in the United States since the National Gallery has risen at a total cost of $20,000,000.

When growth made it no longer practicable for the Los Angeles County Museum to house its art, science, and history wings under one roof, two museums were made from one. While the Division of History and Science started expanding on its own, the LOS ANGELES COUNTY ART MUSEUM burst forth in architectural splendor. The plans of William Pereira Associates called for three buildings set on a shallow reflecting pool. The buildings, connected by covered walks, all open on a large plaza designed to serve as an exhibition area for sculpture, a general meeting place, and the site of social events. The galleries that house the permanent collection surround an atrium and are themselves "planned in the form of a branching tree, starting with the roots of art in prehistory and growing from there in two directions," through the arts of Western civilization and through the arts of the Orient.

William Randolph Hearst was one of the many willing donors who have enriched Los Angeles County with treasures. His gifts, including the Marion Davies collection, were large, impressive, and first-rate. Among the paintings that had belonged to Miss Davies are Sir Thomas Lawrence's *Portrait of Arthur Atherly,* three Bouchers, a Fragonard, and three Greuzes. Other masterpieces owned by the museum are *Portrait of a Young Woman* by Hans Holbein the Younger and Peter Christus' bust-length *Portrait of a Man.* But whether one's interest is in the ancient Egyptian, Greek, and Roman worlds, the Oriental world, the Middle Ages, the Renaissance, the Flemish, the Dutch, the nineteenth- and twentieth-century French, the German Expressionists (Nolde, Beckmann) or John Paul Jones and Stuart Davis, this is an excellent place to come to. The county of Los Angeles has glamor, wealth, and a taste for the superb in art that is nothing short of spectacular.

Stuart Davis' *Premiere,* by the way, is his impression of a trip to the supermarket which he and six other American artists took for *Fortune* magazine in 1956 after the editors, musing about the "mellow still lives of the 17th and 18th centuries" began to wonder what a shopping cart full of today's "stridently packaged" groceries would inspire.

There are over half a dozen more art museums in the state that have excellent things to offer. One of them, the FINE ARTS GALLERY OF SAN DIEGO, has a beautiful collection of old masterpieces. A large number of them are Spanish, but Titian, Peter Christus, Rembrandt, Rubens, and Brueghel are superbly represented also. At the ART CENTER IN LA JOLLA the outlook is twentieth-century. The PASADENA ART MUSEUM features German Expressionism with a large and important body of the work of Paul Klee joined by Kandinskys, Feiningers, and Jawlenskys. The SANTA BARBARA MUSEUM OF ART, on the other hand, features two hundred years of the American product in addition to its unusual collection of antique dolls, its drawings, its African and pre-Columbian objects, its Oriental musical instruments, and its Greek, Roman, and Egyptian sculpture. At the E. B. CROCKER ART GALLERY in Sacramento, master drawings, German paintings, and American glass are to be found with rare Korean pottery. And in Oakland, there is a $6,000,000 project designed by Saarinen and Associates to contain three museums that outgrew their quarters: art, natural history, and anthropology. The OAKLAND ART MUSEUM houses the Archives of California Art, which has been called "the finest collection of California paintings in any one place."

California also has three outstanding university museums, the Stanford University Art Gallery, the Fisher Gallery of the University of Southern California in Los Angeles, and the Art Galleries of the University of California at Los Angeles. The University of California at Berkeley is about to add a fourth, of which one wing will be the gift of Hans Hofmann. He is presenting forty-five of his works and $250,000 for the Hans and Maria Hofmann Memorial Galleries, in memory of his late wife and in thanks for the teaching offer from the university that brought him to this country from his native Germany in 1930.

In the northwestern states of Oregon and Washington there are two museums that have faced the challenge of being solitary sources of reference for art in cities far removed from major cultural centers.

When the PORTLAND ART MUSEUM received twenty-seven Renaissance masterpieces from the Kress Collection in 1952, its director made reference to "serious responsibilities." The museum was then sixty years old but, due to a shortage of purchasing funds during most of its existence, it had acquired only two Renaissance paintings before the Kress contribution arrived. The emphasis had been placed on the art school and loan exhibitions that sometimes dealt with such themes as Artists of Oregon and Early Days in the Northwest. It was during one of these temporary shows that Portland had had its first look at some of Kress's paintings. This was nearly twenty years before a selection of them arrived to take up permanent residence.

Largely through gifts, a fine though small permanent collection had previously been accumulated. The first gift, back in 1892, was the inevitable one of casts of classical sculpture, but it was not long before they were supplanted by real antiquities. A striking group of Northwest Coast Indian carvings—from spoon handles to totem poles—was an important addition. And nineteenth- and twentieth-century European and American paintings (including good representation of the moderns) plus examples of pre-Columbian and Chinese art have rounded out what is here.

The SEATTLE ART MUSEUM is, like its nearest neighbor, the recipient of a Kress benefaction. But it is best known for the Oriental collection built up by the museum's director, Richard Eugene Fuller, and his mother. The Fuller family first visited Japan in 1919 and began acquiring the objects that would lead them to provide a museum for Seattle. Although there had been a Fine Arts Society in the city as early as 1908 holding art classes and temporary exhibits in rented rooms or private homes, there was no permanent location for these activities until 1933 when the Fullers donated one, with a magnificent view.

In addition to a well-rounded inventory of pre-Columbian, Egyptian, classical, Byzantine, and medieval works, Seattle has superlative examples of the art of India, Nepal, Indonesia, China, and Japan. The Chinese collection is renowned, and the Japanese ranges from Jomon pottery that may be seven thousand years old and sixth to third century B.C. Haniwa earthenware figures, to *otsu-e, ukiyo-e, netsuke, inro,* and wood carvings of the eighteenth and nineteenth centuries. Seattle, which has been trading with the Orient since its founding little more than a century ago, has also participated in the mainstream of contemporary American art. Native sons Mark Tobey, Morris Graves, and Kenneth Callahan are spotlighted in the museum's coverage of contemporary work.

In the years since the Second World War, New York has become the art center of the world, replacing Paris as the site of creation and the source of inspiration. In no small measure this is due to New York's many well-known museums, each complementing and supplementing the accomplishments of the others, each with its own ambiance.

It has not always been so. Until 1871 there was no art museum in New York. The few sporadic attempts at establishing one had foundered. As early as 1802, three years before the Pennsylvania Academy was begun, seventy-nine New Yorkers started the American Academy of the Fine Arts. But while that of Philadelphia lived on as the oldest art museum in the country, New York's first attempt lasted barely forty years. Colonel John Trumbull was the Academy's autocratic president for half that time, and the elderly painter had little sympathy for the young artists whom the Academy ostensibly meant to serve. Not only were they not allowed to become members of its board, but they could draw from the casts in its possession only during a few inconvenient hours each week, and had to pay dearly for the privilege. At times the door was kept shut even at the appointed hour. Unwilling to put up with this treatment any longer the artists, led by Samuel F. B. Morse, formed their own Drawing Association in 1825.

Three years later it was incorporated as the National Academy of Design, with Morse pointedly defining an "Academy of Art [as] an Association of Artists for the purposes of Instruction and Exhibition." Several evenings a week were regularly devoted to drawing, supplemented by lectures on such topics as anatomy, perspective, and mythology, and, before long, by an art library for members. Today, primarily an art school, the National Academy holds several important annual exhibitions and has a permanent collection of painting, sculpture, and graphic work done by its members since its founding.

While the new academy was flourishing, the older one was folding. Trumbull left his own paintings not to it but to Yale, thus saving them from the fire that destroyed most of the debt-ridden American Academy's property in 1841 and put an end to its program once and for all.

Meanwhile a newcomer had arrived on the New York art scene. In 1838 James Herring, a portrait painter, opened the Apollo Gallery "to provide for the artists a suitable depot for the temporary exhibition of their works . . . and for the lovers of art a place of resort where they may expect to find a rich variety of subjects for study or for sale."

Herring's project developed into the American Art Union, which had an ambitious and popular program "for the promotion of fine arts in the United States." An annual fee of five dollars would make anyone a member, eligible to receive "a large and costly original engraving from an American painting" and sundry other publications each year, as well as free admission to the gallery. Most exciting of all, members could participate in a drawing for works of art purchased by the Art Union during the year. But after little more than a decade it was charged with running a lottery and forced to liquidate its holdings. Its effects were handed over to the New York Gallery of the Fine Arts, the establishment of merchant Luman Reed, who was the first real patron American artists had. He turned the third floor of his home into an exhibition hall for the work of such friends and protégés as Durand, Cole, and Mount. At his death business associates and friends raised $13,000 to buy his collection and continue the New York Gallery's activities. But although they were successful as grocery wholesalers, they were not able to cope with the financial intricacies of struggling artists and an indifferent public, and by 1858 the New York Gallery was defunct, its effects going to the New-York Historical Society.

There was still no real art museum in New York. But for that matter, there were at this time only three in the entire country—the Pennsylvania Academy, the Wadsworth Atheneum of Hartford, and the Boston Athaeneum, which was to revert to a library after the founding of the Museum of Fine Arts. Corcoran's projected gallery in Washington would not open for more than a decade. And the next art museum to appear, the Buffalo Fine Arts Academy of 1862, would not "take" for another ten years.

Addressing a group of fellow Americans in Paris at a Fourth of July celebration in 1866, therefore, lawyer John Jay (grandson of the first Chief Justice, and active supporter of such liberal causes as Irish Relief and abolition) stated that the time had come "to lay the foundation of a National Institution and Gallery of Art." Presumably because they were not only prominent citizens of their own country, but also admirers of the museums they were visiting abroad, he suggested that "the American gentlemen then in Europe were the men to inaugurate the plan." They listened with interest, formed a committee, and wrote a letter to the Union League Club of New York, to which many of them belonged. (Jay was one of the founders who had organized the League after breaking with the very social Union Club in 1863 over its Confederate sympathies.) They requested the League to "institute the best means for promoting this great project." A Union League Art Committee, consisting of a publisher, several artists, and an art dealer, was appointed to take it from there.

Recognizing from the beginning that the success of their project hinged upon their obtaining a broad base of support, men with a variety of interests ("artists, editors, architects, lawyers, merchants and others," according to the New York *Times*) were invited to a meeting in November of 1869. William Cullen Bryant opened the meeting. It had been called "to consider the subject of founding in this city a Museum of Art . . . which shall be in some measure worthy of this great metropolis and of the wide empire of which New York is the Commercial Center."

Perhaps some of those present had a glimpse of the future greatness of the METROPOLITAN MUSEUM OF ART. The Reverend Dr. Bellows of All Souls' Church accurately anticipated a time when "through the redundant wealth with which our prosperity threatens to possess us" the museum would "be able to outbid the world in any market for those great recondite works of Art which are so necessary to the cultivation of every people." It did come to pass. The $2,300,000 bid by the Metropolitan in 1961 for Rembrandt's *Aristotle Contemplating the Bust of Homer* made headlines as the highest price ever paid for a painting.

But Dr. Bellows' prediction must have seemed unreasonable to most of the men listening that rainy evening. Even Bryant modestly anticipated merely "an annual revenue which would bring to the Museum every stray statue and picture of merit for which there should be no ready sale to individuals, every smaller collection in the country which its owner could no longer conveniently keep."

Those who believed it was impossible to solicit enough money for first-rate works probably felt justified when the first year's fund-raising efforts produced only $106,000—less than half of the $250,000 goal. Nevertheless, the Metropolitan was chartered in 1870, and the following year made its first purchase—174 European paintings. That year also the state legislature empowered the city to issue the "Museums of Art and Natural History Stock" as a means of financing the construction and maintenance of these two institutions on city land. The Metropolitan, meanwhile, had moved into the first of two temporary locations—Allen Dodworth's Dancing Academy (the second would be the Salvation Army Training School on Fourteenth Street). Three days before the subscribers' opening in February 1872, the support of both press and artists was ensured by fortifying them with punch and oysters at a private showing. The museum's first president, John Taylor Johnston, wrote of "our great success in getting together the Artists and Pressmen." He had "felt very apprehensive of the effect of inviting the disaffected Artist element and the gentlemen of the Press, [but] it all worked *very* [sic] well."

Meanwhile, an event had been taking place in Cyprus, halfway around the world, that would be as important to the future greatness of the Metropolitan Museum as the activities in New York. General Louis Palma di Cesnola, an Italian nobleman who had chosen to throw his lot in with the Union army during the American Civil War, had been rewarded for his services with the consulship at Cyprus. Impressed with the history of the Mediterranean island that had been at the crossroads of commerce in the ancient world, Cesnola started excavating almost as soon as he arrived in 1865.

One day in 1870, after reading a magazine article about the efforts being made in New York to found an art museum, the consul wrote a letter to Johnston in which he offered to sell his collection to the new institution at a price to be determined by impartial arbitration and on easy terms. "I have the most valuable and richest private collection of antiquities existing in the world," he wrote in the year that Heinrich Schliemann began his more famous excavations in the Troad. "In six years I opened eight thousand ancient Phoenician, Greek, Assyrian, and Egyptian tombs, from which I extracted and brought to light vases of a hundred different shapes . . . mortuary lamps . . . bronzes . . . glassware of such iridescence that it forms the great attraction of all visitors, more than one thousand objects such as tear bottles, ointment cups . . . plates, bottles, etc. etc., bracelets, rings, beads."

Cesnola's antiquities, which he so much wanted his adopted country to own, went to the Metropolitan for less than the British Museum had offered, and became the cornerstone of the renowned classical collection. And Cesnola himself went to the Metropolitan without salary, to unpack, classify, and arrange his material. He stayed on and became its first salaried director and professional museologist in 1879, a post he held for a quarter of a century.

The next year the Metropolitan opened at its new building in Central Park. Although the city had built the structure (at a cost of $500,-000) and was to maintain it, and although the museum had to pay only a token "rental" of one annual report every May 1, funds for other activities were still scarce. The trustees and director themselves had packed and transported every item being moved from the temporary quarters in the heart of the city at Fourteenth Street to the "suburbs" at Eighty-second Street. The New York *Evening Post* reported that "The Museum of Art, considering that it is the result of only nine years' work, is almost a miracle in this age of work for pay." At the gala opening a plea for more money was a feature of the program. "Ye millionaires of many markets" were urged by one speaker "to convert pork into porcelain, grain and produce into priceless pottery, the rude ores of commerce into sculptured marble, and railroad shares and mining stocks into the glorified canvases of the world's masters, that shall adorn these walls for centuries. The rage of Wall Street is to hunt for the Philosopher's Stone, to convert all baser things into gold, which is but dross; but ours is the higher ambition to convert your useless gold into things of living beauty that shall be a joy to a whole people for a thousand years."

Eventually the money came; at first a trickle, before long a deluge. The first sizable bequest, of over $4,000,000, was the completely surprising legacy of Jacob S. Rogers, whose sole contact with the staff had been his eighteen annual visits to pay his ten-dollar membership fee, and his single request for a copy of the Metropolitan's *Charter, Constitution, Lease and By-Laws*.

J. P. Morgan was the most generous of the early benefactors. He had been an active contributor from the beginning; he was later a trustee and president. His many gifts were of both art and money. After his death, his collection, which was then in storage in the museum's basement, was dispersed. Just under half of it—six thousand objects—went to the Metropolitan.

The treasure house in the park kept on growing until it was truly the colossus of American art museums. A recent building program (costing more than $11,000,000 with the city footing about half the bill) has added a new library wing, a reconstructed Spanish Renaissance patio, and air conditioning. Renovations of the Egyptian, Near Eastern and Far Eastern halls have been completed, while the Costume Institute is taking its turn at being remodeled.

The entire history of man's creativity can be studied here as nowhere else in the country. The classical galleries, unmatched even by Boston, range from one of the finest examples of archaic Greek sculpture, a seventh-century B.C. figure of a young man, to frescoes from the walls of a villa near Herculaneum, the equivalent of which cannot be seen anywhere except in their original location at the foot of Mt.

Vesuvius, whose eruption in 79 A.D. preserved a wealth of late Roman art. The Egyptian collection, started with purchases financed by the sale of duplicates of Cesnola's Cypriote objects, was added to by excavations begun during Morgan's term as museum president. One of the remarkable results is a complete Fifth Dynasty tomb. The collections of arms and armor, musical instruments, textiles, and prints and drawings are exceptional. As for the painting collection, it has been said that it is more nearly comprehensive than that anywhere else in the country. Many canvases are from the bequests of Jules Bache, Benjamin Altman, and Mr. and Mrs. Henry O. Havemeyer. A few of the best known are *The Harvesters* by Pieter Brueghel the Elder, Rubens' *Venus and Adonis,* Vermeer's *Young Woman with Water Jug,* Franz Hals' *Yonker Ramp and His Mistress,* El Greco's *View of Toledo,* Manet's *Woman with a Parrot* and *Boy with a Sword,* Grant Wood's *The Midnight Ride of Paul Revere,* and Picasso's 1906 *Portrait of Gertrude Stein.*

The superlative medieval collection is for the most part situated at the northern tip of Manhattan in THE CLOISTERS. It is almost entirely the gift of John D. Rockefeller, Jr., whose interest in the period began with his purchase of the Unicorn Tapestries for his home on West Fifty-fourth Street. Through an architect friend Mr. Rockefeller met the eccentric American sculptor, George Grey Barnard, who had opened a museum in Washington Heights in 1914 to display fragments of medieval architecture and sculpture he had accumulated while walking through the European countryside. Rockefeller purchased a number of items from Barnard and when, in 1922, the sculptor put his museum up for sale, Rockefeller supplied the funds for the Metropolitan to purchase it. He owned about sixty wooded hilly acres overlooking the Hudson River which he was hoping to develop into a park for the city, and in 1930 four acres were reserved in Fort Tryon Park for the new home of The Cloisters. Rockefeller worked closely with the architect Charles Collens of Boston, and with James J. Rorimer, now director of the Metropolitan, then a young medieval scholar. The result of their efforts makes an important statement about medieval architecture without being either a copy or a composite. It is built around elements—doorways, stained glass windows, capitals—primarily from the cloisters (central courtyards) of five old French monasteries. Modern materials—inconspicuous light fixtures, simple hardware, red roof and floor tiles copied from some that were dug up, hand-hewn granite, unpolished limestone—were chosen to blend in with and be subordinate to the old. Even the shrubbery surrounding the building and the herb garden in one cloister were carefully planned (from manuscript illuminations, paintings, and tapestries) to duplicate as closely as the more rigorous New York climate will permit, what was grown in and around the monasteries of southern France.

An example of the meticulous labor and scholarship that went into this project is the twelfth-century Romanesque chapter house from Nôtre-Dame-de-Pontaut, which was reassembled on the rocky shores of the Hudson "stone for stone and brick for brick," as Rorimer put it when he was The Cloisters' director. Its floors and plaster vaults are the only modern aspects of a totally authentic medieval meeting and discussion chamber.

Just a short walk south from the Metropolitan, there is a museum that is cherished by Manhattanites but too often missed by weekend visitors, even frequent ones. The FRICK COLLECTION, housed in a mansion on Fifth Avenue at Seventieth Street, is neither encyclopedic nor controversial. It is not overwhelming in the way the Metropolitan is; it can be "felt" and comprehended (although certainly not fully appreciated) in a single visit. It is not "disturbing" in the way the Guggenheim is. Its atmosphere is so restful that a short stay becomes a way of getting out of rather than "into" New York. Its paintings, sculpture, drawings, and decorative arts range from the fourteenth through the nineteenth centuries. Chamber music can be heard there on Sundays during the winter. And its Art Reference Library is one of the best in the country. Henry Clay Frick loved this mansion and everything in it. For him, too, it was a means of escaping turbulence.

As a young man in Pennsylvania, Frick gained such an important and controlling position in the coke industry so vital to the manufacture of steel that Andrew Carnegie made sure to gain control of him. Carnegie did it by giving him shares of his steel organization in which Frick became an aggressive officer. It was Frick's anti-union policies that finally brought about the notorious Homestead strike of 1892. The strike lasted five months during which time non-union men were employed and protected by three hundred Pinkertons. When the Pinkertons and strikers fought a violent battle, some were killed, others were wounded, and the governor called out the National Guard. When the non-union employees continued to work, the strike was broken. Later Frick and Carnegie split. Through it all and for years afterward, Frick's need for serenity was provided by art.

What could be more serene than the eight decorative Boucher panels painted for Madame de Pompadour, or the four seasons interpreted by the same artist for the same lady, or the marvelous Fragonards commissioned and then rejected by Madame du Barry? These (which include that most lovely account of a gentleman's graceful assault on a porcelain lady called *Storming the Citadel*) plus a group of smaller panels were bought from the Morgan estate.

Bellini, El Greco, Hals, Rembrandt, Turner, Whistler? Piero della Francesca, Holbein, Van Dyck, Vermeer, Gainsborough, Goya? They are all—superbly—here. Rembrandt's *The Polish Rider* is universally considered one of his finest works, and his *Self-Portrait* from his later years, one of his most penetrating. George de la Tour's dramatic, candlelit *The Education of the Virgin* is, quite apart from its religious theme, a universally meaningful statement of a relationship between a mother and her child. The three Vermeers are treasured reminders of the relative scarcity of that artist's canvases. Ingres' *Portrait of the Comtesse d'Haussonville* is one of his best-known works. Houdon's statue of *Diana* greets the visitor as he enters the Oval Room. And an exquisite group of French painted enamels of the late fifteenth, sixteenth, and early seventeenth centuries, from Limoges and elsewhere, can be found in a small room at the end of the West Gallery.

There are no jarring notes in this museum; just beauty and harmony. The curative powers of art have been tested here by many a nervous New Yorker.

The SOLOMON R. GUGGENHEIM MUSEUM is not restful. It is exciting. It is magnificent. It quite literally, physically upsets your equilibrium; it makes you think on your feet. Outside of the lobby, the cafeteria, and the elevators, there is no place in it where the visitor can stand on a level floor. Designed by Frank Lloyd Wright to represent "the first advance in organic architecture," the circular building encloses "one great space on a continuous floor." The galleries are partitioned sections of a ramp, over a quarter of a mile long, that winds gracefully upward in a widening spiral toward a dome 92 feet high. The key word to the Guggenheim's exhibits, which change regularly, is "impact." And its basic aim, to generate an interest in contemporary twentieth-century art without attempting comprehensive documentation or cross-sectional representation, is supplementary to rather than competitive with the aims of the city's other art museums.

The permanent collection includes 120 paintings by Vasily Kandinsky, the largest group owned by any museum in the world (there were originally fifty more, which were sold when the trustees realized that an exhibit of 170 Kandinskys would never be physically possible); 170 works of Paul Klee, the largest group owned by any museum in America; the largest number of Brancusi sculptures owned by any museum in New York; and important selections of works by Franz Marc, Marc Chagall, Robert Delaunay, and Albert Gleizes. No one should come here expecting to see all or even most of them at any one time. Properly accredited students, however, can gain access to any of them by special arrangement.

Léger, de Kooning, Mondrian, Dubuffet, Pollock, Bonnard, and Seurat are among the modern painters here. Archipenko, Arp, Naum Gabo, Antoine Pevsner and Lipchitz are among the sculptors.

On October 23, 1963, the Guggenheim announced "the most important gift of works of art to be willed to the museum since its original founding" twenty-six years earlier as the Museum of Non-Objective Art. The gift consisted of a portion of the collection of Justin K. Thannhauser, a dealer. It included thirty-four Picassos (*Woman Ironing* among them), four Cézannes, three Renoirs, Degas pastels and bronzes, two Manets, two Gauguins, and two Modiglianis. "The significant effect on the general character of the museum," as reported in the New York *Times* by John Canaday, "is that its boundaries are pushed back into the early impressionist period." Its basic aim, however, and the effectiveness with which it is fulfilled, will not be altered.

The story of modern art in New York does not, of course, begin at the Guggenheim. It begins at the Armory Show of 1913, where modern art was introduced to America.

Organized by a group of artists reacting against the conservatism of the National Academy of Design (which apparently had lost sight of its own origins), the show was at first intended as a display of the work of progressive young American painters and sculptors. But its scope was expanded; until more than a third of the thirteen thousand or so works in the halls of the 69th Regiment Armory were of European origin. Although before that time some Americans were already familiar with the new achievements of European art, and there had even been two or three *avant-garde* showings in New York, it was the Armory Show, and particularly its European canvases, that dramatically forced Fauvism, Cubism, and Expressionism upon the consciousness of layman, collector, critic, and artist.

Several important modern collections were launched by purchases from the Armory Show. Miss Lillie P. Bliss and Mrs. Cornelius J. Sullivan were two affluent ladies who bought the new art. John Quinn, a lawyer, bought works by Segonzac, Redon, Brancusi, Derain, Duchamp, and Duchamp-Villon which cost him, all together, less than $6000. From this beginning Quinn built up an astounding collection—Seurat, the young Picasso, Braque, Matisse, Rousseau—in little more than a decade. He died in 1924, stipulating in his will that his paintings (except for Seurat's *The Circus,* which was to go to the Louvre as its first work by that artist) be sold, the income from the sale to go to his sister. Aline Saarinen quotes him as having "rejected the idea of 'leaving these things to the Metropolitan. They would not be appreciated in New York.'" It seemed true. He had been a major lender to a Postimpressionist show held—under duress—at the Metropolitan, and found that his were the paintings most frequently and violently castigated by friends, critics, and the public. Although the Metropolitan had made a purchase from the Armory, it had been a fairly conservative one—a Cézanne. Nevertheless this was the first Cézanne to be bought by an American museum.

It was the Quinn sale, three years after his death, that led Miss Bliss and Mrs. Sullivan to lament New York's lack of museum hospitality to modern art, and then to resolve that they would remedy the situation. They foresightedly chose, as the third partner in this undertaking, their friend Mrs. John D. (Abby Aldrich) Rockefeller, Jr., who had recently become a collector of American art, both modern and primitive. A luncheon at the Rockefeller home set in motion the events that culminated in the opening of the MUSEUM OF MODERN ART, in rented quarters on the fourteenth floor of an office building, in November of 1929.

The Modern was an instant success, with nearly fifty thousand visitors in the first month alone. A house given by the Rockefellers was the second home of the expanding collection—which received Miss Bliss's bequest of a score of Cézannes and many other works after her death—and when the historic present building on Fifty-third Street went up in 1939, Rockefeller-owned land was under it.

In addition to achieving international fame for its paintings and sculptures, the museum has pioneered in the definition of industrial design, photography, and cinema as art. The architecture and design collection, housed in a new gallery named for Philip L. Goodwin (long-time trustee and co-architect with Edward Durrell Stone of the museum's building) contains thousands of architectural models, examples of furniture and decorative objects. Such twentieth-century masters as Louis C. Tiffany, Matisse, Mies van der Rohe, Eero Saarinen, and Charles Eames are represented. And the film library, the most extensive in the country, provides unlimited material for daily screenings in a pleasant auditorium. Other assets of the Modern are an outstanding department of drawings and prints, a broad program of traveling exhibits, an art lending service, an excellent library, and a cafeteria opening on the recently enlarged sculpture garden. Works by sculptors Brancusi (*Bird in Space*), Calder, Lachaise (*Standing Woman*), Lehmbruck (*Kneeling Woman*), Lipchitz, Maillol, Moore, and others are in the garden and elsewhere in the building. Among the best-known paintings are Van Gogh's *Starry Night*, Cézanne's *Still Life with Apples* and *The Bather*, Chagall's *I and My Village*, Rousseau's *The Sleeping Gypsy*, Malevich's *White on White*, Mondrian's *Broadway Boogie-Woogie*, Dali's *The Persistence of Memory*, Picasso's *Les Demoiselles d'Avignon*, Léger's *Three Women*, Orozco's *Zapatistas*, and Bacon's *Painting, 1946*.

The John D. Rockefeller, Jrs. provided not only land and money to support the Modern, but a son and the wife of another son as well. Mrs. John D. (Blanchette) Rockefeller III has been an active trustee and a generous donor. Nelson Rockefeller, himself a well-known collector of contemporary and primitive works, has been active for more than twenty years as president, chairman, trustee, and donor. The governor recently presented the museum with Matisse's *Dance*, a study done in 1909 in preparation for a mural commissioned by a Russian collector and now in the Hermitage Museum in Leningrad. The subject derives from an earlier work, *The Joy of Life*, that belongs to the Barnes Foundation.

Also serving the cause of modern art in New York is the WHITNEY MUSEUM OF AMERICAN ART, which had its beginning in the Greenwich Village studio of Mrs. Gertrude Vanderbilt Whitney. The award-winning sculptress held small informal exhibitions of work by her friends and fellow artists, first in her studio off MacDougal Alley and then in adjacent larger quarters around the corner on Eighth Street. Aided by her secretary and long-time associate, Mrs. Juliana Force, she expanded the activities of the Whitney Studio into the Whitney Studio Club, which hundreds of young artists were to call home in the years before and during the 1920s. Many of today's "names" received their first showings there as unknowns. Building up a discriminating collection of the work of her contemporaries, beginning with the purchase in 1908 of canvases by Henri, Luks, Lawson, and Shinn, Mrs.

Whitney and Mrs. Force then organized exhibitions for both European consumption and the American hinterlands.

In 1929, when Mrs. Whitney considered giving up the galleries, she offered her collection of more than six hundred works to the Metropolitan. The Metropolitan chose not to accept what was the most complete record of twentieth-century work in America up to that time.

This refusal of works by Gifford Beal, John Steuart Curry, Stuart Davies, Max Weber, Mahonri Young, Yasuo Kuniyoshi, Reginald Marsh, Reuben Nakian, Henry Schnakenberg, Eugene Speicher, William Zorach, and others resulted in the founding of the Whitney Museum. With Mrs. Force as director and three painters as curators, it opened at enlarged and remodeled quarters on Eighth Street in 1931. There, and since 1954 on Fifty-fourth Street adjoining the Modern, it has held pace-setting annual exhibitions of painting, sculpture, and drawing. It has published works by and about contemporary artists. And it has circulated substantial segments of its more than sixteen-hundred-object collection to museums and colleges throughout the country. Never favoring one "ism" over another, the Whitney respects the artist's independence and freedom. Art critic Forbes Watson, who was friend and adviser to Mrs. Whitney, wrote that "the aim was simple, to stimulate current creative forces by showing and buying the works of current creative artists." A special point is made each year of purchasing at least one work by an artist under thirty. This is known as the Juliana Force Purchase. Among those so honored have been Jack Madson, George Tooker (*The Subway*), and Robert Vickrey. The Whitney still has the most complete record of twentieth-century American art anywhere.

It moves yet again in 1966, to Seventy-fifth Street and Madison Avenue, where a building designed by Marcel Breuer will permit greater display (only 20 per cent of the collection is now on view at any one time) and where it will be within walking distance of the Frick, the Metropolitan, the Guggenheim, and a number of Madison Avenue dealers' galleries as well.

Not within walking distance but certainly worth a few minutes in the subway is the BROOKLYN MUSEUM, which ranks among the top ten art institutions in the country. Known best for its Egyptian collection and library, the Brooklyn is also famous for the way in which it has explored the relationship between ethnology and art with important exhibits representing indigenous America, Oceania, and Africa. Exciting, too, are its Oriental, American decorative arts, fashion, and industrial design displays. American Colonial and Victorian period rooms (including the reconstructed oak-timbered Schenck House originally built in Brooklyn in about 1675); European and American painting and sculpture; nineteenth- and twentieth-century drawings and water colors; an important new installation illustrating the art and method of the modern print maker; a sculpture garden containing architectural ornaments from New York buildings now vanishing under the wrecker's ball; and an excellent gift shop which frequently holds sales exhibitions of folk crafts new to this country—all are features offered by this dynamic intellectual center to its responsive community.

Manhattan's remaining art museums cover a wide range of specialized interests. The JEWISH MUSEUM, which has a contemporary outlook and features important changing exhibits of painting and sculpture, offers the best collection in the hemisphere of ceremonial art reflecting the long history and wide dispersal of the Jewish people. The HISPANIC SOCIETY MUSEUM with its paintings, sculpture, decorative arts, and library of over one hundred thousand volumes, is an essential study center for anyone seriously interested in the history and culture of the lands in which Spanish and Portuguese are or have been spoken. In a smaller way, the same purpose is served for the student of the Orient by the gallery and library of ASIA HOUSE, a building provided by John D. Rockefeller III. The MUSEUM OF PRIMITIVE ART was founded by Nelson Rockefeller and received most of his own collection. When it opened in 1957, its director, Dr. Robert Goldwater, defined its interests as the "artistic achievements of the indigenous civilizations of the Americas, Africa, and Oceania, and the early phases of the civilizations of Asia and Europe."

The Primitive is one of three museums that have recently moved into the vicinity of the Modern. Newest is the MUSEUM OF EARLY AMERICAN FOLK ARTS, with changing exhibitions of painting, sculpture, and such objects as weather vanes, ship figureheads, carved toys, and store signs. Only a few years older is the MUSEUM OF CONTEMPORARY CRAFTS, dedicated to exhibiting, with startling effectiveness and originality, the work of today's artisans in weaving, embroidery, jewelry making, wood carving, ceramics, and anything else that can be beautifully handmade. The museum publishes *Craft Horizons* magazine and sends out traveling exhibitions. Its parent body, the American Craftsmen's Council, operates America House directly across the street, which sells everything from a bookmark to a pot-bellied stove, all hand-crafted.

Although its future is at the moment uncertain, the COOPER UNION MUSEUM is worth noting not only because of its importance as a source of research for the decorative arts, with its collection of about one hundred thousand items (prints and drawings, wallpapers, textiles, eighteenth-century ceramics, woodwork, metalwork, glass, leather, and enamels), but also because of its unique history. The museum grew out of the founding in 1859 by Peter Cooper of the first free college-level institution in the country designed, according to its charter, "to improve and instruct those classes of the inhabitants of the city of New York whose occupations are such as . . . to deprive them of proper recreation and instruction."

New York's newest is Huntington Hartford's GALLERY OF MODERN ART, which in March of 1964 opened its doors, set back from a white and green Vermont marble façade, and ended the mystery that had been puzzling the city's residents for more than four years. Inside there was a Tchelitchew retrospective, the first significant over-all look at the Russian-born painter's work since fifteen years before his death in 1958. In addition, there were more than seventy paintings and several pieces of sculpture gathered by Mr. Hartford, reflecting the collector's frequently expressed belief that there is a valid alternative to the present-day dominance of abstract art. Among them were Dalis, paintings by the nineteenth-century Englishman Burne-Jones, and others by the representational Americans Whistler, Sargent, Marsh, Henri, and Cassatt. There were sculptures by Renoir, Rodin, Houdon, Epstein, and Jo Davidson, and a study of the late President John F. Kennedy by Robert Berks, which was acquired by Mr. Hartford just in time for the opening. Described as having an interior of "wall-to-wall luxury," the Gallery features a cocktail-espresso lounge on the eighth floor, with walls and a bar of ebony, and some Oceanic objects gathered by Mr. Hartford. A Polynesian restaurant known as the Gauguin Room is dominated by a pair of tapestries reproducing works by the artist. A gold and red auditorium in the basement seats 154 persons, and has an expanding stage to permit live as well as screened events. Shortly after its opening the Gallery announced the start of a film collection and regular screenings.

Manhattanites, for the most part, are still unaware that important art museums are to be found well beyond the city limits, in that vast territory sometimes spoken of vaguely as "upstate." One such place, the ALBRIGHT-KNOX ART GALLERY, traces its origin back to the founding of the Buffalo Fine Arts Academy more than a century ago. Its growth was steady, although slow, during its first half-century. Then John Joseph Albright, a former director and president, donated the handsome neoclassic building that stimulated the Gallery's burst of energy in the years that followed. With fewer than fifty objects in its possession, with a small purchase fund, generous patrons, and dynamic directors, Buffalo was prepared (despite some lingering conservatism that would soon explode into controversy) to take advantage of the awakening field of modern art; and little time was spent in lamentation over the old masters that were priced beyond reach of the city's rich, but not Morgan-rich, industrialists.

One of the first exhibitions held in the new building was the first showing anywhere in the country of contemporary German painting, followed in short order by a French Impressionist display and the first International Exhibit of Pictorial Photography (arranged by Alfred Steiglitz, who forced the recognition of photography as a fine art). Pavlova danced at an opening of a show of paintings by Ballet Russe designer Léon Bakst, and Sarah Bernhardt emoted at a display of works borrowed from the Luxembourg Museum in Paris. There was never a dull moment; and the Gallery reached its hundredth birthday feeling more vigorous than ever. Shortly after its centennial, a new modern wing was acquired, featuring a glass-walled auditorium and exhibition halls looking out onto a sculpture garden; all of it the $1,400,000 gift of Seymour H. Knox.

The modern paintings the Gallery has acquired since the mid-twenties are distinguished both individually and as a group. De Chirico, Feininger, Gris, Kokoschka, Miró, Rouault, Tanguy, Vuillard, Gorky, Pollock, Hofmann, Kline, and Rothko are just some of the names here. And the sculptures are equally fine. Recently bronzes by Barlach and Giacometti have been added to a collection that ranges from 3000 B.C. (ancient Mesopotamia, Cambodia, India, and China) to the present (Rodin, Epstein, Brancusi, Renoir, Matisse, Picasso, Moore, Lehmbruck, and Nicholson).

Additional paintings include examples of the work of Buffalo's native sons Charles Burchfield, Lars Sellstedt and Thomas Le Clear; canvases by Gainsborough, Hogarth, Lawrence, Romney, and Reynolds; and Picasso's *La Toilette*. There was such a furor among the trustees over this Picasso from the John Quinn sale that vice-president and donor A. Conger Goodyear, who had made the purchase, was forced to resign. The trustees, however, kept the painting; and Goodyear went on to New York where he was invited to conspire with the ladies who were establishing the Museum of Modern Art.

Another gleaming upstate gallery is the elegantly modern MUNSON-WILLIAMS-PROCTOR INSTITUTE of Utica, which was helped along on its way to distinction in the 1930s by a quiet, discerning professor of art appreciation from nearby Hamilton College. The young Edward Wales Root, son of diplomat Elihu Root, was introduced to the contemporary art world in 1907 when he held an editorial job on the old New York *Sun*. His first purchase, a Lawson, was made more out of compassion for the impecunious painter than out of commitment to the new school of American realism. But it marked the turning point of his life, and the origin of a collection that gave early recognition to many young artists.

Root worked closely with the Institute, guiding it to buy the works of the about-to-be-discovered, and consequently providing it with much that would gain both in recognition and value; paintings by Baziotes, Gatch, O'Keeffe, I. Rice Pereira, Pollock, Rothko, Tobey, and others. At his death in 1956, 228 paintings from his own collection and a library of seven hundred volumes were left to the Institute.

Paintings from Albers to Zorn and sculptures from Arp to Zorach represent primarily the twentieth century in America; but small groups of earlier American art and some works by Europeans who have influenced American ideas are also included.

One painter whose works are here in bulk is Arthur B. Davies, a native of Utica, who more than anyone else was responsible for the Armory Show's inclusion of European art. The Institute sponsored a Davies centennial retrospective in 1962. Fittingly, it was the originator of the fiftieth anniversary re-creation of the Armory Show, which in 1963 reminded the public and the press of what it had been like when modern art was young.

In the five Atlantic states directly south of Washington there are well over a dozen first-rate art museums in which a variety of exciting galleries can be found. At the VIRGINIA MUSEUM OF FINE ARTS in Richmond, where the range extends from ancient Egypt to Ben Shahn, with important glimpses of Rembrandt, Watteau, Salvatora Rosa, Reynolds, Lawrence, Copley, Picasso, and Braque, there is a good collection of fifteenth- to eighteenth-century European tapestries and a remarkable collection of imperial Russian jewelry—ornamental conversation pieces—created by Carl Fabergé. Five of the fantastic Easter eggs (of crystal and gold, encrusted with precious stones, and literally full of surprises) that were designed for Czar Nicholas II, are here. In those good old days of conspicuousness, this master jeweler's workshop created employment for seven hundred craftsmen.

Williamsburg, Virginia, is the home of the marvelous ABBY ALDRICH ROCKEFELLER FOLK ART COLLECTION of more than six hundred paintings plus drawings, metal and wood sculpture, and objects —all of the late eighteenth and early nineteenth centuries. Because most of them date from about a century later than the Colonial Williamsburg restoration, they are displayed just beyond that restricted area in their own museum.

The NORTH CAROLINA MUSEUM OF ART in Raleigh was brought into existence as the result of a unique million-dollar appropriation by the state legislature for the purchase of a collection. A matching gift in paintings from the Kress Foundation plus William Valentiner's guidance helped make these galleries rich in European masterworks and eighteenth-century American portraits. Boucher's *The Abduction of Europa*, Nattier's portraits of *Madame de Vintimille* as a vestal virgin and *Mademoiselle de Beaujolais* as the goddess Diana, a David self-portrait, Rubens' *The Bear Hunt*, Rembrandt's *Esther's Feast*, and a *St. Jerome in His Study* by the fifteenth-century German, Stephen Lochner, are only a few of the paintings that make Raleigh worth a special visit.

Not to slight South Carolina, the Kress people extended their generosity to the COLUMBIA MUSEUM OF ART in 1954. And in 1958, the Foundation brought a gift to Georgia.

When the ATLANTA ART ASSOCIATION received thirty-odd Italian paintings spanning a period of four centuries, it had already established itself as an artistic center whose influence was felt far beyond its immediate community. The Association has been an important source of encouragement to artists from an eight-state area (North Carolina, South Carolina, Georgia, Florida, Tennessee, Alabama, Mississippi, and Louisiana) for whom exhibits are regularly held. Atlanta's galleries include examples of Oriental, Early American, and contemporary art, and pre-1830 decorative arts.

One of Florida's most impressive cultural attractions was put there by John Ringling, a man who loved the circus, collected magnificent baroque paintings, and left a beautiful memorial to himself and his wife in Sarasota. A. Everett Austin came from the Wadsworth Atheneum to the JOHN AND MABLE RINGLING MUSEUM OF ART as its first director. He renovated the galleries, refined the collection, imported an eighteenth-century theater from Italy, installed it on the premises, and established America's first circus museum nearby, not far from the Ringling residence. Today the museum conducts an opera season, a drama season, and chamber music recitals as part of its regular activities. And in the midst of all this excitement, there are the remarkable paintings. Richly representing the seventeenth century, with a particular emphasis on Rubens, the collection goes back to the end of the fifteenth and extends through the eighteenth. Piero di Cosimo's famous documentary illustration of *The Building of a Palace* is from the earliest period here. The Rubenses include four (out of eleven) heroic paintings on a religious theme that were used as designs, or cartoons, for a series of Brussels tapestries. The largest of them shows *Abraham Receiving Bread and Wine from Melchizadek*. Also here are Rubens' portrait of *The Archduke Ferdinand* and a painting depicting Lot's flight from Sodom accompanied by his family and guided by angels, one of the most famous in the Sarasota group. Other Ringling masterpieces—there are hundreds of them—are Veronese's *The Rest on the Flight into Egypt,* El Greco's *Christ on the Cross,* Poussin's *The Ecstasy of St. Paul,* Jan Steen's *The Rape of the Sabine Women,* which underwent restoration in 1959, two Canaletto views of Venice, and Gainsborough's outsized equestrian portrait of *General Philip Honywood.*

A brief additional list of notable art museums would include New Orleans' ISAAC DELGADO MUSEUM OF ART with its Kress galleries, its paintings of the Barbizon school, its paintings by Southern artists, and its growing contemporary collection; the J. B. SPEED ART MUSEUM in Louisville, Kentucky, with its historic Kentucky portraits, including work by Matthew Jouett, Chester Harding, and John J. Audubon; the JOHN HERRON ART INSTITUTE of Indianapolis, Indiana, with its representative collection of European and American painting, its pre-Columbian ceramics and sculpture, its small Chinese collection, and its group of Turner paintings; Iowa's DES MOINES ART CENTER with its European and American paintings and sculptures and its contemporary works; Wisconsin's MILWAUKEE ART CENTER with its modern (Saarinen) architecture, its early through contemporary American collection, and its European moderns; the BUTLER INSTITUTE OF

AMERICAN ART of Youngstown, Ohio, with its paintings by Copley, Earl, Stuart, Whistler, Homer, Eakins, Ryder, Burchfield, Wyeth, Shahn, and its portraits of Southwest Indians; the TAFT MUSEUM of Cincinnati (an 1820 house—a fine example of Federal architecture —that became the home of Charles Phelps Taft, lawyer, newspaper publisher, half-brother and adviser to William Howard Taft) with its Rembrandts, Halses, Turners, and Goyas, its Chinese porcelains, its French Renaissance enamels, crystal, and jewelry, and its Duncan Phyfe furniture; the CRANBROOK ACADEMY OF ART GALLERIES of Bloomfield Hills, Michigan (designed by Saarinen), with its pre-Columbian, Chinese, European, and contemporary collections; and Pittsburgh's CARNEGIE INSTITUTE MUSEUM OF ART, with its important triennial international exhibitions of contemporary painting and sculpture, and its history of receptiveness to a wide variety of schools.

New Jersey's NEWARK MUSEUM, which pioneered during its early years when John Cotton Dana was its director in new methods of display and in expanding the institution's public services, is concerned both with science and art. Highlighting its art galleries is an excellent collection of American painting, sculpture, and decorative works.

Far to the west of our westernmost museums, there is the HONOLULU ACADEMY OF ARTS. Originally established in 1927 for the purpose of providing continuity with Hawaii's rich, multi-racial cultural heritage, it has built up fine collections of Oriental and Pacific Islands art. In 1952 the arrival of a Kress Collection, hailed by the Academy's director as an event of "unique importance," brought this unique American city into direct contact with the Renaissance. Western culture, in the form of European and American painting and sculpture, is today, of course, better represented than ever.

Finally, tribute must be paid to the American Federation of Arts which, not itself a museum, has been an important partner in the work of our museums. Founded "to foster production and cultivate the appreciation of art in America," the Federation organizes and circulates exhibits both in the United States and abroad. Many of its domestic shows have gone into towns where there are no permanent galleries. The Federation's headquarters are in Manhattan. *Art News, Art in America, Who's Who in American Art,* and the *American Art Directory* are among the many publications it sponsors.

Observing life in America in an article written for the *Saturday Review* a few years ago, D. W. Brogan took notice in the deliberately borrowed vernacular of *Variety* that there are "no hix in the stix." "In the past generation," he wrote, "there has been a cultural revolution that has resulted in a narrowing of the gap between Manhattan and the rest of the country."

But was it really a revolution? The phenomenon described by Mr. Brogan had its start, in terms of our own short history, a long time ago. And the best evidence that this is so is the story of our museums.

Chapter III

SCIENCE

THERE was a time not too long ago when one could say with fairness of the science museum in America (while remaining aware of a few outstanding exceptions to the epithet): "A dead file of moth fodder." Others preferred the term "dead circuses." But the most evocative image by far was of "a menagerie that doesn't eat." Zoologists, botanists, and geologists, classifying and labeling the objects of their specialization with the kind of earnest pedantry that reflects itself as dullness, had cluttered up the halls. And when research biologists, more interested in the revelations of the laboratory than the effectiveness of exhibits, left the clutter where it was, dreariness quickly set in.

Contrastingly, today's exhibits are not only a vital means of popular education but quite often a lively form of entertainment. And this, in a sense, is as it was meant to be from the beginning. The keepers of our earliest collections, whether members of an academy or managers of an enterprise hopefully intended to make a profit, were guided by lively impulses. This liveliness prevailed right up to the time of Darwin.

In 1824 the *Cincinnati Literary Gazette* published a verse catalogue of the Western Museum, a local establishment where one Joseph Dorfeuille presided over a cabinet of minerals, fossils, archaeological specimens, and later, a waxworks called the Inferno:

> Wend hither, ye members of polished society—
> Ye who bright phantoms of pleasure pursue—
> To see of strange objects the endless variety,
> Monsieur Dorfeuille will expose to your view.
>
> Lo, here is a cabinet of great curiosities
> Procured from the Redmen who once were our foes;
> Unperished tokens of dire animosities,
> Darts, tomahawks, war-cudgels, arrows and bows,

And bone-hooks for fishes and old earthen dishes,
   To please him who wishes o'er such things to pore,
Superb wampum sashes, and mica-slate glasses,
   Which doubtless the lasses much valued of yore.

Of the Western Museum, only the poetry remains. But the institution did help pave the way for the Cincinnati Museum of Natural History which survived some hazardous periods and finally achieved the excellent health it now enjoys.

America's first museum, that of the Library Society of Charleston, South Carolina, established in 1773, took "into . . . consideration, the many advantages and great credit that would result . . . from a full and accurate Natural History of the [province], and being desirous to promote so useful a Design . . . appointed a Committee . . . to collect and prepare Materials for that Purpose." The Committee asked "to be furnished . . . with the Specimens of all the various Fossils, Minerals, and Ores, the different Soils, Earths, Clays, Marles, Stones, Sands, Shells, & the Productions of this Province, with the best Accounts of their several Natures, Qualities, Situations and Uses. . . . Of the Animal Tribe they [wished] to have every species. . . . Of Vegetables, they [requested] every Kind, from the loftiest Tree in the Forest, to the smallest Plant of the Fields. . . . A complete Specimen of any Tree or Plant, will be two small Branches of each, one having the Flower in full bloom, and the other the ripe Fruit. . . . At the same Time the Society [asked] to be furnished with the best Accounts that can be given of the Uses and Virtues, either in Agriculture, Commerce, or Medicine, of which such Tree or Plant is possessed . . . the Soil in which it most commonly grows . . . the Season in which it flowers, and when it bears its fruit."

The popular study of natural history at this time was full of wonder and erroneous notions that caused delight. Collecting was done mostly for its own sake, the motivation being acquisitiveness plus some other need that varied with the collector. In Salem, Massachusetts, in 1799, a group of wealthy sea captains who had been indiscriminately amassing "natural and artificial curiosities" on their voyages to the East, satisfied a desire for status by associating themselves with the world of scholarship. They established a museum.

What is today the PEABODY MUSEUM OF SALEM was founded by the East India Marine Society, an exclusive organization "of such Ship Masters only as have had a Register from Salem and who have navigated those Seas at or beyond the Cape of Good Hope." The quality of the material they brought home pretty much depended upon the degree of sophistication of the people with whom they traded. The mandarins and merchants of China were for the most part unwilling to give up their best pieces of porcelain and bronze to *nouveau riche* seamen bewildered by the difference between a rarity and a souvenir. The Pacific Islanders, on the other hand, had no way of knowing that their simplest everyday utensils would one day be regarded as highly valuable ethnological specimens. The excellent Polynesian collections were, therefore, easily assembled. At a later time in the museum's history other travelers, more knowledgeable about the Orient, would send back a fine collection of Japanese ethnological objects as well as some good Chinese, Siamese, Tibetan, and Korean pieces.

The East India Marine Society began to need money in the 1860s at just about the same time the nearby Essex Institute, interested both in local history and science, was facing a similar problem. It was then that George Peabody, a banker, provided financial aid and a plan to merge the East India collections and the Essex natural history materials into a new organization. Four brilliant young Essex zoologists came along as part of the package; the Essex Institute meanwhile returned with pleasure to the pursuit of local history.

In the years that followed, as Walter Muir Whitehill describes them in his definitive history of the Peabody, "when Science—with a capital S—was in the ascendant, these 'artificial curiosities' (that is, the ethnology collections) were tolerated, but zoology was the real enthusiasm of the day. With the passing of the popular hysteria which was created by the Darwinian evolutionary theory, the handiwork of mankind began again to assume its proper place."

Today's exhibits are divided into three main groups: maritime history, ethnology, and local natural history. The Polynesian objects are still outstanding: a big carved Hawaiian war god is one of three in existence; stuffed birds, including the first penguin to arrive in the United States, abound; and the prevailing atmosphere in this historic building still known as East India Marine Hall is again nautical—with its instruments, tools, ship models, figureheads, paintings, and library of manuscripts, books, and maps.

In their histories, archives, and collections, our science museums tell the extraordinary story of the development of science itself in the not quite two centuries since the Charleston Museum was founded. The insatiable curiosity and omnivorous collecting with which that story begins were already apparent in the middle of the eighteenth century when Harvard College began accumulating "curiosities natural and artificial" such as "two compleat Skeletons of different sexes" and scientific instruments of European manufacture. Harvard's one-room Museum was destroyed by fire in 1765. Rising almost immediately from the ashes, it received "a curious Coralline on its natural bed" from John Hancock and, after a while, "a number of bottles, containing curious reptiles." When it became known that "vermin" were causing the decay of several specimens "not withstanding that the Librarian, who is the Keeper of that room, has used his utmost endeavors," the museum received "three gallons of high wines" to be used as a preservative.

Harvard's Mineral Cabinet was begun in 1794 with a gift of fifty fossils to a lecturer in "Natural Philosophy" who did not let the fact that he was "less acquainted with that branch of natural history than perhaps any other" deter him from holding classes in which he "endeavored to [teach] some idea of the riches hitherto locked up in vast store-houses under our feet." His Cabinet was literally a cabinet, of "elegant mahogany," whose "front" was "glazed" so that specimens could "be easily seen by the ordinary visitants." However, "the curious in this science [could] at any time have a nearer access to them."

Throughout the civilized world at this period, the "curious" in the natural sciences were under the influence of Linnaeus, who had devised, and promulgated in a multitude of publications, a binomial system for the classification of plant and animal life. Every thing living was to be identified in terms of both a genus and a species, and its affiliations were, in these pre-Darwinian days, determined on the basis of evidence derived from minute observation of each specimen's external appearance. This apparently precise system afforded an opportunity to bring order to man's relatively meager comprehension of the world around him.

Art critic John Canaday recently took note of the "direct relationship, which seems to have been inspired by some beneficent god of coincidence, between what artists want to say at a certain time and the means an age offers them for saying it." This relationship is as true for scientists as for artists. The deists of the eighteenth and early nineteenth centuries, to whom the natural world was proof of God's reality and the wonders of nature reason for His worship, embraced Linnaean classification without reservation. Here was a scientific means of demonstrating order in nature, and the existence of order in nature was the most valid proof of the existence of the Deity. An advertisement for Rembrandt Peale's Baltimore Museum expressed the equation this way: "Natural History is well adapted to unfold to our view the attributes of the Great Creator. . . . The Mind, contemplating the wonderful works of God, is expanded and elevated to the Almighty's throne in wonder, love and praise." A few years later Rubens Peale invited the public to the same museum, where they would be able to "look through nature, up to NATURE'S GOD."

With avidity, layman joined scientists in the hunt for more and more specimens, of any- and everything, to observe and classify. Amateurs and professionals banded together to discuss subjects of mutual interest, and formalized their association by forming academies or societies of natural history. When collections outgrew the homes or places of business where the work of describing and labeling had been carried on they gravitated to rooms rented by the academies. The work continued; and museums began to take shape.

The ACADEMY OF NATURAL SCIENCES in Philadelphia started this way, and so did the MARYLAND ACADEMY OF SCIENCES in Baltimore. The museum of Philadelphia's Academy was begun in 1812 when two thousand mineral specimens were purchased for $750 and stored in the home of a founding member. Well past the middle of the century when the museum, in its own building, was "acknowledged to be the finest on this continent," it could still be said that "the entire work of classification and arrangement devolves upon the members, whose ordinary vocations permit them to devote to it only the leisure hours which others spend in amusement." Those busy members had eagerly sought to reach and instruct the public long before this became a normal function of similar institutions. They saw to it that the Academy opened its halls "on Tuesday and Friday afternoons for the gratuitous admission of visitors." Years later, attempting to clarify their exhibits, they would hit upon a display technique that, understandably, could not survive the new spirit of scientific inquiry just around the corner. "The visitor will notice," the 1862 handbook declared, "that the labels attached to these specimens are bordered with various colors. These designate the portion of the globe from which they were obtained, and as far as practicable follow the color of the inhabitants. Thus— Red . . . America; Brown . . . Europe; Black . . . Africa; Yellow . . . Asia" and when it became a matter of obvious impracticability to pursue this color scheme further, they settled for "Green . . . Polynesia."

The first official display of John James Audubon's bird paintings was held here in 1824, and Audubon Hall is a highlight of the Academy's museum today, featuring exhibits on avian evolution, biology and habits. In addition there is the Philadelphia Bird Hall, which serves local watchers as an encyclopedia of the distinguishing characteristics and seasonal migrations of nearly three hundred species. A darkened room in the Mineral Gallery displays fluorescent stones; and in another corner the original cabinet of minerals with which the museum began may still be seen.

Baltimore's Academy was organized because some gentlemen of the city felt the need for a club where they could discuss science and literature with other gentlemen; where they could accumulate collections and build a library. The infant academy flourished under the presidency of Robert Gilmor from 1822 until "in an unfortunate hour nearly the whole of [its] valuable property was consumed by fire." But the organization was rebuilt. Several important civic institutions would grow out of it, and one member, Johns Hopkins, would found the great university bearing his name. Today, having survived a period of dormancy, the Academy has an active program of advanced science seminars for selected students as well as symposiums for teachers, and it circulates exhibits to schools throughout the state. It also maintains a popular planetarium. Its exhibit facilities are temporarily limited within its borrowed quarters, but it has embarked on the construction of a $3,000,000 Maryland Science Center which will greatly expand the services it offers.

Fire was only one of the hazards encountered by these fledgling groups. In San Francisco in 1853, when settlers were arriving daily by boat and wagonload, and when many were perishing on interminable voyages around Cape Horn, or through the jungles of the Panamanian Isthmus, or across the American desert, "a little band of lovers of science" met to organize the CALIFORNIA ACADEMY OF SCIENCES. They had "but few books of reference, fewer types [i.e., specimens] for comparison, and [were] beset by the cares and trials incident to the unsettled condition of society." Unsettled it was indeed. San Francisco, the only real metropolis west of the Mississippi, with more schools, newspapers, and libraries than could be found in all that vast area, was still a rough and rowdy town. Seven years earlier its total population had numbered only two hundred. When statehood was achieved in 1850 it took nearly six weeks for the good news to reach home. Neither railroad nor telegraph yet linked the Pacific with the

Atlantic; nor, for that matter, was there even a pony express. Nevertheless the Academy's founders "were still able to do much good work in their various lines of scientific research," and one early member went on to be "employed . . . in conchology in the Smithsonian Institution."

Among the founders was one Dr. Andrew Randall, elected president of the Academy at its first meeting and re-elected to the same office for two successive years. There is no telling how many times he might have served in that exalted capacity had he not run up against a certain gambler named Joseph Hetherington. They quarreled, and Hetherington shot and fatally wounded Dr. Randall, who was buried three days later. Meanwhile Hetherington, having been apprehended by the Vigilance Committee, was sentenced to be hanged. On the day between the funeral and the hanging, the Academy held its regularly scheduled meeting. No tribute to the late president was written into the minutes, nor even a mention of the violent episode. But some new acquisitions for the library were very carefully recorded.

Despite this unruffled dedication to the world of learning, it took twenty years for the Academy to open its museum to the public, in an old church. After a long period of struggling in those "wholly inadequate accommodations," fortune smiled on San Francisco's scientists, and a generous benefaction supported the construction of a new building to which the expanding collections were brought in 1891. At about this time the Academy's first expedition in search of display material took place, to Baja California, Mazatlan, and Panama. In 1905 the schooner *Academy* departed for the Galapagos; seventeen months later the explorers returned to find their museum and the work of fifty-three years casualties of the earthquake and fire that had leveled most of the city. But their determination was stronger than their sense of loss. With the Galapagos specimens as a starter, the Academy revived its museum.

Since 1916 the Academy's home has been in Golden Gate Park, where it presides over what is actually a series of adjoined museums and related facilities—a Science Museum, Hall of Botany, the Morrison Planetarium, a large reference library, and the recently remodeled Steinhart Aquarium. The Academy produces "Science in Action," a weekly television show from which a dozen alligators once escaped, and publishes *Pacific Discovery,* a popular science magazine. It is an important center of scientific research; publication of research results being a tradition that goes back to the year of its founding. At that time, due to "the isolated condition of the Academy from other societies," a resolution was passed to the effect that "every publication of new species . . . through the daily papers of this city [will be regarded] as substantial evidence of priority of discovery."

Some popular exhibits are the Foucault pendulum that demonstrates the turning of the earth, the horological collection of virtually every type of timepiece invented by man, a chronological display of cameras that begins with a seventeenth-century magic lantern and features portrait photography of a hundred years ago, and a cross-section of a giant redwood whose rings have been marked to indicate many of the important dates of history since the Dark Ages when this tree first sprouted.

Professor Louis Agassiz, who taught zoology and geology at Harvard, was the most popular public speaker in the country in the middle of the nineteenth century. Students crowded his classes. The public flocked to hear him speak, rushed to read his statements, and subscribed large sums to sponsor his scientific publications, often several years in advance of their actual appearance. When he proposed to publish a *Natural History of the Fishes of the United States,* he mailed out more than six thousand circulars in which he explained the importance of obtaining fish from inland waterways all over the country and gave detailed instructions for catching and transporting them. Specimens began arriving in Cambridge by the barrel after thousands of laymen and scientists (whose names he had culled from the mailing list of the Smithsonian and the records of various scientific societies and colleges) had gone fishing for Dr. Agassiz.

This and other collections he was accumulating at a substantial cost to himself were to form the nucleus of Harvard's Gray Museum of Comparative Zoology, financed by the estate of Francis Calley Gray according to the terms of his will. It opened in 1860. Among Agassiz' first students there were Albert S. Bickmore, who within a decade would be the moving force behind the formation of New York's American Museum of Natural History, and the group that would go on via the Essex Institute to reorganize the Peabody of Salem. They all left their professor as the result of a disagreement so basic that it marked a milestone in the history of the natural sciences. The issue was special creation versus evolution.

Only a few years earlier, in 1859, Darwin had published his cogently marshaled evidence in support of a theory of evolution through natural selection. Prior to that time it had been universally believed that the various species of plant and animal life were separate and immutable; that each literally had been formed by God on the appropriate day of the biblical creation. The impact of Darwin's revolutionary view of life was, of course, cataclysmic. Opposition came from many sources. In the United States, the opposing group found a leader—to the extreme distress of his protégés—in Louis Agassiz. He refused even to consider the possibility that special creation was no longer tenable. And his authority not only gave weight to the fundamentalist views of the lay public but also helped perpetuate them.

These events had several consequences in the museum world. As Darwinism prevailed among the scientists, "the religious meaning for the study of natural history, with much of the wonder and glory, officially disappeared," and with it the motivation for the lay interest that had kept natural history societies lively for so long. The amateur was excluded further as professional research, with its more sophisticated tools and terminology, moved into the laboratory. As one observer noted, "scientific men took up the microscope and the scalpel and gave their thoughts to problems which in their very nature do not lend themselves to popular interest. . . . The interests of Biology superseded those of Botany and Zoology. Few biologists [were] interested in a whole bird, or at least not in the outside of a whole bird."

And so, while science advanced, natural history academies and their museums went into a protracted period of decline. The "whole bird," ignored and standing in an exhibit case pressing up against another whole bird, grew dusty.

At a time when most other science institutions were doing their work with an almost total disregard for the public, the AMERICAN MUSEUM OF NATURAL HISTORY was blazing a trail of public service that would eventually be an inspiration and guide to museums everywhere. The first to make the public a founding partner, it was also the first to act as mediator and explicator between the research laboratory and the man in the street. It was the first to seek out its audience and use new devices for putting across its message.

Not every museum would immediately follow in its footsteps. The older ones, with their limited incomes and newly pedantic orientation, would be among the last to catch up. And not every one that came into being after the American Museum's founding in 1869 would be cast in its mold. A trend was not yet apparent; but one had been set in motion. Eventually, no museum would be satisfied with the job it was doing unless it was matching up to the new criteria that had been established for it.

This New York landmark was first envisioned by Dr. Albert Smith Bickmore while he was a student of Agassiz' at Harvard. Dr. Bickmore was a determined man. He had to be. He persuaded the senior Theodore Roosevelt, New York *Sun* publisher Charles Dana, J. P. Morgan, the City Council, and others with money and authority, to support his idea. After he was set up in temporary quarters in a city-owned building that is now part of the Central Park Zoo, the city provided land on what is now Central Park West. And the first unit of a building that would be added to constantly for more than fifty years was given a fashionable opening in December 1877, with Dr. Bickmore as its first director and President Rutherford B. Hayes as guest of honor.

From these early years on, the American Museum pioneered in both exhibit and research techniques. The first adult education program to be illustrated with lantern slides was given here, Bickmore himself discoursing on the subject of coral islands. The first habitat group—in which mounted specimens are displayed in lifelike attitudes with props and painted backgrounds simulating their natural environment—was constructed here by a Mrs. Mogridge, formerly of the British Museum. It showed two robins hovering over eggs in a nest built on apple boughs. And it was here that the famous comparative anatomist, Samuel Harmstead Chubb, mounted animal skeletons in natural positions for the first time.

Not quite a hundred years ago most museums were still planning expeditions to collect anything and everything. But the American Museum was sending groups into the field with very specific goals. Fewer specimens were brought back, but increasing amounts of information concerning their life processes and natural habitats were gathered. This data was obtained through the use of many pieces of ponderous equipment which, modernized and streamlined, now routinely accompany researchers on their trips: still and motion picture cameras, X-ray apparatus, tape recorders, and portable chemistry and meteorology laboratories. Whenever necessity demanded it, staff members invented special equipment to meet special needs. At a time when movie cameras were designed primarily to turn out silent entertainments, explorer and taxidermist Carl Akeley created a panoramic ciné camera that could turn fast enough to keep up with running animals.

The latest field research trend is to maintain permanent expeditions in areas that merit intensive study. The American Museum has four such research stations: the Lerner Marine Laboratory at Bimini in the Bahamas, the Archbold Biological Station at Lake Placid, Florida, the Kalbfleisch Field Station on Long Island, and the Southwestern Research Station in Arizona, not far from the New Mexico border. At this last one, on the eastern slope of the Chiricahua Mountains, are geologic formations representing more than four billion years—from the pre-Cambrian to the Quaternary eras—of history that can be read only in rocks. A mountain road winds its way up from a desert plateau through progressively colder and more humid areas until the climate, flora and fauna near 10,000 feet are those of the Hudson Bay region. An astounding range of plant and animal life, in living and fossil form, is encompassed within the neighboring territory. The station has provided source material for more realistic habitat groups, for the identification of new species, for research and for publication. The facilities here, as at the other field stations, have been used by hundreds of scientists from every part of the world, but they are not open to ordinary visitors.

Today only half of the museum's twenty-three acres of floor space is devoted to exhibits. The remainder is divided between laboratories, libraries, storage areas, and administrative and publications offices. Recently added to the tens of millions of research specimens available here are one million termites preserved in alcohol; the collection of Dr. Alfred E. Emerson, emeritus professor of zoology at the University of Chicago and a museum associate. Of the 1802 known living species of termite, 1645 are now under the same roof as the gigantic Tyrannosaurus, the huge mastodons, and the life-size replica of a sulphur-bottom whale.

Anticipating its approaching centennial, the American Museum of Natural History is in the midst of an extensive remodeling program. The visitor will find many areas closed for this purpose. He will also be struck by contrast: cluttered old-style cabinets in semi-dark halls, and around the next bend a startlingly effective, well-lit brand-new display of the Biology of Man, or one of Ocean Life, or North American Birds, or the Hall of Men of the Montaña. In the latter, the effect of actually standing alongside real Indians and real animals in a South American rain forest is heightened by sound recordings—rain teeming onto large leaves, screeching monkeys, and falling trees.

The pioneering in display techniques continues.

As the need for factual information about local natural resources arose and increased for those engaged in farming, quarrying, and other occupations, state governments were prompted to assess the "animal, mineral and vegetable wealth" within their borders. In the 1830s such surveys were begun in Massachusetts, Connecticut, and Michigan. Eventually other states followed suit. (In the next fifty years so many geologists would be in the field that in order to give coherence to the nation's understanding of its own endowments the United States Geologic Survey would be started under the Smithsonian's jurisdiction.) New York's Geological and Natural History Survey took place in 1836.

Among the questions the New York survey intended to answer was whether, as rumor had it, coal was to be found in the westernmost part of the state. Geologist James Hall reported that it was not. But his report on the rock strata did support another idea, the recently enunciated theory that the earth's surface and structure underwent gradual changes throughout its history and that these changes were produced by the same forces of nature as could be observed in the present. This view of geologic evolution, called uniformitarianism, conflicted with the older doctrine of catastrophism, which held that all of the earth's changes had been brought about by cataclysmic events, such as the biblical flood.

Once out in the field, surveying scientists accumulated not only notes, but also specimens in wholesale lots—rocks, fossils, minerals, insects, animal skins, skeletons, and dried plants. Large quantities of this material begin filling up three rooms of Old State Hall in Albany, and in 1843 the New York Legislature authorized the formation of a State Cabinet of Natural History. Two years later it would be open free of charge to the public for four hours every day—the first such public institution in the country. At about the same time, a Survey of Agriculture was being conducted, adding botanical specimens to the Cabinet. And when the governor decided that it would be nice to have an Antiquarian Collection also, the people of the state were asked to help "in furnishing the relics of ancient masters of the soil." One of those who generously complied, donating a group of Indian artifacts, was Lewis Henry Morgan, a young lawyer whose friendship with the Senecas had led to his honorary membership in their tribe. An assignment from the state to purchase additional artifacts started Morgan on the way to becoming the first American ethnologist.

The State Cabinet became the NEW YORK STATE MUSEUM OF NAT-

URAL HISTORY, eventually administered by the State Education Department. Its exhibits, based upon indigenous inhabitants, flora and fauna, geology, history and prehistory, have been effectively modernized and its orientation today is toward providing information and aids to students and teachers.

Geologic surveys were leading to museums in many places across the continent. California, which owed its existence as a state to its mineral wealth, had seen a number of privately sponsored expeditions in the years before the legislature officially created one in 1860. Legislative tight-fistedness, however, terminated this project after a dozen years. But the need for mineralogical information continued to be strongly felt by the mining industries, and a Bureau of Mines was established. Today the CALIFORNIA DIVISION OF MINES AND GEOLOGY, in San Francisco, possesses thousands of rock and mineral specimens, a research laboratory, and an important reference library. Its extraordinary collection dates from 1880 when a local geological society presented the Bureau of Mines with some 1300 specimens on condition that they be adequately displayed and open free to everyone. One of the side effects of the public's reaction was that, on several occasions, thieves came to steal the gold.

Gold is still the main attraction: replicas of famous nuggets, crystallized gold, placer, and high-grade vein gold specimens. In addition there are about fifty specimens of California's uranium-bearing rocks and minerals. There are models that illustrate the workings of a cement plant, a quicksilver mine, and a gold mill. And the Dana system of mineral classification is illustrated in a group of forty display cases containing two thousand specimens.

In the 1860s Henry A. Ward, a young man whose passion for rock collecting was leading him to much broader interests, came to Albany to visit the State Cabinet and meet James Hall whose work in invertebrate paleontology had attracted world-wide attention. From there the young man returned home to Rochester and met Louis Agassiz, in town for a lecture. As a result of this second meeting, Ward was given an assistantship at Cambridge that marked the beginning of his professional ascent.

It was a stroke of luck that transported him to Paris and the School of Mines as the companion of a rich friend, and from there on trips to the Middle East and throughout Europe. Wherever he went, he gathered specimens for a geological cabinet he was by now planning to form in his native city. When financial need forced him to sell off some duplicate rocks and fossils, the transaction quickly suggested commercial possibilities.

Starting to support himself by marketing specimens, he found he could get twice the price for one bearing a label in the handwriting of a well-known European professor. And there was no shortage of scholars happy to earn a bit of extra income identifying objects for the American entrepreneur.

His next step was to set about gaining entree to the more important continental cabinets and museums; to ask for and receive permission to make casts of fossils and unique artifacts such as the recently unearthed Rosetta Stone. In cases and crates, his varied treasures came home to Rochester, eventually followed by Ward himself. He had decided to set up an establishment. It was to be patterned after one he had seen in Bonn, where a Dr. Kranz was successfully merchandising geological and zoological specimens to museums and universities throughout Europe.

Having assembled the most extensive geological cabinet in the country, he sold it to the University of Rochester for $20,000 raised by public subscription, and with this capital went into business. He called it Ward's Natural Science Establishment. He built Cosmos and Chronos Halls, designed workrooms where display specimens were prepared for sale, and furnished a showroom that was virtually a museum in itself. Scientists, taxidermists, and Henry Ward went on expeditions to remote corners of the world, bringing back animals for stuffing, skeletons for mounting, rocks, fossils, and all manner of objects for which a buyer could be found. Many an American geologist, zoologist, paleontologist, and botanist got his first practical field, laboratory, and museum experience at Ward's, and went on.

In Europe there were enough institutions to provide steady trade for Dr. Kranz. But in America in the 1860s and '70s museums were few and far between, and universities only slightly more numerous. Ward realized that he would have to enlarge the market for his services. At the Paris Exposition of 1855 he had noticed the impact of natural science exhibits on people who were seeing such things for the first time. He resolved to effect the same impact on his fellow countrymen. Combining scientific proselytizing with good business he set up exhibits wherever he could, preferably in cities where natural science societies were already in existence. It was his hope to turn every visiting display into the nucleus of a permanent collection, thereby not only making a sale but gaining a permanent client for his Establishment. He frequently succeeded. The California Academy of Sciences purchased $16,000 worth of specimens after being told what a terrible bother it would be to have to ship the cumbersome miscellany back East. The San Franciscans were as shrewd about raising the money as the science merchant had been in negotiating the deal. They invited the wealthiest men in town, railroad magnates Charles Crocker and Leland Stanford, to be honored guests at a meeting held to discuss the purchase. Crocker and Stanford found themselves persuaded to put up $8000 apiece, and furthermore to forego the profit that would have been theirs had the shipment gone back to Rochester on their railroad.

In all, more than seventy museums made substantial purchases from Ward's, including Agassiz' Museum of Comparative Zoology which spent $61,272. Other customers included museums at Princeton, the University of Virginia, the U. S. Military Academy, St. Louis, Chicago, Buffalo, and the American Museum of Natural History, which bought $24,594 worth of specimens and acquired for its staff an alumnus of the Establishment, a young explorer named Akeley.

According to his grandson's biography of him, Ward once exhibited a gorilla that "too closely resembled a somewhat misshapen man" for the comfort of those still a bit shaken by the news from Mr. Darwin. Yielding to an atmosphere of offended sensibilities, Ward sold it with other zoological displays to a Mr. Vassar of Poughkeepsie, who had previously ordered a complete $8000 geological cabinet for his new school for young ladies. But, as Roswell Ward tells us, "when . . . the trustees saw it, the Gorilla was forced to submit to convention. For years it stood in the Vassar Cabinet, modestly clothed in short pants."

Despite everything, Ward was not a good businessman. Whatever profits he made, and some that he only anticipated, were plowed back for new acquisitions. He constantly overextended his credit, and financial disaster was almost always just around the corner. Finally there came a time when museums conducted their own expeditions and prepared their own specimens.

Some years after his death, Ward's Establishment came under the administration of the University of Rochester, where it is today an important supplier of scientific equipment to schools.

Even the UNITED STATES NATIONAL MUSEUM OF THE SMITHSONIAN INSTITUTION availed itself of Ward's facilities, acquiring some stuffed apes and a brilliant young naturalist who had been an employee of the Rochester Establishment. "One of the most conspicuous objects in the Museum," wrote a moralizing observer of the Smithsonian in the eighties, is "the large case of stuffed orang-utans represented with startling fidelity by the chief taxidermist . . . Mr. William T. Hornaday, as climbing about the branches of a tree, and engaging in one of those quarrels which too frequently mar the beauty of character that ought to be displayed by the acknowledged head of brute creation." Hornaday had killed the beasts for Professor Ward "in the wilds of Borneo" and "a full account of all the incidents connected with their capture and preservation" was given in an "entertaining and valuable narrative" of his travels called *Two Years in the Jungle*. A later work of Hornaday's, published as a report of the National Museum, became a classic in its field. Entitled *The Extermination of the American Bison*, it was probably the greatest single influence in preventing the accomplishment of that calamity.

The "national attic" is aptly nicknamed. It presides over mosquitoes, mastodons and motorcycles, costumes, coins and computers, skeletons, stamps and steam locomotives. There are displays of household equipment from Colonial times to the present, electronics and atomic energy devices, business machines, antique scientific instruments, the process of petroleum manufacture and the process of lithography. Here are the flag that flew over Fort McHenry and inspired Francis Scott Key's verse tribute to the Star-Spangled Banner; the only remaining parts—a boiler and safety valve—of the first American steam locomotive (built in 1825 by Colonel John Stevens of New Jersey); the first American automobile—an 1893 Duryea—driven by an internal combustion engine; life masks of Abraham Lincoln; mementos of Admiral Peary's polar excursions; the first plane to fly across the United States (it took eighty-four days in 1911); a section of a Roman aqueduct; a group of African animals bagged by Theodore Roosevelt on an expedition undertaken immediately following his Presidency in cooperation with the Institution; the largest clear crystal ball—$12\frac{7}{8}$ inches in diameter and $106\frac{3}{4}$ pounds in weight—in the world; a group of portraits of Union soldiers as they looked fifty years after the conflict; and a colossal elephant whose mounting required over five tons of clay, wire, and wood.

It was a national attic from its inception. When the Institution was established, visitors were already familiar with the "heterogeneous cabinet" that had been accumulating in the Patent Office. "Such diverse objects as the femur of a Missouri Mastodon, Washington's knee breeches, and the oriental spoils of the Wilkes expedition around the world" had been added to mechanical models representing "the inventive faculty of this Yankee race." When the Patent Office finally became impossibly cluttered, everything was "trundled over" to the new Smithsonian building, completed in 1855. And the cabinet's heterogeneity was further enhanced as "Smithsonian men (the name National Museum . . . was rarely heard) . . . went westward and northward and southward, and came back with car-loads of Indian relics and modern implements of savagery, skins, shells, insects, minerals, fossils, skeletons, alcoholic preparations, herbaria, and note-books,— the last crammed with novel information."

After the Philadelphia Centennial, carloads of a different sort arrived. The government exhibits of foreign countries were dismantled and, "due to clever persuasion on the part of its officers," presented to the National Museum, "[giving] us an enormous mass of . . . most precious objects, representing resources and humanity 'from China to Peru.' "

What to do with this latest accumulation presented a problem once again. It was solved with the construction of another new "fireproof building, which was nearly enough completed in the spring of 1881 to serve as the ball-room at the inauguration of President Garfield." But even now there was not room enough for everything. The Department of Geology, with its immense stores of rocks and thousands of fossils, could find exhibit space only for "few objects of interest." Among those that pleased visitors were "pictures of scenery and structure near the Grand Cañon of the Rio Colorado [and] models of that profound gorge." Some departments were so occupied with pruning and classifying their holdings that their exhibit activities were, perforce, minimal. This was true, apologized an annual report, of the marine invertebrates, which were "rapidly being reduced to order; the arrearages of many years fast being made up." But the Department of Anthropology was highly praised by knowledgeable observers. It was said that "the National Museum is distinguished among all other American cabinets, and rivaled elsewhere only by those at South Kensington, London, for the attention it has paid to the *illustration of man by his works*." Its displays of Japanese, Chinese, Eskimo, and American Indian costumes were so popular that they were shown in the main hall to "first catch the eye of the visitor as he enters."

Adequate space is still a problem for the National Museum. Recently divided into two separate and distinct divisions of the Smithsonian—one of Natural History, and one of History and Technology —it continues to grow and grow. In addition there are, under the jurisdiction of the Smithsonian, such independent research branches as the Bureau of American Ethnology, the Canal Zone Biological Area, and the Astrophysical Observatory. The collections of the NATIONAL AIR AND SPACE MUSEUM, now located partially in the old Aircraft Building and partially in two or three other temporary places, are still another asset. A glass, steel and concrete building big enough for all the air and space materials should be ready at about the same time the first American arrives on the moon. Lindbergh's *Spirit of St. Louis* and *Freedom 7*, the capsule in which Alan B. Shepard, Jr., became the first American in space, are two of the history-making vehicles that will share the new quarters with exhibits explaining the science and technology behind them.

The natural history collections remain where they have been for more than fifty years. But the newest of the Smithsonian structures on the Mall is the Museum of History and Technology Building, unveiled early in 1964. Before being moved into it, the displays belonging to the halls of First Ladies Dresses, Power Machinery, Health, Textiles, and Graphic Arts were thoroughly renovated in such a way that, only partially dismantled, they could smoothly enter this two-block long rectangular enclosure of nearly 14,000,000 cubic feet of space.

Not far away is the oldest Smithsonian building of them all, made of red brick and well into its second century of service. Besides administrative offices and several research laboratories, it houses an exhibit and directory intended as a guide to the Institution's staggering number of activities.

The complexity of the Smithsonian is balanced by the simple, astoundingly fortuitous, single circumstance that brought it into being. Never was a great scientific institution so casually conceived as when an Englishman named James Smithson sat down to make a will in 1826 leaving all but a fraction of his fortune to his nephew. After adding a provision for one John Fitall, "formerly my Servant, but now employed in the London Docks," he paused, apparently to reflect a while upon the outcome of his generosity. It then occurred to Smithson that his nephew might die "without leaving a child or children." In that case, he decided—and no one knows just why—his estate would go to the United States of America, a country he had never seen and to which he had no ties. The money would be used, he stipulated, "to found at Washington, under the name of Smithsonian Institution, an establishment for the increase and diffusion of knowledge among men." Very little more is known about Smithson. He was the natural son of the Duke of Northumberland. He was elected to membership in the Royal Society, one year after his graduation from Oxford, as "a gentleman well versed in various branches of Natural Philosophy, and particularly in Chymistry [sic] and Mineralogy." Resenting the country of his birth because of his illegitimacy—according to those who have speculated on this matter—he spent much of his time traveling through Europe doing research in the sciences he loved. And he died three years after writing his will, followed shortly by his unmarried—and childless—nephew.

When the prospective recipient learned of the intended benefaction, a number of years late due to legal complications in England, there were those who attempted to interfere with fate. The proud John C. Calhoun led the fight against accepting the bequest, claiming "it was beneath [our] dignity to receive presents from anyone." Many words later, English gold sovereigns were delivered to the mint in Philadelphia, there to be converted into more than half a million American dollars. The Institution was founded. Its money was treated as a loan to the Treasury. And from the 6 per cent interest it earned, the Smithsonian was expected to get along. But the new organization proved so useful that in a very few years Congress instructed it to undertake special research assignments, for which additional money was appropriated. Subsequently, healthy donations from a variety of sources were added to the endowment fund; while eagerly, and sometimes with abandon, providers came forth with many of the fifty-odd million catalogued objects that have made their way into one or another of the collections.

When the men of eighteenth-century Charleston spoke of obtaining material for a natural history of their province they meant precisely that: the history of their own natural environment in terms of local animal, mineral, and vegetable evidence. In the early part of the nineteenth century, universities offering courses in this study called it "Natural Philosophy" and gave it a religious tone. Today the term "Natural History" when used as part of the name of a museum is an inexact one. Generally, it refers to an institution whose scope is the evolutionary sciences, which are geology, biology, anthropology, and their various specialties and subdivisions. These are often referred to as "earth sciences" and "life sciences." Attempting to clear up the ambiguity, some institutions have called themselves museums of "Natural Science."

No two natural history museums are exactly alike. They may contain departments of botany, ornithology, entomology, ichthyology, genetics, embryology, ecology, mineralogy, petrology, ethnology, archaeology, paleontology—and more, or less. They may cover the entire range of the diversity of nature, or they may limit themselves to reporting on their own natural surroundings.

Albert Eide Parr, a long-time observer, found it impossible even from the vantage point of director of the American Museum "to discover any unifying philosophy of museum functions, or generally accepted guiding principles of organization." He noted furthermore that although "within themselves the natural sciences have a very clearly defined logical structure, [this] seems to have little to do with their organization in museums."

Despite this lack of common orientation, they all manage to achieve their major purpose: to help man grasp the meaning of his relationship to the world of nature.

During the Second World War, in 1943, when the CHICAGO NATURAL HISTORY MUSEUM (then known as the Field Museum) was fifty years old, an anniversary bulletin was published in which Stanley Field pointed out that "our soldiers and sailors who are now having the exciting experience of seeing strange and exotic regions and races will, on their return, retain their world-wide interest" and that they and other "thinking people will turn more and more to the natural history museums in their quest for knowledge about races, regions, and customs. . . . Field Museum is a microcosm of the basic realities of this world. Embraced within the scope of the four great natural sciences to which it is devoted—anthropology, botany, geology, and zoology —are the fundamental elements of everything in life, and the causative factors that make people and other living things what they are."

It was Chicago's enthusiastic reaction to the World's Columbian Exposition of 1893 that led both to the founding of the museum and its organization around four basic departments. Anthropological, botanical, and geological exhibits had come to the big fair from all parts of the world. Its zoological exhibit had come directly from Ward's Natural Science Establishment, valued at $100,000. By gift and purchase, these four categories of materials went into the new museum.

Accommodated first in the Exposition's Palace of Fine Arts Building and then in a new home at the south end of Grant Park, the museum cost Marshall Field a total of $9,430,000. His original gift was over a million dollars; the rest he bequeathed in his will.

Two years before its fiftieth anniversary, an exhibit policy of selectivity displaced open storage, the practice of showing everything. With a large part of its acquisitions in storerooms to which research scientists were given keys, Chicago Natural History tidied up its halls. In one of them the story of the American Indian from the time of his arrival from Asia to the time of his discovery by European explorers is told in terms of dioramas and beautifully mounted archaeological artifacts. In another, the "Peoples of the World" are brought together in a series of life-size sculptures in bronze and stone by Malvina Hoffman. Elsewhere a Melanesian collection of tools, weapons, utensils, ornaments, art, and clothing, catalogued as "the finest and most complete in the world," is featured. A pair of African elephants mounted by Carl Akeley, who spent twelve years on the staff perfecting his skills as a taxidermist, are in the great hall on the main floor and introduce animal life exhibits that range from invertebrates to apes. Plant-life exhibits represent aspects of the vegetable kingdom from bacteria to orchids to foodstuffs and other plant products. And fossils, the largest collection anywhere of meteorites whose dates of fall have been recorded, minerals, and gems all help illustrate the earth's history. The research collections have grown over the years and the library has been assiduously acquiring publications of learned societies, academies, and universities from all parts of the world.

Although the method of arranging exhibits used in Chicago—according to the department to which they belong—would continue to be practical for many directors, the innovation introduced by New York's BUFFALO MUSEUM OF SCIENCE would always seem ideal from the visitor's point of view. Walking through Buffalo's halls, where displays are arranged in such a way that they tell a continuous story, is like moving through the chapters of a book. The beginning sections are devoted to the constitution of matter, the structure of the earth, the heavens, and lower forms of life; the middle to higher forms of life; and the conclusion to the story of man and society. This was only one of many new ideas put into effect in 1929 when the Buffalo Society of Natural Sciences installed its collections and first began to conduct its activities in a permanent home.

The Society, organized in 1861, had pioneered in educational work from the outset. An important result of this pioneering is Buffalo's museum-methods training program, open each year to a limited number of college graduates. It is so highly regarded that its influence has extended beyond the United States into South America. And still earning respect for its work with children is the Junior Division of Education, which boasts more than twenty-five clubs and classes ranging in appeal from the first grade through high school.

Planned under the influence of similar thinking, "at a time when a new vision of museum usefulness had emerged and new methods were available," the CRANBROOK INSTITUTE OF SCIENCE of Bloomfield Hills, Michigan, arranged its exhibits in a sequence beginning "with illustrations of the nature of the cosmos and its building units of elements and minerals" and ending with "man and his cultural development." Cranbrook's mineral collections are particularly fine. Among the more striking specimens are black opals from Nevada, tourmalines from California, large copper crystals from Michigan, and a gigantic example of crystalline perfection—a white topaz from Brazil weighing one hundred pounds. The minerals come from a variety of places, but Michigan is particularly well represented. In other halls the state's prehistoric past and its present plant and animal life are considered. Elsewhere, "The World of Physics," "The World of Numbers," "The Societies of Animals," and "The Organization of Life" help vivify the presentation of general science. And outside the building there is a trail, worth following, of glacial boulders. The library is selective; the planetarium and observatory are small. Whatever collections the Institute cannot show are available to the specialist.

One of the best places in the country to study the relationship of animals to their total environment—not only the vegetation and terrain, but the birds, insects, reptiles, fish, and other animals around them—is Colorado's DENVER MUSEUM OF NATURAL HISTORY. In this relatively small institution where the emphasis is on beautiful displays rather than extensive research, mammals and birds have been a primary concern ever since the first organizing meeting was held in 1897. Archaeology, geology, and botany are by no means neglected here, but it is the animals of North and South America and the Arctic—the bison, deer, bears, peccaries, mountain lions, and monkeys—that the casual visitor is likely to go away remembering. And of course this is a good place to learn about Colorado's own mammals and birds, as well as its fish, rocks, minerals, and vegetation.

Several years ago when the museum opened its Laysan Island exhibit, the Denver *Post* found in it both a moral and a reminder of what happens when man gratuitously upsets nature's balance. Laysan Is-

Charles Willson Peale (left) with his sons Rembrandt, Rubens and Raphael. A detail from *Exhuming the First American Mastodon* by Charles Willson Peale.

The Peale Museum, Baltimore, as it looks today. Built in 1814, it was the first structure in this country specifically designed to house a museum.

1

The Alms House after it became the New York Institution in 1816. Among its tenants were John Scudder's American Museum and the New-York Historical Society.

P. T. Barnum's American Museum in 1851.

This view of opening day at the American Museum of Natural History on Central Park West appeared in the New York *Daily Graphic,* December 22, 1877.

Professor Bickmore giving one of his illustrated lectures at the American Museum of Natural History.

Birds at the American Museum as they once were exhibited.

American Egret Group in the American Museum's new Hall of North American Birds.

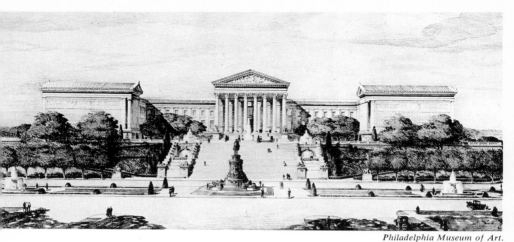

Architect's rendering of the Philadelphia Museum of Art.

Louis XVI Reception Room in the Philadelphia Museum of Art.

An art gallery at the New-York Historical Society, about 1860.

6

Gallery 15: Seventeenth-century Dutch and Flemish works of art at the Toledo Museum of Art, today.

Two galleries in the Museum of Modern Art, New York. Paintings are Léger's *Three Women (Le Grand Déjeuner);* and *The Sleeping Gypsy* and *The Dream* by Rousseau.

The Museum of Modern Art, photos by George Cser

8

land is an atoll in the Pacific, 850 miles northwest of Honolulu. It was famous for its birds—hundreds of thousands of sea birds, two varieties of the albatross, and five species of small birds found no place else in the world. Although hunters used to come regularly to the island, pillaging it in the name of millinery fashion, the birds survived. But when a group of people, humane while ignorant of the laws of nature, decided to put rabbits on the island as a means of providing meat either for those who came to mine the phosphate rock or for sailors who might be shipwrecked there, the birds were doomed. The rabbits, separated by an ocean from wolves, coyotes, and all their other natural enemies, proliferated. Overrunning the island, they ate its vegetation, destroyed the feeding grounds, and desecrated what had been, for hundreds of years, a sanctuary. All of this happened prior to 1912. Toward the end of that year an expedition of the United States Biological Survey was sent out to kill the rabbits. Signed on as its cook was Alfred E. Bailey, a college sophomore bent on collecting bird specimens; the future director of Denver's museum. The expedition was not completely successful. Some of the rabbits escaped and they and their progeny spent the next ten years turning Laysan into a wasteland. The birds died of starvation and disease; and with them, finally, the rabbits. Slowly, over the years, the island renewed its vegetation. Other birds came there. But of the five species unique to the atoll, three were now extinct. They would live again only as inanimate displays made from Dr. Bailey's collection. The Laysan Island exhibit commemorates the whole fantastic episode.

Reflecting a basic concern with local environment are the widely separated SAN DIEGO NATURAL HISTORY MUSEUM, the UTAH FIELD HOUSE OF NATURAL HISTORY in Vernal, the DALLAS MUSEUM OF NATURAL HISTORY, and Connecticut's STAMFORD MUSEUM AND NATURE CENTER.

As a result of explorations and interpretations of the area around it, San Diego has assembled fine exhibits and research collections of plants, shells, insects, mammals, birds, minerals, reptiles, fish, and fossils. Baja California has been the source of much of what the museum owns. The nearby Salton Sea—inland and about 235 feet below sea level—is the site of a wildlife refuge to which the museum regularly conducts bird-watching excursions.

The small Utah city of Vernal is in the heart of oil, livestock, and grain country. The Field House was opened there as the official state museum in 1948, the idea for it having been initiated by the Lions Club a few years earlier. In exhibits of rocks and fossils of the nearby Uinta Mountains and Basin there is a record of one billion years of earth history.

The Dallas Museum in Fair Park, accommodated in a large two-story building that was erected for the Texas Centennial of 1936, has effective displays and habitat groups in which the state's own animal life predominates. It also has important research collections that are much more general.

And the Nature Center in Stamford is a cultural, educational, and recreational community enterprise "dedicated to the idea of conservation." Set in ninety-three acres of woodlands, it consists of trails, a farm for children, a lake, ponds, a seal pool, and a small zoo in addition to buildings that house general exhibits, a small planetarium, an observatory, an art gallery, and a theater.

Although dedication to the people of Pittsburgh and the surrounding regions, together with a sense of relationship to the land itself, has motivated many policies at the Natural History Museum of the CARNEGIE INSTITUTE, the work of the scientific branch of this complex organization is broad in its scope. Its paleontologists have studied and reconstructed Pennsylvania's prehistory—the dragonflies with two-foot wings, the six-foot long amphibians, and the forests that decayed into coal—but the fossil that helped them popularize paleontology is a dinosaur that came out of Wyoming. Purchased by Mr. Carnegie immediately after its discovery in 1898, it is known as *Diplodocus carnegiei*, and replicas reside in London, Paris, Madrid, Mexico City, and Leningrad. Keeping it company in Pittsburgh's Dinosaur Hall are some very impressive relatives plus a group of ammonites, those Mesozoic mollusks of which Pittsburgh has one of the largest collections in the world. North American mammals, American Indians, and the story of transportation are some of the other subjects treated here. And to bring the life of the sea to a city that is an important inland port, there is Marine Hall where great game fish, small tropical fish, the coast of Maine, the Bay of Naples, and the Gulf Stream are all suddenly visible and quite beautiful.

A similar outlook of responsibility to its local supporters, scientific interest in its surroundings, and far-reaching investigation of nature prevails at the LOS ANGELES COUNTY MUSEUM. What makes this museum unique is a combination of circumstances. Money, good taste, and scholarship have mingled here just as easily as the sophisticated metropolis itself was juxtaposed with an area now famous for its dramatic prehistory. Expansion is an understatement for this institution's remarkable growth. The art division having been accommodated in its own new expensive complex of structures, the science and history divisions spread out on their own; the first step including plans for a new vertebrate paleontology research wing that is proudly pointed to as the most modern in the country. Financed initially by a grant of $130,000 from the National Science Foundation plus an appropriation from the county, this facility has made possible the dusting off, studying, and assembling of some marvelous specimens of ancient life that had previously been stored in basement rooms—*Allosaurus,* a twenty-five-foot carnivorous dinosaur; extinct rhinoceroses, camels, sabertooth cats, whales, seals, and many others. In addition to its preparation laboratory and reference gallery, the new wing provides working areas for visiting scientists and students. Elsewhere, the invertebrate paleontology and mineralogy displays were allotted more room. But the most exciting aspect of the expansion was a plan to build a two-million-dollar Rancho La Brea Science Museum in Hancock Park.

The splendid remains of prehistoric plants and animals found in the tar pits of Rancho La Brea were given to the Los Angeles County Museum by Captain G. Allan Hancock even before the doors first opened in 1913. Now, about to enter a great hall of fossils on the very site of their discovery, are the Pleistocene mammoths, mastodons, birds, and reptiles that once lived here. In another unit the dramatic struggle of these huge beasts after their entrapment in the tar will be cycloramically presented. And nearby the entire story of the excavations will be told. The Observation Pit, where animal bones preserved in place in the tar have been an attraction to the curious for years, will continue to function as an important display.

Minerals, gems, birds, plants, marine zoology, entomology, and anthropology materials round out the acquisitions of Los Angeles. The reference collections of every department are available to any person qualified to use them.

In upstate New York, interpreting the region is regarded as a primary function of the ROCHESTER MUSEUM OF ARTS AND SCIENCES. But the scope of its achievements ranges from exhibits showing the area as it looked three hundred million years ago to displays of present-day birds, fish, and mammals; from exhibits of the history of New York State—scenes at an Iroquois village, the French meeting the Indians before English colonization, downtown Rochester and the Erie Canal as they looked in 1838—to a science education program that has concerned itself variously with geology, anthropology, biology, the space age, and local industry.

Bausch & Lomb, Eastman Kodak, General Dynamics, Ritter, and Xerox are just some of the industrial organizations located in Rochester. In 1940 Edward Bausch contributed money that made a new museum building possible. Since then other industrial leaders from the area have eagerly helped in the job of exploring ways to increase the public's understanding of science.

To enlarge its program of service, the museum has acquired more land and made plans for a science center comprising a planetarium, exhibits that deal with the physical sciences, an industrial wing, an auditorium, and Bausch Hall, its present home.

An enormously successful center, in which great attention is given to interrelationships, is the bright, shining, modern BOSTON MUSEUM OF SCIENCE on the banks of the Charles River. A successor to the New England Museum of Natural History, and operated by the 130-year-old Boston Society of Natural History, it combines under one roof a planetarium, natural history exhibits, science and industry displays, and a health museum. Children from kindergarten through high school love it here; they can pet live animals as well as admire mounted ones. And adults who would rather look under the hood of a car than anywhere else can pursue that interest one step further. They can also visit the Hall of Medical Science, study the history of land, sea, and air transportation, get brought up to date on space age communications, and find out about Massachusetts birds and New England game fish.

Research is not an important aspect of the work done here. The Boston area, where universities and laboratories abound, has such a high concentration of research facilities that the museum wisely decided to focus its efforts on stimulating the young, developing a program for the schools, and helping the bewildered adult reorient himself in the quickly changing world of scientific discovery.

Organized differently, but offering a similar program, is St. Louis' MUSEUM OF SCIENCE AND NATURAL HISTORY, which deals with aeronautics and outer space, atoms and molecules, human cells and reproduction, and the history of civilization.

Two widely separated institutions concerned with the natural history, archaeology, and culture history of their areas, with research and study, and with the operation of a modern planetarium, are the NEW JERSEY STATE MUSEUM at Trenton and the BERNICE P. BISHOP MUSEUM in Honolulu.

New Jersey minerals, birds, mammals, fish, shells, reptiles, plants, and insects and New Jersey Indian artifacts are among the impressive collections newly housed in one unit of the multimillion-dollar complex known as the State Capital Development program. The materials are mostly local, but the principles they illustrate are general.

The Bishop Museum of course covers a much larger geographical area. It is a clearing house of scientific information not only on Hawaii but all the islands of the Pacific. Expeditions and research have resulted in excellent zoological, botanical, and anthropological exhibits. Its department of entomology, having amassed the most extensive collection of Pacific Island insects anywhere, is now involved in studies related to disease and public health. The National Science Foundation has been providing financial assistance both for this project and for a program of Polynesian archaeological field work. But the aspect of the museum most popular with visitors is the work of its ethnologists—exhibits such as "Emblems of Royalty in Old Hawaii" with its displays of cloaks, capes, and helmets made of feathers, and "The Story of Ancient Hawaii," which tells of its Polynesian past.

As many of the newer science museums began to concentrate increasingly upon exhibition and public education, the center of natural science research shifted, with a few outstanding exceptions, to the university. University museums, although frequently open to the public, are basically places "where the materials of the earth in all their manifestations, of animate and inanimate origin, indigenous and extraterritorial, are collected and catalogued by competent scholars while in pursuit of their own specialized fields of research."

It sometimes happened that one university museum was chosen to be the sole, official repository of a state-owned collection. The Michigan State University Museum at East Lansing and the University of Massachusetts Scientific Collection at Amherst are two that were. Texas, on the other hand, decided that the best way to help present displays and provide research materials relating to its natural and human resources was by distributing aid among several of its university museums.

Some schools maintain a group of museums, begun with specimens accumulated over the years by teachers in different departments. The University of Michigan at Ann Arbor put a number of them, each separately administered, under the roof of one building. But not all of its collections could be so contained. At Harvard there are half a dozen distinguished museums—one of mineralogy dating from the first cabinet of 1794, one of geology, one of botany, the Gray Herbarium, Agassiz' Museum of Comparative Zoology, and the Peabody Museum of Archaeology and Ethnology.

The same George Peabody who benefited Harvard and the museum at Salem is responsible for the PEABODY MUSEUM OF NATURAL HISTORY at Yale. (America's first international banker, he was also the first American philanthropist interested equally in education and charity. The bank he established became well known under the name of the man who had been his junior partner, Junius Spencer Morgan.) Yale of course owned a mineral cabinet that dated from the early years of the nineteenth century, when the townsfolk of New Haven raised the money to pay for it. Anticipating a museum, Yale professors had been acquiring zoological specimens even before Peabody's $150,000 gift arrived in 1866. The donor's nephew, Othniel Charles Marsh, a brilliant paleontologist who had ridden out West to gather Plains Indians artifacts and dinosaur fossils when the Union Pacific Railroad was making its earliest runs, was appointed the first director. Hounding European collectors with a persistence that could not be ignored, he got them to part with choice specimens which then traveled to Connecticut. Somehow he even acquired the skeleton of the last quagga in captivity, a South African horse-zebra that died in the London Zoo in 1872 at about the same time its wild relatives were becoming extinct in their native habitat. He also put together the first complete sequence of fossil horses—a unique example of fifty million years of equine evolution that began with *Eohippus,* the "dawn horse." The diminutive creature was named—a few months before Marsh himself found the fossil evidence of its existence—during a conversation he was enjoying with a visiting Englishman, Darwin's friend and defender, Thomas H. Huxley.

Yale's Peabody concentrates on anthropology, zoology, geology and their subdisciplines. Its excellent ornithology and oceanography facilities have recently been expanded.

For a Philadelphia exhibit hall, Carleton Coon wrote this eloquent description of man: "A rare animal among millions of other animals, appearing in the world a million years ago. A defenseless animal lacking tusks, horns, claws. With his cunning brain and his useful hands, making beasts his servants; discovering and harnessing the forces [of nature]. Growing in numbers, changing the face of the earth. Changing and taming everything but himself."

Written by an anthropologist, these phrases suggest the three basic areas with which anthropology is concerned—physical anthropology, or the study of human origins, evolution and variations; archaeology, or the discovery and study of man's buried civilizations; and ethnology, the study of man's technology and behavior in society.

The flowering of anthropology in America is directly attributable to our museums. As Western civilization pressed on across the continent, inevitably altering and frequently obliterating the indigenous life in its path, Indian handicrafts—from weapons to wearing apparel, from cooking vessels to ritual paraphernalia—began accumulating in museums, where their availability piqued the curiosity of staff members trained in the natural sciences. Applying a familiar technique, museum men made field trips to accumulate more artifacts, and returned with extensive collections of data as well as arrowheads. These natural scientists whose previous areas of specialization may have been in geology or biology became engrossed in studies of this ethnological material, and turned into the first generation of anthropologists in America. Only after the twentieth century was under way did they gravitate to universities, founding departments and offering formal training to subsequent generations of students. Eventually most of the leadership in anthropological research came from these departments.

It is not surprising, therefore, that one of the leading anthropology museums in America is the UNIVERSITY MUSEUM, affiliated with the University of Pennsylvania. Its credo, stated by director Froelich Rainey, is that "the interpretation of research in the study of man is second only to the research itself."

Serving both the lay public and the professional community, this institution has been particularly successful in its approach to primitive art; presenting objects in terms of their cultural context without weakening their esthetic impact. Since only a small part of its huge and famous collection of native Pacific and African art can be displayed at one time, most of it is either in storage for study or out on loan. Outstanding collections of art and artifacts can also be found in the Egyptian, Babylonian, North and South American, Oriental, and Mediterranean sections. Authentic reproductions of many of these ancient and primitive items are made in the museum's own workshop, and a substantial mail order business distributes them to schools and interested individuals all over the world. Other exhibits interpret early man, physical anthropology, and general ethnology.

Its halls were first opened in 1899 to display the results of pioneering expeditions to Mesopotamia, Borneo, the Ryukyu Islands, Peru, and Florida. This early enthusiasm for field research has continued. In a single year University Museum teams may be in such far-flung places as Afghanistan, San Salvador, Arctic Canada, New Britain Island, and Egypt, giving the institution the reputation of having the most active field program in anthropology in the world.

The most renowned and extensive collection of American Indian material anywhere in the world is at the MUSEUM OF THE AMERICAN INDIAN: THE HEYE FOUNDATION in New York. It was begun with the private accumulation of George G. Heye, and has been augmented since by gifts, purchases, and the results of staff expeditions. Although not affiliated with any university, it is a center for research available to qualified scholars. A separate storage unit now houses 90 per cent of its four million objects. Explaining the policy of admission to this research facility, director Frederic J. Dockstader explained that "small boys wanting to build a copy of an Indian canoe, or a textile designer wishing to see a Zuni pattern, are [considered] just as much students as are the more wooly-headed academicians."

The public is welcomed at the main building, where displays designed to interpret the major tribes show objects, rare and ordinary, made and used by Indians from every part of the Americas: wampum belts, masks of the Iroquois False Face Society, unusual colored baskets and beadwork from the Southeast, equipment of the peyote cult, a complete representation of Pueblo pottery, a whale boat, and carved objects from the northwest coast, plus a fascinating arrangement of effigies, pottery, sculpture, jewelry, masks, textiles, and feather work from Middle and South America and the West Indies.

Through its studies, exhibits, and publications the museum hopes to promote a better understanding of the diverse cultures of Indian tribes throughout the hemisphere and to persuade the public to share its concern for these peoples' future as well as their past. A shop near the main entrance sells authentic contemporary Indian handicrafts in addition to surplus artifacts, and books ranging from the general to the technical. The public can also bring specimens for identification.

A brief list of additional sources for Indian exhibits and research would include the Florida State Museum at the University of Florida in Gainesville, which, thanks to a recent major gift, has materials representing all the North American native civilizations; the Arizona State Museum of the University of Arizona in Tucson and the Museum of Northern Arizona in Flagstaff, both important agencies for field research in their areas; the Heard Museum of Anthropology and Primitive Art in Phoenix; the state-maintained Museum of New Mexico in Santa Fe with its Hall of Ethnology and Laboratory of Anthropology where exhibits of Navaho and Pueblo art and artifacts ranging from the pre-Spanish to the contemporary are featured; and the Thomas Gilcrease Institute of American History and Art in Tulsa, Oklahoma, with its study collection of documents and artifacts. Important general anthropology museums are also located at the University of California in Berkeley, Indiana University in Bloomington, the University of Michigan in Ann Arbor, and Beloit College in Wisconsin.

Not especially research-oriented, the WOOLAROC MUSEUM in Bartlesville, Oklahoma, tells the story, with a local emphasis, of man in the New World from the time of the earliest known Indians through the days of the pioneer settlers and cowboys. Artifacts from the pre-Columbian Spiro Mound site in Oklahoma are here, along with objects made by Plains and southwestern tribes, and a gallery of paintings portraying life in the early West. The museum is located two miles inside the gate of a 4000-acre former ranch on which deer, steers, buffalo, and other beasts have found a home. A warning to motorists is appended to the Woolaroc's brochure: *"Stay in your car. The wild animals along the drive are dangerous. First aid facilities are available at the museum."* So are—safe—picnic facilities.

INDIAN CITY, U.S.A. in Anadarko, Oklahoma, is an open-air museum featuring villages of the Caddo, Pawnee, Comanche, and other Plains tribes, authentically reconstructed under the guidance of the Anthropology Department and Stovall Museum of the University of Oklahoma. Guided tours start in the Lodge, which contains artifacts and introductory displays, proceed through the seven tribal villages, and are followed by a performance of Indian dances.

And filling a need even in a community which also supports a museum of natural history and a famous zoo, is San Diego, California's, MUSEUM OF MAN which was founded in 1915 to retain for the city some of the exhibits from the Panama-California Exposition. In recently modernized galleries, it concentrates on telling about the past and present of man in the Americas through a dramatic series of changing exhibits. Man in other parts of the world is not neglected. In the Native Music Room visitors may try their ability on African drums or on Indian tom-toms. A blowgun range, part of an extensive display of primitive weaponry, offers the visitor an exotic means of testing his marksmanship.

A type of museum uniquely developed in the United States, relatively small, and characterized by its subservience to the natural phenomena near which it is located, is the trailside. Originated quite casually in 1915 when the chief ranger at Yosemite mounted some birds and mammals for his office, it began to gain importance a few years later when the National Park Service—today the largest proprietor of trailsides in the world—was formed.

Recently Ralph Lewis, chief of the Park Service's Museums Branch, began applying the term "site museum" to the exhibit facilities under his jurisdiction. A site museum, he said, is "closely associated with a place having scientific or historic significance." It preserves "the more perishable features of the site . . . provides facilities for students," and concentrates on exhibits that are interpretive.

A new site museum in the Visitor Center at GRAND CANYON NATIONAL PARK was unveiled in June 1957. Various devices there illustrate how rock was eroded to form the gorge, how its structure and the area's climate changed during eons of continued geologic action, how the canyon's appearance is altered during the course of the day and the year, and how it has in different ways exerted a fascination upon the men who encountered it—Indians, Spaniards, and Americans.

At DINOSAUR NATIONAL MONUMENT a museum has been built up and around an exhibit constructed, as Rembrandt Peale might have exclaimed, by Nature herself. Back in 1909 a Carnegie Museum paleontologist on a field trip near Vernal, Utah, discovered what was hailed as "the richest of all dinosaur bone halls." And during the next thirteen years hundreds of giant reptiles were dug out of rock by museum representatives who were dispatched there. Public interest in this seemingly incredible excavation was so intense that the area itself was declared a national monument. But then, to protect and preserve the remaining fossils, the national monument was officially closed.

Thirty years later the Park Service decided to cut into the rock—not to remove anything but to make an "in-place exhibit" of whatever fossil bones would be revealed. Four paleontologists worked with air-powered jackhammers and rotary rock drills, displacing a thousand tons of stone. As dinosaur bones appeared they were set in relief with small pneumatic chipping hammers, followed by careful hand tooling. Tourists who arrived while all this was going on were encouraged to express their reactions to exposed tail vertebrae, foot bones, necks, and skulls. Many of them refused to believe in the reality of what they saw. The perspiring scientists were told it was all a "fake." One man whose pre-Darwinian convictions could not be shaken said, "You're making them out of concrete!" Nevertheless, there were quite a few on-the-spot conversions to evolution. "I never believed it before," said an elderly man, "but I believe it now."

Plans were soon made for a permanent museum building with glass-paneled walls that would enclose the fossil-filled dinosaur quarry. By 1958 visitors could walk along a gallery, see the bones "in place" clearly but unobtrusively labeled, and watch a Park Service paleontologist chiseling around them to bring them into clearer relief. Supplementary displays were created to elaborate on dinosaurs and their times, the prehistory of this particular quarry, and the methods and purposes of paleontology. But the prize exhibit remains the rock itself. There is nothing anywhere quite like the visitor's excited sense of participation as he watches the uncovering of one more bone right before his eyes.

Back in the twenties when the idea of trailsides was new, the American Museum of Natural History pioneered in applying the concept to a nature preserve within easy reach of Manhattan. Bear Mountain State Park, on the western bank of the Hudson River a few miles below West Point, was given both the first of six trailside museums and the first of many miles of nature trails. The hiker, at the outset, encountered a sign announcing that "a friend somewhat versed in Natural History is taking a walk with you." Then, coming upon shrubs, herbs, trees, and a selection of temporarily caged mammals, reptiles, and insects, he found them all identified with chatty labels written by the same friend. All in all the idea was a success, and quickly spread to city parks and botanic gardens throughout the country.

Years afterward, one of the scientists responsible for designing Bear Mountain's facilities founded the ARIZONA-SONORA DESERT MUSEUM. Near Tucson, only 60 miles from Mexico, and named for the bordering

states of the two countries, it considers itself an international site where
—"inasmuch as plants and animals know no political boundaries"—the
flags of both North American nations are flown.

In 1951, newly-created Tucson Mountain Park was a cluster of old
adobe buildings set in a cactus forest on a slope of desert surrounded
by volcanic mountains. Looking at it, naturalist William H. Carr had a
vision of an outdoor educational center where the public could become acquainted "with their rich but vanishing heritage in wildlife,
plant life and scenic values." With support from the people of Tucson,
Carr was able to build a "Desert Museum, botanical trails, a zoo, all in
one, containing only objects and live things native to the surrounding
Sonoran Desert."

Almost every exhibit here is alive and uniquely presented. The botanical trails introduce the desert's plants—ironwood, palo verde, and
cacti of all sizes—and explain their adaptation to a dry, hot, sunny
environment. Outdoor animal pits house bears, javelinas, prairie dogs,
mountain lions, bobcats, coyotes, and others. Nickels and dimes
dropped by visitors into trailside donation boxes paid first for a man-
made moat-surrounded island on which several coati mundis cavort,
and then for a prairie dog village from which a few residents escaped.
(The dogs set up housekeeping in the middle of a well-traveled path,
but proving themselves domesticated, they were allowed to stay.) Hundreds of birds of more than fifty species—golden eagles, hawks, wood
ducks, burrowing owls, jays, and quail among them—inhabit specially
designed enclosures lushly planted to provide shade; it is so pleasant
an oasis that many wild birds have tried to make their way inside.

In the Amphibian Room are "living dioramas"—frogs, toads, salamanders, and aquatic insects splashing in miniature pools, streams,
and rivers in front of simulated rocks and painted backgrounds that
can be raised for feeding and handling. In separate small tanks one
can get a closer look at individual animals that might be temporarily
hidden in the larger dioramas. The cool Aquarium Building contains
surprising proof that even in the desert fish can survive, and a Reptile
Room shows off Gila monsters and coral snakes.

But this is more than a zoo. One of the Desert Museum's most popular features is the Watershed Exposition. On "Water Street U.S.A." the
Southwest's most vital natural resource is the center of attention. Electrically and mechanically operated displays explain rainfall, drainage,
evaporation, erosion, soil conservation, and other aspects of "the use,
abuse and management" of water. From a nearby control tower a member of the staff oversees, via telescope, everyone walking along Water

Street, answering their questions by means of push-button-operated two-way microphones. Other push-buttons switch on tape recordings that serve as oral labels. The written labels here and throughout the Desert Museum are ingenious too, requiring the visitor to work a bit for his information.

Equally unique is the Desert Tunnel, constructed in 1957 to show the underground life of the desert's plants and animals. On one side of a darkened sixty-foot subterranean passageway living plant roots press against a glass wall, to be seen when a visitor presses a button that illuminates both a descriptive label and the exhibit itself. Two openings allow children and adults to view the plant above through a periscope. This is probably the only place in the world where a tree and its root system can be observed simultaneously from below ground level. On the other side of the tunnel are dens where the desert's nocturnal creatures cool off during the hot daylight hours. Behind a glass wall, ring-tailed cats, a kit fox, a porcupine, a pack rat, prairie dogs, and diamondback rattlesnakes burrow in caves cut into thick plaster that has been painted and textured to resemble the natural rock of the surrounding countryside. A beehive's inhabitants busily construct honeycombs, and the denizens of a bat cave hang upside down amidst plaster stalactites.

In addition to all this, the Desert Museum has the answer to a photographer's prayer—a Wildlife Blind from which mule deer, badgers, bobcats, assorted birds, and even coyotes may be captured on film as they come to a brightly lit pipe-fed waterhole only about a dozen feet away. Every convenience is provided for the humans inside as well—carpeting on walls and floors to deaden man-made sounds, comfortable chairs in which to wait, and plenty of reflectors and strobe lights to illuminate the camera bugs' quarry.

In California the PALM SPRINGS DESERT MUSEUM is trying, in a booming luxury vacationland, to preserve a piece of desert as it was before automobiles, tourists, and opportunists arrived. One resident has been quoted as saying, "With more traffic, more freeways, more lodges and more golf courses, we'll have to go to the Desert Museum to see the desert." The museum's building, in the town itself, focuses on the geology, zoology, anthropology, and archaeology of the area. But the major exhibit is its Native Desert Reserve, a fifty-acre "sample of virgin terrain wherein many species of plants and animals of the desert [can] be found living in their native habitat." Nature trails for walking and horseback riding go past the varied features of the landscape, and afford good views of wildlife as well as the mountainous countryside, while a desert garden displays and identifies examples of local flora.

Elsewhere in California, desert flora is the specialty of the SANTA BARBARA BOTANIC GARDEN, and a substantial concern of the 200-acre garden adjoining the HENRY E. HUNTINGTON LIBRARY AND ART MUSEUM in San Marino. The Huntington is a good example of the way horticulture can be effectively integrated with a museum of an entirely different persuasion. Others are Nashville's TENNESSEE BOTANICAL GARDENS AND FINE ARTS CENTER and the READING PUBLIC MUSEUM AND ART GALLERY in Pennsylvania. And buildings of historic interest are featured at the nation's two most important botanic gardens, in St. Louis and New York.

The first botanic garden in the United States was established by John Bartram, a self-educated botanist, near his Philadelphia home in 1728. Here on the banks of the Schuylkill River he presided over both native plants and those he obtained, by an exchange of specimens, from Europe. Bartram's garden is now one of Philadelphia's public parks, but it is no longer of horticultural significance.

Several other botanic gardens made brief appearances on the early American scene and then disappeared. One of them was started in New York City by David Hosack who, following undergraduate work at Columbia College and Princeton, studied botany and medicine in Edinburgh and London. Upon his return to New York he practiced medicine, advocating such advanced and unpopular techniques as vaccination and the use of the stethoscope. As a professor of materia medica and botany at Columbia he conceived the idea of a "garden, where plants useful to agriculture and medicine might be cultivated" and in 1801 invested $4807.36 in twenty acres of mid-Manhattan land. Here he established the Elgin Botanic Garden, with the stated purpose of collecting and cultivating "the native plants of the country, especially such as were possessed of medicinal properties or were otherwise useful." But in less than ten years his garden proved so costly that he was forced to sell it to the state despite its value to his students, at a loss, for $74,288.75. After four years of paying for its upkeep the state became discouraged and deeded the land to Columbia College, gratis. Hosack in this indirect way became the alumnus most beneficent to his alma mater. What was once the Elgin Botanic Garden is now occupied by the buildings of Rockefeller Center, Columbia University being the wealthy landlord.

Making up for the loss of the Elgin, the city now has two major public gardens. In The Bronx's internationally respected NEW YORK BOTANICAL GARDEN a huge conservatory, consisting of eleven attached greenhouses, contains foliage from tropical as well as desert climates. Outdoor herb and rock gardens and native plant displays blend with a waterfall, a meandering river, and the charming terraced Snuff Mill which—a tobacco factory more than a century ago—serves as a restaurant today. The museum building features seasonal displays, an herbarium of about three million preserved and classified plants, and a vast library. Classrooms and a lecture hall are used with great success for courses ranging from the care of house plants, to flower arranging, to plant identification, to a serious study of the fundamentals of botany.

At the other end of the city is the BROOKLYN BOTANIC GARDEN, among whose outstanding attractions are its Japanese gardens. One of them is formally planted, with a picturesque wooden bridge (*torii*) and other decorative adjuncts. Recently a "plant-less" garden was dedicated with the gong of a temple bell and the chant of a sutra by a New York Buddhist priest. For twenty-five cents visitors are given a pair of paper sandals and a chance to view this re-creation of the five-hundred-year-old stone garden at Kyoto's Ryoanji Temple. Here, in an area about the size of a tennis court, where fifteen moss-covered stones from Kyoto of varying shape and size rest on crushed white North Carolina granite, meditation is gracefully invited.

The MISSOURI BOTANICAL GARDEN ranks with the New York and is the only one in America to have achieved more than a century of uninterrupted activity, having made its appearance in St. Louis in 1859. Its displays of living plants, especially its orchids and species from the Southwest, are famous. And it is equally noted for its active research, joint university programs, collecting trips, large herbarium, library, and study courses for adults and children. On its grounds is the historic Shaw House, built in 1849.

In an age when the only wild animals most Americans are likely to have close contact with are plush, washable nursery toys, zoos have become an increasingly popular reminder of the wildlife that civilized man has all but elbowed off the face of the earth. In addition to displaying exotic and local animal life, today's zoos are engaged in various research projects, often as joint programs with nearby universities.

These frequently deal either with aspects of conservation or the problems of breeding and rearing wild animals in captivity.

The New York Zoological Society recently established, at its BRONX Zoo, a Wildlife Survival Center where an attempt is being made at propagating species of animals close to extinction in their natural habitats. In explaining the new program the Society's president, Fairfield Osborn, cited as a precedent the successful mission of fifteen buffalo selected from the zoo's herd in 1907 for a trip to Oklahoma's Wichita Game Preserve, where they were called upon to begin repopulating the national parks with their vanishing species. Within half a century their admirable efforts resulted in about eight thousand descendants; more than realizing the hopes of William T. Hornaday, who was the zoo's director at the time of their journey. Among the animals to be included in the new project are okapis, mountain gorillas, Galapagos tortoises, white-tailed gnus, and such extraordinary rarities as the Prjevalsky horse of the Mongolian plains and the Arabian oryx. Ideally the program will be conducted in co-operation with several other zoos, and "self-maintaining breeding herds" will be developed and returned to replenish their native lands. Zoo director William G. Conway has voiced his hope that, "as political revolutions in Africa outrun the Africans' game-preserving techniques, we may soon be returning to Africa the animals for which Africa is famous." The survival center will be open to the public, so that visitors can learn more about what Osborn refers to as the "contemporary obligations of zoos."

The contemporary trend in zoo display is to substitute moats or panes of glass for walls and wire cages and to show the animals in as nearly a natural setting as practicable. At the SAN DIEGO ZOO on ninety-three acres in Balboa Park a normally subtropical climate makes it possible for five thousand or so animals to be exhibited out of doors throughout the year. In a 90-foot-high bird enclosure through which visitors walk on a series of inclined ramps, "birds, tropical vegetation and people share the intimacy and joy of the natural scene."

The PHILADELPHIA ZOO was the first real animal garden in America. Once the residence of a cow that accompanied General Sherman through Georgia (named Atlanta of course), it pioneered in uncaging its less domesticated beasts and is known for its apes, monkeys, reptiles, large water fowl collection, modern Bird House, million-dollar Carnivora House, and charming zoo for children. Other zoos of importance are in Washington, D.C., Chicago, St. Louis, and Detroit.

Animals and plants whose natural habitat is water are displayed in aquariums; important ones being the Steinhart at the California Academy of Science in San Francisco, the Shedd in Chicago, the Waikiki in Honolulu (maintained by the University of Hawaii), the New York Aquarium (now located in Coney Island, it is operated by the New York Zoological Society) and the Fairmount Park Aquarium in Philadelphia. The nation's capital is building an aquarium, at a cost of $10,000,000, despite the objection of a budget-minded congressman that "there are ten million better ways to spend ten million dollars than on a glorified bathtub for fish."

Recognizing the "social consequences of science and industry," a museum that would eventually become one of the most popular in the country as well as Chicago's foremost tourist attraction articulated a philosophy, in 1933, of being "concerned as much with man as a social being as with his scientific discoveries and industries." Invention was regarded as the "result of social and economic pressures" combined with "the genius of man"; chemistry and engineering as "means to an end." This was the outlook of the applied science museum when it finally arrived in America in a big way, its inspiration and example taken from Europe.

But a little more than a century earlier, when chemists and physicists "were still known as philosophers and were rarely to be found outside their laboratories," a group of practical-minded Americans had involved themselves in a bold experiment based upon a similar outlook. In 1824, at a time when industry was still in its infancy, they founded the FRANKLIN INSTITUTE of Philadelphia, resolving "at a numerous and highly respectable meeting of Mechanics, Manufacturers and others, friendly to the promotion of the Mechanic Arts" to extend "a knowledge of Mechanical Science to . . . members and others at a cheap rate." It was decided that "the best mode of attaining this object [would] be by the establishment of Popular Lectures, by the formation of a cabinet of Models and Minerals, and of a library, and by offering premiums on all useful improvements in the Mechanic Arts." Initiating a revolutionary research program, they soon announced plans to test, in "experimental workshops," the new ideas of inventors and industrialists.

At a time when roads were bad and sales outlets limited, the Institute held the country's first exhibition of American manufactured products, with three hundred exhibitors filling the hall. In the years before the United States Patent Office began to publish claims and special data describing new patents, the Institute provided such information as a regular feature of its Journal. It sponsored Pennsylvania's first engineering and architectural schools. It pioneered in public education by providing young men with free evening instruction related to their occupations, and paving the way for the establishment of Philadelphia's first public high school.

When explosions of boilers, particularly on steamboats, became a matter of public concern, the Institute appointed a committee to detect the causes. It was then that the federal government appropriated its first research grant—$1500—for the benefit of industry. A by-product of this project was the invention of the first machine in America that could test the strength of iron and copper. (This machine is now on display at the Institute's museum.) Standardization of weights and measures, control and prevention of fires in public places, standardization of screw threads, and regulation of railroad signals are some of the problems that were dealt with in the years that followed.

Today the research continues in new fields: electronics, nuclear physics, cosmic radiation, and biochemistry. Offering complete scientific and engineering facilities to industry, the Institute serves the future. Its science museum—telling the stories of aviation, space, transportation, chemistry, steel, oil, electricity, communications, the human heart, the universe, and the weather—serves the present and the past. As part of its tribute to Benjamin Franklin there are exhibits of presses from his printing shop and the apparatus he used in his experiments with electricity. And there is a library of over two hundred thousand volumes available to both scientist and student. For a fee the library provides an information service, in a variety of languages, to industry and research groups. Its collections include a file of five million patents from the United States and elsewhere.

And so the relationship between applied science and the museum was actually tested with success quite early in this country. But it was not until Chicago's MUSEUM OF SCIENCE AND INDUSTRY—taking its inspiration from Europe, expanding what it saw there, adapting it to its own needs, and involving industry as a full-time partner in large-scale exhibition—gave the public as lively a show as it could find anywhere, that the imagination of the public was fully captured. From the time Chicago first dedicated itself to a demonstration of the statement inscribed in the museum's Central Rotunda, that "science discerns the laws of nature" and "industry applies them to the needs of man," a new kind of museum began to evolve. It started one day in Germany, in 1920, when an American schoolboy, William Rosenwald, took his father to Munich's Deutsches Museum.

The automated exhibits, the helpfulness of the attendants, the invitation to touch displays, the real coal mine, and the brilliance of its director, Dr. Oskar von Miller, had already made the Deutsches Museum internationally famous. Julius Rosenwald, chairman of Sears, Roebuck and Company, had some idea of what to expect. And when he arrived there, he immediately understood his son's excitement. Furthermore, he began to brood about the fact that in the country of Morse, Bell, Edison, McCormick, Westinghouse, and Ford, there was no place where one might go for an effective interpretation of science applied to industry. He began to formulate a plan.

Several years later, addressing the Commercial Club of Chicago, Rosenwald persuaded its members to share his dream. Presidents of the Illinois Bell Telephone Company, the U.S. Gypsum Company, the Pullman Company, and the Illinois Central Railroad were just a few of those who agreed to help. The city made available the classically designed Fine Arts Building of the 1893 World's Columbian Exposition, which had for a while housed the Field Museum. Voters approved a $5,000,000 bond issue for the building's restoration. And Rosenwald himself, having already put up $3,000,000 for the new museum's furnishings, agreed to pay any reconstruction costs in excess of the voted $5,000,000. As progress continued, it became plain that this was no mere imitation of the Deutsches Museum. What materialized was fourteen acres of a unique educational institution, some of its halls opening in the thirties, its main section in 1940.

The innovation introduced with such huge success by Chicago was simply this: to invite large corporations to set up elaborate exhibits at their own expense in space provided by the museum. A communications display put together by the Illinois Bell Telephone, American Telephone and Telegraph, and Western Electric companies together with the Bell Laboratories; United Air Lines' history of flight exhibit; IBM's "Mathematica"; General Motors' "Motorama"; International Harvester's fully mechanized farm; the Upjohn Pharmaceutical Company's 24-foot model of a human red blood cell; and Union Carbide's two-story model of an atomic reactor were among the results. In September 1961, *Business Week* magazine informed its readers that museum exhibits are "industry's softest sell." The same article reported outlays for Chicago exhibits of up to $1,000,000 by General Motors, International Harvester, RCA, IBM, Swift, and forty-five other major

companies—each obeying the rule against direct advertising and give-
aways, each knowing that education must take precedence over sales
promotion. What it amounted to was an enlightened public relations
program from which the public immeasurably benefited.

Travelers from all over the world have gone down into the museum's
coal mine, have seen replicas of blast and open-hearth furnaces, have
looked at "The Newspaper in America," "Ships Through the Ages,"
and "The Conquest of Pain," and have promised themselves a return
visit to keep up with the changing world of technology.

Chicago's is not the only museum to have worked out an exhibit
plan with industry. The CALIFORNIA MUSEUM OF SCIENCE AND IN-
DUSTRY in Los Angeles, where exhibits explain both the Telstar and
lasers, carries out a similar program. So do the Franklin Institute, the
Boston Museum of Science, and Pittsburgh's Buhl Planetarium. And
New York City will be doing it on an ambitious scale at its brand new
HALL OF SCIENCE.

Medical museums are by no means new. Health museums—institutions centered around the job of presenting public health information
through exhibition—are relatively recent arrivals, dating from the thirties. Both belong to the category of applied science.

The American Museum of Natural History and the Smithsonian
were pioneers in the presentation of health subjects and the biology
of man. But the MAYO FOUNDATION MUSEUM OF HYGIENE AND MEDI-
CINE in Rochester, Minnesota, the CLEVELAND HEALTH MUSEUM,
the DALLAS HEALTH AND SCIENCE MUSEUM, the HINSDALE HEALTH
MUSEUM in Illinois, and Philadelphia's LANKENAU HOSPITAL HEALTH
MUSEUM are specialists in this area.

Cleveland's is the American prototype and mother institution. One
of its main features is its exhibit for teaching sex and human reproduction to school children. It consists of one hundred sculptured models
showing what happens in the stages between conception and birth.
Developed by Dr. Robert L. Dickinson and sculptor Abram Belskie,
the series was first shown at the New York World's Fair of 1939. After
Cleveland demonstrated how such models could be used in the community, they were purchased by other health museums as part of their
standard equipment.

A giant plastic tooth and a transparent woman are two other items
on the list of standard furnishings. The Mayo Clinic claims credit for
the first glass man, predecessor of the transparent woman. Dr. Arthur

H. Bubulian had one made in Germany in 1933 as part of an exhibit the clinic was then preparing for the Chicago World's Fair. Dallas' transparent woman, named "Visi-Belle," is of more recent German manufacture. Made at the Deutsches-Gesundheits Museum in Cologne, she cost $15,000 and she talks. She has a gentleman friend named "Visi-Bill."

Heredity, hearing, the circulatory system, mental well-being, cancer, and nutrition are other common subjects for illustration at the health museum. And film programs, lectures, and publications are frequently offered on a variety of medical problems.

Whereas the health museum, concentrating on education, does not collect specimens or engage in research, the medical museum does. One of them that is more than a century old is the MEDICAL MUSEUM OF THE ARMED FORCES INSTITUTE OF PATHOLOGY in Washington, D.C.

Shortly after its founding during the Civil War, it issued a circular urging medical officers "diligently to collect, and to forward to the office of the Surgeon General, all specimens of morbid anatomy, surgical or medical, which may be regarded as valuable." General Daniel Edgar Sickles of the Union army answered this request after his right leg, severely wounded at Gettysburg, was amputated. He put the leg into a miniature coffin and sent it off to the museum where, stripped to its splintered bone, it became a cherished exhibit. Whenever he could he came by to pay it a visit, often bringing friends.

Hundreds of thousands of tourists still stare at it each year. The other specimens they view represent only a fraction of what the Institute has acquired. Its enormous collection of diseased eyes, pieces of tissue removed during operations, and tumorous hearts are in the Walter Reed Army Medical Center. Walter Reed himself was once the museum's curator.

An example of the applied science museum in still another field is the AMERICAN MUSEUM OF ATOMIC ENERGY in Oak Ridge, Tennessee. Operated for the United States Atomic Energy Commission by the Oak Ridge Institute of Nuclear Studies, it is concerned primarily with a demonstration of the peaceful uses—in medicine, agriculture, and industry—of atomic power.

And the field of rockets and missiles is importantly documented at New Mexico's ROSWELL MUSEUM in a memorial to the American physicist Robert H. Goddard whose inventions and experiments guided us into the space age. Actual rockets, combustion chambers, gyroscopic control systems, his drawings and photographs, and his rocket launching tower are all here.

To support the age-old belief "that there must be a very much greater power than man responsible for the wonderful things which are daily occurring in the universe" and to provide instruction, Charles Hayden made a gift to the American Museum of Natural History that resulted in the opening, in 1935, of the fourth planetarium in the United States. For now that it had become possible to reproduce an orderly universe inside a room, the museum could both re-create the sense of wonder that was felt by man when he took his first thoughtful look up at the heavens, and satisfy a rapidly increasing public desire to understand basic astronomical principles.

Professional astronomy in America had come a long way since the early nineteenth century when a widely used textbook was proclaiming that "the studies connected with astronomy tend to prepare the soul for the employments of the future world." But when this religious orientation gave way to a mathematical approach, the esthetic and emotional appeal inherent in the subject as well as the growing demand of the layman for digestible information were overlooked almost entirely. The same nineteenth-century textbook had also said that "astronomy displays before us the extent and grandeur of God's universal empire." And for most people this remained true. The universe, after all, provides a rather awe-inspiring spectacle, even to the professional observer. A theater that could explain with authority all that was known of the cosmos while depicting the beauty of the still unknown was bound to be a success. The planetarium was such a theater.

The huge instrument that projects those bright celestial images is itself called a planetarium. Long before its invention, men had been making models representing the planets in motion. After 1543, the year Copernicus published the theory upon which modern astronomy is based—that the planets, of which the earth is one, move around the sun—globes were made and then joined together by gears to illustrate the calculated motion of the planets, the moon, and other satellites, and to demonstrate the succession of day and night, the changing of the seasons, and the phenomenon of eclipse. The first such device that did all of these things with consistent reliability was constructed by a clockmaker in 1682 for Christiaan Huygens, the Dutch mathematician and physicist who designed it. A similar moving model of the solar system—a mechanical planetarium—was made in England about twenty years later. And when another one was made with some additions and improvements for Charles Boyle, the fourth Earl of Orrery, the instrument was referred to by Sir Richard Steele as an "orrery." The term has stuck. A great number and variety of orreries are in use today, at planetariums and in schools, as invaluable teaching aids.

Throughout the eighteenth and nineteenth centuries, orreries were constructed in Europe and in the United States; small, large, simple, and complex. David Rittenhouse of Philadelphia made several that were particularly fine. One of them, built in 1769, shows the relative positions of the planets with great accuracy, demonstrates the movements of the moon, and computes the year, month, and day of past and future eclipses. The mechanism, neatly contained in a cabinet, became the property of the University of Pennsylvania.

But not satisfied with an outside view of the solar system, men had made several attempts to provide an instructive inside view. These were called celestial globes, and they were of two kinds. One variety consisted of a sphere with pin-holes in it representing the stars. The viewer, looking into it through an opening designed for that purpose, would see a pin-point of light on the opposite interior wall. The most famous of these, built in 1699 by Erhardt Weigel, a professor of astronomy at the University of Jena, Germany, was acquired by Philadelphia's Franklin Institute. The other kind of celestial globe, first constructed in Germany somewhat earlier, was big enough for the observer to get into. Weigel built one of these also. It had a diameter of ten feet and it contained devices that simulated meteors, rain, hail, thunder, lightning, and volcanoes.

Cambridge University acquired a similar but larger device in 1758 when Professor Roger Long finished what was described as "an enormous astronomical machine . . . a hollow sphere, about 18 feet in diameter [that] can be made to rotate, while about thirty persons conveniently attend a scientific lecture in the interior and contemplate the orderly march of the constellations painted on the moving concavity above them, the stars being pierced through the metal according to the several magnitudes, so that the light penetrates and each assumes a curious radiated or rather stellated form." The sphere was turned by hand from the outside while spectators stood on a stationary platform at its center. When the machine was considered no longer useful 116 years later, and it became clear that no museum wanted it, it was destroyed.

Then, at the Chicago Academy of Sciences in 1912, the same idea was used again. Dr. Wallace W. Atwood designed a motor-driven celestial sphere that would continue to be popular even after Chicago could boast one of the country's finest modern planetariums. Atwood's globe was, in fact, a close forerunner of the modern planetarium.

When Dr. Oskar von Miller, director of Munich's Deutsches Museum, came to the optical firm of Carl Zeiss in Jena with a request for an astronomical exhibit that would bring the heavens indoors, both he and the Zeiss engineers were thinking in terms of a large, rotating, perforated globe similar to Atwood's. But after experiments with this approach failed to produce the illusion of natural mystery that was desired, Dr. Walter Bauersfield, a member of the firm and a leading authority on optical apparatus, came up with a new idea. He thought of projecting images of the stars upon the interior surface of a fixed dome. By the special arrangement of many small projectors, a complete photograph of the sky could be thrown, section by section, onto the white underside of a great sphere. He and his associates spent five years developing an unbelievably complicated instrument that would reveal to the naked eye not only the stars, but the sun, the moon, and the planets; all in their proper places for any instant of any year of any century. The first model, which could show the skies—past, present, or future—for only one place on earth, was ready to perform in the summer of 1924. (Soon the machine would be adjusted to project these phenomena for any terrestrial position.)

The first American city to order the remarkable Zeiss projector was Chicago. Max Adler, who was a board member of Sears, Roebuck and Company, donated the ADLER PLANETARIUM AND ASTRONOMICAL MUSEUM believing that "the popular conception of the universe is too meager; the planets and the stars . . . too far removed from general knowledge." He went on to say, at the presentation ceremony in the spring of 1930, that "in our reflections, we dwell too little upon the concept that the world and all human endeavor within it are governed by established order, and too infrequently upon the truth that under the heavens everything is interrelated, even as each of us to the other."

Chicago's planetarium, which seats close to five hundred under a dome that is 68 feet in diameter, is the principal feature of a museum whose collections of antique instruments—astronomical, navigational, and mathematical—is considered the finest in the world; globes, astrolabes, nocturnals, sundials, hourglasses, clocks, calendars, and telescopes being just some of these items. There is also an observatory.

The FELS PLANETARIUM was the next to open its doors. Samuel S. Fels, whose soap-manufacturing business formed a solid foundation for his philanthropy, bought the costly Zeiss invention for the Franklin Institute to which the planetarium was added. The first demonstration was given by a director "impressively attired in a wing collar and frock coat." And the occasion was made even more gala by "a musical interlude furnished by violin soloist Iso Briselli, and the Curtis String Quartette." During the following three decades, five million people came to see similar demonstrations without the strings. The original projector, "the most versatile teaching aid ever devised," had to be replaced at the end of its twenty-ninth winter with a later model; the cost this time donated by the Samuel S. Fels Fund.

Another feature of the Institute's astronomical program is its observatory where visitors are invited to gain a working knowledge of observation techniques through the use of a 10-inch refracting telescope and a 24-inch reflecting telescope—the largest in the world devoted entirely to public use.

In Los Angeles, commemorating the generosity of Griffith J. Griffith (blacksmith, newspaperman, owner of ostrich farms, rancher, and real estate investor), the GRIFFITH OBSERVATORY AND PLANETARIUM has many exceptionally fine exhibits and a dome that is 75 feet in diameter.

New York's HAYDEN PLANETARIUM has a dome of the same size and a seating capacity of 814, making it the country's largest. In 1958 the Hayden acquired its second Zeiss projector which weighs two and a half tons without its mounting, is 12 feet long, contains 150 lenses, and, having arrived in parts from West Germany, took nearly a month to assemble. On the first floor of the building audiences gather to watch demonstrations of a large orrery set in the ceiling. This room is called the Hall of the Sun. Moving around the sun at carefully calculated relative speeds, and rotating upon their axes at the same time, the planets make their journey above the heads of the spectators. Since one minute in this exhibit is engineered to equal one month, the earth completes a revolution around the sun every twelve minutes, while Saturn takes nearly six hours. Set in the floor of the same room is a reproduction of the Aztec Calendar Stone. Other rooms contain paintings and photographs of astronomical phenomena, an impressive collection of large meteorites (including the largest in any museum, weighing 68,085 pounds), sundials, compasses, astrolabes, and, of course, space age exhibits.

At the opening demonstration of Pittsburgh's BUHL PLANETARIUM AND INSTITUTE OF POPULAR SCIENCE, the director "took his place at the control board . . . the room became dark to the accompaniment of the music of the organ; and the stars illuminated the dome. Mr. Stokely then presented the Planetarium's first production, 'Stars Over Pittsburgh.'" Dedicated to the popular interpretation of science the Buhl, like every similar institution, would seek out its methods somewhere between the cinema and the university lecture hall; and, having mastered them, would move directly toward its serious goals.

The goals grow more serious every day. Historically, astronomy was the first of the sciences. Now as rockets are pointed to the moon, it is clearly a science the public must understand in order to deal with its own future.

Three "theaters of the sky" built more recently than the Buhl are the MORRISON PLANETARIUM of San Francisco's California Academy of Sciences, the MOREHEAD PLANETARIUM of the University of North Carolina at Chapel Hill, and the CHARLES HAYDEN PLANETARIUM of Boston's Museum of Science. When, just after the Second World War, the California Academy learned that the Zeiss company, isolated behind the Iron Curtain, could not supply a projector, its scientists decided to make one themselves. During the war, the Academy had converted some of its facilities into a workshop that turned out 10,000 optical parts and repaired range finders, sextants, azimuth circles, gun sights, and periscopes for the U. S. Navy. With this experience behind it, and with help where it was needed, they created a projector that they could proudly proclaim unexcelled by any other in the world. It took four years of work, 321 lenses, four miles of wiring, and $140,000.

In the meantime a new Zeiss factory was opened in West Germany and orders were once again being filled. In addition a machine from the Spitz Laboratories of Delaware proved its excellence, becoming the choice of the Longway Planetarium in Flint, Michigan, and the United States Air Force Academy in Colorado Springs. And a unique projector, designed and built by the Korkosz brothers of Springfield, Massachusetts, caused excitement when it was first demonstrated at the Charles Hayden, for which it was commissioned.

Kilohani, an Hawaiian word translated as "observing the heavens," took on a new meaning in Honolulu when a planetarium was added to the Bishop Museum. In St. Louis the building itself found a new shape when a concrete structure, enclosing a domed auditorium, exhibition space, and an observatory, arose in Forest Park and outlined a hyperbola against the sky.

But whatever its location or external appearance may be, or wherever the instrument inside it may come from, the planetarium continues to penetrate "the mystery" without destroying "the majesty," which Dr. Philip Fox, first director of the Adler, once pointed out is its basic aim.

"Science," Plato said, "is nothing but perception."

The gap between the men of science—the perceivers—and the majority of us who do not perceive is wide and getting wider. The museum alone cannot close that gap. But it can and does provide a marvelous opportunity for each of us, on our own level, to increase our own perception.

The more we penetrate the mystery, the more we will feel the majesty. The science museum in America is proof that this is so.

Chapter IV

HISTORY

ONE summer day nearly two centuries ago, a young delegate to the Continental Congress in Philadelphia received a letter from Paris, from a former teacher who was the American Minister to France. "I sincerely wish you may find it convenient to come here," the older man had written. "The pleasure of the trip will be less than you expect, but the utility greater. It will make you adore your own country, its soil, its climate, its equality, liberty, laws, people, and manners. My God! how little do my countrymen know what precious blessings they are in possession of, and which no other people on earth enjoy. I confess," said Thomas Jefferson in his note to James Monroe, "I had no idea of it myself."

From St. Augustine to Juneau, from Williamsburg to Boise, from Worcester to Honolulu, the history of these "precious blessings" is told in close to two thousand museums and monuments. There is no part of the country that has neglected to preserve, display, and enshrine the remembrance of its past.

Although the Charleston Museum—which now boasts both an important library containing research files of early newspapers, and two historic houses—is indisputably the oldest in the country, its members did not exclusively or even systematically concentrate on state and local history until many years after its founding. A greater late-eighteenth-century influence on the movement to preserve the past was Pierre Eugène du Simitière, who maintained a museum in his Philadelphia home. He died in 1784 shortly after his project was begun; but his insistence upon keeping a record of contemporary events from documentary sources, portraits, and military relics had already set an example for serious amateurs.

John Pintard, whose American Museum in New York would eventually become P. T. Barnum's showcase, was an amateur possessed of high and scholarly hopes. To Secretary of State Jefferson, Pintard explained that his plan was "a patriotic one" that might "prove a public benefit," inasmuch as its purpose was "to collect and preserve whatever relates to our country in art or nature, as well as every material which may serve to perpetuate the Memorial of national events and history." It was August 26, 1790, the eve of the transfer of the government seat to Philadelphia, and Pintard requested "any supernumerary papers, Gazettes, &C. in your Department not worth the trouble and expence [sic] of removal," promising that any materials donated would be kept in a place that would "always be open to the curious."

Pintard had been planning his museum for some while. A year earlier, while on a business trip to Boston (he was—unsuccessfully—a merchant), he had paid a call on the Reverend Jeremy Belknap of the Federal Street Church. Belknap was then engaged in writing a three-volume *History of New Hampshire*. Pintard, who agreed to sell subscriptions to this work, described to its author his hope of establishing what he thought might be called the American Antiquarian Society. Belknap liked the idea but nothing much was done about it until, quite coincidentally, the day after Pintard wrote to Jefferson. On August 27, 1790, Belknap wrote to Ebenezer Hazard of New York: "When Mr. Pintard was here, he strongly urged the forming a Society of American Antiquarians. Several other gentlemen have occasionally spoken to me on the same subject. Yesterday I was in company where it was again mentioned, and it was wished that a beginning could be made. This morning I have written something, and communicated it to the gentlemen who spoke of it. How it will issue, time must determine. If it should come to any thing, you shall hear farther."

It is a safe bet that Hazard did "hear farther," for during the following year the Massachusetts Historical Society, the oldest in the country, was born out of the interest of Mr. Belknap and his cohorts in the "antiquities of America." The new group was dedicated to "the preservation of books, pamphlets, manuscripts and records, containing historical facts, biographical anecdotes, temporary projects and beneficial speculations." Such preservation was described as an activity which "conduces to mark the genius, delineate the manners and trace the progress of society in the United States, and must always have a useful tendency to rescue the true history of this country from the ravages of time and the effects of ignorance and neglect."

For a number of years the Boston group maintained a cabinet, largely of natural history specimens, but when a more appropriate organization arose on the local scene to deal with the subject it happily abandoned this chore. (It still supports a cabinet keeper, however, who cares for a decorative arts collection and a group of portraits that are usually on loan to other galleries. But the nation's first historical society, renowned for its library and its possession, editing and publishing of the Adams papers, today has no museum.)

In the meantime Pintard and Belknap had continued their association by correspondence. To cement their relationship the Bostonian sent the New Yorker a gift—a second-edition copy of the Bible John Eliot had translated and transliterated for the Indians of Massachusetts more than a century earlier. In his letter of thanks Pintard tells of his museum, wherein he hoped to "deposit [the Indian Bible], with your permission and in your name." In a later letter Pintard wrote, "My passion for American history increases, tho' I have but detached moments and scant means of gratifying it." As for the museum, he said, "It makes small progress with a small fund, and may possibly succeed."

But "scant means" and a "small fund" were a good combination for an eventual downfall. The American Museum fell into other hands, and Mr. Pintard, having failed in his own business ventures, spent about a year in debtor's prison. It was not until a merciful new law permitting bankruptcy enabled him to renew his efforts at commerce that Pintard landed back on his feet and began again to pursue the memorabilia of history. This time he was successful. He founded the NEW-YORK HISTORICAL SOCIETY. And its museum, which would serve as a model to hundreds of state and local organizations as they came into being, was another of his ideas. In the late fall of 1804, Pintard and eleven prominent "Persons" gathered "in the Picture Room of the City Hall of the City of New York" and "agreed to form themselves into a Society . . . to collect and preserve whatever may relate to the natural, civil or ecclesiastical History of the United States in general and of this State in particular."

During the next twenty years Pintard worked hard to advance the career of what he liked to refer to as his "brat." He had no money, but he gave his energy, time, and his own books—several of which, including the Eliot Indian Bible, were outright gifts. What he did not contribute, he sold to the Society at cost. With his friend and fellow founding member, Mayor DeWitt Clinton, he obtained a rent-free room in the old City Hall. This was the Society's first home. Soon after that he lobbied in the state capital for a lottery that would benefit both the Society and the city's Board of Health, which wanted money for the "exterpation of Wolves & Panthers." Perhaps due to DeWitt Clinton's efforts—he was by then a state senator—the bill passed the first legislative chamber. But all the efforts of another Society member, Assemblyman Samuel L. Mitchill, could not get it through the second. In a condition described as "mortification," Mitchill wrote to Pintard "that the bill . . . for the destruction of wild beasts, and for the encouragement of history, was this day debated and finally rejected."

The Albany legislature made another gift to the Society instead; one that would outlast mere money. This was a hyphen which, in the papers of incorporation, somehow crept into the space that customarily divides "New" from "York." And for sentimental reasons, the gentlemen-historians have scrupulously remained hyphenated ever since.

Even without the lottery money, the Society managed to acquire nearly five hundred books and pamphlets, more than 150 maps, charts and prints, and a multitude of manuscripts, oil portraits, and early newspapers before the end of its first dozen years. A catalogue finally became necessary and among the things it listed was—a gift from Pintard—one of three known copies of the first plan of New York, run off the press of the city's first printer, William Bradford, in about 1731. And an 1809 dedication copy of *Knickerbocker's History of New York* was recorded as having been donated "by the Author," Washington Irving, who fifty years later would be eulogized as a "most distinguished, and most cherished" member. (A memorial service, which featured an address by William Cullen Bryant on the life and works of the deceased, would take place before "one of the largest, most intelligent and appreciative audiences of both sexes"; on stage would be a full-length portrait of Irving, draped with purple and surrounded by evergreens and "three symbolical urns.")

As the acquisitions grew (Pintard wrote to his daughter in 1816 that "it is astonishing what a fund of Historical materials have been collected already") larger quarters were needed, and the founder was able to put another of his dreams into effect: housing the several literary and cultural organizations of the growing city under one roof. For this purpose he obtained the Alms House, whose occupants were being moved to Bellevue Hospital. Promptly rechristened the New York Institution, it contained such short-lived groups as the American Academy of Fine Arts, the new Lyceum of Natural History (this predecessor of the American Museum of Natural History was ultimately destroyed by fire), the Literary and Philosophical Society, and John Scudder's American Museum (the commercial remnant of Pintard's earlier attempt).

For a while, zoology, botany, and "vegetable philosophy" were mixed in with the Society's pursuit of history, but the members soon realized that much more could be accomplished if they limited themselves to their primary purpose.

By now DeWitt Clinton was governor of New York and a friend of his, Dr. David Hosack, was president of the Society. John Trumbull was vice-president. And the Society faced a staggering debt of $7500, which led some members to propose the sale of its library as a means of achieving solvency. Although Pintard was himself a creditor, being owed $3000, he was so upset by this suggestion—an idea so contrary to all his dreams and principles—that he never again appeared at a meeting. Hosack resigned his office, and so did Trumbull. But two years later Hosack was back in office, and once again the Society tried lobbying for funds in the state capital. This time there were results. A grant that would cover two thirds of the debt was made, contingent upon the members' success in finding the balance. Somehow they managed to raise enough to pay back all but about $1400 still due Pintard. By refusing to recognize his claims, for which he could not produce vouchers, they were able to balance their account books and retain the library.

It was now 1828; the Society had almost finished weathering its first quarter of a century. Most of the original members were no longer active. But new ones were coming forth; and later generations would attempt to make up for the shabby treatment of Mr. Pintard. Shortly after its golden anniversary, the Society moved into its own building, and Pintard's visage appeared on one side of a medal commemorating the event. He also appeared on the centennial medal. And shortly after the centennial, the Society moved again—into the first section of the structure on Central Park West which, substantially enlarged, is its residence today. Located here is the great library and a portrait collection whose subjects range from New Amsterdam burghers (including Governor Peter Stuyvesant) and prominent colonials, through American statesmen, artists, and writers (Aaron Burr, Charles Willson Peale, Edgar Allan Poe, Calvin Coolidge among them) and officers and members of the Society. There are eighteenth- and nineteenth-century American miniatures, including portraits by West, Inman, Peale, and Sully, and likenesses of most of the ladies who belonged to the original "Four Hundred," the most elevated social set in town. There are fine examples of New England and New York furniture and decorative objects of the seventeenth through nineteenth centuries.

And there are period rooms of major significance. These include, from the Beekman family's home, the parlor where Nathan Hale was tried and sentenced, and the bedroom where British spy Major John André spent the night before his journey north to meet Benedict Arnold. The Beekman coach, which is here, is the oldest New York conveyance in existence. It was used before the Revolution and then by Washington during his Presidency. The museum has a whole group of vehicles that come out of the city's past. Here also are an accumulation of toys and fashions covering a period of more than three hundred years; posters and other materials relating to the history of advertising in this country; nearly five hundred of Audubon's original water colors of the birds of America; and over two hundred drawings of scenes from Indian life by a long-time member of the Society, George Catlin. A gallery designed to resemble the deck and cabin of a sailing vessel contains exhibits tracing the history of the city's port; a Naval History Gallery recalls, with models, uniforms, paintings, and engravings, important engagements on the high seas. The history of the city and state are arranged chronologically, beginning with Indian culture and the age of exploration, and continuing through Dutch and English colonial life, to the Revolutionary and Federal periods.

Some of the items that may be on view have been owned by the Society for a century, such as Washington's army cot; a copper globe, made in Rome in 1542, depicting Verrazano's discoveries in North America; and the original tombstone of printer William Bradford from the Trinity Church graveyard. (When it was in danger of being irreparably damaged by weather, a new stone was erected in New York's oldest cemetery, and the original was presented to the Society by the church. The exchange was part of the special service held at Trinity in celebration of the two-hundredth anniversary of the birth of the printer.) Also to be found here are what remains of the first two outdoor statues in America. In 1770 a marble representation of Sir William Pitt was placed at the intersection of Wall and William streets; seven years later, when they occupied the city, British troops decapitated this friend of the Yankees and hacked off his arms. The redcoats were perhaps acting in retaliation for the fate that had befallen a gilded lead statue of George III on horseback that had stood at Bowling Green. In the evening of the day New Yorkers heard the Declaration of Independence for the first time, the regal tyrant was taken down and melted for bullets. Four of George's remaining fragments, his marble base, and the torso of Sir William are what reside with the Society.

When, in 1954, the New-York Historical Society celebrated its Sesqui-Centennial with an appropriately festive dinner, "looking down with an approving smile on the proceedings below was" a portrait of John Pintard. In *Knickerbocker Birthday,* an entertaining history of the Society published that year, director R. W. G. Vail reported that, after the dinner, he "gathered up his notes, smiled up at the portrait of the Founder, waved him a salute and said: 'Wasn't it a lovely evening, Sir? I hope you enjoyed it too. Good-night, Mr. Pintard.'"

Groups dedicated to the preservation of local—as opposed to state or national—memorabilia began to appear in the third decade of the nineteenth century. The earliest was the PILGRIM SOCIETY of 1820, the year that marked the bicentennial of the landing of the first party from the *Mayflower.* Founded by "a respectable number of the inhabitants of [Plymouth, who were] impelled by a sense of duty and pious gratitude to divine Providence," it proposed "to commemorate this great historical event, and to perpetuate the character and virtues of our ancestors to posterity."

The anniversary celebration that was the new organization's first project was addressed by Daniel Webster, whose speech was "all that could be anticipated or conceived . . . correct in all its historical statements, powerful in argument, rich in description, and pathetic and eloquent in action." Afterwards, there was an "elegant, though simple repast," at which "treasures both of the land and the sea" were served. In a gesture that was "among other affecting memorials calling to mind the distresses of the Pilgrims," every diner was served with "five kernels of parched corn . . . alluding to the time in 1623 when that was the proportion allowed to each individual on account of the scarcity."

Four years later, when "the funds of the Pilgrim Society [were] thought sufficient to warrant the trustees in commencing the building of a monumental edifice," a public museum was erected. At the ceremony of the cornerstone it was said that "in good earnest have we laid the foundation of [a monument to the Pilgrims] where for ages their descendants may repair and trace their feeble beginnings, and contemplate the astonishing results, that a beneficent Deity has annexed to the resolute, unwearied, conscientious performance of the duties of piety and benevolence."

Today Pilgrim Hall's library contains books, manuscripts, and other documents that record the history of the early settlers and the colony they founded. In the museum are the patent issued to the colony in 1621; a sword that was used by Captain Myles Standish; Bibles that belonged to John Alden and William Bradford; the basketwork cradle made for the first Pilgrim baby (Peregrine White, born on the *Mayflower* while it was anchored in Provincetown Harbor); utensils and furniture used by the founding fathers; a second-edition copy of Eliot's Indian Bible; the only known portrait of a member of the *Mayflower* company (the subject, Governor Josiah Winslow, was painted in 1651, probably during a trip back to England); and models of the fort, first meeting house, an early dwelling, and the *Mayflower* itself.

A year later, the citizens of Salem established the Essex Historical Society, now the ESSEX INSTITUTE. Its first president, Dr. Augustus Holyoke, was ninety-three at the time. Eight years later he died, leaving to the Society what was literally the accumulation of a lifetime. A long line of successors generously did likewise with the assets of lifetimes that were only somewhat briefer. And so the Institute's library and galleries would be described as "bulging at the seams" and "checkmated," even long after its maritime, ethnological, and natural history acquisitions had been sent across the street to the Peabody Museum as the result of a mid-nineteenth-century decision to concentrate on the history of Essex County, on portraits, Massachusetts decorative arts and furnishings, and on historic houses that are masterpieces of early Federal architecture.

At about the same time, three neighboring New England states became interested in historical preservation, followed by two states further to the west. Only two years after Maine, separating from Massachusetts, became a state, the MAINE HISTORICAL SOCIETY was founded. Among its members was Henry Wadsworth Longfellow, whose sister bequeathed the Longfellow family house in Portland, along with its furnishings, and a provision for the construction of a separate library building in the rear. The RHODE ISLAND HISTORICAL SOCIETY of 1823, a year younger than that of Maine, began with two natural history cabinets, one in Newport and one in Providence. But after two decades natural history gave way to state history; the pruned cabinets were amalgamated, and the Society moved into its first building on the Brown University campus. A century later it was fortunate enough to receive the John Brown House in Providence, a luxurious dwelling described by John Quincy Adams, shortly after it was built in 1786, as "the most magnificent and elegant private mansion that I have ever seen on this continent." Also in 1823, the bicentennial of the first set-

tlement in the area created an opportunity for the formation of the
NEW HAMPSHIRE HISTORICAL SOCIETY in Concord, whose earliest efforts were devoted to the publication of source material relating to the
state's history. Library and museum collections accrued, however, and
for many years two buildings were maintained, one for each function.
The present building contains the excellent library as well as several
early eighteenth-century rooms. And the eagerly awaited new museum
wing will at last make room for exhibits stressing the economic and
industrial development of the state.

During this period, too, the HISTORICAL SOCIETY OF PENNSYLVANIA
was formed in Philadelphia, pursuing the publication of source materials and the development of a library more than the expansion of its
cabinet. Today, although it has fine portraits, relics of the state's past,
and mementos of its founder William Penn, it is most renowned for a
huge collection of over half a million rare books, pamphlets, and newspapers and more than four million manuscripts, including at least
25,000 Penn items and about 400 letters written by George Washington. Cincinnati's HISTORICAL AND PHILOSOPHICAL SOCIETY OF OHIO,
founded in 1831 and the first trans-Appalachian organization of its
kind, likewise concentrates on its library activities. Under a unique
arrangement with the Taft Museum, selections from the Society's collection of paintings, prints, and photographs are shown in the Taft's
galleries in May and June of each year. The Society has recently
moved into a new wing of the Cincinnati Art Museum, where its books
and manuscripts are more accessible than previously.

The library resources of historical societies frequently take precedence over their museum functions. This is true not only of Massachusetts, Pennsylvania, and Ohio, but of the majority of the privately
financed groups that developed in the Atlantic states before the end
of the nineteenth century. It is true of New-York, despite its fascinating galleries. The point of view was best summed up by a librarian of
the AMERICAN ANTIQUARIAN SOCIETY who demanded to know
whether the organization that employed him was to be "of literary character, intended for scientific uses and the gratification of enlightened
curiosity," or "a mere museum of articles for idle and unprofitable in-
spection." (This was the country's third historical society. Its name is
the one that Pintard had originally thought of and mentioned to
Belknap at their first meeting. It was founded in 1812 by the Worcester, Massachusetts, printer and patriot, Isaiah Thomas, and for many
years it held onto a conglomeration of objects of doubtful historical

value. However, its documentary reference collection—a treasure house of books, newspapers, and all sorts of things published in early America—was always considered its most important concern, and its ethnological specimens, plaster casts of Michelangelo's *Moses* and *Christ,* and other objects were disposed of during its second half-century.)

In the states that took shape in the Northwest Territory and the region of the Louisiana Purchase, historical societies were formed almost before there was any history to document. The pioneers who settled each successive frontier lost no time in providing what they considered all the amenities of civilized government; and historical societies were plainly among the amenities. The year of Nebraska's entry into the Union was the year its historical society was founded, while Minnesota didn't even wait for statehood, forming a society during the year it attained territorial status. The Wisconsin constitutional convention was the occasion for an early attempt to start a history association there, but it was three years later during the 1849 legislative session that the STATE HISTORICAL SOCIETY OF WISCONSIN actually came into being. It had twenty-five vice-presidents, each of whom was a legislator sent by his county. The governor was its president. And meetings were scheduled to coincide with the annual legislative sessions. By the time the fourth meeting was held the group's total achievement consisted of a fifty-volume library. At that fourth meeting too, dues were doubled (to one dollar) and six new members admitted, including one Lyman Copeland Draper, a short, energetic man recently arrived from various points east.

As a boy growing up in newly settled western New York, Draper had been fascinated by stories of the Revolution and the War of 1812 told by his father, grandfather, and other men. Provided by a generous relative (the husband of one Cousin Lydia) with a college education of sorts (mostly at a new Baptist school in Ohio) and then with a regular income (which he earned by serving as caretaker of his benefactor's property and Cousin Lydia's companion), he spent all of his free time recording the stories of the soldiers and settlers who had built up the Appalachian frontier. He would travel for several months a year, conversing with pioneers and their families, and obtaining old journals and letters from them. In one nine-year period, his travels having cost his patron about $4000, he acquired 10,000 pages of documents, letters, and reminiscences, and filled nearly 10,000 pages more with transcripts of interviews. He continually hoped to turn this material into a book, or better yet a series of books, and he endlessly outlined such projects. But one of a rich variety of psychosomatic ailments always made its appearance just in time to keep him from writing more than a paragraph. The only activity that could allay this recurrent assortment of symptoms was collecting manuscripts and interviews, and so he was almost constantly engaged in what he referred to as the "pious—and, I may add—thankless labor of rescuing from forgetfullness and neglect the memories of an interesting band of worthies." The implied promise that he would immortalize these memories in printed books proved a sufficient inducement to entice from the worthies and their descendants a valuable hoard of material. (He did at one time manage co-authorship, with a hired writer-researcher, of *A Helping Hand for Town and Country: An American Home Book of Practical and Scientific Information Concerning . . . The Many Important Interests Pertaining to Domestic Economy and Family Health,* a sort of encyclopedia dealing with such things as growing strawberries and raising cattle.)

When, after the sudden death of his patron, he was faced with the necessity of supporting himself as well as his cousin and her adopted daughter, he took the advice of a friend and came to Madison in the hope of being appointed state librarian. This plan fell through but Draper stayed on, confident that in a state and city that were "on the high road to prosperity" he would be able to turn his pastime to profit.

On meeting him, the historical society's recording secretary wrote, "I think that Mr. Draper, who is engaged in historical researches . . . will be of service to us in our Society." The new member lost no time in proving this to be an understatement. With the aid of his friend, who had gotten him on the executive committee, he drew up a new charter less than two months after joining the group. Next he got $500 out of the legislature for what he confidently claimed would "necessarily [become] the best Historical Library in the North West extant." In the new charter he had included a provision for honorary members "in every part of the world, distinguished for their literary or scientific attainments and known especially as friends or promoters of American history," and he proceeded to build the society's library by flattering kings and explorers, novelists and military men, artists and clergymen with this honor as he had earlier built his own collection by flattering frontiersmen with the promise of publication. In less than three months he mailed out six hundred membership certificates, and received in return an equal number of books and pamphlets, with promises of more to come.

Lyman Draper had provided a job for himself, and at its next meeting an appreciative organization resolved to give him a salary. Since most of the members were still sitting in the legislature, it was only a matter of weeks before that body voted a $500 stipend, doubled a year later. Whenever anything more was needed for the organization it was to the Statehouse that Draper applied. For the first time, the public was footing the bill for an historic society. And shortly before his retirement in 1887, Draper was able to boast that of the seventy-seven societies in the country Wisconsin had the third largest library. After his death a few years later it was augmented by his own valuable collection of more than three thousand volumes.

His influence was strongly felt in Iowa, Michigan, Minnesota, and Kansas, where a number of Draper's ideas and innovations regarding scholarship, administration, and legislative aid were directly applied.

Shortly before the turn of the century Wisconsin spent $620,000 for its Society's own building, which was envied for both its handsome exterior and spacious interior at a time when organizations in other states were coping with a chronic money problem and shortage of space. Renovation a few years ago expanded the exhibit space in its museum. As an adjunct to its exceptionally active program of bringing history to the public, the museum uses a historymobile, a vehicle that has reached nearly two hundred towns and an audience of over 150,-000 children and adults in a single year. And it maintains, elsewhere in the state, several historic houses and a museum village.

The advantages of rapid growth—which came as the result of appealing to a legislature for funds—over waiting generations for a substantial endowment to show up, had become apparent. As the middle and then the western portions of the country were divided into states, Wisconsin's example was widely imitated. The NEBRASKA STATE HISTORICAL SOCIETY in Lincoln, founded when that thirty-seventh state entered the Union in 1867, developed a similar close relationship with the legislature. An important recent advantage of this closeness was the working out of a highway salvage program, a kind of archaeological rescue operation intended to prevent bulldozers (usually intent only on breaking ground for new highways) from plowing back any relics of the past inadvertently uncovered. In its functionally modern building whose doorway proclaims "the spirit of a people lives in its history" and "here open to all is the history of this people," exhibits concentrate on a chronological presentation of the human experience in Nebraska beginning with the prehistoric Indian hunters of more than ten thousand years ago. One popular display is the furnished interior of a pioneer's sod house. In a land where trees were virtually nonexistent, homes were built of bricks cut out of the hard-packed dry earth, and stoves burned hay. This one-room "soddie" is equipped with a table, chairs, bedstead, chamber pot, and a piece that functioned as a writing table, cupboard, and dresser. The society also maintains exhibits at the state fair grounds, and operates the restored home of William Jennings Bryan whose furnishings, largely contributed by members of the Bryan family, include the decorated ostrich egg which the orator-jurist-politician received during one of his three presidential campaigns and which once again hangs—as it did when he was in residence—from the parlor chandelier.

It was a convention of newspaper editors and publishers that created the KANSAS STATE HISTORICAL SOCIETY, after a few earlier false starts, in 1875. One of the journalist-founders was also state auditor, and it was his Topeka office that served as the group's first headquarters. The first president, who was chief justice of the state supreme court, donated a portion of his library as a start toward building its collections. Today Kansas boasts one of the largest and most remarkable newspaper collections in the country. Its library and manuscript holdings in state, Indian, pioneer, and Western history are extensive, and the Society has been the official repository for all state archives since early in this century. Communicating its conviction that "the Kansas past is a story of great events as exciting and interesting as any novel" are exhibits that include period rooms such as an 1860 bedroom, an elaborate turn-of-the-century parlor, an old general store, and— the influence of the founders is apparent—an early print shop. A military gallery shows, in relics, uniforms, prints, and posters, the state's part in the nation's wars. Other displays explain Indian crafts, recall the first explorations of Europeans in the area, demonstrate how railroads opened a continent, and illustrate more than a century of changing agricultural technology. A special exhibit, "Kansans Famous on TV," takes as its stern purpose correcting the misconceptions promulgated by television Westerns.

That the very existence of an historical society promotes the preservation of things that would otherwise be neglected or scattered, is demonstrated by the experiences of the one in Chicago. About twelve

years after the CHICAGO HISTORICAL SOCIETY was founded in 1856 the
Tribune glowingly reported that, having "passed into the 3d lustrum of
its existence, [the organization] formally celebrated last night, the inauguration of its new building at the corner of Dearborn and Ontario
Streets. . . . The walls covered with bookcases and adorned with portraits added greatly to the charm of the scene."

The group's fourth lustrum was marred by the famous fire and the
destruction of its supposedly fireproof building, but a few years later
the *Tribune* happily announced that on the same site there had arisen
a "new and decidedly cozy-looking little building . . . [with] a few
hundred volumes toward a library."

A reporter for the *Herald* started a feature story in 1886 by describing this same structure as a "queer old brick building of one high story,
severely plain in exterior, rather uninviting, and, on the whole, cheap
and cheerless." He thought "the gorgeous green stone apartment house
next door seem[ed] a palace in comparison," but his enthusiasm returned the moment he stepped "just inside the door [and met] one of
the queerest and quaintest specimens in the collection—a round-
headed, white-haired old man, whose face is sure to wear a smile of
welcome." This was the secretary and librarian, who garrulously
showed the visitor around the premises. "There, sir, is a razor with
which one of the greatest men that ever lived was shaved. I mean
George Washington. . . . There is no doubt that it was Washington's
razor, as it was given to one of Judge Gillespie's ancestors by an intimate of Washington's family. Here is a lancet with which the Father
of His Country was bled. It comes from a Mrs. Lewis, whose grandfather Tyndall was a revolutionary soldier, attached to Washington's
staff, and picked up the instrument just after a camp surgeon had used
it in bringing blood from the veins of the Commander-in-Chief. . . ."

The reporter was also shown such local treasures as the first map
of Chicago village, printed in 1830, and the original manuscript of the
fire proclamation issued by Mayor Mason ("The faith and credit of
the City of Chicago is hereby pledged for the necessary expenses for the
relief of the suffering. . . . With the help of God, order and peace
and private property shall be preserved. . . . It is believed the fire has
spent its force and all will soon be well").

Concluding his story, the newspaperman wrote: "Yet there are many
thousands of people in Chicago who have never heard of this quaint
old building and its rich stores, and whose hearts were never made
lighter by brief converse with the white-haired secretary. Need the

Herald add that admission is free to all and that the fare to Ontario by Mr. Yerkes' streetcars is but a nickel?"

When it was almost fifty years old the society was given a unique gift. "Chicago has received from one of its pioneer residents perhaps the oddest bequest ever made," reported the *Tribune*. "Ossian Guthrie has bequeathed to Chicago and the world through S. H. Kerfoot Jr. and the Chicago Historical Society, all his knowledge of the first settlement of the city and of the surrounding country. . . . Instead of writing the history, Mr. Guthrie hit upon the plan of showing [the sites] to the Historical Society, represented by Mr. Kerfoot . . . and telling the stories.

"He declares he expects to live twenty-five years, but would not take any chances of dying without leaving the world a record of Marquette's historic camps, churches and cabins that he has gained in fifty years of investigation.

"He insisted on making the bequest personally to be sure it was correct, and the Chicago Historical Society arranged an expedition to accompany him to record the stories and to photograph and mark the historic sites. . . .

"Mr. Guthrie started his bequest by giving to Mr. Kerfoot and his companions a view of the site of Marquette's winter camp of 1674 and 1675, where the adventurous pioneer erected the first cabin ever built in what is now Chicago. . . . Mr. Guthrie located the site of Marquette's cabin in 1847, when he was in charge of the Brideport pumping station, but not until he had spent fifty years of careful research did he give out the story as authentic. . . .

"During the last part of the bequest the party advanced in a thunderstorm, and when they saw the spot where Father Marquette launched his canoes, Mr. Guthrie orally signed his bequest and turned over his historic knowledge to Mr. Kerfoot in trust for Chicago."

But not everyone was as imbued as Mr. Guthrie with the importance of preserving material that a later age might find significant. At least one prominent Chicagoan had remained unimpressed by all the benign journalistic propaganda. Corporation lawyer Robert Todd Lincoln refused to part with the private papers of his parents, explaining that "the idea of placing them in the custody of the Historical Society would strike me with favor if there was any thing of sufficient consequence to include in such a collection. I have not examined any of my mother's papers, and do not believe that anything will be found among them of sufficient importance for preservation. The papers left by my father were few in number, and have been for some years in the custody of Mr. Nicolay, who is, with Col. Hay, engaged in preparing a biography." (John George Nicolay and John Hay had been President Lincoln's private secretaries. They had begun planning the biography, with Lincoln's co-operation, nearly thirty years before their massive ten-volume work was published in 1890. They were the only ones to whom the President's son permitted access to these papers, which he later willed to the Library of Congress with the proviso that they remain sealed until twenty-one years after his own death. He died in 1926. When the papers were at long last made available in 1947 there were 194 bound volumes.)

The Lincoln papers got away from the Society, but not the Lincoln mementos and other historical objects and rare books accumulated by a Chicagoan who had served the Confederacy. Charles Frederick Gunther was five years old when his family left Germany in 1842. At the age of ten he delivered mail on horseback in Pennsylvania for twenty-five cents a day. He eventually found employment as a clerk in a country store, in a drugstore, as a cashier in a bank, as an employee of an ice company in Memphis, and as a steward on a Confederate troopship. In 1863 he took a job as a traveling salesman for a Chicago confectionery wholesaler, and toward the end of the decade he decided to open a retail candy store in that city. After it went up in flames along with the rest of the town, he rebuilt and expanded. As a result of his advanced use of newspaper advertising, and the popularity of candies he invented, including the caramel, his business prospered. Financially secure, he began to travel. He collected works of art, Washington and Lincoln relics, and rare manuscripts; placing some of his acquisitions in his elaborately appointed emporium on State Street to make it a tourist attraction. He became a civic leader, and was on the board of the historical society for twenty years. Before he died in 1920 he had offered his entire collection to the city if it would provide a fireproof building to contain it. But the city failed to act, and after his death the collection was sold by his wife and son to the privately supported historical society for $150,000.

The Society now needed a larger museum. During the next few years plans for a new building were discussed. A campaign to raise a million dollars had been scheduled to begin on the day after the stock market crash of 1929. It began as scheduled. And despite the depression years that followed, the goal was achieved. A marble and brick building opened in Lincoln Park three years later. Displays range from a record of the city's development, including souvenirs of the famous fire, to the story of Abraham Lincoln told in terms of dioramas, correspondence, the table on which the Emancipation Proclamation was signed, the White House piano, and replicas of the living room of his Springfield house and the room in which he died. An outstanding Civil War exhibit features posters, photographs, prints, and the uniforms, weapons, and battle flags of both Union and Confederate forces. Other exhibits illustrate other aspects of national history.

What was true of natural science in the early nineteenth century was also true of history—it was more a gentleman's avocation than a scholar's profession. But for historical societies and history museums this continued to be so long after the biological and earth sciences became professionalized. Perhaps out of sentiment, and lacking the discipline trained professionals might have mustered, the gentlemen-historians accumulated keepsakes and unrelated objects, attempting to illuminate for themselves their own recent past and that of their forebears. This approach greatly complicated the task of those who later attempted to make order out of chaos and displace the boredom of the viewing public with comprehensibility.

Toward the end of the century, when history began developing into a distinct field of study, the few American professionals there were, were concentrating on European history and America's European roots. Meanwhile, the American documents and objects being gathered helter-skelter by the amateurs were beginning to pile up. And it was this abundance of material that would prove so enormously valuable to the professionals when, in the next century, they turned to their own country with fresh eyes. From the 1930s on this accumulation was recognized as a rich source of the stuff that makes history come alive. It would subsequently be acknowledged that the gentlemen-amateurs of the societies had "performed a distinguished role . . . as gatherers and curators."

From the point of view of some of their contemporaries, however, the habits of these gentlemen left much to be desired. At a time when science museums were beginning to make their collections comprehensible to the public, the American Historical Association, meeting in Washington in 1888, was told that the "historical museums now in existence contain, as a rule, chance accumulations, like too many natural-history museums of the present, like all in the past." The speaker was the Smithsonian's Assistant Secretary, George Brown

Goode, first to urge a closer relationship between professionals and museums. A "most enthusiastic friend" of museums, he nevertheless dared not hope that they could "be made as useful to history as they are to physical science." Yet he was "confident" that museums could "be made in [historians'] hands a most potent instrumentality for the promotion of historical studies." He told the Association that because "the art of museum administration [was] still in its infancy, and no attempt [had] yet been made to apply it systematically to the development of a museum of history," it was "impossible" to anticipate "what the limits of historical museums are to be."

Three quarters of a century later another Smithsonian man, G. Carroll Lindsay, would observe that "documents unfortunately do not provide a complete index to human intellectual processes and attitudes," and consequently "to arrive at even a general impression of a historical era, one must study not only what was written, but also what was sat upon, eaten from, ridden on, and lived in and with"; the "sort of thing [that] is found most easily and in greatest quantity and variety in museums."

The OHIO STATE MUSEUM in Columbus has passed through all the phases that characterize the evolution of a modern institution. Its exhibits once reflected the fact that for the members of the historical society who managed the museum "the historical object had little or no apparent relationship to the life of the community and its people as evidence of taste, custom, art, craftsmanship, occupation, manufacturing, trade, and livelihood." But now there are a series of interpretive displays illustrating the cultural backgrounds and domestic life of the people of Ohio as well as their economic and political development. A carefully planned program of acquisition, with emphasis on the manufactures of state industries (especially pottery and glass) accompanied this reorientation. And so history now flows from the present scene back to the time of Revolutionary War General "Mad Anthony" Wayne (who negotiated the first treaty with Indians in which their land rights were recognized by the U. S. Government) and then forward again through the pioneers, the Civil War, and two world wars.

Because the original historical society demonstrated an interest in archaeology that persisted, the museum now possesses the definitive collection of Ohio prehistoric Indian materials. Unique among history institutions, it has excellent natural history exhibits and study collections. And its library is a distinguished one. In addition, the historical society maintains at other locations throughout the state, "fifteen prehistoric Indian sites; three natural history areas; three museums; thirteen historic houses, one grist mill, and one early Friends Meeting House; seven sites of forts, four battlegrounds, three monuments, the tombs of two Presidents of the United States, one reconstructed Indian mission village of the Moravian Church, one reconstructed log fort of the Indian Wars, one sternwheel steamboat, the remains of an old iron furnace, and the elm under which the Indian chief Logan is said to have spoken his famous speech." The most important source anywhere of material relating to Rutherford B. and Lucy Hayes is maintained at Fremont where the twenty-five acre Hayes estate, containing everything from a library and papers to Lucy's gowns and the family carriage, is open to the public.

A concept of living history began to be formed on the day the first historic house museum in America opened. In 1851 New York State acquired the stone farmhouse that had been used by Washington as his Newburgh headquarters. By the end of the decade Washington's home at Mount Vernon was similarly preserved and opened for public display. Among the next five structures to be saved were the general's Valley Forge and Morristown headquarters. And by the turn of the century the number of buildings was trebled; these included homes both in the eastern states and in the Midwest. "Then," as Laurence Vail Coleman noted, "came the automobile—four cars registered in 1895, eight thousand in 1900, nearly half a million in 1910." As an ever larger audience was able to come to them, the number of historic houses increased correspondingly, "from about twenty open in 1895 to nearly a hundred in 1910." When the number of cars reached twenty-three million in the early thirties, there were over four hundred historic houses. Today one thousand houses await the passengers of over seventy million vehicles.

Coleman, who considered himself a "collector" of old houses—he accumulated his memories and snapshots of buildings as other hobbyists collect stamps—noted that "some buildings are distinguished from the moment they are finished," while others "achieve importance by withstanding the assaults of time and so gaining values that they did not have while in company with many of their kind." Some "have greatness thrust upon them by acts of man that create hallowed associations." Many of them "come down the years to us bearing messages." These are the buildings that tell us how our ancestors lived, prayed, fought, played, worked—in shop and mill; in farmhouse and court-house; in inn and tavern; in fort, school, and church. They tell us how a nation was built—from the log cabins of the Appalachians to the missions of California, from the mansions of patroons and plantation owners to the tenements of industrializing cities, from the villages of New England to the hastily built and just as quickly abandoned "boom" towns that became "ghost" towns, from governors' palaces to land grubbers' "soddies." They tell of crucial events in the life of the nation, or of divine inspiration in the life of one man; depending upon whether they are the homes where statesmen, artists, merchant princes, or popular entertainers lived and died. Collected within them are the utensils and furniture of bygone days, the manuscripts of writers, the scrap-books of humorists, and the correspondence of heads of state.

An organization that has been responsible for the rescue and management of close to fifty houses in five states is the SOCIETY FOR THE PRESERVATION OF NEW ENGLAND ANTIQUITIES, founded in 1910 by William Sumner Appleton, whose family had lived in Massachusetts and New Hampshire since 1626. The group's letterhead describes its purpose as "acquiring and preserving for posterity buildings, places and objects of historical and other interest." In the museum at its Boston headquarters is a wide range of antique furnishings, glass, pottery, silver, pewter, costumes, and dolls. The museum, and a library that has an outstanding collection of architectural prints and photographs, are in a wing adjacent to one of the Society's finest properties, the carefully restored 1795 HARRISON GRAY OTIS HOUSE, whose ceilings, wallpapers, mantels, and furniture have been singled out as exceptional. Its handsome early Federal design is the work of the master architect and Boston statesman, Charles Bulfinch. It was the home of a lawyer and orator who became congressman, senator, and mayor of Boston.

Two of the Society's earliest properties are the wooden REBECCA NURSE HOUSE (Mrs. Nurse was hanged as a witch in 1692) in Danvers, Massachusetts, and the "SCOTCH"-BOARDMAN HOUSE of 1651 in Saugus, Massachusetts. Home of six generations of the Boardman family and believed to have been built to house a group of Scotch Covenanter prisoners captured by Oliver Cromwell in 1650 and subsequently brought here to operate the nearby ironworks, the Boardman House has been left unfurnished to facilitate study of such early architectural features as the wood sheathing, the staircase, and the sponge-painted walls. In Portsmouth, New Hampshire, the society maintains the 1784 GOVERNOR JOHN LANGDON MEMORIAL MANSION. A Revolutionary leader, Langdon was the first president of the United States Senate, and he served as the new country's acting president until Washington's election. This is one house in which the Father of His Country did indisputably sleep, having been entertained here by Langdon in 1789. In correspondence Washington commended both house and host. The fine period furniture and the magnificent and extensive gardens are among its notable features.

The Society also comes to the aid of other groups with problems about old houses. It has, for instance, frequently been called in by Ipswich to lend its authority to various campaigns for the rescue of many of that town's seventeenth-century buildings, such as the time the Ipswich historians, represented by the wife of their president, needed help in preventing the bulldozing of a 1680 house. With only ten minutes to spare and fifty dollars to buy a day's time from the wrecker who had been scheduled to start demolition, the president's wife succeeded in delaying disaster. But it was not until the Smithsonian Institution, having been authoritatively assured of the value and authenticity of the structure, agreed to have the house removed piece by piece for reconstruction in the new Museum of History and Technology in Washington, that disaster was permanently averted. The local water and light department had unwittingly caused all the fuss when it hired the demolition crew to clear the land. It proved its good faith and interest in history, however, by paying the boss wrecker his $1200 fee even though his services were no longer required. The job was done manually by specialists instead, under the watchful eye of the Smithsonian's New England architectural adviser.

Among other buildings owned by the IPSWICH HISTORICAL SOCIETY is one of the oldest in the country, the JOHN WHIPPLE HOUSE of 1640, to which John Whipple II and John Whipple III made additions in 1670 and 1700. (John Whipple II became quite wealthy, partly as a result of being licensed to "still strong water for a year, and to retail not less than a quart at a time, and none to be drunk in his house.") The historical society purchased the old timber and wattle house in 1898. Layers of plaster were removed from the walls to reveal the original sheathing, old casement windows that had been sealed by later inhabitants were renovated, fireplaces were opened and suitable furnishings moved in.

The ASSOCIATION FOR THE PRESERVATION OF VIRGINIA ANTIQ-
UITIES, which maintains a group of Colonial and early Federal build-
ings throughout the state, has its headquarters in the JOHN MARSHALL
HOUSE built in Richmond in 1790 for the first chief justice of the
United States Supreme Court. In Fredericksburg there is the MARY
WASHINGTON HOUSE of 1772 where the first President's mother lived.
Built about a decade earlier by Washington's youngest brother,
Charles, there is the RISING SUN TAVERN which was a meeting place
during the Revolution and continued to serve the public into the next
century. At Ashland the Association maintains SCOTCHTOWN, the
home of Patrick Henry during the crucial 1770s.

Richmond is also the home of the Confederate Memorial Literary
Society which maintains both the CONFEDERATE MUSEUM and the
ROBERT E. LEE HOUSE. Built in 1844, the Lee House is furnished
with mid-century Victoriana and such mementos as the camp bed and
washstand of the general who came home to his family after surrender-
ing to Grant. The house that serves as the Literary Society's museum
was built more than forty years prior to the conflict and is an excellent
piece of Federal architecture. It was designed by Robert Mills of
South Carolina, who had studied with Jefferson and was later responsible for the Washington Monument. But the fact that it served as the
White House of the Confederacy and not its architectural greatness
accounted for its ultimate preservation. In it, each of the seceding
states is now represented by one room where uniforms, flags, weapons,
and other articles are on display. The Virginia Room contains the
sword and the coat of the uniform worn by Lee at Appomattox, as well
as General J. E. B. Stuart's plumed hat; the Mississippi Room has
the suit worn by Confederate President Jefferson Davis when he was
taken prisoner shortly after the fall of Richmond. In the Florida Room
is Nina, a doll that served as a blockade runner, her hollow head containing quinine for the wounded. The Solid South Room is opposite
the entrance and contains the original Great Seal of the Confederate
States as well as paintings of episodes from the war. Davis lived in this
house all through the war until he left the city; he left just a few hours
before the house was occupied by Union forces. In 1870 the house
began twenty years of service as a city school. And in the 1890s it was
fireproofed and signed over to the society.

Historic houses throughout the South memorialize both the Colonial
period and the later conflict. Charleston has some of the most magnificent eighteenth-century mansions to be seen anywhere on the conti-

nent. Two of them that are maintained by the Charleston Museum are the luxuriously furnished 1770 HEYWARD-WASHINGTON HOUSE and the equally elegant JOSEPH MANIGAULT HOUSE of twenty years later. In addition to its old homes and the oldest museum in America, Charleston has the CONFEDERATE MUSEUM, a project of the city's chapter of the United Daughters of the Confederacy, who describe it as "symbolic of the end of a great era." Here can be found the first cannon made in the Confederate States (out of the iron from the oldest locomotive belonging to the South Carolina Railroad) and the first Confederate flag raised on Fort Sumter. The local Daughters still recall their pleasure in being able to provide Metro-Goldwyn-Mayer with a sample of old cloth and a button to serve as the basis of the Confederate uniforms reconstructed for Hollywood's troops in *Gone With the Wind*.

The energy and dedication of one woman were responsible for the restoration of two New England historic houses and the establishment of two galleries. The four units are known as the FRUITLANDS MUSEUMS. Miss Clara Endicott Sears, descendant of several colonial governors of Massachusetts, spent her summers near the town of Harvard at a house on the top of Prospect Hill, from which she enjoyed a view of mountains across the Nashua River Valley. She also liked to look at an old wooden farmhouse nearby. It was not an ordinary farmhouse, having been inhabited for several years by Bronson Alcott, his family, and some of the Transcendentalists whom he led in an attempt at communal living that ultimately proved unsuccessful. After buying and restoring the structure in 1914, Miss Sears described the feelings that motivated her: "As I looked down on it from my terrace on the hill, pitying its infinite loneliness, the thought came to me that I must save it. If for a time it had borne the semblance of a New Eden, then that time must be honored, and not forgotten. I longed to see it smiling again upon the valley. . . ." After furnishing it with memorabilia of the Transcendentalists and of Bronson's famous daughter, Louisa May Alcott, Miss Sears turned her attention to another old wooden building. This one had been in use in a nearby Shaker settlement from 1794 until the time in the twentieth century when the religious community dwindled away. Having had it moved to her property, she equipped it with the sturdy, ingenious furnishings of these simple people as well as examples of their weaving and herb industries. Some years later she added a brick building to display her accumulation of local Indian artifacts, and in the 1940s, when Miss Sears was past eighty, another brick building went up. This one would house two more collections: primitive New England nineteenth-century portraits, and landscapes of the Hudson River school.

In Philadelphia some of the preservation work begun by individuals and such civic groups as the Junior League has been continued by the Museum of Art, which now maintains the group of city-owned houses known as the COLONIAL CHAIN. All of these are in Fairmount Park; the ones that originally stood elsewhere having been moved by various sponsors starting in the late nineteenth century. The Museum of Art began its work on this project in the 1920s.

The LETITIA STREET HOUSE, long thought to have belonged to William Penn, was moved to Fairmount Park in 1883 from the location which now gives it its name; and even with its earliest claim to fame removed, it remains a fine example of an early eighteenth-century city dwelling, decorated in Queen Anne style. CEDAR GROVE, of the same period, was presented to the city with its original furnishings by a twentieth-century descendant of the family that first occupied it; and the Georgian Colonial building was moved stone by stone in 1927. The most famous house in Fairmount Park is probably MOUNT PLEASANT, built in 1761 and purchased eighteen years later by Benedict Arnold as a wedding gift to his wife. BELMONT, made of stone and brick and added to at least four times in the middle of the eighteenth century and then again a century later, was restored in 1927 under the museum's supervision. SWEETBRIER's restoration a year later, also supervised by the museum, was sponsored by the Junior League, and the house has served as that group's headquarters.

Also concerned with old dwellings is Massachusetts' Essex Institute. Two of the houses it cares for—both of them still on their original sites and both the work of the early Federal master builder Samuel McIntire—are the three-story wooden PEIRCE-NICHOLS HOUSE of 1782 and the brick PINGREE HOUSE (adjacent to the Institute) of 1804. Salem minister William Bentley wrote of McIntire that "he was descended of a family of carpenters who had no claims on public favor and was educated at a branch of that business. By attention he soon gained a superiority to all of his occupation & the present Court House, the North & South Meeting Houses, and indeed all the improvements for nearly thirty years past have been done under his eye."

One of the distinguishing characteristics of a McIntire house is the decorative carving on the mantels, pediments, and gateposts. As a sculptor in wood he "had no rival in all New England." Successful mercantile establishments were the sources of the wealth that ownership of a house by McIntire symbolized. One of the early magnates who admired the builder was Jacob Crowninshield whose clipper ships ranged the seas to Africa, the Indies and China. In the twentieth century, the wife of one of his descendants, Mrs. Francis B. Crowninshield, refurbished the Peirce-Nichols and Pingree mansions.

Moved to the Essex Institute Garden were a QUAKER MEETINGHOUSE of about 1688, the LYE-TAPLEY SHOE SHOP that was serving the wives of prosperous Salem merchants before 1800, and the small JOHN WARD HOUSE, portions of which were built before 1700. Here also is the CROWNINSHIELD-BENTLEY HOUSE, built in 1727 for John Crowninshield, later occupied by Dr. Bentley. A few years ago emergency action became necessary when plans to replace this structure with a parking lot became known. Energetic fund raising made possible its removal from the original site at 106 Essex Street to the Institute's garden at number 126. There it was restored as a memorial to Mrs. Francis B. Crowninshield.

A town's entire history lives again in the buildings that remain from its past. Salem was settled only a few years after the landing at Plymouth, and several organizations have preserved its architectural record, which ranges from Puritan through Colonial to Georgian styles. The WITCH HOUSE of 1642 (the residence of a judge who considered it his duty to deal harshly with those accused of witchcraft) is today maintained by the city as a museum to recall the time when more than two hundred alleged practitioners of the black art were arrested in one year.

Salem in the nineteenth century was the birthplace of Nathaniel Hawthorne. The mid-eighteenth-century HAWTHORNE HOUSE, where he was born and where he lived and wrote at several periods, is maintained by the House of Seven Gables Settlement Association. The Association has its headquarters in a 1668 building known as the HOUSE OF THE SEVEN GABLES and believed to have inspired the novel for which it is named. In addition to its fine New England furnishings, it has the secret staircase and garden that figure importantly in the story. The Association's RETIRE BECKET HOUSE also dates from the middle of the seventeenth century, as does its HATHAWAY HOUSE, which functions as an inn.

Elsewhere in the city the National Park Service maintains the old CUSTOM HOUSE of 1819 (where Hawthorne worked for a while when hack writing failed to support him and his family between novels) and the adjacent DERBY HOUSE and WHARF of 1761–62. Together these comprise the SALEM MARITIME NATIONAL HISTORIC SITE, illustrating the maritime history of the city and reflecting the way of life of a wealthy merchant.

A different tradition is reflected in the buildings of Newport, Rhode Island. Here a group of early churches testifies to the true freedom of worship that attracted a wide variety of religious dissidents following the city's founding in 1639 by refugees from the Massachusetts Bay Colony. The Preservation Society of Newport County maintains TRINITY CHURCH of 1726 and the TOURO SYNAGOGUE of 1763. Trinity is the city's oldest important eighteenth-century building. Architecturally it is derived from Christopher Wren's London churches. It has a rare, early, graceful spire and fine interior woodwork and chandeliers. Touro Synagogue, the first Jewish house of worship in North America, is considered a masterpiece of Colonial design. It is the work of Peter Harrison, the country's first architect. The NEWPORT HISTORICAL SOCIETY building contains the Sabbatarian Meeting House of 1729, the oldest Seventh Day Baptist church in the country.

The Historical Society owns a late seventeenth-century building that is the oldest house in the city. It also owns houses in other Rhode Island towns. But it is the Preservation Society that has done the most to record the Newport story. Its offices are in the Brick Market, another Peter Harrison structure. The Brick Market is a former grain market made of brick. It functioned at one time as the city hall, at another time as a theater. Among the Preservation Society's additional responsibilities is the WHITE HORSE TAVERN, built in 1673. One can still dine there. It is the oldest tavern in the country still in use.

The city's more recent role as the favorite resort of the new and very rich has not been neglected by the Society either. There is a magnificent mansion designed by status-symbol architect Richard Morris Hunt for Cornelius Vanderbilt in 1895; other noted European and American architects collaborated on the design and furnishing of some of the rooms. This Italian Renaissance palace is known as THE BREAKERS. From its sloping lawns there is a cliff-side view of the Atlantic Ocean. It is particularly elegant at night, when elaborate crystal chandeliers throw their light on high, ornate ceilings. The nearby BREAKERS STABLE, with its many fine carriages used in the days when driving was a fashionable pastime, has remained almost as it had been half a century ago. Then there is THE ELMS, a French château built in 1901 for Edward J. Berwind, a Philadelphia coal magnate, with its park and gardens, its gazebos, its bronze and marble statues and French landscaping. During summer evenings the gardens are illuminated, while playing fountains and background music stimulate visions of an opulent past.

THE OLDEST HOUSE in the country is the pride of the St. Augustine Historical Society, which maintains it and several other buildings that have come down from the time of the Spanish colonization of this Florida city, the first permanent settlement in the United States. The Oldest House, whose thick walls are made of locally quarried coquina rock, was built shortly after the city was founded in 1565. About a hundred years later the Spanish, fearing attack by the English who had settled in Charles Town to the north, began turning what had been a small wooden fort into the imposing CASTILLO DE SAN MARCOS, a project that would be continually worked on until past the middle of the following century. In 1702 the Castillo served its purpose for the first time; the entire Spanish population of St. Augustine—several hundred—withdrew into it, pulled up the drawbridge, and stayed put until the governor of South Carolina and his army, unable to penetrate the thick coquina walls, returned home. The Castillo and FORT MATANZAS are maintained by the National Park Service as national monuments. There are exhibits interpreting the military significance of these two Spanish colonial fortifications, as well as displays of Indian archaeological material from the area.

The Spanish were also responsible for the oldest public building in the country, the PALACE OF GOVERNORS in Santa Fe, New Mexico, which served as the seat of provincial and territorial government from the time it was completed in 1612 until 1907; the only interruption being the Pueblo Revolt that gave the town back to the Indians in 1680 for thirteen years. In 1821 the Mexicans forced out the Spanish, and Mexico's governors occupied the palace. They remained there until Santa Fe became United States territory. After that the building was the residence of territorial governors. The elongated adobe structure is now occupied jointly by the Historical Society of New Mexico, the Museum of New Mexico, and the School of American Research, an institution devoted to archaeology and anthropology.

The oldest wooden frame house in the United States was built by

Jonathan Fayerbanke in 1636 in a Massachusetts town then known as Contentment. For eight generations members of the Fairbanks family lived here (modernizing the spelling of their name at some point), while nearby U.S. 1 grew from a footpath into a road and Contentment became Dedham. East and west wings were added to the house in 1648 and 1654. Each of the resulting three sections is separate; but all shared the generous kitchen, whose activities centered about a large hearth of imported English brick. In 1903 members of the family got together to preserve their ancestral FAIRBANKS HOMESTEAD, and it was refurbished, mostly with family heirlooms, a few years later. Now, every August, members of the Fairbanks Family Association come to Dedham for their annual reunion. A tenth-generation descendant is the house's present curator-director. Despite its age, only minor repairs and routine maintenance have ever been necessary, so sturdily did Jonathan Fayerbanke build.

Americans traveling in Europe, knowing how few buildings in their own country can claim even three centuries of useful life, are astounded to visit five-hundred-year-old homes still being lived in. Their awe increases as they realize that their home towns or states may not contain any structures much more than one century old.

The oldest house in the state of Washington, Vancouver's COVINGTON HOUSE, dates back only to the early 1840s. Oregon City in the neighboring state features the 1846 McLOUGHLIN HOUSE. Dr. John McLoughlin was the physician and trader who as chief factor of the Hudson's Bay Company had encouraged the settlement of the Northwest.

From the next generation come two other Oregon homes. In Newberg is MINTHORN HOUSE, where Herbert Hoover lived as a boy. And in the state capital there is the fine late Victorian residence of Asahel Bush, the man who brought the Democratic party to Oregon. (BUSH HOUSE belongs to the Salem Art Museum, whose holdings center about Oregon artist Frank Heath.)

In the same state is Jacksonville which has a population of about a thousand, a city hall that first saw service as a general store a little more than a hundred years ago, and a local history museum in a courthouse that was built in 1884. Here are the BEEKMAN BANK, just as it was during the town's boom years, and the C. C. BEEKMAN MANSION, still furnished as lavishly as only a bank director could manage during the height of a gold rush. Jacksonville has been described as a community "pursuing the past with vigor." Here "progress means not bulldozers and high-rise buildings, but preserving the pioneer character of the village."

The Utah State Historical Society of Salt Lake City is located in "Silver King" THOMAS KEARNS' MANSION, which dates from 1900. There are, of course, older buildings in the city. LION HOUSE, known as the "Mount Vernon of the West," was built by the city's founder, Brigham Young, in 1856. On the top floor of this adobe-walled multiple residence there are twenty rectangular bedrooms, each under its own gable roof; on the second floor are the parlors; and on the first the many kitchens that were necessary to feed a plurality of wives and children.

While centuries of reverence for its own history turned Salem into a city whose very streets are museum pieces, a Virginia town of the same period allowed its past to grow shabby. Then over a period of four decades, a selected portion of that past was reconstructed. The result is COLONIAL WILLIAMSBURG. It stands as a tribute to the vision and energy of the Reverend William A. R. Goodwin, and to the sponsor he had the temerity and good fortune to interest in it.

The story begins with Dr. Goodwin's return to the town where he had been rector of Bruton Parish Church twenty years earlier. It had been a quiet place then. And once it had been the capital of the Virginia colony; a bustling center of political and intellectual life. When Goodwin came back in 1923 to join the faculty of the College of William and Mary, the town was at the end of a wartime boom. An influx of munitions workers and military personnel had been accommodated in hastily constructed buildings which, together with telephone poles, gasoline stations, billboards, and jerry-built shacks would remain as souvenirs once the boom receded. But Goodwin, who had been responsible for removing all the Victorian accretions from his 1715 Bruton Parish Church and restoring its Colonial mien, could still feel "the presence and companionship of the people" who had lived in the town long ago. He pictured them "going into or coming out of the old houses." And he was determined that Williamsburg would be restored.

It was less than a year after Goodwin's return that his path first crossed John D. Rockefeller, Jr.'s. They met during the course of a meeting in New York to raise funds for a Phi Beta Kappa memorial hall at the College of William and Mary, where the nation's first honorary fraternity had been founded. Two years later the Rockefeller family would be driving through Williamsburg and Goodwin would be chosen by the college president to guide them. He showed them the town through his eyes; as it had been and as he hoped it could be again. A few months later Rockefeller visited again, and Goodwin rose to the occasion a second time. And, at a banquet celebrating the dedication of the Phi Beta Kappa Memorial Hall, the clergyman was given the first intimations that the dream of his life could come true. Rockefeller was willing to commission detailed architectural sketches illustrating Goodwin's ideas for the restoration of Williamsburg. He made clear that he was not committed to any further action and he insisted that his participation be kept confidential. But this hesitant beginning belied the extent to which his interest had been aroused. In subsequent correspondence he requested photographs of every single building Goodwin thought he would include in the plan, an appraisal of the relative importance of each, memoranda regarding their ownership, availability for purchase, and probable prices. Goodwin, quietly overjoyed, replied: "It is as though one had, for a long time, been collecting bits of glass with a thought that some day they might be worked into a mosaic."

An architect was chosen. An eighteenth-century map that showed the layout of the town and the location of every building was uncovered. To keep local curiosity at a minimum, the surveying that was necessary to confirm the measurements on the map was done at night. Goodwin wrote Rockefeller of his progress: "I wish you could be here and have some of the real fun that I am getting out of what we are doing. Last night the full moon joined in to help us. We found three College boys who wanted some exercise and with a long steel tape we measured the Duke of Gloucester Street from the Church to the Paradise House, the Court Green and part of the Palace Green, and plotted in the houses. I had a sword—which had come out of the Great War—which I used to stick in the partly frozen ground at the end of the tape line measurements. There were few people on the street and we were able to accomplish a great deal."

Within months Goodwin became the largest single buyer of real estate in town, while the man whose money he was using continued to remain anonymous. Not even the architect knew who was paying him for the maps and plans he was drawing. The reason for secrecy was simple. Rockefeller was not yet fully committed. He still left open the possibility of reselling the property Goodwin was acquiring should the restoration prove unfeasible. But this was the project that would become, according to his biographer, of all his benefactions, the one that gave him the greatest satisfaction.

Eventually the press took note of the incongruity of an Episcopal clergyman, in command of large sums of money, buying acres and acres of land. When reporters joined the crush of real estate agents and property owners at Goodwin's office, a public statement was obviously called for. Goodwin managed to reveal nothing more than "that he had recently been able to enlist the interest of others in the preservation of some of Williamsburg's historic sites."

After a year of investigation and acquisition, Rockefeller agreed "to restore Williamsburg, so far as that may be possible, to what it was in the old colonial days and to make it a great centre for historical study and inspiration." At a town meeting held in June 1928, the community was acquainted with what the future had in store for it. Goodwin revealed his plans and the name of his secret sponsor.

It has taken more than $80,000,000 to tear down or move seven hundred modern buildings, restore close to one hundred buildings of the eighteenth century, reconstruct over four hundred others on their original foundations, and replant nearly one hundred acres of gardens and greens. With scrupulous accuracy, archaeological and documentary evidence were used as the basis for this twentieth-century rebuilding of an eighteenth-century town. Authenticity has been the sole guidepost. Once when a house that had already been partially reconstructed was discovered to be six feet away from its original position, Rockefeller authorized the spending of $6000 to move it. "No scholar," he explained, "must ever be able to come to us and say we have made a mistake." Another time he declared that it was not always easy for him to adhere to the doctrine of authenticity. "Sometimes I suffered a good deal in applying this principle. In some instances I had a feeling that the appearance of the town deteriorated with the erection of new buildings, but those buildings were there in the eighteenth century. For example, the Raleigh Tavern had a yard next to it that gave it a good setting, and then we discovered that in the eighteenth century a brick house had stood within four feet of it. It broke my heart to do it but we built that brick house just where it had stood. After all, two thousand people had lived in the town in the eighteenth century, and there could be no compromise with fact. We stuck absolutely to what *was*."

One critic with whom many others seem to agree has complained that this fidelity to the eighteenth century has created in effect a "superbly executed vacuum [in which] nothing else is permitted to exist . . . [where] a Greek Revival house or other later structure, good or bad, on a spot that once held a colonial building, must [make way for] a newly created colonial substitute, constructed with exquisite taste, painstaking accuracy and alarming artificiality." The same critic points out that "the continuous panorama of change that is *real* history" could have been illustrated by the preservation of an old building along with "whatever valid accretions of later history or art it may have acquired." The final argument appears to be that "galloping restorationitis" does not teach the viewer "to differentiate between real and fake, original and imitation, or to make the essential value judgments involved."

Williamsburg's directors realize that "without a basic devotion to truth, a restoration can easily degenerate into a tourist trap," and they place their confidence in "the spirit of historical accuracy." The pros and cons of a museum town in which the guides are in the costumes of their forebears, where one can dine on Colonial specialties such as peanut soup and fruit shrub at a reconstructed tavern, or watch a craftsman produce handbills in an old print shop or repair saddles at a boot shop, where a fife and drum corps concertizes and the militia marches, will be debated for years to come. But the influence of this first museum town has spread throughout the country, paving the way for both pseudo-historical and other authentic reconstructions and restorations.

Colonial Williamsburg is largely a reconstruction; that is, the majority of its exhibits have been rebuilt on their original sites as they were in the eighteenth century. OLD DEERFIELD in Massachusetts is a preservation, made possible by those who lived, worked, or visited in the town and came to love it. Settled in 1669, it was, for decades, the focus of Indian attacks which culminated in a raid in 1704 that left more than half the settlers imprisoned or dead. In the eighteenth century the town was built up again and became a prosperous agricultural and trading center, whose farmers, craftsmen, and merchants had the means and innate good taste to construct solidly and beautifully. By a town vote Deerfield declared its independence from England on June 25, 1776, more than a week before the Philadelphia declaration. Dr. Bentley, of Salem, visited Deerfield in 1782 and wrote: "The street is one measured mile, running north and south—about sixty houses on the street are in better style than in any of the towns I saw." Today there are fifty-four houses on the same street. Half of them were among those admired by Bentley; only a fourth of them were built after 1825.

George Sheldon, a Deerfield farmer, founded an historical society in 1870 and subsequently wrote a two-volume town history and genealogy of over 1300 pages. This farmer-historian was president of his POCUMTUCK VALLEY MEMORIAL ASSOCIATION until he died in his ninety-ninth year, at which time he was succeeded by a son. When the son died in his eighties, the woman who was his stepmother (a Boston schoolteacher whom George Sheldon had married when he was a widower of seventy-eight and she a spinster of forty-five) took over, holding the post until her death ten years later. The Association owns the FRARY HOUSE, the oldest local building, a survivor of the Indian raid of 1704 and a popular tavern during Revolutionary days. Its library and fine collections of early New England objects are housed in a brick building that originally accommodated one of the town's schools, the Deerfield Academy.

Of the old buildings here, the largest group is owned by the HERITAGE FOUNDATION. Only six of these are open to the public; either as period houses or galleries for the display of excellent collections of lighting devices, furniture, textiles, ceramics, treenware, and other Early American decorative arts. The remaining eighteenth-century houses owned by the Foundation are actually being lived in while being preserved.

Realizing that Deerfield's special ambiance would be destroyed if the area became a tourist attraction, no attempt has been made to circle the town with motels or highways, or to make the project self-supporting by commercializing it in any way.

OLD STURBRIDGE VILLAGE, also in Massachusetts, has been described as a re-creation. Although all of its thirty or so buildings have been restored to their original condition, it is not a restoration. Nor is it a reconstruction. There was no original old town here from which to work. Old Sturbridge is the work of two brothers who for years accumulated antique tables and chairs, mirrors and clocks, hinges and saws, china and glass, tinware, pottery and everything else that was produced and used in the workshops, homes, and barns of early America. And by the 1940s Albert B. and J. Cheney Wells decided that their collections should be displayed to the public, preferably in a setting that would indicate the original function of each object. Gradually they evolved the idea of re-creating a New England village. First they scoured the area near their Southbridge home for a typical village setting, and found a 200-acre site that was ideal, with a river, ponds, hills, rocks, fields, woodland—all the elements that might have attracted settlers two centuries earlier. Then they started collecting structures settlers built elsewhere in the vicinity, and moved them. Finally there emerged a representative New England town that might have been here in the first half-century of nationhood, those pre-industrial years when an agricultural community with its own grist mill and saw mill, blacksmith shop, and general store could be largely self-sufficient. Everything is here—covered bridge and neat white church, barn and tavern, craftsmen's shops and houses, all properly furnished. As at Williamsburg, people in period costume pursue the occupations of their ancestors. The illusion is perfect, and visitors observe that "the place *looks* like a New England Village. Houses sit well on the ground; brooks spring up opportunely; rubbish is skillfully accumulated in likely places; the ox driver knows how to drive oxen."

Just north of Boston is a town that was the scene of the first ironworks in America from about 1646 to 1670. It has now become the SAUGUS IRONWORKS RESTORATION, the iron and steel industry having been responsible for giving a second life to what it considers the industry's birthplace. Seven waterwheels dip into the Saugus River that provided power for the forge and the rolling and slitting mill (where wrought-iron bars were rolled into flats, and some flats slit into rods to make nails). At the river's edge are the warehouse and wharf, where the finished products were stored and shipped, only a few yards from the blast furnace. Overlooking the scene from a high bank is the restored ironmaster's house, and near it a museum building displays finds made by the archaeological crews during long years of research at the site.

Near Dearborn, Michigan, there is a fabricated community that could never have existed in reality. GREENFIELD VILLAGE is a projection of the predilections and interests of one individual. Since that individual was Henry Ford, it is not surprising that he felt entitled to pursue his preferences on a grand scale. Ford was a sentimentalist, and when he put together the community that he hoped would represent all of America's yesterdays, he named it for the nearby township where Mrs. Ford had been born and raised. Then he moved to his village several buildings that he himself had lived or worked in: the simple farmhouse where he was born in 1863, restored and furnished as he remembered it; a small brick shed where, at the age of thirty-three, he built his first automobile, the "quadricycle"; the grade schools he attended; the two jewelry stores where he repaired watches as a young man; and the Edison Illuminating Company shop where he was an engineer for eight years.

The Village of nearly a hundred homes and shops of the seventeenth, eighteenth and nineteenth centuries occupies more than 260 acres. Ford's lifelong friendship with Thomas Edison is recalled by a group of buildings associated with the inventor's career: the Menlo Park laboratory where Edison worked in the 1870s and '80s (the incandescent light and the phonograph were invented here), the boardinghouse (in which several of Edison's assistants lived) that was the first private home in the world to be electrically lighted; the Florida laboratory from Fort Myers that was Edison's last workshop; even the depot where the young inventor was removed from a train after setting fire to a baggage car during a chemical accident, and the Ontario home where his parents were married.

Among the other heroes of Mr. Ford whose lives are represented here are Lincoln, by the Logan County courthouse where he practiced as a young lawyer, and by the theater seat he was sitting on when he was slain; William Holmes McGuffey, by the Pennsylvania log cabin in which the educator was born in 1800; and the Wright brothers, by their homestead and Cycle Shop, brought from Dayton, Ohio. A street on which artisans still practice the trades of early America has a carding mill, a blacksmith shop (in the shade—of course—of a spreading chestnut tree), a pottery shop, a wheelwright's shop, and a cooper's establishment from Kingston, New Hampshire, where it was built in 1785. There are a grist mill, which in the 1830s had been producing whole wheat flour, corn meal, and buckwheat flour in Monroe, Michigan; a powered silk mill that was the first in America, having been in use in Connecticut in 1810; and a glass plant that has been reconstructed, incorporating parts of an 1825 factory from Sandwich on Cape Cod.

A Pennsylvania covered bridge leads to the Village's "residential section." Here are a house of 1652 in which King Charles II's customs collector lived near Baltimore; the even older one-room Plympton House from Massachusetts; the dwelling of a wealthy New Hampshire sea captain of the mid-eighteenth century; Noah Webster's Connecticut home of 1822; the red farmhouse from Lancaster, Massachusetts, in which Luther Burbank was born in 1849; and a building of about 1830 that contains heirlooms from the family of Stephen Foster.

On the fiftieth anniversary of the invention of the incandescent light the Village was dedicated, and Edison himself re-enacted the historic moment of discovery in his old laboratory. The year before, the inventor had been a key participant in the dedication of the cornerstone of the nearby HENRY FORD MUSEUM. On that occasion he inscribed his name and the date—September 27, 1929—in the wet cement. He also left his footprints there alongside a spade that had belonged to Luther Burbank, to symbolize the union of agriculture and industry. It was during the same ceremony that Henry Ford described his plans: "When we are through, we shall have reproduced American life as lived; and that, I think, is the best way of preserving at least a part of our history and tradition." The cornerstone is inside the museum; it marks the point where three major galleries branch off. One gallery, a sort of extension of the Village, is the Street of Shops where one can look into millinery and drug stores, a toy shop containing many penny banks and dolls, and the establishments of a barber, a gun and locksmith, a violin maker, and a carpenter. The Decorative Arts Galleries display chronologically arranged collections of American furniture and accessories of three centuries. And the Mechanical Arts Hall concerns itself with power (examples of every conceivable type of steam, early gas and oil engine); transportation (more than a hundred horse-drawn vehicles, and row upon row of bicycles, automobiles, airplanes, and locomotives); agriculture (the development of farm implements); and electricity (the most comprehensive exhibit anywhere explains the development of generators, motors, electric lighting, the telephone, telegraph and radio, and the beginnings of television). "I am collecting the history of our people as written into things their hands made and used," Ford said. "A piece of machinery or anything that is made is like a book, if you can read it."

Minden, Nebraska, is the scene of another village that never existed, created by another farm boy turned industrialist. Harold Warp was born there, the youngest of twelve children, shortly after the turn of the century. He left the rural community in the twenties for Chicago, where his invention of a plastic window material was the beginning of a highly productive manufacturing enterprise. But he remained attached to his background, and in 1948 when the one-room rustic schoolhouse (where some of his lessons were learned from an older brother who taught there) was put up for sale, Harold Warp was the buyer. That was the beginning of his PIONEER VILLAGE, opened five years later "just 192 miles west of Omaha and 358 miles east of Denver." A reflection of the way one man remembers his early years on a

Nebraska farm, it is dedicated "as a memorial to my parents and all of America's other pioneers." With the aid of a brother-in-law who was an auctioneer and an authority on antiques of the Midwest, Warp laid out a plan to illustrate the way of life of the early homesteaders, and "preserve one item of a kind of all the things the people used in settling and building our nation." In a sign posted over the main entrance to the village he explains, "For thousands of years man lived quite simply. Then, like a sleeping giant, our world was awakened. In a mere hundred and twenty years of eternal time, man progressed from open hearths, grease lamps and ox carts to television, super-sonic speed and atomic power. We have endeavored to show you the actual development of this astounding progress as it was unfolded by our forefathers and by ourselves. . . ." At the end of his message Warp adds, "We kindly ask that you help us protect these items so that we, our children, and our children's children may also have the privilege of seeing them."

More than twenty buildings have been moved to or built on a twenty-acre site. Among the ones brought here are the small stone land office where Warp's father filed his homestead claim in the 1870s, the train depot from which his mother and her family entered the area, a pony express station and barn, and Minden's first church, St. Paul Lutheran. A general store patterned after one that stood in a nearby town has been reconstructed and stocked with appropriate merchandise. And eleven acres of sod plus the labor of six men over a period of three weeks went into the reconstruction of a sod house which, in 1870, could have been built for under forty dollars.

Other buildings serve as exhibit galleries. An old country schoolhouse was moved to the village green and turned into a china shop whose shelves are lined with the precious bric-a-brac that pioneer wives brought with them on the long trip west in covered wagons. A fire house contains hand-, horse-, steam-, and gasoline-operated equipment. A home appliance exhibit follows the chronological development of such devices as clothes washers and irons. An agricultural exhibit does the same for farm equipment. Antique automobiles, aircraft, and "the world's largest collection of antique farm tractors" are elsewhere. In one large L-shaped structure devoted to shops and homes there are five kitchens from 1830 to 1930, and a doctor's office, barber shop, shoe shop, broom factory, loom shop, toy shop, and smithy. Also on the village grounds are a steam locomotive of 1889, and the "oldest steam merry-go-round," which still provides nickel rides to all comers. Every one of the thirty thousand or so items on display has been restored to its original good working condition, and many of them will show off at the push of a button.

In Cooperstown, New York, pioneer life from a generation earlier and in a very different setting has been recorded. This village with a permanent population of under 3000 was founded by William Cooper in 1786. During an exploratory visit through the beautiful "rough and hill country" near Lake Otsego the previous year, with "nothing but the melancholy wilderness" around him, he "formed . . . plans for future settlement, and meditated upon the spot where a place of trade or village should afterwards be established." By the end of the century he was the benevolent landlord in a productive farm community that had lawyers and doctors, a tavern and a distillery, a courthouse and jail (Cooper was the judge), a public library, a school, roads, and a clergyman. The Presbyterian church would come a few years later. The founder's son, James Fenimore Cooper, would immortalize the lake and other nearby landmarks in a series of novels, and would picture the town's future as "a place of resort, for those who live less for active life than for its elegance and ease." The region did indeed become a summer resort, and among those attracted to it in the nineteenth century was Edward Clark, partner in Isaac Singer's sewing machine company. In the twentieth century it was his grandson, Stephen C. Clark, who made possible the memorial to the region's early days that is the FARMERS' MUSEUM AND VILLAGE CROSSROADS.

The Farmers' Museum is located in an outsize barn. Here are the home and farm implements of a New York pioneer family; a series of displays illustrating, month by month, the chores of the farmer's year; and demonstrations of such homely crafts as broommaking, woodworking, spinning, and weaving. The Village Crossroads contains a dozen buildings, moved here from within a hundred-mile area, representative of the period from 1783 to 1840. Horses are still shod in the 1827 smithy, and broadsides and an occasional newspaper are still turned out at the printing office of 1829. A small working farm has a 1797 homestead, where samples of country cooking are always available in the kitchen. In the farmyard near the old log barn, pigs, oxen, geese, cows, and horses are allowed to wander. The uncostumed guides who demonstrate the old equipment, which visitors are encouraged to try out, are elderly inhabitants of the region who themselves were farmers, blacksmiths, or storekeepers, and who can recall from their youth stories about the pioneer years they are helping to interpret for a new generation.

A selection of folk art that ranges from portraits to weather vanes can be seen in Fenimore House, which completes this complex of museums belonging to the New York Historical Association, a private organization established just before the turn of the century. The Association's large-scale program includes scholarly research, working with the schools, educating the public, and publishing. A spokesman has expressed the hope that the Village Crossroads, Farmers' Museum, and the galleries in Fenimore House "will change as many people as possible from tourists into Americana enthusiasts, from casual passers-by into interested amateur historians. . . . The crux of our message is precisely how much of what counted most in the American experience was unspectacular."

A different aspect of upstate New York history is memorialized at the ADIRONDACK MUSEUM at Blue Mountain Lake. At first settled only by the loggers and trappers who earned their livelihood by working hard in these picturesque hills, the region became a fashionable resort before the turn of the century. Among those who kept returning was Harold K. Hochschild, whose delight in the area led him to investigate its history and write a 612-page volume on the subject. Later with several friends, relatives, and a group of year-round residents of a nearby village he founded the Adirondack Historical Association and its museum, whose theme is the relationship of man to the Adirondacks. A variety of structures clusters about the main building, where a large relief map of the lake country orients the visitor. A log cabin nearby was an extension of a hotel that stood on this site in the 1870s. A one-room cottage is typical of a rustic camp of around 1900, and contrasts vividly with the bedrooms, dining salon, and parlor in a private railroad car used by a wealthy Victorian as a conveyance to this retreat. At a tiny railroad station a locomotive and one car are all that remain of a line that extended only three quarters of a mile, operating from 1900 to 1929. At the end of a path is what appears to be a miniature log cabin, formerly the home of a well-known mountain hermit. An aquarium houses local fish. Two vehicle buildings display the varied modes of summer and winter travel in the mountains: surrey, sleigh, buckboard, coach, peddler's cart, motor car (a 1909 Maxwell), and the bobsled that won the Lake Placid Olympics of 1932. Collections of logging equipment, hunting and fishing gear, and such basic items as stoves for heating and cooking and a varied assortment of lamps from boats, trains, and dwellings are here too. The harsh mountain winter makes it impracticable for the museum to remain open for more than four months each year, yet about twenty thousand visitors, described by the director as "a steady flow of constantly changing country and city dwellers who travel the highways," find their way here every summer.

At Old Chatham in New York, near the Massachusetts border, are a re-created village and the SHAKER MUSEUM. The United Society of Believers in Christ's Second Appearing had originated in England during a Quaker revival in the middle of the eighteenth century. Subsequent persecution there sent Mother Ann Lee and eight of her followers to Albany at the time of the Revolution; and before long there were nineteen religious communities spread out from Maine to Indiana. The "Shaking Quakers" got their popular name from the ecstatic trembling produced by some of their emotional rituals, but they became better known and respected as a result of one of their major tenets, "consecrated work," which was applied for the most part to agriculture. Celibate, the sect was in need of converts to insure survival. Although diminished, the sect has survived. Today's "members sit in late Victorian rockers in front of a last-year's television set, with an 1815 candlestand alongside."

In the 1930s a New York banker, John S. Williams, who had a farm in Old Chatham, began purchasing quantities of Shaker-made objects as an outgrowth of his interest in preserving early American farm implements. By the mid-fifties Williams (who has been president of the board of the Heye Foundation Museum of the American Indian) had enough to start a museum. His dairy barn was ingeniously renovated (cattle and tons of fodder having been moved out) to contain reconstructed rooms and the bulk of his collection. Half a dozen buildings in the adjoining courtyard complete the most extensive interpretive treatment this sect has received. Their well-known functional furniture, and especially the sturdy Shaker chair, are on display throughout. There are a blacksmith shop, a broom shop (they invented the flat broom; earlier, sweeping had been done with a bundle of straw tied around a handle), a kitchen, and a foundry. The Shakers were the first growers and merchandisers of seed on a commercial scale, and there is a seed room where preparation, packaging, and labeling were carried on. They were responsible for many innovations in the processing and packaging of herbal remedies and other nineteenth-century pharmaceuticals, and a medicine room contains the equipment for this industry. There are a textile building with looms and spinning equipment, a schoolroom where orphans and foundlings taken in by the community were taught and proselytized, a Brother's and a Sister's bedroom, an office and a dining room. The furnishings of a laundry include a washing machine patented in 1858 and used continuously for ninety years without major repairs. A Sisters' Work Room, reconstructed, illustrates the many domestic skills of these women, which included rug making, quilting, dressmaking, and millinery. The museum's director reports that this so delighted some present-day Sisters and an Eldress that they insisted on being photographed here.

New York City's RICHMONDTOWN RESTORATION on Staten Island is still under construction. When completed it will contain about forty buildings—among them a basketmaker's shop, a carriage factory, two old jails, a parsonage, three courthouses, and a tavern and its carriage shed—that date from the Dutch and English colonial period to the time of the Civil War. Once known as Cocclestown (probably because of the clam and oyster shells that were found by the area's settlers), Richmondtown was the capital of Staten Island from the time of its settlement before 1700 until the island joined New York City as the Borough of Richmond in 1898. The Staten Island Historical Society's Museum was opened in 1935 in a County Clerk's and Surrogate's Office that was put up in 1848, used until 1920, abandoned, and finally restored by WPA workers. A number of buildings, some of them close to three hundred years old, have already been restored and opened to the public. Some have been, or are scheduled to be, moved from elsewhere on the island. Visitors can see the Voorlezer's ("lay reader's") House built prior to 1696 by Dutch settlers as a church and school. It is believed to be the oldest elementary school building in the United States. Also to be seen are the "Treasure House," built by a tanner in 1700, where a cache of British gold coins was discovered a hundred years ago and where Major André is reported to have written his will; the Lake-Tyson House (about 1700), moved here from two miles away and restored at a cost of about $75,000; and a little country Grocery Store. St. Andrew's Church on a nearby hillside, with its charming early eighteenth-century graveyard, contains communion silver presented by Queen Anne. A courthouse built in 1846 contains, among other things, a collection of old fire-fighting apparatus. Visitors can watch the work of restoration going on; they can see archaeological crews uncovering old foundations; and they can look at a scale model showing the restoration as it will be after the $4,000,000 provided jointly by the city's Department of Parks and the Staten Island Historical Society have been spent. The Society's members, who initiated the project, speak of it in words that would not have sounded strange coming from John Pintard. They say it is "an undertaking that will soon prove itself to be a noteworthy and stimulating example of patriotic and historical enterprise."

Some museum communities have been developed as a result of the efforts of state governments. In California, SUTTER'S FORT STATE HISTORICAL MONUMENT consists of a reconstructed adobe-walled fort and the village (also reconstructed) of stores, homes, and warehouses that it protected. The originals were put up in 1839 by John A. Sutter as a trading post to serve new settlers. The community found its niche in history when one of Sutter's men discovered gold forty miles upstream in the American River. After that, Sutter's employees deserted as fast as they could; his land was overrun by squatters, and he went into bankruptcy.

The Pennsylvania Historical and Museum Commission maintains at Ambridge the seventeen buildings of OLD ECONOMY, the third and longest lasting settlement of the Harmony Society. Among the homes, shops, and gardens of this 1825 community are the thirty-five room Great House of handmade brick, a three-story music hall, a granary, a post office, and a community kitchen. Art galleries display local contemporary paintings as well as a collection that once belonged to this celibate separatist sect.

The PENNSYLVANIA FARM MUSEUM OF LANDIS VALLEY in Lancaster, devoted to rural Americana of all periods, is another Commission project. Most of the objects on exhibit (and in storage) were accumulated by two brothers born here in the 1870s who shared a lifelong compulsion to acquire used home and farm implements. George and Henry Landis were known to their neighbors as "The Penny Men" because they regularly offered one cent for items left unsold at the end of local auctions. They spent the last years of their strange lives in a huge house with twenty cats and more than 250,000 objects. Two Conestoga wagons, a dozen spinning wheels, a thousand pairs of wrought-iron hinges, and such curiosities as a washing machine to be run by dog-power were among their assorted possessions. So vast is the collection that it will furnish a rural village now being planned. Unlike most restorations elsewhere in the country, this one will represent the continuum of rural life through several periods of time and history. Some buildings are already here: a country store, a tavern, and a Victorian farmhouse with barn and sheds. A farmhouse from the Federal period has been moved here and is being restored. At an annual Harvest Days weekend held here in early October local farm families dress the way their ancestors did and demonstrate farm and crafts equipment from the museum's collections.

THE HENRY FRANCIS DU PONT WINTERTHUR MUSEUM near Wilmington, Delaware, occupies a mansion surrounded by woodland and gardens. Mr. du Pont had been a collector of American and European decorative objects for several years when in 1927 he fell heir to the residence built by his great-aunt and great-uncle, nearly a century earlier, in the style of a French château. Shortly after that he began to formulate a plan for a museum. He enlarged the house and prepared it to receive about eighty period rooms plus half as many display areas in which the highest standards of American craftsmanship would be represented. Complete in every detail from paneling to lighting fixtures, furniture, porcelain, glass, silver, pewter, and fabrics, these rooms, which were in homes between 1640 and 1840, are a delight to the antique lover and historian alike. There are simple rustic ones as well as sophisticated urban ones. The aim has been to "foster an understanding of American culture by studying and encouraging others to study the early American arts as a chapter in the development of the West's artistic tradition; as an embodiment of the ideals, values and techniques of American craftsmanship; and as social documents throwing important light on the history of the American people." All visitors are taken on guided tours, planned in advance, that point up the influence of different regional styles, national backgrounds, and European imports on American design. These aims are reinforced through a graduate course in early American culture conducted for future museologists in conjunction with the University of Delaware, a program that applies the research techniques of the historian to the field of the decorative arts.

BOSCOBEL, near Garrison, New York, is a mansion that illustrates one period and one European influence flawlessly. Completed in 1805, believed by some to have been designed by Robert Adam, and furnished with Adam pieces and other examples of the finest English and American work of that time, it was built for Staats Morris Dyckman. The house continued to be lived in by his descendants until 1920, when it entered upon three decades of decline. In 1956 it was just another abandoned ruin, about to be sold to a wrecker, when rescuers appeared. A group dedicated to its restoration found that for thirty-five dollars it could be theirs. Since then it has been moved to a new location a few miles north of the original. Still overlooking the Hudson River, it now stands renovated in all its glory. From the second-story library to the basement kitchen, from the butler's pantry to the music room, every part of the mansion is as elegant as it must have been a century and a half ago. And its setting in a thirty-six acre park once more justifies its name which, taken from the Italian *bosco bello,* means "beautiful wood."

The proprietor of the largest number of historic places in the nation is the federal government, with the Department of the Interior acting as managing agent through its National Park Service. Although the first old houses to receive federal protection did so before the end of the nineteenth century (appropriately these were some Indian cliff dwellings and pueblos of the Southwest), it was in 1933 that the first systematic program for the conservation of our historic resources on a national scale was initiated. The record shows that practical economic considerations were responsible for this giant step forward, and not a sudden popular or even governmental awakening to its merits. In that depression year plans were hastily made to conduct a Historic American Buildings Survey with relief funds from the Civil Works Administration; its purpose, to provide employment. A graphic record of over fourteen hundred structures throughout the country was produced by hundreds of out-of-work architects, draftsmen, and photographers, participating in a field program that ran from the beginning of January to the end of April of the following year. With the exception of a section of the Northwest where the rigors of winter and a lack of architects made the program unfeasible, the country was divided into districts, the chief officers of which were selected by the American Institute of Architects. Working personnel were chosen by the local CWA branches. The National Park Service co-ordinated and supervised the program, providing supplies and instructions, while office facilities were furnished free by interested local people and organizations. The measured drawings, photographs, and written data that resulted were deposited in the Library of Congress as a permanent reference source. It was this inter-organizational co-operation that

was eventually responsible for turning an expedient measure into a
national policy.

When the initial expenditure of under $200,000 ran out, the un-
finished work was voluntarily brought to completion by the participants. In about a third of the states, emergency relief funds were used
to continue the program; in many places schools and universities contributed personnel or facilities; and sporadically the Secretary of the
Interior was able to allocate special funds over the next year. The
achievements of even this brief venture motivated the National Park
Service, the American Institute of Architects, and the Library of Congress to formally co-operate, and enabled the Secretary of the Interior
to persuade Congress, in 1935, that the work should be specifically
financed. In "An Act to provide for the preservation of historic American sites, buildings, objects, and antiquities of national significance,"
it was declared "national policy to preserve" such places and objects
"for the inspiration and benefit of the people of the United States."

But there were limits to what the federal government could directly
manage, and in 1949 forty national, regional, and state organizations
sponsored a bill authorizing the formation of the National Trust for
Historic Preservation. The bill passed Congress and the Trust became
a legal entity able to take title to donated properties. These properties
would either be operated by the Trust itself or by another organization
delegated to do the job. The Trust has turned historic preservation
into a well-rounded program that includes scientific research and
study, restoration, maintenance, and interpretation. It is not a government agency. Although it works with the National Park Service it is
privately financed. Its work is supported by memberships, gifts, and
bequests.

The value of the National Trust is constantly being demonstrated.
Recently, in Virginia, a superhighway was scheduled to be built across
property on which there stood a house of modest proportions built in
1940 by Frank Lloyd Wright. The house's owner, Mrs. Robert A.
Leighey, alerted Secretary of the Interior Stewart L. Udall, who in turn
called upon the American Institute of Architects and the National
Trust. Letters from these organizations were then sent to the governor
of Virginia. And the federal government's concern was publicly demonstrated when Secretary Udall made a televised visit to the house,
which has the distinction of being one of the few small ones Wright
designed. (It has been said that he undertook such commissions in
order to dispel the impression that he worked exclusively for the rich.)

As a result of all these actions the state of Virginia decided to pay Mrs. Leighey $31,000 as opposed to the $25,605 that had originally been offered. Furthermore, the bulldozing was postponed long enough to allow the structure to be moved. Mrs. Leighey deeded the house to the National Trust, and contributed her $31,000 as payment of a bit more than half the moving costs. The house will be permanently located at Woodlawn, an estate near Mount Vernon that had belonged to George Washington and that the Trust now supervises.

Although the National Park Service is best known for the park system that called it into being in 1916, its largest classes of properties are its historic sites, monuments, and memorials which commemorate every aspect of the national record. They include the place where Coronado entered Arizona in 1540; about thirty cemeteries, battlefields, and military parks recalling the Civil War; the site near Beatrice, Nebraska, of the first farm claimed under the Homestead Act in 1862; and the scene of the first successful flight of the Wright brothers near Kitty Hawk in North Carolina.

The ninety-one acre JEFFERSON NATIONAL EXPANSION MEMORIAL PARK in St. Louis commemorates the exploration and pioneer days that resulted in settlement of the trans-Mississippi two thirds of the country. A huge stainless steel Gateway Arch, designed by Eero Saarinen to symbolize St. Louis as the gateway to the West, towers over a group of early nineteenth-century houses: a courthouse, a cathedral, and an old rock house of the Missouri Fur Company. A Visitor Center under the arch is a museum illustrating a century of westward expansion, recalling the roles played by explorers, trappers, prospectors, ranchers, and others who pushed the frontier before them as they moved across the land.

Federal encouragement of the preservation movement also comes in the form of a certificate and a bronze plaque that proclaim a place to be a national landmark. Some that have been recently marked in this way are the birthplaces of Presidents Kennedy and Wilson (in Massachusetts and Virginia, respectively), the Robie House designed by Frank Lloyd Wright in Chicago (funds are being raised privately for its preservation and maintenance), Sandy Hook Light (an 85-foot-high white lighthouse in New Jersey, constructed between 1762 and 1764, and still watched for by ships on their way in and out of New York Harbor), and Woodchuck Lodge, the Catskill Mountain home of naturalist-writer John Burroughs.

FORT OSAGE near Buckner, Missouri, an early nineteenth-century trading fort, "has been designated a National Historic Landmark. . . . This site possesses exceptional value in commemorating and illustrating the history of the United States." The place where the first government outpost in the Louisiana Territory was to stand was selected by Lewis and Clark during their first exploration. Clark supervised the building of the fort four years later, and his original notes were the basis of a reconstruction by the Jackson County Park Department with assistance from the Native Sons of Kansas City. When the government left the trading business to private enterprise in the 1820s the fort was closed, and its logs taken by settlers to build their homes. Plans were made for its revival in the 1940s when archaeological investigation disclosed some of its boundary lines and the substructure of an old building.

Our cities, too, have enjoyed preserving the records of their lives. Philadelphia's ATWATER KENT MUSEUM uses collections of prints, paintings, old photographs, local folk art, and Frankliniana to depict the evolution of that city from the time it was an Indian village before the arrival of William Penn. Baltimore has the PEALE MUSEUM, reopened in 1931 to do a similar job. The MUSEUM OF THE CITY OF NEW YORK has extensive research and library facilities in addition to a costume gallery, theater and music collections, and dioramas showing the development of the communications industries and the world of finance. It has old prints, pictures and photographs, groups of furnishings, silver and glass, fire-fighting equipment, and period settings showing New Yorkers at home from 1700 to 1906.

The DETROIT HISTORICAL MUSEUM, opened in 1951 on the 250th anniversary of the city's founding, presents the "Streets of Detroit," where visitors can walk on wooden sidewalks along an 1840 cobblestone street, or on flagstone sidewalks along an 1870 cedar plank street, passing by appropriate shops and store fronts. The museum is run by the city's historical commission, with the co-operation of the Detroit Historical Society, which initiated the project. Two of its branches are the FORT WAYNE MILITARY MUSEUM on the shores of the Detroit River, and the DOSSIN GREAT LAKES MUSEUM on Belle Isle. The former is a restored military post. Built at a strategic location commanding the waterway, it had been planned in the 1830s when border difficulties with Canada made defense seem necessary. But by the time of its completion in 1848 the problem had been peacefully resolved and the fort never saw action, although it was a troop training center during the Civil War. Exhibits tell of Detroit's growth from a small fortified trading post to a major industrial center contributing to national defense, and there are displays of military equipment used in the area over a period of two and a half centuries. The Dossin building is the marine division of the Detroit Historical Museum. It is concerned with the story of the Great Lakes, their recreational value, and their economic importance.

Seattle's MUSEUM OF HISTORY AND INDUSTRY, located in a park along a scenic lake shore, is a project of the Seattle Historical Society. It gave it to and operates it for the city. Here are pioneers' gear, Eskimo artifacts, and Victorian street lights. A favorite, if bulky, object on constant display is an old cable car. The Boeing Airplane Company contributed to an aviation wing, and the Puget Sound Maritime Historical Society co-operated on a maritime division. A library of Northwest Americana and an active program for eight- to twelve-year-olds are other features.

The WESTERN RESERVE HISTORICAL SOCIETY of Cleveland was founded in 1867 and boasts of being the city's first cultural organization. It took its name from the northeastern section of the state that had originally been the Western Reserve of Connecticut. Its original plan was to concentrate on regional information and materials, but its collections expanded in all directions, and now include a Napoleonic Gallery as well as a pioneer cabin, an Egyptian mummy as well as Great Lakes ship models. Here too are dolls, clocks, costumes, cigar-store Indians, fine antique furniture in period rooms (a Victorian bedroom is complete down to a shaving mirror and marble-topped washstand), and a new auto-aviation wing.

In contrast to these urban history museums is one that serves a small Massachusetts town both as a community center and a means of recording its past. The WENHAM HISTORICAL ASSOCIATION AND MUSEUM consists of a cluster of structures and a varied group of collections, highlighted by more than three thousand dolls and figurines representing every era and culture from 1500 B.C. to the present. A seventeenth-century house is furnished as though it had been in continuous use until recently. And two cobblers' shops, displays of agricultural tools and ice-cutting equipment (Wenham Lake was a productive source of ice blocks, shipped around the globe, in the days before refrigeration), and libraries of agricultural and local history add to the value of what is here. An adjacent building is used for meetings and temporary exhibitions.

Patriotism is a problematic emotion. Purely expressed, it is—to use Cervantes' word—sweet. Sentimentalized, it gets lost in bathos. In America, patriotism should be sweet and easy. There is no need here to strain to create an effect. Who needs brass bands when there is the Liberty Bell? Who needs bombast when there is the Declaration of Independence? If we visited only Andrew Jackson's Hermitage, if we went no further than Philadelphia, if we stayed only in Boston, if we looked around just in Washington, D.C., we could feel, without anyone giving us a slogan, how "sweet is the love of one's country."

A group of buildings in downtown Philadelphia known as INDEPENDENCE NATIONAL HISTORIC PARK consists of Independence Hall, where the Declaration was adopted and the Constitution written; Carpenters' Hall, where the first Continental Congress met in 1774; the Episcopal church of 1695, where Washington and other founders worshiped; and Congress Hall, where the Congress met for ten years after the capital was moved here in 1790.

In Boston there are Paul Revere's House, Old South Meeting House, Faneuil Hall; in Lexington the Monroe Tavern; in Quincy the homes of the Adams family.

In Washington, D.C., there are the White House, the monuments to Presidents Washington, Jefferson and Lincoln, and the Capitol; and in Virginia, Washington's home at Mount Vernon and Jefferson's Monticello.

Our past is alive. We thank all those who ever cared about preserving it.

Chapter V

CHILDREN

A TTEMPTS have been made, from time to time, to spread the rumor that children's museums "display dismembered children . . . as an art museum displays sculptured torsos." The discrepancy upon which this story was based is obvious. Most museums are categorized according to their collections. Only these special and particularly marvelous places for the young are categorized according to their audience.

In the last decade of the last century, when the Brooklyn Institute of Arts and Sciences (out of which the Brooklyn Museum and Botanic Garden would grow) was under the direction of Franklin W. Hooper, who had stood beside the open grave of Louis Agassiz and made "a young man's impassioned vow to devote his life to the building of a great museum," it moved from temporary quarters in the Adams House in Bedford (now Brower) Park to a permanent home. The collections were reappraised and "some of the things considered not quite up to standard were left [behind] to make a Museum For Children." But it was immediately "realized that what was not good enough for adults was surely not good enough for . . . new minds [and] waking imaginations." And so a unique institution was conceived to "delight and instruct the children who visit it . . . to stimulate their power of observation and reflection . . . to bring [boys and girls] whether attending school or not, into direct relation with the most important subjects . . . in their daily life, in their school work, in their reading, in their games, in their rambles in the fields, and in the industries that are being carried on about them or in which they themselves later may become engaged."

Just a few years after its opening in 1899, the Brooklyn Children's Museum hired Anna Billings Gallup, a thirty-year-old teacher of nature studies, as curator in chief. It was she who, leading her enthusiastic visitors through the halls, unlocked cases for them, and let them handle exhibits which until that time had been austerely labeled "Do Not Touch." Other innovations—equally startling—soon followed. Displays were expressly designed for touching; some of them had movable parts. And there were live animals that could be fondled. Here was a place at last where, by his own experience, a child could directly satisfy his curiosity about the world around him; a place where ideas that somehow remained remote when presented in a classroom, came suddenly and dramatically alive; a place where a child felt at home. It was the first of its kind in this country or, for that matter, anywhere.

Many years later, when Helen V. Fisher became director, it still remained necessary to explain that "a children's museum is not a 'miniature adult museum,' nor a junior version of one." Emphasizing the importance of interpretation, Miss Fisher would point out that "our collections are not necessarily gathered for their intrinsic worth or rarity . . . but to . . . be of use to us in interpreting various subjects and conveying ideas." While the adult museum, by acquiring important collections and sponsoring original research, adds to general knowledge, the children's museum "can direct the child's interests, even into future productive fields."

Scientifically oriented, Brooklyn's program encompasses three broad fields: natural history, cultural history, and the physical sciences. The Natural History Department has both living and mounted mammals, birds and reptiles; and it has excellent study collections of insects and shells. The Cultural History Department presides over Indian artifacts, clothing from many parts of the world, early Americana, an outstanding group of dolls from other times and other places, transportation exhibits, and household objects that are either antique or foreign or both. Every one of these things may be handled and examined closely by visiting school classes that come by appointment. The Science Department maintains demonstration collections for illustrating the basic laws of physics and performing simple experiments in chemistry. It provides instruction in mineralogy and astronomy and operates a small planetarium. In addition there is a good-sized library. Since a large part of the program is devoted to work with school groups, there is, as an extension of this work, a loan collection of over five thousand items which, carried by truck, circulate from one local classroom to another.

"In Brooklyn," Helen Fisher said, "we do not make any effort to whip up extracurricular interests in the below-average child, because this generally entails lessened advantages for the above-average, thereby netting a sad level of mediocrity. This is not to say that only gifted children are welcome at our museum; it simply means that any child who has the spark of interest for a club is not below-average and is worth encouraging to become above-average."

A variety of clubs and workshops meet regularly, attended by students from every borough of the city. Registration is limited and the curators are able to work individually with each child. There are museum-conducted field trips that are followed up by seminars. Right here many a career—in biology, anthropology, archaeology, mineralogy, ornithology, and astronomy—has been started. And programs like one given for junior and senior high school students by Dr. Roman Vishniac, called "Careers in Microbiology," are a regular feature. (Dr. Vishniac, a biologist who is the world's foremost microphotographer, donated a unique and extraordinarily beautiful selection of his work for permanent exhibition in a new science gallery. The exhibit includes thirteen microphotographs enlarged from color transparencies. The birth of an amoeba, light from a rabbit's brain, and an image seen through the eye of a wasp are among the phenomena he has captured on film.)

For qualified boys and girls twelve years old and older, there is an excellent junior curator program. "These are honorary positions," a handsome brochure declares, "achieved through competition for excellence of work and effort in the Science, Natural and Cultural History, Library, and Exhibits Departments. After a try-out period, the most promising candidates are selected for a one-year tenure as Junior Curators. Their activities range from care of the collections and engaging in 'research,' to developing projects or exhibits in fields of their special interests."

Every weekday afternoon there are films selected for various age groups. And on Saturdays a story hour, a live animal program, two planetarium shows, a gallery talk, and other special events make their appeal to children from four to fourteen. A monthly publication lists all of these activities and classifies them according to age level. There are usually some that are suitable for pre-schoolers. But whatever his age, the visitor's sense of freedom is assured. A protective policy decrees that "this is a child's world" to which "adults are not admitted . . . so that children may relax in an atmosphere of their peers."

The impact of this turn-of-the-century innovation in Brooklyn was, of course, hardly apparent to anyone outside the world of the museum. But within it the repercussions were numerous and frequent. Pedagogi-

cal arguments were begun that are still unsettled. It took fourteen years
for the experiment to be repeated in another part of the country.
However, when the second children's museum finally opened in Boston it was an immediate and continuing success. Indianapolis, Detroit, and Hartford followed the lead shortly thereafter. The idea was
decidedly catching on. Today there are about two hundred such places
organized in a variety of ways to serve a variety of purposes. Whereas
Indianapolis' exhibits range from a transportation gallery (that includes a history of fire fighting), to a prehistory gallery, to a collection
of African culture objects, exhibits elsewhere may be limited to the
study of nature.

To Boston, in 1962 when he was thirty years old, came Michael
Spock, son of the adviser to millions of American mothers, as its new
director. "I want a museum to do more than just display some objects,"
he told an interviewer. "I want the exhibits designed on an intuitive
level so that the objects say something." One of the first exhibits he
prepared was called "What's Inside?" It allowed a child to step into a
huge simulated drop of water and see tremendously enlarged protozoa
swimming all around him. Similarly, a child could step inside a city
street and see what lies beneath the sidewalk; or inside the human circulatory system. In this way Michael Spock proved to himself that "a
museum has one advantage over books and films: it gives you information through direct experience with real objects and real places. It
is the only medium where *all* the senses may be excited."

The American Museum of Natural History deals with the needs of
elementary and high school students not through a separate set of exhibit facilities but through its Department of Public Instruction whose
teachers use the adult displays (supplemented by expendable demonstration collections) as the basis of their lectures. Technically this is
not the same as a children's museum. But to compensate for this technical lapse, there is a small Natural Science Center which—crowded
with local turtles, frogs, snakes, salamanders, skunks, fish, and other
live animals in addition to mounted specimens and plants, and directed to youngsters eight years old and older—delightfully fits the
definition. To high school and college students, the main branches of
the museum offer opportunities for studying the research methods of
staff scientists whom the young men and women are allowed to assist.
And there is an entire program planned especially for the handicapped
and the blind. (Brooklyn, Boston, and for that matter nearly all the
institutions that cater to youth have made it a point to provide for the

disabled child, not only on their own premises but by sending out live animal and other displays to hospitals.)

Similarly, the California Academy of Sciences takes care of its budding scientists through its adult facilities, an excellent junior curator program, and a separate junior museum. Thus a large institution can serve its junior participants by creating a special department to help them make special use of adult materials, or it can create a semi-autonomous children's branch with collections of its own, or it can do both. One of the first general museums to "set aside [an area] for exhibitions planned, labeled and installed to be attractive to young people" was Newark's. When it moved into its new building in 1926, the junior department really came into its own "with a Life Membership of 10¢, entitling all members to participate in daily activities in Science, Art, Nature and Crafts, the only additional expense being a registration fee for the Saturday morning activities."

Another way in which one of these organizations gets founded is as a school-system museum controlled by a board of education. These direct the greater part of their activities toward the classroom. The one in Cambridge, Massachusetts, provides all the visual aid materials for the geography, history, and nature study classes of the public schools. In St. Louis the Board of Education supports one whose basic function is to supply teachers with audio-visual study exhibits for the classroom. And Detroit's, which is virtually owned and operated by the city's school system, not only sends its collections out but receives and instructs classes whose visits are scheduled on a regular basis during school hours.

Sometimes a children's museum is affiliated with another community agency such as a library, or playground, or recreation commission. Here activities are directed toward the leisure hours. The emphasis is on clubs and hobby groups, and members are encouraged to become collectors and set up their own exhibits. This is the way San Francisco's Josephine D. Randall Junior Museum is run.

Finally, there are the totally independent children's museums directed by their own boards, such as Boston's and Hartford's and the local nature centers that are going up everywhere. Boston's displays extend to anthropology, art, and biology. Hartford is second only to Brooklyn in the size and diversity of its collections.

Because it is the only natural science museum in its immediate area, about one third of Hartford's general attendance is adult. To begin "on an adult level," said Director Jane B. Cheney, a woman who knows

how to get things done, "might have been impossible . . . but by gradual community education, firmness of planning, and honest answering
of an unfelt need, what was essentially 'good for the kiddies' has become good for everyone." Mrs. Cheney and her staff have planned
their programing to rise from the level of nursery school to college
and graduate school. There is a summer Science Academy for elementary and junior high school children. And there is an in-service
training program in the natural sciences for elementary school teachers. In addition, teachers can find assistance in presenting American
history, geography, ethnology, ornithology, and biology. Natural history exhibit materials are borrowed for classroom use constantly.

For the general visitor, there are displays covering these areas plus
galleries for sea life, rocks and minerals, plants, and artifacts of the
Southwest and Plains Indians.

Although most junior museums emphasize science and nature, the
arts are being increasingly well provided for. The Art Institute of Chicago has opened a $250,000 children's division. And the Metropolitan
Museum of Art continues to increase the activities of its superb little
people's halls which were opened in 1941.

Realizing that the patrons of its junior wing are "the advanced students, artists, designers, and interested laymen, the Museum patrons
of the future," the Metropolitan wisely illustrates for these children,
by means of beautifully mounted exhibits, subjects that are richly represented in the collections on view in its main galleries. Furthermore,
these are all subjects considered important by the New York City
school system with which the Metropolitan's staff regularly consults.
And so an "Age of Discovery" display, beginning with Marco Polo and
continuing through the early seventeenth century, contained late
medieval, Renaissance, late pre-Columbian, and Near and Far Eastern
art objects taken from the main collections as well as photographs and
maps, and ship models borrowed from other institutions. In this way
antique jars and vases, animal figures, tools and implements that could
not be meaningful to a child in the context of a large gallery, were made
to stand out and relate to the history of the period that produced them.
Additional instruction was provided by means of peepholes, push-
buttons that controlled recorded messages, spices that could be sniffed,
and a large map on which a series of lights traced the voyages of Columbus and Vasco Da Gama.

A number of years ago, the Metropolitan's Junior Museum presented a special exhibit that is still remembered as a splendid example of what such an institution-within-an-institution can do. Planned for the age level between seven and twelve, and called "How to Look at Paintings," it opened in September and remained on view through June. Its purpose was not to present a history of art, but to introduce and illustrate the basic elements of painting, such as color, line, shape, and arrangement, and to show the tools, materials, and techniques of the artist. The exhibit began by explaining how one artist might approach his subject with the intention of representing it as it really is while another might want to paint it as an element in a decoration, while still another might wish to tell a story, or depict a dream, or capture a mood. Elsewhere, grouped to show the subjects artists choose, were landscapes, seascapes, cityscapes, portraits, still lifes, religious themes, and genre paintings. To demonstrate that artists have always liked to portray their own occupation, a series of peepholes was arranged with color slides showing Vermeer's *The Artist in His Studio,* Matthew Pratt's *The American School,* and an Egyptian wall painting, a Greek vase painting, a Persian portrait, and a medieval illuminated page, each dealing with a similar scene. At the peepholes there were earphones through which recorded footnotes could be heard. In other parts of the exhibit recordings were used effectively to dramatize Grant Wood's *The Midnight Ride of Paul Revere* with a reading of stanzas from the Longfellow poem, and to musically support *The Parade* of Saul Steinberg with Strauss' *Radetzky March.* To test the effect of these displays on their own creativity, school classes could use the Studio Room in which, year after year, youngsters have expressed themselves in crayon and paint.

"Russia, we are told," said Dr. M. Graham Netting (director of the Carnegie Museum) at a national symposium in Rochester, "is opening museums—and good ones—in hundreds of towns and cities to educate youth, even though the elderly wear shoddy clothes." Dr. Netting was not sounding a note of alarm over a cold war advantage; he was merely illustrating his larger point about the museum's role in firing "the rockets of youthful imagination."

If for no other reason than the enormous success it has had in this role, Ohio's Dayton Museum of Natural History would have to be considered one of the nation's most important. Here youngsters are encouraged to actually work along with the staff; which is why this institution, housed in a beautifully modern structure designed by Richard

Neutra, has been referred to as a "nursery for naturalists." A fourth grader who qualifies for the title of junior naturalist will attend classes and may be assigned the job of cleaning animal cages. At thirteen he may become a junior curator. And if he should continue to prove worthy, the job of junior staff member, and a salary under a dollar an hour, await him.

Once, a fourteen-year-old asked to be allowed to operate on a newly acquired skunk in order to prevent it from offending with its protective odor. Permission was granted and both the young doctor and his mammalian patient were prepared for surgery. For more than a year afterward the skunk smelled almost as good as the children. But that was probably because, pitying him in his condition, they gave him all kinds of preferential and exceedingly gentle treatment. Inevitably, there came a time when the skunk was handled roughly and panicked. And spraying the air around him with his still potent, foul juices he proved the operation an unqualified failure. Far from discouraged, however, the boy who had wielded the scalpel grew up to become a highly respected teacher of biology.

Communities that do not offer this kind of special opportunity to children may be surprised to learn how easily some of these centers were started. Boston's was begun with only two exhibits, one of birds, the other of minerals and shells, in an old house provided by the Park Department. When Duluth, Minnesota, opened what is now known as the A. M. Chisholm Children's Museum, which covers the fields of geology, history, Indian lore, industry, and general science, its collections consisted of items belonging to two staff members and some stuffed birds rescued from local attics. The Cape Cod Museum of Natural History, which occupies quarters over the Town Hall in Brewster and provides the local schools with loan exhibits, has been supplied by children and their teachers with wildlife, plants and shells from nearby wooded areas and beaches. The point to be made is that nothing more than an excellent sampling of local plant life, animals, arrowheads, dolls, Colonial furniture, or whatever the community is uniquely equipped to provide, is ever needed. One good exhibit in a library or school lobby can be the beginning.

Another way of beginning is for parents to get together to provide animal lending libraries. These are small collections of tame animals that can be borrowed either by individual children or by schools and hospitals in the area. In several cases an animal lending library has grown into a permanent enterprise. The Lake Erie Junior Nature and Science Center of Cleveland was established in just this way.

Different still is Piedmont Center, which occupies the ground floor of an old tenement renovated by some volunteer workers of Worcester, Massachusetts. It is the successful result of a happy notion to put underprivileged children of a crowded city neighborhood in direct touch with nature. The Worcester Natural History Society, which maintains it, also operates the Rice House Children's Museum elsewhere in town. Rice House has a planetarium, and its exhibits may be borrowed by the schools.

Helping local communities in the job of "influencing children powerfully by giving them knowledge and happiness and bringing them closer to God as they draw closer to Nature" is a startlingly energetic, fast-talking, scrappy, bright-eyed proselytizer named John Ripley Forbes. Combining the unshakable persistence of a man accustomed to having a cause with the buoyant aspect of a salesman anticipating a marvelous day, he "runs all over the country setting up museums" (a job which no one before him "has ever been crazy enough to do") and joyously applies himself to the intricacies of raising money. He is a minister's son who equally loves children and the world of nature. "The over-privileged child," he says, "needs to get close to nature and understand it, to have the satisfaction of working on a research project or assuming responsibility for the care of an animal, as much as the slum child." Insisting upon the importance of live animal exhibits, he has been a controversial figure in an academic world where the art of the taxidermist is emphatically preferred to the ambiance of the zoo keeper. He supports his point of view by telling the story of an afternoon when, entertaining a group of spastics at the San Mateo County Junior Museum in California, he placed a rabbit in the lap of a badly crippled boy who touched it and uttered his first sound. No stuffed leporid, Forbes makes clear, could have had the same emotional effect. Forbes is the founder and director of the Natural Science for Youth Foundation which stimulates, guides, and assists towns and cities interested in establishing centers where boys and girls can discover, begin to love, and finally understand the plant and animal life around them.

As a boy, he went regularly to the Boston Children's Museum where there was an inspired curator named Madalene Sawyer. Then his family moved to Stamford, Connecticut, and he discovered that one of his neighbors was Dr. William T. Hornaday. Before long he persuaded the older naturalist to come and look at the birds and small mammals he had mounted in his attic. When Dr. Hornaday told Forbes' mother, "I came to see a boy's collection, but I have seen a scientific museum," he made the statement that determined the fourteen-year-old's future career.

At Dr. Hornaday's suggestion, Forbes entered Iowa State College and studied zoology. Later he transferred to Bowdoin. Graduated into the depression in 1935, he realized that the only way he could possibly get a job was by creating one; and he promptly organized and raised money for a children's museum in Stamford with Dr. Hornaday as honorary president and himself as curator. But he was fired when he fought with the board of directors over his insistence upon having live animals and his refusal to use precious, limited space for "things like an African heads-and-horns collection" which he considered valueless trophies.

He joined an expedition led by Donald Baxter MacMillan to Baffin Island in the Arctic to collect birds, raising the $750 necessary to pay his share of the expenses by calling on alumni of Bowdoin and telling them his story. Upon his return, he set up a live animal display for the Boston Children's Museum, did a bit of lecturing, and read somewhere that R. A. Long, a Missouri lumber magnate, had died leaving his seventy-four-room house to Kansas City to be converted into exhibit halls. There was just one catch; no money was left to remodel the place or furnish it with acquisitions. Quite literally playing the role of *deus ex machina,* Forbes got into his car and drove straight to Kansas City, having first visited a loan company where a persuasive monologue netted him one hundred dollars to finance his mission. Arriving at his destination, he located the office of the museum association's president and, walking in unannounced, said, "I've come to work." While the man behind the desk considered the implications of this announcement, Forbes amplified his proposal. "I'll raise the money to set up a first-class institution, open a children's program, and go without pay until you can afford me." It was then that the cautious president conceded to himself that he had nothing to lose and agreed to Forbes' terms of employment.

The stranger in town did precisely what he had promised. He opened a campaign that brought in $35,000. He got the WPA to remodel the Long mansion. He scoured attics and storerooms for usable specimens; and what he could not beg or borrow, he purchased. He wound up with 160,000 assorted objects; among them a stuffed whale, a buffalo, a polar bear, extinct birds, fossils, a collection of Indian artifacts, and a group of African mammals. Within a few months he developed a program that attracted a thousand children a week. The general museum that he brought to life today continues to serve both the young and adult communities with satisfying success.

During the Second World War Forbes, drafted, found himself in a medical unit at an army air corps base in Alabama. Assigned to rehabilitating airmen whose nerves were shot, he took them either fishing or on nature walks. On his days off, he traveled through the rural South bringing to the school children exhibit materials and films for which he had written to museums all over the country. His letterhead said "The William T. Hornaday Memorial Foundation."

The idea for the Foundation, which would perpetuate the ideals of his mentor, had occurred to Forbes shortly after Hornaday died. He organized it and put it on paper in 1939, with Laurance Rockefeller, Roy Chapman Andrews, Eleanor Roosevelt, Laurence Vail Coleman, Anna Billings Gallup, Fairfield Osborn, and Austin H. MacCormick among its sponsors and advisers. It remained little more than a letterhead (supported by limited private funds) until it was incorporated under the laws of New York State in 1944. But what a letterhead it was! It made possible Forbes' work in Geneva County, Alabama, where thirty-one schools received two dozen birds from the American Museum of Natural History, entomological materials from Chicago's Field Museum, and Indian collections from the Denver Art Museum, plus a "glass-eyed raccoon and a balding skunk." It gave impetus (after the Army relocated Forbes in Tennessee) to the formation of the Nashville Children's Museum Association, the leasing of a building from the city for a dollar a year, Forbes' flight to New York's American Museum (on a three-day pass) which resulted in a gift of $300,000 worth of specimens, and other gifts from all over including a sizable one from the Smithsonian. When Jacksonville, Florida, learned how Nashville had achieved its excellent institution, which is today the largest and most modern of its kind in the state, a committee of Floridians sent Forbes an appeal for help. He strenuously requested a two-week furlough, got it, and vigorously answered the plea.

By the time Fort Worth, Texas, read about him in Eleanor Roosevelt's column, Forbes was out of the Army. Working hand in hand with the city, he guided it in its ambitious program and eventually in the building of a million-dollar model museum—the first of its kind in the Southwest. Next he gave encouragement to Charlotte, North Carolina, which boasts an excellent planetarium and a fine collection of invertebrate fossils gathered by boys and girls and their parents, digging together along the coast. Then he helped out ten centers in northern and central California; he worked with the developers of a handsome center in Savannah, Georgia; he founded the exemplary Mid-Fairfield County Youth Museum in Westport, Connecticut; and he gave advice to Kalamazoo, a city that has worked hard to achieve a top place in this field.

The original Hornaday Foundation has undergone reorganization and reincorporation several times. Now known as the Natural Science for Youth Foundation, it can be contacted either through the half-million-dollar museum in Westport or at its office in New York. Administered by a board of trustees on an annual budget well under $75,000, it offers its services completely free to any community requesting them. It sets up a non-profit sponsoring organization within the community, provides a five-year projection of needs, helps raise money, gives advice on acquisitions, provides professional exhibit aid, works with architects on building plans, helps hire personnel, works within the curriculum of the local schools, arranging for them to bring their classes for natural science instruction, and remains on active call as a consultant on just about any problem that might arise. Mr. Forbes' services are paid for by the Foundation; not the community. Furthermore, all of his expenses are met by the Foundation. The Foundation does not, however, donate money to the community. This is not its purpose. Its purpose is to organize the museum and make it self-sufficient.

Working with "people genuinely interested in children," Forbes has been responsible for about 25 per cent of the natural science youth centers in America. Some of these have combined social science and history with their basic program. But the Foundation will not lend its aid to the establishment of an institution whose major concern is something other than the world of nature. Art centers for children will have to find their own benefactor.

Forbes considers his Mid-Fairfield County project a kind of prototype. Furthermore he has a personal stake in this one since he lives close by and his own children are among those who benefit from its activities. On fifty-one acres of land that has been laid out in a series of nature trails, it serves the families and schools of thirteen towns. When money was being raised for its Hornaday Memorial Wing, Forbes decided that he himself would like to contribute. Why, after all, should the joys of philanthropy escape him? He thought he would like to give $5000. The fact that he did not have it available hardly bothered him at all. He got off some letters to a number of people of means, explaining to them his desire to be a donor. When, bit by bit, $4500 came in, John Ripley Forbes dipped into his own bank account for the remainder. "At last," he said, writing a check, "I've become a philanthropist."

"The whole art of teaching," wrote Anatole France, "is only the art of awakening the natural curiosity of young minds for the purpose of satisfying it afterwards." Hartford has used these words to illuminate its pursuits.

"This is a child's world," says Brooklyn, "a world where young minds may seek knowledge at their individual pace, in their own time. They may compare the birds that prey and the birds that wade, Andromeda and the Milky Way, gold ore and fool's gold . . . and in making these comparisons they are led in turn to new curiosities and new avenues of discovery."

Ideas about the art of teaching, respect for young minds—these concerns have reached out from the world of the museum and touched communities all over America.

Chapter VI

AN INFINITE VARIETY

VISIT the world's most unusual museum, the BARTON MUSEUM OF WHISKEY HISTORY in the heart of Kentucky's vacationland; Bardstown, Nelson County, Kentucky."

This invitation appears on the first page of an inexpensively printed brochure. On the next page it is noted that the museum was "founded and dedicated to the public by Mr. Oscar Getz, President of Barton Distilling Company on April 22, 1957. It represents a life time of collecting by Mr. Getz and depicts graphically the famous 170 year history of the distilling industry in the United States."

The story of George Washington's commercial distillery on his Mount Vernon estate; a replica of Abraham Lincoln's "license to keep a tavern" and sell liquor at New Salem, Illinois, dated March 1833; a parchment document for a patent on an improved distilling method signed by President James Monroe and Secretary of State John Quincy Adams, dated 1822; one of the first books on whiskey distilling, dedicated to Thomas Jefferson whose efforts in getting farmers to make whiskey from grain laid the foundation of this early American industry; the original Booz bottle, manufactured by E. C. Booz in 1854, from which the expression "booze" was derived; a Hayner combination-lock bottle made to protect the owner's bourbon from children and servants; a Whiskey Rebellion exhibit; a Carrie Nation exhibit; prohibition items; curios, advertisements, old newspaper stories, old tax stamps; and a whiskey history library are among the featured attractions.

In a corner of the brochure there is this appeal: "Send your old whiskey artifacts and memorabilia to the Museum, so that others may enjoy them."

Probably the only museum in the world that sells popcorn and pink lemonade is the CIRCUS WORLD MUSEUM of Baraboo, Wisconsin. Maintained by the State Historical Society of Wisconsin and located on the site of the former winter quarters of the Ringling Brothers Circus, it features among its many colorful mementos an eighteen-ton calliope. As an added attraction, "you can have yourself photographed in a cage with a living, roaring, black-maned African lion assuring you and your children a triumph of indescribable sensations and novel photographs."

The Ringling Circus originated in Baraboo and the museum occupies some of the old circus buildings. Its collection of baroquely decorated wagons has been called "the biggest and the best." When the Ringling Brothers and Barnum and Bailey Combined Show, Inc., comes to town at the beginning of the summer, the museum participates in a mammoth parade. The parade of 1963 was hailed as the first major one "staged in the United States in 40 years."

Owned and operated by the state of Florida, the RINGLING CIRCUS MUSEUM of Sarasota is on the same grounds as the Ringling Museum of Art and the Ringling mansion. Proud of its claim that its "circus wagon collection is unequalled anywhere in the world," it also boasts of calliopes, costumes, lithographs, posters, and "a storehouse of relics and documents that . . . illustrate the history of the circus in a manner both academic and entertaining."

At HAGANS CLOCK MANOR MUSEUM in Bergen Park, Colorado, "you will see one of the most famous permanent exhibitions of its kind in the world." Here is "the world renowned Gebhard Clock, the Astronomical Clock that performs more Artful Timekeeping Functions with Mechanized Hand Carved Figures than the Average Mind Can Conceive—Thirty years of work in planning and production by Christian Gebhard—one of the 19th Century's foremost horological geniuses. The clock is 10 feet high, 10 feet wide, and 3 feet deep, and has 15,000 parts, 26 separate and distinct mechanical and astronomical movements. The twelve Apostles, angels, trumpeter, rooster and many other moving and performing figures will delight and astound the fortunate viewer. This World Wonder Clock cannot be fully described or appreciated unless viewed in person. Then it leaves one in a quandary as to how far ahead such men as Gebhard were as compared to the average."

The remarkable timepieces that are here date from 900 A.D. to the present. The collection was compiled by Orville R. Hagans, a dedicated horologist, and his wife. Mr. and Mrs. Hagans own and operate the museum. In addition to clocks and watches, they have tools and machines of the trade used centuries ago, and a library of rare books and manuscripts.

In New York there is a good collection at New York University's clock museum.

Do you prefer Sandwich glass to clocks? Then visit the SANDWICH GLASS MUSEUM on Cape Cod. Although a glass factory was built here in 1825, the town was never industrialized. Although the factory closed in 1888, the town held onto its tradition. Many of its homes have collections, and its museum is filled with marvelous examples of the craft.

And at the MUSICAL MUSEUM in Deansboro, New York, "you are welcome to play the fully restored antique musical instruments—to try a tune on an antique pipe organ, crank an organ grinder's organ, listen to an 'eartube' Edison phonograph, or drop a nickel in yesterday's juke box which plays perforated metal discs." There is "an amazing machine which will play two violins with piano accompaniment from the paper roll. It was invented in 1904, and made use of electric magnets and solenoids." There is an antique shop "specializing in old lamps" and "musical gift items." Old sheet music and recordings of the various old machines can be bought. The museum workshop specializes in "expert and careful restorations." There is a Music Box Restaurant and there are "No Tiring Stairs to Climb Anywhere."

In Vermont, at the SHELBURNE MUSEUM, there is a collection of—collections. The china, glass, dolls, hat boxes, woodworking tools, prints, pewter, cigar-store Indians, furniture, primitive paintings, and a multitude of other American arts and crafts, manufactures and implements are the highly personal accumulation of a highly individual woman who was once called "the damnedest grande dame." Mrs. J. Watson Webb had been collecting objects for all of her sixty years when the opportunity arose to create a museum for the magnificent antique carriages that had been in her husband's family for several generations. With the purchase of eight acres of countryside near the Webb family estate in Shelburne, and the erection of a large horseshoe-shaped vehicle barn, Electra Webb was in business. Now she could display all of her own collections as well as the carriages and sleighs. Hearing that an old schoolhouse or an inn had outworn its welcome elsewhere in the state, she would have it moved onto her property. When a 168-foot two-lane covered bridge, the last in Vermont, was about to be replaced with one of steel, she moved it thirty-five miles.

Since no stream crossed her property, she had a lily pond made to fit under the bridge.

Now twenty acres and about thirty structures stand as a memorial to one woman's acquisitive instincts and good taste in old things. Some of the buildings are period houses, furnished by Mrs. Webb with items she had previously acquired. Of the thousands of chairs and tables, old clothes and old teacups stored in a large attic, she invariably found just the right ones to make a room look lovely and lived in (although her lack of adherence to a single style or period did cause these houses to be considered anachronisms by historians). Other buildings serve as galleries devoted to such things as Hats and Fragrance, Quilts and Rugs, Duck Decoys, and mounted game animals bagged by Mrs. Webb herself on hunting trips in northern Canada and Alaska.

But perhaps the high points of a visit that must inevitably be a half-day's ramble are the two-story Colchester lighthouse and the S.S. *Ticonderoga*, a plush Victorian steamboat; both moved here to dry land from Lake Champlain. It took over two months to transport the 892-ton, 220-foot-long sidewheeler two miles overland to Shelburne, where it now towers over such earlier structures as a blacksmith shop, a sawmill, a steam locomotive, and a diminutive private railroad station.

"On the heavily-traveled highways of mid-America in Oklahoma City" the NATIONAL COWBOY HALL OF FAME AND WESTERN HERITAGE CENTER stands, dedicated to "the hardships and struggles, the ideals and aspirations of [the] indomitable pioneers who carved our civilization from a rugged wilderness." Even before the builders' plans materialized, the sponsors were anticipating a "towering Hall of Fame of Great Westerners" with bronze portrait plaques honoring "the trail blazers and empire builders . . . the colonizers and captains . . . the men who, with self-tutored brilliance, composed state constitutions." They described the "chapel-like quietude" of Heritage Hall, in which each of the western states depicts its scenic grandeur. And armed with a supply of superlatives that gave promise of being inexhaustible, they spoke of a Museum of Western History; a Research Library of Western Americana; an Institute of Western Art; an Institute of Western Music and folklore; a Museum of Western Agriculture, Commerce and Industry; a Rodeo Hall of Fame; and a Hall of Fame of Western Television, Motion Pictures and Dramatic Art to honor "the famous names of the entertainment world who have contributed so much to the popu-

larity of the Western theme . . . [and] the classics from that drama-
tist's art [that] have stirred a thousand Americans." Surrounding all
of this is an "open sanctuary," the Western Flora Gardens—"a composite of the entire West itself—a fanciful wonderland of greenery and
blossom that only God could create."

When the ambitious plans being made in Oklahoma City were announced, others elsewhere felt the project was a bit superfluous. A
spokesman for the PANHANDLE-PLAINS HISTORICAL MUSEUM in Canyon, Texas, said it was "obvious . . . that we already have the outstanding Cowboy Museum of the world." The collections to which he
referred included paintings and sketches of western frontier subjects;
European furnishings and Oriental ceramics that had adorned wealthy
ranchers' homes; extensive archives of mercantile, ranching, and agriculture operations; such Indian crafts and artifacts as blankets, baskets, buckskin work, beadwork, and costumes; documents and objects
relating to cowboy life; and natural history exhibits of local fauna,
with habitat groups and such extinct animals as the great lobo wolf.

There were already, in fact, several other museum tributes to the
men who made the West. In Claremore, Oklahoma, the WILL ROGERS
MEMORIAL had been honoring that state's cowboys and a famous native son since 1938. Thirteen dioramas illustrate scenes from the humorist's life, and scrapbooks, manuscripts, gifts, and personal effects
continue the story. Other galleries in the large stone building tell of
the cowboy and his tools in different parts of the world as well as in
the American West.

A monument to another western hero is located at the east entrance
to Yellowstone National Park in Cody, Wyoming. The BUFFALO BILL
MUSEUM is made up of five log buildings patterned after those on
Colonel William Cody's nearby ranch, plus his boyhood home, moved
here from Iowa. Exhibited are stagecoaches, guns, saddles, furniture,
flags, and photographs of the pioneers and cowboys who settled the
area; objects made and used by the Indians of the Northern Plains;
and of course mementos of the famous scout himself. The museum
constitutes half the domain of the Buffalo Bill Memorial Association,
which is working to make its Buffalo Bill Historical Center in Cody
"the country's outstanding memorial to all the white men and red men
who made our Old West the most colorful and most important era in
the broad development of the United States." Its first move in this direction was its commission, in the 1920s, to Gertrude Vanderbilt
Whitney to create an eight-foot-high bronze equestrian statue of Cody

himself. Mrs. Whitney was instrumental in the Association's acquisition of its forty-acre site, and her family and associates made possible the WHITNEY GALLERY OF WESTERN ART which opened in 1959. Here are the treasures of the Association—beautifully decorated Indian garments, rare books, maps and documents, and "Western Americana Art." There are works by Russell plus everything that was found in Remington's studio at the time of his death in 1909—personal effects, fine Indian gear, cowboy accouterments, and more than a hundred oil paintings, sketches, and drawings. The Association, which has begun to create a Fine Arts Center for the Cody area, hopes to foster contemporary art related to western history, and to establish a children's museum devoted to the art and lore of the Old West.

An hour away from Denver, Colorado, the Central City Opera House Association has been managing a revived ghost town since 1932. When gold-bearing quartz was discovered here in 1859, a cluster of communities sprang up around Central City, and the section was known for a while as "the richest square mile on earth." When the surface gold was exhausted, and it became necessary to dig into the rock, experienced miners arrived from Ireland, Germany, Italy, and elsewhere on the continent, and "introduced their culture, their patterns of life. They insisted on music, books, good theater, for these had always been part of their lives. Soon after their arrival, good drama, given in a log theater, became regular recreation." Tickets were paid for in gold dust, and scales were standard box office equipment. A fire in 1874 destroyed most of the town, but brick and stone buildings immediately started to replace the log ones, and in 1878 the new $18,000 Opera House, financed by subscription from the townsfolk, opened. Although opening night was a glittering success, the mining days were just about over. When a new theater in Denver drew the visiting troupes and their audience away, the last hope for Central City's survival disappeared.

Years later a daughter-in-law of one of the builders of the Opera House arranged to have the old theater donated to the University of Denver, where she was a professor of English. Following her lead, others joined a movement to have it restored. A production of *Camille*, starring Lillian Gish and produced especially for the gala reopening by Robert Edmond Jones, was presented before an audience dressed in period costume.

That was the beginning of the Central City Festival. Every year since (with the exception of the war years) it has continued; and a deserted mining camp became a popular summer resort. Many of the surrounding Victorian houses have been restored. Others have been refurbished to complete the telling of the Central City story—the COEUR D'ALENE MINING MUSEUM, a THEATRE MUSEUM, an ANTIQUE VEHICLE MUSEUM, and the TELLER LAW OFFICE MUSEUM which displays paintings of Central City in its heyday along with some of the gold that made it what it was.

Exhibit after exhibit concerned with the history of Christianity can be found at the BIBLE MUSEUM maintained by the Open-Church Foundation in Gloucester, Massachusetts. The collection contains first- and second-century Greek translations on parchment and a rare English Bible of 1577 known as the "Breeches Bible." In it, Adam and Eve "knew that they were naked, and they sewed fig tree leaves together, and made themselves breeches." There is a Martin Luther Bible published in 1710. There is a John Eliot Indian Bible. The history of the Bible is traced, and highlighting a collection dealing with Judaism, there is a Torah, smuggled out of Nazi-occupied Poland, that is believed to be five hundred years old.

The only research museum in the world devoted entirely to the study of coins and medals is the AMERICAN NUMISMATIC SOCIETY which was organized by twelve New Yorkers in 1858. "Devoted to the advancement of numismatic knowledge, especially as it relates to history, art, archaeology, and economics . . ." it not only engages in the collection of coins, medals, tokens, decorations, and paper money, but also maintains a library covering all phases of the field. The Society's collections of ancient Greek and Roman, Byzantine, Far Eastern, and Islamic coins are of special importance; but the medieval and American collections are also good. Among the great collections bequeathed to the Society was that of Edward T. Newell, the Society's president from 1916 until his death in 1941. He left more than 87,000 pieces, many of them from the time of Alexander the Great and his successors. The Society's public exhibits concentrate on telling the story of coins from ancient times to the present and the story of medallic art from the Renaissance to today. The library is the most comprehensive on its subject in America. And there is an active publications program.

Devoted more to display are two comparatively small collections.

One is at the MONEY MUSEUM OF THE NATIONAL BANK OF DETROIT where there are exhibits of ancient, medieval and modern coinage, paper currency, rare gold coins, and primitive media of exchange; and the other is at the CHASE MANHATTAN BANK MONEY MUSEUM in New York, where exhibits range from the Babylonian to the modern. Wooden nickels, Spanish pieces of eight, the rare American Silver Dollar of 1804 (of which only fifteen were minted), personal checks written by Presidents of the United States, and primitive barter items and trinkets from all over the world are among the materials displayed here.

A unique institution that combines "exhibit space, meeting halls, a center devoted to foreign cultures and commerce, and a showcase for city planning" is Philadelphia's COMMERCIAL MUSEUM. It originated seventy years ago in the mind of Professor William P. Wilson, who foresaw the expansion of international trade. Wilson, director of the University of Pennsylvania's School of Biology, visited the World's Columbian Exposition at Chicago where the array of raw materials and manufactured products from every corner of the earth led him to conceive of a permanent means of bringing "before our manufacturers, dealers and consumers, all the varied products of the world, that they may make the best selection for their own special interests." Wilson persuaded Philadelphia's civic and business leaders to purchase Chicago's exhibits when the fair ended and to provide facilities for their display. Ten thousand dollars bought twenty-four railroad carloads of slightly used materials originally valued at half a million dollars. Among the purchases were two hundred jars of reptiles, snakes, and centipedes from Colombia, a paper exhibit from logs to finished product from Germany, medicinal plants from Persia, and rare woods from Mexico, New South Wales, Paraguay, and elsewhere. President McKinley referred to the new enterprise as a "world-industrial object-lesson" when it opened officially in 1897.

In the next three decades an active and multi-faceted program of encouraging foreign trade was pursued. A Foreign Trade Bureau to advise businessmen was established, specialized periodicals were published, and meeting rooms and exhibition facilities for trade shows and other organizations were provided. Meanwhile an educational program was bringing cabinets of display material to hundreds of schools throughout the state. Classes were receiving instruction in the museum's galleries, and illustrated lectures were being given to the community at large. These were all pioneering efforts in the years before any other advisory groups existed to deal with the businessman, before the federal government's Department of Commerce appeared on the scene, and when international trade was a thing of the future. During this period Dr. Wilson himself continued to spearhead the program he had set in motion, and visits by him and by other staff members to fairs and expositions around the world produced acquisitions for the museum that were literally measured by the ton. The Paris Exposition of 1900 alone resulted in the arrival of five hundred tons of specimens in Philadelphia, much of it rare sculpture, costumes, and musical instruments from French Africa which, acquired before the rush for African artifacts, are today considered to be of exceptional quality and value.

But after a remarkable record of accomplishment, the museum began to decline. The death of Dr. Wilson in 1927, the Depression, years of civic corruption and neglect, and finally the presence of other agencies serving the businessman's interests were all factors. Convention Hall, which had been built in 1930 to expand the museum's facilities, began immediately to deteriorate to the point where buckets were needed to catch rain water and tar melting off the roof. But in the 1950s, under a new city administration, its renascence began. Extensive remodeling of the convention and commercial display facilities, rejuvenation of the library, and a $1,500,000 renovation of the museum building itself, have already taken place. And a $14,900,000 modernization of the entire Trade and Convention Center of which the museum is a part is under way. Under a new exhibit policy the museum has become "a showcase [for] the cultures and commerce of foreign countries as well as the Philadelphia area . . . a research and information center for foreign trade and commerce . . . an educational center with an international orientation for the schools and the adult community . . . [as well as] a center to which all foreign visitors would be welcomed, given hospitality and program assistance." "The Philadelphia Panorama" is a permanent exhibit that illustrates the past, present, and projected future of an old city revitalizing itself. Among the best shows of recent years, some of which have entered the permanent galleries in condensed form, have been "Japan Today," "Festival of France," "Festival of Italy," "Ships and Their Stories," "Musical Instruments of Asia-Africa," and "African Crafts." The two African shows made use of newly appreciated treasures that had been gathering dust in the museum's cases for more than six decades.

"I will have the best equipped & largest Laboratory extant, and the facilities incomparably superior to any other for rapid & cheap development of an invention, & working it up into Commercial shape with models patterns & special machinery—In fact there is no similar institution in Existence. We do our own castings forgings Can build anything from a ladys watch to a Locomotive." These words were written by Thomas Edison in 1877 about a cluster of buildings he was putting up in West Orange, New Jersey. His notebook continues: "Inventions that formerly took months & cost a large sum can now be done 2 or 3 days with very small expense . . ."

During the forty-four years he worked here he patented over five hundred inventions—electric motors and generators, incandescent and fluorescent lamps, the Edison alkaline storage battery, the Kinetophone which gave voice to silent films in 1913, and the first long-playing record. The fluoroscope was not patented in order to make it more quickly available to the medical profession.

In 1956 the laboratory, presented to the government by Thomas A. Edison, Inc. (now part of the McGraw-Edison Company), became a national monument. Glenmont, the nearby estate Edison had purchased in 1876 (a many-gabled twenty-three-room house set in a landscaped park, luxuriously appointed with cut velvet curtains, oak paneling, and damask-covered walls) was given to the nation in 1959 by the McGraw-Edison Company and the Edison family. Both were combined into the EDISON NATIONAL HISTORIC SITE in September 1962.

Among the inventions on display within the laboratory structures (on sixteen acres of land) are the first phonograph, some early motion picture equipment, and various types of lamps. The "Black Maria," a tar-papered shack that was the first motion picture studio, is now a theater where old and recent films dealing with the inventor's career are shown. In the library are the cot where he took the naps that enabled him to work day and night, and his own collection of scientific and technical books along with his notebooks, patents, correspondence, and memoranda. Here too is his desk, its contents undisturbed since his death in 1931. The story of his life and achievements are told in a comprehensive exhibit that was originally prepared for the Chicago World's Fair of 1933.

Although there is a case on record of a business executive destroying a collection of old products manufactured by his company, businessmen for the most part have looked with favor upon the idea of setting up company museums. Although they have sometimes proved difficult to maintain, company museums have provided valuable collections and historical records of a wide variety of services and products from the collar to the shoe, from the telephone to the typewriter, from firearms to furniture.

On the banks of the Brandywine near Wilmington, Delaware, is the HAGLEY MUSEUM, which illustrates a portion of the nation's industrial history. "The Brandywine serves as a symbol of an industrial childhood. What happened along the banks of the Brandywine was happening in various degrees up and down the Atlantic coast. The story of this river is the story of industry's role in the making and maintaining of a great new nation." Mills located here ground flour in pre-Revolutionary days. With the arrival in 1802 of Pierre Samuel du Pont and his son, Eleuthère Irénée, one of the nation's best-known companies had its inception, manufacturing gunpowder. Exhibits trace the development of industry in this area: the Stone Age techniques of the Delaware Indians, the waterwheel- and turbine-powered mills, the elaborate complex of buildings of Irénée du Pont's Eleutherian Mills, the expansion of the iron and steel industry in the nineteenth century, and the development of the textile and papermaking industries. An explosives display shows how "the Du Pont experience exemplifies the interaction of national and corporate growth" and how explosives serve in peace and war. Other exhibits illustrate working conditions a hundred years ago as well as the assembly line and mass production. A Black Powder Exhibit Building demonstrates the various steps in the manufacture of this commodity by showing the interiors of an early refinery, a graining mill, a dry house, a glazing mill, and a powder magazine. On grounds that "offer a rare combination of historical interest and natural beauty" there are several old mill buildings, homes occupied by the early Du Ponts, the first office of the company and an old barn. The Eleutherian Mills Library, which contains family manuscripts and business and industrial records goes beyond the Du Pont family; it is a research source for the industrial history of the whole Middle Atlantic States area.

Over a thousand pieces of antique furniture are in the BAKER MUSEUM FOR FURNITURE RESEARCH, located in a wing of the company's factory in Holland, Michigan. The collection was begun by the company's founder, who had bought "pieces which interested him for their color, for their style or just because they were freaks" on his trips abroad. When Mr. Baker found his chief designer paying frequent visits to the room where he had stored his "bunch of junk" he decided to open it "for the study and convenience of students of furniture design and for the furtherance of public interest in the furniture arts and crafts." The collection is displayed under conditions unique for old furniture of museum quality—unrestored, unreconstructed, and neither in chronological nor in "period room" arrangements. There are rows of old chairs, showing the results of years and years of being sat upon. There is a curious table, surely one of Mr. Baker's "freaks," that opens up to become library stairs. An eighteenth-century gadget that might find a market today is an exercising chair of which the seat is a bellows that causes the sitter to bounce up and down. A provincial gallery shows that American, French, Italian, and English country cabinet work share a "certain family resemblance." Books and other study materials have been included for the inspiration of those interested in interior design. And a recent addition has been a room of modern chairs and other furniture created by Finn Juhl, the Danish architect. When the museum opened in 1940, a writer for the New York *Sun* spoke of "visitors [being] instructed, enlightened or amused." They still are.

In the first steel and glass office building in this country (1930, J. D. Leland, architect), the Worcester Pressed Steel Company of Massachusetts operates the JOHN WOODMAN HIGGINS ARMORY. It is named for the company's former president whose love of metal craftsmanship and especially of its culmination in the art of the armorer inspired him to provide it. A chronological arrangement tells the story of the development of armor from steel plates combined with mail, through full armor and decorative armor, to modern armor which is applied to vehicles instead of people. Displays of tools and weapons include Stone Age axes and arrowheads, early shields, swords, lances, crossbows, and other paraphernalia of the medieval knight. An armorer's workshop is complete with forge, anvils, hammers, and other implements. There are artistic iron-crafted objects such as stirrups, strongboxes, locks, and keys; and the Golden Age of armor is further illustrated in paintings, tapestries, stained glass windows, armorial banners, wood carvings, and furniture. The importance of achieving good design in modern pressed metal products is emphasized: "The fact that armor was functional was not a handicap to beauty. . . . Though we excel the past in efficiency, science, understanding and speed of output, we must not lose the feeling . . . that lamps and pots should be beautiful as well as serviceable. Indeed modern machines and modern steels and other metals open new vistas for craftsmanship.

. . . We need to restore zeal and pride of workmanship to present-day workers with machines. . . . Arms and the man we sing and, in praising the artist-craftsmen of long ago, we urge recognition for those of our day who succeed them."

Crane & Co. of Dalton, Massachusetts, began manufacturing fine rag papers for currency, bonds, stock certificates, and social and business correspondence in 1801. One hundred and twenty-nine years later the CRANE MUSEUM, tracing the history of papermaking in America, was opened in the Old Stone Mill, which once utilized the waters of the nearby Housatonic River. Displays include a scale model of the vat house of the first Crane mill (where rags were washed before being turned into the fine final product) and some of the hand molds used by early members of the Crane family.

The GEORGE EASTMAN HOUSE OF PHOTOGRAPHY was opened in 1949 in Rochester, New York, in the former residence of the man who founded the Eastman Kodak Company. It maintains a permanent collection of photographs, motion pictures, apparatus, documents, and books; organizes exhibitions for rental; conducts research in the history of photography and cinematography; and publishes. It is supported through membership and an annual grant from the company. There are three permanent exhibitions: three hundred examples of "The Art of Photography" from the era of Daguerre to the present; a display of popular photographic work known as "Pictures for All"; and visitor-operated devices explaining "The Science and Technology of Photography." Special exhibitions of outstanding camera work by individuals or groups are held several times a year. Films from the Motion Picture Archives of over three thousand titles are shown in a small theater. Always on display are significant pieces from a collection of cameras, lenses, and photographic equipment that is believed to be the largest in the world.

In Corning, New York, the CORNING MUSEUM OF GLASS displays antique and contemporary examples illustrating 3500 years of glass history. A Hall of Science and Industry, glass-blowing demonstrations, an exhibit relating the history of illumination, and a kitchen with virtually all of its equipment made of glass are other features.

The IBM GALLERY OF ARTS AND SCIENCES in New York is home base for an art collection of over five hundred items which spend most of their time circulating to museums, schools and other company exhibit halls elsewhere in the country. IBM got into the art business during the New York World's Fair of 1939, when it acquired for display there a contemporary work from each of the seventy-nine nations with which it had contact. There are ancient and modern Mexican works, American and British portraits, and a group of American contemporary paintings that is recent but not quite *avant-garde*. Old clocks, vintage typewriters, early calculating machines, and models of Leonardo da Vinci inventions and his drawings of them constitute the science collection.

Not just a single company, but the motion picture, television, radio, and recording industries are represented in the HOLLYWOOD FILM MUSEUM. It is sponsored by a star-studded list of individual donors, and located on land contributed by Los Angeles County. The more than $6,000,000 structure, not far from the Hollywood Bowl, will house frequently changing exhibits of great film productions of the past; a reference library; a theater; and demonstrations of how movies, television and radio shows, and recordings are made.

A museum "devoted to the culture of the sea and its tributaries—its conquest by man and its influence on civilization" was started in 1930 in Newport News, Virginia, by Archer M. Huntington. THE MARINERS MUSEUM was dedicated by its founder to his father, who had established in the late nineteenth century the Newport News Shipbuilding and Drydock Company (which in recent years has constructed the liner *United States* and the nuclear-powered aircraft carrier *Enterprise*). Everything from the sea and for the sea that can be imagined, and a lot more, are here: ship's figureheads; builder's half-models; sailors' rope craft and scrimshaw; prints of historic naval actions, reviews, and disasters; portraits of mariners from Columbus, Magellan, and Vespucci to Perry, Farragut, and Dewey; shackles, collars, and leg irons; and navigational instruments and timepieces. Among the examples of lifesaving equipment are a breeches buoy, lifecars, lifeboats, and a lightship. Naval armaments range from bow and arrow and boomerang through boarding pikes and cutlasses to firearms and cannon. Among the china-, glass-, and silverware used on board ship or decorated with marine subjects are Staffordshire statuettes, Liverpool jugs, Lowestoft dinnerware, early English and Dutch goblets, and Bristol glass rolling pins. A tattooing display—inks, lotions, needles, patterns, and a male figure completely covered with designs—came from a shop on the Norfolk waterfront. Among the small craft that are displayed in the exhibit halls, on a lake, or in a roofed boat shelter, there are Portuguese fishing vessels, dugouts from North and South America, a sampan from Shanghai, Eskimo kayaks and a umiak, several birchbark canoes, and a pair of circular bull boats (one of cowhide, the other of bullhide, both made by an Indian named Crow's Heart). Among the more sophisticated small craft are a racing shell, a pleasure barge, a yacht, and a fishing sloop. And in a group of World War II Axis vessels there are a 17-foot Japanese suicide launch made of plywood, a 36-foot Japanese two-man midget steel submarine used for salvage operations, and a German one-man torpedo-shaped submarine.

Among the relics of famous ships are planking and lanterns from the *Maine;* a bronze bolt, a piece of ballast and a piece of the rudder from H.M.S. *Bounty;* copper rivets made by Paul Revere for the *Constitution* ("Old Ironsides") and pieces of its original oak hull; and pieces of the spars and rigging and the 10-foot main cabin skylight from the schooner yacht *America,* for which the "America's Cup" is named. These fragments are exhibited with models, pictures, documents, and other illustrative material pertaining to the well-known vessels from which they came.

There are scale models of the *Merrimac* both before and after iron sheathing transformed that steam frigate into the Confederate ironclad *Virginia,* and of the *Monitor.* The famous engagement, which took place not far from where the museum is located, is illustrated in a "sight and sound" diorama that is part of a "Sea Power in the Civil War" exhibit.

Other displays tell of whaling and fishing, navigation and safety, the Chesapeake Bay area, shipbuilding through the ages, marine engineering, and underwater exploration. The museum sponsors an annual marine photography exhibition, and has a research library of over 40,000 volumes. It is located in an 880-acre park that is a popular recreational area for the community. Commanding works of sculpture by the founder's wife (Anna Hyatt Huntington) and others stand near the museum entrance.

The KENDALL WHALING MUSEUM of Sharon, Massachusetts, was founded by Henry Plimpton Kendall in 1957 to display to the public the literature and objects he spent years accumulating. Here are tools for catching, cutting up, and processing whales; samples of whale products such as oil for light, fuel, and lubrication, and ambergris for perfume; and a completely outfitted whaleboat with eighty-three essential pieces of equipment for a six-man crew. Two galleries display scrimshaw—decoratively carved teeth of the sperm whale, and such useful objects as sewing cabinets, walking sticks, and even piecrust crimpers made of whalebone. Scrimshaw, it is explained, is "the only important indigenous folk art, except that of the Indians, that we have ever had in America." Paintings and prints of whaling life, models of whaling vessels, a substantial library of logs, account ledgers, personal diaries and assorted books and manuscripts, and over two thousand photographs complete Mr. Kendall's remarkable collecting achievement.

Similar exhibits are to be seen on the Massachusetts island of Nantucket, whose WHALING MUSEUM occupies a former candle factory, and in the port of New Bedford, where the WHALING MUSEUM is one stop along the "Moby Dick Trail." Here in the town from which Melville shipped on a voyage that would provide material for his greatest novel, are exhibits showing the shops of the coopers, sailmakers, blacksmiths, and others whose products were needed to equip a whaler for its years-long adventure. A model of a whaler, large enough to be boarded and complete with rigging (which visitors are requested not to climb), and the whaleboat sent out by such a parent ship are major attractions.

On Long Island, the WHALING MUSEUM OF SAG HARBOR in the mansion of a ship owner recalls with similar items the days when this port too was an important center for the industry.

Also on Long Island is the VANDERBILT MUSEUM, end product of the travels of one seagoing man, William K. Vanderbilt, Jr., who presented to Suffolk County the ship models, shells, marine specimens of every description, and curios he had gathered from every part of the world, along with the paintings, tapestries, and other luxurious furnishings of his summer mansion in Centerport.

MYSTIC SEAPORT, an ambitious preservation project in Mystic, Connecticut, is on the site that was once occupied by the Greenman Brothers, master shipbuilders. Today, restored by the Marine Historical Association, are an 1833 countinghouse, an apothecary shop, a figurehead carver's establishment, a print shop, a weaver's, a clock shop, and the Peters Smithship Shop. There are several vessels that can be boarded: the whaler *Charles W. Morgan,* the square-rigger *Joseph Conrad,* and the schooners *Australia* and *Louis A. Dunton.* Cobblestoned Seaport Street, which runs along the harbor, contains the restored buildings and the museum in which ship models, navigational instruments, and graphic art are displayed. And a planetarium shows audiences what early navigators saw in the sky.

One of New York City's two maritime museums is located on Wall Street in the SEAMEN'S BANK FOR SAVINGS, and its most popular feature is a collection of antique coin banks, many in the form of sailors and ships. Marine oil paintings, ship models, and scrimshaw are also on display. And at the SEAMEN'S CHURCH INSTITUTE, a home for merchant seamen, there are more than three hundred ship models as well as figureheads, paintings, photographs, and other objects relating to seafaring.

The SAN FRANCISCO MARITIME MUSEUM features scale models of Pacific Ocean craft, and has a thirty-two-acre outdoor marine and transportation museum. And the full-rigged ship *Balclutha* serves as a "floating museum."

The MARINE LABORATORY MARINE MUSEUM of the University of Florida in Miami ranges the field from mammals to sponges, and serves as a research and identification center.

"When a section of Roman aqueduct, 1900 years old and weighing 3½ tons, is acquired by a transport museum in the American Middlewest," wrote a reporter for the St. Louis *Post-Dispatch* a few years ago, "it highlights the idea that the museum is thinking about its theme in broad and imaginative terms."

A "Showcase of Transportation History" (covering the transportation of water as well as people) is to be found at the NATIONAL MUSEUM OF TRANSPORT in St. Louis. It "presents a distinguished display of more than fifty locomotives and railway cars, a city transit collection representing periods from the horsecar to the motorbus, highway vehicles, and many smaller related items. Here visitors feel the vitality of history by sitting in the cab of a steam locomotive, boarding a double deck bus, or walking into the first railway tunnel bored west of the Mississippi."

The museum originated in the rescue of an old mule-drawn streetcar scheduled for scrapping after many years of dead storage. It was born at a propitious time, in 1944, when railroad lines were rapidly converting from steam to diesel locomotives, when public transportation systems were shifting from trolleys to buses, and transportation companies were glad to co-operate with the new institution and provide obsolete equipment; in most cases, at no cost. It soon outgrew its suburban quarters, and it is now moving to a forty-acre site, across the river, in East St. Louis (thereby becoming a resident of Illinois). Its collections are expanding to include "communications and waterway, pipeline, animal powered and air transportation." It is the only place in the country where a Roman aqueduct could be at home with a Douglas DC-7, an electric railway car, a mid-nineteenth-century locomotive, and the first diesel locomotive in regular service. A walnut-paneled "swank business car" has a lounge, two staterooms (each with bath), kitchen, and a dining room whose table is set with the Delaware and Hudson Line's monogrammed linen, china, glassware, and silver. And for those New Yorkers who long nostalgically for the old double-deck Fifth Avenue buses, both the open and closed models are waiting here.

A fascinating museum that temporarily fell victim to the present-day economic difficulties of the industry it celebrates "opened in July 1953 and operated continuously until May 1958 when [it was] forced to close . . . due to unsatisfactory earnings of the company." The BALTIMORE AND OHIO TRANSPORTATION MUSEUM in Baltimore, Maryland, houses historic equipment in a group of historic railroad structures. It is entered through the Mount Clare Station, probably the oldest in the world, where the first tickets for regularly scheduled passenger trains were sold (seventy-five cents for a twenty-six-mile round trip) in May of 1830. A 22-sided roundhouse built in 1884 serves as the showcase for the locomotives and cars. A third building, which once was an employees' circulating library, contains model bridges, exhibits illustrating the development of rail track and locomotive headlights, historical dioramas, signal equipment, railroad lamps, timepieces, photographs, rail documents, antique toy trains, railroad paintings (many of which were commissioned by the B. & O.), railroad insignia and "tail-end" signs, and the blue china designed by Staffordshire for the B. & O. dedication in 1827.

Among historic locomotives the favorite is a slightly enlarged operating replica of the *Tom Thumb,* designed by Peter Cooper to convince the B. & O. to use steam power instead of horses. The line did in fact use it in 1830, becoming the first railroad to have a train powered by an American-built locomotive. The *Atlantic* was completed in 1832, and saw service for sixty years before being retired to the exhibition grounds; it is still operable. The *John Hancock* of a few years later, also in service for many decades and still operable, was the first locomotive to have a cab for the engineer. Here are a replica of the first locomotive on the B. & O. to have a horizontal boiler, the *Lafayette;*

the locomotive that, when it was new and shiny, won first honors at the Philadelphia Centennial Exposition as the finest and largest ever built, the *Mogul; Old 592,* capable of 100 miles per hour, which rushed pictures of the Dempsey-Tunney fight from Philadelphia to New York, and another time delivered Enrico Caruso to a New York engagement in record time; and the first streamlined diesel-electric locomotive operated in this country. Known as No. 51 (No. 50, not streamlined, is in St. Louis), it made its first run on the B. & O. in May 1937. Rolling stock includes a baggage car of Civil War vintage; a Union Army iron freight car that hauled ammunition; early gondola and hopper cars; and the Imlay coach with a canopied observation platform, a stagecoach adapted to the railroad. Non-rail vehicles include a Conestoga wagon, old fire engines, and other pre-automobile items.

A plaque near the entrance to the Mount Clare building is "in honor of Samuel Finley Breese Morse, inventor of the electric telegraph, and in commemoration of the one hundredth anniversary of the transmission of the prophetic message 'What Hath God Wrought!' . . . sent by Morse himself on May 24, 1844, from the chamber of the Supreme Court, then located in the basement of the Capitol in Washington, D.C. It was received by Alfred Vail, loyal friend and associate of Morse, in the Pratt Street Station of the Baltimore and Ohio Railroad . . . The line conveying this first telegram was erected on the railroad's right-of-way between the two cities."

In a place of honor is "The First Stone of the Baltimore and Ohio R.R." laid on July 4, 1828, by Charles Carroll of Carrollton, last surviving signer of the Declaration of Independence, whose dedication speech contained the statement: "I consider this the most important act of my life, second only to my signing of the Declaration, if even it be second to that."

The collection was begun sixty years before the museum opened, when historic material and replicas were shown at the 1893 Chicago fair. They were used again in St. Louis in 1904. When the B. & O., the nation's first common carrier railroad, marked its centennial in 1927 with the "Fair of the Iron Horse," the collections, much expanded, were shown again. Individual pieces traveled to other fairs, and went on television and motion picture duty. Six years after closing the museum was reopened to the public for a very special event, the "Star-Spangled Banner" Sesquicentennial celebrated during the summer of 1964. Its doors now seem to be open permanently.

Companies, historic societies, and just plain train lovers are responsible for several other museums.

St. Louis also has the MISSOURI PACIFIC LINES MUSEUM in the Missouri Pacific building; collections here include iron and steel rails, headlights, link and pin couplers, surveying equipment; photographs and advertising posters; railroad commemorating stamps from around the world; passes, timetables, and early publications on railroading in Kansas and Missouri.

The COLORADO RAILROAD MUSEUM in Golden, concerned with that state's railroad history, displays locomotives, railway cars, and streetcars.

The State Historical Society of Wisconsin maintains the NATIONAL RAILROAD MUSEUM in Green Bay, which grew out of a private collection. The OHIO RAILWAY MUSEUM in Worthington is a project of a group of "Railfans" who provide loving care and restoration for the old equipment they own. They operate some of it on Sundays between May and November.

The UNION PACIFIC HISTORICAL MUSEUM in Omaha, Nebraska, includes Lincolniana and Indian artifacts in a collection of railroading items put on display by that famous company.

In East Haven, Connecticut, is the BRANFORD TROLLEY MUSEUM, whose founding, inspired by "sentiment and fun," began with the acquisition of twenty-eight acres that included some trolley tracks, poles, and electric rigging formerly part of the regular run between New Haven and the shore towns along Long Island Sound. The collection here includes a crane car, a trolley rotary snowplow, open trolleys, and a pre-World War I passenger car, as well as horse-drawn vehicles of earlier vintage, and a relatively recent car that can manage 80 miles per hour. Photographs and models of electric railway systems and cars are in the main building, named for Frank Sprague who reportedly started in Richmond, Virginia, the first successful city-wide electric railway system. Perhaps the most luxurious trolley car in existence is here—a parlor car with wall-to-wall carpeting, cushioned chairs, and an electric stove built in 1904 to carry Connecticut transportation officials over the trackage under their jurisdiction.

Kennebunkport, Maine, has the SEASHORE TROLLEY MUSEUM, begun in 1939, where more than seventy-five trolleys from England, Australia, New Zealand, Italy, Japan, and the United States are displayed and operated. Similar items are on display at the ILLINOIS ELECTRIC

RAILWAY MUSEUM, on the grounds of a hardware manufacturing company in North Chicago.

Vintage automobiles can be seen in the world's largest auto museum, the LONG ISLAND AUTOMOTIVE MUSEUM in Southampton, New York, which has more than one hundred vehicles including steam-driven jalopies, early trucks, and fire engines. Collecting old cars is a popular hobby, and one authority estimates that there are about eighty motorcar museums, whose contents are of varying quantity and quality, in the country today. Among them is the MUSEUM OF MOTORING MEMORIES in Natural Bridge, Virginia, where costumes of 1900–1940 and license plates, advertisements, and "assorted automobiliana" compete with antique and classic cars for the visitor's attention.

The new WRIGHT MEMORIAL MUSEUM at Kitty Hawk, North Carolina, displays the 1902 glider in which the brothers practiced before constructing their biplane, and reconstructions of the wooden structures that were their workshop, hangar, and living quarters while they were working on the biplane of wire, cloth, and wood that they successfully tested on the nearby sand dunes. In December, 1963, on the sixtieth anniversary of man's first powered flight (that lasted twelve seconds), a new airport was dedicated here, and a replica of the first Wright Flyer was presented to the museum by Astronaut John Glenn.

Although there is no comprehensive armed forces museum in this country, there are quite a few museums devoted to specific aspects of military and naval history.

The UNITED STATES MILITARY ACADEMY, WEST POINT MUSEUM, in New York, displays flags, uniforms, small arms, and other equipment, along with propaganda devices and military posters.

At Fort McClellan in Alabama the WOMEN'S ARMY CORPS MUSEUM, founded in 1955, tells the story of the WACS in photographs, newspaper clippings, scrapbooks, uniforms, insignia, trophies, flags, and documents.

At Fort Sill, Oklahoma, is the U. S. ARMY ARTILLERY AND MISSILE CENTER MUSEUM, established in 1934 and expanded within the last decade. Historic buildings, some of which date from the founding of the military reservation in 1870, include the First HQ School of Fire for Field Artillery and the Old Post Guardhouse. Small arms, swords and uniforms, horse-drawn vehicles, and other early equipment, and artifacts of Plains Indians and frontier settlers tell the story of the establishment of the post here, and of the use of artillery in the last hundred years.

The U. S. ARMY QUARTERMASTER CORPS MUSEUM at the Quartermaster School in Fort Lee, Virginia, contains examples of military garb and equipment, flags, insignia, military horse equipment, paintings and prints of quartermaster generals, and uniforms of various eras.

In the same state are the Marine Corps Schools at Quantico, with its U. S. MARINE CORPS MUSEUM displaying equipment and illustrating the history of the corps.

At the Wright-Patterson Air Force Base near Dayton, Ohio, is the AIR FORCE MUSEUM, containing "thousands of items of historic and interesting equipment relating to the development of aviation . . . fittingly situated within sight of the 'Birthplace of Aviation.'" Organized in 1923 "to provide for the collection, preservation, and display of the aircraft and accessories" of the First World War, it was expanded after World War II to preserve new types of equipment, and it now has 98,000 square feet of display space. Both the exhibits here and the documents in the museum's research section have proved valuable as evidence in presenting the government's case in patent infringement suits.

It is the "largest and most complete military aviation museum in the world." Wright engines are here with jet engines, propellers, gliders, helicopters, instruments, radar, experimental and test equipment, wind tunnels, scale models, and operating models of aircraft and equipment. German and Japanese aircraft, accessories, and paintings are among the World War II additions. "Flight and Fantasy" is an introductory exhibit, presenting "man's fervent desire down through the ages to break the bonds of earth." A full-scale reproduction of the first military airplane, along with the Wright 1909 Flyer and some of the Wrights' equipment recalls the earliest era in aviation. "Warriors with Wings" illustrates the "U. S. Army's aerial participation in World War I"; "Patience and Progress" is a display relating developments between the wars, when technology advanced but military preparedness was minimal. Exhibits on the Second World War emphasize precision high-altitude daylight bombing, long-range fighter escort, and aircrew survival. "Our Independent Air Force in Action" tells about achievements during the Berlin Airlift and the Korean conflict, breaking the sound barrier, the ram-jet engine, and other technological achievements of the decade from 1945 to 1954. The "Aerospace" displays bring the coverage up to date. And hanging in an Art Gallery are paintings and drawings having to do with air force activities.

The NAVAL AVIATION MUSEUM at the Naval Air Station in Pensacola opened in 1963. It has since put together the most comprehensive exhibit of its kind in the country. In 1914 when the U.S.S. *Mississippi* arrived in Pensacola Bay with seven aircraft, as many pilots, and twenty-five enlisted men—the nation's entire complement of personnel trained in naval aviation—this aspect of military operations was begun. The station here is now the world's largest. In the museum are photographs, scale models (including one of the first aircraft carrier, U.S.S. *Ranger*), reconstructions of early aircraft, and other materials pertaining to the forty-year history of naval aviation. And a survival exhibit demonstrates how pilots are trained to cope with environments from the equator to the Arctic.

The Navy Yard in Washington, D.C., was once named the Naval Gun Factory, and on its waterfront stands an old building, known a century ago as the Breech Mechanism and Gun Shop. Now it houses the brand-new UNITED STATES NAVAL HISTORICAL DISPLAY CENTER, a museum intended for the inspiration of servicemen as well as for the information of laymen. From a diorama of the famous Revolutionary engagement between the *Bon-Homme Richard* and the *Serapis* to a spigot that only a short time ago dispensed Cuban water at the naval base at Guantanamo, the nation's naval history emerges. Uniforms of all periods, a case of tinned food found at the Antarctic fifty years after Captain Robert F. Scott left it there, tools used to build the *Monitor,* a death mask of Admiral Dewey, model ships of varied vintages, and a model drydock—these are among the tangible remains of our Navy's past. Temporarily present are twenty-four ship models from the collection of President Kennedy, ultimately intended for the Kennedy Memorial Library in Cambridge, Massachusetts. And the Presidential yacht *Honey Fitz,* escorted by a patrol boat renumbered PT-109, stands at the dock just outside the museum building.

Also in the capital is the TRUXTON-DECATUR NAVAL MUSEUM, maintained by the Naval Historical Foundation, which emphasizes the exploits of the Marine Corps and the Coast Guard.

The U. S. NAVAL ACADEMY MUSEUM at Annapolis, Maryland, deals with naval history in terms of art and ship models; it is primarily a teaching collection designed for midshipmen.

At Port Hueneme, California, the U. S. Navy maintains the SEABEE

MUSEUM, which tells the story of that branch of the service, and displays carvings made by Seabees during the Second World War.

One hundred years after Abner Doubleday laid out a rough diamond in a Cooperstown, New York, cow pasture in 1839, and explained the rules of a new game to an audience that could not have suspected its future greatness, the NATIONAL BASEBALL HALL OF FAME AND MUSEUM was opened in that very town and dedicated "to the pioneers who were the moving spirits of the game in its infancy . . . to the players who have been elected to the Hall of Fame . . . [and] to all America." The project began when Stephen C. Clark, whose family was living in the Cooperstown area when the game originated, purchased Doubleday's baseball. (Subsequently Clark would become the prime sponsor of the Farmers' Museum and Village Crossroads that make the town a mecca for Americana as well as sports fans.) Clark soon hit upon the idea of displaying the historic baseball with other relics of the sport in a public room in the town. Then the presidents of both major leagues and the baseball commissioner became interested in expanding the project, and members and fans of all leagues—major, minor, college, and high school—contributed funds and materials. In a building that has been expanded several times "are gathered treasured mementoes representing more than a century of baseball's glorious past. Devotees of baseball from all over the world daily stream through the hushed rooms, filled with nostalgia as they examine priceless relics of the sport they love." The Hall of Fame is the "rarest of accolades" that "represents the ultimate goal of every player . . . fewer than a hundred players out of the ten thousand who have trod major league diamonds have been elected . . . [They are] the cream of the cream, the stars that shine with a brilliance destined never to be dimmed." Lockers contain the uniforms of Lou Gehrig and Babe Ruth. There are photographs of every President, from William Howard Taft on, throwing out the first ball of the season for an American League team in Washington, and the baseball autographed by each. The statistical achievements of major league players of past and present line the walls of one large room. A display honors members of the "200 Home Run Club." Trophies and accounts of Little League and other youngsters' baseball activities are shown. An exhibit that shows how gloves, bats, and balls are manufactured; the home plate and cornerstone from old Ebbets Field; and an assortment of objects of nostalgic or historic significance are all here. Any baseball argument imaginable can be settled in the library, which contains the box scores of thousands of major and minor league games, the world's largest collection of books on baseball, and a historian "on duty at all times to answer questions raised by fans, sports writers and announcers."

The NATIONAL SKI HALL OF FAME is in Ishpeming, Michigan, where one of the first ski clubs in the country was formed in 1887 and where the National Ski Association was formed in 1904. Two floors of exhibits honor with plaques, photographs, and trophies male and female greats in the sport. And skiing equipment of the past and present is shown. A replica of the oldest known ski in the world, found in Sweden and believed to be more than four thousand years old, was a gift from the Swedish Ski Association. The 12- and 14-foot long hickory boards that were in use a hundred years ago, and the broomstick-type poles that went with them, can be seen as well as skis made for horses, old photographs of skiers and their garb, and historical records.

The NATIONAL MUSEUM OF THOROUGHBRED RACING in Saratoga, New York, with its trophies, and paintings of horses, is opposite the famous race course in the town where the first thoroughbred race in the United States took place in 1863. In Goshen, New York, the HALL OF FAME OF THE TROTTER has Currier & Ives prints and famous sulkies and high-wheelers in a fifty-year-old stable. And there is a library in a new wing.

The NATIONAL PROFESSIONAL FOOTBALL HALL OF FAME is a recent arrival in Canton, Ohio, the town where professional football was begun with the election of Jim Thorpe as first president of the league. Thorpe is, of course, one of those honored here with a bronze bust and a painting, while trophies, balls, uniforms, and pictures illustrate varied aspects of the game.

At the Newport Casino, where the annual invitation tennis tournament is played, is the NATIONAL LAWN TENNIS HALL OF FAME AND TENNIS MUSEUM. The Casino was designed by Stanford White in 1881. Displayed are trophies, equipment, and pictures of famous players in action.

And in Indianapolis is the MOTOR SPEEDWAY MUSEUM with its Auto Racing Hall of Fame, displaying cars that figured in important races in the past, and honoring famous manufacturers as well as racers.

More than one hundred communities throughout the country have general museums that offer some combination of programs in art, science, and history, with special instruction for children. One of the best of these is the NEWARK MUSEUM.

The idea for it was John Cotton Dana's. As librarian of the city of Newark he turned one room of the library building into an "Art Museum," the other into a "Science Museum." Between 1902 and 1908, he held fifty-six exhibitions. One of them, given over to Japanese prints and other Oriental objects that belonged to George T. Rockwell, was such a success that it made clear the need for a full-fledged museum. The Newark Museum Association was therefore chartered in 1909. The Rockwell Collection was then procured and paid for by the city. The important Edward N. Crane Memorial Collection of Tibetan objects was acquired. And a science collection that had been previously given to the library by a local physician, Dr. William S. Disbrow, was turned over to the new organization. During the next decade, one lively exhibit was held after another. Then in 1922 the city bought a plot of land and the wealthy merchant, Louis Bamberger, made known his intention of putting up a museum building at his own expense. "It is the greatest pleasure of my life," he said.

It was Mr. Dana's show from that point on. One of the first things he did was announce the need for "a new kind of museum worker." He explained that this would be "an intelligent person, preferably young, who has added, by apprenticeship, to a native good sense and sympathy and a sound formal education a certain skill in social manner and in the task of so introducing dead objects to fairly sensitive human beings as to make that introduction stimulative, suggestive, and even educative to those human beings who form, of course, the museum's visiting public." To fill the need for this new kind of worker, he started the first museum apprentice course in the country.

Eventually the subject of history was added to the program. The museum prospered and expanded; Mr. Dana all the while illustrating his philosophy that "much can be done . . . with simple things—objects of nature and daily life—as well as with objects of great beauty." He believed furthermore that "a museum should also reflect our industries—be stimulating and helpful to our workers and promote interest in the products of our own time."

Having housed a German applied arts display in 1912, the first exhibit of industrial art in an American museum, Newark's galleries reviewed "Aviation: A Newark Industry" in 1932, and fifteen years later the "Pottery and Porcelain of New Jersey, 1688–1900." And this was the first American museum to exhibit American primitive painting and sculpture.

American art is an important aspect of Newark's collections. The eighteenth, nineteenth, and twentieth centuries are well represented, as are artists of the city of Newark and the state of New Jersey. There are works by Bellows, Guy Pène du Bois, Sloan, Glackens, George Luks, Robert Henri, Hopper, Sheeler, Georgia O'Keeffe, Kuniyoshi, Ben-Zion, and Joseph Stella (his five-part *New York Interpreted*). Copley, Ralph Earl, Sully, Thomas Cole, Edward Hicks, Joseph Pickett (*George Washington Under the Council Tree*), Inness, Ryder, Sargent, and Prendergast are among the others on the roster.

The ethnological collections are from America, Africa, and Oceania, and the science department covers the fields of ornithology, entomology, conchology, general zoology, botany, and mineralogy. There is an excellent Junior Museum, and there is a small planetarium.

The GRAND RAPIDS PUBLIC MUSEUM is a general museum concerned with "the story of nature in Michigan and beyond," "the story of man in all ages and places," "Memory Lane" (a Grand Rapids street of 1895 that has a barbershop, harnessmaker's shop, pharmacy, millinery shop, general store, gunsmith's shop, and fire station), programs for children, and a planetarium.

Ethnic, racial, and religious chauvinism in the "melting pot" account for a varied group of American museums. Art and history collections pertaining to the Negro are at the GEORGE WASHINGTON CARVER MUSEUM of Tuskegee Institute in Alabama (African and American Negro art); the HOWARD UNIVERSITY GALLERY OF ART in Washington, D.C. (African Negro sculpture is shown as part of a general teaching collection of American painting, sculpture and graphic work, and European graphics); and the archives of the ASSOCIATION FOR THE STUDY OF NEGRO LIFE AND HISTORY in the same city. The CARNEGIE LIBRARY of Wilberforce University, an African Methodist Episcopal school near Xenia, Ohio, contains art and memorabilia of William Wilberforce (1759–1833), British member of parliament and abolitionist who worked for the cessation of the slave trade throughout the empire. The Ohio Historical Society maintains the HARRIET BEECHER STOWE HOUSE in Cincinnati as a museum of the history of the Negro in Ohio, and the PAUL LAURENCE DUNBAR HOUSE in Dayton, furnished with the possessions of the Negro poet.

Washington's new MUSEUM OF AFRICAN ART, the only one in the

country concerned exclusively with this subject, is located in the Capitol Hill residence of Frederick Douglass, a former slave who was the first Negro to become a statesman in this country. A sculpture garden in the brick patio displays African work in juxtaposition with European and American art that it has influenced. The museum is a project of the Center for Cross-Cultural Communication, a non-profit institution established by a former Foreign Service officer whose official concerns for a ten-year period had been cultural exchange programming. The purpose and hope of the new gallery is "to foster a better understanding of the African peoples, their culture and their art."

In Chicago the POLISH MUSEUM OF AMERICA is about to get a modern, two-million-dollar lake-front building that will be a "MONUMENT to the lives, efforts and contributions" of immigrants of that nationality "who helped to make this our beloved, the United States of America, the greatest country on the face of the earth." It began more than thirty years ago with archives and objects of the Polish Roman Catholic Union of America. It is now dedicated to "ALL American Polonia." There is a memorial to Paderewski that includes a reconstruction of the New York hotel room in which the pianist-composer died. (Authentically furnished, it contains the chair the artist was accustomed to take on tour with him and his piano, as he left it, with a Chopin work on its rack.) There is a collection of letters, manuscripts, paintings, medals, coins, and other memorabilia of General Kosciuszko, the man who fought for liberty in the Revolutionary War and returned to his own country to battle for Polish independence. There are documents of General Pulaski, whose shorter life saw him engaged in the same struggles, and who initiated the use of cavalry in the American Revolution before his death in that cause in 1779. The Helen Modjeska collection contains costumes, masks, costume sketches, playbills and photographs of the Shakespearean actress who achieved fame in two countries. Other exhibits are of folk art, including Easter eggs, dolls, and wood carvings; reminders of the pioneer life of Polish immigrants; and paintings by Polish artists. In the archives and library divisions are manuscripts, documents, books, newspapers, magazines, photographs, maps, films, and recordings relating to Polish literature and history.

Norwegian contributions to the United States are documented at the NORWEGIAN-AMERICAN HISTORICAL MUSEUM of Luther College, Decorah, Iowa; at the BELOIT HISTORICAL MUSEUM in Wisconsin; and by the NORWEGIAN-AMERICAN HISTORICAL ASSOCIATION of St.

Olaf College in Northfield, Minnesota. And in 1938 the AMERICAN-SWEDISH HISTORICAL MUSEUM of Philadelphia was dedicated by the Crown Prince of Sweden during the tercentenary anniversary of the settlement of the Delaware Valley by Swedes. It was financed by the contributions of more than twenty thousand descendants of Swedish immigrants. The name of John Morton—a Revolutionary hero who cast the deciding vote in the Pennsylvania delegation for ratification of the Declaration of Independence—appears over the doorway of the building. (Sweden, furthermore, was the first European country to recognize the United States.) Exhibits here honor the "Swedish Nightingale," Jenny Lind; Fredericka Bremer, novelist and feminist who wrote of her travels in mid-nineteenth-century America; and John Ericsson, inventor and marine engineer who designed and built the *Monitor*. Handicrafts, folk arts, and the achievements of other Swedish-Americans are also on display.

In Philadelphia, too, is the CARL SCHURZ MEMORIAL FOUNDATION, concerned with the promotion of cultural relations between Americans and German-speaking peoples, and exhibiting art and handicrafts of German and German-American workers.

The GARIBALDI AND MEUCCI MEMORIAL MUSEUM on Staten Island, New York, is in the house where Antonio Meucci, inventor of a forerunner of Bell's telephone, lived and died. It recalls the Risorgimento wars in paintings, prints, photographs, guns, sabers, uniforms, and military decorations.

The LOVELY LANE MUSEUM OF THE BALTIMORE CONFERENCE METHODIST HISTORICAL SOCIETY in Maryland is concerned with Methodist church history and displays costumes, archives, and religious objects.

The PRESBYTERIAN HISTORICAL SOCIETY of Philadelphia has portraits, communion tokens, and archives illustrating the history of that church in the United States.

Materials pertaining to the Lutheran Church in America are on display at the CONCORDIA HISTORICAL INSTITUTE in St. Louis. They include Reformation and Lutheran medals and coins; and costumes, crafts, and works by Lutheran artists.

Aspects of Jewish history are illustrated in the JEWISH MUSEUM of Hebrew Union College in Cincinnati and the JEWISH MUSEUM of the Jewish Theological Seminary in New York, both of which show contemporary work by Jewish artists as well as ceremonial objects. Both touch on such matters as biblical archaeology and synagogue architecture through the ages. At the B'NAI B'RITH MUSEUM in Washington, art is combined with social history. There might at one time be, in addition to a show of paintings that recall East European Jewish communities, displays of "Jewish contributions to the American Labor Movement"; the latter featuring personal mementos of Samuel Gompers and documents relating to the pioneer work of Jewish unions in creating a program of social welfare.

One of the newest categories of museum to make its presence felt throughout the country is the Presidential library. The pioneer in this field was Franklin D. Roosevelt who, in 1938, outlined a plan to house his mass of documents, correspondence, pictures, and just plain things on his family estate at Hyde Park, New York, in a museum and library building for which the funds would be privately raised. The next year legislation was enacted that would set a precedent for the National Archivist to take title to and co-ordinate the activities of this and every future Presidential library. Until that time the papers of Presidential administrations were centralized in the Library of Congress; but this proved unwieldy, and administrations from that of Hoover on can now be studied at sites related to the lives of the Presidents and selected by them.

The FRANKLIN D. ROOSEVELT LIBRARY AND HOME, now maintained by the National Park Service, was not only the first but is the only one to have been opened during the administration to which it refers. On display in the house where the President was born are family furnishings, carriages, cars, the largest collection of American naval prints and paintings, ship models, and all of the gifts, mementos, and "oddities" that Roosevelt acquired. Objects still continue to arrive weekly. The million-dollar separate library building contains more than 20, 000,000 manuscripts and 33,000,000 books. A million-dollar addition, to be paid for with donations raised by the Eleanor Roosevelt Memorial Foundation, will increase the library's facilities for research, exhibits, and discussions by 50 per cent. The average annual attendance here is 200,000, although this figure has been doubled in some years. It opened in 1940.

The HARRY S. TRUMAN LIBRARY at Independence, Missouri, displays political cartoons, murals by Thomas Hart Benton, and a reproduction of the President's White House office. Research materials center on American foreign policy in the twentieth century and the history and problems of the Presidency. A coin collection that was originally put together by Truman's Secretary of the Treasury, John W. Snyder, and valued at $50,000, includes an example of every coin minted in this country, arranged chronologically according to the Presidential administration in which it was struck. When thieves stole the original collection in 1962, a leading coin dealer, Stack's of New York, organized a drive to replace it, and on Mr. Truman's eightieth birthday in May 1964 a nearly complete replacement set—about 450 coins contributed by more than 150 collectors—was presented.

The DWIGHT D. EISENHOWER LIBRARY at Abilene, Kansas, and the HOOVER PRESIDENTIAL LIBRARY in West Branch, Iowa, have been established in the last few years, and public contributions are being sought for the KENNEDY PRESIDENTIAL LIBRARY AND MUSEUM in Cambridge, Massachusetts, which will be the first of the Presidential libraries to attempt a representation of "a complete record of a Presidential era," Mr. Kennedy having reportedly requested members of his administration to preserve their personal as well as official papers for inclusion.

Walter Muir Whitehill, writing in 1962 about the "magnetism of the presidency" that draws large numbers of Americans annually to these library-museums, commented that "no independent historical society has or is likely to have a legitimate popular attraction as potent as the memory of Franklin D. Roosevelt or the living presence of Harry S. Truman."

There are other libraries that attract the museum-goer. Foremost among them is the LIBRARY OF CONGRESS, whose prints and photographs division has been hailed as a "storehouse of offbeat art treasures" and "the biggest and mixedest graphic grab bag in this country if not in the world"—posters, architectural drawings, engravings, over 70 million feet of motion picture film, photographs, and fine historic and contemporary prints being just a few categories represented.

Original documents of American history—the Declaration of Independence, the Constitution, and the Bill of Rights among them—are in the NATIONAL ARCHIVES.

In New York the PIERPONT MORGAN LIBRARY is noted for its Byzantine enamels, its drawings and etchings by old masters including Rembrandt, its illuminated manuscripts from the sixth to the sixteenth centuries, its old, rare and beautiful books and fine bindings (from cuneiform tablets through the Gutenberg Bible to the present), and its autographed manuscripts of Dickens' *Christmas Carol,* Thackeray's

Classical Gallery, New Wing, Cleveland Museum of Art.

A typical exhibit in the main gallery at the Cranbrook Academy of Art, Bloomfield Hills, Michigan.

9

The Panoroll, a ninety-foot moving mural that portrays sixty million years of mammal evolution in fifteen minutes. In the Fossil Mammal Hall, Carnegie Museum, Pittsburgh.

Carnegie Museum.

Chicago Natural History Museum.

School children confront the prehistoric past at the Chicago Natural History Museum.

Harvey Croze. Cranbrook.

The orrery just outside of the exceptional Mineral Hall at the Cranbrook Institute of Science, Bloomfield Hills, Michigan.

Chicago Museum of Science and Industry

The coal mine at the Chicago Museum of Science and Industry.

The Arizona-Sonora
Desert Museum showing the
Desert Tunnel outside and in.

Arizona-Sonora Desert Museum
photo by Ray Manley.

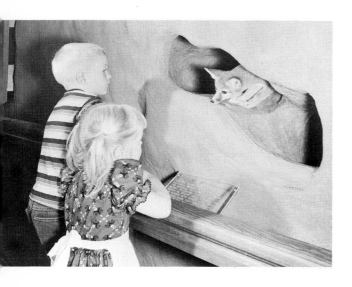

The late Anna Billings Gallup, who started the children's museum movement in Brooklyn, with John Ripley Forbes, its most active advocate today.

An astronomy demonstration in the Brooklyn Children's Museum Planetarium.

Courtesy of the Brooklyn Children's Museum

The Buffalo Bill Museum and Whitney Gallery of Western Art, Buffalo Bill Historical Center, Cody, Wyoming.

A sister's bedroom, Shaker Museum, Old Chatham, New York.

Louis B. Frohman, Bronxville.

Interior of a sod house, Nebraska State Historical Society Museum, Lincoln.

Nebraska State Historical Society.

Front parlor of the Harrison Gray Otis House (1795), Boston.

The Society for the Preservation of New England Antiquities.

"The Farmer's Year" exhibit, Farmers' Museum, Cooperstown, New York.

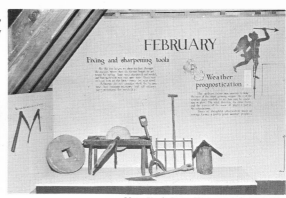

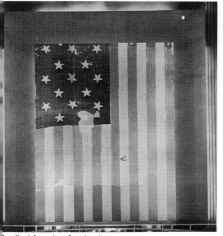

The original Star-Spangled Banner, Flag Hall, Museum of History and Technology, Washington, D.C.

The Ancient Wing of he John Woodman Higins Armory, Worcester, Massachusetts.

Main Gallery of the Mariners' Museum, Newport News, Virginia.

Façades, U.S.A.

Harvey Croze, Cranbrook.

Cranbrook Academy of Art, Bloomfield Hills, Michigan.

Carnegie Instit

Carnegie Institute Building, Pittsburgh.

Museum of Science, Boston, Massachusetts.

Museum of Science, Science Park, Boston.

National Park Serv

Dinosaur Quarry Visitor Center, Dinosaur National Monument, Vernal, Utah.

California Academy of Sciences.

Steinhart Aquarium, California Academy of Sciences, San Francisco.

The Whitney Museum, O. Winston L

Scale model of the new building of the Whitney Museum of American Art, New York, scheduled for completion in 1966.

Vanity Fair, and Balzac's *Eugenie Grandet.* The NEW YORK PUBLIC LIBRARY has outstanding collections of prints, stamps, paintings, rare editions and fine bindings, and theatrical and dance materials that include photographs, programs, and costume and set sketches.

The FREE LIBRARY OF PHILADELPHIA has 8000 prints relating to common law; a group of rare bookplates; Fraktur (these are birth, baptism, and marriage certificates issued by the Pennsylvania German community illustrated by local primitive artists); and drawings and other graphic works by Dickens.

In Texas the SAN ANTONIO PUBLIC LIBRARY has the Harry Hertzberg Circus Collection of 20,000 photographs, paintings, prints, route books, scrapbooks and other assorted items relating to the American circus, including a miniature circus under canvas.

The BOSTON PUBLIC LIBRARY has a print collection; murals by Puvis de Chavannes and Sargent; paintings by Copley, Greuze, and Homer; sculpture and dioramas illustrating Dickens' London, *Alice in Wonderland,* and the *Arabian Nights.* The BOSTON ATHENAEUM has prints and photographs of New England. The ENOCH PRATT FREE LIBRARY of Baltimore has prints of that city and a collection of unusual bookplates. The ST. LOUIS PUBLIC LIBRARY has a costume collection in addition to photographs of Mississippi steamboats, river life, nineteenth-century buildings in the city, and the Louisiana Purchase Exposition of 1904. The CALIFORNIA STATE LIBRARY in Sacramento has historical materials, maps, and old prints.

The JOSIAH C. TRENT LIBRARY at the Medical Center of Duke University in Durham, North Carolina, has portraits, etchings, and drawings on medical subjects, and a collection of medical instruments.

Libraries elsewhere have non-book collections that range from the H. C. BULL MEMORIAL LIBRARY AND MUSEUM of Cokato, Minnesota, with about 2000 items of pioneer handicrafts and implements, and the PONCA CITY LIBRARY in Oklahoma with its Indian Museum of costumes, basketwork, beadwork, and Catlin drawings; through the CHICAGO PUBLIC LIBRARY's Memorial Hall displays of Civil War objects and the BILL MEMORIAL LIBRARY of Groton, Connecticut, with mounted butterflies and birds, and local historical documents and objects; to the BERKSHIRE ATHENEUM in Pittsfield, Massachusetts, which displays scrimshaw, first editions, correspondence, and some personal effects of Herman Melville in the city where *Moby Dick* was written.

Elsewhere, a charming tiled gallery surrounding an interior garden court is devoted lovingly to "the art of the book"; this is LA CASA DEL

LIBRO in Old San Juan, Puerto Rico, which occupies the first Spanish building to be restored as part of the preservation project that has turned a run-down district into the pride of a city.

The only structure in the country combining a library, a museum, and a mausoleum is the GENERAL DOUGLAS MACARTHUR MEMORIAL in Norfolk, Virginia, the hero's adopted home town. MacArthur never saw the city's tribute to him, having died less than two months before the Memorial Day dedication of the $650,000 rebuilt courthouse. The money for it was raised by public subscription, and the Memorial is expected to be a major tourist attraction in the city where the general's mother had lived, and where he would have been born had not military orders transferred his father to Little Rock, Arkansas. A marble rotunda containing the sarcophagus (encircled by the flags of thirty regiments the general once commanded) is surrounded by nine rooms with displays ranging from his famous cap and corncob pipes, to service medals and ribbons, editorial cartoons, and various papers and other mementos.

Little Rock has turned the building in which the general was born into the ARKANSAS ARTS CENTER in MacArthur Park.

With startling energy, frequent sensitivity, and occasional vulgarity, our museums—as America itself—have grown. Each year, pushed along by people taking delight in their own enthusiasms, new museums are born. There is no end to collecting; no end to the impulse to leave something behind—a souvenir or a whole heritage—for a future generation.

ACKNOWLEDGMENTS AND
BIBLIOGRAPHIC NOTES

WE thank Barbara W. Tuchman for the refuge she provided by endowing the Wertheim Study at the New York Public Library. We thank the staff there, the staff at the Metropolitan Museum of Art library, and the staff at the American Museum of Natural History library. We thank the many museum directors, curators, and public relations people who answered our queries and sent us gracious letters; and we apologize for resisting the strong urge to write each of them a personal note of appreciation. We thank that best of all editors, Margaret Cousins, for her patience and advice. And we thank Shirley Burke, our agent, for being always a friend.

In addition to books and periodicals, we consulted hundreds of handbooks, catalogues, annual reports, bulletins, and other publications of the museums themselves; the oldest of them reliably preserved at the Central Research Library of the New York Public Library. Where sources are adequately identified in the body of the text we have not duplicated them here. The lists that follow are, of necessity, selective.

Chapter I: BACKGROUND

The most complete appraisal of the American museum until 1939 is Laurence Vail Coleman's *The Museum in America* (Washington, D.C.: The American Association of Museums, 1939) which we found an invaluable source. Two other books by the same author that were additionally valuable to us are *College and University Museums* (Washington, D.C.: American Association of Museums, 1942) and *Museum Buildings* (Washington, D.C.: American Association of Museums, 1950).

Two sources for the early years of America's first museum are *The Charleston Museum: Its History, Collections, Activities,* Leaflet No. 24, (Charleston, South Carolina: The Charleston Museum, 1949) and *Charleston Library Society Rules and By Laws* (Charleston, South Carolina: 1785).

Sources for the story of Charles Willson Peale's Philadelphia Museum include *Peale's Museum Gallery of Oil Paintings . . . Catalogue of the national portrait and historical gallery* . . . (Philadelphia: M. Thomas & Sons, 1854); Jessie Poesch, ed., *Titian Ramsey Peale and His Journals of the Wilkes Expedition,* Memoirs, Vol. 52, (Philadelphia: American Philosophical Society, 1961); and Charles Willson Peale and A. M. F. J. Beauvois, *A Scientific and Descriptive Catalogue of Peale's Museum* (Philadelphia: 1796).

Among sources for our description of the contrast between the development of the museum in the Old World and in America are Charles Schuchert, "The Rise of Natural History Museums in the United States," *Peabody Museum of Natural History, Bull. 1, No. 1, Addresses delivered on the occasion of the dedication of the New Museum Building* (New Haven, Connecticut: Peabody Museum, 1925) and L. C. Everard, "Museums and Exhibitions," *Encyclopedia of the Social Sciences* (New York: Macmillan, 1933). Walter Pach's statement regarding this contrast is in *The Art Museum in America* (New York: Pantheon, 1948).

Information about Messrs. Pintard, Baker, Savage, Scudder, and Barnum was drawn in part from Robert M. and Gale S. McClurg, "Tammany's Remarkable Gardiner Baker," *New-York Historical Society Quarterly* (New York: New-York Historical Society, April 1958) and Loyd Haberly, "The American Museum from Baker to Barnum," ibid. (July 1959).

James Flexner's description of the tastemakers of early America is from his foreword to Mary Bartlett Cowdrey's *American Academy of Fine Arts and American Art Union* (New York: New-York Historical Society, 1953).

The description of the founding of the Philadelphia Academy of Natural Sciences was based partly upon material from J. H. Slack, M.D., ed., *Handbook to the Museum of the Academy of Natural Sciences of Philadelphia* (Philadelphia: 1862); and W. S. W. Ruschenberger, M.D., surgeon, USN, *A Notice of the Origin, Progress and present condition of the Academy of Natural Sciences of Philadelphia* (Philadelphia: 1852).

The story of the Columbian Institute of Washington is based upon material found in George Brown Goode, "Genesis of the United States National Museum," *Annual Report,* Smithsonian Institution Bull. 101 (Washington, D.C.: 1897), pp. 273–380.

Rembrandt Peale's activities in Baltimore were recalled in *Rendezvous for Taste: Peale's Baltimore Museum, 1814 to 1830* (Baltimore: Municipal Museum, 1956).

Sources for early museums in Boston include *The New England Museum of Natural History, Milestones, 1830–1939* (Boston: The Boston Society of Natural History, 1930); *Catalogue of the . . . collection of the Boston Museum and Gallery of Fine Arts* (Boston: 1844); and several guidebooks: Abel Bowen, *Picture of Boston* (Boston: 1829, 1838), Edward Stanwood, *Boston Illustrated* (Boston: 1875), and *King's Handbook of Boston* (Boston: 1878).

Among sources for our description of the founding and activities of the Smithsonian Institution are Goode, op. cit., and C. G. Abbot, *The Smithsonian Institution* (Washington, D.C.: Government Printing Office, 1941).

New York City's instructions to the American and Metropolitan Museums after granting them fiscal benefits are quoted in Laurence Vail Coleman, *The*

Museum in America, Vol. I (Washington, D.C.: *American Association of Museums,* 1939).

The quotation from the Constitution of the American Association of Museums as well as the story of its founding were drawn from its *Proceedings,* Vol. 1, "Organization and Minutes, first meeting" (Washington, D.C.: American Association of Museums, 1907).

John D. Rockefeller, Jr.'s involvement with trailside museums is described by his biographer, Raymond B. Fosdick, in Chapter XVI of *John D. Rockefeller, Jr. A Portrait* (New York: Harper & Brothers, 1956).

References for the internal structure of museums include Everard, op. cit.; S. A. Barrett, "Training for Museum Work," *Papers & Reports, 21st Annual Meeting* (Washington, D.C.: American Association of Museums, 1926); and *Careers in Museum Work* (Chicago: The Institute for Research, 1939). Current museum placement information can be obtained from individual institutions or the American Association of Museums (2306 Massachusetts Ave. N.W., Washington 8, D.C.).

The museologist who said, "examples set by museum collections have no appreciable influence . . ." was John Cotton Dana in *Should Museums Be Useful?* (Newark, New Jersey: The Newark Museum, 1927).

The American Association of Museums' definition of a museum was reported by Gay Talese, "What Is Museum? Heckscher Asks," New York *Times* (June 7, 1962).

Chapter II: ART

A. Selected Book List:

Behrman, S. N. *Duveen.* New York: Random House, 1952.

Cairns, Huntington and John Walker, eds. *Great Paintings from the National Gallery of Art.* New York: Macmillan Company, 1952.

Carter, Morris. *Isabella Stewart Gardner and Fenway Court.* Boston: Houghton Mifflin, 1940.

Cartwright, W. Aubrey. *Guide to Art Musems in the United States: East Coast—Washington to Miami.* New York: Duell, Sloan and Pearce, 1958.

Faison, S. Lane, Jr. *A Guide to the Art Museums of New England.* New York: Harcourt Brace and Company, 1958.

Fosdick, Raymond B. *John D. Rockefeller, Jr. A Portrait.* New York: Harper & Brothers, 1956.

Gardner, Helen. *Art Through the Ages.* New York: Harcourt, Brace and Company, 1948.

Gilbert, Dorothy B., ed. *American Art Directory.* American Federation of Arts. New York: Bowker, 1961.

Harvey, George. *Henry Clay Frick, The Man.* New York: The Frick Collection, 1936.

Howe, Winifred. *A History of the Metropolitan Museum of Art.* 2 vols. New York: The Metropolitan Museum of Art, 1913–1946.

Newmeyer, Sarah. *Enjoying Modern Art.* New York: Mentor, 1957.

Noble, W. H., Jr. *Philadelphia's Treasure Houses*. Philadelphia: University of Pennsylvania Press, 1950.

Pach, Walter. *The Art Museum in America*. New York: Pantheon, 1948.

Roberts, George and Mary. *Triumph on Fairmount*. Philadelphia: J. B. Lippincott Company, 1959.

Saarinen, Aline. *The Proud Possessors*. New York: Random House, 1958.

Seymour, Charles, Jr. *Art Treasures for America, An Anthology of Paintings and Sculpture in the Samuel H. Kress Collection*. Prefaces by John Walker and Guy Emerson. New York: Phaidon Press for the Samuel H. Kress Foundation, 1961.

Shoolman, Regina and Charles E. Slatkin. *The Enjoyment of Art in America*. Philadelphia and New York: J. B. Lippincott Company, 1942.

Spaeth, Eloise. *American Art Museums and Galleries—An Introduction to Looking*. New York: Harper & Brothers, 1960.

Walker, John. *National Gallery of Art, Washington*. New York: Harry N. Abrams, Inc., 1956.

Wecter, Dixon. *The Saga of American Society—A Record of Social Aspiration 1607–1937*. New York: Charles Scribner's Sons, 1937.

1913–1963. Armory Show: 50th Anniversary Exhibition. Utica and New York: Organized by Munson-Williams-Proctor Institute; Sponsored by the Henry Street Settlement, New York, 1963.

B. *Other Sources:*

Material on Robert Gilmor, Jr., including quotation from his diary, is from the *Maryland Historical Magazine*, Vol. 17, No. 4 (Baltimore: December 1922) and Vol. 51, No. 1 (Baltimore: March 1956); *Journal of the Walters Art Gallery*, Vol. 12, No. 19 (Baltimore: 1949). *A Century of Baltimore Collecting— 1840 to 1940*, a catalogue to an exhibition held at the Baltimore Museum of Art from June 6 to September 1, 1941, provided additional material.

Francis Henry Taylor's appraisal of Henry Walters is from "The Walters Gallery Revisited" in *Parnassus*, Vol. 6 (December 1934).

The conversation between Eli Price and Fiske Kimball is from George and Mary Roberts, *Triumph on Fairmount* (Philadelphia: J. B. Lippincott Company, 1959).

The critic who described the "Boston Plan" was William Howe Downes, whose article on "The New Museum in Boston" appeared in *Art and Progress*, Vol. 1, No. 2 (December 1909).

The plan to reconstruct the monuments of the world on a site in Washington was described by John Walker in *The National Gallery of Art, Washington* (New York: Harry N. Abrams, Inc., 1956).

All the quoted material relating to A. E. Austin, Jr. is from *A. E. Austin, Jr., A Director's Taste and Achievement* (Hartford: Wadsworth Atheneum, 1958).

Important sources for the section on the National Gallery of Art are Walker, ibid.; Huntington Cairns and John Walker, eds., *Great Paintings from the National Gallery of Art* (New York: Macmillan Company, 1952); and Charles Seymour, Jr., *Art Treasures for America, An Anthology of Paintings and Sculp-*

ture in the Samuel H. Kress Collection. Prefaces by John Walker and Guy Emerson (New York: Phaidon Press for the Samuel H. Kress Foundation, 1961).

Frank Jewett Mather, Jr.'s criticism of "The W. A. Clark Collection" appeared in *The Arts,* Vol. 13, No. 4 (April 1928).

Andrew Wyeth's letter to Jerry Bywaters appeared in John Canaday, "Wyeth Painting Is Bought for $58,000," New York *Times* (September 25, 1962).

Henry De Young's statement about where he "got the museum bug" is from Marjorie C. Driscoll's article "The Story of San Francisco's Treasure House and Its Contents," *The M. H. De Young Memorial Museum, Golden Gate Park, San Francisco* (published under the auspices of the Park Commission, November 1927).

The major source for the story of the Metropolitan Museum of Art in New York, and its antecedents, was Winifred Howe, *A History of the Metropolitan Museum of Art,* Vol. I (New York: The Metropolitan Museum of Art, 1913).

The purpose behind the Whitney Museum was described by Forbes Watson in *Juliana Force and American Art* (New York: Whitney Museum of American Art, 1949).

Dr. Robert Goldwater's summation of the scope of the Museum of Primitive Art appeared in an interview in *The New Yorker* (March 16, 1957).

It was Ada Louise Huxtable who spoke of "wall to wall luxury" in "Architecture: Huntington Hartford's Palatial Midtown Museum," New York *Times* (February 25, 1964).

Chapter III: SCIENCE

The science museum epithets in the opening paragraph were recalled by Carlos E. Cummings, M.D., in *Your Guide to the Buffalo Museum of Science* (Buffalo: 1939).

The story of Cincinnati's early Western Museum was told in *The Journal of the Cincinnati Society of Natural History,* Vol. XXII, No. 4 (April 1945).

The prospectus of the Library Society of Charleston is quoted by William Martin Smallwood in *Natural History and the American Mind* (New York: Columbia University Press, 1941) pp. 109–110.

The quoted material regarding Harvard's Musaeum and Mineral Cabinet is from I. Bernard Cohen, *Some Early Tools of American Science: An Account of the Early Scientific Instruments and Mineralogical and Biological Collections in Harvard University* (Cambridge: Harvard University Press, 1950).

John Canaday wrote of the relationship between artists and their age in the New York *Times* (January 5, 1964).

The history of the Maryland Academy of Science was given in its *Journal,* Vol. I, No. 1 (Baltimore: January 1930).

The quoted material relating to the early years of the California Academy is from an address by Col. Charles F. Crocker, which was published in a booklet called *Laying the Corner-Stone of the Building of the California Academy of Sciences* (San Francisco: July 12, 1889). An account of the shooting of Dr. Randall by Mr. Hetherington is given in *Pacific Discovery,* Vol. VI, No. 2 (San

Francisco: California Academy of Sciences, March–April 1953). The quotation regarding the Academy's publications is from the same source.

Biographical information about Louis Agassiz was drawn largely from Edward Lurie, *Louis Agassiz, A Life in Science* (Chicago: University of Chicago Press, 1960).

The quotation beginning "the religious meaning for the study of natural history" is from G. Evelyn Hutchinson, "Dedication of the Oceanographic and Ornithological Laboratories, Peabody Museum of Natural History Yale University," *Curator,* Vol. III, No. 2 (New York: The American Museum of Natural History, 1960); and the quotation beginning "scientific men took up the microscope" is from Nevin M. Fenneman, "The Museum Situation in Cincinnati," *Journal of the Cincinnati Society of Natural History,* Vol. XXII, No. 2 (November 1, 1917).

A good summary of the history of the American Museum of Natural History, which we drew upon, can be found in Alden Stevens, "The First Ninety Years; The American Museum Celebrates an Anniversary," *Natural History Magazine* (New York: American Museum of Natural History, April 1959). Also helpful was the article "Theodore Roosevelt Park: 1807–1958," *Curator,* Vol. III, No. 2 (1960).

In addition to Roswell Ward's *Henry A. Ward, Museum Builder to America,* Publications Vol. XXIV (New York: The Rochester Historical Society, 1948), a series of articles by Julian D. Corrington in *Nature Magazine* (August 1957, March 1958, June 1958) provided useful information.

The quoted material about the early years of the Smithsonian is from *A Handbook to the National Museum at the Smithsonian Institute* [sic] *Washington,* (New York: Brentano Brothers, 1886). Biographical material on James Smithson, such as there is, appears in *Sons of Science—The Story of the Smithsonian Institution and Its Leaders* by Paul H. Oehser (New York: Henry Schuman, 1949).

The statement by Albert Eide Parr regarding the functions of natural history museums is from "Museums and Museums of Natural History," *Curator,* Vol. V, No. 2 (1962).

The quoted definition of the university museum is from Hutchinson, op. cit. Information about the Yale Peabody Museum was taken, in part, from S. Dillon Ripley, "Dedication of the Oceanographic and Ornithological Laboratories . . ." op. cit., and from Karl K. Turekian, ibid.

Froelich Rainey's credo for the University Museum can be found in "Tradition and Change," *University Museum Bulletin,* Vol. 18, No. 4 (Philadelphia: 1954).

Ralph H. Lewis used the term "site museum" and defined it in "Site Museums and National Parks," *Curator,* Vol. II, No. 2 (1959). "Dinosaur Monument and the People: A Study in Interpretation" by Gilbert F. Stucker, in *Curator,* Vol. VI, No. 2 (1963) was an important source for that story.

The first nature trail of the American Museum of Natural History was described by Laurence Vail Coleman in *Contributions of Museums to Outdoor Recreation* (Washington, D.C.: American Association of Museums, 1928).

The complete stories of the founding of the Arizona-Sonora Desert Museum and the setting up of two of its major exhibits have been told by William H. Carr in three booklets: *The Desert Speaks* (1956; revised 1961); *Water Street U.S.A.* (1959); and *Tunnel in the Desert* (1957). All are published by the museum, Tucson.

The story of David Hosack and the Elgin Botanic Garden was told by William Martin Smallwood, op. cit.

Plans for the New York Zoological Society's Wildlife Survival Center were described by Fairfield Osborn in "Another Noah's Ark—For New York," the New York *Times Magazine* (October 27, 1963), and in news articles in the New York *Times* on August 28, 1962, p. 33 and October 4, 1963, p. 1.

The brief quote beginning "birds, tropical vegetation" is from Fairfield Osborn, "A Zoo of Zoos," the New York *Times Magazine* (November 4, 1962).

The outlook of the Chicago Museum of Science and Industry was summed up under the heading of "The Social Consequences of Science and Industry" by Waldemar Kaempffert in a booklet he wrote called *From Cave-Man to Engineer. The Museum of Science and Industry founded by Julius Rosenwald; An Institution to Reveal the Technical Ascent of Man* (Chicago: Museum of Science and Industry, 1933).

The quotation, physicists "were still known as philosophers and were rarely to be found outside their laboratories," is from Thomas Coulson, "The First Hundred Years of Research at the Franklin Institute," *Journal of the Franklin Institute,* Vol. 256, No. 1 (July 1953). The *National Gazette and Literary Register* of February 10, 1824, carried a notice describing the founding meeting of the Franklin Institute; this and other information about the history of the Institute were recorded in *A Book Issued to Commemorate the Centenary of the Franklin Institute of Pennsylvania* (Philadelphia: 1924). Coulson, op. cit., also provided useful historic information.

The impact of the Deutsches Museum upon Julius Rosenwald and his subsequent appeal to the Commercial Club of Chicago were related by Kaempffert, op. cit.

The story of General Sickles' leg was told by W. A. Swanberg in his biography *Sickles the Incredible* (New York: Charles Scribner's Sons, 1956) Chapters XX and XXI.

The nineteenth century astronomy text referred to is Elijah H. Burritt, *The Geography of the Heavens and Class Book of Astronomy* (New York: F. J. Huntington and Co., 1839, fifth ed.). Excerpts from it were quoted in Joseph Miles Chamberlain, "A Philosophy for Planetarium Lectures," *Curator,* Vol. 1, No. 1 (1958).

Professor Roger Long's "enormous astronomical machine" was described in Smyth and Chambers, *Cycle of Celestial Objects* (Oxford; 1881, pp. 208–9) and quoted in Philip Fox, *Adler Planetarium and Astronomical Museum of Chicago: An Account of the Optical Planetarium and a Brief Guide to the Museum* (Chicago: The Lakeside Press, R. R. Donnelly & Sons Co., 1933).

Roy K. Marshall's "The Planetarium," *Sky and Telescope,* Vol. III, No. 1 (Cambridge: Harvard College Observatory, November 1943); Chamberlain, op. cit.; and Fox, op. cit., were all good sources of information for the planetarium section.

Max Adler's statement appeared in both Chamberlain, op. cit. and Fox, op. cit.

Descriptions of the first presentations of the Fels and Buhl Planetariums are from *The Institute News*, Vol. XXVII, No. 4 (Philadelphia: The Franklin Institute, December 1963) and *Dedication of the Buhl Planetarium and Institute of Popular Science* (Pittsburgh; 1939), respectively.

Chapter IV: HISTORY

An invaluable, scholarly and thorough appraisal of historical societies is Walter Muir Whitehill's *Independent Historical Societies: An enquiry into their research and publication functions and their financial future* (Boston: The Boston Athenaeum, distributed by Harvard University Press, 1962), a book to which we are deeply indebted as an important source.

A beautifully made volume that provided us with some general background information is *The American Heritage Book of Great Historic Places* by the editors of *American Heritage,* narrative by Richard M. Ketchum, Introduction by Bruce Catton (New York: American Heritage Publishing Co., Inc., in co-operation with Simon and Schuster, Inc., 1957).

Thomas Jefferson's letter to James Monroe is in *The Life and Selected Writings of Thomas Jefferson,* edited and with an Introduction by Adrienne Koch and William Peden (New York: Random House, The Modern Library, 1944, p. 366).

Pintard's letter to Jefferson and his correspondence with Rev. Belknap are quoted in Whitehill, op. cit.

The major source for the section dealing with the New-York Historical Society was R. W. G. Vail, *Knickerbocker Birthday; A Sesqui-Centennial History of the New-York Historical Society 1804–1954* (New York: The New-York Historical Society, 1954).

Descriptions of some early activities of the Pilgrim Society come from James Thacher, *History of the Town of Plymouth* . . . (Boston: Marsh, Capen & Lyon, 1835, 2nd ed.).

The description of the Essex Institute as "bulging at the seams" and "checkmated" is from Whitehill, op. cit., as is the query of the librarian of the American Antiquarian Society regarding the purposes of that institution.

Sources for the growth of historical societies in the Middle West, and especially in Wisconsin, were Whitehill, op. cit., and William B. Hesseltine, *Pioneer's Mission. The Story of Lyman Copeland Draper* (Madison, Wisconsin: The State Historical Society of Wisconsin, 1954). Also helpful was James C. Olson, "The Nebraska State Historical Society in 1953 (With a Glance Backward to 1878)," *Nebraska History,* Vol. XXXIV, No. 4 (December 1953).

The various newspaper accounts that contribute to the story of the Chicago Historical Society are quoted by Paul M. Angle in *The Chicago Historical Society 1856–1956 An Unconventional Chronicle* (New York–Chicago–San Francisco: Rand McNally & Company, 1956).

Recognition of the role of the gentlemen-amateurs of early historical societies was given in "The Ohio Historical Society Collections," *Antiques Journal* (June 1960).

Dr. Goode's address to the American Historical Association was "Museum-History and Museums of History," a paper read before the American Historical Association meeting in Washington, December 26–28, 1888, reprinted in *Report of the United States National Museum. Part II*. Annual Report of the Board of Regents of the Smithsonian Institution for the year ending June 30, 1897. (Washington, D.C.: Government Printing Office, 1901) pp. 65–81. G. Carroll Lindway appraises the relationship between museums and historical research in "Museums and Research in History and Technology," *Curator,* Vol. V, No. 3 (New York: American Museum of Natural History, 1962).

The story of the Ohio Historical Society was drawn in part from "The Ohio Historical Society Collections," *Antiques Journal* (June 1960).

Important sources for the section dealing generally with historic houses are Laurence Vail Coleman, *The Museum in America* (1939) and *Historic House Museums* (1933), both published in Washington, D.C., by the American Association of Museums; and the same author's article "Collecting Old Houses," *The Scientific Monthly* (November 1935) pp. 461 ff.; Elise Lathrop, *Historic Houses of Early America* (New York: Robert M. McBride & Company, 1927); and Arthur C. Parker, *A Manual for History Museums* (New York: Columbia University Press, 1935).

Among the sources for individual historic houses or groups of them are *Old-Time New England* Vol. XXXVIII, No. 4 (Boston: Society for the Preservation of New England Antiquities, April 1948); John H. Fenton, "Ipswich Battling for Its Old Homes," New York *Times* (September 8, 1963), p. 86; Lathrop, op. cit.; American Heritage, op. cit.; Harriet E. O'Brien, *Lost Utopias. A brief description of three quests for happiness . . . recorded and preserved by Clara Endicott Sears . . .* (Boston: Perry Walton, 1929); *The Chain of Colonial Houses. Fairmount Park* (Philadelphia: The Associate Committee of Women of the Pennsylvania Museum of Art, 1932); Ralph Friedman, "Oregon Town in Pursuit of the Past," New York *Times* (April 21, 1963); Patricia L. Tull and Helena B. Stites, comp., "Museums and Collections in Utah open to the public," *Utah Historical Quarterly,* Vol. XXI (Salt Lake City: Utah Historical Society, 1953); Philip Brady, "Visit to the Old Fairbanks House in Dedham," New York *Times* (May 10, 1964).

Whitehill, op. cit., quotes Clara Endicott Sears on her reasons for preserving the Alcott home. William Bentley's account of Samuel McIntire appears in American Heritage, op. cit. p. 30.

Our primary source for the story of the establishment of Colonial Williamsburg is Raymond B. Fosdick, *John D. Rockefeller, Jr. A Portrait,* Chapter XV (New York: Harper & Brothers, 1956). The case against "galloping restorationitis" was stated by Ada Louise Huxtable in "Dissent at Colonial Williamsburg," New York *Times* (September 22, 1963). The Williamsburg director who spoke of "basic devotion to truth" was Edward P. Alexander in "Historical Restorations," in William B. Hesseltine and Donald R. McNeil, eds., *In Support of Clio, Essays in Memory of Herbert A. Kellar* (Madison: State Historical Society of Wisconsin, 1958).

Helpful accounts of the collections at a group of preservation projects were provided by Alice Winchester and the Staff of *Antiques Magazine*, eds., *The Antiques Treasury of Furniture and Other Decorative Arts at Winterthur, Williamsburg, Sturbridge, Ford Museum, Cooperstown, Deerfield, Shelburne* (New York: E. P. Dutton & Company, Inc., 1959). Dr. Bentley's description of Deerfield's main street appeared here. Whitehill, op. cit., tells the story of the Pocumtuck Valley Memorial Association and its founder; and Whitehill is the visitor who observed that Old Sturbridge *"looks* like a New England village." Basic information was provided by the individual museum communities themselves.

Sources for the New York Shaker Museum included Richard Shanor, "Museum Gateway," New York *Times* (April 26, 1964) and Robert F. W. Meader, "The Story of the Shaker Museum," *Curator*, Vol. III, No. 3 (1960).

Sources for the account of the federal government's role in preserving national sites include J. Thomas Schneider, "Historic American Buildings Survey (Recording the Historic Structures and Early Architecture of the United States and Possessions by Measured Drawings, Photographs and Manuscripts)," *Report to the Secretary of the Interior on the Preservation of Historic Sites and Buildings* (Washington, D.C.: United States Department of the Interior, 1938); David Finlay, "Present and Future Role of the National Council for Historic Sites and Buildings," *National Council for Historic Sites and Buildings. Quarterly Report.* Vol. 1. No. 1, 2 (1949); and *Criteria for Evaluating Historic Sites and Buildings,* a report by the Committee on Standards and Surveys (Washington, D.C.: National Trust for Historic Preservation, 1956).

The story of the Frank Lloyd Wright house being saved in Virginia was told by Ben A. Franklin, "A Wright House in Virginia Saved," New York *Times* (July 31, 1964).

Material about the Wenham Historical Association and Museum was provided by the museum itself, and Whitehill, op. cit.

Chapter V: CHILDREN

In discussing the term "children's museum" in "Children's Museums: A Definition and a Credo," *Curator*, Vol. III, No. 2 (New York: American Museum of Natural History, 1960), Helen V. Fisher wrote, "This admittedly anomalous term leads the humorists to ask if we display dismembered children in our halls as an art museum displays sculptured torsos." Subsequent statements by Miss Fisher are from the same article.

Sources for the early years of the Brooklyn Children's Museum included Rebecca Hooper Eastman, *The Story of the Brooklyn Institute of Arts and Sciences 1824–1924* (Brooklyn: 1924); Frederick A. Lucas, "A History of the Museum," Annual Report for 1907, reprinted in *The Brooklyn Museum Quarterly,* Vol. XII, No. 1 (January 1925); and Peter Farb, "An Island of Nature," *National Parent Teacher,* Vol. 54 (April 1960).

Michael Spock expressed himself about the Boston Children's Museum in an interview with Jerry Talmer for an article, "Sons of the Famous," New York *Post* (May 21, 1963).

The quotation describing Newark's children's museum is from *A Survey: 50 Years of the Newark Museum,* Vol. 11, New Series (Newark, New Jersey: The Museum, 1959).

Sources for the Junior Museum of the Metropolitan Museum of Art included Louise Condit, *The New Junior Museum* (New York: Metropolitan Museum of Art) and "How to Look at Paintings," *Hobbies,* No. 63 (December 1958).

The statement by Dr. M. Graham Netting is from "Museums—Launching Pads for Scientists," *Understanding Science in the Space Age, Discussions and Addresses at a National Symposium* (Rochester: Museum of Arts and Sciences, 1963).

Material on the Dayton Museum of Natural History, including the story of the young man and the skunk, was drawn from Allan W. Eckert, "Dayton's Nursery for Naturalists," *Coronet* magazine (June 1961).

Biographical material about John Ripley Forbes and all information pertaining to the history of the Natural Science for Youth Foundation was provided by Mr. Forbes during an extensive interview.

Other references for this chapter included A. E. Parr, "Why Children's Museums?" *Curator,* Vol. III, No. 3 (1960), and Eleanor Moore, *Youth for Museums* (Philadelphia: University of Pennsylvania Press, 1941).

Chapter VI: AN INFINITE VARIETY

Most of the museums described in this chapter themselves provided the information on which our accounts are based.

The reference to Mrs. J. Watson Webb as "the damnedest grande dame" is quoted by Aline Saarinen in *The Proud Possessors* (New York: Random House, 1958).

The spokesman for the Panhandle-Plains Historical Museum of Canyon, Texas, was J. Harold Dunn in "A Purpose for the Panhandle-Plains Historical Museum," *Panhandle-Plains Historical Review,* Vol. XXIX (1956). An additional source for that museum and others in the state was Carl E. Guthe, "Texas Museums," ibid. A helpful source for institutions in the neighboring state was S. F. de Borhegyi, "A Survey of Oklahoma Museums 1893–1957," *The Chronicle of Oklahoma,* Vol. XXXV, No. 2 (Oklahoma City: Oklahoma Historical Society, Summer 1957).

The laying of the cornerstone of the Hollywood Film Museum, and its plans for the future, were reported by Murray Schumach in the New York *Times:* "Hollywood Plans," (October 20, 1963), "Ground-Breaking Ceremonies Held for Coast Movie Museum," (October 21, 1963), and "Movie Museum Gains Support" (January 29, 1964).

The collections of the Kendall Whaling Museum were described by Philip Brady, "Whaling Era Preserved in Bay State Muséum," New York *Times* (August 9, 1964).

George McCue, writing in the Music and Arts Section of the *Sunday Post-Dispatch,* made reference to the imagination of the National Museum of Transport in St. Louis; his article, "Bright Prospects for Transport Museum," appeared on July 1, 1962.

A major source for the Newark Museum is *A Survey: 50 Years of the Newark Museum*, New Series, Vol. 11 (Newark, New Jersey: The Museum, 1959).

We found useful information about presidential libraries in a group of articles in the New York *Times:* Ben A. Franklin, "Kennedy Chose Site at Harvard for Presidential Library Oct. 19," (November 30, 1963); Lincoln Grahlfs, "Truman Library Seeks Rare Coins," (October 8, 1963); Donald Janson, "Truman Gets Coin Collection to Replace Stolen One," (May 7, 1964); Merrill Folsom, "Roosevelt Shrine Will Be Expanded," (February 3, 1964). It was Walter Muir Whitehill who spoke of the "magnetism of the presidency" in *Independent Historical Societies* . . . (Boston: The Boston Athenaeum, distributed by Harvard University Press, 1962).

The description of the Library of Congress as a "storehouse of offbeat art treasures" and a "graphic grab bag" was offered by John Canaday, "Surprise Cache," New York *Times* (June 16, 1963).

Information about the General Douglas MacArthur Memorial was largely drawn from Ben A. Franklin, "Norfolk Museum Is General's Tomb," New York *Times* (April 6, 1964) and "M'Arthur Rites in Norfolk Today," ibid. (April 11, 1964).

APPENDIX

We acknowledge with gratitude our indebtedness to The American Association of Museums whose *Museums Directory of the United States and Canada* was the source we relied upon most heavily in compiling this appendix. Our dependence upon the *Directory* saved us hours, possibly weeks, of work. For those wishing to consult its detailed entries, it is available in many libraries and can be purchased directly from the Association, 2306 Massachusetts Avenue N.W., Washington 8, D.C.

Additional information for this Appendix came from regional, state and city directories ("Our Philadelphia Museums," a brochure made available by Station WFLN, Philadelphia, and *Philadelphia Guide; New England Museums & Historic Houses,* published by The New England Council, The Museum of Fine Arts, Boston, and The Society for the Preservation of New England Antiquities; *Museums of New York City* published by the Museums Council of New York City; and others like these) and, of course, the hundreds of individual museum publications we have by now accumulated.

KEY

† See discussion in text; check Index for page reference.
* Of more than routine interest.
** One of the county's outstanding museums.
Survey Indicates collections of broad scope, covering most major areas of subject; designation has been used for art and natural history.
Exhibitions Where this is the only designation, it indicates that temporary shows are the major activity.
Kress Indicates that a museum has been the recipient of a group of Renaissance paintings from the Samuel H. Kress Foundation; see discussion in text; check Index for page reference.

Most museums will arrange to admit visitors by appointment at other than regular visiting hours.

ALABAMA

Anniston

REGAR MEMORIAL MUSEUM OF NATURAL HISTORY. (108 E. 10th St.) Natural history, history, art exhibitions. Winter: Mon.–Fri. 2–6; Sat. 9–6; Sun. 2–5. Summer: Mon.–Sat. 9–6, Sun. 2–5.

Birmingham

ARLINGTON HISTORICAL SOCIETY. (331 Cotton Ave.) Historic house, 1842; Civil

War, ante-bellum collections. Mon.–Sat. 9–5, Sun. 2–5.

BIRMINGHAM MUSEUM OF ART. (2000 8th Ave. N.) *Survey.* Mon.–Sat. 10–5; Thurs. 10–9; Sun. 2–6.

Fort McClellan

WOMEN'S ARMY CORPS MUSEUM. (United States Women's Army Corps Center.) Documentary history of the WACS. Mon.–Fri. 7:30–4:30. †

Mobile

HISTORIC MOBILE PRESERVATION SO- CIETY. (350 Oakleigh Pl.) Historic house, 1883; local history. Winter: Wed. 10–4; Summer: Mon.–Sat. 10–4; Sun. 2–5.

Montgomery

FIRST WHITE HOUSE OF THE CONFED- ERACY. (Washington and Union Sts.) Historic house; Confederate memora- bilia. Daily 9–4:30.

MONTGOMERY MUSEUM OF FINE ARTS. (440 S. McDonough St.) Paintings, graphics. Tues.–Sat. 10–5; Thurs. eve. 7–9; Sun. 2:30–5.

STATE OF ALABAMA DEPARTMENT OF ARCHIVES AND HISTORY. State history, archaeology and arts. Daily 8–4.

Moundville

MOUND STATE MONUMENT. Archaeo- logical site museum. Daily 9–5.

Tuscaloosa

GORGAS HOUSE. (University of Ala- bama.) Historic house, 1830. Home of Dr. William Gorgas. Mon.–Sat. 9–12, 2–5; Sun. 3–5.

Tuskegee Institute

GEORGE WASHINGTON CARVER MU- SEUM. African and American Negro his- tory and art. Mon.–Sat. 10–12, 1–4; Sun. 1–4. †

University

ALABAMA MUSEUM OF NATURAL HIS- TORY. Anthropology, archaeology. Daily 8–5.

ALASKA

Anchorage

ANCHORAGE LOG CABIN MUSEUM. (5th and G Sts.) Alaskan natural history. Mon.–Sat. 9–6.

College

UNIVERSITY OF ALASKA MUSEUM. An- thropology, natural history, Eskimo arti- facts. Summer: daily 9–5; Winter: Mon.– Sat. 10:30–5; Sun. 1–5.

Juneau

ALASKA HISTORICAL LIBRARY AND MU- SEUM. Territorial and state history and natural history. Mon.–Fri. 8:30–12, 1–5; some eves. 7–10.

Kodiak

KODIAK MUSEUM, Kodiak and Aleutian Islands Historical Society. (Mill Bay Rd.) Local history and archaeology. Sun. and by appt.

Sitka

SHELDON JACKSON JUNIOR COLLEGE MUSEUM. Alaskan, Eskimo, and North- west Coast Indian history and anthro- pology. Summer: daily 10:30–12, 2–4.

SHELDON JACKSON JUNIOR COLLEGE ART MUSEUM. *Survey* and Indian and Eskimo art. Summer: Mon.–Sat. 10–12, 1–2:30.

ARIZONA

Ajo

ORGAN PIPE CACTUS NATIONAL MON- UMENT. Local natural history. Daily 8–5. *

Camp Verde

MONTEZUMA CASTLE NATIONAL MON- UMENT. Park museum, archaeology. Daily 8–5. *

Clarkdale

TUZIGOOT NATIONAL MONUMENT. Park museum, archaeology. Daily 8–5. *

Coolidge

CASA GRANDE NATIONAL MONUMENT. Prehistoric Indian ruins, Pueblo Indian artifacts. Daily 8–5. *

Dos Cabezas

CHIRICAHUA NATIONAL MONUMENT. Park museum, geology. Daily 8–5. *

Flagstaff

MUSEUM OF NORTHERN ARIZONA. (Fort Valley Rd.) Natural history, anthropology. Mon.–Sat. 9–5, Sun. 1:30–5. †*
WALNUT CANYON NATIONAL MONUMENT. (Rt. 1.) Park museum, archaeology. Summer: daily 7–7. Winter: daily 8–5. *
WUPATKI CRATER NATIONAL MONUMENT. (Tuba Star Route.) Park museum, anthropology, geology. Daily 8–5. *

Grand Canyon

GRAND CANYON NATIONAL PARK. Tusayan Museum, Visitor Center, Yavapai Museum. Natural history. Daily 8–5. **

Holbrook

PETRIFIED FOREST NATIONAL MONUMENT RAINBOW FOREST MUSEUM. Local natural history. Summer: daily 6 A.M.–8 P.M. Winter: daily 8–5. *

Moccasin

PIPE SPRING NATIONAL MONUMENT. Historic house, 1869; Mormon pioneer items. Summer: daily 8–7. Winter: daily 8–5. *

Phoenix

DESERT BOTANICAL GARDEN OF ARIZONA. (Papago Park.) Botanic garden, herbarium: desert flora. Daily 9–5.
THE HEARD MUSEUM OF ANTHROPOLOGY AND PRIMITIVE ART. (22 E. Monte Vista Rd.) Pre-Columbian, Navaho objects. Oct.–June: Tues.–Sat. 10–5; Sun. 1–5. †*
THE PHOENIX ART MUSEUM. (1625 N. Central Ave.) *Survey.* Tues.–Sat. 10–5, Sun. 1–5.
PHOENIX COLLEGE PLANETARIUM. (1202 W. Thomas Rd.) Planetarium, observatory. 2d and 4th Mon. and Fri. eves.

PUEBLO GRANDE MUSEUM. (4619 E. Washington St.) Preservation project: Hohokam village; archaeology, anthropology. Mon.–Fri. 9–5, Sun. 1–5.

Prescott

OLD GOVERNORS MANSION. (West Gurley.) Historic house: residence of territorial governors 1864–67.
PRESCOTT HISTORICAL SOCIETY, SHARLOT HALL MUSEUM. (West Gurley.) Local history, maintains Old Governors Mansion. Mon.–Fri. 9–12, 1–5; Sun. 1–5.
SMOKI MUSEUM. (N. Arizona Ave.) Archaeology. Summer: Mon.–Sat. 10–4:30, Sun. 1–5.

Roosevelt

TONTO NATIONAL MONUMENT. Park museum, archaeology. Daily 8–5. *

Superior

BOYCE THOMPSON SOUTHWESTERN ARBORETUM. Desert flora. Daily 8–5.

Tempe

ARIZONA STATE UNIVERSITY COLLECTION OF AMERICAN ART. American primitive, Indian art. Mon.–Fri. 8–10; Sat. 8–5; Sun. 2–5.

Tonalea

NAVAJO NATIONAL MONUMENT. Park museum, ethnology. Daily 8–5. *

Tucson

ARIZONA PIONEERS' HISTORICAL SOCIETY. (949 E. 2d St.) Local history. Mon.–Fri. 8–4, Sat. 8–1.
ARIZONA-SONORA DESERT MUSEUM. (Tucson Mountain Park.) Natural history, zoo, botanic garden. Daily 10–5. †**
SAGUARO NATIONAL MONUMENT. (Rt. 8) Botanic garden. Daily 8–5. *
TUCSON ART CENTER. (325 W. Franklin St.) *Exhibitions.* Mon.–Sat. 10–5, Sun. 2–5.
UNIVERSITY OF ARIZONA, ARIZONA STATE MUSEUM. Anthropology. Mon.–Sat. 10–5, Sun. 2–5. *
UNIVERSITY OF ARIZONA ART GALLERY.

(Speedway at Palm Rd.) *Kress,* contemporary collections. Mon.–Sat. 10–5, Sun. 2–5. *

Tumacacori

TUMACACORI NATIONAL MONUMENT. Historic house: 18th-century Spanish mission. Daily 9–5. *

ARKANSAS

Fayetteville

UNIVERSITY OF ARKANSAS, ARTS CENTER GALLERY. Painting, sculpture, graphics; teaching collection, exhibitions. Mon.–Sat. 8 A.M.–11 P.M.

UNIVERSITY OF ARKANSAS MUSEUM. Archaeology, natural history, local history. Mon.–Fri. 9–5; Sat. 9–4; Sun. 2–5.

Hot Springs

HOT SPRINGS NATIONAL PARK MUSEUM. (Central and Reserve Aves.) Natural history, nature trail. Daily 8–5.

Little Rock

THE ARKANSAS ARTS CENTER. (MacArthur Park, E. 9th and Commerce Sts.) *Exhibitions.* Tues.–Sat. 10–5, Sun. 2–5. †

ARKANSAS HISTORY COMMISSION. (Old State House) State history. Mon.–Fri. 8–4.

State College

ARKANSAS STATE COLLEGE MUSEUM. Natural history; archaeology, Woodland Indian artifacts; botanical garden. Mon.–Fri. 8–12, 1–5; Sat. 8–12; Sun. 1–5.

CALIFORNIA

Arcadia

LOS ANGELES STATE AND COUNTY ARBORETUM. Natural history, herbarium. Daily 9–sundown.

Bakersfield

KERN COUNTY MUSEUM. (3801 Chester Ave.) Local history, natural history. Preservation project: pioneer community. Mon.–Fri. 8–5; Sat., Sun. 10–6.

Berkeley

REGIONAL PARKS BOTANIC GARDEN. (Tilden Regional Park) Botanical garden: California wild flora. Daily 8–5.

UNIVERSITY OF CALIFORNIA HERBARIUM. (3016 Life Science Bldg.) Teaching, research collection. Mon.–Fri. 8–12, 1–5; Sat. 9–2.

UNIVERSITY OF CALIFORNIA, MUSEUM OF PALEONTOLOGY. (Earth Sciences Bldg.) Plant, vertebrate and invertebrate fossils. Teaching collection, research. Mon.–Fri. 8–5, Sat. 9–12.

UNIVERSITY OF CALIFORNIA, ROBERT H. LOWIE MUSEUM OF ANTHROPOLOGY. (Bancroft Way and College Ave.) Archaeology, ethnology; primitive art. Tues.–Fri. 11–3; Sat., Sun. 1–5. †*

Bloomington

SAN BERNARDINO COUNTY MUSEUM. (18860 Orange St.) Local history, natural history. Mon.–Sun. 1–5.

Cazadero

FORT ROSS STATE HISTORICAL MONUMENT. (19005 Coast Highway No. 1) Preservation project: military structures restored to 1812 period. Daily 9–5.

Claremont

THE CHILDREN'S INTERNATIONAL ART GALLERY. (Harper Hall, McAllister Bldg., College and 9th Sts.) Children's paintings from around the world. Mon.–Fri. 9–9.

POMONA COLLEGE GALLERY. (College and 3rd Sts.) *Exhibitions.* Daily 2–5.

RANCHO SANTA ANA BOTANIC GARDEN. (1500 N. College St.) California flora. Mon.–Sat. 8–5, Sun. 10–5.

Concord

DIABLO VALLEY COLLEGE SCIENCE CENTER. (Golf Club Rd.) Botanical garden; planetarium; natural history, technology, and applied science.

Davis

UNIVERSITY OF CALIFORNIA ARBORETUM. Botanical garden. Daily, to sundown.

Death Valley

DEATH VALLEY NATIONAL MONUMENT, DEATH VALLEY MUSEUM. Park museum: natural history. Daily. *

Fresno

ACADEMY OF CALIFORNIA CHURCH HISTORY. (1530 N. Fresno) Maintains Spanish missions in Central California: San Luis Obispo, San Miguel, Jolon, Carmel, San Juan Bautista, Monterey. Missions open daily; Fresno archives open by appt.

FRESNO COUNTY HISTORICAL SOCIETY, ROEDING PARK MUSEUM. (4191 N. Blackstone) Local history. Weekends 1–4:30.

M. THEO. KEARNEY MANSION. (Kearney Park) Historic house; late Victorian.

ROEDING PARK ZOO. (890 W. Belmont St.) Mon.–Sun. 8–sundown.

Imperial

CALIFORNIA MID-WINTER FAIR ZOO. Daily, daylight hours.

IMPERIAL COUNTY PIONEER MUSEUM. Local history. Weekends 12–5.

Independence

EASTERN CALIFORNIA MUSEUM. Local history, natural history. Mon.–Sat. 10–12, 1–5; Sun. 1–5.

La Canada

DESCANSO GARDENS. (1418 Descanso Dr.) Botanical gardens. Daily 8–sundown.

La Jolla

ART CENTER IN LA JOLLA. (700 Prospect St.) European and American contemp., Japanese prints.

UNIVERSITY OF CALIFORNIA, T. WAYLAND VAUGHAN AQUARIUM-MUSEUM. Natural history, oceanography, herbarium. Mon.–Fri. 9–5; weekends 10–6.

Lakeport

LAKE COUNTY MUSEUM. Local furnishings, Indian items. Mon.–Fri. 1–4. Sat. 10–12, 1–4.

Lompoc

LA PURISIMA MISSION STATE HISTORICAL MONUMENT. Spanish mission and period items; Indian artifacts. Daily 8:30–4:30.

Long Beach

LA CASA DE RANCHO LOS CERRITOS (4600 Virginia Rd.) 1844 Historic house, furnished 1866–86 period; ranch implements; archaeology. Wed.–Sun. 1–5.

LONG BEACH MUSEUM OF ART. (2300 E. Ocean Blvd.) Art of southern California. Winter: Tues.–Fri. 10–5; weekends 1–5; Fri. eve. 7:30–10.

MARITIME AND COMMERCE MUSEUM. Branch of California Museum of Science and Industry, Los Angeles.

Los Angeles

CALIFORNIA MUSEUM OF SCIENCE AND INDUSTRY. (700 State Dr.) Principles and applications of science. Daily, 10–5. †**

GRIFFITH OBSERVATORY AND PLANETARIUM. (Griffith Park) Astronomy. Daily (except Mon.) 2–10. †**

GRIFFITH PARK ZOO. Daily 10–6.

LOS ANGELES COUNTY MEDICAL ASSOCIATION, INSTRUMENTS MUSEUM. (634 S. Westlake Ave.) Medical exhibits; prints and cartoons of medical subjects. Mon., Wed. 9–9; Tues., Thurs.–Sat. 9–5.

LOS ANGELES COUNTY MUSEUM OF ART. (Wilshire Blvd., Hancock Park) *Survey.* Daily (except Mon.) 10–5. †**

LOS ANGELES COUNTY MUSEUM. Science and History Alliance. (Exposition Park) Local history, natural history; historic photographs; La Brea Tar Pits (paleontology). Daily (except Mon.) 10–5. †**

MUNICIPAL ART GALLERY. (Barnsdall Park, 1649 N. Vermont Ave.) *Exhibitions.* Mon.–Fri. 1–9, weekends 1–5.

SOUTHERN CALIFORNIA HISTORICAL SOCIETY. (1909 S. Western Ave.) Regional history. Mon.–Fri. 9–5.

SOUTHERN CALIFORNIA PHARMACEUTICAL ASSOCIATION, LTD. (701 S. St. Andrews Pl.) Documentary history of pharmaceutical items. Mon.–Fri. 8:30–4:30.

SOUTHWEST MUSEUM. (10 Highland Park) Archaeology, ethnology, Indian art. Daily (except Mon.) 1–5.

SPACE AGE MUSEUM. Branch of California Museum of Science and Industry, Los Angeles.

TOWER GALLERY. (City Hall) Art; exhibitions. Mon.–Fri. 10–4, weekends 11–5.

UNIVERSITY OF CALIFORNIA AT LOS ANGELES, ART GALLERIES. (405 Hilgard Ave.) European and American graphics, 19th and 20th centuries; exhibitions. Mon.–Fri. 12:30–5, Sun. 1:30–4:30. †*

UNIVERSITY OF CALIFORNIA, BOTANICAL GARDEN. (405 Hilgard Ave.) Daily 8–5.

UNIVERSITY OF CALIFORNIA, DEPARTMENT OF ASTRONOMY. Planetarium; meteorological exhibits. Teaching and research collection.

UNIVERSITY OF CALIFORNIA HERBARIUM. (405 Hilgard Ave.) Mon.–Fri. 8–5.

UNIVERSITY OF SOUTHERN CALIFORNIA, FISHER GALLERY. (University Park) Survey. Mon.–Fri. 1–5 during University semester. †*

WILLIAM S. HART HOME. Maintained by Los Angeles County Museum.

Manzanita Lake

LASSEN VOLCANIC NATIONAL PARK, LOOMIS VISITOR CENTER. Park museum: geology. Summer, daily 8–6. *

Mariposa

MARIPOSA COUNTY HISTORICAL SOCIETY. Local history; preservation project: store fronts. Summer, daily 10–5.

Merced

APPLEGATE ZOO. (2525 O St.) Daily, daylight hours.

Mineral

LASSEN VOLCANIC NATIONAL PARK, LOOMIS MUSEUM. Park museum, geology. Summer, daily 8–6. *

Monterey

COLTON HALL. (522 Pacific St.) 1849 historic house where first state constitution was written; early state history. Daily 10–5.

OLD CUSTOM HOUSE STATE HISTORICAL MONUMENT. (Alvarado St.) Historic house, 1827; early local history. Daily 10–5.

OLD MONTEREY JAIL. (550 Pacific St.) Historic house, 1854. Daily 10–4:30.

PACIFIC BUILDING. (Scott and Calle Principal) Historic house, 1847; local history. Daily (except Thurs.) 10–5.

Nevada City

NEVADA COUNTY HISTORICAL SOCIETY MUSEUM. (214 Main St.) Local history, gold rush items. Summer: daily 10–4.

New Almaden

NEW ALMADEN MUSEUM. (21570 Almaden Rd.) Historic house: adobe Carson House, 1845; local industrial history, electronics. Daily (except Mon.) 9–5.

North Hollywood

CAMPO DE CAHUENGA. (3919 Lankershim Blvd.) Local history, civic arts center. Mon.–Fri. 8–4, 7–10.

Oakland

CHILDREN'S FAIRYLAND. (Lakeside Park) Natural history. Tues.–Sat. 10–4:30; Sun. 10–5; Mon. 12:30–5.

MILLS COLLEGE ART GALLERY. (MacArthur Blvd.) Graphics, textiles. Wed., Fri., Sun. 2–5.

OAKLAND ART MUSEUM. (Municipal Auditorium, 10th and Fallon Sts.) California art, 19th and 20th century; Oriental; exhibitions. Daily 10–5.

OAKLAND PUBLIC MUSEUM. (1426 Oak St.) Natural history, anthropology. Mon.–Sat. 9:30–5, Sun. 10–5.

ROTARY NATURAL SCIENCE CENTER. (Lakeside Park) Children's museum: natural history, botanical garden; Daily (except Mon.).

SNOW MUSEUM. (274 19th St.) Natural history: varied exhibits, incl. African and American mammals, insects. Daily 10–5.

THE JUNIOR CENTER OF ART AND SCIENCE. (3612 Webster St.) Children's museum; aquarium. Daily (except Mon.) 9–5.

Pacific Grove

PACIFIC GROVE MUSEUM OF NATURAL HISTORY. (165 Forest Ave.) Local natural history; botanical garden. Daily (except Mon.) 10–5.

Paicines

PINNACLES NATIONAL MONUMENT.

Park museum; natural history. Daily 8–5. *

Palm Springs

PALM SPRINGS DESERT MUSEUM, INC. (135 E. Tahquitz Dr.) Natural history of the desert; geology, zoology, archaeology, ethnology; wildlife sanctuary, nature trails. Oct.–May: Mon.–Sat. 10–5, Sun. 1–4. Tues., Fri., Sat. eves (Nov.–Apr.) 7:30–9·30. †*

Palo Alto

PALO ALTO HISTORICAL ASSOCIATION. (1213 Newell Rd.) Local history; exhibitions, archives. Daily (except Sun.) 9–5.
PALO ALTO JUNIOR MUSEUM. (1451 Middlefield Rd.) Children's museum, general collections, zoo. Mon.–Fri. 10–12, 1–5; Sat. 10–12.

Palos Verdes Estates

MARINELAND OF THE PACIFIC. Daily 10–sundown.

Pasadena

THE PASADENA ART MUSEUM. (46 N. Los Robles Ave.) 20th-century art, American painting. Tues. 10–9; Wed.–Sat. 10–5; Sun. 2–5. †*
PASADENA PUBLIC LIBRARY, PASADENA HISTORICAL ROOM. (285 E. Walnut St.) Regional history. Wed. and Fri. 2–5.

Placerville

PACIFIC SOUTHWEST FOREST AND RANGE EXPERIMENT STATION; INSTITUTE OF FOREST GENETICS. Botanical garden, arboretum, herbarium; especially pines, other conifers. Mon.–Fri. 8–4:30.

Pomona

ADOBE DE PALOMARES. (491 Cucamonga Ave.) Historic house, 1850–54; ranch implements. Tues. 9–12, Wed.–Sun. 2–5.

Port Hueneme

SEABEE MUSEUM. (United States Navy, Construction Battalion Center) History of the Seabees. Mon.–Fri. 8–4:30, weekends 12:30–4:30. †

Redwood City

CALVARY LIBRARY MUSEUM. (1321 Hudson St.) Religious coins, stamps, art; Bibles. Sun. 1–4.
RAILWAY AND LOCOMOTIVE HISTORICAL SOCIETY, INC., PACIFIC COAST CHAPTER. (978 Emerald Hill Rd.) Railroad equipment, photographs.

Richmond

RICHMOND ART CENTER. (Civic Center) Folk art; exhibitions. Mon.–Thurs. 9–4:30, 7–9:30; Fri. 9–4:30; Sun. 2–5.

Riverside

RIVERSIDE MUNICIPAL MUSEUM. (7th and Orange Sts.) Local history, natural history, Indian. Mon.–Sat. 9–5.

Sacramento

CALIFORNIA STATE LIBRARY. (Library and Courts Bldg.) State history; old prints, maps, manuscripts. Mon.–Fri. 8–5. †
E. B. CROCKER ART GALLERY. (216 O St.) German painting, Korean ceramics, American glass, graphics. Daily (except Mon.) 10–5. †
SACRAMENTO JUNIOR MUSEUM, INC. (4500 Y St.) Science, nature center, planetarium. Daily (except Mon.) 9–5.
SUTTER'S FORT STATE HISTORICAL MONUMENT. (2701 L St.) Preservation project: early California history, discovery of gold 1839–1848. Daily 10–5. †*

San Diego

CABRILLO NATIONAL MONUMENT. Historic lighthouse, 1855; history museum; California gray whale observatory. Daily 9–5:30. *
THE FINE ARTS GALLERY OF SAN DIEGO. (Balboa Park) Survey. Tues.–Sat. 10–5, Sun. 1–5:30. †*
HISTORICAL SHRINE FOUNDATION OF SAN DIEGO COUNTY. (2482 San Diego Ave.) Historic home and courthouse, 1856. Wed.–Sun. 10–5.
JUNIPERO SERRA MUSEUM. (Presidio Park) Local history: Spanish, Indian items; pioneer equipment. Mon. 10–5; Tues.–Sat. 9–5; Sun. 12–5.
SAN DIEGO MUSEUM OF MAN. (Balboa

Park) Anthropology, New World. Mon.–Sat. 10–4:45; Sun. 12–4:45. †

SAN DIEGO NATURAL HISTORY MUSEUM. (Balboa Park) Marine and medical exhibits; children's museum. Daily 10–4:30. †

SAN DIEGO ZOOLOGICAL GARDEN. Zoo, children's zoo. Daily 9–5. †**

San Fernando

SAN FERNANDO MISSION. (15151 San Fernando Mission Blvd.) Historic Franciscan mission, 1797. Mon.–Sat. 9:30–5; Sun. 11–5.

San Francisco

CALIFORNIA ACADEMY OF SCIENCE. (Golden Gate Park) Natural history; aquarium, planetarium, junior museum; science and technology. Daily 10–5. †**

CALIFORNIA DIVISION OF MINES AND GEOLOGY. (Ferry Bldg.) Mineralogy. Daily 9–4. †*

CALIFORNIA HISTORICAL SOCIETY. (2090 Jackson St.) Historic Whittier Mansion, 1894–96, Victorian furnishings; local history. Daily (except Mon.) 10–4.

CALIFORNIA PALACE OF THE LEGION OF HONOR. (Lincoln Park) Art museum: *Survey*, decorative arts. Mon.–Sat. 10–5. †*

JOSEPHINE D. RANDALL JUNIOR MUSEUM. (Roosevelt Way and 16th St.) Natural history, model aircraft and railroad displays. Mon.–Sat. 10–5. †

M. H. DE YOUNG MEMORIAL MUSEUM. (Golden Gate Park) *Survey*. Daily 10–5. †*

MUSEUM OF RUSSIAN CULTURE. (2450 Sutter St.) Russian history, esp. recent. Tues. 5–9.

SAN FRANCISCO MARITIME MUSEUM. (Foot of Polk St.) Ship models, relics; other maritime items; full-rigged ship. Daily 10–5; weekend evenings. †*

SAN FRANCISCO MUSEUM OF ART. (Veterans Bldg., Civic Center) Contemporary art, exhibitions. Tues.–Fri. 12–10; Sat.–Mon. 1–6. †*

SAN FRANCISCO PUBLIC LIBRARY. (Civic Center) Costumes; Oriental art objects. Winter: Mon.–Fri. 9–9, Sat. 9–6, Sun. 1–5.

SAN FRANCISCO ZOOLOGICAL SOCIETY.

(Great Hwy. and Sloat Blvd.) Zoo. Daylight hours.

SCHLAGE LOCK COMPANY. (2201 Bayshore Blvd.) Locks and keys: for company use only.

THE SOCIETY OF CALIFORNIA PIONEERS. (456 McAllister St.) City and State history in paintings and graphic work. Maintains birthplace, in Mallorca, Spain, of Fr. Junipero Serra. Mon.–Sat. 10–4.

STRYBING ARBORETUM AND BOTANIC GARDEN. (Golden Gate Park) Mon.–Fri. 8–4:30, weekends 10–5.

WELLS FARGO BANK HISTORY ROOM. (22 Montgomery St.) History of Wells Fargo Company in California; company museum. Mon.–Fri. during banking hours.

San Jose

ROSICRUCIAN EGYPTIAN, ORIENTAL MUSEUM AND ART GALLERY. (Rosicrucian Park) Babylonian and Egyptian art. Mon.–Fri. 9–12, 1–5; Sat. 1–5, Sun. 12–5.

THE ROSICRUCIAN SCIENCE MUSEUM AND PLANETARIUM. (Rosicrucian Park) Museum: Wed., Sun. 1–5. Planetarium: daily.

SAN JOSE STATE COLLEGE ART GALLERY. Contemp. painting, graphics, crafts. Mon.–Fri. 10–4, Sun. 1:15–5.

YOUTH SCIENCE INSTITUTE. (16260 Alum Rock Ave.) Natural history, paleontology, small animals. Tues.–Fri. 9–4:30, Sat. 10–5.

San Marino

HENRY E. HUNTINGTON LIBRARY AND ART GALLERY. (1151 Oxford Rd.) 18th-century British paintings, 18th-century French furnishings; botanical garden. Tues.–Sun. 1–4:30 (except Sept.). †*

San Mateo

SAN MATEO COUNTY JUNIOR MUSEUM, INC. (Coyote Pt.) Nature center. Tues.–Sat. 9–5, Sun. 1–5. †

San Pedro

CABRILLO MARINE MUSEUM. (3720 Stephen White Dr.) Sea life, ship models, fish. Daily 9–5.

San Rafael

JUNIOR MUSEUM OF MARIN. (76 Albert

Park Lane) Natural history. Sept.–June, Tues.–Sat. 9–5, Sun. 2–5.

PONY EXPRESS HISTORY AND ART GALLERY. (75 Margarita Dr.) Private collection of items relating to founding and history of pony express. By appt. only.

Santa Ana

CHARLES W. BOWERS MEMORIAL MUSEUM. (2002 N. Main St.) General museum: art, state history, regional archaeology and anthropology. Tues.–Sat. 10–4:30, Sun. 1–5, Thurs. eve. 7–9.

Santa Barbara

SANTA BARBARA BOTANIC GARDEN. (Mission Canyon) Esp. ornamental plants of California; historic Old Mission Dam, 1807; open-stone aqueduct. Daily, daylight hours.

SANTA BARBARA HISTORICAL SOCIETY. Historic Old Mission; early California history. Tues.–Sat. 2–5.

SANTA BARBARA MUSEUM OF ART. (1130 State St.) *Survey;* Oriental instruments; doll display. Tues.–Sat. 11–5, Sun. 12–5.

SANTA BARBARA MUSEUM OF NATURAL HISTORY. (2550 Puesta Del Sol Rd.) Archaeology, anthropology, mineralogy, paleontology of Pacific Coast; planetarium; children's museum. Mon.–Sat. 9–5, Sun. 1–5.

SANTA BARBARA PUBLIC LIBRARY, FAULKNER MEMORIAL ART GALLERY. (40 E. Anapamu St.) Exhibitions, local art. Mon.–Fri. 10–9, Sat. 10–6.

Santa Clara

UNIVERSITY OF SANTA CLARA, DE SAISSET ART GALLERY AND MUSEUM. Art (painting, decorative arts, Indian artifacts); history; mineralogy. Tues.–Sat. 2–4:30.

Santa Cruz

SANTA CRUZ MUSEUM. (1305 E. Cliff Dr.) Natural history: seashore birds, minerals, shells. Daily (except Mon.) 1–5.

Santa Rosa

SANTA ROSA JUNIOR COLLEGE, JESSE PETER MUSEUM AND NORTH COAST HER-

BARIUM. Area natural history: seed plants, minerals, birds. Mon. and Thurs. 2–4:30 and by appt.

Stanford

STANFORD UNIVERSITY ART GALLERY. Teaching collection: Oriental, Italian 18th century. Tues.–Sat. 1–5, Sun. 12–4.

STANFORD UNIVERSITY MUSEUM. Teaching collection: classical archaeology; Egyptian materials. Daily, 1–5.

STANFORD UNIVERSITY, NATURAL HISTORY MUSEUM. Teaching and research collections. Mon.–Fri. 9–12, 1–5.

Stockton

PIONEER MUSEUM AND HAGGIN GALLERIES. (Victory Park, Pershing Ave.) Art, local history, minerals. Daily (except Mon.) afternoon.

SAN JOAQUIN COUNTY SCIENCE CENTER AND JUNIOR MUSEUM. (1305 Occidental St.) Natural history, Indian materials. Mon.–Fri. 9–5.

UNIVERSITY OF THE PACIFIC, PONY EXPRESS MUSEUM. History; teaching collections. Hours vary.

Three Rivers

SEQUOIA NATIONAL PARK, GIANT FOREST MUSEUM. Park museum: natural history, nature walks, trailsides. Daily: winter 9–6; summer 8–7. *

Tulelake

LAVA BEDS NATIONAL MONUMENT. Park museum: natural history. Daily: winter 8–5; summer 8–7. *

Twentynine Palms

JOSHUA TREE NATIONAL MONUMENT. (74485 Palm Vista Dr.) Park museum: archaeology, geology, herbarium. Daily 8–5. *

Ventura

VENTURA COUNTY PIONEER MUSEUM. (77 N. California St.) Local history. Mon.–Fri. 8–4:30.

Visalia

TULARE COUNTY MUSEUM. (Mooney's

Grove) Local history, Indian artifacts, pioneer objects. Winter: daily 9–6.

Weaverville

TRINITY COUNTY, JAKE JACKSON HISTORICAL MUSEUM. (Main St.) Local history, gold rush objects; in jail of old courthouse.

Whittier

PIO PICO STATE HISTORICAL MONUMENT. (6003 Pioneer Blvd.) 1801 historic house; home of last Mexican governor of California. Wed.–Sun. 10–5.

Yosemite

YOSEMITE NATIONAL PARK, Happy Isles Nature Center, Mariposa Grove Museum, Pioneer Yosemite History Center, Yosemite Museum. Park museums: nature center, natural history, pioneer and local history, botanical garden, nature walks, art and ethnology. Daily: winter 8–5; summer 8–6. †**

Yreka

SISKIYOU COUNTY HISTORICAL SOCIETY. (910 S. Main St.) Local history. Tues.–Sat. 9–5, Sun. 1–5.

COLORADO

Bayfield

THE GEM VILLAGE MUSEUM, INC. Anthropology, geology, mineralogy, archaeology, paleontology. Daily 6:30–9:30 P.M.

Bergen Park

HAGANS CLOCK MANOR MUSEUM. (Hwys. 68 and 74) Clocks of all countries and ages. Daily (except Mon.) 10–5. †

Boulder

BOULDER PIONEER MUSEUM. (1655 Broadway) Local history, period rooms and shops. Daily 2–5.
UNIVERSITY OF COLORADO MUSEUM. (Broadway between 15th and 16th) Natural history, arts, anthropology, graphics,

science. Teaching collections. Mon.–Fri. 8–5, Sat. 9–12, Sun. 3–5.

Canon City

CANON CITY MUNICIPAL MUSEUM. (612 River St.) Mounted game, birds; minerals; Colorado paintings. Mon.–Sat. 8–5, Sun. 1–5.

Central City

CENTRAL CITY OPERA HOUSE ASSOCIATION. (Eureka St.) Preservation project: gold mining community. Summer festival. Daily 9:30–6. †*

Colorado Springs

CHEYENNE MOUNTAIN ZOOLOGICAL PARK. Zoo. Daylight hours.
COLORADO COLLEGE MUSEUM. (Palmer Hall, Tejon and San Rafael) Natural history, Indian artifacts, archaeology. Mon.–Fri. 8:30–12, 1–4:30.
COLORADO SPRINGS FINE ARTS CENTER. (30 W. Dale St.) Santos, Navaho sand paintings, European painting, exhibitions. Winter: Tues.–Sat. 9–5; Sun. 1:30–5; Summer: Mon.–Sat. 9–5; Sun. 1:30–5. †*
PIONEERS' MUSEUM. (25 W. Kiowa St.) Local history. Tues.–Sat., 10–5, Sun. 2–5.
TRIANON. European paintings, tapestries, decorative arts in mansion of 1907 copied from Grand Trianon, Versailles; gardens.

Cripple Creek

CRIPPLE CREEK DISTRICT MUSEUM. Local history, railroad and mining items. Summer, daily 9–5.

Denver

BOTANIC GARDEN FOUNDATION. (909 York St.) Botanical garden, herbarium.
COLORADO STATE MUSEUM. (E. 14th Ave. and Sherman St.) State history, archaeology, mineralogy, Indians. Mon.–Sat. 9–5, Sun. 10–5.
DENVER ART MUSEUM. (1343 Acoma) *Survey;* primitive art of Africa, Oceania and the Americas. Tues.–Sat. 9–5, Sun. 2–5. †*
DENVER MUSEUM OF NATURAL HISTORY. (City Park) *Survey;* botanical

garden; planetarium. Winter: Mon.–Sat. 10–4:30, Sun. 12–5; Summer: Mon.–Sat. 9–5, Sun. 12–5. †*

DENVER ZOOLOGICAL GARDEN. (City Park Zoo) Daily, daylight hours.

Durango

DURANGO PUBLIC LIBRARY MUSEUM. (1188 2d Ave.) Archaeology, geology; pioneer history; wood exhibit illustrating dendrochronology. Mon.–Sat. 9:30–9, Sun. 9:30–12.

Estes Park

ROCKY MOUNTAIN NATIONAL PARK, MORAINE PARK VISITOR CENTER. Park museum: history, nature trails. Summer, daily 8–8. *

Fruita

COLORADO NATIONAL MONUMENT. Park museum: trailside. Daily 8–5. *

Georgetown

HOTEL DE PARIS. Historic house, 1875; Victorian furnishings. Summer: Mon.–Fri. 9–5, weekends 9–6.

Golden

BUFFALO BILL MUSEUM. (Lookout Mt.) Local history, mementos of Col. Wm. Cody. Daily 8–6.

COLORADO RAILROAD MUSEUM, INC. (17555 W. 44th Ave.) Railroad and electric railway equipment of Colorado. Daily 8–9. †

COLORADO SCHOOL OF MINES MUSEUM (Maple and 16th Sts.) Geology, mineralogy. Daily 8–5.

JEFFERSON COUNTY MUSEUM. (Washington Ave.) Local history, 1877 house. Mon.–Fri. 2–4:30.

Greeley

MEEKER HOME. (1324 9th Ave.) Historic house, 1870; local history. Mon.–Sat. 1–5; Summer: 9–12, 1–5.

Julesburg

JULESBURG HISTORICAL MUSEUM. (320 Cedar) Local history, Pony Express and Union Pacific displays. Mon.–Sat. 2–4.

La Junta

OTERO JUNIOR COLLEGE, KOSHARE INDIAN KIVA MUSEUM. (18th and Santa Fe Ave.) Indian art and crafts.

Las Animas

THE KIT CARSON MUSEUM. (Earl's Court) Local history. Mon.–Sat. 1–5.

Loveland

LOVELAND MUSEUM. (5th and Lincoln) Local history. Winter: Mon.–Fri. 8:30–5, Sat. 8:30–4; Summer: Mon.–Fri. 8:30–8:30, Sat. 8:30–4:30, Sun. 2–5.

Meeker

THE WHITE RIVER MUSEUM. (565 Park) Historic house, built after Meeker Massacre of 1879; local history. Mon.–Sat. 9–12, 1–5.

Mesa Verde National Park

MESA VERDE NATIONAL PARK MUSEUM. Archaeology. Winter: daily 8–5; Summer: daily 7:45–6. *

Montrose

BLACK CANYON OF THE GUNNISON NATIONAL MONUMENT, WAYSIDE EXHIBIT. Herbarium. Daily 8–5. *

UTE INDIAN MUSEUM. (Chief Ouray State Historical Park, Rt. 550) Indian artifacts, interpretive exhibits. May 30–Oct. 31, daily 9–5.

Sterling

OVERLAND TRAIL MUSEUM. Local history; mementos of ox caravan journey to California and Colorado gold fields. Summer: daily (except Mon.) 8:30–4:30.

Trinidad

TRINIDAD STATE JUNIOR COLLEGE MUSEUM. Archaeology, paleontology of Colorado and New Mexico; teaching collections. Mon.–Fri. 9–4.

United States Air Force Academy

UNITED STATES AIR FORCE ACADEMY. Planetarium; teaching purposes. †

CONNECTICUT

Branford

SWAIN-HARRISON HOUSE. (112 W. Main St.) House of 1680, maintained by Soc. for the Preservation of New England Antiq., for members only.

Bridgeport

BARNUM INSTITUTE OF SCIENCE AND HISTORY, THE P. T. BARNUM MUSEUM. (804 Main St.) Personal effects of P. T. Barnum; mementos of Tom Thumb, Jenny Lind; local history. Winter: Mon.–Fri. 2–5; Summer: Mon.–Fri. 2–4.

BEARDSLEY PARK ZOO. Daylight hours.

MUSEUM OF ART, SCIENCE AND INDUSTRY. (Ninety Acres Park) Planetarium; general collections; children's; historic Captain Brooks House. Mon.–Fri. 9–5:30, weekends 10–6.

Clinton

STANTON HOUSE. Historic house. Tues.–Sun. 2–5.

Colebrook

COLEBROOK HISTORICAL SOCIETY. Local history; house 1804; household and farming equipment. June–Sept., weekends 2–5.

Danbury

THE DANBURY SCOTT-FANTON MUSEUM AND HISTORICAL SOCIETY, INC. (43 Main St.) Historic Barnum House, Revolutionary Period costumes, furnishings. Tues., Thurs., Sat. 2–5.

East Haven

BRANFORD TROLLEY MUSEUM. (Sprague Memorial Bldg., River St.) Electric railway cars and equipment; some operative. Summer, 10–5; cars operate weekends 1–6. †

Essex

PRATT HOUSE. (20 West Ave.) Historic house of 1725, maintained by the Soc. for the Preservation of New England Antiq. American furniture. Summer: Mon.–Fri. 1–4.

Farmington

FARMINGTON MUSEUM. (High St.) Historic Stanley-Whitman House of 1660; period furnishings, local history. April–Nov., Tues.–Sat. 10–12, 2–5, Sun. 2–5; Dec.–Mar., Fri.–Sun. 10–12, 2–5.

HILL-STEAD MUSEUM. Historic house, 1900. Art, decorative arts, French Impressionist works. Wed., Thurs., Sat., Sun. 2–5.

Greenwich

AUDUBON CENTER OF CONNECTICUT. (Riversville Rd. and John St.) Nature center. Tues.–Sat. 9–5, Sun. 1–5.

THE BRUCE MUSEUM. (Bruce Park) Art, natural history, zoo. Mon.–Fri. 10–5, Sun. 2–5.

PUTNAM COTTAGE. (245 E. Putnam Ave.) House of 1692, used by Gen. Israel Putnam during Revolutionary War; local history. Mon., Thurs.–Sat. 10–5.

Groton

BILL MEMORIAL LIBRARY. (Monument St.) Butterflies, birds, historical collection. Mon., Tues., Thurs.–Sat. 2:30–5:30, Wed. eve. 7–9. †

GENERAL DYNAMICS CORP., ELECTRIC BOAT DIV., THE SUBMARINE LIBRARY. (Thames St.) Submarine history, models, paintings. Mon.–Sat. 9–5.

MONUMENT HOUSE. (Monument St.) Revolutionary period equipment, uniforms, furnishings. Summer: 2:30–4:30.

Guilford

THE GUILFORD KEEPING SOCIETY. (Boston St.) Thomas Griswold House, 1736; local history, documents, costumes, furnishings. Fri.–Sun. 1–5.

HENRY WHITFIELD HOUSE. (Whitfield St.) Furnishings, textiles, 1639 house. Apr.–Oct. daily (except Mon.) 10–12, 1–5; Dec.–Mar. daily (except Mon.) 10–12, 1–4.

HYLAND HOUSE. (84 Boston St.) 1660 house, furnishings. Summer, daily 11–5.

Hamden

THE HAMDEN HISTORICAL SOCIETY,

INC. (Mt. Carmel Ave.) Jonathan Dickerman House of 1770, furnishings. Sat. 1:30–5.

Hartford

CONNECTICUT HISTORICAL SOCIETY. (1 Elizabeth St.) Furniture and decorative arts, paintings by Connecticut artists; state history; historic Old State House (880 Main St.) Summer: Mon.–Fri. 1–5; Winter: Mon.–Sat. 1–5.

CONNECTICUT STATE LIBRARY MUSEUM. (231 Capitol Ave.) State history; Colt collection of firearms; archaeology. Mon.–Fri. 9–5, Sat. 9–1.

THE MARK TWAIN LIBRARY AND MEMORIAL COMMISSION. (351 Farmington Ave.) Winter: Tues.–Fri. 2–5, Sat. 10–5; Summer: Tues.–Sat. 10–5, Sun. 2–5.

TRINITY COLLEGE MUSEUM. (Summit St.) Teaching collection: natural history. Daily 8:30–4.

WADSWORTH ATHENEUM. (25 Atheneum Sq. N.) Art: *Survey.* Tues.–Fri. 10–5, Sat. 9–5, Sun. 1:30–5:30. †**

Litchfield

LITCHFIELD HISTORICAL SOCIETY. (South and East Sts.) Local history, portraits; Historic Tapping Reeve House and First Law School, 1774, period furnishings. Summer: Tues.–Sat. 2:30–5:30, Thurs. 11–1; Winter: Thurs. 11–1, 2:30–5:30. House: May 15–Oct. 15, daily (except Wed.) 2–5.

Madison

MADISON HISTORICAL SOCIETY. (Boston Post Rd.) Local history; Nathaniel Allis House, 1739; Summer: Mon.–Fri. 10–5, Sat. 10–12.

Manchester

LUTZ JUNIOR MUSEUM. (126 Cedar St.) Natural history, history, Indians, aquarium. Daily (except Mon.) 2–5.

Meriden

MERIDEN HISTORICAL SOCIETY, INC. (424 W. Main St.) Historic Andrews Homestead, 1760; period furnishings. Sun. 2–5.

Middletown

WESLEYAN UNIVERSITY, DAVISON ART

CENTER. (High St.) Art: teaching collection; fine prints. Historic Alsop House. Mon.–Fri. 9–5, Sat. 9–12, 1–4, Sun. 2–4 (closed weekends when school is not in session).

Mystic

DENISON HOMESTEAD. (Pequot-Sepos Rd.) Historic house 1717, kitchen equipment and other period furnishings; costumes, decoys. Summer: daily (except Mon.) 1–5.

MARINE HISTORICAL ASSOCIATION. (Mystic Seaport, Greenmanville Ave.) History of Mystic port; planetarium. Preservation project: ships, 19th-century buildings. Daily 9–5. †*

PEQUOT-SEPOS WILDLIFE SANCTUARY. (Pequot-Sepos Rd.) Nature center; aviary, zoo, woods. Tues.–Sat. 10–5, Sun. 1–5.

New Britain

THE CHILDREN'S MUSEUM OF NEW BRITAIN. (Hawley Memorial Library, High St.) Natural history, aquarium, animals. Mon.–Fri. 2:30–5:30; Sat. 10–12:30, 1:30–4.

NEW BRITAIN MUSEUM OF AMERICAN ART. (56 Lexington St.) 18th–20th-century American graphics, paintings. Daily (except Mon.) 2–5:30.

New Canaan

NEW CANAAN HISTORICAL SOCIETY. (10 Cherry St.) Historic Hanford-Silliman House (Oenoke Ave.). Local history library. House: some afternoons. Library: Mon.

New Haven

THE EDWARD CLARK STREETER COLLECTION OF WEIGHTS AND MEASURES. (333 Cedar St.) University museum. By appt.

NEW HAVEN COLONY HISTORICAL SOCIETY. (114 Whitney Ave.) American and local history. Historic Morris House of 1680 and 1780 with period furnishings (325 Lighthouse Rd.). Mon.–Fri. 9–12, 1–5; Sun. 2–5.

WINCHESTER GUN MUSEUM. (275 Winchester Ave.) Company museum

(Olin-Mathieson Chemical Corp.): guns. Mon.–Sat. 9–4.

YALE UNIVERSITY ART GALLERY. (1111 Chapel St.) *Survey*. Tues.–Sat. 10–5, Sun. 2–5. †*

YALE UNIVERSITY COLLECTION OF MUSICAL INSTRUMENTS. Sun., Thurs. 2–5 (during school year).

YALE UNIVERSITY HERBARIUM. (Osborn Botanical Laboratory) Mon.–Fri. 9–5.

YALE UNIVERSITY, PEABODY MUSEUM OF NATURAL HISTORY. (170 Whitney Ave.) Anthropology, geology, oceanography. Mar.–Oct. Mon.–Sat. 9–5; Nov.–Feb. 9–4:30, Sun. 2–4:30. †*

New London

CONNECTICUT COLLEGE, CONNECTICUT ARBORETUM. Botanical garden, herbarium. Daylight hours.

CONNECTICUT SOCIETY OF THE SONS OF THE AMERICAN REVOLUTION. (Huntington St.) Nathan Hale School House; Nathan Hale and Revolutionary War items. By appt.

HEMPSTED HOUSE. (Hempsted St.) Historic house, 1678–1728. Colonial furnishings. May 15–Oct. 15 Mon.–Sat. 10–12, 1–5; Sun. 2–5.

LYMAN ALLYN MUSEUM. (100 Mohegan Ave.) American and Connecticut art; decorative arts; historic Deshon-Allyn House of 1829, Federal period furnishings (613 Williams St.). Tues.–Sat. 1–5, Sun. 2–5.

NEW LONDON COUNTY CHILDREN'S MUSEUM. (Williams St.).

NEW LONDON COUNTY HISTORICAL SOCIETY. (11 Blinman St.) Historic Shaw Mansion; local history; ms. collection of Revolutionary maritime material. Tues.–Sat. 1–4.

New Milford

NEW MILFORD HISTORICAL SOCIETY. (55 Main St.) Local history; Boardman House; Litchfield County Bank Building (arrowheads and other Indian artifacts). Wed., Sat. 2–5.

North Haven

NORTH HAVEN ART GALLERY. (38 Warner Rd.) Historic house of 1685; work by Connecticut artists. Exhibitions. Daily 2–6.

Norwich

THE NORWICH FREE ACADEMY, SLATER MEMORIAL MUSEUM. (108 Crescent St.) Art: Oriental, American; miscellaneous. Mon.–Fri. 10–4, Sun. 2–5.

SOCIETY OF THE FOUNDERS OF NORWICH, CONN., INC. (348 Washington St.) Local history; Leffingwell Inn, 1675; Historic Joseph Carpenter Shop, Colonial silversmith (71 E. Town St.). All year Tues.–Sat. 9:30–12:30, 2–5:30; summer, Sun. 2–5:30.

Old Lyme

LYME ART ASSOCIATION, INC. *Exhibitions*. June 15–Sept. 15 Mon.–Sat. 10–5, Sun. 1–5.

LYME HISTORICAL SOCIETY, FLORENCE GRISWOLD ASSOCIATION. Historic house of 1817; period furnishings. Summer, daily (except Mon.) 2–5.

Ridgefield

LARRY ALDRICH MUSEUM. (Main St.) Contemporary painting, sculpture garden, library; "Old Hundred," bldg. of 1783, exhibitions. Sat. 12–6, Sun. 2–6.

Sharon

SHARON HISTORICAL SOCIETY. Antique implements, furniture; historic Gay-Hoyt House. Mon.–Sat.

South Coventry

NATHAN HALE HOMESTEAD. (South St.) House, 1776. May 15–Oct. 15 daily 1–5.

South Woodstock

QUASSET SCHOOL MUSEUM. One-room school built 1748, furnished with mid-19th-century equipment.

Southington

POWERS AUTO MUSEUM. (Rt. 10) Antique automobiles, other Americana; farm tools, toys. May 1–Nov. 15 daily 9–7.

Stamford

THE STAMFORD HISTORICAL SOCIETY, INC. (713 Bedford St.) House, 1901;

early American furnishings, implements, needlework. Tues.–Fri. 1–4.

THE STAMFORD MUSEUM AND NATURE CENTER. (High Ridge and Scofieldtown Rds.) Hecksher Farm; animals. Overbrook Natural Science Center. Planetarium; herbarium; natural history *survey*. Tues.–Sat. 9–5, Sun. 2–6. †*

Stonington

STONINGTON HISTORICAL SOCIETY. Local history; old lighthouse. Summer: daily (except Mon.) 11–4:30.

Stratford

STRATFORD HISTORICAL SOCIETY MUSEUM. (967 Academy Hill) Local history. Historic Judson House, 1723; period furnishings, kitchen equipment. Summer: Wed., weekends 11–5; winter: Thurs.–Sat. 1–5.

Wallingford

NEHEMIAH ROYCE HOUSE. (538 N. Main St.) Period furnishings, lean-to style house, 1672. Maintained by Soc. for the Preservation of New England Antiq. Summer: daily (except Sun.) 3–5.

WALLINGFORD HISTORICAL SOCIETY, INC. (180 S. Main St.) Historic Samuel Parsons House. Sun. 2–5.

Warehouse Point

THE CONNECTICUT ELECTRIC RAILWAY ASSOCIATION, INC. (North Rd. Rt. 191) Trolley cars, engines; some operative. Wed. and weekends 2–sundown.

Washington

GUNN MEMORIAL LIBRARY MUSEUM. (Washington Green) American military items; Indian collection. Tues., Thurs.–Sat. 2–5.

Waterbury

MATTATUCK HISTORICAL SOCIETY. (119 W. Main St.) Local history. Tues.–Sat. 10–5, Sun. 2–5.

WATERBURY COMPANIES, INC. (835 S. Main St.) Company museum; metal and glass buttons. By appt.

Waterford

HARKNESS MEMORIAL STATE PARK.

(R.D. 2, Great Neck Rd.) Park museum; art gallery (bird paintings); gardens. May 30–Oct. 12, 10–6.

West Hartford

THE CHILDREN'S MUSEUM OF HARTFORD, INC. (950 Trout Brook Rd.) Natural history. Mon.–Sat. 9–5, Sun. 2–5. Closed weekends during summer. †*

Westport

MID-FAIRFIELD COUNTY YOUTH MUSEUM. (10 Woodside Lane) Natural history; nature trails; wildlife sanctuary; planetarium; animals. Mon.–Sat. 9–5, Sun. 2–5. †*

Wethersfield

BUTTOLPH-WILLIAMS HOUSE. (249 Broad St.) House, 1692; period furnishings, kitchen equipment. May 15–Oct. 15, daily 12–4:30.

WEBB HOUSE. (211 Main St.) Historic house. Mon.–Sat. 10–5, Sun. 11–5; Nov.–Feb. 10–4.

WETHERSFIELD HISTORICAL SOCIETY. (150 Main St.) Local history and archives; household and farm implements; equipment for spinning and weaving; historic Old Academy Museum, 1804 house. Tues.–Sat. 1–4:30.

Wilton

THE CRAFT CENTER MUSEUM, INC. Contemporary and early American crafts; metal work, leatherwork, woodwork.

Windsor

THE WINDSOR HISTORICAL SOCIETY. (96 Palisado Ave.) Local history; Historic Fyler House, 1640; period furnishings. May–Oct. Tues., Fri. 2–4:30.

Winsted

WINCHESTER HISTORICAL SOCIETY. (Prospect St.) Historic house; portraits, early 19th-century. Summer, daily 1–5.

Woodbury

THE GLEBE HOUSE. Associated with Judge Samuel Seabury; built 1690, added to 1750; documents related to Seabury. Mon., Tues., Thurs.–Sat. 10–5, Sun. 1–5.

DELAWARE

Dover

THE DELAWARE STATE MUSEUM. (316 S. Governors Ave.) State history, crafts and industries; Indian artifacts; Old Presbyterian Church of 1790. Tues.–Sat. 11–5, Sun. 2–5.

Newark

UNIVERSITY OF DELAWARE, ART DEPARTMENT GALLERY. Paintings, sculpture, prints. Daily 8 A.M.–9 P.M.

Odessa

THE CORBIT HOUSE. (Main St.) Historic house; decorative arts of 18th and 19th centuries. Tues., Thurs., Sat. 10–5; Sun. 2–5.

Wilmington

HAGLEY MUSEUM. (Barley Mill Rd. and Brandywine Creek) Preservation project; old bldgs. of Eleutherian Mills; history of American industry. Company Museum. Tues.–Sat. 9:30–4:30, Sun. 1–5. †*
HISTORICAL SOCIETY OF DELAWARE. (Market St.) Local history. Mon.–Fri. 10–5 (except Aug.).
THE WILMINGTON SOCIETY OF THE FINE ARTS, DELAWARE ART CENTER. (2301 Kentmere Pkwy.) English 19th-century, American paintings; exhibitions. Mon.–Sat. 10–5, Sun. 2–6.

Winterthur

THE HENRY FRANCIS DU PONT WINTERTHUR MUSEUM. American decorative arts and interior design, Colonial to present. Tues.–Sat. 9:30–4:30 (all visitors get guided tours; advance reservations necessary). †**

WASHINGTON, D.C.

AMERICAN PHARMACEUTICAL ASSOCIATION MUSEUM. (2215 Constitution Ave., N.W.) Pharmaceutical antiques. Mon.–Fri. 9–4:30.
THE AMERICAN UNIVERSITY, WATKINS GALLERY. (Massachusetts and Nebraska Aves., N.W.) Contemporary European and American painting. Daily (except Sat.) 2–5.
ARTS CLUB OF WASHINGTON. (2017 I St., N.W.) Exhibitions; in historic James Monroe House, 1802. Daily 11–5.
THE ASSOCIATION FOR THE STUDY OF NEGRO LIFE AND HISTORY, INC. (1538 9th St., N.W.) Old and rare books relating to Negro history. Weekdays 8:30–5. †
B'NAI B'RITH MUSEUM. (1640 Rhode Island Ave., N.W.) American-Jewish history, art; exhibitions. Mon., Tues., Thurs., Fri. 1:30–5; Sun. 10–5. †
THE CHILDREN'S MUSEUM OF WASHINGTON, INC. (1714 19th St., N.W.) Natural history, history.
COLUMBIA HISTORICAL SOCIETY. (1307 New Hampshire Ave.) History of District of Columbia; in Historic Christian Heurich House, 1892; period furnishings. Daily (except Sun.) 2–4.
THE CORCORAN GALLERY OF ART. (New York Ave. and 17th St., N.W.) 19th- and 20th-century American art, 19th-century French painting; European decorative arts. Tues.–Fri. 10–4:30, Sat. 9–4:30, Sun. 2–5. †*
DECATUR HOUSE. (748 Jackson Pl., N.W.) Designed by B. H. Latrobe, 1818. Wed. and Sat. afternoons.
DEPARTMENT OF COMMERCE AQUARIUM. (14th St. and Constitution Ave., N.W.) United States fish, frogs, etc. Daily 8:30–4:30.
THE DUMBARTON OAKS RESEARCH LIBRARY AND COLLECTION. (1703 32nd Ave., N.W.) Byzantine art, pre-Columbian art; research; gardens. (Dept. of Harvard University.) Tues.–Sun. 2–5. †*
FEDERAL BUREAU OF INVESTIGATION EXHIBIT AREAS. (Dept. of Justice Bldg., Pennsylvania and 9th Aves.) Memorabilia of famous FBI cases; firearms demonstration. Mon.–Fri. 9:30–4.
HOWARD UNIVERSITY GALLERY OF ART. (6th and Howard Pl., N.W.) American painting, graphics; African Negro art; European graphics. Wed.–Sun. 2–5. †
KENILWORTH AQUATIC GARDENS. (42d and Douglas Sts., N.E.) Water plants. Daylight hours.
LIBRARY OF CONGRESS. Photographs, prints; musical instruments. Exhibition

halls: Mon.–Sat. 9 A.M.–10 P.M., Sun. 11:30 A.M.–10 P.M. †*

LINCOLN MUSEUM. (511 10th St., N.W.) Historic Ford's Theatre, 1863–65, where Lincoln was shot; collection of Lincolniana. Mon.–Sat. 9–9, Sun. 12:30–9.

MEDICAL MUSEUM OF THE ARMED FORCES INSTITUTE OF PATHOLOGY. (Independence Ave. at 9th St., S.W.) Pathological specimens, surgical equipment. Daily 9–5. †

MUSEUM, NATIONAL SOCIETY, DAUGHTERS OF THE AMERICAN REVOLUTION. (1776 D St., N.W.) Furnishings, costumes, objects of art. Mon.–Fri. 10–3.

MUSEUM OF THE SOCIETY OF THE CINCINNATI. (2118 Massachusetts Ave.) Revolutionary War items. Mon.–Sat. 2–4.

NATIONAL ARCHIVES. (Constitution Ave. between 7th and 9th Sts.) Original copies of national documents. Mon.–Sat. 9 A.M.–10 P.M.; Sun. 1–10.

NATIONAL GALLERY OF ART. (6th St. and Constitution Ave.) *Survey; Kress,* American primitive, old masters, graphics. Mon.–Sat. 10–5; Sun. 2–10. †**

NATIONAL HISTORICAL WAX MUSEUM. (26th and E Sts., N.W.) Tableaux. Daily 9–9.

NAVAL HISTORICAL DISPLAY CENTER. (Navy Yard) Ship relics; model vessels. Mon.–Fri. 1–4. †

THE OCTAGON, NATIONAL HEADQUARTERS OF THE AMERICAN INSTITUTE OF ARCHITECTS. (1741 New York Ave.) Historic house, 1798; architecture displays. Tues.–Sat. 9–5, Sun. 2–5.

OLD STONE HOUSE. (3051 M St., N.W.) Historic house, 1764–65; period furnishings. Wed.–Sun. 1–5.

PAN AMERICAN UNION. (Constitution Ave. at 17th St., N.W.) Painting and sculpture from Latin America. Mon.–Sat. 8:30–4.

PETERSEN HOUSE. (516 10th St., N.W.) Historic house, 1849, 1876; where Lincoln died. Mon.–Fri. 9–5:30, Sun. 12:30–5:30.

THE PHILLIPS GALLERY. (1600 21st St., N.W.) Modern art. Mon. 11 A.M.–10 P.M.; Tues.–Sat. 11–6; Sun. 2–7.†*

POSTAL HISTORY MUSEUM. (12th St. and Pennsylvania Ave., N.W.) History of American postal service. Mon.–Fri. 10–4.

RED CROSS NATIONAL HEADQUARTERS MUSEUM. (17th St. between D and E)

History of Red Cross from Civil War through World War II. Mon.–Fri. 8:30–4:45.

ROCK CREEK NATURE CENTER. (Glover Rd., N.W., Rock Creek Park) Park museum; natural history; planetarium; Children's museum. Tues.–Fri. 10–5, Sat. 9:30–5, Sun. 1:30–5.

SCOTTISH RITE TEMPLE. (1733 16th St., N.W.) Masonic history, mementos. Mon.–Fri. 9–4:30, Sat. 9–12.

SMITHSONIAN INSTITUTION, FREER GALLERY OF ART. (Jefferson Dr. at 12th St., N.W., on the Mall) Oriental art, work of Whistler. Daily 9–4:30. †*

SMITHSONIAN INSTITUTION, NATIONAL AIR AND SPACE MUSEUM. (Independence Ave. at 10th St., N.W.) Aeronautic and astronautic collections. Daily 9–4:30, Apr.–Aug. 9 A.M.–10 P.M. †*

SMITHSONIAN INSTITUTION, NATIONAL COLLECTION OF FINE ARTS. (Temporarily in Museum of Natural History Bldg.) Paintings, decorative arts. Daily 9–4:30. †

SMITHSONIAN INSTITUTION, NATIONAL ZOOLOGICAL PARK. (3000 Connecticut Ave., N.W.) Zoo. Daily 9–sundown. †

SMITHSONIAN INSTITUTION, UNITED STATES NATIONAL MUSEUM, MUSEUM OF HISTORY AND TECHNOLOGY. (Constitution Ave. between 12th and 14th Sts., N.W., on the Mall) National history; history of industry; science and technology. Daily 9–4:30, Apr.–Aug. 9 A.M.–10 P.M. †**

SMITHSONIAN INSTITUTION, UNITED STATES NATIONAL MUSEUM, MUSEUM OF NATURAL HISTORY. (Constitution Ave. at 10th St., N.W., on the Mall) *Survey;* American ethnology and archaeology. Daily 9–4:30, Apr.–Aug. 9 A.M.–10 P.M. †**

THE TEXTILE MUSEUM. (2320 S St., N.W.) Rugs and other textiles from Europe, Asia, Africa, and the Americas, 2000 B.C. to present. Oct.–May: Tues.–Sat. 1–5. †

TRUXTON-DECATUR NAVAL MUSEUM. (1610 H St.) United States naval, Coast Guard, Marine Corps, and maritime history. Tues.–Fri. 12–5, Sat. 10:30–5. †

UNITED STATES BOTANIC GARDEN. (Maryland Ave. between 1st and 2nd Sts., S.W.) Sun.–Fri. 9–4, Sat. 9–12.

THE UNITED STATES CAPITOL. Historic house; paintings. Mon.–Sat. 9–4:30. †*

UNITED STATES DEPARTMENT OF THE

INTERIOR MUSEUM. (C St. between 18th and 19th Sts., N.W.) Activities and concerns of dept.; geology, Indian affairs, conservation. Mon.–Fri. 8–4.

UNITED STATES NATIONAL ARBORETUM. (28th and M Sts., N.E.) Mon.–Fri. 8–4:30; weekends 10–7 (April, May); 9–5 (Oct., Nov.).

UNITED STATES TREASURY DEPARTMENT EXHIBIT ROOM. (15th and Pennsylvania Ave.) Dept. history and activities; incl. Coast Guard, Printing and Engraving, Internal Revenue, Mint, Narcotics, Secret Service, etc. Mon.–Fri. 9:30–1:30.

THE WASHINGTON GALLERY OF MODERN ART. (1503 21st St., N.W.) Contemp. American; exhibitions. Daily (except Mon.). †

THE WHITE HOUSE. (1600 Pennsylvania Ave.) Half a dozen period rooms open to the public. Mon.–Fri. 10–2; Sat. 10–1. †**

FLORIDA

Bradenton

THE ART LEAGUE OF MANATEE COUNTY. (209 9th St.) Local art; exhibitions. Winter: Mon.–Fri. 9–5, Sat. 9–12, Sun. 2–5. Summer: Mon.–Fri. 9–12.

Cape Kennedy

AIR FORCE SPACE MUSEUM. (Space Center) Missiles, vehicles, rockets, other Space Age memorabilia.

Clearwater

SEA-ORAMA. (Marina, 71–75 Causeway Blvd.) Gulf marine life. Tues.–Sat. 10–5, Sun. 2–5.

Coral Gables

UNIVERSITY OF MIAMI, JOE AND EMILY LOWE ART GALLERY. Painting, primitive art; exhibitions. Tues.–Sat. 10–5, Sun. 2–5 (except Aug.).

Daytona Beach

DAYTONA BEACH HISTORICAL MUSEUM OF THE HALIFAX HISTORICAL SOCIETY. (145 N. Halifax Ave.) Local history, costumes, autos. Thurs.–Sat. 2–5.

Fernandina Beach

FORT CLINCH MUSEUM. Local history, natural history; Park museum. Daily 9–5.

Fort Lauderdale

FORT LAUDERDALE ART CENTER. (625 Las Olas Blvd.) Paintings, graphics; exhibitions. Tues.–Sat. 10–5, Sun. 2–5.

Fort Myers

EDISON WINTER HOME. (2341 McGregor Blvd.) Historic house, built by Thomas Edison, 1886; chemical laboratory; botanical garden. Daily 9–4.

Gainesville

UNIVERSITY OF FLORIDA, FLORIDA STATE MUSEUM. (Seagle Bldg.) State history, prehistory; natural history. Anthropology, geology, paleontology, American Indian coll. Mon.–Sat. 9:30–5, Sun. 1–5. †*

Hialeah

HIALEAH FIRE ENGINE MUSEUM. (1022 E. 27th St.) Historic fire equipment. Daily 9–6.

Homestead

EVERGLADES NATIONAL PARK, FLAMINGO VISITOR CENTER. Park museum: natural history. Daily 9–5. *

ORCHID JUNGLE. (26715 S.W. 157th Ave.) Botanical garden: orchids and related flora. Daily 8–5:30.

Jacksonville

CUMMER GALLERY OF ART. (829 Riverside Ave.) Survey; 18th-century European furniture.

FORT CAROLINE NATIONAL MEMORIAL. (Rt. 1) Park museum: commemorates massacre of French colonists by Spanish, 1565. Daily 8:30–5. *

JACKSONVILLE ART MUSEUM, INC. (1550 Riverside Ave.) Exhibitions.

JACKSONVILLE CHILDREN'S MUSEUM. (1061 Riverside Ave.) Art, nature center, science, planetarium. Summer: Mon.–Fri. 8:30–4; Winter: Tues.–Sat. 9–4:30. †

JACKSONVILLE MUNICIPAL ZOO. (8605 Zoo Rd.) Daily 8–5.

Key West

EAST MARTELLO GALLERY AND MUSEUM. (S. Roosevelt Blvd.) Local history, art; house 1861. Winter: daily (except Mon.) 9–5; Summer: 9:30–5.

MUNICIPAL AQUARIUM. (Whitehead St.) Fish, turtles. Daily 8–5:30.

Lake Worth

LAKE WORTH ART LEAGUE, INC. (Lucerne Ave. W. of M St.) *Exhibitions.* Nov. 15–Apr. 15 daily 3–5.

Maitland

RESEARCH STUDIO, INC. Art; exhibitions. Daily (except Mon.) 2–5.

Marathon

SOUTHEAST MUSEUM OF THE NORTH AMERICAN INDIAN. (U.S. 1) Archaeology, ethnology. Mon.–Sat. 9–6, Sun. 1–6.

Miami

BASS MUSEUM OF ART. (21st St. and Collins Ave.) *Survey;* exhibitions; musical instruments; ecclesiastical vestments. Tues.–Sat. 10–11:30, 1–5; Sun. 1–5.

CRANDON PARK ZOO. (4000 Crandon Blvd., Key Biscayne) Daily 9:30–5.

FAIRCHILD TROPICAL GARDEN, PALM PRODUCTS MUSEUM. (10901 Old Cutler Rd.) Botanical garden: palms; useful and decorative palm products. Mon.–Fri. 10–5, weekends 1–5.

MIAMI MUSEUM OF MODERN ART. (2000 N. Bayshore Dr.) Contemp. paintings, graphics, sculpture; primitive, Oriental. Mon.–Sat. 10–5, Sun. 12–5.

THE MIAMI SEAQUARIUM. (Virginia Key) Aquarium. Daily 9–5:30.

MIAMI SERPENTARIUM. (12655 S. Dixie Hwy.) Herpetology. Daily 9:30–5:30.

MONKEY JUNGLE. (S.W. 216th St.) Zoo: tropical jungle, monkeys and apes. Daily 9:30–5:15.

MUSEUM OF SCIENCE AND NATURAL HISTORY, INC. (3280 S. Miami Ave.) Natural history; anthropology; planetarium; aquarium. Mon. 9–5, 8–10; Tues.–Sat. 9–5; Sun. 2–5.

PARROT JUNGLE. (11000 S.W. 57th Ave.) Aviary: parrots and related birds. Daily 9:30–5.

UNIVERSITY OF FLORIDA, THE MARINE LABORATORY MARINE MUSEUM. (1 Rickenbacker Causeway) Marine animals; research. Mon.–Fri. 8:30–5. †

VIZCAYA: DADE COUNTY ART MUSEUM. (3251 S. Miami Ave.) Decorative arts, in Deering mansion, 1914–16. Daily 10–5.

Orlando

CENTRAL FLORIDA MUSEUM. (810 E. Rollins Ave.) History, natural history, planetarium. Tues.–Sat. 10–5, Sun. 2–5.

Palm Beach

THE HENRY MORRISON FLAGLER MUSEUM. (Whitehall Way) Furnishings, in 1902 mansion. Daily (except Mon.) 10–5.

SOCIETY OF THE FOUR ARTS. (Four Arts Plaza) Art exhibitions, tropical gardens. Dec.–Mar., Mon.–Sat. 10–5, Sun. 2–5.

Pensacola

NAVAL AVIATION MUSEUM. (Naval Air Station) History of naval aviation. Guided tours: Main Gate, daily 1:30. †

PENSACOLA ART CENTER. (407 S. Jefferson St.) Mon.–Sat. 9:30–4:30, Sun. 1:30–4:30.

PENSACOLA HISTORICAL MUSEUM. Old Christ Church, 1832. Local history.

St. Augustine

CASTILLO DE SAN MARCOS AND FORT MATANZAS NATIONAL MONUMENTS. Spanish colonial fortifications. Daily 8:30–5:30. †*

LIGHTNER MUSEUM OF HOBBIES. (King St.) 40 rooms of "collections." Mon.–Sat. 9–9, Sun. 11–9.

ST. AUGUSTINE HISTORICAL SOCIETY. (22 St. Francis St.) Local history. Preservation of historic houses: The Dodge House (54 St. George St.); The Fornells House (Spanish and Hypolita Sts.); The Llambias House (St. Francis St.); The Oldest House (14 St. Francis St.); The Tovar House (St. Francis St.); The Triay House (Spanish and Cuna Sts.). Daily 9–6. †

St. Petersburg

ST. PETERSBURG HISTORICAL MUSEUM. (335 2d Ave.) State and local history; pioneer items; Civil War relics. Mon.–Sat. 11–5, Sun. 2–5.

THE SCIENCE CENTER. (1039 Arlington Ave., N.) Children's museum: history, natural history, physical sciences. Mon.–Fri. 9–5, Sat. 9–5, 7:30–10.

Sarasota

THE JOHN AND MABLE RINGLING MUSEUM OF ART. (5401 Bay Shore Rd.) *Survey;* theatrical history; baroque art and decorative arts. Mon.–Sat. 9:30–4:30, Sun. 12:30–4:30. †*

RINGLING CIRCUS MUSEUM. (5401 Bay Shore Rd.) Circus history in prints, equipment, costumes, wagons. Mon.–Sat. 9:30–4:30. †*

RINGLING RESIDENCE. (5401 Bay Shore Rd.) Furnishings. Mon.–Sat. 9:30–4:30.

SARASOTA ART ASSOCIATION, INC. (Civic Center) Contemp. art; exhibitions. Mon.–Sat. 10–5, Sun. 2–5.

Stuart

HOUSE OF REFUGE MUSEUM. (Hutchinson Island) Local art and history; aquarium; marine and naval exhibits. Building of 1875. Elliott Museum of Vehicular Evolution (Florida transportation). Daily (except Mon.) 1–5.

Tallahassee

FLORIDA STATE UNIVERSITY, ART GALLERY. European paintings, 17th century. Mon.–Fri. 9:30–4:30, Sat. 9–12, Sun. 1–4.

FLORIDA STATE UNIVERSITY, UNIVERSITY MUSEUM. Anthropology, archaeology (Prehistoric Peruvian, local). Mon.–Fri. 9–4:30, Sat. 9–12, Sun. 1–4.

TALLAHASSEE JUNIOR MUSEUM. (104 W. Madison St.) Natural history, animals, Indian exhibits. Tues.–Sat. 9–4:30.

Vero Beach

McKEE JUNGLE GARDENS. Botanical gardens: tropical plants. Daily 8–5.

West Palm Beach

NORTON GALLERY AND SCHOOL OF ART.

(1401 S. Olive Ave.) Chinese objets d'art; modern French and American painting and sculpture. Tues.–Sat. 10–5, Sun. 1:30–5:30.

Winter Park

ROLLINS COLLEGE, BEAL-MALTBIE SHELL MUSEUM. (Holt Ave.) Marine items: shells. Mon.–Sat. 1–5, Sun. 2–5.

ROLLINS COLLEGE, THE MORSE GALLERY OF ART. American and European work; exhibitions. Daily 2–5.

GEORGIA

Albany

ALBANY AREA JUNIOR MUSEUM, INC. (516 Flint Ave.) History, science. Mon.–Fri. 10–12, 2–5.

Athens

UNIVERSITY OF GEORGIA, GEORGIA MUSEUM OF ART. (Jackson St.) American art; exhibitions. Mon.–Fri. 9–5:30, Sat. 9–12.

Atlanta

ATLANTA ART ASSOCIATION GALLERIES. (1280 Peachtree St., N.E.) *Survey, Kress,* contemp. American. Mon. 1–5; Tues. 10–5, 7–9; Wed.–Sat. 10–5; Sun. 2–6. †*

ATLANTA MUSEUM. (537–39 Peachtree St., N.E.) Local and other historic items. Mon.–Sat. 9–5.

ATLANTA PUBLIC LIBRARY, FINE ARTS DEPARTMENT GALLERY. (126 Carnegie Way, N.W.) *Exhibitions.* Mon.–Fri. 9–9, Sat. 9–6.

ATLANTA PUBLIC SCHOOL, CHILDREN'S MUSEUM AND PLANETARIUM. (176 10th St., N.E.) General; zoo. Mon.–Fri. 9–3.

EMORY UNIVERSITY MUSEUM. (Bishops Hall) Teaching collections; archaeology, local natural history. Mon.–Fri. 10–12, 2–5.

Augusta

AUGUSTA MUSEUM. (500 Block Telfair St.) Local history. Mon.–Sat. 2–6.

GERTRUDE HERBERT MEMORIAL INSTITUTE OF ART. (506 Telfair St.) European painting; historic house (Nicholas

Ware Mansion, 1818). Mon.–Sat. 10–5, Sun. 4–6.

Calhoun

NEW ECHOTA. Preservation project: Cherokee capitol, 1825; mission house; tavern. Daily (except Wed.) 9–5.

Columbus

COLUMBUS MUSEUM OF ARTS AND CRAFTS, INC. (1251 Wynnton Rd.) *Survey.* Tues.–Sat. 10–5, Sun. 3–6.

Fort Benning

THE INFANTRY MUSEUM. American and foreign military exhibits from 1775 to present. Mon.–Fri. 10–5; Sat., Sun. 12:30–5.

Fort Oglethorpe

CHICKAMAUGA AND CHATTANOOGA NATIONAL MILITARY PARK, CHICKAMAUGA BATTLEFIELD VISITOR CENTER, OCHS MUSEUM. Military, Civil War, gun exhibits. Daily, 8–5. *

Indian Springs

INDIAN CHIEF WILLIAM McINTOSH HOME. (Rt. 23) Creek Indian house, 1800–21.

Jefferson

CRAWFORD W. LONG MEMORIAL MUSEUM. Medical; tribute to Dr. Long; story of anesthesia. Daily (except Wed.) 9–5.

Macon

MACON YOUTH MUSEUM, INC. (483 College St.) Anthropology. Mon.–Fri. 9–12, 1–5:30; Sat. 9–12.
OCMULGEE NATIONAL MONUMENT. Anthropology. Daily 8:30–5. *

Marietta

KENNESAW MOUNTAIN NATIONAL BATTLEFIELD. Civil War. Mon.–Fri. 8:30–5, Sun. 10–6. *

Midway

MIDWAY COLONIAL MUSEUM. Local history. Daily (except Mon.) 9–5.

Pine Mountain

IDA CASON CALLAWAY GARDENS. Arboretum; herbarium; foliage of Appalachians. Daily 9–dusk.

Richmond Hill

FORT McALLISTER. Confederate house. Daily 9–5.

Savannah

GEORGIA HISTORICAL SOCIETY. (501 Whitaker St.) State history, archives. Mon.–Fri. 9–5:30.
THE JULIETTE GORDON LOW BIRTHPLACE. (10 Oglethorpe Ave., E.) Birthplace of founder of Girl Scouts of America.
OWENS-THOMAS HOUSE. (124 Abercorn St.) Historic house decorated in Regency style. Mon. 2–5, Tues.–Sat. 10–5, Sun. 3–6.
TELFAIR ACADEMY OF ARTS AND SCIENCES, INC. (121 Barnard St.) American painting, American and English decorative arts. Mon. 12–5, Tues.–Sat. 10–5, Sun. 2–5.
YOUTH MUSEUM OF SAVANNAH, INC. (4405 Paulsen St.) Natural history, planetarium. Tues.–Sat. 10–5, Sun. 2–5. †

Spring Place

CHIEF VANN HOUSE. 1804 house of Scotch-Cherokee. Daily 9–5.

Toccoa

JARRETT MANOR. Historic house. Daily 9–5.

Warm Springs

FRANKLIN D. ROOSEVELT WARM SPRINGS MEMORIAL. Historic house. Daily 9–5 (9–6 in summer).

Washington

WASHINGTON-WILKES HISTORICAL MUSEUM. Confederate history. Daily (except Thurs.) 9–12, 2–6.

West Point

CHATTAHOOCHEE VALLEY HISTORICAL SOCIETY. (309 E. 9th St.) Local history.

HAWAII

Hawaii National Park

THOMAS A. JAGGAR MEMORIAL MUSEUM. Park museum. Ethnology, volcanology, herbarium. Daily 7:30–4.

Honolulu

BERNICE P. BISHOP MUSEUM. Natural history, anthropology; planetarium. Weekdays (except Tues.) 9–4:30; Sat. 10–1, Sun. 2–5. †*

CHILDREN'S MUSEUM OF NATURAL HISTORY. (1201 Ala Moana Blvd.) Mon.–Fri. 9–4, Sat. 9–12.

HAWAIIAN MISSION CHILDREN'S SOCIETY. (553 S. King St.) History and historic houses. Mon., Fri., Sat. 9–1; Tues., Thurs. 9–3.

HONOLULU ACADEMY OF ARTS. (900 S. Beretania St.) *Survey;* Oriental, Oceanic art. Daily 10–4:30 (except Thurs.) 10–9:30, Sun. 3–6. †

HONOLULU ZOO. (Kalakaua and Kapahulu Aves.)

UNIVERSITY OF HAWAII, WAIKIKI AQUARIUM. (2700 Kalakaua Ave.) Tues.–Sat. 10–5, Sun. 1–5.

Kekaha, Kavai

KOKEE NATURAL HISTORY MUSEUM. (Napli-Kena Forest Reserve) Archaeology. Tues.–Sun. 11–4. Inquire for winter hours.

Lihue

KAUAI MUSEUM. (Rice Street) Local art and history. Mon., Thurs., Fri. 10–5. Inquire about Sat., Sun.

Wailuku

HALE HOIKEIKE. (Main St.) Historic house; pre-missionary and missionary items. Mon.–Sat. 10–3:30.

IDAHO

Arco

CRATERS OF THE MOON NATIONAL MONUMENT. Geology. Daily 8–5; in summer 7–7. *

Boise

BOISE GALLERY OF ART. (Julia Davis Park) Idaho artists; exhibitions. Wed.–Sun. 12–5.

THE IDAHO HISTORICAL SOCIETY. (610 Parkway Dr.) State history. Mon.–Fri. 9–5, Sat. 11–5, Sun. 1–5.

Pocatello

IDAHO STATE COLLEGE MUSEUM. Archaeology, anthropology. Mon.–Fri. 8–5; Wed. eve. 7:30–9:30.

Sandpoint

BONNER COUNTY MUSEUM. (210 S. 1st Ave.) Local history and natural history. Summer 9–5; other times by appt.

ILLINOIS

Aurora

AURORA HISTORICAL SOCIETY, INC. (304 Oak Ave.) Local history; old carriages. Sun., Wed., Fri. 2:30–5 and by appt. Carriage house open Sun. May to Nov.

Bloomington

BLOOMINGTON MUNICIPAL ZOO. Daily 8–5; 8–8 in summer.

Cairo

CAIRO HISTORICAL ASSOCIATION. (2700 Washington Ave.) Historic house, 1870s furniture. Daily 8–8.

Carbondale

SOUTHERN ILLINOIS UNIVERSITY MUSEUM. Anthropology, history, natural history, industry. Mon.–Fri. 8:30–4:30, Sat. 9–12, Sun. 2:30–4:30.

Charleston

EASTERN ILLINOIS UNIVERSITY, PAUL SARGENT GALLERY. Paintings, ceramics, student exhibits. Mon., Tues. 2–5; Wed., Thurs. 2–5, 7–9; Sun. 12:30–5.

Chicago

ADLER PLANETARIUM AND ASTRONOMICAL MUSEUM. (900 E. Achsah Bond Dr.)

Daily 10–5; Tues., Fri. eves. until 9:30. †**

THE ART INSTITUTE OF CHICAGO. (Michigan Ave. at Adams St.) *Survey;* Impressionist. Mon.–Sat. 9–5, Sun. 12–5. †**

CHICAGO ACADEMY OF SCIENCES. (2001 N. Clark St.) Natural history. Daily 10–5.

CHICAGO HISTORICAL SOCIETY. (North Ave. and Clark St.) City history, Lincolniana. Mon.–Sat. 9:30–4:30, Sun. 12:30–5:30. †**

CHICAGO NATURAL HISTORY MUSEUM. (Roosevelt Rd. and Lake Shore Dr.) *Survey;* anthropology, primitive art. Daily 9–4, 5, or 6; depending on time of year. †**

CHICAGO PUBLIC LIBRARY, MEMORIAL HALL. (78 E. Washington St.) Civil War materials. Mon.–Sat. 9–5. †

COMPTOMETER CORPORATION. (5600 W. Jarvis Ave.) Company museum; office machines. During business hours by appointment.

GARFIELD PARK CONSERVATORY. (300 N. Central Park Ave., Garfield Park) Botanical garden. Daily 9–5.

GEORGE F. HARDING MUSEUM. (4853 S. Lake Park Ave.) Armor, weapons; ship models; works by Frederic Remington. Tues.–Fri. and Sun. 1–4.

JOHN G. SHEDD AQUARIUM. (1200 S. Lake Shore Dr.) Daily 9 or 10–5 or 4, depending on time of year. †*

LINCOLN PARK ZOOLOGICAL GARDENS. (100 W. Webster St.) Zoo. Daily 9–5; weekends 10–6 in summer. †

MUSEUM OF SCIENCE AND INDUSTRY. (57th St. and S. Lake Shore Dr.) Science, technology, industrial history. Mon.–Sat. 9:30–4; until 5:30 in summer; Sun. 10–6. †**

THE POLISH MUSEUM OF AMERICA. (984 Milwaukee Ave.) Polish-American history. Tues.–Fri. 1–4, weekends 1–5. †

RAVENSWOOD-LAKEVIEW HISTORICAL ASSOCIATION. (4546 N. Lincoln Ave.) Local history; Chicago's north side. Mon.–Fri. 9–9, Sat. 9–5:30.

UNIVERSITY OF CHICAGO, ORIENTAL INSTITUTE. (1155 E. 58th St.) Oriental archaeology and art. Daily (except Mon.) 10–5. Closed 12–1 Tues., Wed. *

V. MUELLER AND CO., HISTORICAL INSTRUMENT COLLECTION. (320 S. Honore St.) Company museum; surgical instruments.

Decatur

DECATUR ART CENTER. (125 N. Pine St.) 19th- and 20th-century works. Tues., Thurs., weekends 2–5; Wed., Fri. 7–9.

Elgin

LAURA DAVIDSON SEARS ACADEMY OF FINE ARTS. (210 Academy Pl.) Early American.

Evanston

REST COTTAGE. (1730 Chicago Ave.) Home of Frances E. Willard, organizer and president of National Women's Christian Temperance Union. Mon.–Sat. 9–12, 1–5. Closed Wed. afternoon.

Freeport

STEPHENSON COUNTY HISTORICAL SOCIETY. (1440 S. Carroll Ave.) Local history and industry; historic house, 1857. Fri., Sat., Sun. 1:30–5 and by appt.

Galena

THE GALENA HISTORICAL SOCIETY. (211 S. Bench St.) Museum; historic houses: reconstructed J. R. Grant Leather Store of 1861, and Old Firehouse #1. April 27–Nov. 15, 9–5.

GALENA MARKET HOUSE STATE MEMORIAL. (Commerce St.) Restored town market; history of architecture in state. Daily 1–5.

ULYSSES S. GRANT HOME STATE MEMORIAL. (Bouthiller St.) Historic house. Daily 9–5.

Hinsdale

DU PAGE GRAUE MILL CORPORATION. (York Rd. at Salt Creek) Furnishings, implements, vehicles of 1850–75; still-operative old water-powered grist mill. May 15–Oct. 15 daily 1:30–8:30; opens Sun. 11:30.

HINSDALE HEALTH MUSEUM. (40 S. Clay St.) Public health and medicine. Mon.–Sat. 9–5, Sun. 1–5. †*

Jacksonville

THE DAVID STRAWN ART GALLERY. (331 W. College Ave.) Local history, period room, Indian crafts, art. Weekdays 3–5, 7–9; weekends 3–5.

Kankakee

KANKAKEE COUNTY HISTORICAL SOCI-
ETY. (8th Ave. and Water St.) Indian
artifacts. Weekends 2–5 and by appt.

Knoxville

KNOX COUNTY HISTORIC SITES, INC.
(Public Square) Courthouse where Stephen Douglas presided; jail. By appt.

Macomb

WESTERN ILLINOIS UNIVERSITY ART
GALLERY. Teaching collection. Mon.–
Fri. 10–4.

Metamora

METAMORA COURTHOUSE. Historic
house; Lincoln practiced law here for 12
years. Daily (except Sun.) 9–12, 1–5.

Nauvoo

NAUVOO STATE PARK MUSEUM. Fossils,
Indian artifacts, period rooms recalling
German and French settlers. Tues.–Fri.
1–4, weekends 10–12, 1–4.

North Chicago

THE ILLINOIS ELECTRIC RAILWAY MU-
SEUM. (2500 S. Commonwealth Ave.)
Trolley cars and equipment. Sat. 9–5. †

Peoria

ARTS AND SCIENCE FEDERATION OF PE-
ORIA AREA. (Glen Oak Pavilion) Civic
arts center; science exhibits. Mon.–Sat.
10–4, Sun. 1–5. In summer Tues.–Sun.
12–8.

Quincy

HISTORICAL SOCIETY OF QUINCY AND
ADAMS COUNTY. (425 S. Twelfth St.)
1835 historic house; local history. Mon.–
Fri. 10–12, 2–5 (except Fri.), and by
appt.

River Forest

TRAILSIDE MUSEUM OF NATURAL HIS-
TORY. (738 Thatcher Ave.) Exhibits in-
clude live animals of area. Daily (except
Thurs.) 10–12, 1–5.

Rockford

BURPEE GALLERY OF ART. (737 N.
Main St.) Contemp. American. Tues.–
Sat. 9–5, Sun. 2–5.

NATURAL HISTORY MUSEUM. (813 N.
Main St.) Birds; invertebrate fossils of
area. Tues.–Sat. 1–5; Sun. 2–5.

Rockton

ROCKTON TOWNSHIP HISTORICAL SOCI-
ETY. (Macktown Forest Preserve) 1839
historic house; pioneer implements and
Indian relics. June–Oct., Sun. and Wed.
2–4:30.

Springfield

ILLINOIS STATE HISTORICAL SOCIETY.
(Centennial Bldg.) Civil War; Lincoln.
Mon.–Fri. 8:30–5, Sat. 8:30–12.

ILLINOIS STATE MUSEUM OF NATURAL
HISTORY AND ART. (501 S. Second St.)
Science: archaeology, ethnology. Natural history. Art: contemporary, Japanese
prints, decorative arts. Mon.–Sat. 8:30–
5, Sun. 2–5.

Urbana

UNIVERSITY OF ILLINOIS, KRANNERT
ART MUSEUM. *Survey;* Malayan textiles.
Mon.–Sat. 9–12, 1–5; Sun. 2–5.

UNIVERSITY OF ILLINOIS, MUSEUM OF
NATURAL HISTORY. (Natural Hist. Bldg.,
Green and Mathews Sts.) Teaching col-
lection. Mon.–Sat. 8–5.

Vandalia

VANDALIA HISTORICAL SOCIETY MU-
SEUM. (212 Gallatin Ave.) Local history.
Tues.–Sat. 1–5.

Wadsworth

LAKE COUNTY MUSEUM OF HISTORY.
(Rt. 41 and Wadsworth Rd.) Local history, pioneer, agricultural, Civil War.
May to Nov. Tues.–Sat. 10–5 (summer
until 8), Sun. 12–5.

Wilmette

THE WILMETTE HISTORICAL COMMIS-
SION. (Village Hall) Costumes. 1st Sun.
every month 2:30–5.

INDIANA

Aurora

HILLFOREST HISTORICAL FOUNDATION, INC. (213 Fifth St.) Ohio River Valley history; historic house. Daily (except Mon.) 1–5.

Bedford

LAWRENCE COUNTY HISTORICAL SOCIETY MUSEUM. (Courthouse Basement) Local history. Mon., Tues., Thurs., Fri. 9–4; Wed., Sat., 9–12.

Bloomington

INDIANA UNIVERSITY MUSEUM OF ANTHROPOLOGY. Daily 1–4.

INDIANA UNIVERSITY MUSEUM OF ART. Survey. Mon.–Fri. 9–5, Sat. 9–12.

Evansville

EVANSVILLE MUSEUM OF ARTS AND SCIENCES. (411 S.E. Riverside Dr.) Art. Natural history. History. Planetarium. Tues.–Sat. 9–5, Tues. eve. 7–10, Sun. 12–5.

Fort Wayne

ALLEN COUNTY–FORT WAYNE HISTORICAL MUSEUM. (1424 W. Jefferson St.) Local history; 1844 homestead. Tues.–Sat. 10–12, 1–5; Sun. 2–5.

FORT WAYNE ART MUSEUM. (1202 W. Wayne St.) Exhibitions. Tues.–Sat. 1–5, Sun. 2–5.

LINCOLN NATIONAL LIFE FOUNDATION. (1301 S. Harrison St.) Lincolniana: paintings, photographs, prints, medals, plaques. Mon.–Fri. 8–4:30.

Indianapolis

THE ART ASSOCIATION OF INDIANAPOLIS, INDIANA, THE JOHN HERRON ART INSTITUTE, MUSEUM. (110 E. 16th St.) Survey. Tues.–Sat. 9–5, Sun. 1–6; Fri. eves. (Sept.–May) 7:30–10:30. †*

BUTLER UNIVERSITY, J. I. HOLCOMB OBSERVATORY. Planetarium. Weekends 3–5, 7–9.

ELI LILLY AND COMPANY. (740 S. Alabama St.) Company museum; pharmaceuticals.

HOOSIER SALON ART GALLERY. (610 State Life Bldg., 15 E. Washington St.) Exhibitions; Indiana artists. Mon.–Fri. 9–4:30, Sat. 9–12.

INDIANAPOLIS CHILDREN'S MUSEUM. (3010 N. Meridian St.) Anthropology, geology, natural history. Sept.–May Tues.–Sat. 9–5, Sun. 2–5. †*

INDIANA STATE MUSEUM. State history, natural history. Mon.–Fri. 8:15–4:45.

Kokomo

HOWARD COUNTY HISTORICAL SOCIETY. (Courthouse) Local history and industry. Mon., Wed., Fri. 12–4.

Lafayette

LAFAYETTE ART ASSOCIATION GALLERY. (658 Main St.) Exhibitions. Tues.–Sun. 1–5.

TIPPECANOE COUNTY HISTORICAL ASSOCIATION. (909 South St.) Local history; 1851 historic house. Tues.–Sun. 1–5.

Mishawaka

MISHAWAKA CHILDREN'S MUSEUM. (410 Lincoln Way East) School days 8–12, 1:30–4:30.

Muncie

BALL STATE TEACHERS' COLLEGE ART GALLERY. Teaching collection. Weekdays 2–5, 7–9; weekends 1:30–4:30.

Notre Dame

UNIVERSITY OF NOTRE DAME, THE UNIVERSITY ART GALLERY. Teaching collection: Survey, pre-Columbian. Daily 1–5.

Peru

MIAMI COUNTY HISTORICAL SOCIETY. (11 N. Huntington St.) Local history, pioneer and circus items. Mon.–Sat. 9–4:30.

Plymouth

MARSHALL COUNTY HISTORICAL CENTER. (215 W. Garro St.) Local history. Tues., Thurs.–Sat. afternoons.

Richmond

ART ASSOCIATION OF RICHMOND. (Mc-

Guire Hall, Whitewater Blvd.) 20th-century paintings; exhibitions. Daily 9–12, 1–4:30.

EARLHAM COLLEGE, JOSEPH MOORE MUSEUM. Natural history. Mon.–Fri. 9–4, Sun. 1–5; Sun. only in summer.

JULIA MEEK GAAR WAYNE COUNTY HISTORICAL MUSEUM. (North 11th and "A" Sts.) 1865 Quaker Meeting House, Indian artifacts, pioneer items. Tues.–Sun. 1–5.

South Bend

NORTHERN INDIANA HISTORICAL SOCIETY. (112 S. Lafayette Blvd.) History and natural history of area. Tues., Wed., Thurs., Sat. 9–5.

SOUTH BEND ART ASSOCIATION. (620 W. Washington St.) Contemp. regional work; exhibitions. Tues.–Sat. 9–5, some Sun. 2–5.

Terre Haute

HISTORICAL MUSEUM OF WABASH VALLEY. (1411 S. 6th St.) Local history and archaeology. Wed., Fri. 2–4; Sun. 2–5.

SHELDON SWOPE ART GALLERY. (25 S. 7th St.) Objets d'art. Tues.–Sat. 9:30–5, Sun. 2–5.

Wabash

WABASH COUNTY HISTORICAL MUSEUM. (Memorial Hall) Newspapers; Civil War, county archives. Mon., Wed., Fri., Sat. 9–12. Tues., Thurs. 9–4:30.

IOWA

Cedar Rapids

CEDAR RAPIDS ART ASSOCIATION. (Public Library, 3d Ave. and Fifth St., S.E.) Local art; exhibitions. Mon.–Fri. 12–6, Sat. 1–5.

Cherokee

SANFORD MUSEUM AND PLANETARIUM. (117 E. Willow St.) Archaeology, geology; planetarium. Mon.–Fri. 9–12, 1–5; Sat. 9–12; Sun. 2–5.

Clarion

4-H HISTORICAL BUILDING. (Hwy. No. 3) 4-H Club history and emblems, in house where emblem originated in 1907. Summer months Mon.–Sat. 1–5, Sun. 11–5.

Davenport

CHILDREN'S ZOO. (12th and Wilkes Sts.) Mon.–Sat. 1–dusk; Sun. in summer 10–dusk.

DAVENPORT MUNICIPAL ART GALLERY. (120 W. Fifth St.) Survey. Tues.–Sat. 10–5, Sun. 2–5. Closed July, Aug.

DAVENPORT PUBLIC MUSEUM. (704 Brady St.) Anthropology, archaeology, natural history. Tues.–Sat. 9–5, Sun. 2–5. †

Decorah

LUTHER COLLEGE, THE NORWEGIAN-AMERICAN HISTORICAL MUSEUM. (520 W. Water St.) History; historic houses of pioneer era. April to Nov. Mon.–Sat. 9–6, Sun. 1–6. †

Des Moines

DES MOINES ART CENTER. (Greenwood Park) Contemp., European, American, decorative. Tues., Wed., Fri., Sat. 11–5; Thurs. 11–9; Sun. 1–6. †

STATE DEPARTMENT OF HISTORY AND ARCHIVES. (Historical Bldg., E. Twelfth and Grand Ave.) State history and archives.

Fort Dodge

BLANDEN MEMORIAL ART GALLERY. (3d Ave., S.) Contemp. work. Thurs. 2–4:30, Sun. 1:30–5.

Iowa City

STATE UNIVERSITY OF IOWA MUSEUM OF NATURAL HISTORY. Teaching collection. Mon.–Sat. 8–5, Sun. 1–5.

McGregor

EFFIGY MOUNDS NATIONAL MONUMENT, VISITOR CENTER. Archaeology; Indian mounds. Daily 8–5. *

Marshalltown

CENTRAL IOWA ART ASSOCIATION. (Fisher Community Center, 709 S. Center St.) 19th-cent. French; exhibitions. Daily 8:30–5.

Mason City

MASON CITY PUBLIC LIBRARY. (2d and S. Penna.) Regional art. Mon. 12:30–9, Tues.–Fri. 9–9, Sat. 9–5:30, Sun. 3–5 (in summer until 8).

Mt. Ayr

RINGGOLD COUNTY HISTORICAL SOCIETY. (Courthouse) Local history. Daily 8–5.

Mt. Pleasant

IOWA WESLEYAN COLLEGE MUSEUM. Art, archaeology, entomology; teaching collection. Herbarium.

Nashua

CHICKASAW COUNTY HISTORICAL MUSEUM. 1890 historic house. Daily 9–5:30.

Sibley

ALBERT W. McCALLUM MUSEUM. (City Park) 1871 homestead; Civil War equipment. May–Oct. Sun. 2–5; and by appt.

Sioux City

SIOUX CITY ART CENTER. (Commerce Bldg., 5th Fl.) Contemp. Midwestern; exhibitions. Tues.–Sat. 11–5; Tues., Thurs. eves. 7–9, Sun. 2–5.

SIOUX CITY PUBLIC MUSEUM. (2901 Jackson St.) 1889 historic house; local archaeology, history and natural history. Mon.–Sat. 9–4:30, Sun. 2:30–4:30.

Waterloo

GROUT HISTORICAL MUSEUM. (Park Ave. at South St.) Local history, natural history; planetarium. Tues.–Fri. 1–5, Sat. 10–4.

KANSAS

Abilene

DWIGHT D. EISENHOWER LIBRARY. Presidential library. Daily 9–5. †*

Atchinson

ST. BENEDICT'S COLLEGE MUSEUM. Natural history, teaching collection. Mon., Tues., Thurs., Fri. 2–5.

Colby

SOD TOWN, PRAIRIE HISTORICAL MUSEUM. (Rt. 24) Pioneer history, natural history.

Council Grove

OLD KAW MISSION. Historic house.

Dodge City

BOOT HILL MUSEUM, INC. (Boot Hill) Local history; old street as it looked 1872–78. Daily 7 A.M.–10 P.M. in summer, 8–6 in winter.

Emporia

KANSAS STATE TEACHERS COLLEGE, BIOLOGY DEPARTMENT MUSEUM. (12th and Commercial) Teaching collection; Kansas ornithology and mammalogy. Mon.–Fri. 7:30–5.

Fort Riley

FIRST TERRITORIAL CAPITOL OF KANSAS. 1855 historic house. Mon.–Sat. 8–5, Sun. 1:30–5.

Fort Scott

OLD FORT HISTORICAL MUSEUM. (101 Blair Ave.) Historic house: Fort Scott Headquarters, 1842. Local history, implements, furnishings, manufactures. Daily 8–5.

Hays

FORT HAYS KANSAS STATE COLLEGE MUSEUM. Archaeology, geology; teaching collection. Weekdays 8–5, weekends 2–5. In summer weekdays only 2–5.

Highland

IOWA, SAC, AND FOX INDIAN MISSION MUSEUM. Restored mission; local history, pioneer period. Apr.–Nov. daily (except Mon.) 1–6.

Jetmore

HOUSE OF YESTERDAY. (Main St.) Local and state history. Daily (except Sun.) 2–4.

Kansas City

OLD SHAWNEE MISSION. (3403 W. 53rd St.) Historic house; Kansas Historical Society.

THE WYANDOTTE HISTORICAL SOCIETY MUSEUM. (Memorial Bldg., 7th St. and Barnett Ave.) Philippine ethnological, Delaware, and Wyandotte Indian artifacts. Tues. 1–4, Sat. 9–12.

Larned

FORT LARNED HISTORICAL SOCIETY. Military and pioneer objects, prehistoric and Indian artifacts. Preservation project; Santa Fe Trail Post buildings. Daily 7 A.M.–8 P.M. in summer, 9–5 in winter.

Lawrence

UNIVERSITY OF KANSAS MUSEUM OF ART. European and American. Mon.–Sat. 9–5, Sun. 1:30–5.

UNIVERSITY OF KANSAS MUSEUM OF NATURAL HISTORY. *Survey.* Mon.–Sat. 8–5, Sun. 1:30–5.

UNIVERSITY OF KANSAS, SNOW ENTOMOLOGICAL MUSEUM. Research collections. Mon.–Fri. 8–12, 1–5; Sat. 8–12.

Manhattan

KANSAS STATE UNIVERSITY, ZOOLOGICAL MUSEUM. (Fairchild Hall) May to Nov. daily.

RILEY COUNTY HISTORICAL MUSEUM. (Memorial Auditorium Bldg., 110 block Poyntz Ave.) Local history and old furnishings. Tues.–Sun. 2–4:30.

SUNSET ZOO. (Sunset Park) Daily.

North Newton

BETHEL COLLEGE, THE KAUFFMAN MUSEUM. Natural history, 1874 Mennonite log cabin, and misc. Mon.–Fri. 8:30–5; Sat. 8:30–12; Sun. 11–5.

Oberlin

DECATUR COUNTY INDIAN AND HISTORICAL MUSEUM. (258 S. Penna.) Local history, sod house, pioneer items. Mon.–Sat. 9–12, 1–5; Sun. 2–6; in summer 8 A.M.–9 P.M.

Pittsburg

KANSAS STATE TEACHERS COLLEGE,

MUSEUM OF NATURAL HISTORY. Anthropology, zoology, geology, costumes; teaching collection. Weekdays 8–4.

Pratt

KANSAS FORESTRY, FISH AND GAME COMMISSION. (Hwy. K–64 and Lake Rd.) Aquarium; zoo. Daily 8 A.M.–9:30 P.M.

Salina

SMOKY HILL HISTORICAL MUSEUM. (Oakdale Park) Local history; old country store. Daily (except Mon.) 1–5.

Scott City

EL QUARTELEJO INDIAN MUSEUM. (W. 5th St.) Plains Indian artifacts; reconstructed pueblo.

Topeka

GAGE PARK ZOO. (6th–10th and Gage Sts.)

KANSAS STATE HISTORICAL SOCIETY. (Memorial Bldg.) State history, anthropology, archaeology. Weekdays 8:15–5; Sat. 8:15–4 (in summer until noon); Sun. 1–4:30. †

WASHBURN UNIVERSITY, MULVANE ART CENTER. Contemp. Midwestern. Weekdays 10–5, Sun. 2–5.

Wichita

WICHITA ART ASSOCIATION. (401 N. Belmont Ave.) *Exhibitions.* Daily (except Mon.) 1–5.

WICHITA ART MUSEUM. (619 Stackman Dr.) American art; graphics. Daily (except Mon.) 1–5.

KENTUCKY

Bardstown

BARTON MUSEUM OF WHISKEY HISTORY. (Barton Rd.) Company museum. Mon.–Sat. 10–5, Sun. 12–5. †

MY OLD KENTUCKY HOME STATE SHRINE. (Federal Hill, Rt. 3) House where song was written, restored to 1852; outdoor theater presents "The Stephen Foster Story." Daily 8–5 (in summer until 7:30).

Bowling Green

WESTERN KENTUCKY STATE COLLEGE, KENTUCKY MUSEUM. (U.S. 68 and 23) Misc.: pioneer relics, costumes, zoological, and more. Weekdays 9–12, 1–5; Sat. 9–12; 1–4:30; Sun. 2–4.

Covington

BEHRINGER MUSEUM OF NATURAL HISTORY. (Devou Park) Archaeology, geology, zoology. Tues.–Sat. 9–5, Sun. 1–5.

Danville

DANVILLE AND BOYLE COUNTY HISTORICAL SOCIETY, SHELBY MUSEUM. (Old Courthouse, Constitution Sq.) Material relating to state's first governor, Shelby. Daily in summer 10–6.

POST OFFICE. (Constitution Sq.) 1792 log structure. Daily in summer 10–6.

Frankfort

KENTUCKY HISTORICAL SOCIETY. (Old State House.) Daily 8:30–4:30 (Sun. opens at 9).

LIBERTY HALL. (218 Wilkinson St.) 1797 house where state's first senator, Brown, lived. Tues.–Sat. 10–5, Sun. 2–5.

OLD GOVERNOR'S MANSION. (High St.) 1798 historic house; period furnishings. Weekdays 11–4.

ORLANDO BROWN HOUSE. (202 Wilkinson St.) 1835 historic house; American furniture. Tues.–Fri. 10–5, Sun. 2–5.

Henderson

AUDUBON MEMORIAL MUSEUM. (Audubon State Park) Natural history; aquarium; botanical garden; zoo.

Hodgenville

ABRAHAM LINCOLN BIRTHPLACE NATIONAL HISTORIC SITE. Park museum; Lincoln and frontier materials. Daily 8–5; 8–6 in summer. *

Lexington

ASHLAND. (E. Main and Sycamore Rd.) 1811 home of Henry Clay; furnishings. Daily (except Mon.) 9:30–4:30.

HUNT MORGAN HOME. Local art; exhibitions. Mon.–Sat. 10–4, Sun. 2–5.

UNIVERSITY OF KENTUCKY, KENTUCKY

LIFE MUSEUM. (Higbee Mill Pike) State history from pioneer days to 1900; 19th-cent. implements and furnishings. Weekdays 9–5, Sat. 9–12.

UNIVERSITY OF KENTUCKY, MUSEUM OF ANTHROPOLOGY. Eskimo and Navaho; state archaeology. Mon.–Sat. 9–4:30.

UNIVERSITY OF KENTUCKY, UNIVERSITY ART GALLERY. (Fine Arts Bldg., Rose St.) Teaching collection. School yr. weekdays 12–4; Sat. 10–3; Sun. 3–5.

Louisville

ART CENTER ASSOCIATION. (2111 S. 1st St.) Local art; exhibitions. Mon., Thurs., Fri. 9–5; Mon., Tues., Thurs. eves. 6–10.

FARMINGTON. (3033 Bardstown Rd.) 1810 historic house. Tues.–Sat. 10–4, Sun. 2–5.

THE FILSON CLUB. (118 W. Breckinridge St.) State history. Oct.–June, Mon.–Fri. 9–5, Sat. 9–12.

J. B. SPEED ART MUSEUM. (2035 S. 3d St.) Art relating to state; European. Oct.–July, Tues.–Sat. 10–4, Sun. 2–6. †

THE JUNIOR ART GALLERY. (301 Library Place) Prints and sculpture; exhibitions. Daily (except Sun.) 9–5.

KENTUCKY RAILWAY MUSEUM. (Upper River Rd.) RR equipment. June–Labor Day, weekends 1–6; rest of Sept., Sun. 1–6.

THE LOUISVILLE MUSEUM. (743 S. 5th St.) Natural history. Mon.–Fri. 9–5.

UNIVERSITY OF LOUISVILLE, ALLEN R. HITE ART INSTITUTE. (Belknap Campus) Graphics, paintings. By appt.

Middlesboro

CUMBERLAND GAP NATIONAL HISTORICAL PARK. Park museum; history of Cumberland Gap. Daily 8–5 (until 6 in summer). *

Paris

CANE RIDGE SHRINE. (Rt. 3) 1801 Great Western Revival commemorated in historic house. Daily.

DUNCAN TAVERN HISTORIC CENTER. (Public Sq., Hwy. 68) Historic houses, period furnishings, pioneer items. Daily 10–12, 1–5.

Richmond

EASTERN KENTUCKY STATE COLLEGE,

COLLEGE MEMORIAL MUSEUM. (Lancaster Ave.) Misc., mostly American. Mon.–Fri. 9–12, 2–5; Sat. 9–12.

Springfield

LINCOLN HOMESTEAD PARK. (Rt. 1) Francis Berry House, where Lincoln's parents were married. Daily 7:30–6:30.

LOUISIANA

Arabi

CHALMETTE NATIONAL HISTORICAL PARK. Park museum; military. Daily 7:30–5. *

Baton Rouge

LOUISIANA STATE UNIVERSITY ART MUSEUM. English and American portraits; period rooms.
LOUISIANA STATE UNIVERSITY, DEPARTMENT OF GEOLOGY MUSEUM. Local paleontology; research, Mon.–Fri. 8–5, Sat. 8–12.
LOUISIANA STATE MUSEUM, HERBARIUM. Louisiana plants. Mon.–Fri. 8–5, Sat. 8–12.
LOUISIANA STATE UNIVERSITY, MUSEUM OF NATURAL SCIENCE. Botany, zoology, research. Mon.–Fri. 8–5; Sat. 8–12; Sun. 2–5.
STATE OF LOUISIANA ART COMMISSION. (208 Old State Capitol) Contemporary art; exhibitions. Mon.–Sat. 10–5, Sun. 1–5.

Franklin

OAKLAWN MANOR. (Irish Bend) 1827 historic house; paintings, furniture, gardens. Daily 8–6.

Many

HODGES GARDENS, EXPERIMENTAL AREA AND WILDLIFE REFUGE. (Hwy. 171) Arboretum; botanical garden. Daily 8–dusk.

Marksville

MARKSVILLE PREHISTORIC INDIAN MUSEUM. (Overton St.) Mound-builder Indians. Mon.–Sat. 10–4, Sun. 10–6.

New Orleans

GALLIER HALL. (St. Charles and Lafayette Sts.) 1843 historic house. Weekdays 9–5.
ISAAC DELGADO MUSEUM OF ART. (Lelong Ave., City Park) Survey; Kress. Tues.–Sat. 10–6, Sun. 12–7. †*
LOUISIANA HISTORICAL ASSOCIATION'S CONFEDERATE MUSEUM. (929 Camp St.) Military; La. history. Tues.–Sat. 10–4.
LOUISIANA MUSEUM OF TULANE UNIVERSITY. (6823 St. Charles Ave.) Art; anthropology; geology, zoology, herbarium; state and city historic prints and maps; architectural history of New Orleans. Mon.–Fri. 9–5, Sat. 9–12.
TULANE UNIVERSITY, NEWCOMB COLLEGE ART GALLERY. (60 Newcomb Pl.) 19th- and 20th-century graphics, decorative arts. Weekdays 9–5, Sat. 9–12.

St. Francisville

AUDUBON MEMORIAL STATE PARK, OAKLEY HOUSE. (State Hwy. 965) Historic house; Audubon. Mon.–Sat. 9–4:45, Sun. 1–4:45.

Shreveport

FORD PARK CHILDREN'S ZOO. (South Lakeshore Dr.)
LOUISIANA STATE EXHIBIT MUSEUM. (3015 Greenwood Rd.) Natural history, history, art of state.
THE R. W. NORTON ART GALLERY. (4700 block, Creswell Ave.) Americana.

MAINE

Bangor

BANGOR HISTORICAL SOCIETY. (159 Union St.) Local history, Civil War; historic house of 1834. Mon.–Sat. 2–4.

Bar Harbor

ROBERT ABBE MUSEUM OF STONE AGE ANTIQUITIES. Local archaeology. July–Sept. daily 9–5.

Brunswick

BOWDOIN COLLEGE MUSEUM OF FINE ARTS. (Walker Art Bldg.) Survey. Mon.–Sat. 10–12, 2–4; Sun. 2–4.

PEJEPSCOT HISTORICAL SOCIETY. (12 School St.) Local history, costumes, textiles, crafts. Summer: Mon.–Fri. 1–5, Sat. 9–1.

Caribou

THE NYLANDER MUSEUM. (S. Main St.) Natural history of Maine; mineralogy, stratigraphy. Contemp. Maine art. Mon.–Fri. 9–5.

Castine

WILSON MUSEUM. Anthropology. French and American early Stone Age artifacts; Indian materials. Summer; Wed., Sat. 2–5.

Dresden

POWNALBOROUGH COURT HOUSE. (Rt. 128) Original pine interior in building of 1760. Summer: daily.

Farmington

THE NORDICA HOMESTEAD. House, built about 1810; home of Lillian Nordica, opera singer. Family furnishings, opera costumes, programs. Summer: Mon. 12–5, Tues.–Sun. 10–12, 1–5.

Gorham

BAXTER HOUSE. (South St.) Built 1798. Wed., Sat. 2:30–5.

Houlton

AROOSTOOK HISTORICAL AND ART MUSEUM OF HOULTON. (109 Main St.) Local history; prints. Tues., Sat. 1–5.

Islesford

ACADIA NATIONAL PARK, ISLESFORD HISTORICAL MUSEUM. (Little Cranberry Island) Park museum: local history, crafts. Summer. *

Kennebunk

THE BRICK STORE MUSEUM. (117 Main St.) Historic house, 1825; local history, early mercantile materials. April 1–Oct. 15, Tues.–Sat. 10–4:30.

Kennebunkport

KENNEBUNKPORT HISTORICAL SOCIETY. (North St.) Local history. Summer.

SEASHORE TROLLEY MUSEUM. Old trolley cars, operative. Summer daily 10–5; Sept.–May, Sun. and holidays 12–5. †

Kittery Point

LADY PEPPERRELL HOUSE. Period furnishings, house of 1760. Maintained by Soc. for Preservation of New England Antiq. Summer daily (except Sun.) 10–4.

Machias

BURNHAM TAVERN. Revolutionary period furnishings in house of 1770. June–Aug., Wed. 2–5.

New Harbor

GALLERY OF MODERN ART. *Exhibitions* of modern painting and sculpture. Summer daily 9–5.

Ogunquit

MUSEUM OF ART OF OGUNQUIT. (Shore Rd.) Modern American painting, sculpture, graphics, ceramics; exhibitions. June (last week)–mid-Sept. daily.

Orono

UNIVERSITY OF MAINE ART GALLERY. (Carnegie Hall) Contemp. European, American (and Maine) paintings and graphics; exhibitions. Mon.–Fri. 9–5, Sat. 9–12.
UNIVERSITY OF MAINE HERBARIUM. (Rm. 317, Deering Hall) Flora of Maine and Canada. Mon.–Fri. 8–12, 1–5.

Portland

MAINE HISTORICAL SOCIETY. (485 Congress St.) Paintings of Maine subjects; Historic Wadsworth-Longfellow House built 1785, family furnishings. Society: Mon.–Fri. 10–5, Sat. 10–12; House: June–Sept. daily (except Sun.) 9:30–4:30. †
PORTLAND MUSEUM OF ART. (111 High St.) Daily (except Sun.) 10–4:30.
PORTLAND SOCIETY OF NATURAL HISTORY. (22 Elm St.) State natural history. Tues.–Sat. 10–5.
VICTORIA SOCIETY OF MAINE WOMEN. (109 Danforth St.) Historic Victoria Mansion, 1859; period furnishings. June 15–Oct. 1 daily (except Sun.) 10:30–4:30.

Rockland

WILLIAM A. FARNSWORTH LIBRARY AND ART MUSEUM. (Elm St.) Contemp. Maine artists. Tues.–Sat. 10–5, Sun. 1–5.

Saco

YORK INSTITUTE. (Main St.) Local items: portraits, furnishings, costumes. Tues., Sat. 2–5.

Searsport

PENOBSCOT MARINE MUSEUM. Maine marine and maritime items. Daily 9–5.

Skowhegan

HISTORY HOUSE. (Elm St.) Local history, archives. June 20–mid-Sept. Mon., Wed., Fri. 2–5.

South Berwick

HAMILTON HOUSE, 1785; gardens. Maintained by Soc. for the Preservation of New England Antiq. June 15–Sept. 15: Wed.–Sat. 1–5.

JEWETT MEMORIAL. (Rt. 103) Birthplace of Sarah Orne Jewett. Maintained by Soc. for the Preservation of New England Antiq. June 15–Sept. 15: Wed.–Sat. 1–5.

South Windham

PARSON SMITH HOMESTEAD. (River Rd.) Historic farmhouse, 1764. Maintained by Soc. for the Preservation of New England Antiq. July 1–Oct. 15: Sun., Mon. 1–5.

Standish

DANIEL MARRETT HOUSE, 1789. Maintained by Soc. for the Preservation of New England Antiq. June 15–Sept. 15: Wed., Sun. 1–5.

Thomaston

MONTPELIER. (High St.) Replica of old house, original furnishings; home of Maj. Gen. Henry Knox. May–Nov. daily 10–6.

Waterville

COLBY COLLEGE ART MUSEUM. American art, 19th century; exhibitions. Mon.–Sat. 10–12, 1–5.

COLBY COLLEGE, DEPARTMENT OF GEOLOGY. Maine minerals. By appt. during school sessions.

Wiscasset

THE LINCOLN COUNTY MUSEUM. (Federal St.) Local history, early industries and crafts; in jail bldg. of 1809–11. Maine Art Gallery in Academy Bldg. of 1807; Maine artists, exhibitions. Lincoln County Fire Museum (in barn of Sortwell-Nickels House); old equipment. Summer: Mon.–Sat. 9–5, Sun. 2–5. Winter: Wed., Sat., Sun. afternoon. Art Gallery: July and August only.

NICKELS-SORTWELL HOUSE. (Main and Federal Sts.) Federal period furnishings; house of 1807. Maintained by Soc. for the Preservation of New England Antiq. June 15–Oct. 15. Tues.–Sat. 11–5, Sun. 2–5.

York

ELIZABETH PERKINS HOUSE; JEFFERDS' TAVERN; OLD SCHOOL HOUSE. June 15–Sept. 7: Tues.–Sat. 10:30–5:30, Sun. 1:30–5:30.

OLD GAOL MUSEUM. (Rt. 1-A) Dungeons, furnishings, in jail of 1653. Mon.–Sat. 9:30–5:30, Sun. 1:30–5:30.

WILCOX HOUSE. 18th-century furnishings. Mon.–Sat. 9:30–5:30.

MARYLAND

Accokeek

NATIONAL COLONIAL FARM. Agricultural history; Preservation project; Colonial farming methods. Daily 9–5.

Annapolis

BRICE HOUSE, 1773. Mar.–Nov. Tues.–Fri. 2–5.

CHASE-LLOYD HOUSE, 1769. Mon.–Fri. 10–12, 2–4.

HAMMOND-HARWOOD HOUSE, 1774. (Maryland Ave. and King George St.) Mar.–Oct. Mon.–Sat. 10–5, Sun. 2–5; Nov.–Feb. Mon.–Sat. 10–4, Sun. 1–4.

U. S. NAVAL ACADEMY MUSEUM. Teaching coll.; naval history. Mon.–Sat. 9–5, Sun. 11–5. †

Baltimore

THE BALTIMORE MUSEUM OF ART. (Wyman Park) *Survey;* French 19th and 20th century; Colonial period rooms; Tues. 2–5, 8–11; Wed.–Sat. 10–5, Sun. 2–6. †*

BALTIMORE AND OHIO TRANSPORTATION MUSEUM. (Pratt and Poppleton Sts.) Antique vehicles, especially railroad locomotives, rolling stock and equipment. Not open to public at present. †

ENOCH PRATT FREE LIBRARY. (400 Cathedral St.) Bookplates, prints of Baltimore. Mon.–Fri. 9–9, Sat. 9–5:30. †

FORT MCHENRY NATIONAL MONUMENT AND HISTORIC SHRINE. Park museum. History of War of 1812, in replicas of original documents. Daily 9–5. *

LOVELY LANE MUSEUM OF THE BALTIMORE CONFERENCE METHODIST HISTORICAL SOCIETY. (2200 St. Paul St.) Methodist church history, archives. Maintains John Evans House (Rt. 407, near Rt. 27, in Carroll County). Mon.–Fri. 9–4; Sun. after church. †

BALTIMORE ZOO. (Druid Hill Park) Daily 10–5.

MARYLAND ACADEMY OF SCIENCES. (400 Cathedral St.) Planetarium; natural history; archaeology, astronomy. (New Maryland Science Center will expand facilities.) Mon.–Sat. 9–4:45, Thurs. eve. 7–10. Planetarium shows Thurs. 7:15 and 9; Sat. 1 and 2. †

MARYLAND HISTORICAL SOCIETY. (201 W. Monument St.) City and state history; costumes, decorative arts, furniture. Winter: Mon.–Fri. 9–5, Sat. 9–1. Summer: Mon.–Fri. 9–4, Sat. 9–1; closed Sat. in Aug.

NATURAL HISTORY SOCIETY OF MARYLAND. (2101–3 Bolton St.) *Survey.* Maintains Maryland House (City Park); natural history displays. May–Oct. daily 9–5.

THE PEALE MUSEUM. (225 N. Holliday St.) Municipal museum: city history, art. First museum bldg. 1814. Tues.–Sat. 10:30–4:30, Sun. 1:30–5:30. Summer, closed Sun.; Aug., closed Sat. †*

THE WALTERS ART GALLERY. (Charles and Centre Sts.) Decorative arts: antique, European, Oriental; paintings and sculpture through 19th century. Mon. 1:30–5, 7:30–10; Tues.–Sat. 11–5; Sun. 2–5. (Closes at 4 during July and August). †*

Great Falls

CHESAPEAKE AND OHIO CANAL MUSEUM. Park museum. History and natural history of canal and region. June–Labor Day, daily; Sept.–May, weekends.

Hagerstown

HAGER HOUSE. Local history.

WASHINGTON COUNTY MUSEUM OF FINE ARTS. (City Park) American and European art. Tues.–Sat. 9–5, Sun. 1–6.

Hollywood

SOTTERLEY MANSION. 18th-century house and furnishings. June–Sept. 11–6.

Monkton

BREEZEWOOD FOUNDATION, INC. (Hess Rd.) Siamese sculpture. Apr.–Oct. 1st Sunday 2–6.

Sharpsburg

ANTIETAM NATIONAL BATTLEFIELD SITE MUSEUM. Park museum. History, Civil War; memorabilia of Lee, Jackson. Daily 8–5. *

Towson

HAMPTON NATIONAL HISTORIC SITE. (Society for the Preservation of Maryland Antiquities) Preservation project; house 1783–90, period furnishings. Tues.–Sat. 11–5, Sun. 1–5. *

Westminster

SHELLMAN HOUSE. (Historical Society of Carroll County, Inc.) (206 E. Main St.) Historic house, 1807; dolls, Indian materials. Mon.–Sat. 2–5.

MASSACHUSETTS

Abington

DYER MEMORIAL LIBRARY. (Centre Ave.) Pre-Revolutionary ceramics; old glass; military materials. Mon., Tues., Thurs.–Sun.

Amesbury

WHITTIER HOME. (86 Friend St.)

Family furnishings, mss. of John Greenleaf Whittier. Tues.–Sat. 10–5.

Amherst

AMHERST COLLEGE, MEAD ART BUILDING. American art; textiles; teaching coll. Sept.–June 15: Mon.–Sat. 9–5, Sun. 11:30–5. June 15–July, Sun. 9–12, 2–4. †

THE JONES LIBRARY, INC. (Amity St.) 19th-century paintings; exhibitions. Winter: Mon., Fri. 10–5:30; Tues.–Thurs. 10–9:30; Sat. 10–7. Summer: Mon., Wed., Thurs. 10–5:30; Tues., Fri. 10–8.

UNIVERSITY OF MASSACHUSETTS, KNOWLTON HERBARIUM. Also botanical garden. Massachusetts flora; Hawaiian materials. Mon.–Fri. 9–5.

UNIVERSITY OF MASSACHUSETTS, MUSEUM OF ZOOLOGY. (Morrill Hall) Mon.–Fri. 8:30–5, weekends 8:30–12.

UNIVERSITY OF MASSACHUSETTS SCIENTIFIC COLLECTION. Entomology, zoology, mineralogy, geology, herbarium. Mon.–Fri. 8–5, Sat. 8–12. †

ABBOT ACADEMY, JOHN-ESTHER ART GALLERY. Junior museum of art. Mon.–Fri. 2–4:30.

Andover

PHILLIPS ACADEMY, ADDISON GALLERY OF AMERICAN ART. Teaching collection; exhibitions. Paintings, furniture. Mon.–Sat. 9–5, Sun. 2:30–5. †

PHILLIPS ACADEMY, ROBERT S. PEABODY FOUNDATION FOR ARCHAEOLOGY. Archaeology of North America; research. Mon.–Fri. 9–4:30, weekends 1:30–4:30.

Arlington

ARLINGTON HISTORICAL SOCIETY. (7 Jason St.) Historic Jason Russell House; Revolutionary period items; local history. Apr.–Oct. Tues.–Sat. 2–5.

Attleboro

ATTLEBORO MUSEUM, INC. (Capron Park) Art; exhibitions. Daily (except Mon.) 2–5.

BRONSON MUSEUM. (8 N. Main St.) Archaeology (Mass. Arch. Soc.) Mon., Tues., Thurs. 9–5.

Barnstable

CROCKER TAVERN. (Main St.) Historic wooden house, about 1754. Maintained by Soc. for the Preservation of New England Antiq. June–Oct. 15, Mon., Thurs., Sat. 10–5.

Belchertown

BELCHERTOWN HISTORICAL ASSOCIATION. (Maple St.) Mid-May–mid-Oct., Wed., Sat. 2–5.

Beverly

BEVERLY HISTORICAL SOCIETY. (117 Cabot St.) Historic John Cabot House, 1781. Local history, archives, minerals, artifacts. Sept.–June: Mon., Wed., Fri., Sat. 10–4. Summer: daily (except Sun.) 10–4. John Balch House (448 Cabot St.), 1636; and Reverend John Hale House (39 Hale St.), 1694, are open June 15 to Sept. 15 only.

Boston

BOSTON ATHENAEUM. (10½ Beacon St.) Library; prints and photographs of New England; exhibitions. Oct.–June: daily (except Sun.) 9–5:30; Summer: Mon.–Fri. 9–5:30. †

BOSTON MARINE SOCIETY. (88 Broad St.) Paintings, models, archives, maritime and merchant marine subjects. Mon.–Fri. 9–4.

BOSTON PUBLIC LIBRARY. (Copley Sq.) Prints, murals, paintings, sculpture. Mon.–Fri. 9–9, Sat. 9–6, Sun. 2–6. Closed Sun. June–Sept. †

THE BOSTONIAN SOCIETY. (206 Washington St.) Historic Old State House, 1713. City history, antiquities, prints, maritime subjects. Daily (except Sun.) 9–4.

CHILDREN'S ART CENTRE. (36 Rutland St.) Exhibitions, classes. Mon.–Fri. 9–5, Sat. 9:30–12. Closed Aug.

CHRISTIAN SCIENCE PUBLISHING SOCIETY, MAPPARIUM. (1 Norway St.) Huge globe of world; viewed from inside. Mon.–Fri. 8:30–4:30, Sat. 8:30–4.

FANEUIL HALL. (Dock Sq. at Market St.) Historic house built 1742. "Cradle of Liberty." Paintings, portraits. 1st floor: market. 2nd floor: Armory of the Ancient and Honorable Artillery Company; military museum, items from all American wars. Hall open Mon.–Fri. 9–5, Sat. 9–12, Sun. 1–5; Museum open Mon.–Fri. 10–4. †

INSTITUTE OF CONTEMPORARY ART. (Newbury St.) Contemp. art; *exhibitions*. Weekdays (except Mon.) 11–6, Sun. 2–5, Thurs. eve. 6–9.

ISABELLA STEWART GARDNER MUSEUM. (280 The Fenway) European art, esp. Renaissance; decorative arts. Tues., Thurs., Sat. 10–4; 1st Thurs. 10–10; Sun. 2–5. Tours only, Mon., Wed., Fri. 11 and 2. Closed August (except for tours, Mon.–Fri., 11 and 2). Music program: Tues., Thurs., Sat. 2:45; Sun. 3; 1st Thurs. 8:45. †*

MASSACHUSETTS HISTORICAL SOCIETY. (1154 Boylston St.) Prints, portraits; exhibitions of American history materials. Mon.–Fri. 9–4:45. †

MUSEUM OF FINE ARTS. (465 Huntington Ave.) *Survey;* especially fine Oriental, classical, American 18th and 19th century. Tues.–Sat. 10–5, Tues. until 10 P.M. (Oct.–May), Sun. 1:30–5:30. †**

MUSEUM OF SCIENCE. (Science Park) Physical, natural sciences; medicine, industry; nature center; aquarium; Charles Hayden Planetarium. Tues.–Sat. 10–5, Sun. 1–5. Fri. until 10 P.M. †**

NEW ENGLAND CONFERENCE METHODIST HISTORICAL SOCIETY. (745 Commonwealth Ave.) Methodist history. Mon.–Sat. 9–6.

OLD SOUTH MEETING HOUSE. (Washington and Milk Sts.) Built 1729; location of signals for Paul Revere, 1775. Oct.–May daily (except Sun.) 9–4; June–Sept. until 5. †

PAUL REVERE HOUSE. (19 N. Sq.) Period furnishings, house built 1680. Daily (except Sun.) 10–4. †

SOCIETY FOR THE PRESERVATION OF NEW ENGLAND ANTIQUITIES. (141 Cambridge St.) Regional decorative arts, architectural prints and photographs; toys, needlework. Maintains historic houses in Mass., Me., N.H., Conn., R.I. Headquarters in Harrison Gray Otis House of 1795. Weekdays 10–4. †*

Bourne

BOURNE HISTORICAL SOCIETY, APTUCXET TRADING POST. (Aptucxet Rd., Cape Cod Canal) Replica of old Pilgrim-Dutch-Indian trading post of 1627. Indian artifacts, Pilgrim items. July, Aug. daily, 10. Sept.–June daily (except Mon.).

Boxford

BOXFORD HISTORICAL SOCIETY, HOLYOKE-FRENCH HOUSE. Period furnishings, family heirlooms, old shoemaker's shop, farm implements, in house built 1760. May–Oct.: Sun. 3–5.

Braintree

BRAINTREE HISTORICAL SOCIETY, GENERAL SYLVANUS THAYER BIRTHPLACE. (786 Washington St.) Daily (except Mon.) 1:30–4, Sat. 10:30–4. Oct. 13–Apr. 18: Tues., Thurs., Sat. 1:30–4.

Brewster

CAPE COD JUNIOR MUSEUM OF NATURAL HISTORY, INC. (Town Hall) Cape Cod specimens. During school hours. †

Brockton

BROCKTON PUBLIC LIBRARY. (304 Main St.) 19th-century New England art. Mon.–Sat. 9–9 (closes Sat. at 6, July, Aug.).

Brookline

ANTIQUE AUTO MUSEUM. (15 Newton St. at Larz Anderson Park) Daily (except Mon.) 1–5.

EDWARD DEVOTION HOUSE. (347 Harvard St.) House of 1750. Wed. 2–4.

Cambridge

CAMBRIDGE HISTORICAL SOCIETY. (159 Brattle St.) Historic Lee-Nichols House of about 1660. Thurs. 3–5.

CAMBRIDGE MUSEUM FOR CHILDREN. (359 B'way) Nature center. Mon.–Fri. 8:30–2:30.

COOPER-FROST-AUSTIN HOUSE. (21 Linnaean St.) Furnished in period 1657 (oldest house in Cambridge). Maintained by the Soc. for the Preservation of New England Antiq. June–Oct.: Mon., Thurs. 2–5, Tues. 7–9. Nov.–May: Thurs. 2–5, Tues. 7–9.

HARVARD UNIVERSITY, BOTANICAL MUSEUM. (Oxford St.) Mon.–Sat. 9–4:30, Sun. 1–4:30.

HARVARD UNIVERSITY, BUSCH-REISINGER MUSEUM. (Kirkland St. and Divinity Ave.) Germanic art and culture; Middle Ages, Renaissance to Modern.

Mon.–Sat. 9–5; closed Sat. during July and Aug. †*

HARVARD UNIVERSITY, FOGG ART MUSEUM. (Quincy St.) Art *survey*, Oriental. Mon.–Sat. 9–5, last Sun. of Nov.–May 2–5; closed Sat. during July and Aug. †*

HARVARD UNIVERSITY, GEOLOGICAL MUSEUM. (Oxford St.) Mon.–Fri. 9–4:30, Sat. 9–1, Sun. 1–4:30.

HARVARD UNIVERSITY, GRAY HERBARIUM. (22 Divinity Ave.) Plants of the world, over 1,500,000 specimens. Mon.–Fri. 9–5. †

HARVARD UNIVERSITY, MINERALOGICAL MUSEUM. (Oxford St.) Mon.–Sat. 9–4:30, Sun. 1:30–4:30. †

HARVARD UNIVERSITY, MUSEUM OF COMPARATIVE ZOOLOGY. (Oxford St.) Natural history. Mon.–Sat. 9–4:30, Sun. 1–4:30. †

HARVARD UNIVERSITY, PEABODY MUSEUM OF ARCHAEOLOGY AND ETHNOLOGY. (Divinity Ave. off Kirkland St.) Primitive art; anthropology. Africa, North and South America, Oceania, Asia, Europe. Mon.–Sat. 9–4:30, Sun. 1–4:30. †**

THE LONGFELLOW HOUSE. (105 Brattle St.) Built 1759; Washington's headquarters 1775–76; home of poet 1837–1882. Furnished as when Longfellow died; portraits, garden. Mon.–Fri. 10–5, Sat. 12–5, Sun. 1–5 (closes at 4 Nov.–Apr.).

MASSACHUSETTS INSTITUTE OF TECHNOLOGY, FRANCIS RUSSELL HART NAUTICAL MUSEUM. (77 Massachusetts Ave.) Rigged models, half models, marine items. During school hours.

MASSACHUSETTS INSTITUTE OF TECHNOLOGY MUSEUM. (Rm. 7–345, 77 Massachusetts Ave.) Art gallery, exhibitions. Sept.–June, Mon.–Fri. 10–5, weekends, 2–5.

Chatham

CHATHAM HISTORICAL SOCIETY, INC. (Stage Harbor Rd.) Historic house, 1752. July, Aug.: Wed., Fri. 2–5.

Concord

CONCORD ANTIQUARIAN SOCIETY. (Lexington Rd. and Cambridge Tpk.) Period rooms; Emerson Study, Thoreau Room. Diorama of Battle of Concord; herb garden. April 19–Nov. 11: Mon.–Sat. 10–5, Sun. 2–5.

CONCORD ART ASSOCIATION. (Lexington Rd.) Exhibitions; local art. Tues.–Sat. 11–5, Sun. 2–5.

ORCHARD HOUSE. (Lexington Rd.) Alcott family home, 19th century; the family combined two houses built 1650 and 1730. Alcott furniture, memorabilia, manuscripts. Apr. 19–Nov. 11: Mon.–Sat. 10–5, Sun. 2–6.

RALPH WALDO EMERSON HOUSE. (Cambridge Tpk.) Built 1828; Emerson home 1835 to 1882; his furnishings, manuscripts. Tues.–Sat. 10–11:30, 1:30–5:30, Sun. 2:30–5:30. Closed Dec. 1–Apr. 18.

Cummington

WILLIAM CULLEN BRYANT HOMESTEAD. Family furnishings, in house of 1794 where *Thanatopsis* was written. Mid-June–mid-Sept.: Mon., Wed. and Fri. 2:30–5.

Dalton

CRANE MUSEUM. (off Rt. 9) Company museum: papermaking equipment, history; old company bldg., mill. June–Sept. Mon.–Fri. 2–5. †

Danvers

DANVERS HISTORICAL SOCIETY MUSEUM. (13 Page St.) Local history, furnishings, crafts, textiles, uniforms. Historic Page House, 1754. By appt.

REBECCA NURSE HOUSE. (149 Pine St.) Period furnishings, built 1678. Mid-June–mid-Oct. Mon.–Sat. 10–5. Maintained by Soc. for the Preservation of New England Antiq. †

Danversport

SAMUEL FOWLER HOUSE. (166 High St.) Federal period furnishings, house built 1810. Maintained by the Soc. for the Preservation of New England Antiq. Mid-Apr.–mid-Sept. Mon., Wed. and Thurs. 2–5.

Dartmouth

CHILDREN'S MUSEUM, INC. (Russells Mills Rd.) Natural history, nature trails, animals, Indian artifacts. Weekends 2–4.

Dedham

DEDHAM HISTORICAL SOCIETY. (612

High St.) Local history, furnishings. Mon.–Sat. 2–5 (closed Sat. during July and Aug.).

THE FAIRBANKS HOMESTEAD. (East St. and Eastern Ave.) Oldest wood frame house in the U.S. Family furnishings 1636–1903. May–Oct. daily (except Mon.) 9–12, 1–5. †

Deerfield

DEERFIELD ACADEMY, HILSON GALLERY FOR CREATIVE ART. Junior museum, contemp. painting. Daily 2–5. Closed Mar., July, Aug., Dec.

HERITAGE FOUNDATION. Historical Society. Museum: furniture, ceramics, glassware, textiles, paintings and portraits. Historic Houses: Asa Stebbins House, 1790s (period furnishings); Ashley House, 18th century (fine period furnishings); Dwight-Barnard House; Sheldon-Hawks House, 1734 (sewing room, dresses, fabrics); Wilson Printing House, 1816 (hand press, publications). All: Daily 9:30–12, 1:30–4:30; Sun. 1:30–4:30. †*

INDIAN HOUSE MEMORIAL. (Old Deerfield St.) Replica of 1698 bldg.; and historic early 18th-century Bloody Brook Tavern, a hewn timber house. Crafts center; demonstrations, weaving, ceramics. May to Nov. daily (except Tues.) 9:30–12, 1–5, Sun. 1:30–5.

POCUMTUCK VALLEY MEMORIAL ASSOCIATION. (Old Deerfield and Memorial Sts.) Historical society. Memorial Hall, 1799: furniture, decorative items, signs, textiles. Apr.1–Jan.1 daily 9:30–12, 2–5. Frary House, 1689: Revolutionary tavern. Apr.–Oct. Tues.–Sat. 9–12, 1:30–5, Sun. 2–5. †

Dorchester

DORCHESTER HISTORICAL SOCIETY. (195 Boston St.) Local history. Historic House of 1683; Blake House (Edward Everett Sq.). Apr.–Oct. 2nd Sat. 2–4; and by appt.

Duxbury

DUXBURY RURAL AND HISTORICAL SOCIETY. Local history, Civil War. June–Sept. daily (except Mon.) 2–6.

JOHN ALDEN HOUSE. (Alden St.) June–Sept. daily 9–5.

East Gloucester

NORTH SHORE ARTS ASSOCIATION OF GLOUCESTER. (E. Gloucester Sq.) Exhibitions. Summer: Mon.–Sat. 10–5:30, Sun. 2:30–5:30.

Edgartown, Martha's Vineyard

DUKES COUNTY HISTORICAL SOCIETY, INC. (School and Cooke Sts.) Historic Thomas Cooke House, 1765; whaling items; local history; marine items incl. lighthouse tower. June–Sept.: Tues.–Sat. 10–12, 2–4:30; Sun. 2–4:30. Oct.–May: Mon., Wed., Sat. 1–4.

Fall River

FALL RIVER HISTORICAL SOCIETY. (451 Rock St.) Local history; textile industry; marine items; furnishings. Mon.–Fri. 9–4:30, Sat. 9–12; closed July, Aug.

Falmouth

FALMOUTH HISTORICAL SOCIETY. (Village Green) Historic house, 1790; whaling, local history, portraits, pottery, furniture. Mid-June–mid-Sept. Daily 2–5.

Fitchburg

FITCHBURG ART MUSEUM. Paintings, sculpture, graphics; decorative arts; French Provincial furniture. Exhibitions, esp. fine arts and crafts, contemp. art. Tues.–Sat. 9–5, Tues. eve. 6–9, Sun. 2–5.

FITCHBURG HISTORICAL SOCIETY. (50 Grove St.) American primitive paintings; local antiques. Mid-Sept.–mid-June, Thurs. and Sun. 2–4.

Gloucester

"BEAUPORT." (Eastern Pt. Blvd.) Period rooms, different styles; Massachusetts furnishings. Maintained by Soc. for the Preservation of New England Antiq. June–Sept. Mon.–Fri., guided tours only, 2:30, 3:30 and 4:30.

CAPE ANN SCIENTIFIC, LITERARY AND HISTORICAL ASSOCIATION. (27 Pleasant St.) Historic Capt. Elias Davis House, 1804; period furnishings, ship models, fishing industry, domestic implements. Mid-June–mid-Sept. Daily (except Mon.) 11–4, Sun. 2–5. Historic White-Ellery House, about 1700 (Rt. 128, traffic circle at entrance to Gloucester); period furnishings, interesting construction in very old, unrestored house. Mid-June–mid-Sept. daily (except Mon.) 3–5.

HAMMOND MUSEUM, INC. (Hesperus Ave.) Gothic, Renaissance art, architectural fragments, tapestries, furnishings; building in castle form. July–mid-Sept. daily (except Sun.) guided tours only, 10, 11, 12 and 2.

OPEN-CHURCH BIBLE MUSEUM. (58 Middle St.) Rare historical Bibles; all English translations. July–Sept. daily 2–5. †

SARGENT-MURRAY-GILMAN-HOUGH HOUSE. (49 Middle St.) Paneled interior, fine antiques in house of 1768. Summer, weekdays 11–5.

Groton

GROTON HISTORICAL SOCIETY. (Main St.) Historic Gov. Boutwell House of 1851; local history. June–Oct. Sat. 3–5.

Hadley

FARM MUSEUM, MASSACHUSETTS SOCIETY FOR PROMOTING AGRICULTURE. Old barn, 1782; historic farm implements. May–mid-Oct. Tues.–Sat. 10–5, Sun. 1:30–5.

PORTER-PHELPS-HUNTINGTON HOUSE. (128 River Dr., Rt. 47) House of 1752, household articles 17th–19th centuries, family papers. Apr.–mid-Oct., daily 1–5.

Hanover Center

SAMUEL STETSON HOUSE. (Rt. 139) Built 1694–1716. Maintained by Soc. for the Preservation of New England Antiq. June–Oct.: Mon., Wed., Fri. 10–5.

Harvard

FRUITLANDS MUSEUMS. (Prospect Hill) Historic farmhouse, Shaker House, American Indian Museum, Picture Gallery. May 30–Sept. daily (except Mon.) 1–5. †

Haverhill

HAVERHILL HISTORICAL SOCIETY. (240 Water St.) "The Buttonwoods," historic house of 1814; Indian relics, household items, 18th and 19th centuries. Tues., Thurs., Sat. 2–5. John Ward House; period furnishings in house of

1643. Apr.–Oct. Tues., Thurs., Sat. 2–5.

JOHN GREENLEAF WHITTIER HOMESTEAD. (Rt. 110; 305 Whittier Rd.) Family furnishings, house built 1688. Tues.–Sat. 10–6, Sun. 1–6.

Hingham

HINGHAM HISTORICAL SOCIETY. (18 Bradford Rd.) Historic house of 1650, period furnishings. Summer: Tues.–Sat. 11:30–4:30.

Holliston

HOLLISTON HISTORICAL SOCIETY, INC. (760 Washington St.) Local history; historic house, 1825. Mon., Wed.–Sat. 6–8 P.M., Sun. 1–3.

Holyoke

HOLYOKE MUSEUM. ("Wistariahurst," Cabot at Beech Sts.) Egyptian, American Indian art; children's museum. Mon.–Sat. 10–12, 1–5.

Ipswich

EMERSON-HOWARD HOUSE. (41 Turkey Shore Rd.) Built 1648. Maintained by the Soc. for the Preservation of New England Antiq. Mid-June–Sept., Mon.–Thurs. 2–5.

IPSWICH HISTORICAL SOCIETY. (53 S. Main St.) John Whipple house, built 1640; later additions. 17th- and 18th-century furnishings, garden. Waters Memorial (John Heard House) of 1795; 18th- and 19th-century furnishings, china, guns. Apr.–Nov. Tues.–Sat. 10–5, Sun. 1–5. †

LAKEMAN-JOHNSON HOUSE. (16 East St.) Early 19th-century home of sea capt. Maintained by Soc. for the Preservation of New England Antiq. Mid-June–Sept. Tues., Thurs. and Sat. 10–5.

Jamaica Plain

CHILDREN'S MUSEUM, BOSTON. (60 Burroughs St.) Science, nature, dolls, history, ethnology. Tues.–Sat. 9–5, Sun. 2–5. †*

Kingston

MAJOR JOHN BRADFORD HOUSE. (Landing Rd.) Period furnishings, house of 1674. Summer, daily 10–5.

Lenox

PLEASANT VALLEY SANCTUARY (320–W). Nature center, aviary, botanical garden. May–Oct. daily 10–5.

Lexington

LEXINGTON HISTORICAL SOCIETY. Buckman Tavern (opposite Battlegreen) built 1690. Minute Men met here Apr. 19, 1775; period rooms, bar. Hancock-Clarke House (35 Hancock St.) built 1698. Where Paul Revere woke Samuel Adams and John Hancock; 8 period rooms, museum of Revolutionary items. Munroe Tavern (1332 Massachusetts Ave.) built 1695. British headquarters, April 1775; period rooms, historical items. Apr. 19–Oct. 12: Mon.–Sat. 10–5, Sun. 1–5. †*

Lincoln

DE CORDOVA AND DANA MUSEUM AND PARK. (Sandy Pond Rd.) Contemp., New England art. Tues.–Sat. 10–5, Sun. 2–5.

Longmeadow

COLTON HOUSE. (787 Longmeadow St.) Frame house, 1734. Maintained by Soc. for the Preservation of New England Antiq. Mid-June–mid-Oct.: Mon., Tues., Wed. 3–5.

LONGMEADOW HISTORICAL SOCIETY. (697 Longmeadow St.) Local history. Mid-May–mid-Oct. Fri. 2–5, Sat. 7–9.

Lowell

WHISTLER HOUSE, PARKER MEMORIAL GALLERY. (243 Worthen St.) James McNeill Whistler born here; Whistler prints; contemp. art and crafts. Gallery open Tues., Thurs., Sun. 1:30–5 (closed Aug.). House open daily except Mon.

Lynn

LYNN HISTORICAL SOCIETY, INC. (125 Green St.) Local history; primitive paintings; historic Hyde-Mills House, 1838; 18th-century shoemaker's shop; period furnishings. Mon.–Fri. 10–4.

Malden

MALDEN PUBLIC LIBRARY AND ART GALLERY. (36 Salem St.) 17th–19th-century paintings, graphics. Mon.–Fri. 10–9; Sat. 10–6.

Manchester

MANCHESTER HISTORICAL SOCIETY. (12 Union St.) House, 1830. Local history. Summer: Wed. 2–5.

Marblehead

MARBLEHEAD HISTORICAL SOCIETY, JEREMIAH LEE MANSION. (161 Washington St.) House of 1768, National Landmark; fine construction, furnishings. Primitive paintings. May 15–Oct. 12 daily (except Sun.) 9:30–4. *

MARBLEHEAD ARTS ASSOCIATION, KING HOOPER MANSION. (8 Hooper St.) House of 1728, period rooms, garden; art exhibitions. Daily (except Mon.) 2–5.

HOOPER-PARKER HOUSE. (181 Washington St.) Merchant's house, 1770; fishermen's supplies, counting room. Maintained by Soc. for the Preservation of New England Antiq. Mid-June–mid-Sept. Mon., Wed., Fri. 2–4.

Marshfield

HISTORIC WINSLOW HOUSE. (Careswell and Webster Sts.) Furnishings in house of 1699. Summer: daily 10–5.

Medford

MEDFORD HISTORICAL SOCIETY. (10 Governors' Ave.) Misc. items relating to local history; ship building, rum distilling. Mon. 1–5.

PETER TUFTS HOUSE. (350 Riverside Ave.) Brick house, 1678. Maintained by the Soc. for the Preservation of New England Antiq. June–Oct.: Mon., Thurs., Fri. 2–5. Nov.–May: Mon., Thurs. 2–5.

ROYALL MANSION. (15 George St.) 18th-century furnishings. May–mid-Oct. Daily (except Mon. and Fri.) 2–5.

TUFTS UNIVERSITY, BARNUM MUSEUM. Circus history; Barnum memorabilia; posters, etc. Sept.–May weekends 2–5.

Nantucket

MARIA MITCHELL ASSOCIATION, MUSEUM OF NATURAL SCIENCE. (7 Milk St.) Natural history, local flora and fauna; aquarium; astronomical observatory. Mid-June–mid-Sept., Mon.–Fri. 10–12,

2–5; Sat. 10–12. Historic Maria Mitchell House (1 Vestal St.), built 1790; birthplace of astronomer-educator; Quaker furnishings, toys.

NANTUCKET HISTORICAL ASSOCIATION. Historical Museum, Friends Meeting House of 1838. (Fair St.) Marine items, costumes, portraits. Old Jail (Vestal St.). Old Wind Mill (Mill Hill) of 1746. Oldest House (Jethro Coffin House) of 1686 (Sunset Hill Rd.). 1800 House (Mill St.). Mid-June–mid-Sept. daily 10–5.

WHALING MUSEUM, Nantucket Historical Association. (Broad St.) Gear, rigged boat, scrimshaw, etc. June–mid-Oct. daily 10–5. †

New Bedford

NEW BEDFORD FREE PUBLIC LIBRARY. (Pleasant St.) Prints: Bierstadt, local artists, whaling subjects; Quaker material. Mon.–Fri. 9–9, Sat. 9–6.

SEAMAN'S BETHEL. (15 Johnny Cake Rd.) Church of whaling days.

SWAIN SCHOOL OF DESIGN, WILLIAM W. CRAPO GALLERY. (19 Hawthorn St.) Exhibitions. Mon.–Sat. 10–4, Mon. and Wed. eves. 7–9, Sun. 2–5.

WHALING MUSEUM AND OLD DARTMOUTH HISTORICAL SOCIETY. (18 Johnny Cake Hill) Marine and whaling items; prints; whale ship and equipment. Daily 9–5; Sun. 2–5. Closed Mon. Sept.–May.

Newbury

SHORT HOUSE. (39 High Rd.) Wooden house of 1733; paneling, antique furnishings. Maintained by Soc. for the Preservation of New England Antiq. Mid-June–Sept. Tues.–Sat. 10–12, 2–5.

SWETT-ILSLEY HOUSE. (4–6 High Rd.) Old woodwork, fireplaces in house built before 1670. Maintained by Soc. for the Preservation of New England Antiq. Tues.–Sat. Closed Jan., Feb.

TRISTRAM COFFIN HOUSE. (16 High Rd.) Interiors, period furnishings in house built 1651. Maintained by Soc. for the Preservation of New England Antiq. Mid-June–mid-Sept. Mon., Wed., Fri. 2–5.

Newton

JACKSON HOMESTEAD. (527 Washington St.) History of Newton in house built 1809. Sept.–June: Mon.–Fri. 2–4. July, Aug.: Wed. 2–4. Oct.–May "Open House" 3rd Sun. 3–5.

North Andover

NORTH ANDOVER HISTORICAL SOCIETY. (153 Academy Rd.) Local history, industries, decorative arts. Parson Barnard House (179 Osgood St.), built 1715; period rooms, furnished according to documentary evidence in inventories of early owners. Wed., Fri., Sat. 2–5. (Closed Oct.–Apr.).

North Oxford

THE CLARA BARTON BIRTHPLACE. (Clara Barton Rd. between Rts. 12 and 20) American Red Cross items; period furnishings in house built 1805. Daily (except Mon.) 10–12, 1–5.

Northampton

NORTHAMPTON HISTORICAL SOCIETY MUSEUM. (240 Main St.) Local and regional history; arts and crafts; dolls, valentines. Tues., Thurs. 2–5. Cornet Joseph Parsons House. (58 Bridge St.) Antique furnishings. Wed., Fri., Sun. 2–5. Isaac Damon House. (46 Bridge St.) Home of architect and bridge-builder. Jenny Lind items; furniture, tools. Summer: Wed., Sat. 2–5.

SMITH COLLEGE MUSEUM OF ART. (Elm St. at Bedford Terrace) 18th–20th-century paintings, graphics, sculpture; esp. French. Winter: Mon.–Sat. 9–5, Sun. 2:30–4:30. Summer daily 2:30–4:30. †*

Norwell

JACOBS FARMHOUSE. (Main St. and Jacobs Lane, Assinippi) House of 1726; old fire equipment in barn. Maintained by Soc. for the Preservation of New England Antiq. June–Sept. Mon., Tues. and Fri. 2–5.

Orange

ORANGE HISTORICAL SOCIETY. (41 N. Main St.) Local history. Mon.–Sat. 1–5.

Paxton

WENDELL PHILLIPS PARKER NATURE TRAINING SCHOOL. (Asnebumskit Pond) Nature center, wildlife sanctuary. July, Aug.

Pembroke

PEMBROKE HISTORICAL SOCIETY, INC. (Centre St.) Shipbuilding tools, local history; Bryantville Schoolhouse of 1847. July, Aug. Sun. 2–5.

Petersham

HARVARD UNIVERSITY, FISHER MUSEUM OF FORESTRY. (Athol Rd.) Dioramas relating to New England land use, forest management; Indian tools; forest soils. Mon.–Sat. 10–5, Sun. 2–5.

PETERSHAM HISTORICAL SOCIETY. (N. Main St.) Local history and art; furniture, tools. June–Sept. Wed. 2–4.

Pittsfield

THE BERKSHIRE ATHENAEUM. (44 Bank Row) Library; Melville Room. Mon.–Fri. 9–9, Sat. 9–6. Mid-June–mid-Sept. Mon., Wed., Fri. 9–9; Tues., Thurs., Sat. 9–6. †

THE BERKSHIRE MUSEUM. (39 South St.) Art *survey*. Local history and natural history. Exhibitions. Tues.–Sat. 10–5, Sun. 2–5. Closed Mon.

Plymouth

ANTIQUARIAN HOUSE, PLYMOUTH ANTIQUARIAN SOCIETY. (126 Water St.) Household furnishings, in home of 1809–1830. Spooner House (27 North St.) occupied 1750–1950 by one family. Harlow Old Fort House (119 Sandwich St.), built 1677; period furnishings, demonstrations of household occupations such as dyeing, spinning, candle making, weaving, fireside cooking. Mid-June–mid-Sept. 10–5, Sun. 1–5 (Old Fort open May 30–Sept. 30).

THE JABEZ HOWLAND HOUSE, PILGRIM JOHN HOWLAND SOCIETY, INC. (33 Sandwich St.) Built 1667. May–mid-Oct. daily (except Tues.) 9–5.

PILGRIM HALL. (Court St.) Pilgrim mementos, history, local history. First public museum bldg. in America. Mid-Apr.–mid-Oct. daily 10–4, Sun. 1–4; winter Sun. only. †

PLIMOUTH PLANTATION, INC. (Warren Ave.) Replicas of early Pilgrim houses, *Mayflower II*, Pilgrim Village. Mid-April–Nov. daily 9–5; open summer eve. until 8 or 9.

Princeton

ANTIQUE AUTO MUSEUM. (Rt. 31) Also other vehicles, incl. baby carriages, fire trucks. Apr.–mid-Nov., Sun. Mid-June–mid-Sept. daily. Closed Dec.–Mar.

Provincetown

PROVINCETOWN ART ASSOCIATION. (460 Commercial St.) Exhibitions, contemp. art. Summers: Mon.–Sat. 10–6, 7–10; Sun. 2–6.

Quincy

ADAMS NATIONAL HISTORIC SITE. (135 Adams St.) Adams family residence for four generations, built 1781; family furnishings. Apr. 19–Nov. 10 daily 9–5. †*

COL. JOSIAH QUINCY HOUSE. (20 Muirhead St., Wollaston) Fine furnishings in merchant's house built 1770. May–mid-Oct. Tues., Thurs., Fri., Sun. 1–5.

JOHN ADAMS BIRTHPLACE. (133 Franklin St.) Built 1681; and JOHN QUINCY ADAMS BIRTHPLACE. (141 Franklin St.) Built 1663. Apr. 19–Sept. 30 daily (except Mon.) 10–5. †*

Reading

PARKER TAVERN. (103 Washington St.) Built 1694; 17th-century furnishings. June–Sept., Sun. 2–5.

Rockport

THE OLD CASTLE. (Old Castle Lane, at Granite and Curtis Sts.) Built 1678, leanto added 1792. Period furnishings, utensils. July–Aug. weekends 2–5.

SANDY BAY HISTORICAL SOCIETY AND MUSEUM. Sewall-Scripture House (40 King St.). Victoriana, marine items, local history. July, Aug. daily 2–5.

Salem

ESSEX INSTITUTE. (132 Essex St.) Early American and local history, archives, decorative arts, clocks, tools, toys, paintings. Historic John Ward House of 1684; Lye-Tapley Shoe Shop; Pingree House of 1804; Crowninshield-Bentley House. All in garden or adjacent. And Peirce-Nichols House of 1782 (80 Federal St.). Tues.–Sat. 9–4:30, Sun. 2–5. †*

HOUSE OF SEVEN GABLES SETTLEMENT

ASSOCIATION. (54 Turner St.) House of Seven Gables, 1668; Hathaway House, 1682; Hawthorne House, where novelist was born, mid-18th century; Retire Beckett House. Period furnishings, paintings; guest rooms available. Summer daily 9:30–7. Labor Day–June 30, 10–5. †

PEABODY MUSEUM OF SALEM. (161 Essex St.) Ethnology, natural history, maritime and marine items, primitive art. Mon.–Sat. 9–5, Sun. 2–5. Nov.–Feb.: Mon.–Sat. 9–4, Sun. 2–4. †*

SALEM MARITIME NATIONAL HISTORIC SITE, CUSTOM HOUSE. (168 Derby St.) and DERBY HOUSE (172 Derby St.) Park museum. Maritime history of Salem; custom house of 1819, wealthy merchant's home of 1762, period furnishings, imported china. Daily 10–5. †*

ROPES MEMORIAL. (318 Essex St.) Family furnishings of 18th and 19th centuries in house built in 1722; garden. May–Dec. Mon.–Sat. 10–12, 2–5.

WITCH HOUSE. (310 Essex St.) Reminders of Salem witch hunt in house built 1642. June–Oct. daily 10–6. †

Sandwich

SANDWICH HISTORICAL SOCIETY, GLASS MUSEUM. (Rt. 130 Town Hall Sq.) Sandwich glass. May–Oct. daily 10–5. †

Saugus

SAUGUS IRONWORKS RESTORATION. (244 Central St.) Preservation project. Reconstruction of buildings from 1646 iron industry; Iron Master's House, period furnishings; operating mills, forge, other demonstrations. Mid-May–mid-Oct. daily (except Mon.) 9–4. †

"SCOTCH"-BOARDMAN HOUSE. (17 Howard St.) Unusual construction, house built 1651. Maintained by the Soc. for the Preservation of New England Antiq. June–Sept. Mon.–Thurs., Sat. 10–5. †

Scituate

SCITUATE HISTORICAL SOCIETY. (First Parish Rd.) Local history; historic Cudworth House. July–Sept. 2–6.

Somerville

SOMERVILLE HISTORICAL SOCIETY. (Central St. and Westwood Rd.) Local history, Revolutionary and Civil War items; staircase designed by Bulfinch. Holidays only, Apr.–Oct. 2–4.

South Carver

RAILWAY AND LOCOMOTIVE HISTORICAL SOCIETY MUSEUM, EDAVILLE RAILROAD. Railroad history. May–Oct.

South Hadley

MOUNT HOLYOKE COLLEGE, DWIGHT ART MEMORIAL. *Survey.* Mon.–Fri. 9–5:45; Sat. 9–12, 2–5:30; Sun. 2:30–4:30. †

South Lancaster

THAYER MUSEUM, INC. (Main St.) Birds of North America, stuffed and mounted; habitat groups. Mon., Wed., Sat. 1–5.

South Natick

HISTORICAL, NATURAL HISTORY AND LIBRARY SOCIETY. (Eliot St.) Local history and natural history. Sept.–June: Wed., Sat. 2:30–5; July, Aug. Wed. only.

South Sudbury

GARDEN IN THE WOODS. (Raymond Rd.) Botanical Garden; wild flower sanctuary. Mon.–Sat. daylight hours.

Springfield

CONNECTICUT VALLEY HISTORICAL MUSEUM. (William Pynchon Memorial Bldg.) Local history and business history; miniatures. Tues.–Sat. 1–5, Sun. 2–5; closed Aug.

GEORGE WALTER VINCENT SMITH ART MUSEUM. (222 State St.) Decorative arts, Oriental, American. Tues.–Sat. 1–5, Sun. 2–5.

MUSEUM OF FINE ARTS. (49 Chestnut St.) *Survey;* Oriental bronzes, pottery, porcelain. Tues.–Sat. 1–5, Sun. 2–5. Closed Sun. July; closed Aug.

MUSEUM OF NATURAL HISTORY. (236 State St., the Quadrangle) Natural history, ethnology, aquarium, planetarium. Tues.–Sat. 1–5, Tues. eve. 8–10, Sun. 2–5; closed Sun. during July and Aug.

SPRINGFIELD ARMORY MUSEUM. (Federal St.) Small arms, other military items. Tues.–Sat. 1–4.

TRAILSIDE MUSEUM. (Forest Park)

Nature Center, aquarium, children's museum. Daily 11–4:30.

Zoo. (Forest Park) Aviary; tropical animals. Daily 11–4:30.

Stockbridge

BERKSHIRE GARDEN CENTER, INC. Botanical Garden. Daily 9–5.

CHESTERWOOD STUDIO MUSEUM. Sculpture of Daniel Chester French, in his studio of 1897. Summer daily 10–6.

MISSION HOUSE. (Main St.) Period furnishings, garden in house built 1739 by first missionary to local Indians. Mid-May–Oct. Mon.–Sat. 10–6, Sun. 2–6.

Sturbridge

OLD STURBRIDGE VILLAGE. (Mass. Tpk., Rts. 15 and 20) Re-creation of New England rural community; preservation project. Crafts demonstrations. Daily 9:30–5:30. †*

Swampscott

SWAMPSCOTT HISTORICAL SOCIETY. (99 Paradise Rd.) House, 1634; scattered items of marine interest. Daily 10–5.

Swansea

MARTIN HOUSE. (22 Stoney Hill Rd.) 17th- and 18th-century furnishings in house built 1728. Mid-May–Oct. daily 10–6.

Taunton

OLD COLONY HISTORICAL SOCIETY. (66 Church Green) Local history, industry, Indian relics, portraits; house of 1853. Mon.–Fri. 10–12, 2–4; Sat. 10–12.

Templeton

NARRAGANSETT HISTORICAL SOCIETY, INC. (Templeton Common) Local history, costumes, archives. Old country store of about 1810. July–mid-Sept. Tues., Sat. 2–5. 1st Sun. 2–5.

Topsfield

TOPSFIELD HISTORICAL SOCIETY. (1 Howlett St., off Village Common) 17th-century furnishings in Parson Capen House, built 1683. Mid-May–mid-Oct. Tues.–Sat. 10:30–4:30, Sun. 12–5.

Townsend Harbor

CONANT HOUSE. (South St., off Rt. 119) Construction details, furnishings in house built about 1720; cooperage and grist mill of about 1840. Maintained by Soc. for the Preservation of New England Antiq. July–Oct. Mon., Wed., Fri. 2–4.

Waltham

GORE PLACE. (52 Gore St.) Federal period furnishings, house built 1805. Tues.–Sat. 10–5, Sun. 2–5.

LYMAN HOUSE. (Lyman and Beaver Sts.) Known as "The Vale." Samuel McIntire designed it; 1793. Ballroom, bow parlor, garden. McIntire stable, greenhouses; two McIntire pieces of furniture. Maintained by Soc. for the Preservation of New England Antiq. End May–beg. Sept. Thurs.–Sat. 11–5.

WALTHAM PRECISION INSTRUMENT COMPANY. (221 Crescent St.) Antique watches; company museum. Daily 9–3.

Watertown

ABRAHAM BROWNE HOUSE. (562 Main St.) Restored house of about 1698. Maintained by Soc. for the Preservation of New England Antiq. May–Oct. Mon.–Fri. 2–5; Nov.–Apr. Tues. and Fri. only 2–5.

PERKINS SCHOOL FOR THE BLIND MUSEUM. (175 N. Beacon St.) Junior museum; education and welfare of the blind. Mon.–Fri. 8:30–5.

Wellesley

WELLESLEY COLLEGE, BOTANICAL GARDEN AND ARBORETUM. Teaching coll. Daily 8:30–4.

WELLESLEY COLLEGE, JEWETT ARTS CENTER. Survey. Mon.–Thurs. 8:30–5, Sat. 8:30–12, 2–5; Sun. 2:30–5:30.

WELLESLEY COLLEGE ZOOLOGY MUSEUM. Zoology, ornithology. Teaching collection. Class hours.

Wenham

WENHAM HISTORICAL ASSOCIATION AND MUSEUM, INC. (Main St. Rt. 1A) Local history; antique dolls. 19th-century cobbler's shop. Claflin-Richards House, about 1664. Mon.–Fri. 1–4; last Sun. every month. 2–4. †

Westfield

WESTFIELD ATHENAEUM, EDWIN SMITH HISTORICAL MUSEUM and JASPER RAND ART MUSEUM. (6 Elm St.) Local history; archives of Western Hampden Historical Society. Art; exhibitions. Mon., Tues., Thurs., Fri. 8:30 A.M.–9 P.M. Wed., Sat. 8:30–6.

Williamstown

STERLING AND FRANCINE CLARK ART INSTITUTE. (South St.) 19th-century American, French painting; silver; sculpture. Daily (except Mon.) 10–5. Closed Feb. †

WILLIAMS COLLEGE, LAWRENCE ART MUSEUM. *Survey;* American furniture, painting, sculpture. Mon.–Sat. 10–12, 2–4; Sun. 2–5. †

Winthrop

WINTHROP IMPROVEMENT AND HISTORICAL ASSOCIATION, DEANE WINTHROP HOUSE of 1637. (40 Shirley St.) Local history. Tues., Wed., Fri. 2–5.

Woburn

RUMFORD HISTORICAL ASSOCIATION, RUMFORD HOUSE. (90 Elm St.) House built 1714; portraits, antique furnishings. Daily 10–3.

Woods Hole

BIOLOGICAL LABORATORY AQUARIUM.

Worcester

AMERICAN ANTIQUARIAN SOCIETY. (Park Ave. and Salisbury St.) American history; library; archives. Mon.–Fri. 9–5. †

JOHN WOODMAN HIGGINS ARMORY, INC. (100 Barber Ave.) Arms, armor through history; modern pressed steel products. Company museum. Mon.–Fri. 9–4:30, Sat. 9–12. †

PIEDMONT CENTER. Nature center for underprivileged children. Daily 1–9. †

RICE HOUSE CHILDREN'S MUSEUM. (41 Elm St.) Natural history; planetarium. Mon.–Sat. 10–5. †

WORCESTER ART MUSEUM. (55 Salisbury St.) *Survey.* Mon.–Sat. 10–5, Sun. 2–5. Nov.–Apr. Tues. until 10 P.M. †*

WORCESTER HISTORICAL SOCIETY. (39 Salisbury St.) Local history, industries, farm and household implements, costumes. Tues.–Sat. 2–5. Closed Aug.

WORCESTER NATURAL HISTORY SOCIETY. (21 Cedar St.) Science, industry, natural history. Maintains Rice House and Piedmont Center (above). Mon.–Sat. 9–5, Sun. 2–5.

Yarmouth Port

COLONEL JOHN THACHER HOUSE. (Thacher Lane and King's Hwy.) Period furnishings, house built 1680. Maintained by Soc. for the Preservation of New England Antiq. Mid-June–Sept. daily (except Sun.) 10–12, 2–5.

HISTORICAL SOCIETY OF OLD YARMOUTH. (Strawberry Lane) 1830 period furnishings in historic house. End June–Sept. daily (except Sun.) 2–5.

WINSLOW CROCKER HOUSE. (King's Hwy.) Woodwork, period furnishings in house built about 1780. Maintained by Soc. for the Preservation of New England Antiq. Mid-June–mid-Sept. daily (except Sun.) 10–12, 2–5.

MICHIGAN

Adrian

SIENA HEIGHTS COLLEGE, STUDIO ANGELICO. Art gallery; demonstrations of techniques, exhibitions. Mon.–Fri. 9–8, Sun. 2–8.

Albion

ALBION COLLEGE ART MUSEUM. Graphics; African, American Indian art. School year: Mon.–Fri. 10–12, 2–5; Sat. 9–12, Sun. 2:30–5.

STARR COMMONWEALTH FOR BOYS, BRUECKNER MUSEUM. Modern representational painting, for high school students. Daily (except Mon.) 8–5.

Ann Arbor

ANN ARBOR HIGH SCHOOL, ARGUS PLANETARIUM. (601 W. Stadium Blvd.) By appt. to groups only.

UNIVERSITY OF MICHIGAN, EXHIBIT MUSEUM. (Washtenaw at N. University) Anthropology, natural history, planetarium, American Indian material. Mon.–Sat. 8–5, Sun. 1:30–5:30.

UNIVERSITY OF MICHIGAN HERBARIUM. Michigan flora. Mon.–Fri. 8–5.

UNIVERSITY OF MICHIGAN, KELSEY MUSEUM OF ARCHAEOLOGY. (434 S. State St.) Roman, Near Eastern materials. Mon.–Fri. 1–5, Sun. 3–5.

UNIVERSITY OF MICHIGAN, MUSEUM OF ANTHROPOLOGY. (University Museums Bldg.) American and Far Eastern archaeology and ethnology; primitive art. Research. Public by appt. only. †

UNIVERSITY OF MICHIGAN, MUSEUM OF ART. (Alumni Memorial Hall) *Survey;* exhibitions. Mon.–Sat. 9–5, Sun. 2–5; Oct.–May Wed. eve. 7–10.

UNIVERSITY OF MICHIGAN, MUSEUM OF PALEONTOLOGY. (Washtenaw and N. Univ. Aves.) Research coll. Mon.–Fri. 8–5.

UNIVERSITY OF MICHIGAN, MUSEUM OF ZOOLOGY. (Washtenaw and N. Univ. Aves.) Also herbarium. Research, teaching coll. Mon.–Fri. 8–5, Sat. 8–12.

Battle Creek

KINGMAN MUSEUM OF NATURAL HISTORY. (Leila Arboretum) Archaeology, ethnology (American Indian); mineralogy, astronomy. Mon.–Fri. 8–5; Sat. 8–12, 1–5; Sun. 2:30–5.

Bay City

BAY COUNTY HISTORICAL SOCIETY MUSEUM. (2d floor, County Bldg.) County history; logging, cooper's, and carpenter's tools. Mon.–Fri. 2–5.

Bloomfield Hills

CRANBROOK ACADEMY OF ART, GALLERIES. (Lone Pine Rd.) *Survey;* pre-Columbian, Chinese; decorative arts. Daily (except Mon.) 2–5. †*

CRANBROOK INSTITUTE OF SCIENCE. (500 Lone Pine Rd.) Anthropology, geology, natural history; planetarium. Daily 2–5. †*

Copper Harbor

FORT WILKINS STATE PARK MUSEUM. Natural history. May–Sept. daily 7 A.M.–10 P.M.

Dearborn

DEARBORN HISTORICAL MUSEUM. (915 Brady St.) Historic McFadden-Ross House of 1833; military items; local history. Commandant's Quarters (21950 Michigan Ave.) Mon.–Thurs., Sat. 9–5; Fri. groups by appt. only.

THE HENRY FORD MUSEUM AND GREENFIELD VILLAGE. Art; folk art; industrial history (vehicles, power, agriculture); decorative arts. Preservation project. Mid-June–Labor Day daily 9–6:30. Otherwise daily 9–5; weekends to 5:30. †*

Detroit

CITY OF DETROIT ZOOLOGICAL PARK AND AQUARIUM. (8450 W. 10 Mile Rd.) Mid-May–early Nov. Mon.–Sat. 10–5, Sun. 9–6.

DETROIT ARTISTS MARKET. (110 Madison Ave.) Sales exhibitions of local artists and craftsmen. Daily (except Sun.) 10–5. Closed Aug.

DETROIT HISTORICAL MUSEUM. (5401 Woodward St.) Local history; military, maritime, industrial. Indian artifacts. Tues.–Fri., Sun. 1–10, Sat. 9–6. †*

DETROIT HISTORICAL MUSEUM, DOSSIN MUSEUM OF GREAT LAKES HISTORY. (Belle Isle) Marine history, ship models. Wed.–Sun. 10–7. †*

DETROIT HISTORICAL MUSEUM, FORT WAYNE MILITARY MUSEUM. (6053 W. Jefferson) Reconstructed fort; military equipment. April–Oct.: Wed.–Sun. 1–7. †*

THE DETROIT INSTITUTE OF ARTS. (5200 Woodward Ave.) *Survey;* period rooms; theater arts; Archives of American Art. Tues.–Fri. 1–10, weekends 9–6. Closes at 6 during July and Aug. †*

DETROIT PUBLIC SCHOOLS, CHILDREN'S MUSEUM. (67 E. Kirby Ave.) Art, history, natural history, planetarium. Mon.–Fri. 1–5, Sat. 9–4:30; July: Mon.–Fri. 1–4. †*

NATIONAL BANK OF DETROIT, THE MONEY MUSEUM. (Fort and Woodward Sts.) Numismatics; historical media of exchange. Mon.–Thurs. 10–4:30, Fri. 10–5:30. †

PEWABIC POTTERY. (10125 E. Jefferson) Company museum. Pottery since 1900; tiles, vases, plates, etc. Mon.–Fri. 8–4:30.

WAYNE STATE UNIVERSITY, MUSEUM OF ANTHROPOLOGY. (451 W. Kirby Ave.) Research and teaching coll.

East Lansing

MICHIGAN STATE UNIVERSITY, BEAL-GARFIELD BOTANIC GARDEN. 900 acres on campus. Daily.

MICHIGAN STATE UNIVERSITY, BEAL-DARLINGTON HERBARIUM. Mon.–Fri. 8–5.

MICHIGAN STATE UNIVERSITY, KRESGE ART CENTER. *Survey.* Mon.–Fri. 8–5; Tues. eves. 6–9; Sat. 10–4, Sun. 2–6.

MICHIGAN STATE UNIVERSITY MUSEUM. Natural history, history; agriculture, anatomy, archaeology, folk and primitive art; research. Mon.–Fri. 8–5, weekends 1–5. †

Escanaba

DELTA COUNTY HISTORICAL SOCIETY MUSEUM. (Ludington Park) Local history; fishing, lumbering, pioneer and Indian materials. June–Aug. Mon.–Fri. 1–5.

Flint

FLINT INSTITUTE OF ARTS. (DeWaters Art Center, 1120 E. Kearsley St.) *Survey;* Italian Renaissance furnishings. Mon.–Sat. 10–5, Tues.–Fri. eves. 7–10; Sun. 1–6.

GENESEE COUNTY MUSEUM AND HISTORICAL SOCIETY. (411 Courthouse) Local history: model lumber camp; lighting devices. Mon.–Fri. 8–5.

Garden City

NANKIN MILLS NATURE CENTER. (33175 Ann Arbor Trail) Arboretum. Daily 1–5.

Grand Rapids

GRAND RAPIDS ART GALLERY. (230 E. Fulton St.) Contemp. painting, sculpture. Tues.–Fri. 10–5, Sun. 2–5.

GRAND RAPIDS PUBLIC MUSEUM. (54 Jefferson Ave.) Art, history, natural history. Mon.–Sat. 10–5, Sun. 2–5. †*

Grayling

HARTWICK PINES STATE PARK, LOGGING CAMP MUSEUM. Park museum; logging tools.

Harbor Springs

CHIEF BLACKBIRD HOME MUSEUM.

(368 E. Main St.) Indian items. Daily 10–6.

Hastings

CHARLTON PARK AND BARRY COUNTY MEMORIAL MUSEUM. Indian mission, camp site, early settler's home, shop; farming implements, handicrafts, Indian items. Sun. 1–5; Mon.–Sat. tours by appt.

Holland

THE BAKER MUSEUM FOR FURNITURE RESEARCH. (E. 6th St.) Antique furniture; design research. Mid-May–Sept. daily (except Sun.) 10–4. †

NETHERLANDS MUSEUM. (12th St. and Central Ave.) Local history, Dutch background of community. Daily (except Sun.) 9–12, 1–5.

Houghton

ISLE ROYALE NATIONAL PARK. Park museum. Natural history, herbarium, archaeology, geology, zoo. Daily 8–5. *

MICHIGAN COLLEGE OF MINING AND TECHNOLOGY, A. E. SEAMAN MINERALOGICAL MUSEUM. Research. Mon.–Fri. 9–12, 1–5, Sat. 9–12.

Huron City

WILLIAM LYON PHELPS MEMORIAL MUSEUM. Pioneer log cabin; church; mementos and library of Prof. Phelps of Yale. July, Aug. daily (except Mon.) 3–5.

Ishpeming

NATIONAL SKI HALL OF FAME AND SKI MUSEUM. (Mather Ave.) Ski equipment, photographs, trophies. Weekends 2–4. †

Kalamazoo

THE KALAMAZOO INSTITUTE OF ARTS. (509 Jasper St.) *Survey.* Mon.–Fri. 9–5, Sat. 9–3.

KALAMAZOO NATURE CENTER. Live animals, trails, natural history, planetarium; children's museum. †*

KALAMAZOO PUBLIC MUSEUM. (314 S. Rose St.) Anthropology, local history, planetarium. Daily (except Sun.) 9–6.

Lansing

MICHIGAN HISTORICAL MUSEUM. (505

N. Washington) History; Indian, pioneer items. Mon.–Fri. 10–5, Sun. 2–5.

POTTER PARK ZOO. (City Hall) Daily 10–10.

Ludington

MASON COUNTY MUSEUM. (3–5 E. Filer St.) Local history. Fri., Sat. 2–5.

Mackinac Island

FORT MUSEUM. History. Mid-June–mid-Sept. daily 10–12, 1–5.

Manistee

MANISTEE COUNTY HISTORICAL MUSEUM. (1st St. Dr.) Logging material; county history. Mid-June–mid-Oct. daily (except Mon.) 1:30–5.

Marquette

MARQUETTE COUNTY HISTORICAL SOCIETY MUSEUM AND J. M. LONGYEAR RESEARCH LABORATORY. (213 N. Front St.) Archaeology, Indian and pioneer items; minerals; logging, shipping. Historic John Burt House of 1857 (212 Craig St., South Marquette); Officers' Quarters at Fort Wilkins of 1844 (Keweenaw Peninsula). Mon.–Fri. 9–12, 1–5; children only Fri. aft.

Midland

THE MIDLAND ART ASSOCIATION. (1710 W. St. Andrews Dr.) *Exhibitions.* Mon.–Fri. 3–5, 7–9, Sat. 1–5.

MIDLAND COUNTY HISTORICAL ASSOCIATION. (Midland Rm., Grace A. Dow Memorial Library, 1710 W. St. Andrews Dr.) County history, Indian items. Mon.–Fri. 2–5; Tues., Wed., Thurs. 7–9.

Monroe

MONROE COUNTY HISTORICAL MUSEUM. (Sawyer Bldg., 320 E. Front St.) Local history. Summer daily (except Mon.) 1–5; winter Wed., Thurs. 1–5.

Muskegon

THE HACKLEY ART GALLERY. (296 W. Webster Ave.) Painting, prints. Mon.–Sat. 9–5, Sun. 2:30–5:30.

MUSKEGON COUNTY MUSEUM. (1259 Marquette Ave.) Local history, archaeology, geology. Mon.–Fri. 12–5, Sun. 2:30–5.

Pontiac

THE GOVENOR MOSES WISNER HOME. (405 Oakland Ave.) 1848 mansion of Michigan's gov.

Saginaw

THE SAGINAW MUSEUM. (1126 N. Michigan Ave.) Art: graphics, prints, contemp. and European. Daily (except Mon.) 1–5, Tues. and Thurs. eves. 7–9.

Sault Ste. Marie

CHIPPEWA COUNTY HISTORICAL SOCIETY. The Agency House, built by Indian Agent Henry Rowe Schoolcraft in 1827 (705 Portage Ave.). Bishop Baraga Museum, residence of first bishop of local diocese, 1853–66 (E. Portage Ave.). The John Johnston House, a French-Canadian log building of 1815 (415 Park Place). July 1–Labor Day, daily 11–5.

Traverse City

CLINCH PARK AQUARIUM, ZOO. (Grandview Pkwy.)

CLINCH PARK, CON FOSTER MUSEUM. (Grandview Pkwy.) Natural history; geology. Records of lumbering and Astor Fur companies. May 30–Sept. daily 10–10.

MINNESOTA

Ada

NORMAN COUNTY MUSEUM. Local history. Tues. 3–5, Fri. 7–9, Sat. 3–5.

Austin

HORMEL FOUNDATION ARBORETUM. Native Minnesota trees; nature trails. By appt. only.

MOWER COUNTY PIONEER AND HISTORICAL CENTER. (Fairgrounds) Preservation project: church, school, house of pioneer days. June–Aug., Sun. afternoons and by appt.

Bemidji

BELTRAMI COUNTY HISTORICAL SO-

CIETY. Indian materials; picture collections; Log Homestead and Log School. During county fairs only, 10–10.

Benson

SWIFT COUNTY HISTORICAL SOCIETY MUSEUM. (Basement, Public Library, 1415 Kansas Ave.) Local history, family biographies. Mon.–Fri. 9–12, 1–5.

Blue Earth

FARIBAULT COUNTY HISTORICAL SOCIETY. Historic Wakefield House, 1880. Daily (except Mon.) 2–5.

Brainerd

CROW WING COUNTY HISTORICAL SOCIETY. (County Courthouse) Indian materials, guns; old country schoolhouse. Summer: Tues.–Fri. 1–5. Winter: Tues. and Fri. 1–5.

Cokato

H. C. BULL MEMORIAL LIBRARY AND MUSEUM. (W. 5th St.) Pioneer implements. Daily during school year, 8:30–4. †

Crookston

HOLTE MEMORIAL MUSEUM. (Community Theatre Bldg.) Local history. Mon.–Fri. 2–5.

Detroit Lakes

BECKER COUNTY HISTORICAL SOCIETY. Local history and natural history. Mon.–Fri. 2–5.

Duluth

A. M. CHISHOLM MUSEUM. (1832 E. 2d St.) Children's museum: natural history, Indians, science. Mon.–Fri. 9–5, Sat. 9–12; first Sun. each month 2:30–5. †
ST. LOUIS COUNTY HISTORICAL SOCIETY. (2228 E. Superior St.) Regional history; paintings and drawings of Chippewa Indians; Indian materials. Mon.–Fri. 10–12, 2–5; first Sun. of each month 2:30–5.
UNIVERSITY OF MINNESOTA, TWEED GALLERY. Art: 19th century. Barbizon painting; exhibitions. Tues.–Fri. 8–12, 1–5; weekends 2–5.

Excelsior

UNIVERSITY OF MINNESOTA LANDSCAPE ARBORETUM. Daily except Sun. 8–sundown.

Fairmount

MARTIN COUNTY HISTORICAL SOCIETY. (300 E. Blue Earth Ave.) Pioneer, county history. May–Aug. afternoons daily (except Mon.).

Faribault

RICE COUNTY HISTORICAL SOCIETY. (Rice County Fairgrounds) Pleasant Valley Schoolhouse; Holy Innocents Church; Alexander Faribault House. May–Nov.

Grand Marais

COOK COUNTY HISTORICAL SOCIETY. Pioneer history; Maple Hill Church; Chippewa City Church Historic Houses.

Grand Rapids

ITASCA COUNTY HISTORICAL ROOM. (Itasca County Courthouse) County history. Mon.–Fri. 12:30–4:30.

Henderson

SIBLEY COUNTY HISTORICAL SOCIETY. Local history; historic Poehler House. May–Oct. Sun. 2–5.

Little Falls

MORRISON COUNTY HISTORICAL SOCIETY. (E. B'way and 2d St.) Wed.–Fri. 10–5.

Madison

LAC QUI PARLE COUNTY MUSEUM. Pioneer implements, period rooms; Indian items. Fri. 2–5.

Mankato

BLUE EARTH COUNTY HISTORICAL SOCIETY. (606 S. Broad St.) Local history, natural history. Daily 1–5.

Minneapolis

ELOISE BUTLER WILD FLOWER GAR-

DEN. (Theodore Wirth Park) Apr.–mid-Sept.: 9–6. Mid-Sept.–Oct.: 9–5 daily.

HENNEPIN COUNTY HISTORICAL SOCIETY. (2303 3d Ave.) Pioneer items, period schoolroom and kitchen. Daily (except Mon.) 1:30–4:30.

THE MINNEAPOLIS INSTITUTE OF ARTS. (201 E. 24th St.) *Survey;* Chinese bronzes, jades. Summer: Tues.–Fri. 12–5, Sat. 10–5, Sun. 2–5. Winter: Tues.–Thurs. 12–9, Fri. 12–5, Sat. 10–5, Sun. 1–5. †*

MINNEAPOLIS PUBLIC LIBRARY. (300 Nicollet Ave.) Picture collection; all subjects; reproductions. Mon.–Fri. 9–9, Sat. 9–5.

MINNEAPOLIS PUBLIC LIBRARY, SCIENCE MUSEUM AND PLANETARIUM. (300 Nicollet Ave.) Astronomy, geology, natural history. Mon.–Sat. 9–5:30.

UNIVERSITY OF MINNESOTA, ANTHROPOLOGY MUSEUM. (325 Ford Hall) Minnesota archaeology, ethnology; research. Mon.–Fri. 9–4 during school sessions.

UNIVERSITY OF MINNESOTA, COLLEGE OF PHARMACY. Botanical garden; medicinal plants; research. Mon.–Fri. 8–5, Sat. 8–12.

UNIVERSITY OF MINNESOTA, MUSEUM OF NATURAL HISTORY. (17th and University Ave.) Ornithology, zoology, herpetology. Field trips, expeditions. Mon.–Sat. 9–5, Sun. 2–5.

UNIVERSITY OF MINNESOTA, UNIVERSITY GALLERY. (310 Northrop Memorial Auditorium) Modern American art; exhibitions. Mon.–Fri. 9–4:30.

WALKER ART CENTER. (1710 Lyndale Ave. S.) Contemp. art, jade; decorative arts. Tues.–Thurs. 10–10; Fri., Sat. 10–5; Sun. 12–6. †*

Montevideo

CHIPPEWA COUNTY HISTORICAL MUSEUM. (Courthouse) Maintains Lac Qui Parle Mission in Watson and restored log cabin at County Fairgrounds, Montevideo. Wed.–Fri. 1–5.

Moorhead

CLAY COUNTY HISTORICAL SOCIETY. (County Courthouse) Costumes, Indian items. Mon.–Fri. 2–5.

Northfield

NORWEGIAN-AMERICAN HISTORICAL

ASSOCIATION. (St. Olaf College) History of Norwegian immigrants in America; research. †

Owatonna

STEELE COUNTY HISTORICAL SOCIETY. (Chamber of Commerce Bldg.) Local history; crafts, textiles, natural history. Mon.–Fri. 8:30–4:30, Sat. 9–12.

Pipestone

PIPESTONE NATIONAL MONUMENT. Park museum. Archaeology, ethnology, geology; Indian quarries. Daily 8–5. *

Redwood Falls

REDWOOD COUNTY HISTORICAL SOCIETY. (1115 E. Bridge St.) History of Sioux revolt, 1862; history of Sears, Roebuck Company, and historic house where company was founded; county history. Summer: by appt.

Rochester

MAYO FOUNDATION MUSEUM OF HYGIENE AND MEDICINE. (103 First Ave.) Medical history; instruments. Mon.–Sat. 10–12, 1:30–4; Sun. 2–5. †

OLMSTED COUNTY HISTORICAL SOCIETY. (214 Third Ave. S.W.) County history, natural history; Indian items; graphics. Mon.–Fri. 9–5, Sat. 8–12.

ROCHESTER ART CENTER. (320 E. Center) Local art; exhibitions. Mon.–Sat. 9–5, Sun. 2–5.

Roseau

ROSEAU COUNTY HISTORICAL SOCIETY. Local history, natural history. Mon.–Fri. 1–5.

St. Paul

FOREST HISTORY SOCIETY, INC. (2707 W. 7th Blvd.) Forest products; research. Mon.–Fri. 8–5.

MINNESOTA HISTORICAL SOCIETY MUSEUM. (Cedar St. and Central Ave.) State history; archaeology, ethnology; Indian life. Pioneer life: period log cabin, parlor, newspaper office. Military relics; Charles A. Lindbergh, Sr., Home, (Little Falls). Mon.–Fri. 8:30–5, Sat. 12:30–4:30. †

ST. PAUL ARTS AND SCIENCE CENTER.

St. Paul Art Center: exhibitions. Science; natural history. Performing arts.

ST. PAUL GALLERY AND SCHOOL OF ART. (476 Summit Ave.) Contemp. art; crafts of all periods. Tues.–Sat. 9–5; Wed., Thurs. eves. 7–9; Sun. 1–5.

ST. PAUL INSTITUTE SCIENCE MUSEUM. (51 University Ave.) Natural history; archaeology, folk art, paleontology, zoology. Tues.–Sat. 9–4:30, Sun. 1–5.

ST. PAUL'S COMO ZOO. (1224 N. Lexington) Daily 8–8.

St. Peter

NICOLLET COUNTY HISTORICAL SOCIETY. (Courthouse) Local history. Daily (except Sun.) 2–5.

South St. Paul

DAKOTA COUNTY HISTORICAL MUSEUM. (Municipal Bldg.) Local history, art exhibitions. Tues., Thurs., Sun. 2–5.

Waconia

CARVER COUNTY HISTORICAL SOCIETY. Furnishings, clothing, implements, decorative arts of 1880s and '90s; local natural history. Tues. and Fri. eves.; last Sun. of each month.

Winona

WINONA COUNTY HISTORICAL SOCIETY MUSEUM. (125 W. 5th St.) County history; lumbering; newspapers. Mon.–Fri. 1–5. Steamboat Museum on 1898 river boat. (Levee Park) May–Sept. daily 10–12, 1–5.

WINONA STATE COLLEGE, ART MUSEUM. Paintings, graphics, ceramics. Mon.–Fri. 9–5.

MISSISSIPPI

Aberdeen

EVANS MEMORIAL LIBRARY. Old South history. Mon.–Sat. 9–5.

Biloxi

JEFFERSON DAVIS SHRINE AND MEMORIAL GARDENS. Historic house: last home of Davis; gardens. Daily 9–5.

Jackson

LIVINGSTON PARK ZOO. (2918 W. Capitol St.) Daylight hours.

MISSISSIPPI GAME AND FISH COMMISSION, WILDLIFE MUSEUM. (111 N. Jefferson St.) Zoo. Mississippi vertebrates; paintings of wild flowers. Mon.–Fri. 8–4:30, Sat. 8–12.

OLD STATE CAPITOL MUSEUM. (State and E. Capitol Sts.) State archaeology and history. Mon.–Sat. 8:30–4:30, Sun. 1–5.

Laurel

LAUREN ROGERS LIBRARY AND MUSEUM OF ART. (5th Ave. and 7th St.) 19th- and 20th-century European and American painting; Indian basketry; exhibitions. Tues.–Sat. 10–12, 2–5; Sun. 2–5.

Oxford

MARY BUIE MUSEUM. (510 University Ave.) Art objects and historical items belonging to local family; paintings by Mrs. Buie. Revolutionary and Confederate relics. Tues.–Fri. 10–12, 2–5; weekends 2–5.

Pascagoula

MISSISSIPPI STATE UNIVERSITY MUSEUM. Geology, paleontology. Mon.–Fri. 8–4:30, Sat. 8–12.

Tupelo

NATCHEZ TRACE PARKWAY MUSEUM SYSTEM. Preservation project: Indian trail, 18th- and 19th-century trade route and post road. Daily. Mt. Locust (Natchez), house of 1780. Mar. daily; April–Oct. weekends, 9:30–6. Ridgeland Visitor Center (Jackson). Daily 9–4:45.

University

UNIVERSITY OF MISSISSIPPI MUSEUM. Archaeology; American Indian, classical. Geology; herbarium; art exhibitions. By appt.

Vicksburg

OLD COURT HOUSE MUSEUM. Local history, building of 1858. Mon.–Sat. 8–5, Sun. 2–5.

VICKSBURG NATIONAL MILITARY PARK. Park Museum. Civil War. Daily 8:30–4:30. *

MISSOURI

Alley Spring

THE OLD MILL. (Alley Spring State Park) Historic house. Daily 8–6.

Altenburg

CONCORDIA LOG CABIN SEMINARY. (Main St.) Local and church history; early settlers' furnishings; seminary of 1839. Open 24 hours daily.

Arrow Rock

ARROW ROCK STATE PARK, ARROW ROCK TAVERN (at start of Santa Fe trail) 1837; CALEB BINGHAM HOME; and old jail. Daily 8–5.
OLD TAVERN. (Main St.) Period furnishings, tavern of 1834. Daily 7–7.

Cape Girardeau

SOUTHEAST MISSOURI STATE COLLEGE MUSEUM. (Kent Library Bldg.) Minerals, Indian artifacts. Mon.–Fri. 8–4.

Columbia

STATE HISTORICAL SOCIETY OF MISSOURI. (Univ. of Mo. Library Bldg.) State history, archives. Art gallery; Bingham and Benton paintings, cartoons. Mon.–Fri. 8–12, 1–5, Sat. 8–12.
UNIVERSITY OF MISSOURI HERBARIUM. (208 Lefevre Hall) Weekdays.
UNIVERSITY OF MISSOURI MUSEUM OF ANTHROPOLOGY. (15 Switzler Hall) Archaeology, Indian ethnology; research. Daily (except Sun.) 8–12, 1–5.

De Soto

WASHINGTON STATE PARK MUSEUM. Natural history; petroglyphs; nature walks. May–Sept.

Diamond

GEORGE WASHINGTON CARVER NATIONAL MONUMENT, VISITOR CENTER. Park museum. Memorabilia of Carver; herbarium. Daily 8–5. *

Florida

MARK TWAIN MEMORIAL SHRINE. (Mark Twain State Park) Birthplace (1835) of Twain enclosed in memorial bldg. Mss. and first eds. Summer daily (except Mon.) 10–4.

Florissant

FLORISSANT HISTORICAL SOCIETY MUSEUM. (St. Francois St.) Local history. Weekends 12–6.

Hannibal

MARK TWAIN HOME BOARD, MARK TWAIN MUSEUM. (208 Hill St.) First eds., furniture, letters relating to author and his family. Mark Twain Boyhood Home; John M. Clemens Law Office, where author's father practiced; Pilaster House, where Clemens family lived. Summer daily 7:30–6. Oct.–May 8–5.

Hermann

GENTNER HOUSE. (108 Market St.) Period furnishings, house of 1850. Apr.–Oct. first Sun. every month.
HISTORIC HERMANN MUSEUM, RIVER BOAT ROOM. (4th and Schiller Sts.) History of German settlers in area; river lore; school bldg. of 1871. First Sun. every month; third weekend in May, Maifest.

Hermitage

HICKORY COUNTY HISTORICAL SOCIETY. Local history, implements. Daily (except Sun.) 8–4.

Independence

HARRY S. TRUMAN LIBRARY. (Hway 24 and Delaware) Presidential library and museum. Mon.–Sat. 9–4:30, Sun. 2–5. †*
JACKSON COUNTY HISTORICAL SOCIETY. (217 N. Main St.) Local history; County Jail, Marshal's House. Daily (except Mon.) 10–4.

Jefferson City

COLE COUNTY HISTORICAL SOCIETY. (109 Madison) Bingham paintings; 19th-century furnishings; local history. Mon.–Fri. 1–4.

MISSOURI STATE MUSEUM. (Capitol Bldg.) State history; archaeology; agriculture, industry, mineralogy, transportation. Murals by N. C. Wyeth, T. H. Benton. Daily 8–5.

Joplin

SPIVA ART CENTER. (406 Sergeant St.) Paintings, graphics, American glass; exhibitions. Wed.–Sat. 1–5; Fri. eve. 7–9. Sun. 2–5.

Kansas City

J. A. FOLGER AND Co. Company museum: coffee pots.

KANSAS CITY MUSEUM ASSOCIATION. (3218 Gladstone Blvd.) Natural history, Indian ethnology, archaeology, paleontology; planetarium. Mon.–Sat. 9–5, Sun. 2–6.

LIBERTY MEMORIAL. (100 W. 26th St.) First World War memorial; relics. Daily 9–5.

SWOPE PARK ZOOLOGICAL GARDENS. (6701 Lister Ave.) Zoo. Daily 10–6.

WILLIAM ROCKHILL NELSON GALLERY OF ART AND MARY ATKINS MUSEUM OF FINE ARTS. (4525 Oak St.) *Survey;* English ceramics; classical sculpture. Tues.–Sat. 10–5, Sun. 2–6. †*

Kirksville

NORTH EAST MISSOURI STATE TEACHERS COLLEGE, E. M. VIOLETTE MUSEUM. History, Indian items, agriculture. Mon.–Fri. 1–4.

Laclede

GENERAL JOHN J. PERSHING BOYHOOD HOME MEMORIAL SHRINE. Restored house, furnishings; where Pershing lived 1860s–1882. Daily (except Mon.) 10–4.

Lamar

HARRY S. TRUMAN BIRTHPLACE MEMORIAL SHRINE. Restored home. Daily 10–4.

Lebanon

BENNETT SPRING STATE PARK NATURE MUSEUM. Park museum. Natural history, nature walks. May–mid-Sept. Daily 8–6.

Lexington

CIVIL WAR BATTLE OF LEXINGTON STATE PARK, ANDERSON HOUSE. Park museum. Civil War relics; hospital. Daily (except Mon.) 10–4.

Liberty

WILLIAM JEWELL COLLEGE MUSEUM. Natural history; herbarium; local flora and fauna. Mon.–Fri. 7:30–5:30.

Miami

UNIVERSITY OF MISSOURI ARCHAEOLOGICAL RESEARCH CENTER. (Van Meter State Park) Park museum. Indian sites being excavated. June–Aug.

O'Fallon

FORT ZUMWALT STATE PARK, LOG CABIN. Park museum; ruins of log cabin built 1798. Daily.

Rolla

PHELPS COUNTY HISTORICAL SOCIETY, INC. (506 E. 6th St.) Phelps County Stone Jail. Local history, archives.

Ste. Genevieve

STE. GENEVIEVE MUSEUM. (City Sq.) Local history; folk art, pioneer relics (first permanent white settlement west of Mississippi R.) Winter daily 1–4; summer 10–3.

St. Joseph

JESSE JAMES HOUSE. Mementos of Jesse and Frank James. Daily 9–5.

PONY EXPRESS MUSEUM. (Pony Express Stables) History of Pony Express and city. June–Aug. Tues.–Sat. 10–5, Sun. 2–5.

ST. JOSEPH MUSEUM. (301 S. 11th St.) Local history, natural history, archaeology, ethnology. Tues.–Sat. 10–5 (Sept.–Apr. 1–5); Sun. 2–5.

St. Louis

CAMPBELL HOUSE MUSEUM. (1508 Locust St.) Costumes; decorative arts, in house of 1851. Mon.–Sat. 10–5, Sun. 1–5.

CHEROKEE CAVE AND MUSEUM. (3400 S. B'way at Cherokee) Anthropology, geology; art, antiques, costumes; DeMeniel Mansion. Daily 10–5.

CITY ART MUSEUM OF ST. LOUIS. (Art Hill, Forest Park) *Survey.* Wed.–Sun. 10–5, Tues. 2:30–9:30. †*

CONCORDIA HISTORICAL INSTITUTE. (801 DeMun Ave.) History of Lutheran and Reform church; medals, coins; art. †

EUGENE FIELD HOUSE. (634 S. B'way) Boyhood home of poet; period furnishings. Daily (except Mon.) 10–5.

JEFFERSON NATIONAL EXPANSION MEMORIAL. (Riverfront between MacArthur and Eads Bridges) Museum, Gateway Arch, and historic houses in tribute to St. Louis as Gateway to the West. Mon.–Fri. 8–5, weekends 9–5. †*

MISSOURI BOTANICAL GARDEN. (2315 Tower Grove) Tropical, semitropical plants; herbarium; historic Shaw House. Daily 9–5, Fri.–Sun. til 9. †**

MISSOURI HISTORICAL SOCIETY. (Lindell and De Baliviere) City and regional history; Mississippi R., the West. Daily 9:30–5.

MISSOURI PACIFIC LINES MUSEUM. (Rm. 1112, Missouri Pacific Bldg., 13th St.) Company museum. Rail transportation. Mon.–Fri. 10–12, 2–5. †

MUSEUM OF SCIENCE AND NATURAL HISTORY. (2 Oak Knoll Park) Archaeology; industry; health; nature. Tues.–Sat. 9–5, Sun. 1–5.

NATIONAL MUSEUM OF TRANSPORT, INC. (Barrets Station Rd.) Rail and urban transport; river, water transport. May 30–Labor Day, daily 10–8; otherwise 10–5. †*

PLANETARIUM. (Forest Park) Daily (except Mon.) *

ST. LOUIS BOARD OF EDUCATION, DIVISION OF AUDIO-VISUAL EDUCATION. (1517 S. Theresa Ave.) Loan collections for schools; small permanent display. Mon.–Fri. 8–4:45. †

ST. LOUIS ZOO. (Forest Park) Daily. 9:30–5 (Dec.–Feb. til 4:30).

Springfield

SPRINGFIELD ART MUSEUM. (1111 E. Brookside Dr.) American art, ceramics, antiques. Mon.–Sat. 9–5, Tues.–Thurs. eves. 6:30–9:30, Sun. 1–5.

WILSON'S CREEK BATTLEFIELD FOUNDATION, INC. (408 Woodruff Bldg.) Civil War History; maintains 37-acre Bloody Hill site, Wilson's Creek Battlefield. Daily.

Sullivan

MERAMEC STATE PARK NATURE MUSEUM. May–mid-Sept. 8–6.

Van Buren

BIG SPRING STATE PARK MUSEUM. Natural history. Daily 8–5.

Vienna

HISTORICAL SOCIETY OF MARIES COUNTY. Local history. Old Stone Jail; Old Log House. Both of 1855.

MONTANA

Billings

YELLOWSTONE MUSEUM. Local, county history. Tues.–Sat. 10:30–12, 1–5, Sun. 2–5.

Bozeman

MONTANA STATE COLLEGE HERBARIUM. (Lewis Hall) Montana plants. Mon.–Fri. 8–12, 1–5, Sat. 8–12.

MONTANA STATE COLLEGE, MCGILL MUSEUM. Agriculture, anthropology, history, mineralogy. Daily 2–4.

Browning

MUSEUM OF THE PLAINS INDIAN. Plains ethnology, archaeology, art, artifacts. Maintained by Bureau of Indian Affairs, fed. govt. June–mid-Sept. daily 8–5. *

Butte

MONTANA SCHOOL OF MINES. (W. Park St.) Teaching coll., mineralogy. Mon.–Fri. 9–5, Sat. 9–12.

Crow Agency

CUSTER BATTLEFIELD NATIONAL MONUMENT. Park museum. History; Indian, military items; mementos of Battle of the Little Bighorn. Daily 8–5. Memorial Day–Labor Day, 7–7. *

Dillon

BEAVERHEAD COUNTY MUSEUM. (15 S. Montana) Local history, natural history.

Summer: daily 9:30–11, 1–5, 7–9. Winter: daily (except Sun.) 9:30–11:30, 1–5.

Ekalaka

CARTER COUNTY MUSEUM. (County High School, Basement) Local history, natural history. Daily (except Mon.) 1–4.

Fort Benton

FORT BENTON MUSEUM. Illustrating early trade routes, Lewis and Clark expedition, founding of fort. June–Labor Day: daily 10–12, 1:30–5, 7–9.

Great Falls

C. M. RUSSELL GALLERY. (1201 4th Ave.) Painting, sculpture, graphics; exhibitions. June–Aug.: Mon.–Sat. 10–4, Sun. 1–4. Sept.–May: Sun. 2–4:30.

Hamilton

BITTER ROOT VALLEY HISTORICAL MUSEUM. (Chamber of Commerce and Library) Western Montana history, archives; Indian items; pioneer cabin, furnishings. Mon.–Sat. 9–5, Sun. 1–5.

Helena

HISTORICAL SOCIETY OF MONTANA. (Roberts at 6th Ave.) State and Great Plains history, art, artifacts. June–Sept. daily 7–9. Oct.–May: Mon.–Fri. 8–5, weekends 1–5.

LAST CHANCE GULCH RESTORATION ASSOCIATION. (212 S. Park Ave.) Old Fire Bell Tower (Watch-Tower Hill); period furnishings, gold rush 1864–1880. Tourist season, and by appt.

Lewistown

CENTRAL MONTANA MUSEUM. (E. Main St.) Local history. Mon.–Sat. 8:30–5:30.

Missoula

MONTANA STATE UNIVERSITY MUSEUM. History, natural history, Indian artifacts, geology, botany, zoology. Mon.–Fri. 1–3.

Moiese

NATIONAL BISON RANGE. Wildlife Refuge: buffalos, elk, deer. Daily. *

Stevensville

REV. A. J. RAVALLI PHARMACY. Catholic mission pharmacy of 1841; pioneer items.

Virginia City

VIRGINIA CITY–MADISON COUNTY HISTORICAL MUSEUM. Local, state and western history. Summer: daily 8–6; fall: daily 11–5. And by appt.

West Glacier

GLACIER NATIONAL PARK, NATURALISTS' WORKSHOP. Park museum. Natural history, zoology, ethnology, herbarium. Daily. *

Wisdom

BIG HOLE BATTLEFIELD NATIONAL MONUMENT. Park museum. Guns, frontier period relics. May 26–Oct. sunrise–sundown. *

NEBRASKA

Beatrice

HOMESTEAD NATIONAL MONUMENT. (Rt. 1) Park museum. Palmer-Epard Pioneer Cabin; history of American land policy. Summer daily 7–7; winter 8–5. †*

Bellevue

SARPY COUNTY HISTORICAL SOCIETY. (1805 Hancock St.) Preservation project. Restoration of sites in oldest town in state; log cabin of 1856; local history. Summer: Sun. 2–5.

Brownville

BROWNVILLE HISTORICAL SOCIETY MUSEUM. Local history; The Carson House, 1860, period furnishings in home of pioneer banker. May–Oct. Sun. 2–5.

Chadron

MUSEUM OF THE FUR TRADE. Trader's equipment; Indian trade items; Plains Indian crops; James Bordeaux Trading Post of 1846–72, restored. June–Sept. Daily 8–6; and by appt.

Crawford

NEBRASKA STATE HISTORICAL SOCIETY, FORT ROBINSON MUSEUM. (U.S. 20) Interpretation of military post; regional history. May–Sept. Mon.–Sat. 8–5, Sun. 1–5.

Fairbury

JEFFERSON COUNTY MUSEUM. (612 4th St.) Local history, paleontology; Oregon Trail and Pony Express items. Thurs., Sat. 2–5.

Fort Calhoun

WASHINGTON COUNTY HISTORICAL MUSEUM. Local history. May–Dec. Sun. 3–6.

Franklin

FRANKLIN COUNTY MUSEUM. Local history. Sun. 2–5.

Gering

SCOTTS BLUFF NATIONAL MONUMENT. Park museum. Oregon Trail history, Indian artifacts, paleontology. Summer daily 8–8; winter 8–5. *

Grand Island

STUHR MUSEUM OF THE PRAIRIE PIONEER. Outdoor and indoor historical exhibits; arboretum.

Hastings

HASTINGS MUSEUM, HOUSE OF YESTERDAY. (14th and Burlington Ave.) Natural history; transportation; planetarium. Mon.–Sat. 8–5, Sun. 1–5.

Lincoln

LINCOLN MUNICIPAL ZOO. (1300 S. 27th St.) Daily 9–4:45.
NEBRASKA STATE HISTORICAL SOCIETY. (1500 R St.) State history, archives; newspapers; archaeology, ethnology. Mon.–Sat. 8–5:30, Sun. 2–5. †*
UNIVERSITY OF NEBRASKA ART GALLERIES. (Merrill Hall) Modern American paintings. Mon.–Sat. 8–5, Tues. eve. 7–10, Sun. 2–5.
UNIVERSITY OF NEBRASKA STATE MUSEUM. (101 Merrill Hall, 14th and U St.) Natural history; archaeology, geology; mineralogy; ethnology; health and hygiene; herbarium; planetarium. Mon.–Sat. 8–5, Sun. 2–5.
UNIVERSITY OF NEBRASKA STATE MUSEUM HERBARIUM. (314 Bessey Hall) Great Plains, Nebraska plants; teaching coll. Daily 8–5.

Minden

THE HAROLD WARP PIONEER VILLAGE. (Hway 6, 34, 10) Preservation project: pioneer buildings, history, implements. Daylight hours. †*

Nebraska City

ARBOR LODGE STATE HISTORICAL PARK. Morton Family Mansion, 1855; home of J. Sterling Morton, originator of Arbor Day. Arboretum; carriage house. Mid-Apr.–Oct. daily 1–5:30.
JOHN BROWN'S CAVE. Illustrating the story of abolition and John Brown. Apr.–Oct. daily 10–5.

North Platte

D.A.R. MUSEUM. (Memorial Park) Historic house of 1862, old furnishings, costumes, drawings. June–Aug. daily 12–5.

Omaha

JOSLYN ART MUSEUM. (2218 Dodge St.) *Survey;* art of the West; exhibitions. Tues., Wed., Fri., Sat. 10–5; Thurs. 10–9; Sun. 2–6. †*
OMAHA PUBLIC LIBRARY. (1823 Harney St.) Numismatics. Daily 9:30–4:30.
UNION PACIFIC HISTORICAL MUSEUM. (15th and Dodge Sts.) Company museum. Rail transportation; Indian items. Mon.–Fri. 9–5.

Red Cloud

WILLA CATHER PIONEER MEMORIAL. Memorabilia of author. June–Aug. 2–4.

Valentine

CHERRY COUNTY HISTORICAL SOCIETY, INC. (S. Main St., Hway 20 and 83) Local history; needlework, Indian items, portraits.
FORT NIOBRARA NATIONAL WILDLIFE REFUGE. Natural history; area fossil bones; history of military reservation; birds. Daily 6–9. *

Wayne

WAYNE COUNTY HISTORICAL MUSEUM. (510 Pearl St.) Pioneer items, local history. Tues., Thurs. 3–5.

York

DAUGHTERS OF AMERICAN REVOLUTION MUSEUM. (222 W. 10th St., Library basement) Pioneer items, military relics (Civil War, Spanish-American War, World War I); local history. During school semesters Mon.–Sat. 10–8.

NEVADA

Baker

LEHMAN CAVES NATIONAL MONUMENT. Park museum. Mineralogy. May 30–Sept. 7 daily 8–5; otherwise 9–4. *

Boulder City

LAKE MEAD NATIONAL RECREATION AREA. (601 Nevada Hway) Park museum. Anthropology, archaeology, geology, herbarium. Mon.–Fri. 8–12, 1–5. *

Carson City

NEVADA STATE MUSEUM. State history, military items, natural history, Indian artifacts, archaeology. U. S. Mint Bldg. Mon.–Sat. 8:30–4, Sun. 1–4.

Reno

NEVADA ART GALLERY, INC. (643 Ralston St.) Western art. Daily (except Fri.) 1–4.

NEVADA HISTORICAL SOCIETY. State history; natural history; Indian baskets; cattle brands; costumes; dolls. Tues.–Sat. 10–4.

NEW HAMPSHIRE

Center Sandwich

SANDWICH HISTORICAL SOCIETY. Old Country Store, 1850. Local history, implements, household items, furniture. July–Aug. Mon., Wed., Sat. 2–5.

Concord

THE FRANKLIN PIERCE HOUSE. (52 S. Main St.) Home of Pres. Pierce 1857–1869; period furnishings; Currier prints of early presidents. Apr.–Dec. by appt.

NEW HAMPSHIRE HISTORICAL SOCIETY. (30 Park St.) 17th- and early 18th-century period rooms; state history. Daily 9:30–4:30. †

Cornish

SAINT-GAUDENS MUSEUM. Bronzes, plaster casts of works by Saint-Gaudens; house and studio of the sculptor. Exhibitions. May 30–mid-Oct. daily 10–6.

Dover

WOODMAN INSTITUTE. (182–192 Central Ave.) Historic Damm House, old garrison of 1675; natural history. Daily (except Mon.) 2–6.

Durham

UNIVERSITY OF NEW HAMPSHIRE ART GALLERY. Daily 9–12, 1–5.

Exeter

PHILLIPS EXETER ACADEMY, LAMONT ART GALLERY. Contemp. paintings, graphics; Daumier prints. Mon.–Fri. 9–1, 2–5; Sat. 9–3:30; Sun. 11:30–1, 2–5 during school year.

Francestown

THE FRANCESTOWN VILLAGE IMPROVEMENT SOCIETY MUSEUM. Bixby House. Soapstone articles, an early local industry. Wed. and Sat. afternoon, Sat. eve.

Franklin

DANIEL WEBSTER BIRTHPLACE. (Off Rt. 127) Furnishings, Webster memorabilia, house of 1780. May 30–Oct. 12, daily 9–6.

Hampton

MEETING HOUSE GREEN MEMORIAL AND HISTORICAL ASSOCIATION, INC. (Park Ave.) Local history. Summer, Sat. 1–6.

Hancock

HANCOCK HISTORICAL SOCIETY. History of Hancock and neighboring communities. May 30–Oct. 12, Wed., Sat. 2–5.

Hanover

DARTMOUTH COLLEGE, CARPENTER ART GALLERIES. American and French painting; sculpture, graphics, Chinese art. Daily 2–5. †

DARTMOUTH COLLEGE, JESUP HERBARIUM. (Dept. of Botany, Silsby Hall) Research, teaching collections. Mon.–Fri. 8–5, Sat. 8–12.

DARTMOUTH COLLEGE MUSEUM. Anthropology; local history; biology; paleontology; geology. Research, teaching coll. Mon.–Sat. 9–5; Sun. during school semester 2–5.

Hillsborough

FRANKLIN PIERCE HOMESTEAD. Built 1805. Daily 10–5.

Manchester

THE CURRIER GALLERY OF ART. (192 Orange St.) European and American paintings; American sculpture, decorative arts. Mon.–Sat. 10–5, Sun. 2–5. †*

MANCHESTER HISTORIC ASSOCIATION. (129 Amherst St.) Local history; textile industry; furniture; costumes. Tues.–Fri. 9–4:30, Sat. 10–4.

New Ipswich

BARRET HOUSE. (Main St. Rt. 123) Historic Forest Hall, 1800; ballroom, portraits, carriages, grounds, furniture. Maintained by Soc. for the Preservation of New England Antiq. Mid–June–mid-Oct. Tues.–Sat. 11–5.

NEW IPSWICH HISTORICAL SOCIETY. Local history, minerals. July, Aug. Tues., Thurs. 2:30–5.

Peterborough

GOYETTE MUSEUM OF AMERICANA. (Elm St.) American antiques; furnishings, stagecoaches, old shops. Daily (except Mon.) 1:30–4:30.

SHARON ARTS CENTER. *Exhibitions.* Tues.–Sat. 10–5:30, Sun. 2:30–5.

Plymouth

O. RUNDLE GILBERT'S U. S. PATENT MODEL MUSEUM. (Rt. 3) Working models of 19th-century patent applications. July–mid-Oct.

Portsmouth

BAILEY HOUSE. (386 Court St.) Historic house of 1790; background for Thomas Bailey Aldrich story; Aldrich memorabilia. Mid–June–Sept. daily (except Sun.) 10–5.

GOVERNOR JOHN LANGDON MANSION MEMORIAL. (143 Pleasant St.) House of 1784; furnishings, gardens. Maintained by Soc. for the Preservation of New England Antiq. June–mid-Oct. daily (except Sun.) 1–5. †*

JACKSON HOUSE. (Jackson Hill St.) Period furnishings, house of about 1664. Maintained by Soc. for the Preservation of New England Antiq. Mid–June–mid-Sept. Mon.–Fri. 12:30–4.

JOHN PAUL JONES HOUSE. (43 Middle St.) Decorative arts, city history, house of 1750. June–mid-Sept. daily (except Sun.) 10–5.

MOFFATT-LADD HOUSE. (154 Market St.) Historic house of 1763, furnishings, gardens. Mid–June–end Sept. daily (except Sun.) 10–5.

THE PORTSMOUTH ATHENAEUM. (9 Market Sq.) Library; historical archives; models of clipper ships; paintings relating to Portsmouth. Thurs. 1–3:30.

PORTSMOUTH PUBLIC LIBRARY. (8 Islington St.) Historic house, built after Bulfinch design 1809. Daily 10–8:30.

WARNER HOUSE. (150 Daniel St.) Period furniture, Chinese export porcelain; paintings in fine house of 1716. Mid–June–Sept. weekdays 9–5.

Tamworth

TAMWORTH HISTORICAL SOCIETY. Local history, in house of about 1800. July, Aug. Sat. 2–4.

Wakefield

WAKEFIELD-BROOKFIELD HISTORICAL ASSOCIATION. Local history, antique furnishings. Summer, Sun. 2–4.

Walpole

WALPOLE HISTORICAL SOCIETY, INC. Town history; local art; historic Old Walpole Academy. July and Aug., Sun. 2–5.

Wolfeboro

THE LIBBY MUSEUM. (Rt. 109) Natural history; Indian items; historical objects recalling campaigns of Generals Montcalm and Wolfe. Daily (except Mon.) 10–5.

WOLFEBORO HISTORICAL SOCIETY. Clark House of 1788, with period furnishings; one-room schoolhouse of early 19th century. July, Aug. daily (except Sun.) 2:30–4:30.

NEW JERSEY

Burlington

BURLINGTON COUNTY HISTORICAL SOCIETY. (457 High St.) Local history; Historic James Fenimore Cooper House, of about 1780. Sun. 3–5.

Camden

CAMDEN COUNTY HISTORICAL SOCIETY. (Euclid Ave. and Park Blvd.) Historic Charles S. Boyer Memorial Hall; local history. Mon.–Fri. 12–5.

Clinton

HUNTERDON COUNTY ART CENTER. (Old Stone Mill, Center St.) *Exhibitions.* Tues.–Sat. 1–6, Sun. 2–5.

Cranford

CRANFORD HISTORICAL SOCIETY, INC. (N. Union Ave.) Local history. Tues., Thurs., Sat., Sun. 2–5.

East Orange

ART CENTRE OF THE ORANGES, INC. (16 Washington St.) *Exhibitions.* Nov.–June.

Flemington

HUNTERDON COUNTY HISTORICAL SOCIETY. (Public Library) Local history, Colonial and Revolutionary material. Tues., Thurs. 2–4.

Freehold

MONMOUTH COUNTY HISTORICAL ASSOCIATION. (70 Court St.) Local history; Colonial, Revolutionary items; primitive paintings; china; dolls; toys; furniture; Tues.–Sat. 11–5, Sun. 2–5 (closed Jan.)

Haddonfield

THE HISTORICAL SOCIETY OF HADDONFIELD. (343 Kings Hwy E.) Local history; historic John Gill House of 1841. Tues.–Sat. 2:30–4:30.

Middletown

MARLPIT HALL. (137 Kings Hwy.) Dutch Colonial house, furnishings of 1684. Tues., Thurs., Sat. 11–5, Sun. 2–5 (closed Jan.)

Millville

MILLVILLE HISTORICAL SOCIETY, INC. (Columbia Ave.) Local history; historic Mansion House of 1804.

Montclair

THE MONTCLAIR ART MUSEUM. (Bloomfield and S. Mountain Aves.) Art, anthropology, costumes, decorative arts. Tues.–Sat. 10–5, Sun. 2–5:30.

Morristown

MORRIS JUNIOR MUSEUM. (141 Madison Ave.) Children's museum: art, science. Daily (except Sun.) 10–4:30.

MORRISTOWN NATIONAL HISTORICAL PARK. 18th-century Ford Mansion; Wick House of about 1750, military headquarters; reconstructed Fort Nonsense; Jockey Hollow camp grounds, camp hospital, burying grounds; 18th-century weapons, furniture, prints and paintings. Daily (except Mon.) 10–5. *

Mountainside

WATCHUNG RESERVATION, TRAILSIDE MUSEUM. (Coles Ave. and New Providence Rd.) Park museum. Natural history; pre-Revolutionary copper mine and village site. Mon.–Thurs. 3–5; school classes, 10–3 (during semester only); weekends 1–5. July, Aug. daily (except Fri.) 1–5.

New Brunswick

KILMER MUSEUM OF SURGICAL PRODUCTS. (501 George St.) Johnson and Johnson Company museum. Pharmaceuticals; company products from 1886. For employees only: Mon.–Fri. 9–5.

RUTGERS UNIVERSITY ART DEPT.

(Various university bldgs.) American portraits; Old Master, English, and modern graphics. Mon.–Sat. 9–5.

RUTGERS UNIVERSITY GEOLOGICAL MUSEUM. Mineralogy, paleontology. Mon.–Fri. 9–12, 1–4.

RUTGERS UNIVERSITY, SEROLOGICAL MUSEUM. (New Jersey Hall) Sera and blood samples of animals throughout the world. By appt. only.

Newark

NEW JERSEY BELL COMPANY, PIONEER HISTORICAL MUSEUM. (540 Broad St.) Company Museum. Old and modern telephone equipment. Mon.–Fri. 9–5.

THE NEW JERSEY HISTORICAL SOCIETY. (230 B'way) State history, transportation, furniture and decorative arts; paintings, graphics. Tues.–Sat. 10–4:30.

THE NEWARK MUSEUM. (43–49 Washington St.) General museum. Art: *survey*, decorative arts, American, classical, primitive, Oriental. Ethnology. Science: industry, natural history. Planetarium. Children's museum. Mon.–Sat. 12–5:30, Sun. 2–6; Wed., Thurs. eve. 7–9:30. Summer: Mon.–Sat. 12–5, Sun. 2–6. †*

NEWARK PUBLIC LIBRARY. (5 Washington St.) Print coll., esp. modern American and local work. Mon.–Fri. 9–9, Sat. 9–5.

Newton

SUSSEX COUNTY HISTORICAL SOCIETY. (82 Main St.) Historic house: Hill Memorial Bldg. Local history. Daily 9–5.

North Hackensack

VON STEUBEN HOUSE. Furnishings, house of 1739. Daily (except Mon.) 10–12, 1–5.

Nutley

NUTLEY HISTORICAL SOCIETY MUSEUM. (65 Church St.) Local history, New Jersey birds; costumes. Sun. 2–5.

Oradell

THE HIRAM BLAUVELT WILDLIFE MUSEUM. (637 Kinderkamack Rd.) Natural history. Fri. 10–3; tours by appt. Fri. 3:30–4:30.

Paterson

THE PASSAIC COUNTY HISTORICAL SOCIETY. (Lambert Castle, Valley Rd.) Local history, art, decorative arts, crafts. Wed.–Fri. 1–5, weekends 10–5.

PATERSON MUSEUM. (268 Summer St.) Anthropology; Lenape Indians; archaeology; art; mineralogy, natural history. Mon.–Fri. 1–5, Sat. 10–5.

Plainfield

PLAINFIELD HISTORICAL SOCIETY. (Front St., Plainfield Ave.) Drake House, 1745. Americana, Indian, military items. Mon., Wed., Sat. 2–5.

PLAINFIELD PUBLIC LIBRARY. (8th St. at Park Ave.) Paintings. Mon.–Fri. 9–9, Sat. 9–5 (summer 9–1).

Pomona

LENOX, INCORPORATED. (Tilton Rd.) Company museum. Lenox China. Daily (except Sun.) 9–4:30.

Princeton

PRINCETON UNIVERSITY, ART MUSEUM. *Survey.* Mon.–Sat. 10–12, 2–4:30; Sun. 2–5.

PRINCETON UNIVERSITY, MUSEUM OF NATURAL HISTORY. (Guyot Hall) Paleontology, archaeology, anthropology, geology. Daily, 9–4:30.

Ridgewood

PARAMUS HISTORICAL AND PRESERVATION SOCIETY. (650 E. Glen Ave.) One-room schoolhouse, equipped, of 1872; early household items, agricultural tools, toys, spinning and weaving equipment. Wed. 1:30–4, Sun. 3–5.

River Edge

DEMAREST HOUSE. (E. Main St.) Period furnishings, house of 1678. Tues. 10–4.

Somers Point

ATLANTIC COUNTY HISTORICAL SOCIETY. Historic Somers Mansion of about 1726, period furnishings; Indian artifacts; glassware. Tues.–Sat. 10–12, 1–5, Sun. 2–5.

Springfield

SPRINGFIELD HISTORICAL SOCIETY. (126 Morris Ave.) The Cannonball House of about 1741; decorative arts, graphics, textiles. Sun. 3–5.

Teaneck

BERGEN COMMUNITY MUSEUM. (Fort Lee Rd. at Overpeck Creek) Art, history, natural history, science. Wed., Sat., Sun. 2–5.

Trenton

FREE PUBLIC LIBRARY. (Academy St.) Mon.–Fri. 9–9, Sat. 9–6. July–Aug.: Mon., Fri. 9–9, Tues.–Thurs. 9–5, Sat. 9–1.
LENOX, INCORPORATED. (Prince and Meade Sts.) Company museum. Mon.–Fri. 9–5.
NEW JERSEY STATE MUSEUM. (W. State St.) Natural history; state archaeology, paleontology, geology. Art history. Science and industry. Mon.–Sat. 9–5, Sun. 2–5. †*
OLD BARRACKS. (S. Willow St.) House of 1758, antique furniture. May–Aug.: Mon.–Fri. 10–5 (otherwise 10–4).
WILLIAM TRENT HOUSE. (539 S. Warren St.) House built 1719 by William Trent, city founder; period furnishings, garden. Mon.–Sat. 10–4, Sun. 1–4.

Vineland

VINELAND HISTORICAL AND ANTIQUARIAN SOCIETY. (108 S. 7th St.) Local history. Tues.–Sat. 2–5.

West Orange

EDISON LABORATORY NATIONAL MONUMENT. (Main St. at Lakeside Ave.) Original models of Edison inventions; furnishings in laboratories as inventor left them. Wed.–Sun. 9:30–11, 1:30–4. And Glenmont (Park Way, Llewellyn Park), Edison family residence, original furnishings, garden, conservatory. †*

NEW MEXICO

Abiquiu

GHOST RANCH MUSEUM. Natural history, paleontology; beaver, history of traders and trappers; local wildlife. Daily 10–5.

Alamogordo

WHITE SANDS NATIONAL MONUMENT. Park museum. Natural history. Daily 8–5 (later in summer). *

Albuquerque

RIO GRANDE ZOO. (903 10th St.) Daily 8–5 (May–Aug. to 6:30).
UNIVERSITY OF NEW MEXICO, MUSEUM OF ANTHROPOLOGY. Teaching coll., local ethnology. Mon.–Sat.

Aztec

AZTEC RUINS NATIONAL MONUMENT. Park museum. Archaeology. Daily 8–5. *

Bloomfield

CHACO CANYON NATIONAL MONUMENT. Park museum. Anthropology, natural history, herbarium. Daily 8–5. *

Carlsbad

CARLSBAD CAVERNS NATIONAL PARK. Park museum. Natural history, geology, archaeology, herbarium, cavern paintings. June–Sept. daily 6:30–9. Oct.–May 7:30–5. *
CARLSBAD MUSEUM. Natural history, Indian artifacts. Daily (except Sun.) 1–7.

Gallup

MUSEUM OF INDIAN ARTS. (Hwy. 66) Indian crafts, artifacts. Daily (except Sun.) 9–5.

Gran Quivira

GRAN QUIVIRA NATIONAL MONUMENT. 17th Century mission, prehistoric pueblo ruins. Park museum. Daily 8–5. *

Lincoln

OLD LINCOLN COUNTY MEMORIAL COMMISSION, LINCOLN COUNTY COURTHOUSE STATE MONUMENT. OLD TUNSTALL STORE. WORTLEY HOTEL (daily 8–7; accepts guests). County history, historic houses. Daily 9–4:30.

Pecos

PECOS STATE MONUMENT. Prehistoric

pueblo ruins. Daily 8–5 (Nov.–Mar. closed Mon.).

Portales

EASTERN NEW MEXICO UNIVERSITY, ROOSEVELT COUNTY MUSEUM. (Hwy. 70) History, Indian items, minerals, paintings. Daily 9–4.

Roswell

ROSWELL MUSEUM AND ART CENTER. (11th and Main Sts.) Art of the Southwest; anthropology, geology, archaeology, rocketry. Mon.–Sat. 10–12, 1–5, Sun. 1–5. †*

Santa Fe

BANDELIER NATIONAL MONUMENT. Park museum. Archaeology. Daily 8–5. *

HISTORICAL SOCIETY OF NEW MEXICO. (Palace of the Governors) New Mexico history, Spanish period to present; archaeology, ethnology. †

MUSEUM OF NAVAJO CEREMONIAL ART. (Camino Lejo, off Old Pecos Rd.) Sand painting, Indian crafts. Tues.–Sat. 9–12, 1–4:30; Sun. 2–5. †*

MUSEUM OF NEW MEXICO. (Palace of the Governors) Art, history, archaeology of Southwest. Historic house of 1610. Mon.–Sat. 9–12, 1–5, Sun. 2–5. †*

MUSEUM OF NEW MEXICO, HALL OF ETHNOLOGY. (Washington Ave.) Navajo, other Indian crafts, artifacts, village models, implements. Mon.–Sat. 9–12, 1–5, Sun. 2–5. †*

MUSEUM OF NEW MEXICO, LABORATORY OF ANTHROPOLOGY. (Camino Lejo) Pueblo pottery, Pueblo and Navajo textiles. Mon.–Sat. 9–12, 1–5, Sun. 2–5. †*

MUSEUM OF NEW MEXICO, MUSEUM OF INTERNATIONAL FOLK ART. (Pecos Rd.) Folk art around the world. Mon.–Sat. 9–12, 1–5; Sun. 2–5. †*

MUSEUM OF NEW MEXICO, STATE ART GALLERY. (Lincoln Ave.) Works of Taos, Santa Fe artists. Mon.–Sat. 9–12, 1–5, Sun. 2–5. †*

SCHOOL OF AMERICAN RESEARCH. (Palace of the Governors) Ethnology and archaeology of Southwest, Latin America. Hewett House (116 Lincoln Ave.) from Civil War times.

Taos

KIT CARSON HOME AND MUSEUM. (E. Kit Carson St.) Local history, Indian items; house of 1825. Summer: daily 6:30–8. Autumn and spring, 7–6. Winter 8–5.

UNIVERSITY OF NEW MEXICO, THE HARWOOD FOUNDATION. (Ledoux St.) Paintings by Taos artists; santos; Indian artifacts; Spanish Colonial furniture. D. H. Lawrence Ranch. Daily (except Sun.) 10–5.

Watrous

FORT UNION NATIONAL MONUMENT. Park museum. Santa Fe trail history, ruins of fort 1851–91. Daily 8–5. *

NEW YORK

Albany

ALBANY INSTITUTE OF HISTORY AND ART. (125 Washington Ave.) American paintings from 18th–20th centuries. Tues.–Sat. 9–4:45, Sun. 2–6. †

NEW YORK STATE HISTORY MUSEUM. (State Education Dept.) Shaker collection; transportation, crafts. Mon.–Fri. 8:30–5.

NEW YORK STATE MUSEUM OF NATURAL HISTORY. (State Education Bldg.) State history; natural history, Indian items, geology, anthropology, arboretum. Mon.–Sat. 9–5, Sun. 10–5. †

SCHUYLER MANSION. (Clinton and Catherine Sts.) Period furnishings in Maj. Gen. Philip Schuyler's house of 1762. Mon.–Sat. 9–5, Sun. 1–5.

Amsterdam

GUY PARK HOUSE. (366 W. Main St.) Historic house of about 1773. Mon.–Sat. 9–5, Sun. 1–5.

WALTER ELWOOD MUSEUM. (Perkins St.) Children's museum: science, nature, Indian lore. School days 9–4:30.

Auburn

CAYUGA MUSEUM OF HISTORY AND ART. (203 Genesee St.) Local history, archaeology; American paintings. Tues.–Fri. 1–5, Sat. 9–12, 1–5, Sun. 2–5.

Batavia

HOLLAND LAND OFFICE MUSEUM. (131 W. Main St.) Local history; household items, uniforms, Indian artifacts. May–Nov. Wed.–Sat. 10–5, Sun. 2–5.

Bear Mountain

BEAR MOUNTAIN TRAILSIDE MUSEUMS AND NATURE TRAILS. Park museum. Zoo, aquarium, geology, history, botany. Daily 9–5. †

Binghamton

ROBERSON MEMORIAL CENTER. (30 Front St.) Art, archaeology, natural history, astronomy; exhibitions. Tues.–Fri. 10–5, weekends 12–5.

Blue Mountain Lake

THE ADIRONDACK MUSEUM. History of man in the Adirondacks; period houses; vehicles; lumbering. Mid-June–mid-Oct. daily 10–5, Sun. 1–5. †*

Brooklyn

BROOKLYN BOTANIC GARDEN. (1000 Washington Ave.) Mon.–Sat. 8:30–sundown; Sun. 10–sundown. †*

BROOKLYN CHILDREN'S MUSEUM. (Brooklyn Ave. and Park Pl.) Dolls, science, nature, planetarium, aquarium, anthropology. Sept.–June. Mon.–Sat. 10–5, Sun. 1–5. †**

BROOKLYN MUSEUM. (188 Eastern Pkwy.) Art. *Survey;* Pre-Columbian, Egyptian, Oceanic; American decorative arts; American period rooms; costumes. Mon.–Sat. 10–5, Sun. 1–5. †**

LEFFERTS HOMESTEAD. (Prospect Park, Flatbush Ave. and Empire Blvd.) Fine furnishings in house of 1777. Nov.–May: Mon., Wed., Fri. 1–5 (closed second Wed. of each month).

LONG ISLAND HISTORICAL SOCIETY. (128 Pierrepont St.) Brooklyn and Long Island history in paintings and prints; Tues.–Sat. 9–5 (closed Aug.).

NEW YORK ZOOLOGICAL SOCIETY, NEW YORK AQUARIUM. (Boardwalk at W. 8th St., Coney Island) Winter daily 10–5, summer 10–10. †*

Buffalo

BUFFALO BOTANICAL GARDEN. (S. Park and McKinley Pkwy.) Daily 9–4.

BUFFALO AND ERIE COUNTY HISTORICAL SOCIETY. (Nottingham Court) City and county history; agriculture; archaeology; industry; marine; military. Mon.–Sat. 10–5, Sun. 2–5.

THE BUFFALO FINE ARTS ACADEMY, ALBRIGHT-KNOX ART GALLERY. (1285 Elmwood Ave.) *Survey;* esp. 20th-century American art. Tues.–Sat. 10–5, Sun., Mon. 2–6. †*

BUFFALO MUSEUM OF SCIENCE. (Humboldt Park) Physical and natural sciences; planetarium; zoo; aquarium; anthropology. Mon.–Fri. 10–5, Sun. 1:30–5:30. †*

BUFFALO ZOOLOGICAL GARDENS. (Delaware Park) Daily: bldgs., 10–4, grounds, 8–5 (summer to 7).

Caledonia

BIG SPRINGS HISTORICAL SOCIETY OF CALEDONIA, NEW YORK. Local history. Winter: Sun. 3–6. Summer: Fri. 6–9. Fall: Fri. 1–4.

Canajoharie

CANAJOHARIE ART GALLERY. (97 Church St.) American paintings, sculpture. Mon.–Fri. 10–5:15, Sat. 9–2.

Canandaigua

ONTARIO COUNTY HISTORICAL SOCIETY. (55 N. Main St.) Iroquois Indian items, local history, furnishings. Tues.–Sat. 2–5, 7–8:30.

Canton

HISTORY CENTER OF ST. LAWRENCE COUNTY. (Courthouse) Local history; archives; costumes; pictures. Mon., Fri. 9–4.

Castile

CASTILE HISTORICAL SOCIETY. (17 E. Park Rd.) Local history, Iroquois, Seneca Indian lore. Daily (except Mon.) 2–5.

Centerport

VANDERBILT MUSEUM. (Little Neck Rd.) Marine items; paintings, art objects in 1922 mansion. May–Oct. Tues.–Sat. 10–4, Sun. 12–5.

Cold Spring-On-Hudson

PUTNAM COUNTY HISTORICAL SOCIETY. Local history, furnishings in West Point Foundry Schoolhouse; annual exhibit.

Cooperstown

COOPERSTOWN INDIAN MUSEUM. (1 Pioneer St.) Ethnology, archaeology relating to New York State Indians; dioramas of Indian life; artifacts. Mid-May–mid-Sept. Daily 1–6 (July, Aug. 9–9).

NATIONAL BASEBALL HALL OF FAME AND MUSEUM, INC. (Main St.) Baseball equipment, mementos, trophies. May–Oct. daily 9–9; Nov.–Apr. 9–5. †*

NEW YORK STATE HISTORICAL ASSOCIATION, FARMERS' MUSEUM AND VILLAGE CROSSROADS. Folk art, agricultural and household implements. Preservation project: 18th- and 19th-century homes, shops, church; crafts demonstrations. May–Oct. daily 9–6; Nov.–Apr. Tues.–Sat. 9–5, Sun. aft. †*

NEW YORK STATE HISTORICAL ASSOCIATION, FENIMORE HOUSE. American folk art, Hudson River school; 19th-century arts and crafts. May–Oct. daily 9–6; Nov.–Apr. Tues.–Sat. 9–5, Sun. aft. †*

WOODLAND MUSEUM. Natural history; nature trails, wildflowers, game and birds. Old railroad. Memorial to James Fenimore Cooper and *The Deerslayer*.

Corning

CORNING GLASS CENTER. (Centerway) Glass history; company museum. Science. Art exhibitions. Daily (except Mon.) 9:30–5. †

Croton-on-Hudson

VAN CORTLANDT MANOR. 18th-century Dutch-English Colonial house, furnishings. Daily 9–5.

Deansboro

MUSICAL MUSEUM. Antique instruments, music boxes, phonographs. Daily 10–7. †

Douglaston, Long Island

ART LEAGUE OF LONG ISLAND, INC. (44–21 Douglaston Pkwy.) *Exhibitions.* Oct.–June Tues., Thurs.–Sat. 9:30–12:30; Tues.–Thurs. 1:30–4; Tues. 7:30 P.M.–10 P.M.

East Aurora

THE TOOLHOUSE. (128 Church St.) Company museum. Woodworking tools, carpentry. Sat., Sun. 3–5, Sun. 7–9.

East Hampton

EAST HAMPTON HISTORICAL SOCIETY. (Main St.) Local history, furnishings; historic Clinton Academy of 1784. Late June–early Sept. daily 1:30–5.

GUILD HALL, INC. (Main St.) Local art; exhibitions. Mon.–Sat. 10–5, summer Sun. 3–6.

"HOME SWEET HOME" HOUSE. (14 James Lane) 17th-century bldg., birthplace of John Howard Payne, 1791; 17th–19th-century furnishings, Payne memorabilia. Mon., Wed.–Sat. 10–12, 1:30–4, Sun. 2–5.

East Meadow, Long Island

NASSAU COUNTY HISTORICAL MUSEUM. (Nassau County Park) Local history. Historic bldgs.: schoolhouse, old mill.

Elizabethtown

ADIRONDACK CENTER MUSEUM AND COLONIAL GARDEN. (Court St.) Indian and pioneer items, local history, early farm and household equipment, lumbering, mining. Mid-June–mid-Sept. Mon.–Sat. 9–9, Sun. 12–6.

Elmira

ARNOT ART GALLERY. (235 Lake St.) Painting, sculpture; exhibitions. Daily 2–5, Thurs. 12–5.

CHEMUNG COUNTY HISTORICAL CENTER. (425 E. Market St.) Local history, house of 1848. Mon.–Fri. 1:30–4, Sun. 2–5.

STRATHMONT MUSEUM. (Strathmont Park) Folk and decorative arts; children's museum; exhibitions. Mon.–Sat. 12–5, Sun. 1–5.

Fabius

PIONEER'S MUSEUM. (Highland Forest) Park museum. County history. Winter: 9–5 daily. Summer 9–9.

Flushing

THE BOWNE HOUSE. (37–01 Bowne St.) 17th-century household items, pewter collection in 1661 home, Quaker meeting site. Tues., Sat., Sun. 3–5.

QUEENS COLLEGE ART COLLECTION. (Paul Klapper Library) *Survey.* Mon.–Thurs. 9 A.M.–10:40 P.M., Fri. 9–5, Sat. 9–1 (summer: Mon.–Fri. 9–5).

Fonda

THE MOHAWK-CAUGHNAWAGA MUSEUM. Mohawk Valley archaeology, history; Indian, Colonial material. Site of 17th-century Indian village. June–Sept.: Mon.–Sat. 9:30–11:30, 1:30–4:30, Sun. 12:30–4:30.

Forest Hills

CHILDREN'S MUSEUM IN THE BROOKLYN HOME FOR CHILDREN. (67–35 112th St.) American Indian lore, natural history. Sat. 10–4:30, Tues. for school classes only, by appt.

Fort Anne

FORT ANNE MUSEUM OF HISTORY. (George St.) Reconstructed stockade, blockhouse, barracks; Colonial and Revolutionary military relics; Indian items. July, Aug. daily; June, Sept. weekends; 9–sundown.

Fort Edward

FORT EDWARD ART CENTER, INC. (83 B'way) *Exhibitions.* Oct.–June Mon., Tues., Thurs. 7–9.

FORT EDWARD HISTORICAL ASSOCIATION. (27 B'way) Local history; Old Fort House of 1772–73. May 31–Oct. 1, 1–6.

Fort Johnson

FORT JOHNSON. Period furnishings, house of 1749. May, June, Sept., Oct. daily 1–5. July, Aug. Tues.–Sat. 10–5, Sun., Mon. 1–5.

Fort Plain

FORT PLAIN MUSEUM. Restoration of 1776 fort; Indian burial grounds; Colonial homes. Nelson Greene Memorial House: Indian, military relics. Daily 10–5.

TRYON COUNTY MUZZLE LOADERS, INC. Old fort of 1750–64; district schoolhouse, 1825; blacksmith shop, 1840. Local history.

Garrison

BOSCOBEL MANSION. (Rt. 9D) Period furnishings, in restored early Federal mansion. Daily (except Tues.) 9:30–5. †*

Geneseo

LIVINGSTON COUNTY HISTORICAL SOCIETY, CENTER STREET MUSEUM. Farm and household items; Indian, Civil War relics. June–Oct. Tues., Thurs. 2–5.

Geneva

GENEVA HISTORICAL MUSEUM. (S. Main St.) Local history. Mon.–Fri. 2–4.

GENEVA JUNIOR HIGH SCHOOL, NATURE MUSEUM. (W. North St.) Teaching exhibits, general science, nature center. School days 8–4.

HOBART AND WILLIAM SMITH COLLEGES MUSEUM. Natural history teaching collections.

Glens Falls

THE HYDE COLLECTION. (161 Warren St.) Art: painting, sculpture, graphics, European decorative arts. Sun. 2–4.

Goshen

GOSHEN LIBRARY AND HISTORICAL SOCIETY. (203 Main St.) Local history, archives. Mon., Tues., Thurs., Fri. 3–6, 7–8:30; Sat. 3–6.

HALL OF FAME OF THE TROTTER. (240 Main St.) Currier & Ives prints; trophies; relating to harness racing. Mon.–Sat. 10–5, Sun. 1–5.

Great River, Long Island

BAYARD CUTTING ARBORETUM. Also ornithology. Summer daily 9–sundown.

Herkimer

HERKIMER COUNTY HISTORICAL SOCIETY AND FAIRFIELD SEMINARY ASSOCIATION. Local history; decorative arts, costumes, graphics. Mon.–Fri. 9–5.

Huntington, Long Island

THE HECKSCHER MUSEUM. (Prime Ave.) 19th-century American art; Egyptian materials. Tues.–Sat. 10–12 (also 1–5 in summer), Sun. 1–5.

HUNTINGTON HISTORICAL SOCIETY. (High St. and N.Y. Ave.) Local history, archives incl. tape recordings. Wed.–Fri., Sun. 2–5.

Huntington Station, Long Island

WALT WHITMAN HOUSE. (246 Walt Whitman Rd.) Poet's birthplace; graphics, library. Mon.–Sat. 9–5, Sun. 2–5.

Hyde Park

FRANKLIN D. ROOSEVELT LIBRARY AND HOME. (U.S. 9) Presidential library and museum; historic house of 1867, Roosevelt family furnishings. Tues.–Sun. 10–5 (home); 9–5 (library). †*

VANDERBILT MANSION. Italian and French style furnishings in 1898 house. Daily (except Mon.) 9–5.

Ilion

REMINGTON ARMS MUSEUM. Company's guns, mfd. since 1816. Daily.

Ithaca

CORNELL UNIVERSITY, ANDREW DICKSON WHITE MUSEUM OF ART. (27 East Ave.) American and European paintings; graphics. Tues.–Sat. 12–5, Sun. 2:30–5:30.

CORNELL UNIVERSITY, MARTHA VAN RENSSELAER ART GALLERY. *Exhibitions.* Mon.–Fri. 12–5.

THE DEWITT HISTORICAL SOCIETY OF TOMPKINS COUNTY, INC. (113 E. Court St.) Local history; pioneer, agricultural, household items. Tues., Thurs. 9–5.

Jamaica

QUEENS BOROUGH SOCIETY OF ARTS AND ALLIED CRAFTS, INC. (90–22 155th St.) Art; exhibitions. Old Volunteer Fire House of 1860. Mon., Sat. 10–12.

Jamestown

JAMES PRENDERGAST FREE LIBRARY. (106 W. Fifth St.) Paintings, decorative arts. Mon.–Fri. 9–9, Sat. 9–6.

Johnstown

JOHNSON HALL. (139 Hall Ave.) House of 1763, period furnishings, Indian artifacts. Mon.–Sat. 9–5, Sun. 1–5.

Katonah

JOHN JAY HOUSE. (Jay St., Rt. 22, Bedford Village) Home of first Chief Justice, portraits by Trumbull, Stuart. Mon.–Sat. 9–5, Sun. 1–5.

Kingston

SENATE HOUSE AND SENATE HOUSE MUSEUM. (312 Fair St.) Restored bldg. of 1676; Vanderlyn paintings. Mon.–Sat. 9–5, Sun. 1–5.

Lake Placid

JOHN BROWN FARM. Homestead and grave of abolitionist. Mon.–Sat. 9–5, Sun. 1–5.

Le Roy

LE ROY HISTORICAL SOCIETY. (23 E. Main St.) Local pioneer history, Le Roy House. June–Aug. Sun. 2–5.

Lindenhurst, Long Island

OLD VILLAGE HALL MUSEUM. (215 S. Wellwood Ave.) Local history. Mon., Wed. 2–4, Fri. 7–9.

Little Falls

HERKIMER HOME. Home of Gen. Nicholas Herkimer, built 1764. Mon.–Sat. 9–5, Sun. 1–5.

Liverpool

THE FRENCH FORT. (Onondaga Lake Park) Park museum. Early local history. Winter daily 9–5; summer till 9.

SALT MUSEUM. (Onondaga Lake Park) History of salt industry in Syracuse area. Daily 9–5 (summer till 9).

Lockport

NIAGARA COUNTY HISTORICAL SOCIETY, INC. (215 Niagara St.) Frontier history, Indian lore. Sun., Wed., Sat. 1–5.

Lyons

WAYNE COUNTY MUSEUM. (Courthouse, Church St.) Art, local history. Daily 1–4.

Monroe

OLD MUSEUM VILLAGE OF SMITH'S COVE, INC. (Rt. 6 and 17) Preservation project: 19th-century homes, shops. Daily 10–5.

Mount McGregor

GRANT COTTAGE. Where Grant spent last years. Mon.–Sat. 9–5, Sun. 1–5.

New Paltz

HUGUENOT HISTORICAL SOCIETY, INC. (Huguenot St.) Hugo Freer House of 1712, with Huguenot items; Col. Josiah Hasbrouck House (Rt. 32); Memorial House. Daily (except Mon.) 9–5.

New Rochelle

THOMAS PAINE COTTAGE. (North and Paine Aves.) 18th-century farmhouse. Tues.–Sat. 2–5.

New York

AMERICAN ACADEMY OF ARTS AND LETTERS. (633 W. 155th St.) Paintings: American 19th century; manuscripts. Daily 2–5 (closed Mon.).

AMERICAN FEDERATION OF ARTS. (41 E. 65th St.) Organization of traveling exhibitions. †

AMERICAN INSTITUTE OF GRAPHIC ARTS. (5 E. 40th St.) Arts in printing and publishing. Mon.–Fri. 9:30–5.

AMERICAN JEWISH HISTORICAL SOCIETY. (3080 B'way) Archives, paintings, historical items relating to American Jews. Mon.–Fri. 9–5.

AMERICAN MUSEUM OF NATURAL HISTORY. (Central Park W. at 79th St.) *Survey;* nature center; Hayden Planetarium. Mon.–Sat. 10–5, Sun. 1–5 (Planetarium shows during museum hours and in evening at 8:30, except Mon.; and 5 and 8:30 weekends). †**

AMERICAN NUMISMATIC SOCIETY. (B'way between 155 and 156th Sts.) Coins from ancient times; research. Tues.–Sat. 10–5. †*

AMERICAN SCANDINAVIAN FOUNDATION.

(127 E. 73rd St.) Scandinavian art and literature; exhibitions. Mon.–Fri. 9–5.

ART COMMISSION OF THE CITY OF NEW YORK. (City Hall) Paintings, sculpture, furnishings in City Hall. Mon.–Fri.

THE ASIA SOCIETY; ASIA HOUSE GALLERY. (112 E. 64th St.) Paintings, ceramics, decorative arts, sculpture of Asiatic countries; exhibitions, formal garden, library.

CENTRAL PARK ZOO. (64th St. and Fifth Ave.) Children's zoo. Daylight hours.

CHASE MANHATTAN BANK MUSEUM OF MONEYS OF THE WORLD. (1254 Ave. of the Americas, RCA Bldg.) Company museum. Coins, bills, checks. Mon.–Fri. 10–5. †

THE CITY COLLEGE, ART GALLERY. (Eisner Hall, 139th St. and Convent Ave.) Paintings, graphics. During school session.

COLUMBIA UNIVERSITY, THE COLLEGE OF PHARMACY OF THE CITY OF NEW YORK. (115 W. 68th St.) Apothecary jars.

THE COOPER UNION MUSEUM. (Cooper Sq. at 7th St.) Decorative arts, design. Mon.–Sat. 10–5 (Oct.–Apr. Tues. and Thurs. till 9); closed Sat. June–mid-Sept. †*

FEDERAL HALL NATIONAL MEMORIAL. (15 Pine St.) Bldg. of 1842 on site of old Federal Hall, City Hall; memorabilia of years when New York was first national capital; John Peter Zenger Memorial. Mon.–Fri. 10–4. †*

FRAUNCES TAVERN. (54 Pearl St.) Oldest bldg. in city, 1719; scene of Washington's farewell to his officers. Mon.–Fri. 10–4, Sat. 10–3.

FRENCH INSTITUTE. (22 E. 60th St.) Porcelain. Mon., Wed.–Fri. 10–6, Tues. 10–7.

THE FRICK COLLECTION. (1 E. 70th St.) Paintings, sculpture and decorative arts. Tues.–Sat. 10–5, Sun. 1–5. †*

GALLERY OF MODERN ART. (Columbus Circle) Paintings and sculpture; Pre-Raphaelites, Orozco, Dali; exhibitions. Tues.–Fri. 12–8, weekends 12–6 (closed Mon.). †*

GENERAL GRANT NATIONAL MEMORIAL. (Riverside Dr. at 122nd St.) Grant's tomb, memorabilia. Daily 9–5. *

HISPANIC SOCIETY OF AMERICA. (B'way between 155th and 156th St.) Spanish paintings, furniture, crafts; li-

brary. Tues.–Sat. 10–4:30, Sun. 2–5. †*
HISTORIC LANDMARK SOCIETY, INC.
(29 E. 4th St.) The Old Merchants
House, New York town house with origi-
nal furnishings. Tues.–Sat. 11–5, Sun.
1–5 (closed Aug.).
IBM GALLERY OF ARTS AND SCIENCES.
(16 E. 57th St.) Modern American paint-
ing, prints; models of da Vinci inven-
tions; antique office machines. Company
museum. Mon.–Sat. 9:30–5. †
JEWISH MUSEUM, Jewish Theological
Seminary of America. (1109 Fifth Ave.)
Jewish historical items, ceremonial art;
modern American art. Mon.–Thurs. 1–5,
Sun. 11–6.
LA NAPOULE ART FOUNDATION—HENRY
CLEWS MEMORIAL. (130 B'way) Art:
American, sculpture of Henry Clews; ex-
hibits for American Art Center of Châ-
teau de La Napoule, France. Mon.–Fri.,
Sun. 3–6.
METROPOLITAN LIFE INSURANCE COM-
PANY, ARCHIVES MUSEUM. (1 Madison
Ave.) Company museum. History of
Metropolitan Life. Mon.–Fri. 9:30–4:30.
METROPOLITAN MUSEUM OF ART. (5th
Ave. at 82nd St.) Survey; classical,
Egyptian, armor, musical instruments.
Tues.–Sat. 10–5, Sun. 1–5. †**
METROPOLITAN MUSEUM OF ART, THE
CLOISTERS. (Ft. Tryon Park) Medieval
art, sculpture, architecture, illuminations,
gardens. Tues.–Sat. 10–5, Sun. 1–5. †*
METROPOLITAN MUSEUM OF ART,
COSTUME INSTITUTE. (5th Ave. at 82nd
St.) Costume, design, textile collections;
library. †*
MUSEUM OF THE AMERICAN INDIAN.
(B'way at 155th St.) Archaeology, eth-
nology, anthropology—Indians of North,
Central, and South America. Tues.–Sun.
2–5. †**
MUSEUM OF THE CITY OF NEW YORK.
(1220 5th Ave.) City history. Prints, sil-
ver, decorative arts, paintings, fire equipment, marine items. Tues.–Sat. 10–5,
Sun. 1–5. †*
MUSEUM OF CONTEMPORARY CRAFTS.
(29 W. 53rd St.) American and other
handcrafts; contemporary design. Mon.–
Sat. 12–6, Sun. 2–6. †*
MUSEUM OF EARLY AMERICAN FOLK
ARTS. (49 W. 53rd St.) Painting, sculpture, and related items; exhibitions. Daily
(except Mon.) 11–6.
MUSEUM OF MODERN ART. (11 W.
53rd St.) Painting, sculpture, design, pho-

tography of late 19th and 20th centuries.
Mon.–Sat. 12–7, Sun. 1–7. †**
THE MUSEUM OF PRIMITIVE ART. (15
W. 54th St.) Art of Oceania, Africa, pre-
Columbian America, prehistoric Europe
and Asia. Tues.–Sun. 1–5, Thurs. to
7. †*
NATIONAL ACADEMY OF DESIGN. (1083
5th Ave.) Works by members since
founding in 1825; portraits of all mem-
bers; exhibitions. Daily 1–5. †
NEW YORK BOTANICAL GARDEN. (Bed-
ford Park Blvd., E. of Webster Ave., The
Bronx) Daily 10–sundown. †**
NEW-YORK HISTORICAL SOCIETY. (170
Central Park W., at 77th St.) American,
state and city history; period rooms, fur-
nishings; paintings, portraits. Tues.–Sun.
1–5, Sat. 10–5. †**
NEW YORK PUBLIC LIBRARY. (5th
Ave. at 42nd St.) Picture collection;
prints; fine bindings; stamps. Daily 9
A.M.–9:45 P.M.
NEW YORK UNIVERSITY, HALL OF
FAME FOR GREAT AMERICANS. (181st
St. and University Ave., The Bronx)
Bronze busts. Daily 9–5.
NEW YORK ZOOLOGICAL PARK, BRONX
ZOO. (185th St. and Southern Blvd., The
Bronx) Daily 10–5. †**
THE PIERPONT MORGAN LIBRARY. (33
E. 36th St.) Rare books, fine bindings,
illuminated mss.; prints, paintings. Mon.–
Fri. 9:30–5, Sat. Sept.–May; closed
Aug. †*
POLICE MUSEUM. (Police Academy
Bldg., 235 E. 20th St.) Evidence, weap-
ons, famous crimes, narcotics exhibits.
Mon.–Fri., tours at 10 and 2.
QUEENS BOTANICAL GARDEN. (43–50
Main St., Kissena Corridor Park, Flush-
ing) Gardens, arboretum. Mon.–Sat.
9–sundown, Sun. 11–sundown.
RIVERSIDE MUSEUM. (310 Riverside
Dr.) Contemporary art exhibitions.
Daily 1–5.
SALMAGUNDI CLUB. (47 5th Ave.)
American paintings; exhibitions; discus-
sions. Daily.
SCALAMANDRÉ MUSEUM OF TEXTILES.
(57 E. 57th St.) Company museum. Tex-
tile research. Mon.–Fri. 9–5.
THE SEAMEN'S BANK FOR SAVINGS. (30
Wall St.) Maritime items: paintings, ship
models, antique coin banks. †
SEAMEN'S CHURCH INSTITUTE OF NEW
YORK, MARINE MUSEUM. (25 South St.)
Maritime items: ship models, paintings,

photographs. Mon.–Fri. 10:30–6, weekends 11–4. †

THE SOLOMON R. GUGGENHEIM MUSEUM. (1071 5th Ave.) 20th-century art; bldg. designed by Frank Lloyd Wright. Tues.–Sat. 10–6, Sun. 12–6, Wed. eve. to 9. †*

STATUE OF LIBERTY NATIONAL MONUMENT. (Liberty Island) History of Statue of Liberty, immigration. Daily 9–5. *

THEODORE ROOSEVELT HOUSE. (28 E. 20th St.) Tues.–Sat. 10–5, Sun. 1–5.

TRAPHAGEN SCHOOL OF FASHION, MUSEUM COLLECTION. (1680 B'way) Costumes, textiles. Mon.–Fri. 10–5.

VAN CORTLANDT HOUSE MUSEUM. (Van Cortlandt Park, B'way at 242nd St., The Bronx) Period furnishings, house of 1748. Mon. 12–4:30, Tues.–Sat. 10–4:30, Sun. 2–4:30.

WHITNEY MUSEUM OF AMERICAN ART. (22 W. 54th St.) 20th-century American art. Daily 1–5. †*

WOOD LIBRARY–MUSEUM OF ANESTHESIOLOGY, INC. (137 W. 11th St.) Historic and modern anesthesia equipment; reference library; research. Mon.–Fri. 9:30–4:30.

Newburgh

HISTORICAL SOCIETY OF NEWBURGH BAY AND THE HIGHLANDS. (189 Montgomery St.) Local history; historic Crawford House of 1820–25. Mon.–Wed. 2:30–4:30.

KNOX HEADQUARTERS HOUSE. Period furnishings, Revolutionary headquarters of Gens. Knox, Greene and Gates, 1779–83, bldg. of 1754. Mon.–Sat. 9–5, Sun. 1–5.

WASHINGTON'S HEADQUARTERS AND (STATE) MUSEUM. (84 Liberty St.) Hasbrouck House of 1750–70; furnished with items of 1782–83. First historic house in country to be preserved. Mon.–Sat. 9–5, Sun. 1–5. †*

North Salem

HAMMOND MUSEUM, INC. (Deveau Rd., E. of Rt. 124) "Museum of the humanities," center for performing arts; art, art objects, Oriental garden. Wed.–Sun. 11–5 (closed Feb., Mar.).

North Tarrytown

PHILIPSBURG MANOR. Period furnishings, Dutch Colonial house of 1683. Daily 9–5.

Ogdensburg

REMINGTON ART MEMORIAL. (303 Washington St.) Paintings and bronzes by Frederic Remington; furnishings of Parish family who built home in 1810. Daily (except Sun.) 2–5; mid-June–mid-Sept. 10–12, 2–5.

Old Chatham

THE SHAKER MUSEUM. Preservation project: Shaker furnishings, period rooms. May–Oct. Mon.–Sat. 10–5:30, Sun. 12–6. †*

Oneida

MADISON COUNTY HISTORICAL SOCIETY. (435 Main St.) Higgenbotham Home. May–Oct. daily (except Sun.) 3–5, 7–9.

Orangeburg

TAPPAN ZEE HISTORICAL SOCIETY, ROCKLAND COUNTY. (Kings Hwy.) County history, house of 1775. Sun. 2–5.

Orchard Park

ORCHARD PARK HISTORICAL SOCIETY. (E. Quaker St.) 1820 Quaker meeting house; Quaker items.

Orient, Long Island

OYSTERPONDS HISTORICAL SOCIETY, INC. (Village Lane) Local history, house of 1790; marine items; Revolutionary and War of 1812 relics. July–mid-Oct. Tues., Thurs., Sat., Sun. 2–5.

Ossining

OSSINING HISTORICAL SOCIETY MUSEUM. (Washington School, 83 Croton Ave.) Local history, natural history.

Oswego

FORT ONTARIO. British military post, 1755; later American. Mon.–Sat. 9–5, Sun. 1–5.

OSWEGO COUNTY HISTORICAL SOCIETY. (135 E. 3rd St.) Victorian house, paneling; local history. Tues.–Fri., Sun. 2–4 (winter Wed. only).

Owego

TIOGA COUNTY HISTORICAL SOCIETY MUSEUM. (110–112 Front St.) County history, archives. Tues.–Fri. 10–12, 2–5; Wed. eve. 7–9. Nov.–Apr. Tues.–Fri. 3–5, Wed. 7–9.

Oyster Bay, Long Island

RAYNHAM HALL. (W. Main St.) Historic house. Daily (except Tues.) 10–12, 1–5.

SAGAMORE HILL. Theodore Roosevelt home. Daily (except Tues.) 10–5.

STATE UNIVERSITY OF NEW YORK PLANTING FIELDS ARBORETUM. (Planting Fields Rd.) Mon.–Sat. 8–5, Sun. 9–4:30.

Pawling

QUAKER HILL MUSEUM OF NATURAL HISTORY. (Quaker Hill) Tues.–Fri. 2–5, Sat. 10–5, Sun. 1–6.

Pearl River

AMERICAN CYANAMID COMPANY, LEDERLE LABORATORIES DIVISION. Company museum. Medical history, apothecary art; Old Apothecary Shop, Lederle Old Farm House. Mon.–Fri. 8–4:30.

Penn Yan

OLIVER HOUSE MUSEUM. (200 Main St.) County history; portraits. Fri. 2–4.

Plattsburg

THE KENT-DELORD HOUSE MUSEUM. (17 Cumberland Ave.) Period rooms, paintings by Inman in house of 1789. Mon.–Sat. 10–5.

Poughkeepsie

CLINTON HOUSE. (549 Main St.) House of 1765. Mon.–Sat. 9–5, Sun. 1–5.

DUTCHESS COUNTY HISTORICAL SOCIETY. THE GLEBE HOUSE. (635 Main St.) Daily 2–5.

VASSAR COLLEGE ART GALLERY. Hudson River · school, modern painting. Mon.–Fri. 9–4:30, Sat. 9–5, Sun. 2–5.

Rensselaer

FORT CRAILO. (14 Nelson Ave.) Fortified home of Van Rensselaer family, period furnishings in house of 1704. Mon.–Sat. 9–5, Sun. 1–5.

Riverhead

SUFFOLK COUNTY HISTORICAL SOCIETY. (W. Main St.) Local history, furnishings; old fire engines, other vehicles; ship models; display of bee hives and life cycle of honey bee. Mon.–Sat. 1–5.

Rochester

AMERICAN BAPTIST HISTORICAL SOCIETY. (1100 S. Goodman St.) Baptist ceremonial items, history, archives. Mon.–Fri. 9–12, 1–5.

GEORGE EASTMAN HOUSE OF PHOTOGRAPHY. (900 East Ave.) Photography and cinematography as art, science, history; library; film and photograph library; equipment. Home of George Eastman. Tues.–Sat. 10–5, Sun. 1–6. †*

HIGHLAND AND DURAND EASTMAN PARKS. Arboretum. Botanical Garden. Zoo. Daily 8–5.

HIGHLAND PARK HERBARIUM. (5 Castle Park) Daily 8–5.

ROCHESTER HISTORICAL SOCIETY. (485 East Ave.) Local history, medals, guns, pewter. Mon.–Sat. 9:45–4:30.

ROCHESTER MEMORIAL ART GALLERY. (490 University Ave.) *Survey;* American, folk art. Mon. 1–5, Tues.–Fri. 10–5, Sun. 2–5:30. *

ROCHESTER MUSEUM OF ARTS AND SCIENCES. (657 East Ave.) Indian arts and crafts; anthropology, natural history, aquarium. Mon.–Sat. 9–5, Sun. 2–5 (closed Sun. May–Aug.). †*

SENECA PARK ZOO. Mon.–Sat. 9:30–7, Sun. 9:30–8.

SOCIETY FOR THE PRESERVATION OF LANDMARKS IN WESTERN NEW YORK. (123 S. Fitzhugh St.) Campbell Whittlesey House of 1835, stenciled N.Y. furniture; Orringh Stone Tavern (East Ave.) of 1792; Jonathan Child House of 1838 (Washington St.). Daily (except Mon.) 10–5.

Rome

FORT STANWIX MUSEUM. (117 E. Dominich St.) Regional history, central N.Y.; archaeology.

Sag Harbor, Long Island

OLD SAG HARBOR COMMITTEE, CUSTOMS HOUSE. (Garden St.) 1789 Customs house, first in state; also post office. July 4–Oct. 10, daily 1:30–5.

SUFFOLK COUNTY WHALING MUSEUM OF SAG HARBOR, LONG ISLAND. (Main and Garden Sts.) Marine items, whaling mementos. May 30–Oct. 12, Mon.–Sat. 10–5, Sun. 2–5. †

Saratoga Springs

NATIONAL MUSEUM OF RACING, INC. (Union Ave.) Paintings, trophies relating to horse racing. Daily (except Sun.) 10–5; Aug. daily 10–9.

SARATOGA HISTORICAL MUSEUM AND THE WALWORTH MEMORIAL MUSEUM. (Congress Park) Local history, furnishings, Indian items. May–Oct. daily 9–6.

Schenectady

SCHENECTADY COUNTY HISTORICAL SOCIETY. (32 Washington Ave.) Local history, archives. Mon.–Sat. 12–5, Sun. 1–5.

SCHENECTADY MUSEUM ASSOCIATION. (37 Steuben St.) History; natural history; planetarium; art collection; children's museum. Tues.–Fri. 12–5, Sat. 10–4, Sun. 2:30–5.

Schoharie

THE OLD STONE FORT MUSEUM. (Main St.) Old church of 1772; local history, Indian items. Daily 10–5, June–Aug. 9–6 (closed Nov.–Mar.).

Schuylerville

GENERAL PHILIP SCHUYLER HOUSE. Furnishings of Revolutionary period. Daily (except Sun.) 10:30–4:30.

Seneca Falls

SENECA FALLS HISTORICAL SOCIETY. (37 Fall St.) Local history, military items; Bank Building of 1857. Fri. 2–5, 7–9.

Setauket, Long Island

THE SOCIETY FOR THE PRESERVATION OF LONG ISLAND ANTIQUITIES. The Thompson House; The Sherwood–Jayne House (Old Post Rd.). Mon., Wed.–Fri. 1–5, June–Oct. 12.

Skaneateles

SKANEATELES LIBRARY, JOHN D. BARROW ART GALLERY. (49 E. Genesee St.) Barrow's paintings of local scenes; archaeology, mineralogy. Mon.–Sat. 10–5:30, Wed. 10–1, Tues., Thurs. eves. 7–8:30.

Smithtown, Long Island

SMITHTOWN HISTORICAL SOCIETY. (Rt. 25A) Local history, house of about 1700. June–Sept. Thurs. 2–5.

Southampton, Long Island

THE PARRISH ART MUSEUM. (Job's Lane) European and American painting; annual exhibitions. Mon.–Sat. 10–5, Sun. 2–5; Oct.–Apr. Thurs.–Sat. 10–5.

Staten Island

CONFERENCE HOUSE ASSOCIATION, BILLOPP HOUSE. (Hylan Blvd., Tottenville) Site of British-American peace conference 1776. Daily (except Mon.) 10–5.

THE GARIBALDI AND MEUCCI MEMORIAL MUSEUM. (420 Tompkins Ave., Rosebank) History of Italian Risorgimento; house of 1808, home of Antonio Meucci, inventor. Tues.–Sat. 10–5, Sun. 1–5. †

JACQUES MARCHAIS CENTER OF TIBETAN ARTS. (336 Lighthouse Ave.) Tibetan temple; gardens; material on art and religion of Far East; library. Tues., Thurs. 3–5; 2nd and 4th Sun. of every month (except Jan., Feb.).

STATEN ISLAND HISTORICAL SOCIETY. THE HISTORICAL MUSEUM. RICHMONDTOWN RESTORATION. (Court and Center Sts., Richmondtown) Local history; preservation project: homes, shops, and civic bldgs. 17th–19th century. Tues.–Sat. 2–5, Sun. 2–6. †*

STATEN ISLAND INSTITUTE OF ARTS AND SCIENCES. (75 Stuyvesant Pl., St. George) Natural history, Indian artifacts, work of local artists and craftsmen; nature center; children's museum. Tues.–Sat. 10–5, 7–10; Sun. 2–6.

STATEN ISLAND ZOO. (614 B'way, Barrett Park, W. Brighton) Aquarium, children's zoo. Daily 10–5.

Stillwater

SARATOGA NATIONAL HISTORICAL PARK. Park museum; military items, archaeology. Daily 8:30–5 (June–Aug. to 5:30) (closed Dec.–Mar.). *

Stony Brook, Long Island

SUFFOLK MUSEUM AND CARRIAGE HOUSE. Antique horse-drawn vehicles; natural history; paintings of William S. Mount and others. Wed.–Sun. 10–5:30. Carriage House closed Oct.–Mar.

Syracuse

BURNET PARK ZOO. (Coleridge and S. Wilbur Aves.) Daily 10–6.
DANIEL PARISH WITTER AGRICULTURAL MUSEUM. (State Fair Grounds) History of agriculture, domestic life in state; herbarium; textiles; early industry. Fair week (1st week in Sept.) 9–8; Apr.–Oct. weekends 12–8; and by appt.
EVERSON MUSEUM OF ART. (State and James Sts.) American painting, ceramics. Mon.–Sat. 12–5, Sun. 2:30–5:30 (closed Aug.).
ONONDAGA HISTORICAL ASSOCIATION. (311 Montgomery St.) Local art, history, Indian lore; N.Y. canal memorabilia. Oct.–May daily 2–5.
SYRACUSE UNIVERSITY, JOE AND EMILY LOWE ART CENTER. (309 University Pl.) Contemporary American art; exhibitions. Mon.–Fri. 9–5, 7–10; Sat. 9–5, Sun. 2–6.

Tarrytown

HISTORICAL SOCIETY OF THE TARRYTOWNS. (1 Grove St.) Local hist. Wed. 3–5, 7:30–9; Sat. 10–12.
SLEEPY HOLLOW RESTORATIONS. Sunnyside, home of Washington Irving, built 18th century (W. of Sunnyside La., off Rt. 9). Apr.–mid-Nov. Mon.–Fri. 10–5, otherwise 12–4; weekends 10–5.

Ticonderoga

FORT TICONDEROGA. Colonial and Revolutionary period items, military relics. Mid-May–mid-Oct. daily 8–sundown.

Troy

RENSSELAER COUNTY HISTORICAL SOCIETY. (59 2nd St.) County history, house of 1827; art exhibitions. Mon.–Fri. 10–12, 2–5.
RENSSELAER COUNTY JUNIOR MUSEUM. (108 2nd Ave.) Art; planetarium. Mon.–Fri. 1–5, Sat. 1–3, first Sun. every month 2–4.

Utica

MUNSON-WILLIAMS-PROCTOR INSTITUTE. (310 Genesee St.) American art 18th–20th centuries. Fountain Elms, house of 1850. Exhibitions. Mon.–Fri. 10–10, Sat. 10–6, Sun. 2–6. †*

Valhalla

HAMMOND HOUSE. (County House Rd., Rt. 100C) Colonial farmhouse of 1715; local history, archives. Apr.–Oct. Tues.–Sat. 2–5.

Wading River, Long Island

WADING RIVER HISTORICAL SOCIETY. (N. Country Rd.) Crafts, textiles; house of 1830. Apr.–Dec. first Fri. in month 8–10.

Warwick

WARWICK HISTORICAL SOCIETY, WARWICK VALLEY MUSEUM. (Main St.) Local furnishings, Indian relics, paintings; Old Shingle House of 1764 (Forrester Ave.); Old School Baptist Church of 1810 (Church St.) June–Aug. Tues.–Sat. 2–5.

Watertown

JEFFERSON COUNTY HISTORICAL SOCIETY. (228 Washington St.) Local art, anthropology, furnishings, costumes. Tues.–Sat. 9:30–12:30, 2–5.
ROSWELL P. FLOWER MEMORIAL LIBRARY. (229 Washington St.) 19th-century paintings; dolls and miniature furniture. Mon.–Fri. 8:30 A.M.–9 P.M., Sat. 8:30–6.

Watkins Glen

YORKER YANKEE VILLAGE. (Irelandville Rd.) Preservation project: 19th-century homes, shops; American Dolls' Museum; John Ireland Manor House of 1825. Mid-May–mid-Oct. Tues.–Sat. 9–5, Sun. 12–8.

West Coxsackie

GREENE COUNTY HISTORICAL SOCIETY, BRONK HOUSE. Home of Jonas Bronck, 1663; local history, memorabilia. Daily 9–5.

West Point

UNITED STATES MILITARY ACADEMY, WEST POINT MUSEUM. Arms, equipment, flags, posters, paintings. Daily 10:30–4:30. †*

Westfield

CHAUTAUQUA COUNTY HISTORICAL SOCIETY. Archaeology, agriculture, military; historic McClurg Mansion of 1818. Tues.–Sat. 10–12, 1–4; Sun. 2–4 July, Aug.

Whitehall

SKENESBOROUGH MUSEUM. (Riverside Dr.) Naval, marine history; local art. July–Sept. 10–5, 7–9.

Wyoming

MIDDLEBURY HISTORICAL SOCIETY. (Academy St.) Local history, crafts; Middlebury Academy bldg. of 1817. Summer, Sun. 2:30–5.

Yonkers

HUDSON RIVER MUSEUM. (511 Warburton Ave.) 19th-century Americana and art in Victorian mansion; Indian lore, regional history and natural history, planetarium. Tues.–Sat. 10–12, 1–5; Sun. 2–5 (closed Aug.).
PHILIPSE MANOR. (29 Warburton Ave.) Dutch colonial mansion, furnishings of 1682, early 18th century. Portraits by Stuart, West, Copley, etc. Mon.–Sat. 9–5, Sun. 1–5.
SHERWOOD HOUSE. (Tuckahoe Rd.) Tenant farm house to Philipse Manor.

Youngstown

OLD FORT NIAGARA ASSOCIATION, INC. Preservation project: fort and buildings of 1726, period equipment. Daily 9–4:30; July–Aug. 9–8:45.

NORTH CAROLINA

Asheville

BILTMORE HOUSE AND GARDENS. (Biltmore Estate) Mansion of 1890s, paintings, tapestries, luxurious furnishings; gardens. Daily 9–6.
BLUE RIDGE PARKWAY, CRAGGY GARDENS VISITOR CENTER. (Milepost 364.6) Park museum. Herbarium; flora and fauna of region; nature trails. Mid-May–mid-June, and Labor Day–Oct., Thurs.–Mon. 9–5; mid-June–Labor Day, daily 9–5. *

Blowing Rock

FRANCES L. GOODRICH PIONEER MUSEUM. (Parkway Craft Center) Pioneer implements, local crafts. Daily 9–6 (closed Nov.–Apr.)

Boone

SOUTHERN APPALACHIAN HISTORICAL ASSOCIATION. Colonial life in mountain area; gardens. July, Aug.

Burlington

MCDADE WILDLIFE MUSEUM. (1333 Overbrook Rd.) Wildlife of North and South America, India, Africa, Australia. Geology, archaeology; collection of game hunter. Mon.–Fri. 8–5, Sun. 2–4.

Buxton

CAPE HATTERAS NATIONAL SEASHORE, MUSEUM OF THE SEA. Park museum. Marine items, lighthouses. Items relating to lifesaving, Coast Guard, shipwrecks. Cape Hatteras Lighthouse. *

Chapel Hill

UNIVERSITY OF NORTH CAROLINA, COKER ARBORETUM. Trees, shrubs of southeast; herbarium. Daily.
UNIVERSITY OF NORTH CAROLINA, THE MOREHEAD PLANETARIUM. Astronomy; art collection. Teaching and public. Mon.–Fri. 2–5, 7:30–10; Sat. 10–10; Sun. 1–10. †
UNIVERSITY OF NORTH CAROLINA, RESEARCH LABORATORIES OF ANTHROPOLOGY. (Person Hall) Archaeology, ethnology,

geology, paleontology. Teaching coll. Mon.–Sat. 8:30–5.

UNIVERSITY OF NORTH CAROLINA, WILLIAM HAYES ACKLAND MEMORIAL ART CENTER. (Columbia St.) Paintings, sculpture, graphics, minor arts. Tues.–Fri. 2:30–5, 8–10; Sat. 10–5; Sun. 2–5.

Charlotte

CHARLOTTE CHILDREN'S NATURE MUSEUM, INC. (1658 Sterling Rd.) Geology, paleontology, planetarium, astronomy. Tues.–Sat. 9:30–1, 2–5; Sun. 2:30–5. †*

MINT MUSEUM OF ART. (501 Hempstead Pl.) Italian Renaissance, 18th–20th-century American painting and sculpture; U. S. Mint Bldg. Tues.–Sat. 10–5, Sun. 3–5.

Cherokee

THE MUSEUM OF THE CHEROKEE INDIAN. Spring daily 9–5; summer 8–7.

Currie

MOORES CREEK NATIONAL MILITARY PARK, VISITOR CENTER. (Rt. 1) Park museum. Military, early Revolutionary War items. Daily 8–5. *

Durham

CHILDREN'S MUSEUM ASSOCIATION, INC. (2500 Georgia Ave.) Mineralogy, live animals; medieval weapons. Tues.–Sat. 10–12, 2–5, Sun. 2–5.

DUKE UNIVERSITY, MEDICAL CENTER, JOSIAH C. TRENT LIBRARY IN HISTORY OF MEDICINE. Medical instruments, portraits and graphics. †

Greensboro

GREENSBORO HISTORICAL MUSEUM. (220 Church St.) O. Henry coll. inc. letters, first eds. Pioneer implements. Period rooms; Colonial, pioneer, Victorian. Dolly Madison exhibit. Tues.–Fri., Sun. 2–5.

GREENSBORO JUNIOR MUSEUM. (4301 Lawndale Dr.) Natural history, hobbies. Tues.–Sat. 9–12, 1–5, Sun. 2–5.

GREENSBORO MASONIC MUSEUM. (424 W. Market St.) Ceremonial and historic items of Masonic order. Daily.

GUILFORD COURTHOUSE NATIONAL MILITARY PARK. (New Garden Rd.) Park Museum. Revolutionary War items. Daily 9–5. *

UNIVERSITY OF NORTH CAROLINA, THE WOMAN'S COLLEGE, WEATHERSPOON ART GALLERY. Modern painting, graphics, textiles. Mon.–Sat. 10–5, Sun. 2–6.

Greenville

GREENVILLE ART CENTER. (802 Evans St.) Paintings, sculpture, graphics; exhibitions. Tues.–Sat. 10–5.

Hickory

HICKORY MUSEUM OF ART. (514 3d Ave., N.W.) Paintings; local art; exhibitions. Mon.–Fri. 10–12, 2–5.

Lake Junaluska

LEROY GEORGE MEMORIAL CHILDREN'S NATURE MUSEUM, INC. Nature Center.

WORLD METHODIST BUILDING. Portraits of religious leaders; busts, statuettes, first eds. of John Wesley; church history, research. Mon.–Fri. 9–5.

Leaksville

ROCKINGHAM COUNTY HISTORICAL SOCIETY. Local history. Summer daily 8:30–5.

Manteo

CAPE HATTERAS NATIONAL SEASHORE, BODIE ISLAND VISITOR CENTER. Park museum. Plants, geology, birds, weather of Cape Hatteras. Summer daily 8:30–5:30; irregularly rest of year. *

FORT RALEIGH NATIONAL HISTORIC SITE. Reconstructed fort; history of early Virginia colony. Winter daily 8–4:30; summer later; pageant "Lost Colony" summer only. *

New Bern

NEW BERN FIREMEN'S MUSEUM. (Broad St.) Old fire engines and equipment.

TRYON PALACE RESTORATION. (613 Pollock St.) 18th-century furnishings, paintings, restored mansion of 1760s. Tues.–Sat. 9:30–4, Sun. 1:30–4.

Raleigh

BIRTHPLACE OF ANDREW JOHNSON.

(Pullen Park) Daily (except Sat.) 2–5.

HALL OF HISTORY. (Edenton and Salisbury Sts.) State and local historical items. Mon.–Sat. 9–5, Sun. 2–5.

NORTH CAROLINA MUSEUM OF ART. (107 E. Morgan St.) *Survey.* Tues.–Sat. 10–5, Sun. 2–6.

NORTH CAROLINA STATE MUSEUM. (101 Halifax) State natural history. Mon.–Sat. 9–5, Sun. 1–5.

Rocky Mount

ROCKY MOUNT CHILDREN'S MUSEUM. (Sunset Park) Nature trails, arts and crafts, archaeology, planetarium. Tues.–Sat. 10–12, 2–5; Sun. 2–5.

Salisbury

ROWAN MUSEUM, INC. (114 S. Jackson St.) Local history; early Federal furnishings in historic Maxwell Chambers House of 1819; Civil War items; Revolutionary War weapons. Tues.–Sat. 2–5, Sun. 2–4. Summer Wed., Sat. 2–5, Sun. 2–4.

Southern Pines

MOORE COUNTY HISTORICAL ASSOCIATION. (S.W. Broad St.) Historic Shaw House; local history. Feb.–Apr. 10–4.

Spruce Pine

BLUE RIDGE PARKWAY, MUSEUM OF NORTH CAROLINA MINERALS. (Gillespie Gap) Park museum. Mineralogy; rocks, gems. Commercial uses of minerals. May–Oct. Mon.–Fri. 9–5, weekends 9–6. *

Statesville

ARTS AND SCIENCE MUSEUM. (Pump Station Rd.) North Carolina artists; anthropology; geology. Sun. 2–5.

Wilmington

BRUNSWICK TOWN STATE HISTORIC SITE. (225 Pine Grove Dr.) Preservation project: port town 1726–76. 18th-century English artifacts. Daily 7–6.

NEW HANOVER COUNTY MUSEUM. (County Courthouse) Local history, relics, costumes. Mon., Wed., Fri. 2:30–4:30.

Winston-Salem

OLD SALEM, INC. (614 S. Main St.) Preservation project: restored 18th- and 19th-century bldgs. in 18-block area; incl. John Vogler House of 1819; Miksch Tobacco Shop of 1771; Salem Tavern of 1784; household items, furniture, crafts of period. Mon.–Sat. 9:30–4:30, Sun. 2–4:30. *

NORTH DAKOTA

Bottineau

NORTH DAKOTA SCHOOL OF FORESTRY. Herbarium, zoo; general botany and zoology; teaching collection. School hours.

Fargo

CASS COUNTY HISTORICAL SOCIETY MUSEUM. (North Dakota State College) Local history; pioneer items; natural history. Mon.–Fri. 1–5.

THE FORSBERG HOUSE. (815 3d Ave. S.) Local art, folk art; pioneer and Victorian furnishings. Daily 10–5.

NORTH DAKOTA INSTITUTE. (North Dakota Agricultural College Campus) State history; Indian, pioneer life; minerals, textiles. Tues.–Fri. 1–5.

Grand Forks

UNIVERSITY OF NORTH DAKOTA, ZOOLOGICAL MUSEUM. State fauna; teaching coll. Mon.–Fri. 9–5.

Medora

THEODORE ROOSEVELT NATIONAL MEMORIAL PARK, VISITOR CENTER. Park museum. Local natural history; ranching items of T.R.; Maltese Cross Ranch Cabin, first home of T.R. (Badlands, N.D.) and Elkhorn Ranch Site (Badlands, N.D.). Daily 8–5; summer till 7. *

Valley City

BARNES COUNTY HISTORICAL MUSEUM. (Courthouse) Local history. Early log cabin, early school bldg. Mon. 1–4:30.

Chillicothe

OHIO

Akron

AKRON ART INSTITUTE. (69 E. Market St.) 19th–20th century American art. Tues.–Sat. 12–5, Wed., Thurs. eve. 7–10; Sun. 2–6.

AKRON MUSEUM OF NATURAL HISTORY AND CHILDREN'S ZOO. (500 Edgewood Ave.) Daily 12–8.

STAN HYWET HALL FOUNDATION. (714 N. Portage Path) English antiques, portraits 17th–18th centuries; garden; performing arts. House: Tues.–Sun. 10–4:30; grounds 10–8.

SUMMIT COUNTY HISTORICAL SOCIETY. (550 Copley Rd.) Local history. Daily (except Mon.) 1–5.

Alliance

MT. UNION COLLEGE, CRANDALL ART STUDIOS. (Simpson St.) Exhibitions. Mon.–Fri. 9–4:30, Sun. 2–5.

Brecksville

BRECKSVILLE HISTORICAL ASSOCIATION, SQUIRE RICH HOUSE. (9367 Brecksville Rd.) Period furnishings, local history in house of 1840–45, pioneer period. Sun. 2–5.

Burton

GEAUGA COUNTY HISTORICAL SOCIETY, BOUGHTON HOUSE. (S. Cheshire) Household items, agricultural implements in house of 1858. Tues.–Sat. 10–6, Sun. 1–5.

Canton

CANTON ART INSTITUTE. (1717 Market Ave., N.) *Survey;* 20th-century regional art. Tues.–Sat. 9–5; Tues.–Thurs. eve. 7–9; Sun. 2:30–5.

STARK COUNTY HISTORICAL SOCIETY. (2677 Cleveland Ave., N.W.) County history. Mon.–Fri. 9–4:30, Sat. 9–12.

Celina

MERCER COUNTY HISTORICAL SOCIETY, INC. (126 S. Main St.) Local history; agriculture, military, Indian lore; archives. Tues., Fri., Sun. 1–5.

ADENA STATE MEMORIAL. (Allen Ave. extension) Historic mansion of 1802–07, imported furnishings; home crafts demonstrations. March–Oct. Tues.–Sun. 9–4:30.

MOUND CITY GROUP NATIONAL MONUMENT. Hopewell Indian mound, archaeology. Daily 8–6. *

ROSS COUNTY HISTORICAL SOCIETY, INC. (45 W. 5th St.) Local history; portraits, Indian artifacts; naval art; furnishings; early state history. Mar.–Nov. daily (except Wed.) 1–5.

Cincinnati

ALFRED K. NIPPERT NATURE MUSEUM. (Hamilton County Park District, 1000 Miles Rd.) Zoo; natural history; archaeology; woods; crafts. Summer daily 12–8; spring and fall weekends only.

CINCINNATI ART MUSEUM. (Eden Park) *Survey;* Far Eastern, primitive; musical instruments. Mon., Wed.–Sat. 10–5; Tues. 10–10; Sun. 2–5. †*

CINCINNATI MUSEUM OF NATURAL HISTORY. (1720 Gilbert Ave.) Anthropology; planetarium. Mon.–Sat. 9–5, Sun. 2–5. †

EDEN PARK CONSERVATORY. Mon.–Sat. 10–5, Sun. 10–6.

HEBREW UNION COLLEGE, JEWISH INSTITUTE OF RELIGION, THE JEWISH MUSEUM. (3101 Clifton Ave.) Jewish ceremonial objects, paintings; modern art; archaeology. Mon.–Fri. 9–5. †*

HISTORICAL AND PHILOSOPHICAL SOCIETY OF OHIO. (University of Cincinnati Library, Rm. 205) City and state history, art, archives. Mon.–Sat. 8:30–4:30 (closed Sat. during school vacations, July, Aug.).

MT. AIRY FOREST ARBORETUM. (Eden Park) Daily.

PARK MUSEUM OF NATURAL HISTORY. (Burnet Woods) Trailside museum. Mon.–Sat. 10–5:30, Sun. 2–5:30.

THE TAFT MUSEUM. (316 Pike St.) European painting, 16th–19th centuries; Chinese porcelain; mansion of 1820. Mon.–Sat. 10–5, Sun. 2–5. †*

UNIVERSITY OF CINCINNATI, UNIVERSITY MUSEUM. Paleontology, mineralogy; research only. By appt.

Cleveland

CASE INSTITUTE OF TECHNOLOGY, GEOLOGY MUSEUM. (210900 Euclid Ave.) Mon.–Fri. 9–5.

CLEVELAND HEALTH MUSEUM. (8911 Euclid Ave.) Medicine, hygiene, public health. Daily 9–5, Sun. 1–6. †*

CLEVELAND METROPOLITAN PARK DISTRICT TRAILSIDE MUSEUMS. June–Sept. daily 9–6; otherwise weekends only, 9–6.

CLEVELAND MUSEUM OF ART. (11150 E. Blvd.) *Survey;* European decorative arts; medieval art and objects. Tues., Thurs. 10–6; Wed., Fri. 10–10; Sat. 9–5; Sun. 1–6 (July–Sept. Tues.–Fri. 10–6). †**

CLEVELAND ZOOLOGICAL SOCIETY. (Brookside Park) Zoo. Winter daily 10–5 (summer till 7).

DUNHAM TAVERN MUSEUM. (6709 Euclid Ave.) House of 1832, early furnishings. Daily (except Mon.) 12:30–4:30.

GARDEN CENTER OF GREATER CLEVELAND. (E. Blvd. at Euclid Ave.) Arboretum; botanical garden.

HOWARD DITTRICK MUSEUM OF HISTORICAL MEDICINE. (11000 Euclid Ave.) History of medicine; implements. Mon.–Fri. 1–5.

KARAMU HOUSE. (2355 E. 89th St.) African art. Mon.–Sat. 10–12 midnight; Sun. 2–12 midnight.

LAKEWOOD HISTORICAL SOCIETY. (14710 Lake Ave.) Stone House of 1838, period furnishings. Wed., Sun. 2–5.

NATURAL SCIENCE MUSEUM. (University Circle) *Survey;* aquarium; planetarium; botanical garden. Tues.–Sat. 9–5, Sun. 1–5:30. *

THOMPSON PRODUCTS AUTO ALBUM AND AVIATION MUSEUM. (1845 E. 30th St.) Company (Thompson Ramo Wooldridge, Inc.) museum; transportation. Tues.–Sat. 11–5, Sun. 1–5.

WESTERN RESERVE HISTORICAL SOCIETY. (10825 E. Blvd.) History of Eastern Ohio region; art; furnishings. Tues.–Sat. 10–5, Sun. 2–5. †*

Columbus

COLUMBUS GALLERY OF FINE ARTS. (480 E. Broad St.) *Survey.* Daily 12–5. †*

FRANKLIN COUNTY HISTORICAL SOCIETY AND MUSEUM. (Memorial Hall, 280 E. Broad St.) County history; Indian lore; industrial. Mon.–Fri. 8:30–5.

OHIO STATE MUSEUM. (High St. at 15th Ave.) Archaeology, history, industries of Ohio. Mon.–Sat. 9–5, Sun. 1–5. †**

OHIO STATE UNIVERSITY, GEOLOGICAL MUSEUM. (155 S. Oval Dr.) Mineralogy, paleontology. Research, teaching coll. Mon.–Sat. 8–5.

OHIO STATE UNIVERSITY, SCHOOL OF FINE AND APPLIED ARTS. (108 N. Oval Dr.) Art gallery; exhibitions. Mon.–Fri. 8–5, Sat. 8–12.

Coshocton

JOHNSON-HUMRICK HOUSE MEMORIAL MUSEUM. (Sycamore St. at 3rd) Objets d'art from Europe and the Orient. Mon.–Fri. 1–4:30, Sat. 1–4, Sun. 2–5.

Crestline

CRESTLINE SHUNK MUSEUM. (211 N. Thoman St.) Local history, furnishings, toys in house of 1860. Thurs. aft. and eve.

Dayton

AIR FORCE MUSEUM. (Wright-Patterson Air Force Base) Early aircraft; history of U.S.A.F. Mon.–Fri. 9–4, weekends 1–5. †*

DAYTON ART INSTITUTE. (Forest and Riverview Aves.) *Survey;* pre-Columbian. Tues.–Fri. 12:30–5; Tues. eve. 7–10; Sat. 9–5; Sun. 1–6. †*

DAYTON MUSEUM OF NATURAL HISTORY. (2629 Ridge Ave.) Geology; Indian material; planetarium. Mon., Wed., Fri. 1–6 (summer 10–6); Tues., Thurs. 1–9 (summer 10–9); Sat. 9–6, Sun. 2–6.

THE DAYTON POWER AND LIGHT COMPANY MUSEUM. (1900 S. B'way) Company museum: historical lighting devices. By appt.

PAUL LAURENCE DUNBAR HOUSE. (219 N. Summit St.) Furnishings and personal effects of poet.

HISTORICAL SOCIETY OF THE EVANGELICAL UNITED BRETHREN CHURCH. (1810 Harvard Blvd.) Church archives, historical material. Tues., Thurs., Fri. 8:30–4.

THE NEWCOM TAVERN. Pioneer items in house of 1798. Summer daily (except Sun.) 9–4.

Delaware

DELAWARE COUNTY HISTORICAL MUSEUM. (157 E. William St.) Local and state history. Sun.–Wed. 2–4.

East Liverpool

EAST LIVERPOOL HISTORICAL SOCIETY MUSEUM. (Carnegie Public Library, E. 4th St.) Early ceramics of Eastern Ohio; research. Daily (except Sun.) 10–8.

Elyria

LORAIN COUNTY HISTORICAL SOCIETY MUSEUM. (334 Washington Ave.) Local history. Tues., Sat. 2–5.

Fairport Harbor

FAIRPORT MARINE MUSEUM. (129 2d St.) Great Lakes history, marine relics, ship models, instruments; old lighthouse. May 30–Labor Day, Wed. and Sun. 2–5.

Findlay

FINDLAY COLLEGE MUSEUM. (Grose Hall, 126 College St.) 19th-century American furniture; Indian items; oriental items. Oct.–June, Sun. 2–5.

Fort Recovery

FORT RECOVERY HISTORICAL SOCIETY MUSEUM. (Old Fort St.) Mementos of battlefield, 1791. Sun. 10:15–6:30.

Fremont

THE RUTHERFORD B. HAYES LIBRARY AND MUSEUM. (1337 Hayes Ave.) Family furnishings, photographs in president's home; library. Daily 9–5, Sun. 1–5. †*

Gallipolis

OUR HOUSE. (432 1st Ave.) 1819 tavern. Apr. 16–Sept. 15: 9:30–5 daily (except Mon.).

Gates Mills

GATES MILLS HISTORICAL SOCIETY, SOUTHWICK HOUSE. (Old Mill Rd.) Local history, house of 1836. Daily (except Sun.) 8–6.

Georgetown

GRANT SCHOOLHOUSE. (S. Water St.) Grant and Civil War memorabilia, house of 1804. Daily (except Mon.) 12–5.

Granville

GRANVILLE HISTORICAL MUSEUM. (B'way) Village archives; artifacts; carpenters' tools of early 19th century; house of 1816. Weekends 2–5.

Greenville

DARKE COUNTY HISTORICAL SOCIETY, GARST MUSEUM. (223 W. 3rd St.) County history; 1850 bldg. Tues., Fri., Sun. 1–5.

Hudson

THE HUDSON LIBRARY AND HISTORICAL SOCIETY. (49 E. Main St.) Local history; art exhibitions. Mon., Tues., Thurs., Fri. 10–9; Sat. 10–5.

Ironton

LAWRENCE COUNTY HISTORICAL SOCIETY. (Dean State Forest at Vesuvius Lake) County history, charcoal iron furnace industry. Summer, Sun.

Kent

KENT STATE UNIVERSITY, SCHOOL OF ART. *Exhibitions.* Mon.–Fri. 8 A.M.–10 P.M.

Lebanon

GLENDOWER. (Rt. 42) Greek Revival house, mid-19th-century furnishings; and Warren County historical material. Apr.–Oct. daily (except Mon.) 9:30–5.

Lima

ALLEN COUNTY MUSEUM. (620 W. Market St.) Locomotive file, photographs; archaeology, costumes, Indian artifacts; geology. Daily (except Mon.) 1:30–5.

Lisbon

LISBON HISTORICAL SOCIETY, OLD STONE HOUSE. (E. Washington St.) Local history, furnishings, house of 1805. June–Sept. Fri. 2–5, 7–9, Sun. 2–5.

Mansfield

KINGWOOD CENTER. (900 Park Ave. W.) Botanical garden; civic arts center. Mon.–Fri. 9–5, Sun. 1:30–4:30.

Marietta

CAMPUS MARTIUS MUSEUM. (601 2d St.) Local history, furnishings, paintings. Ohio Company Land Office of 1788, first in state. Rufus Putnam House, fortified log dwelling of 1788. Marine items, incl. steamboat on Muskingum River. Apr.–Oct. daily 9–5; Nov.–Mar. Mon.–Sat. 9–5, Sun. 1–5. *

Massillon

THE MASSILLON MUSEUM. (212 Lincoln Way E.) American folk art, pioneer items; bldg. of 1835. Mon.–Sat. 10–5, Wed. eve. 7–9, Sun. 2–5.

Mentor

THE HOLDEN ARBORETUM. (Sperry Rd.) Woody plants; herbarium; nature walks. Daily (except Mon.) 10–6.

LAKE COUNTY HISTORICAL SOCIETY, PRESIDENT JAMES A. GARFIELD HOME. County, regional history; furnishings in house of 1832. Tues.–Sat. 9–5, Sun. 1–5.

Milan

MILAN HISTORICAL MUSEUM. (10 Edison Dr.) Historic house of 1840, kitchen, toy room, blacksmith shop, old general store; dolls; antique glass; firearms. Mid-Apr.–Oct. daily 1–5.

Newark

LICKING COUNTY HISTORICAL SOCIETY, SHERWOOD-DAVIDSON HOUSE. (6th St. between W. Main and Church) Antique furnishings in house of 1820; local history, Indian items. Sun., Wed. 1–5.

Oberlin

THE LITTLE RED SCHOOLHOUSE. (Vine St.) First public school in Oberlin, early equipment. By appt.

OBERLIN COLLEGE, ALLEN MEMORIAL ART MUSEUM. Teaching coll., exhibitions. School year: Mon.–Fri. 1:30–

4:30, 7–9:30; Sat. 2–4, Sun. 2–6. Summer: Mon.–Fri. 10–12, 2–4; Sat. 2–5, 7–9; Sun. 2–6.

Oxford

MIAMI UNIVERSITY ART GALLERY. Paintings. Mon.–Fri. 8–5, Sun. 2–5.

OXFORD MUSEUM ASSOCIATION. (316 W. High St.) Pioneer furnishings, house of 1850–80. May–Nov. weekends 1:30–5.

Peninsula

JONATHAN HALE HOMESTEAD AND PIONEER FARM MUSEUM. (Oak Hill Rd.) Period furnishings in restored farm and home of 1810; agricultural implements. Tues.–Sat. 10–5, Sun. 1–5.

PENINSULA LIBRARY AND HISTORICAL SOCIETY. Bordner Historical Collection; local history, folk lore; paintings. Mon.–Fri. 12–8.

Point Pleasant

GRANT BIRTHPLACE. (U.S. 52 and 232) Period furnishings. Apr.–Oct. daily (except Mon.) 9:30–5.

Pomeroy

THE MEIGS COUNTY PIONEER AND HISTORICAL SOCIETY, INC. (105 Plum St.) River transportation, photographs of steamboats; local history. Daily.

Port Clinton

OTTAWA COUNTY HISTORICAL MUSEUM. (City Hall, 2d and Adams Sts.) Local history, paintings, geology. Wed., Sat. 6:30 P.M.–8:30 P.M., Thurs., Sat. 3–5.

Powell

COLUMBUS MUNICIPAL ZOO. (Riverside Dr.) Daily 10–6.

Shaker Heights

THE SHAKER HISTORICAL SOCIETY. (Moreland School, Lee and Van Aken Blvd.) Shaker relics, furniture; pioneer life. Thurs. 1–4.

Tiffin

SENECA COUNTY MUSEUM. (28 Clay

St.) County history, pioneer items. Wed., Sun. 2–4.

Toledo

HISTORICAL SOCIETY OF NORTHWESTERN OHIO. (Toledo Public Library) Local history. Daily 10–6.

TOLEDO MUSEUM OF ART. (Monroe St. at Scottwood Ave.) *Survey;* history of writing and books; glass. Tues.–Sat. 9–5, Sun., Mon. 1–5. †*

TOLEDO ZOOLOGICAL SOCIETY. (2700 B'way) Zoo. Natural science museum; Indian artifacts, mineralogy. Aquarium. Peter Navarre Cabin. Summer daily 10–7; winter till 5.

Unionville

SHANDY HALL. (Rt. 84) Family furnishings, 1815–1935. May–Oct.: Tues.–Sat. 10–5, Sun. 2–6.

Upper Sandusky

WYANDOT COUNTY HISTORICAL SOCIETY. (Courthouse) Wyandot Indian culture; pioneer items; Indian Mill Park. Mon.–Fri. 9–11:30, 1–4; Sat. 9:30–12; Sun. 1–4.

Vermilion

GREAT LAKES HISTORICAL SOCIETY MUSEUM. (142 Main St.) Marine collection: ship models, instruments. Daily 10:30–6.

Warren

TRUMBULL COUNTY HISTORICAL SOCIETY, JOHN STARK EDWARDS HOUSE. (259 South St., N.E.) Furnishings, early historical items in house of 1807. Daily, by appt.

West Liberty

CASTLE PIATT MAC-A-CHEEK. Painting, decorative arts; French and Indian War relics in two "French" castles of 1864–79. Feb.–Oct. daily 8–10.

Westerville

OTTERBEIN COLLEGE, WEITKAMP OBSERVATORY AND PLANETARIUM. College and public demonstrations. Tues. 8:30 P.M. by appt. First and third Sat. every month, 7:30 P.M.

Wilmington

THE CLINTON COUNTY HISTORICAL SOCIETY. (149 E. Locust St.) County history, early furnishings, paintings in Rombach Place, house of 1835. Apr.–Nov. Thurs., Sun. 2–5.

Wooster

THE COLLEGE OF WOOSTER, JOSEPHINE LONG WISHART MUSEUM OF ART. Prints, Oriental bronzes, Chinese painting. Mon.–Fri. 8–4:30, Sat. 8:30–12.

Worthington

OHIO RAILWAY MUSEUM. (936 Proprietors Rd.) Transportation; restoration of old equipment. Sat. 1–5, Sun. 10–5.

THE WORTHINGTON HISTORICAL SOCIETY MUSEUM. (137 E. Granville Rd.) Pioneer and Indian items. Sun. 1–5.

Xenia

THE GREENE COUNTY HISTORICAL SOCIETY MUSEUM. (308 E. 2d St.) Local history; Galloway Cabin (S. Monroe St.) Wed., Sat., Sun. aft.

WILBERFORCE UNIVERSITY, CARNEGIE LIBRARY. Negro art, William Wilberforce memorabilia. Mon., Tues., Thurs., Fri. 9–4, 6–9; Wed. 9–11, 1–4, 6–9; Sat. 9–12; Sun. 5–7:30. †

Youngstown

BUTLER INSTITUTE OF AMERICAN ART. (524 Wick Ave.) American and Southwest Indian art; exhibitions. Tues.–Sat. 12–5, Sun. 1–5. †*

Zanesfield

LOGAN COUNTY ARCHAEOLOGICAL AND HISTORICAL SOCIETY, INC. (Dr. Sloan Library) Indian, pioneer items; early local industry. Mon., Tues., Wed., Fri., Sat. 1–5, 7–9.

Zanesville

ART INSTITUTE OF ZANESVILLE, OHIO. (Maple at Adair) *Survey.* Mon.–Thurs., Sat. 1–5, Sun. 2–5.

MUSKINGUM PIONEER AND HISTORICAL SOCIETY. (1145 Maple Ave.) Early state and county items. Daily 9–5.

OKLAHOMA

Ada

EAST CENTRAL STATE COLLEGE MUSEUM. Archaeology, ethnology, geology, history, Indian artifacts, contemporary art. Exhibitions. Mon.–Fri. 8–5:30, Wed. eve. 6:30–9.

Anadarko

THE ANADARKO CITY MUSEUM. (City Hall, Main and First Sts.) Paintings by Indian artists; Indian arts and crafts; early local household equipment; photographs.
INDIAN CITY, U.S.A. Replicas of Indian villages. Daily 9–6. †
SOUTHERN PLAINS INDIANS EXHIBIT AND CRAFTS CENTER. Indian art, 20th century; ethnology. Tues.–Sat. 8–12, 1–5, Sun. 1–5.

Bartlesville

WOOLAROC MUSEUM. Indian art, artifacts; western art. Daily (except Mon.) 10–5. †

Claremore

WILL ROGERS MEMORIAL. (W. Will Rogers Blvd.) Memorabilia of the humorist. Daily 8–5. †

Edmond

CENTRAL STATE COLLEGE, THE LABORATORY OF HISTORY. (400 E. Hurd St.) Contemporary political science; Civil War and World Wars, international affairs; research. During school year, daily, 9–12, 1–5; summer session, 1–5.

Fort Sill

U. S. ARMY ARTILLERY AND MISSILE CENTER MUSEUM. Military equipment, small arms, uniforms; Plains Indians and frontier items. Historic bldgs. of old fort. Wed.–Sun. 10–5. †

Goodwell

NO MAN'S LAND HISTORICAL MUSEUM. (Sewell St.) Local history, ethnology, archaeology, geology, zoology; Indian artifacts; art exhibitions. Mon.–Fri. 9–12, 1–4; Sat. 9–12, Sun. 1–4.

Lawton

MUSEUM OF THE GREAT PLAINS. (Elmer Thomas Park) Local history, anthropology, transportation. Mon.–Sat. 10–5, Sun. 2–5.

Norman

UNIVERSITY OF OKLAHOMA, MUSEUM OF ART. Indian, contemp. American art; exhibitions. Mon.–Fri. 8–5; Oct.–May: Tues., Thurs. eve. 7–9; Sat. 9–12, Sun. 1–5.
UNIVERSITY OF OKLAHOMA, STOVALL MUSEUM. Natural history, anthropology, paleontology. Tues.–Fri. 9–5, Sat. 9–12, Sun. 2–5; closed Sat., Sun. in Aug. †

Oklahoma City

LINCOLN PARK ZOO. Daily 7:30–6.
NATIONAL COWBOY HALL OF FAME AND MUSEUM. (200 Skirvin Tower) History, art, folklore of the West. †
OKLAHOMA ART CENTER. (Plaza Circle, Fair Park) Contemp. American art; exhibitions. Tues.–Sat. 10–5, Sun. 2–5.
OKLAHOMA HISTORICAL SOCIETY. (Historical Bldg.) Indian and pioneer items. Mon.–Fri. 8–4:30, Sat. 8:30–12, Sun. 1:30–4:30.

Okmulgee

CREEK COUNCIL HOUSE, CAPITOL OF THE MUSCOGEE NATION. (Chamber of Commerce) Bldg. of 1878; paintings of prominent Indians; Indian artifacts, culture. Tues.–Sat. 10–4, Sun. 1–4.

Pawhuska

OSAGE TRIBAL MUSEUM. (Osage Agency Reserve) Ethnology. Daily 8–12, 1–5.

Ponca City

PIONEER WOMAN MUSEUM. (801 Monument Rd.) Utensils, costumes, textiles;

bronze statue of the Pioneer Woman. Wed.–Mon. 10–12, 1–5, Sun. 1–5.

PONCA CITY INDIAN MUSEUM. (Ponca City Library) Indian costumes, basketwork, beadwork; prints; Catlin drawings. Mon.–Fri. 10–9, Sat. 10–6. †

Shawnee

POTTAWATOMIE COUNTY HISTORICAL ASSOCIATION. (Hwy. 18) Local history, photographs; machinery, implements. Shawnee Mission Church, pre-territorial period. Fourth Mon. every month, and by appt.

ST. GREGORY'S COLLEGE, GERRER MUSEUM. Ethnology, natural history; 17th-century Italian, 19th-century American painting. Daily 10–5.

Sulphur

PLATT NATIONAL PARK. Park museum. Natural history, zoology, herbarium, geology. Daily 8–5. *

Tahlequah

THE MURRELL HOME. Bldg. of 1840s. Mon.–Sat. 9–5, Sun. 1–6.

Tonkawa

NORTHERN OKLAHOMA JUNIOR COLLEGE, YELLOW BULL MUSEUM. Natural history, paleontology, Indian artifacts. Mon.–Fri. 8–5.

Tulsa

GILCREASE INSTITUTE OF AMERICAN HISTORY AND ART. (2401 W. Newton St.) Western art, archives; Indian art, artifacts. Mon.–Sat. 9–5, Sun. 1–5. †*

PHILBROOK ART CENTER. (2727 S. Rockford Rd.) Indian art, crafts, artifacts; *Kress* coll.; Chinese ceramics, jades; local art; exhibitions. Sun. 1–5; Tues.–Sat. 10–5; Tues. eve. 7:30–9:30. †*

TULSA ZOOLOGICAL GARDEN. (Mohawk Park) Mon.–Sat. 8–4:30, Sun. 8–7.

OREGON

Ashland

LITHIA PARK. Arboretum; zoo.

Astoria

CLATSOP COUNTY HISTORICAL MUSEUM, SOCIETY. Daily 10–5. Winter: Tues.–Sun. 1–5.

LEWIS AND CLARK FORT CLATSOP. Reconstructed Fort of 1805–06.

Burns

MALHEUR NATIONAL WILDLIFE REFUGE. Daily. *

Canyon City

GRANT COUNTY MUSEUM AND HISTORICAL SOCIETY. (Hwy. 395) Joaquin Miller Cabin, 1864. Mon.–Sat. 9–5, Sun. 1–5.

Coquille

COQUILLE VALLEY ART ASSOCIATION. (Myrtle Pt. Hwy.) Oregon artists; textiles.

Corvallis

OREGON STATE COLLEGE, HORNER MUSEUM. (Coliseum) Local history, natural history, Indian items. Mon.–Fri. 9–5, Sat. 10–12, 2–5, Sun. 2–5.

Crater Lake

CRATER LAKE NATIONAL PARK. (Crater Lake 211) Park museum. Natural history; geology, nature center, park flora and fauna; volcanology. Mid-June–mid-Sept. daily 8–6. (Study coll. daily 8–5, by appt.) *

Depoe Bay

THE AQUARIUM. (101 Hwy.) Local marine specimens. Daily 8–5 (summer to 8).

Eugene

LANE COUNTY PIONEER MUSEUM. (704 W. 13th Ave.) Local history. Sun.–Tues. 1–5.

UNIVERSITY OF OREGON MUSEUM OF ART. Oriental, Russian art; *survey;* exhibitions. Daily (except Mon.) 1–5.

UNIVERSITY OF OREGON, MUSEUM OF NATURAL HISTORY. Anthropology, archaeology, geology, zoology, herbarium. Research. Mon.–Fri. 8–5, weekends 1:30–5.

Forest Grove

PACIFIC UNIVERSITY MUSEUM. Indian and pioneer items; historic house of 1850. Thurs. 2–5.

Hood River

HOOD RIVER COUNTY HISTORICAL MUSEUM. (County Courthouse, State, between 3d and 4th) Local history, industrial implements, Indian items. Mon.–Fri. 8–5.

Jacksonville

BEEKMAN BANK AND BEEKMAN MANSION. Gold rush bank and banker's home, 19th century. †

JACKSONVILLE MUSEUM. (206 N. 5th St.) Photographs, equipment, studio of early photographer; mining items; early furnishings. Mar.–Oct. Mon.–Sat. 10–5, Sun. 12–5; Nov.–Feb. Tues.–Sun. 12–4. †

Klamath Falls

COLLIER STATE PARK LOGGING MUSEUM. (U.S. Hwy. 97) Logging equipment, photographs. Daily.

KLAMATH COUNTY MUSEUM. (Klamath and 3d) Local history, anthropology, natural history. Tues.–Sat. 1–5.

Newberg

MINTHORN HOUSE. (115 S. River St.) Home of Herbert Hoover. Tues.–Sat. 8–10, 2–4, Sun. 2–4. †

North Bend

COOS-CURRY MUSEUM. (Simpson Park) Indian items. Tues.–Sun. 11–5 (1–5 winter).

Oregon City

McLOUGHLIN MEMORIAL ASSOCIATION. (713 Center St.) Home of Dr. John McLoughlin, 1846; period furnishings. Tues.–Sun. 10–5 (winter to 4). †

Portland

HOYT ARBORETUM. (4000 S.W. Fairview Blvd.) Daily 8–4:30 (Sept.–May, Mon.–Fri.)

JUNIOR MUSEUM OF PORTLAND, OREGON. (3037 S.W. 2d Ave.) Minerals, dolls, zoo, ceramics, art. Tues., Thurs. 2–10; Wed., Fri. 10–6; Sat. 9–5.

LIBRARY ASSOCIATION OF PORTLAND. (Multnoman County Library, 801 S.W. 10th Ave.) Picture collection; reproductions and color slides of art works. Mon.–Fri. 9–9, Sat. 9–5:30.

OREGON CERAMIC STUDIO. (3934 S.W. Corbett Ave.) Ceramic and textile arts of Northwest; exhibitions. Mon.–Sat. 11–5.

OREGON HISTORICAL SOCIETY. (235 S.W. Market) State history, anthropology, archives, art. Mon.–Fri. 9–5, Sat. 9–12.

OREGON MUSEUM OF SCIENCE AND INDUSTRY. (4015 S.W. Canyon Rd.) Geology, paleontology; technology; planetarium; other natural sciences. Mon.–Fri. 1–5, weekends 12–6.

PORTLAND ART MUSEUM. (S.W. Park and Madison St.) *Survey; Kress;* Northwest coast Indian art; contemp. Oregon art. Tues.–Thurs., Sat., Sun. 12–5, Fri. 12–10. †*

PORTLAND ZOOLOGICAL GARDENS. (4001 S.W. Canyon Rd.) Daily 10–5:30 (summer to 7:30).

Salem

CHAMPOEG STATE PARK. State history, arboretum. Historic pioneer homes. Daily 8–5.

SALEM ART MUSEUM. (600 Mission St.) Oregon and Northwest artists; historic Bush House of 1877–78, Victorian furnishings. Tues.–Sun. 1–5. †

Seaside

SEASIDE AQUARIUM. (200 N. Prom) 9–5:30 (summer 8:30 A.M.–9 P.M.).

The Dalles

SURGEON'S QUARTERS, FORT DALLES. County history, Indian and pioneer items.

Tillamook

TILLAMOOK COUNTY PIONEER MUSEUM. (2106 2d St.) Local history and natural history; Indian, pioneer items; furniture. Mon.–Sat. 9–5, Sun. 1–5 (winter, closed Mon.).

PENNSYLVANIA

Allentown

ALLENTOWN ART MUSEUM. (5th and Court Sts.) European art; *Kress;* exhibitions. Mon.–Sat. 10–5, Sun. 2–5. *

THE LEHIGH COUNTY HISTORICAL SOCIETY. Indian items; historic Trout Hall of 1770.

Ambridge

OLD ECONOMY. Preservation project: homes, shops, gardens of Harmonist settlement. Art, early 19th century, contemp. American. Ohio Valley industry, 19th century. Mon.–Sat. 8:30–5, Sun. 12–6. †*

Athens

TIOGA POINT MUSEUM. (724 Main St.) Local history, natural history. Mon. 7–9 P.M.; Wed., Sat. 2–5.

Berwick

ELAN MEMORIAL PARK. (Old Rt. 11, Bloomsburg) Arboretum, botanical garden. Daily.

Bethlehem

LEHIGH UNIVERSITY ART GALLERIES. Contemp. American and French painting; Chinese porcelain. Mon.–Fri. 9–5, Sat. 9–12.

LEHIGH UNIVERSITY, DEPARTMENT OF GEOLOGY. (311 Williams Hall) Mineralogy; research. Mon.–Fri. 8–5, Sat. 8–12.

Birdsboro

DANIEL BOONE HOMESTEAD. Farm house, blacksmith shop, barn; birthplace of pioneer. Mon.–Sat. 8:30–5, Sun. 12–5.

Bloomsburg

COLUMBIA COUNTY HISTORICAL SOCIETY. (353 College Hill) County history, geology, Indian items. Mon.–Fri. 9–5.

Boalsburg

BOAL MANSION AND MUSEUM, COLUMBUS CHAPEL. (Rt. 322) 16th century Spanish chapel, 17th century altar, paneling, furnishings, paintings. Early Federal mansion, furnishings; May–Oct. daily 10–6.

Carlisle

HAMILTON LIBRARY AND HISTORICAL ASSOCIATION OF CUMBERLAND COUNTY. (21 N. Pitt St.) Local history. Tues. 7–9 P.M.; Wed., Fri. 3–5.

HESSIAN GUARDHOUSE MUSEUM. (Carlisle Barracks) Bldg. of 1777; U.S. military relics, all wars. Sun., Wed. 1–5.

Chadds Ford

BRANDYWINE BATTLEFIELD PARK. (Baltimore Pike, U.S. 1) Washington's Headquarters, Lafayette's Quarters, site of Battle of Brandywine. Daily.

Chester

DELAWARE COUNTY HISTORICAL SOCIETY. (410–412 Market St.) Local history; Old Caleb Pusey House (Upland, Penna.). Old Morton Mortonsen House (Norwood Borough, Penna.). Mon.–Fri. 1–4, Sat. 9–12.

TAYLOR MEMORIAL ARBORETUM. (10 Ridgely Dr.) Daily, daylight hours.

Clarion

CLARION COUNTY HISTORICAL SOCIETY. (Courthouse) Pioneer household items. Wed. 2–4 (closed July).

Columbia

COLUMBIA MUSEUM OF HOROLOGICAL ANTIQUITIES. (333 N. Third St.) Clocks, watches; research; appraisals. By appt.

Cornwall

CORNWALL FURNACE. Iron furnace of 18th and 19th century, made Revolutionary War materials, household and farm equipment. Tues.–Sat. 8:30–5, Sun. 12–5.

Coudersport

POTTER COUNTY HISTORICAL SOCIETY. (308 N. Main St.) Pioneer items; historic house. Mon., Wed., Fri. 2–4.

Dilworthtown

1704 BRINTON HOUSE. (Old West Chester, Wilmington Pike) Transportation and agriculture materials. Apr.–Nov. Tues., Thurs., Sat. 2–5.

Doylestown

BUCKS COUNTY HISTORICAL SOCIETY. (Pine and Ashland Sts.) Early crafts, industries; ceramics. Mon.–Sat. 10–5. Apr.–Sept.: Sun. 1:30–5:30.

Easton

NORTHAMPTON COUNTY HISTORICAL AND GENEALOGICAL SOCIETY. (101 S. 4th St.) Local history, costumes, painting. Thurs., Fri. eve. 7–10, Sat. 2–5.

Ebensburg

THE CAMBRIA COUNTY HISTORICAL SOCIETY. (120 E. High St.) Early county history. Tues., Thurs. 2–5.

Elizabethtown

MASONIC HOMES OF PENNSYLVANIA. (Rt. 241) Arboretum. Daily 8–5.

Elverson

HOPEWELL VILLAGE NATIONAL HISTORIC SITE. (Birdsboro, near Pottstown) Restored iron-making community, 18th and 19th century; antique carriages. Oct.–June, daily 9:30–5:30; July–Sept., weekends to 7:30. *

Ephrata

EPHRATA CLOISTER. Preservation project: nine bldgs. of 18th century German Baptist community; medieval architectural details; illuminated mss. Mon.–Sat. 8:30–5, Sun. 12–5. *

Erie

ERIE PUBLIC MUSEUM. (6th and Chestnut Sts.) Lincolniana, costumes, Indian lore; planetarium. Tues.–Fri. 10–5, Sun. 2–5. Planetarium: Wed. 8, weekends 3, and by appt.

Farmington

FLAGSHIP NIAGARA. Reconstructed ship of Com. Perry. Mon.–Sat. 8:30–5, Sun. 12–5.

PENNSYLVANIA FISH COMMISSION, STATE FISH HATCHERY. (Foot of Chestnut St.) Aquarium; Lake Erie fish. Sept.–May daily 7:30–4:30; June–Aug. to 4.

FORT NECESSITY NATIONAL BATTLEFIELD SITE. French and Indian War relics; pioneer household items; bldg. of 1816. Daily 9–5 (winter 10–5). *

Fort Washington

HOPE LODGE. Pennsylvania Georgian house, Federal and Empire period furnishings. Tues.–Sat. 8:30–5, Sun. 12–5.

Gettysburg

ADAMS COUNTY HISTORICAL SOCIETY. (Courthouse) Local history, Civil War archives. Mon.–Fri. 2–4:30.

GETTYSBURG NATIONAL MILITARY PARK. Park museum. Military memorials; historic houses. Visitor Center interpreting the Gettysburg battle; painting by Philippoteaux, the *Gettysburg Cyclorama.* Cemetery. Daily 8–5. *

GETTYSBURG NATIONAL MUSEUM, INC. Civil War relics; electric map of battlefield; Round Top Museum on battlefield. Daily.

LUTHERAN THEOLOGICAL SEMINARY, LUTHERAN HISTORICAL SOCIETY. Bldg. of 1826; religious historical material. Mon.–Fri. 9–5.

Greensburg

WESTMORELAND COUNTY MUSEUM OF ART. (221 N. Main St.) American art, decorative arts; Penn. Dutch folk art; Victorian period rooms. Tues., Thurs. 1–9; Wed., Fri., Sat. 10–5; Sun. 2–5.

Harrisburg

FORT HUNTER MUSEUM. (5300 N. Front St.) Historic house, built 1789, using ruins of old French and Indian War fort; 19th-century dolls, costumes. Tues.–Sun. 10–5.

HISTORICAL SOCIETY OF DAUPHIN COUNTY. (219 S. Front St.) Indian items;

local furniture. Daily (except Sun.) 1–4:30.

PENNSYLVANIA STATE MUSEUM. (State Museum Bldg.) State history, archaeology. American arts and crafts. Science; ethnology. Mon.–Sat. 8:30–5, Sun. 1–5.

Haverford

BRYN MAWR ART CENTER. (746 Panmure Rd.) Exhibitions. Mon.–Fri. 9–5.

Hershey

THE DERBY PRESBYTERIAN CHURCH, SESSION HOUSE. (248 E. Derry Rd.) Old church of 1732. Daily.

HERSHEY ZOO. (Hershey Park) Daily.

Honesdale

WAYNE COUNTY HISTORICAL SOCIETY. (810 Main St.) Local history. Mon.–Thurs., Sat. 12–5; summer: 10–12, 1–4.

Huntingdon

HUNTINGDON COUNTY HISTORICAL SOCIETY. (330 Penn St.) Local history, Indian items. Wed. 10–5.

THE SWIGART MUSEUM. (Museum Park) Antique automobiles. Mon.–Fri. 12–6, weekends 10–8.

Indiana

MUSEUM OF THE HISTORICAL AND GENEALOGICAL SOCIETY OF INDIANA COUNTY, PENNSYLVANIA. (S. 6th St. and Wayne Ave.) County history. Tues. 1:30–4, 6:30–9 (closed July, Aug.).

Jenkintown

ALVERTHORPE PRINT MUSEUM. Graphics coll. of Lessing J. Rosenwald, in Georgian mansion; park.

Kennett Square

LONGWOOD GARDENS. Botanical garden. Conservatories, daily 11–5; gardens 8–sundown.

King of Prussia

THE KING OF PRUSSIA HISTORICAL SOCIETY. (812 Swedesford Rd.) Old Roberts School of about 1848; preservation project near Valley Forge; pioneer life. By appt.

Lancaster

HISTORICAL SOCIETY OF THE EVANGELICAL AND REFORMED CHURCH. (Fackenthal Library, Franklin and Marshall College) Church pewter; art objects; archives. Daily 8 A.M.–10 P.M.; summer 8–5.

LANCASTER COUNTY HISTORICAL SOCIETY. (230 N. President Ave.) Local history; state papers of James Buchanan. Mon.–Sat. 1–5 (closed first two weeks of Sept.).

PENNSYLVANIA FARM MUSEUM OF LANDIS VALLEY. (Kissel Hill Rd.) Agricultural and household items; rural life. Mon.–Sat. 8:30–5, Sun. 12–6 (winter: Mon.–Fri. 8:30–5; Sat. 10–4:30; Sun. 12–4:30). †*

PENNSYLVANIA GERMAN SOCIETY. (Fackenthal Library, Franklin and Marshall College) History, archives. Mon.–Sat. 8–5.

WHEATLAND. (1120 Marietta Ave.) Home, built 1828, of President James Buchanan. Summer: Mon.–Sat. 9–5, Sun. 10–5; Dec.–Mar. Mon.–Sat. 10–4.

Lebanon

LEBANON COUNTY HISTORICAL SOCIETY. (6th and Walnut Sts.) Local history. Mon. 1–5, 7–9.

Lewistown

MIFFLIN COUNTY HISTORICAL SOCIETY, INC. (N. Main and 3rd Sts.) County history, military. Sept.–June Mon., Thurs. 7–9.

Ligonier

FORT LIGONIER MEMORIAL FOUNDATION, INC. Preservation project: British fort, French and Indian War period.

Lima

JOHN J. TYLER ARBORETUM. (Painter and Forge Rds.) Daily, daylight hours.

McKeesport

CITY OF McKEESPORT ARBORETUM. (Renziehausen Park) Roses. Mon.–Sat. 8–4.

Mercer

MERCER COUNTY HISTORICAL SOCIETY. (119 S. Pitt St.) County history; pioneer items, transportation, textiles; historic Magoffin House of 1852. Tues.–Sat. 1–5, Fri. eve. 7–10:30.

Merion

BARNES FOUNDATION ART GALLERY. (Latch's Lane and Lapsely) 19th and 20th century French, American art. †*
BUTEN MUSEUM OF WEDGWOOD. (246 N. Bowman Ave.) Comprehensive coll. of Wedgwood designs; Oct.–May, Tues.–Thurs. 2–5.

Mont Alto

MONT ALTO STATE FOREST ARBORETUM. Weekdays 8–5.

Morrisville

PENNSBURY MANOR. House built by William Penn, 1683–1700; reconstructed. Gardens. Summer: Mon.–Sat. 8:30–5, Sun. 12–6. Winter: Mon.–Sat. 8:30–4:30, Sun. 12–4:30. *

Nazareth

MUSEUM OF MORAVIAN HISTORICAL SOCIETY. (200 block, E. Center St.) Furnishings, musical instruments, books of 18th century; local and Moravian church history; Whitefield House of 1740. By appt.

Norristown

THE HISTORICAL SOCIETY OF MONTGOMERY. (1654 De Kalb St.) 18th-century portraits, furniture. Sept.–May Mon.–Fri. 10–12, 1–4; Sat. 10–12.

Northumberland

JOSEPH PRIESTLY HOUSE. Restored home of English scientist.

Philadelphia

ACADEMY OF NATURAL SCIENCES. (19th St. and Pkwy.) Natural history; *survey;* botanical garden; birds. Mon.–Sat. 10–5, Sun. 1–5 (to 4 June–Aug.). †**
AMERICAN SWEDISH HISTORICAL MUSEUM. (1900 Pattison Ave.) Folk arts, history. Mon.–Fri. 10–5. †*
ATWATER KENT MUSEUM. (15 S. 7th St.) History of city. Mon.–Sat. 9–5, Sun. 9:30–5. †*
BETSY ROSS HOUSE. (239 Arch St.) Daily 10–4:30.
CARL SCHURZ MEMORIAL FOUNDATION, INC. (420 Chestnut St.) German and German-American art, folk art, crafts. Mon.–Fri. 9–5. †
CEDAR GROVE. (Lansdowne Dr., Fairmount Park) Daily 10–5. †*
COLLEGE OF PHYSICIANS OF PHILADELPHIA, MÜTTER MUSEUM. (19 S. 22nd St.) Anatomy, pathology; teaching coll. Mon.–Fri. 9:30–1, 2–4.
DREXEL INSTITUTE OF TECHNOLOGY. (32d and Chestnut Sts.) 19th-century painting, crafts. Mon.–Fri. 9–9, Sat. 9–1.
EDGAR ALLAN POE HOUSE. (530 N. 7th St.) Daily 10–5.
FAIRMOUNT PARK AQUARIUM. (Belmont, W. Fairmount Park) Daily 8:30–4:30.
THE FRANKLIN INSTITUTE AND FELS PLANETARIUM. (20th and Pkwy.) Science, technology; maritime, aviation, industrial, space. Tues.–Sat. 10–5, Sun. 12–5. Planetarium also Wed., Fri. 8 P.M. †**
FREE LIBRARY OF PHILADELPHIA. (Logan Square, 19th and Pkwy.) Rare books, graphics, illuminations, Fraktur. Mon.–Fri. 9–9, Sat. 9–5, Sun. 2–6. †
GERMANTOWN HISTORICAL SOCIETY. (5214 Germantown Ave.) Conyngham-Hacker House; Germantown folk art; Bechtel House, costumes (52 Germantown Ave.); Boynton House, library (5208 Germantown Ave.). Tues., Thurs., Sat. 1–5.
THE HISTORICAL SOCIETY OF PENNSYLVANIA. (1300 Locust St.) Paintings, state history; library. Mon. 1–9, Tues.–Fri. 9–5. †
INDEPENDENCE NATIONAL HISTORICAL PARK (about five blocks; Information Center at 420 Chestnut St.). Independence Hall, Congress Hall, First Bank of the U.S., Carpenters' Hall; Franklin's home. Daily 8:45–5:15. †**
INSURANCE COMPANY OF NORTH AMERICA. (1600 Arch St.) Fire-fighting equipment, prints. Mon.–Fri. 10–4.
LANKENAU HOSPITAL HEALTH MUSEUM.

(Lancaster and City Line Aves.) Medicine and public health. Daily 9–5. †

LETITIA STREET HOUSE. (Lansdowne Dr., Fairmount Park). †

MOORE INSTITUTE OF ART, SCIENCE AND INDUSTRY. (20th and Race Sts.) Art gallery; teaching coll. Mon.–Fri. 9–4, Sat. 10–12.

MOUNT PLEASANT. (Fairmount Park) Daily 10–5. †

THE PENNSYLVANIA ACADEMY OF THE FINE ARTS. (Broad and Cherry Sts.) American art. Tues.–Sat. 10–5, Sun. 1–5. †*

PHILADELPHIA MARITIME MUSEUM. (219 S. 6th St.) Maritime history of U.S. and Delaware Valley ports; art, models, weapons, relics, tools, whaling items. Mon.–Sat. 10–4 (July–Sept. to 5), Sun. 1–5.

PHILADELPHIA METHODIST CONFERENCE HISTORICAL CENTER AND OLD ST. GEORGE METHODIST CHURCH. (326 New St., 235 N. 4th St.) Church history, old church (two bldgs. joined). Daily 10–4.

PENNBROOK MILK COMPANY, THE DAIRY MUSEUM. (500 S. 27th St.) Old dairy equipment. By appt.

PHILADELPHIA ART ALLIANCE. (251 S. 18th St.) *Exhibitions.* Mon.–Sat. 10:30–9, Sun. 1–6 (July, Aug. Mon.–Fri. 10:30 to 6).

PHILADELPHIA COLLEGE OF PHARMACY AND SCIENCE, GLENTWORTH PHARMACY. (43rd St., Kingsessing and Woodland Aves.) Old pharmaceutical items. Daily 9–5.

PHILADELPHIA MUSEUM OF ART. (Benjamin Franklin Pkwy. at 26th St.) *Survey;* period rooms; Pennsylvania and city decorative and folk art. Daily 9–5. †**

PHILIP H. AND A. S. W. ROSENBACH FOUNDATION. (2010 Delancey Pl.) Decorative arts, paintings, tapestries; library. Wed., Fri., Sun. 2–5 (closed Sun. June and July, closed Aug.).

RODIN MUSEUM. (22nd St. and Pkwy.) Drawings, sculpture by August Rodin. Daily 9–5. †*

STRAWBERRY MANSION. (33d and Ridge Ave., Fairmount Park) Tues.–Sun. 11–5 (closed Aug.). †*

SWEETBRIER MANSION. (Fairmount Park) Daily 9–5. †

TRADE AND CONVENTION CENTER, COMMERCIAL MUSEUM DIVISION. (34th St. and Convention Ave.) Anthropology; industrial products of the world; crafts; raw materials; international exhibitions. Mon.–Fri. 10–5, weekends 1–5. †**

UNIVERSITY OF PENNSYLVANIA HERBARIUM. (34th and Walnut) State flora. Daily 9–5.

UNIVERSITY OF PENNSYLVANIA, MORRIS ARBORETUM. (9414 Meadowbrook Ave.–101 Hillcrest Ave.) 170 acres. Daily 9–5 (summer to 8).

UNIVERSITY OF PENNSYLVANIA, UNIVERSITY MUSEUM. (33rd and Spruce Sts.) Anthropology, archaeology, art, ethnology. Tues.–Sat. 10–5, Sun. 1–5. †**

WAGNER FREE INSTITUTE OF SCIENCE. (17th St. and Montgomery Ave.) Natural history survey. Wed., Fri. 2–5.

WOODFORD MANSION. (33rd and Dauphin Sts., E. Fairmount Park) Colonial mansion. Sept.–July Tues.–Sun. 1–5.

ZOOLOGICAL SOCIETY OF PHILADELPHIA. (34th St. and Girard Ave.) Zoo; children's zoo. Daily 10–5 (summer weekends to 6). †**

Pittsburgh

BLOCK HOUSE. (25 Penn Ave.) Block house from old Fort Pitt, 1764. Tues.–Sun. 9–5.

BUHL PLANETARIUM AND INSTITUTE OF POPULAR SCIENCE. (Federal and Ohio Sts.) Physical science; astronomy. Daily 1–10:30. †*

CARNEGIE INSTITUTE, CARNEGIE MUSEUM. (4400 Forbes Ave.) Natural history: *survey;* anthropology. Powdermill Nature Reserve of 1400 acres (Star Rt. S., Rector, Penna.). Mon.–Sat. 10–5, Sun. 2–5. Tues. 10–10 autumn and spring. †*

CARNEGIE INSTITUTE, MUSEUM OF ART. (4400 Forbes Ave.) American painting; contemp. world art; exhibitions. Mon.–Fri. 10–5, Sun. 2–5; Tues. 10–10 winter. †*

CONSERVATORY AVIARY. (West Park, Northside) Tropical and subtropical birds. Daily 9–5.

THE FISHER COLLECTION OF ALCHEMICAL AND HISTORICAL PICTURES. (717 Forbes Ave.) Paintings, graphics of medicine, alchemy, pharmacology; collection of chmn. of Fisher Scientific Co. Mon.–Fri. 9–4:30.

HISTORICAL SOCIETY OF WESTERN PENNSYLVANIA. (4338 Bigelow Blvd.)

Regional history; glass. Tues.–Fri. 10–4:30, Sat. 10–12.

PHIPPS CONSERVATORY. (Schenley Park) Botanical gardens. Daily 9–5.

UNIVERSITY OF PITTSBURGH, STEPHEN FOSTER MEMORIAL. (Forbes St.) Foster memorabilia; music items. Mon.–Fri. 9–4:30.

Pottstown

POTTSTOWN HISTORICAL SOCIETY, POTTSGROVE MANSION. (W. High St.) 18th-century furnishings; local archives. Mon.–Sat. 9–5, Sun. 1–5.

Pottsville

HISTORICAL SOCIETY OF SCHUYLKILL COUNTY. (14 N. 3d St.) County history in photographs; coal mining, transportation. Tues.–Sat. 9:30–12, 1:30–4:30.

Prospect Park

MORTON HOMESTEAD. Swedish style log house of 17th century. Tues.–Sat. 8:30–5, Sun. 12–5.

Reading

HISTORICAL SOCIETY OF BERKS COUNTY. (940 Centre Ave.) Furnishings, vehicles, textiles, dental and surgical instruments, needlework, local art. Tues.–Sat. 9–4, Sun. 2–5 (closed Sun. in summer).

THE READING PUBLIC MUSEUM AND ART GALLERY. (500 Museum Rd.) American art, natural history, botanical garden. Mon.–Fri. 9–5, Sat. 9–12, Sun. 2–5. †

Red Lion

THE LAUCKS FARM AND CRAFT MUSEUM. Folk arts, agricultural implements, country store. May 30–Labor Day, Sun. and holidays 1–5 and by appt.

Scottdale

WESTMORELAND-FAYETTE HISTORICAL SOCIETY. Local history, anthropology, natural history. Mid-May–mid-Oct. weekends 2–5.

Scranton

EVERHART MUSEUM. (Nay Aug Park) Natural history; North and South American, African, Oceanic primitive and folk art; ethnology; planetarium. Tues.–Sat. 10–5, Sun. 2–5.

LACKAWANNA HISTORICAL SOCIETY. (232 Monroe Ave.) Local history. Tues.–Fri. 10–5, Sat. 10–12.

MUNICIPAL ZOO. (Nay Aug Park) Daily.

State College

PENNSYLVANIA STATE UNIVERSITY, THE MINERAL INDUSTRIES MUSEUM. Mining, esp. in Penna.; geology, metallurgy, ceramics. Mon.–Sat. 9–5, Sun. 1–5.

Stroudsburg

MONROE COUNTY HISTORICAL SOCIETY. (9th and Main Sts.) County history; dolls; furnishings and household items; Indian items. Winter, Tues. 2–4.

Swarthmore

SWARTHMORE COLLEGE, ARTHUR HOYT SCOTT HORTICULTURAL FOUNDATION. Botanical garden, arboretum. Daily.

SWARTHMORE COLLEGE, FRIENDS HISTORICAL LIBRARY. Paintings by Edward Hicks; Quaker items, mss., costumes. Mon.–Fri. 9–5, Sat. 9–12; summer to 4:30 (closed Sat., Aug.).

Titusville

DRAKE WELL MEMORIAL PARK MUSEUM. Early Penna. oil industry items; paintings and photographs; oil history; research. Nov.–Apr. daily 8:30–4:30; May–Oct. Mon.–Sat. 8:30–5; Sun. 12–5. *

Towanda

BRADFORD COUNTY HISTORICAL SOCIETY MUSEUM. (Court St.) Early paintings, portraits; local history. Mon. 2–4, 7–9; Tues.–Fri. 9:30–11:30, 2–4.

University Park

PENNSYLVANIA STATE UNIVERSITY, ART GALLERY. (Hetzel Union Bldg.) *Exhibitions.* Daily 8 A.M.–10 P.M.

PENNSYLVANIA STATE UNIVERSITY, HERBARIUM. Pennsylvania and North American plants. Mon.–Fri. 8–5, Sat. 8–12.

PENNSYLVANIA STATE UNIVERSITY INSECT COLLECTION. (Frear Laboratory) Research, teaching coll. Mon.–Fri. 9–5.

Valley Forge

VALLEY FORGE HISTORICAL SOCIETY, WASHINGTON MEMORIAL MUSEUM. Early American, Revolutionary War and George Washington items; Mon.–Sat. 9–5, Sun. 1–5.

VALLEY FORGE STATE PARK. Washington's Headquarters; camp hospital; restored fortifications. Daily 9–5. †*

Washington

WASHINGTON COUNTY HISTORICAL SOCIETY, LEMOYNE HOUSE. (49 E. Maiden St.) Local history. Mon.–Fri. 1–5.

Washington Crossing

BOWMAN'S HILL STATE WILDFLOWER PRESERVE. (Washington Crossing State Park) Botanical garden; wild plants of Penna. Daily, daylight hours.

WASHINGTON CROSSING STATE PARK. (Rt. 32) Arboretum, botanical garden, nature center. Thompson-Neely House of 1702, where attack on Trenton was planned. House: Mon.–Sat. 10–5, Sun. 1–5. Park: 9–sundown.

Waterford

FORT LEBOEUF. Models of colonial forts. Tues.–Sat. 8:30–5, Sun. 12–5.

Watsontown

WARRIOR RUN CHURCH. Restoration of 19th-century church, earlier graveyard. Tues.–Sat. 8:30–5, Sun. 12–5.

West Chester

CHESTER COUNTY HISTORICAL SOCIETY. (225 N. High St.) Indian, military items; models of local inventions; early shops, kitchen, schoolroom. Mon.–Sat. 1–5, Wed. eve. 7–9 (closed Aug.).

DAVID TOWNSEND HOUSE. (225 N. Matlack St.) Empire furnishings. Apr.–Nov. Tues., Thurs., Sat. 2–5.

Wilkes-Barre

WYOMING HISTORICAL AND GEOLOGICAL SOCIETY. (69 S. Franklin St.) Local history, natural history; industrial, military items. Tues.–Sat. 10–5.

Williamsport

LYCOMING HISTORICAL SOCIETY. (858 W. 4th St.) Local history; Civil War; early lumbering items. Oct.–June, Sun. 2–5.

Womelsdorf

CONRAD WEISER HOMESTEAD. Colonial house, grave, park. Mon.–Sat. 8:30–5, Sun. 12–5.

Wyoming

SWETLAND HOMESTEAD. (885 Wyoming Ave.) Tools and furniture, house of 1797. July–Sept. Tues.–Sun. 12–6.

York

THE HISTORICAL SOCIETY OF YORK COUNTY. (250 E. Market St.) Local history, natural history; American primitive paintings; musical instruments; Indian items. Tues.–Sat. 9–5.

MARTIN MEMORIAL LIBRARY. (159 E. Market) Art exhibitions. Mon.–Fri. 10–9, Sat. 9–6.

RHODE ISLAND

Anthony-Coventry

GENERAL NATHANAEL GREENE HOMESTEAD. (50 Taft St.) Wed., weekends 2–5.

Ashaway

TOMAQUAG INDIAN MEMORIAL MUSEUM. (Burdickville Rd.) New England Indian culture. Daily 10–7 (mid-Oct.–Apr. 2–5).

Block Island

BLOCK ISLAND HISTORICAL MUSEUM. (New Shoreham) Local history, crafts; exhibitions. Mon., Wed., Sat. 11–4.

Bristol

BRISTOL HISTORICAL SOCIETY MUSEUM. (42 Court St.) Local history, documents in old county jail. Wed. 2:30–5.

East Greenwich

THE JAMES MITCHELL VARNUM HOUSE AND MUSEUM. (57 Pierce St.) Period furnishings, coach house; bldg. of 1773. June: Sun. only. July–Sept. Wed., Sun.

VARNUM MILITARY AND NAVAL MUSEUM. (Main and Division Sts.) Military items, all U.S. wars.

Johnston

CLEMENCE-IRONS HOUSE. (38 George Waterman Rd.) Stone-end house of about 1680. Maintained by Soc. for the Preservation of New England Antiq. By appt. during May–mid-Oct.

Kingston

SOUTH COUNTY ART ASSOCIATION. (1319 Kingstown Rd.) Art exhibitions; historic Helme House of 1760. Tues.–Sun. 3:30–5:30.

UNIVERSITY OF RHODE ISLAND, DEPARTMENT OF ZOOLOGY. Rhode Island and New England specimens; reference coll. Mon.–Fri. 8–5, Sat. 8–12.

Lincoln

ELEAZER ARNOLD HOUSE. (449 Great Rd.) Period furnishings in stone-end house of about 1687. Maintained by Soc. for the Preservation of New England Antiq. Mid-June–mid-Oct. Tues.–Sat. 12–5.

Little Compton

LITTLE COMPTON HISTORICAL SOCIETY. (West Rd.) Local historic buildings, furnishings. Late spring–early fall, daily (except Thurs.).

Middletown

WHITEHALL. (Berkeley Ave.) Historic house; delft and English delft. July–Labor Day daily 10–5.

Newport

ART ASSOCIATION OF NEWPORT. (76 Bellevue Ave.) Local art, exhibitions. Mon.–Sat. 10–5, Sun. 2–5.

THE BREAKERS. Summer mansion, 1895; garden. May, weekends; Memorial Day–Oct. daily 10–5; Sun. (July, Aug.) till 9. †*

THE BREAKERS STABLE. (Coggeshall Ave.) Vehicles: carriages, sleighs. July 1–Sept. 5: daily 10–5. †*

NATIONAL LAWN TENNIS HALL OF FAME AND TENNIS MUSEUM, INC. (Newport Casino, 194 Bellevue Ave.) Trophies, equipment. May–Oct. Mon.–Fri. 9–5, weekends 11–5. †

NEWPORT HISTORICAL SOCIETY. (82 Truro St.) State and city history. Tues.–Fri. 9:30–4:30, Sat. 9:30–12. †

NICHOLS-WANTON-HUNTER HOUSE. (Washington St.) Newport furniture, house of 1748. June–Sept. daily 10–5.

PRESERVATION SOCIETY OF NEWPORT COUNTY. (2 Long Wharf) Portraits, decorative arts. Brick Market of 1762. Mon.–Fri. 9–5. †*

TOURO SYNAGOGUE. Oldest synagogue in U.S., 1763. July–early Sept. daily (except Sat.) 10–5. †*

TRINITY CHURCH. Built 1726. Mid-June–early Sept. daily 10–5. †*

WANTON-LYMAN-HAZARD HOUSE. (B'way) Built 1675. July–early Sept. daily 10–5. †*

WHITE HORSE TAVERN. (Farewell and Marlborough Sts.) Authentic furnishings in Colonial tavern, built 1673. Tues.–Sun. †*

North Kingston

CASEY FARM. Farm bldgs. of about 1750. Maintained by Soc. for the Preservation of New England Antiq. June–Sept. Mon., Wed., Sat. 2–5.

North Kingstown

SOUTH COUNTY MUSEUM. Early state farm implements, vehicles. May 31–Oct. 12.

North Smithfield

THE PILGRIM JOHN HOWLAND SOCIETY, INC. (73 Pound Hill Rd.) Maintains Jabez Howland House, Plymouth, Mass., and other Howland family sites. Colonial period furnishings. Daily 9:30–5.

Pawtucket

OLD SLATER MILL MUSEUM. (Roosevelt Ave.) Textile industry. Tues.–Sat. 10–5, Sun. 2–5.

Peace Dale

MUSEUM OF PRIMITIVE CULTURES. (Columbia St. and Kingstown Rd.) North American anthropology. Tues.–Sat. 10–12, 1–5.

Providence

BETSEY WILLIAMS COTTAGE. (Roger Williams Park)

BROWN UNIVERSITY, ANNMARY BROWN MEMORIAL. (21 Brown St.) 16th–18th-century painting; 15th-century books; Renaissance. Mon.–Fri. 9–5, Sat. 9–12 (closed Sat. in summer).

GOVERNOR STEPHEN HOPKINS HOUSE. (Hopkins and Benefit Sts.) Furnishings, house of 1707. Wed.–Sat. 1–4.

RHODE ISLAND HISTORICAL SOCIETY, JOHN BROWN HOUSE. (52 Power St.) State history, art, decorative arts; house of 1786. Mon.–Fri. 9–5, Tues. eve. 7–9, Sun. 3–5 (closed July and Aug.). †*

RHODE ISLAND SCHOOL OF DESIGN, MUSEUM OF ART. (224 Benefit St.) *Survey;* decorative arts. Mon.–Sat. 11–5, Sun. 2–5. †*

ROGER WILLIAMS PARK MUSEUM AND PLANETARIUM. Natural history; planetarium. Mon.–Sat. 9–5, Sun. 2–5 (July, Aug. Mon.–Sat. 9–4). *

Saunderstown

GILBERT STUART MEMORIAL, INC. (Gilbert Stuart Rd.) Bldg. of 1750, Grist Mill of 1757. Mon.–Thurs., Sat., Sun. 10–5.

West Barrington

STEAMSHIP HISTORICAL SOCIETY OF AMERICA, INC. (53 Annawamscutt Rd.) History of steam navigation; library, photographic coll., research. (Exhibits at Mystic Seaport, Conn.) Daily.

Wickford

RICHARD SMITH BLOCK HOUSE. (Post Rd., North Kingston) Antique furnishings, costumes, 18th-century garden in house of 1677. Mon.–Wed., Fri., Sat. 10–5, Sun. 12–5.

SMITH'S CASTLE, COCUMSCUSSOC. Architectural details, furnishings in house of 1680 where Roger Williams lived. Mon.–Wed., Fri., Sat. 11–5, Sun. 2–5.

SOUTH CAROLINA

Beaufort

THE BEAUFORT MUSEUM. (Armory Bldg., Craven St.) Bldg. of 1776; local history, natural history. Thurs.–Tues. 4–6, Wed. 10–12.

Charleston

CAROLINA ART ASSOCIATION, GIBBES ART GALLERY. (135 Meeting St.) Works by state artists; exhibitions.

CHARLESTON MUSEUM. (125 Rutledge Ave.) First museum in U.S. City and state history, natural history, Charleston furniture. Planetarium. Heyward-Washington House (87 Church St.); Manigault House (350 Meeting St.). Mon.–Sat. 10–5, Sun. 2–5. †*

THE CITADEL MEMORIAL MILITARY MUSEUM. (The Citadel, Military College of S.C.) State history, military equipment. Sun.–Fri. 2–5, Sat. 9–5.

CONFEDERATE MUSEUM. (Market and Meeting Sts.) Market Hall, 1841. Confederate relics. Mar. 1–June 4, Mon., Tues., Thurs.–Sat. 10–1. †

Clemson

COLUMBIA MUSEUM OF ART. (Senate and Bull Sts.) Decorative arts; Renaissance, contemp. American painting; graphics. Tues.–Sat. 10–5, Sun. 2–6. †

Florence

FLORENCE MUSEUM. (Graham and Spruce Sts.) American Indian, Oriental, African art, art objects. Tues.–Sat. 10–5, Sun. 2–5.

Greenville

BOB JONES UNIVERSITY ART GALLERY

AND MUSEUM. Religious art; Middle East archaeology. Tues.–Fri. 9–11, 1–5; Sat. 10–5, Sun. 1–3:30 (June–Aug. daily except Mon. 2–4, 5–6).

GREENVILLE MUSEUM OF ART. (106 Dupont Dr.) Painting, design, decorative arts, sculpture; exhibitions. Tues.–Sat. 10–5, Sun. 2–6.

SOUTH CAROLINA BAPTIST HISTORICAL SOCIETY. (Furman University Library) Religious history, memorabilia of Richard Furman, Baptist pioneer. Daily 8 A.M.–10 P.M.

Kings Creek

KINGS MOUNTAIN NATIONAL MILITARY PARK. Park museum. Revolutionary War items; battlefield trail. Mon.–Sat. 8–5, Sun. 9:30–5:30. *

Pawley's Island

BROOKGREEN GARDENS. Botanical garden; ante-bellum rice plantations; garden sculpture. Zoo. Daily (except Mon.) 9–5:30.

Rock Hill

CHILDREN'S NATURE MUSEUM OF YORK COUNTY. (Fewell Park) Natural history, Indian lore, African art. Tues.–Sat. 10–5, Sun. 3–5.

Spartanburg

WOFFORD COLLEGE PLANETARIUM. Mon.–Wed. 8 P.M. during school year; Mon.–Fri. 11:30–12:30 by appt.

SOUTH DAKOTA

Brookings

SOUTH DAKOTA STATE COLLEGE MUSEUM. (Extension Bldg. 204) History: farming, household implements. Sun. 2:30–4:30.

Deadwood

ADAMS MEMORIAL MUSEUM. Mineralogy; pioneer life. Daily 9–5 (summer 8–8).

Hot Springs

JEWEL CAVE NATIONAL MONUMENT VISITOR CENTER. (Wind Cave National Park) Tour of cave; research on cave formations. Memorial Day–Labor Day daily 8–5. *

WIND CAVE NATIONAL PARK. Herbarium; geology, zoology, Indian artifacts. May–Sept. daily 8–5. *

Interior

BADLANDS NATIONAL MONUMENT. Park museum. Geology, archaeology. Daily 8–5 (summer 7–7). *

Keystone

MOUNT RUSHMORE NATIONAL MEMORIAL. Park museum. Tools, models for sculptures. Daily 8–5 (summer 6 A.M.–10 P.M.). *

Madison

LAKE COUNTY HISTORICAL SOCIETY. (Courthouse) Local history, artifacts, zoology. Thurs. 1:30–4:30.

Pierre

SOUTH DAKOTA STATE HISTORICAL MUSEUM. (Memorial Bldg., Capitol Ave.) State history, agriculture, archaeology, ethnology, natural history, transportation, costumes. Mon.–Fri. 8–12, 1–5; June–Aug. Sun. 1–5 also.

Rapid City

BLACK HILLS REPTILE GARDENS. (S. 8th St.) Zoo: snakes. Daily 5 A.M.–9 P.M.

SOUTH DAKOTA SCHOOL OF MINES AND TECHNOLOGY, MUSEUM OF GEOLOGY. (E. St., Joe St.) Mineralogy, paleontology, natural history. Mon.–Sat. 8–6, Sun. 2–8. Winter: Mon.–Fri. 8–5, Sat. 8–12.

Sioux Falls

PETTIGREW MUSEUM. (131 N. Duluth Ave.) Archaeology, history, natural history. Mon.–Sat. 9–12, 1:30–5; Sun. 2–5.

Vermilion

SHERMAN PARK ZOO. Daily 8–sundown. UNIVERSITY OF SOUTH DAKOTA, W. H.

OVER MUSEUM. Anthropology, history, natural history; research American Indian archaeology, ethnology. Mon.–Sat. 9–5, Sun. 2–4:30.

TENNESSEE

Chattanooga

GEORGE THOMAS HUNTER GALLERY OF ART. (10 Bluff View) Exhibitions of work by southern artists. Tues.–Sat. 10–5, Fri. eve. 7–9, Sun. 2–5.

Columbia

JAMES K. POLK ANCESTRAL HOME. Built by the President's father, 1816; period furnishings. Mon.–Sat. 9–12, 1–5, Sun. 1–5.

Gatlinburg

GREAT SMOKY MOUNTAINS NATIONAL PARK. Pioneer museum, farm bldgs., mill; Sugarland Visitor Center; demonstration of cornmeal grinding at mill. Apr.–Oct. daily 9–5. *

Greeneville

ANDREW JOHNSON NATIONAL MONUMENT. Park museum; Andrew Johnson Home, restored to 1869; Andrew Johnson Tailor Shop; cemetery. Daily 8–5. *

Hermitage

THE HERMITAGE. Home, farm, furnishings of Andrew Jackson; family items. Oct.–Mar. daily 8–4; Apr.–Sept. 8–5. *

Hohenwald

MERIWETHER LEWIS NATIONAL MONUMENT VISITOR CENTER. (Natchez Trace Pkwy.) Lewis' grave; history of explorations; maps. Daily 9–5. *

Knoxville

GOVERNOR WILLIAM BLOUNT MANSION. (200 W. Hill Ave.) House, 1792, of signer of Constitution, first state gov.; period furnishings. Mon.–Fri. 9:30–5, Sun. 2–5 (closed Nov.–Apr.).
UNIVERSITY OF TENNESSEE, THE FRANK

H. MCCLUNG MUSEUM. Tennessee Valley archaeology, natural history, Indian ethnology, art gallery.

Maryville

MARYVILLE COLLEGE FINE ARTS CENTER. Contemp. prints; exhibitions. Mon.–Fri. 8:30–4:30, Sat. 8:30–12.

Memphis

BROOKS MEMORIAL ART GALLERY. (Overton Park) Kress; European and American painting; decorative arts. Mon.–Sat. 10–5, Sun. 2–5.
MEMPHIS MUSEUM. (233 Tilton Rd. and Central Ave., Chickasaw Gardens) History, natural history, planetarium. Tues.–Sat. 9–5 (Nov.–Mar. to 4:30); Sun. 1–5.
MEMPHIS ZOOLOGICAL GARDEN AND AQUARIUM. Zoo. Summer: Mon.–Fri. 9:30–5:30, weekends to 6. Winter: Mon.–Fri. 9:30–5, weekends to 5:30.
SOUTHWESTERN AT MEMPHIS, SOUTHWESTERN ARBORETUM. (2000 N. Pkwy.) Daily.
W. C. PAUL ARBORETUM. (800 S. Cherry Rd.) Daylight hours.

Nashville

CHILDREN'S MUSEUM. (724 2d Ave.) Art, natural history, planetarium. Tues.–Sat. 10–5, Sun. 2–5. †*
FORT NASHBOROUGH. (1st Ave. S.) Log replica of first settlement, 1779; implements, furniture. Tues.–Fri. 9–4, weekends 9–12.
GEORGE PEABODY COLLEGE FOR TEACHERS MUSEUM. (21st Ave. S.) European painting, sculpture; contemp. American painting. Mon.–Fri. 9–5, weekends 1–5.
THE PARTHENON. (Centennial Park). Bldg. is replica of Greek Parthenon. Art gallery. American paintings; exhibitions. Mon.–Sat. 9–4:45, Sun. 1:30–5:45.
THE TENNESSEE BOTANICAL GARDENS AND FINE ARTS CENTER, INC. (Cheekwood) Works by state artists; decorative arts; Georgian mansion; gardens. Tues.–Sat. 10–5, Sun. 1–5. Gardens daily, 8 to sundown. †
TENNESSEE STATE MUSEUM. (War Memorial Bldg., Capitol Blvd.) State his-

tory, natural history, military, historical portraits. Mon.–Sat. 8–4:30, Sun. 2–4.

Oak Ridge

AMERICAN MUSEUM OF ATOMIC ENERGY. (Jefferson Circle) Explains scientific principles, potential uses of atomic energy. Mon.–Sat. 9:30–5, Sun. 12:30–6:30. †

Pittsburg Landing

SHILOH NATIONAL MILITARY PARK MUSEUM. History, Civil War battlefield. Daily 8–4:30 (summer to 5:30). *

Sewanee

UNIVERSITY OF THE SOUTH ART GALLERY. Paintings, graphics; exhibitions. Mon.–Sat. 3–5.

Smyrna

SAM DAVIS MEMORIAL. Garden, antique furnishings, firearms, Civil War relics in bldg. of 1810. Mon.–Sat. 8–5, Sun. 1–5.

TEXAS

Abilene

HARDIN-SIMMONS UNIVERSITY ART GALLERY. (Hickory and Ambler Sts.) Local artists; teaching coll. Mon.–Fri. 8–5, Sat. 8–12.

Alpine

BIG BEND HISTORICAL MUSEUM. (Sul Ross State College Campus) Local history, anthropology, geology; botanical garden. Daily 3–5.

Austin

DAUGHTERS OF THE REPUBLIC OF TEXAS MUSEUM. (Old General Land Office Bldg., 11th and Brazos Sts.) Furniture, costumes, flags, branding irons. Tues.–Sat. 9–12, 2–5.

FRENCH LEGATION. (E. 7th and San Marcos Sts.) Official residence of French chargé d'affaires to Republic of Texas; period furnishings 1840; garden. Daily 1–6.

O. HENRY MEMORIAL MUSEUM. (409 E. 5th St.) Furnishings, memorabilia in author's home, built 1886. Mon., Wed.–Sat. 10–12, 2–5.

TEXAS CATHOLIC HISTORICAL SOCIETY, INC. (Congress and W. 16th St.) Catholic, Spanish archives, historical items relating to Texas, Mexico, Southwest. Mon.–Fri. 9–12.

TEXAS FINE ARTS ASSOCIATION, LAGUNA GLORIA GALLERY. (3809 W. 35th St.) Texas and Southwest artists; exhibitions. Tues.–Sat. 10–5, Sun. 2–5.

UNIVERSITY OF TEXAS ANTHROPOLOGY MUSEUM. (Pearce Hall) Texas archaeology. Mon.–Fri. 8–12, 2–5.

Baird

UNIVERSITY OF TEXAS, TEXAS MEMORIAL MUSEUM. (24th and Trinity Sts.) State history, archaeology, paleontology; research, teaching coll. Mon.–Sat. 9–5, Sun. 2–5.

CALLAHAN COUNTY MUSEUM. (3d and Market Sts.) Local history. Mon.–Fri. 1–5.

Beaumont

BEAUMONT ART MUSEUM. (2675 Gulf St.) Gallery; exhibitions. Sept.–June, Tues.–Fri. 10–4, Sun. 2–5.

Big Bend National Park

BIG BEND NATIONAL PARK. Nature trails. Daily. *

Brazos River

THE FORT BELKNAP SOCIETY. Preservation project: restoration of arsenal, commissary, barracks, other structures of fort, 1851; military equipment, costumes, portraits. Sun.–Fri. 8–5; Sat. half-day.

Canyon

PANHANDLE-PLAINS HISTORICAL MUSEUM. (2401 Fourth Ave.) State, regional history, ethnology, paleontology, archives; art, regional and European decorative arts. Mon.–Sat. 9–5, Sun. 2–6. †*

Clifton

BOSQUE MEMORIAL MUSEUM. Pioneer, Indian, local natural history items. Sun. 2–5.

Corpus Christi

CENTENNIAL MUSEUM. (902 Park) Art coll.; exhibitions. Tues.–Fri. 10–5, weekends 2–5.

CORPUS CHRISTI JUNIOR MUSEUM. (1202 N. Water St.) Natural history. Tues.–Sun. 9–12 for school classes; 2–5 for public.

Cuero

DE WITT COUNTY HISTORICAL MUSEUM. (2075 E. Main St.) Local history, Indian artifacts. Mon.–Sat. 1–5.

Dallas

DALLAS HEALTH AND SCIENCE MUSEUM. (Fair Park) Public health, medicine; planetarium. Mon.–Sat. 9–5, Sun. 2–6. †*

DALLAS HISTORICAL SOCIETY. (Hall of State, Fair Park) State and regional history; prints, crafts, archives. Mon.–Sat. 9–5, Sun. 2–6.

DALLAS MUSEUM FOR CONTEMPORARY ARTS. (3415 Cedar Springs Rd.) Contemp. painting, graphics; exhibitions. Tues. 11:30–8, Wed.–Sat. 11:30–5:30, Sun. 2–5. †

DALLAS MUSEUM OF FINE ARTS. (Fair Park) Survey; Texas folk art. Tues.–Sat. 10–5. †*

DALLAS MUSEUM OF NATURAL HISTORY. (Fair Park) Zoology. Mon.–Sat. 8–5, Sun. 12–6. †

DALLAS ZOO AND DALLAS AQUARIUM. (524 S. Marsalis Ave.) Zoo: daily 8 A.M.–9 P.M. Aquarium: Mon.–Sat. 8–5, Sun. 12–6.

MCCORD THEATRE MUSEUM. (Fondren Library, Southern Methodist University) Costumes, programs, pictures, other theatrical items. By appt.

SOUTHERN METHODIST UNIVERSITY, THE A. V. LANE MUSEUM OF ARCHAEOLOGY. Egyptian, Babylonian artifacts. By appt.

Denison

EISENHOWER BIRTHPLACE. (Lamar and Day Sts.) Furnishings, family items in house built 1880. Daily 10–5.

Denton

NORTH TEXAS STATE COLLEGE, STATE HISTORICAL COLLECTIONS. Crafts, transportation. Mon.–Sat. 2–5.

TEXAS WOMAN'S UNIVERSITY, COLLEGE OF HOUSEHOLD ARTS AND SCIENCES, MUSEUM OF HISTORIC COSTUMES. Inaugural gowns of wives of presidents and governors of Texas; historic women's wear. Mon.–Fri. 8–5, Sat. 8–12.

TEXAS WOMAN'S UNIVERSITY, MUSEUM OF ART. (Fine Arts Bldg.) Paintings, graphics, primitive art; exhibitions. Daily 8–12, 1–5.

El Paso

EL PASO MUSEUM OF ART. (1200 block Montana) Survey; Kress; western regional art. Tues.–Sat. 10–5, Sun. 2–5. †*

TEXAS WESTERN COLLEGE, EL PASO CENTENNIAL MUSEUM. (W. College Ave.) Regional archaeology, anthropology, folk art, paleontology; research. Mon.–Fri. 8–5, Sat. 8–12, Sun. 2–5.

Fort Bliss

REPLICA MUSEUM. (U. S. Army Air Defense Center) Military equipment, uniforms, firearms. Replicas of old Fort Bliss bldgs.; history of fort. Tues.–Sun. 10–4.

Fort Stockton

ANNIE RIGGS MEMORIAL MUSEUM. (301 S. Main St.) Pioneer items; art exhibitions. Mon., Tues., Thurs.–Sat. 9:30–11:30, 2:30–5:30; Sun. 3–6.

Fort Worth

AMON CARTER MEMORIAL MUSEUM. (Carter Square) Works by Remington, Russell; western Indian art; gardens. †

FORT WORTH ART CENTER. (1309 Montgomery St.) 19th- and 20th-century American paintings, graphics. Tues.–Sat. 11–9, Sun. 2–9. *

FORT WORTH BOTANIC GARDEN. (3220 Botanic Garden Drive) Daily, daylight hours. Greenhouse closed Sat., open Sun. 2–4.

FORT WORTH CHILDREN'S MUSEUM. (1501 Montgomery St.) Nature center, pioneer items; mineralogy, Texas birds. Planetarium. Tues.–Sat. 9–5, Sun. 2–5. †*

FORT WORTH PUBLIC LIBRARY. (9th and Throckmorten Sts.) Costumes, decorative arts, cartoons, folk art, book plates. Mon.–Fri. 9–9, Sat. 9–6, Sun. 2–6.

FORT WORTH ZOOLOGICAL PARK. ZOO; aquarium. Daily, daylight hours. Zoo bldgs. and aquarium: 9:30–5:30 (summer to 9:30 P.M.).

TEXAS CHRISTIAN UNIVERSITY, NATURAL HISTORY MUSEUM. (University Dr.) Teaching coll. Mon.–Sat. 8 A.M.–10 P.M.

Freeport

BRAZORIA COUNTY MUSEUM. Children's museum: natural history, art, local history. Work with schools; during school hours.

Galveston

GALVESTON HISTORICAL FOUNDATION, INC. (3806 Ave. Q) City history, documents; historic Williams-Tucker House of 1838–40 (3601 Ave. P). June–Aug. daily 2–5; otherwise weekends only.

Goliad

GOLIAD STATE PARK MUSEUM. (Hwy. 183) Park museum. Relics of Mexican War, 1835. Mission Espiritu Santo de Zuniga, restored Spanish chapel, granary, of about 1749. Daily 6 A.M.–8:30 P.M.

Houston

CONTEMPORARY ARTS ASSOCIATION. (6945 Fannin St.) 20th-century European and American works; exhibitions. Mon.–Sat. 9–5, Sun. 2–6. †

HARRIS COUNTY HERITAGE AND CONSERVATION SOCIETY. (Sam Houston Historical Park, 212 Dallas Ave.) Historic Kellum-Noble House, furnishings 1836–50. Tues.–Sat. 10–4, Sun. 1–5.

HOUSTON MUSEUM OF NATURAL HISTORY. Zoology. Daily 9:30–5.

HOUSTON ZOOLOGICAL GARDENS. (Hermann Park) Zoo. 9:30–sundown.

MUSEUM OF FINE ARTS OF HOUSTON, TEXAS. (Main at Montrose Blvd.) *Survey; Kress.* Tues.–Sat. 9:30–5:30, Sun. 10–6, Wed. eves. to 9:30. †*

SAN JACINTO MUSEUM OF HISTORY ASSOCIATION, SAN JACINTO BATTLE MONUMENT. (LaPorte, E. of Houston) State and regional history, memorial to 1836 battle for Texas independence. Tues.–Sat. 9:30–5:30, Sun. 10–6.

Huntsville

SAM HOUSTON MEMORIAL MUSEUM. (1804 Ave. L; Sam Houston State Teachers College) State history; Houston's first Texas home; Steamboat House where he died; period furnishings in houses; personal effects. Daily 9–5.

Jacksboro

FORT RICHARDSON MUSEUM. Local history; farm, military items; Old Fort Richardson Hospital bldg. of 1809. June–Aug. daily 1–5.

Langtry

JUDGE ROY BEAN MUSEUM. House of 1892. Daily 9–6.

LANGTRY FRONTIER MUSEUM. Roy Bean's Opera House of 1901. Daily 9–6.

Lubbock

TEXAS TECHNOLOGICAL COLLEGE, WEST TEXAS MUSEUM. Natural history, anthropology, archaeology, paleontology. Planetarium. Tues.–Fri. 8–12, 1–5, Sat. 8–12, Sun. 3–6.

Midland

COLEPARK ZOO. (Cloverdale Rd.) West Texas mammals. Daily (except Mon.) 9–5:30 (summer to 7:30).

MIDLAND COUNTY MUSEUM. (301 W. Missouri) Local history, military items, natural history. Mon.–Fri. 2–5.

Monahans Sandhills State Park

THE SANDHILLS MUSEUM. Park museum. Anthropology, archaeology, zoology, botanical gardens. Weekends 10–sundown; Mon.–Fri. 4–sundown, June–Aug.

Nacogdoches

OLD STONE FORT. (Stephen F. Austin College Campus) Guns, arrowheads in bldg. of 1779. Daily (except Tues.).

New Braunfels

SOPHIENBURG MEMORIAL MUSEUM. (401 W. Coll St.) Local household items, tools, guns. May–Sept. Mon.–Sat. 3–6; Oct.–May Mon., Fri. 3–6; all year Sun. 2–6.

Orange

ORANGE JUNIOR MUSEUM. (2111 W. Burton St.) History, natural history, aquarium; art exhibitions. Sun.–Fri. 3–5, Sat. 10–12.

San Angelo

FORT CONCHO MUSEUM. (716 Burges St.) Historic house of 1876. History, natural history. Mon.–Sat. 9–5, Sun. aft.

San Antonio

THE ALAMO. (Alamo Plaza) Historic house, chapel of 1744; Historical items, documents. Mon.–Sat. 9–5, Sun. 10–5.

BUCKHORN HALL OF HORNS. (600 Simpson St.) Horned mammals, horn coll. Daily 10–6.

HERTZBERG CIRCUS COLLECTION. (San Antonio Public Library, 210 W. Market St.) Circus items, archives. Tues.–Sat. 9–5:30. †

MARION KOOGLER MCNAY ART INSTITUTE. (6000 N. New Braunfels) 19th- and 20th-century French, American works; Gothic and Renaissance items. Tues., Wed., Fri., Sat. 9–5, Thurs. 9–9, Sun. 2–5. †*

MISSION DE LA PURISIMA CONCEPCION DE ACUNA. (Mission Rd.) Church of 1731, still in use; Spanish architecture, furnishings. June–early Sept. daily 9–5; otherwise weekends only.

O. HENRY HOUSE. (600 Simpson St.) First eds., furnishings in house of 1855 rented by author in 1894–95. Mon.–Sat. 10–6, Sun. 1–6.

SPANISH GOVERNOR'S PALACE. Restored residence, built 1749, used until 1821; furnishings; interior courtyard.

WITTE MEMORIAL MUSEUM. (3801 B'way) History, anthropology, natural history, pioneer items, transportation, regional art. Daily 9:30–5.

San Marcos

SOUTHWEST TEXAS STATE COLLEGE MUSEUM. Art, anthropology, geology, crafts. Tues.–Sat. 10–12, 1:30–4.

Sequin

LOS NOGALES MUSEUM. (S. River and Live Oak Sts.) Restored Juan Sequin post office of 1838; local history. Fri. 2–4; June–Aug. 9–11.

Tyler

GOODMAN MUSEUM. (624 N. B'way) Civil War items; furnishings of about 1900 in historic house. Daily 9–5.

Uvalde

GARNER MEMORIAL. (333 N. Park St.) Personal and family items, portraits of John Nance Garner. Library. Mon.–Sat. 12–5:30.

Waco

BAYLOR UNIVERSITY, ARMSTRONG BROWNING LIBRARY. (Speight at 8th) Paintings, furniture; memorabilia of Robert Browning and Elizabeth Barrett Browning. Mon.–Fri. 9:30–11:30, 2:30–4:30; Sat. 9:30–11:30; Sun. 2–5.

BAYLOR UNIVERSITY, STRECKER MUSEUM. (Pat Neff Hall) Anthropology, geology, zoology. Texas fauna; Indian artifacts. Mon.–Fri. 8–4:30, Sat. 8–11:30.

BAYLOR UNIVERSITY, TEXAS HISTORY COLLECTION. History, archives; military portraits; Texas and Southwest materials; research. Mon.–Thurs. 8 A.M.–9:45 P.M., Fri. 8–5, Sat. 8–12.

HERITAGE SOCIETY OF WACO. (Mill St. and Brazos River) Historic J. W. Mann House, furniture, costumes.

West Columbia

VARNER-HOGG PLANTATION. Plantation House of about 1835; period furniture; Sam Houston memorabilia; items pertaining to J. S. Hogg, Texas gov. 1901–06. Tues., Thurs.–Sun. 10–5.

UTAH

Brigham City

BEAR RIVER MIGRATORY BIRD REFUGE. Wildlife preserve, maintained by Fed. govt. Fish and Wildlife Service. Daily.

Bryce

BRYCE CANYON NATIONAL PARK. Park museum. Geology, herbarium. Daily 8–5. *

Logan

UTAH STATE UNIVERSITY, INTERMOUNTAIN HERBARIUM. Regional flora; research. Mon.–Fri. 8–5, Sat. 8–12.

Moab

MOAB MUSEUM. (125 E. Center) Archaeology, regional mining history. Daily 3–5, 7–9 (Sept.–May Sun., Wed., Thurs. 7 P.M.–9 P.M.).

Provo

BRIGHAM YOUNG UNIVERSITY, SUMMERHAYS PLANETARIUM. First Thurs. every month, 7:30–8:30 P.M.; and by appt. Tues. and Thurs. 1–3 and 7:30–9:30.

Salt Lake City

HOGLE ZOOLOGICAL GARDEN. (2600 Sunnyside Ave.) Zoo. Daily 9:30–4:30, summer to 7.
LATTER-DAY SAINTS MUSEUM. (Temple Sq.) Early church history; pioneer, Indian, western items. Lion House, residence of Brigham Young. Daily 8–5; summer 6:30–9. †
PIONEER MEMORIAL MUSEUM. (300 N. Main St.) Pioneer items, furnishings, implements. Mon.–Fri. 9–5; Sun. 1–5, summer.
UTAH STATE HISTORICAL SOCIETY. (603 E. South, Temple Sq.) Thomas Kearns Mansion of 1900; State, Mormon and western history, archives. Mon.–Fri. 9–5, Sat. 9–1. †

Seney

SENEY NATIONAL WILDLIFE REFUGE. Maintained by Fed. govt. Fish and Wildlife Service. Daily.

Springfield

ZION NATIONAL PARK MUSEUM. Natural history, geology. Daily 7–7; winter 8–5. *

Springville

SPRINGVILLE HIGH SCHOOL ART ASSOCIATION. (120 E. 4th South St.) Contemp. American and other paintings; exhibitions. Daily, school hours; summer daily (except Sat.) 9–8.

Vernal

DINOSAUR VISITOR CENTER, DINOSAUR NATIONAL MONUMENT. Park museum. Paleontology; dinosaur quarry, exhibits in situ. Daily 7–7 (mid-Sept.–May 8–5). †*
UTAH FIELD HOUSE OF NATURAL HISTORY. (Vernal State Park) State natural history. Daily 8 A.M.–9 P.M.; winter 9–6. †

VERMONT

Barre

JOHN SHELBY'S MAPLE MUSEUM. (370 Ayers St.) Maple sugaring equipment, candy kitchen. May–mid-Oct. Mon.–Sat.; also Sun. July–Labor Day.

Bennington

BENNINGTON COLLEGE, THE NEW GALLERY. Contemp. art; teaching coll. Sept.–June daily 9–9.
THE BENNINGTON MUSEUM. (W. Main St.) American crafts, folk art; furniture, uniforms. Daily 9–6; winter 9:30–4:30 (closed Sun. Dec., Jan.; closed Feb.).

Brownington

ORLEANS COUNTY HISTORICAL SOCIETY. Old Stone House, of granite, built 1836; local history, early farm, household items. May–Oct. daily 9–5.

Burlington

UNIVERSITY OF VERMONT, PRINGLE

HERBARIUM. U.S. and Mexican flora; research. Mon.–Fri. 9–5.

Calais

KENT TAVERN. Victorian furnishings. July, Aug. Wed.–Sun. 1–5.

Middlebury

SHELDON MUSEUM. (1 Park St.) 18th and 19th-century furnishings, gun room, nursery in New England home and tavern, country store; local and state history. Mon.–Sat. 10–5; Tues., Thurs. 1–5 Nov.–May.

Montpelier

VERMONT HISTORICAL SOCIETY. (State Library Bldg.) Portraits, pottery, old printing press, Indian items. Mon.–Fri. 8–4:30.

Morrisville

MORRISTOWN HISTORICAL MUSEUM. (Foot of Main St.) Noyes House of 1820, restored and furnished; pitcher and Toby mug coll.; toys, dolls; antique wallpaper. May–Oct. daily 2–5.

Newfane

HISTORICAL SOCIETY OF WINDHAM COUNTY. Local history. May 31–Oct. 12, Sun. 2:30–5:30.

Plymouth

PRESIDENT CALVIN COOLIDGE HOMESTEAD. Family effects, archives. Mon.–Sat. 8:30–5:30, Sun. 12–5:30.

Poultney

POULTNEY HISTORICAL SOCIETY. Local history, art; in Old Melodeon Factory of about 1800. Weekends in Aug., aft.

Proctor

MARBLE EXHIBIT. (Rt. 3, Main St.) Vermont Marble Co. Geology, model rooms, decorative marbles; industrial procedures. May 25–Oct. 20, daily 9–5.

St. Johnsbury

FAIRBANKS MUSEUM. (Main St.) Natural science, primitive art, planetarium, botanical garden. Mid-June–mid-Sept. Mon.–Sat. 9–5, Sun. 2:30–4:30, Mon.–Thurs. eve. 7:30–9:30. Winter: Mon.–Sat. 10–4:30, Sun. 2:30–4:30.

ST. JOHNSBURY ATHENAEUM. (30 Main St.) American painting, Hudson River school. Mon., Wed., Fri. 10 A.M.–9 P.M.; Tues., Thurs., Sat. 10–5.

Shelburne

SHELBURNE MUSEUM, INC. (Rt. 7) Early American homes, shops, steamboat, covered bridge; collections of folk art, textiles, costumes, dolls, decoys, toys. May 25–Oct. 20, daily 9–5. †*

Springfield

THE MILLER ART CENTER. (9 Elm St.) Early American painting, decorative arts; exhibitions. Mon.–Fri. 10–5.

Weston

THE FARRAR-MANSUR HOUSE. (On the Common) Old bar, ballroom, historical murals, local family portraits and heirlooms in Inn of 1797. End June–early Sept. daily (except Mon.) 1–5.

Woodstock

WOODSTOCK HISTORICAL SOCIETY. (26 Elm St.) Furniture, tools, costumes in house built 1807; local history. End May–end Oct. Mon.–Sat. 10–12, 2–5, 7–9; Sun. 2–5:30.

VIRGINIA

Alexandria

GEORGE WASHINGTON NATIONAL MASONIC MEMORIAL. Washingtoniana, Masonic history, portraits, chapel. Daily 9–5.

STABLE-LEADBETTER APOTHECARY MUSEUM. (107 S. Fairfax St.) Old apothecary equipment, jars in bldg. of 1792. Mon.–Sat. 10–5.

Appomattox

APPOMATTOX COURT HOUSE NATIONAL

HISTORICAL PARK, CLOVER HILL TAVERN VISITOR CENTER. Park museum. Restoration of village to 1865; interpretation of Civil War surrender; reconstructed Mc-Lean House, where Lee surrendered to Grant. Daily 9–5:30. *

Arlington

CUSTIS-LEE MANSION. (Arlington National Cemetery) Early 19th-century home, furnishings; home of Washington's foster son. Park museum. Daily 9:30–4:30 (Apr.–Sept. to 6). *
FORT MYER POST MUSEUM. (Headquarters, Fort Myer) Military items. Wed.–Fri. 12–2; weekends 1–5.

Ashland

SCOTCHTOWN. Patrick Henry's home. Daily (except Sun.) 10–5. †

Blacksburg

VIRGINIA POLYTECHNIC INSTITUTE HERBARIUM. Virginia and regional flora. Tues., Thurs. 9–4.

Blue Ridge Parkway

BLUE RIDGE PARKWAY, HUMPBACK ROCKS VISITOR CENTER. Park museum. History; trail through reconstructed mountain farm. Thurs.–Mon. 9–5 May–Sept.; daily July, Aug. *

Boyce

UNIVERSITY OF VIRGINIA, THE ORLAND E. WHITE RESEARCH ARBORETUM. Botanical garden; research in plant adaptation, genetics. By appt.

Boydton

ROANOKE RIVER MUSEUM. Archaeology, costumes, Indian items. Mon.–Sat. 9–5.

Charlottesville

ASH LAWN. (State Rt. 53) Home designed by Thomas Jefferson for James Monroe, 1799; Monroe furnishings.
MICHIE TAVERN MUSEUM. Original furnishings, bar, china, silver, sconces; in bldg. of 1753. Daily summer 8–7; winter 9–5.
MONTICELLO, HOME OF THOMAS JEFFERSON. Built by Jefferson 1769–1809; original furnishings, paintings. Daily 8–5. †**
UNIVERSITY OF VIRGINIA MUSEUM OF FINE ARTS. (Rugby Rd.) Portraits, 18th- and 19th-century American paintings. Mon.–Fri. 9–4:30.

Fort Lee

THE U. S. ARMY QUARTERMASTER CORPS MUSEUM. (The Quartermaster School). Military equipment, uniforms, paintings. Mon.–Fri. 7–4 (winter 8–5); Wed. eve. 7–9; last Sun. every month 2–5. †

Fredericksburg

FREDERICKSBURG AND SPOTSYLVANIA NATIONAL MILITARY PARK. (Lafayette Blvd.) Park museum. Civil War battlefields of Chancellorsville, Fredericksburg, the Wilderness, and Spotsylvania Courthouse; Jackson Shrine (Guinea, Va.) where Gen. died. Daily 9–5. *
HUGH MERCER APOTHECARY SHOP. (1020 Caroline St.) 18th-century bldg. Mon.–Sat. 9–5, Sun. 1–5.
JAMES MONROE LAW OFFICE MUSEUM. Built 1758; where Monroe practiced from 1786. Monroe family effects, furniture. Daily 9–5:30.
KENMORE. (1201 Washington Ave.) 18th-century furnishings in house of 1752, where Washington's sister lived.
MARY WASHINGTON HOUSE. (1200 Charles St.) Period furnishings in house of 1772 where Washington's mother lived. Daily 9–5. †
RISING SUN TAVERN. (1306 Caroline St.) Pewter coll.; Revolutionary tavern, built 1760. Daily 9–5. †

Jamestown

COLONIAL NATIONAL HISTORICAL PARK, JAMESTOWN VISITOR CENTER. Interpretation of first permanent English settlement in New World, 1607; foundations, church tower; artifacts; research. Daily 9–5:30 (fall and winter to 5). *
JAMESTOWN FOUNDATION. Preservation project: restoration of James Fort, Pow-

hatan's Lodge, three colonists' ships. Daily 9–5 (July–early Sept. to 5:30; Nov.–mid-Mar. 9:30–4:30).

Lorton

GUNSTON HALL. Period furnishings, portraits in 18th-century home. Daily 9:30–5.

Luray

SHENANDOAH NATIONAL PARK, DICKEY RIDGE VISITOR CENTER. Park museum. Natural history. Apr.–Oct. daily 8:30–4:30.

Lynchburg

RANDOLPH-MACON WOMAN'S COLLEGE, ART GALLERY. (2500 Rivermont Ave.) American paintings; exhibitions. Gallery: Quinlan St. Sept.–June, weekends 3–5. Exhibition Rm. English–Art bldg. Sept.–June daily 9–9.

Manassas

MANASSAS NATIONAL BATTLEFIELD PARK. Site of First and Second Battles of Bull Run. Daily 8:30–5. *

Mount Vernon

MOUNT VERNON. George Washington's home, restored; Washington family furniture, paintings; greenhouse; gardens, kitchen, stable. Tombs of Washington and Martha Washington. Mar.–Sept. daily 9–5, Oct.–Feb. 9–4. †**

Natural Bridge

MUSEUM OF MOTORING MEMORIES. (U. S. Rt. 11) Antique automobiles, license plates, advertisements. Daily 9–9 (winter 8–10.) †

Newport News

THE MARINERS MUSEUM. Marine archives, models, craft, accessories, relics, paintings and prints. Park, wildlife preserve. Mon.–Sat. 9–5, Sun. 2–5. †*

Norfolk

THE HERMITAGE FOUNDATION MU-SEUM. (7637 N. Shore Rd.) Chinese, Indian art. Tues.–Sat. 1–5, Sun. 2–6.
LAFAYETTE PARK. Botanical garden, zoo. Daily.
MYERS HOUSE. (Bank and Freemason Sts.) Georgian house of 1792, furnishings. Tues.–Sun. 12–5.
NORFOLK MUSEUM. (Museum Plaza) American art, decorative arts; archaeology; natural history; European decorative arts. Tues.–Sun. 12–5, Wed., Fri. eve. 7:30–9:30.

Petersburg

THE CENTRE HILL MANSION MUSEUM. (Centre Hill, Franklin St.) Confederate historical items; historic house of 1823. Tues.–Sat. 10–1, 2–5, Sun. 2:30–5:30.
PETERSBURG NATIONAL MILITARY PARK. Park museum. Civil War battlefield; interpretation of battle; equipment. Daily 8:30–5. *

Portsmouth

NORFOLK NAVAL SHIPYARD MUSEUM. Fed. govt. naval, marine history, archives. Mon.–Fri. 8–4:30 (summer 7–3:30); weekends 1–3.

Quantico

U. S. MARINE CORPS MUSEUM. (Marine Corps Schools) Equipment, flags, weapons. Mon.–Fri. 9–6, Sat. 9–5, Sun. 12–4. †

Richmond

CONFEDERATE MUSEUM. (1201 E. Clay St.) Civil War items; in White House of the Confederacy, built 1816–18. Mon.–Sat. 9–5, Sun. 2–5. †
EDGAR ALLAN POE FOUNDATION. (1918 E. Main St.) Poe mss. in Old Stone House of 1686, oldest house in city.
JOHN MARSHALL HOUSE. (818 E. Marshall St.) House of 1790; original furnishings in home of first Chief Justice; headquarters for the Association for the Preservation of Virginia Antiquities. Mon.–Sat. 10–5. †*
RICHMOND NATIONAL BATTLEFIELD PARK. (3215 E. Broad St.) Park museum. Interpretation of Civil War battlefield. Daily 8:30–5. *

THE VALENTINE MUSEUM. (1015 E. Clay St.) Historic archives, costumes, portraits, decorative arts, Indian artifacts, prints of city and state historic scenes; in Wickham-Valentine House of 1812. Mon.–Sat. 10–5, Sun. 2:30–5.

VIRGINIA HISTORICAL SOCIETY. (428 N. Boulevard) State history, archives, portraits, prints. Tues.–Fri. 9–5, weekends 2–5.

VIRGINIA HOUSE. (Windsor Farms) Reconstructed English Tudor manor house, imported in 1926; 17th-century furnishings, English gardens. Tues.–Fri. 10–4, weekends 2–4. *

VIRGINIA MUSEUM OF FINE ARTS. (Blvd. and Grove Ave.) *Survey;* exhibitions; artmobile. Tues.–Thurs., Sat. 11–5; Fri. 3–5, 8–10 (summer Fri. 11–5); Sun. 2–5. *

Roanoke

ROANOKE FINE ARTS CENTER. (25th at Carolina Ave.) Local, contemp. art; exhibitions. Mon.–Sat. 12–4.

Stratford

STRATFORD HALL. Lee family plantation built 1725. Daily 9–5. *

Washington's Birthplace

GEORGE WASHINGTON BIRTHPLACE NATIONAL MONUMENT. Bldg. of about 1725 restored on original foundations; period furnishings. Daily 8–5. *

Williamsburg

ABBY ALDRICH ROCKEFELLER FOLK ART COLLECTION. American painting, sculpture and crafts in Ludwell-Paradise House. Daily (except Mon.) 12–9. †*

COLONIAL WILLIAMSBURG, INC. Preservation project: restored and reconstructed buildings (shops, homes, public buildings) and gardens of Virginia Colony capital, 18th century; period furnishings; archives. Daily 9–5 (winter 10–5). †**

Winchester

GEORGE WASHINGTON'S OFFICE. 18th-, 19th-century furniture, costumes, prints, guns, Civil War items in log bldg. of

about 1747, used by Washington as surveying office. Daily 9–5.

Woodlawn

WOODLAWN PLANTATION. (U. S. Hwy. 1) Late Georgian furnishings in home of 1805 that was Washington's wedding gift to his adopted daughter, Nelly Custis. Maintained by National Trust for Historic Preservation. Mar.–Oct. daily 10–5 (Nov.–Feb. to 4:30). *

Yorktown

COLONIAL NATIONAL HISTORICAL PARK, MOORE HOUSE. Furnishings of 1750–80s, in house where Cornwallis surrendered. Park museum. Washington's and Rochambeau's headquarters; Revolutionary fortifications. Mar.–Oct. daily 9:30–5:30. *

COLONIAL NATIONAL HISTORICAL PARK, YORKTOWN VISITOR CENTER. Battlefield exhibits; paintings of battle; Revolutionary War items; interpretation of battle of Yorktown. Spring, summer: daily 9–5:30; fall, winter 9–5. *

WASHINGTON

Bellingham

BELLINGHAM PUBLIC MUSEUM. (121 Prospect St.) Local history, regional Indian, Eskimo artifacts. Fri.–Sun. 2–5.

Brewster

FORT OKANOGAN HISTORICAL MUSEUM. Park museum. Indian, pioneer items. May–Nov. Tues.–Sun. 9–5.

Cathlamet

WAHKIAKUM COUNTY MUSEUM. (City Center) Pacific Northwest history; contemp. art exhibitions. June–Sept. Tues.–Sun. 11–4; winter: Wed., Sat. aft.

Chinook

FORT COLUMBIA STATE PARK HISTORICAL MUSEUM. Indian, pioneer items, on site of Lewis and Clark camp. June–Sept. Tues.–Sun. 10–5.

Eastsound

ORCAS ISLAND HISTORICAL SOCIETY. Indian artifacts, pioneer implements in bldg. of adjoining homestead cabins. Daily, summer.

Everett

SNOHOMISH COUNTY MUSEUM AND HISTORICAL ASSOCIATION. (Legion Park) County history; local art exhibitions. Sun. 2–5.

Kelso

COWLITZ COUNTY HISTORICAL MUSEUM. (Courthouse Annex, Church and 5th Sts.) Local history, natural history, anthropology. Period shops, log cabin, ladies' parlor, livery stable. Tues.–Sat. 10:30–4:30, Sun. 2–5.

Longmire

MOUNT RAINIER NATIONAL PARK, LONGMIRE HOUSE. Park museum; nature trails. Daily 8–8 (winter to 5). *
MOUNT RAINIER NATIONAL PARK, MOUNTAIN HOUSE, YAKIMA PARK MUSEUM, AND OHANAPECOSH FOREST HOUSE MUSEUM. Natural history, trails; interpretation of park. Daily 8–6. *

Maryhill

MARYHILL MUSEUM OF FINE ARTS. Paintings, sculpture; Northwest Indian art; ceramics. Apr.–Nov. daily 9–5:30.

Olympia

STATE CAPITOL HISTORICAL MUSEUM. (211 W. 21st St.) State history, natural history; furnishings; Indian artifacts. Tues.–Sun. 1–5.

Port Angeles

OLYMPIC NATIONAL PARK, PIONEER MEMORIAL MUSEUM. (600 Park Ave.) Park museum. Natural history, Northwest Coast history, Indian materials. Daily 8–4:30. July, Aug. 8–6, 7:30–9:30. *

Port Orchard

KITSAP COUNTY HISTORICAL MUSEUM. (Administration Bldg., County Courthouse, 614 Division St.) Local history, archaeology. Mon. 10–3.

Port Townsend

JEFFERSON COUNTY HISTORICAL MUSEUM. (City Hall) Local history, natural history. Wed.–Sun. 12:30–4:30; Sept.–Apr. Sat., Sun.

Pullman

WASHINGTON STATE UNIVERSITY, CHARLES R. CONNER MUSEUM. (Dept. of Zoology) Herpetology, vertebrate zoology; teaching coll. Mon.–Fri. 8–5, Sat. 8–12.
WASHINGTON STATE UNIVERSITY HERBARIUM. Northwest vascular plants; research. Mon.–Fri. 9–12, 1:30–5 during school year.

Seattle

CHARLES AND EMMA FRYE ART MUSEUM. (704 Terry Ave.) 19th-century American, European paintings. Mon.–Sat. 10–5, Sun. 12–6.
MUSEUM OF HISTORY AND INDUSTRY. (2720 Lake Washington Blvd.) State history; industry; ethnology; maritime and aeronautical items. Tues.–Fri. 11–5, Sat. 10–5, Sun. 12–5. †*
SEATTLE ART MUSEUM. (Volunteer Park) *Survey; Kress;* Northwest coast Indian art; ethnology; Oriental arts. Tues.–Sat. 10–5, Thurs. 7–10 P.M., Sun. 12–5. †*
UNIVERSITY OF WASHINGTON ARBORETUM. Daily 8–sundown.
UNIVERSITY OF WASHINGTON, HENRY ART GALLERY. 19th-century American, French painting; ceramics; graphics; exhibitions. Mon.–Sat. 10–5, Wed. 8–10 P.M., Sun. 2–6.
UNIVERSITY OF WASHINGTON, WASHINGTON STATE MUSEUM. (4037 15th St.) Anthropology, Northwest coast Indian ethnology; regional natural history. Mon.–Fri. 9–12, 1–5.
WOODLAND PARK ZOOLOGICAL GARDEN. (5400 Phinney Ave.) Daily.

Seaview

FORT COLUMBIA STATE PARK, D.A.R. MUSEUM. Period furnishings in officer's home. June–mid-Sept. daily 11–5.

Spokane

EASTERN WASHINGTON STATE HISTORI-
CAL SOCIETY. (W. 2316 1st Ave.) Local
history, anthropology, geology; historic
mansion, Grace Campbell Memorial of
1898. Tues.–Sat. 10–5, Sun. 2–5.
JOHN A. FINCH ARBORETUM. (W. 3404
Woodland Blvd.) Regional trees and
shrubs. Mon.–Sat. 8:30–4:30.

Tacoma

POINT DEFIANCE AQUARIUM. (Point
Defiance Park) Salt-water life. Daily 9–5
(summer 9–9).
WASHINGTON STATE HISTORICAL SO-
CIETY. (315 N. Stadium Way) State his-
tory, natural history, Indian materials.

Vancouver

COVINGTON HOUSE. (42d and Main
Sts.) Oldest house in state, 1840s. By
appt. †
FORT VANCOUVER NATIONAL MONU-
MENT. Park museum. History of Hudson's Bay Co. base 1824–46; U.S. fort,
1848; fur trade items. Daily 8–4:30. *

Vantage

GINKGO PETRIFIED FOREST STATE
PARK. Natural history; archaeology, geology, Indian painted rocks. Museum: summer, daily 7–7; winter, weekends 9–5.
Park: daily 7 A.M.–9 P.M.

Walla Walla

WALLA WALLA COUNTY PIONEER
AND HISTORICAL SOCIETY. (City Hall)
County history; Spanish-American War
items. Weekday aft.
WHITMAN COLLEGE MUSEUM OF
NORTHWEST HISTORY. Pioneer and In-
dian items, regional history. Oct.–May,
Wed. 1:30–4:30; June–Aug. Mon.–Fri.
9–12.
WHITMAN NATIONAL MONUMENT. Park
museum. Site of 1836–47 mission. Mon.–
Fri. 8–5, weekends 8:30–5:30.

Wenatchee

NORTH CENTRAL WASHINGTON MU-
SEUM ASSOCIATION. (Chelan and Douglas
Sts.) Anthropology, mineralogy. Tues.–
Sun. 1–5, Thurs.–Sat. eve. 7–9.

White Swan

FORT SIMCOE STATE PARK. Preservation project: original and restored bldgs.
of 1856 fort; local history, anthropology.
Daily (except Mon.) 10:30–5.

Yakima

YAKIMA VALLEY MUSEUM. (2105 Tie-
ton Dr.) Local history; Indian, mineralogy, archaeology colls.; postal history.
Wed.–Sun. 10:30–4:40.

WEST VIRGINIA

Ansted

FAYETTE COUNTY HISTORICAL SO-
CIETY. (Midland Trail) Mountain pioneer, Indian relics.

Buckhannon

UPSHUR COUNTY HISTORICAL SOCIETY.
(Gibson Memorial Library) Local history. Mon.–Sat. 1–5.

Charleston

MUSEUM OF DEPARTMENT OF AR-
CHIVES AND HISTORY. (State Capitol)
State history; Indian mound artifacts;
mounted birds and mammals; firearms;
Colonial kitchen. Mon.–Fri. 9–5, Sun.
1–5.
CHILDREN'S MUSEUM OF CHARLESTON.
(Public Library) Arts and crafts, natu-
ral and physical sciences; planetarium.
Tues.–Fri. 1–5, Sat. 10–3.
WEST VIRGINIA HISTORICAL SOCIETY.
(Rm. 610, Capitol Bldg.) Pioneer relics,
furnishings.

Harpers Ferry

HARPERS FERRY NATIONAL MONU-
MENT. Park museum. Interpretation of
events that took place here; research.
Daily 8–5. *

Huntington

HUNTINGTON GALLERIES. (Park Hills)
Art: paintings, decorative arts, sculpture.
Guns; arboretum. Tues.–Fri. 2–5, Sat.
10–6, Sun. 2–6.

Lewisburg

DAYWOOD ART GALLERY, INC. (301 E. Foster St.) 19th- and 20th-century American painting; glass, china; American and English furniture. Mid-Mar.–mid-Nov. Mon.–Sat. 1–5.

Moundsville

GRAVE CREEK MOUND, THE MOUND MUSEUM. Archaeology. Daily, daylight hours.

Morgantown

WEST VIRGINIA UNIVERSITY ARBORETUM. (Monongahela Blvd.) State flora; research; nature trails. Daily, daylight hours.

Wheeling

MANSION HOUSE MUSEUM AND FRONTIER TRAVEL GALLERY. (Oglebay Inst., Oglebay Park) Local art, firearms, glass; 19th-century period rooms in house of 1832; river lore, ship models. Mid-Apr.–mid-Nov. Mon.–Sat. 9:30–12, 1:30–5, Sun. 2–7.

WISCONSIN

Antigo

LANGLADE COUNTY HISTORICAL SOCIETY. (7th Ave. and Superior St.) Agricultural history, in historic old F. A. Deleglis Cabin. Tues. and Fri. 12–5.

Baraboo

CIRCUS WORLD MUSEUM. Circus memorabilia. Maintained by State Historical Society. †*

Beaver Dam

DODGE COUNTY HISTORICAL SOCIETY. (127 S. Spring St.) Local history, shells, Indian items. Mon.–Sat. 2–5, second Sun. of every month, 2–5.

Beloit

BELOIT COLLEGE, LOGAN MUSEUM OF ANTHROPOLOGY. North American archaeology, ethnology; European, North African paleontology, ethnology; research; teaching coll. Mon.–Sat. 8–5, Sun. 1:30–4. †*

BELOIT COLLEGE, WRIGHT ART CENTER. Contemp. graphics; Oriental ceramics. Mon.–Fri. 8–6, 6–9:30; Sat. 8:30–12, 1:30–4; Sun. 2–4.

BELOIT HISTORICAL MUSEUM. (Beloit Municipal Bldg., 220 W. Grand Ave.) Regional history; Norwegian artifacts; agricultural tools. Tues.–Fri. 1–4.

Cassville

STONEFIELD FARM AND CRAFT MUSEUM. Folk arts, agriculture. Maintained by State Historical Society.

Elkhorn

WALWORTH COUNTY HISTORICAL SOCIETY MUSEUM. (9 E. Rockwell at Washington St.) Local history, furnishings, Indian items; historic Webster House of about 1857. Tues.–Sat. 10–12, 1:30–4:30, Sun. 1:30–4:30.

Fort Atkinson

HOARD HISTORICAL MUSEUM. (407 Merchants Ave.) County history, birds, Indian items. Wed., Fri. 9–12, 1–5.

Green Bay

BROWN COUNTY HISTORICAL SOCIETY. (2632 S. Webster Ave.) Local history; historic Cotton House, restored, of 1840; Henry S. Baird Law Office of 1830. May–Oct. Sun. 2–5; Tues.–Sat. 10–5.

NATIONAL RAILROAD MUSEUM. Transportation history; maintained by State Historical Society.

NEVILLE PUBLIC MUSEUM. (129 S. Jefferson St.) Local art, decorative arts; history; anthropology; geology; natural history. Mon.–Sat. 9–5, Sun. 2–5.

Greenbuch

WADE HOUSE. Inn of 1851, restored. Maintained by State Historical Society.

Hales Corners

ALFRED L. BOERNER BOTANICAL GARDENS. (5879 S. 92d St.) Arboretum;

herbarium; garden. Daily 7:30–sundown (Nov.–Mar. to 4).

Janesville

LINCOLN-TALLMAN MUSEUM. (440 N. Jackson St.) Archives; local history; in bldg. of 1857, visited by Lincoln in 1859; served as Underground Railroad Station. Mid-May–Oct. Mon.–Sat. 9–5, Sun. 11–5.

Kenosha

KENOSHA COUNTY HISTORICAL MUSEUM. (County Courthouse) County history; archaeology; pioneer items. Mon.–Fri. 10:30–5.

KENOSHA PUBLIC MUSEUM. (Civic Center) Natural history, art. Summer: Mon.–Fri. 8–12, 1–5, Sat. 8–12; winter: Mon.–Fri. 8–12, 1–9, Sat. 8–5, Sun. 1:30–4:30.

Keshena

ANGUS F. LOOKAROUND MEMORIAL MUSEUM AND STUDIO. (Menominee Indian Reservation, Hwy. 55–47) Menominee Indian artifacts, crafts. June–Oct. daily.

Madison

HENRY VILAS ZOO. (1317 Wingra Dr.) Daily 2–5.

STATE HISTORICAL SOCIETY OF WISCONSIN. (816 State St.) Pioneer history; Civil War materials; Indian ethnology, archaeology; archives. Mon.–Fri. 8 A.M.–10 P.M.; Sat. 8–5, Sun. 1–5. †**

UNIVERSITY OF WISCONSIN, THE WISCONSIN UNION. (770 Langdon St.) Contemp. Wisconsin art; Japanese prints; exhibitions; student work. Daily 9 A.M.–10 P.M.

UNIVERSITY OF WISCONSIN, WASHBURN OBSERVATORY. Planetarium. First and third Wed. every month.

Manitowoc

LINCOLN PARK ZOO. (Lincoln Park) North American birds, mammals. Daily, daylight hours.

RAHR CIVIC CENTER AND PUBLIC MUSEUM. (610 N. 8th St.) Archaeology, military, Indian items. Mon.–Fri. 9–12, 1–5; Tues., Thurs. eve. 7–9; Sun. 2–5.

Milton

MILTON HOUSE. Restored inn of 1844; Indian, pioneer items; also 1837 log cabin. Daily 10–5.

Milwaukee

CHARLES ALLIS ART LIBRARY. (1630 E. Royall Pl.) Painting, sculpture, ceramics, furniture. Tues.–Sun. 1–5, Wed., Fri. eve. 7–9:30.

MILWAUKEE ART CENTER. (750 N. Lincoln Memorial Dr.) Survey; children's museum. Mon.–Sat. 10–5, Thurs. 10–10; Sun. 1–5. Children's museum: Mon.–Sat. 9–3, Thurs. 9 A.M.–10 P.M., Sun. 1–5. †*

MILWAUKEE-DOWNER COLLEGE, THOMAS A. GREENE MEMORIAL MUSEUM. (2512 E. Hartford Ave.) Mineralogy, paleontology; regional material; research. By appt.

MILWAUKEE COUNTY HISTORICAL SOCIETY. (7th fl., Courthouse) County history; research. Historic Lowell Damon House of 1840s (Wauwatosa Ave. and Rogers St.); Kilbourntown House, Greek Revival style, period furnishings, 1844 (Estabrook Park), and replica of pioneer log cabin. Houses, Sun. aft.

MILWAUKEE COUNTY ZOOLOGICAL PARK. (101 N. 100 St.) Zoo. Daily 9:30–4:30. *

MILWAUKEE PUBLIC MUSEUM. (818 W. Wisconsin Ave.) Anthropology, natural history. Spanish colonial, Oriental, primitive art; decorative arts. Mon.–Fri. 9–5, Sun. 1–5.

TERRACE AVENUE MUSEUM. (2246 N. Terrace Ave.) China; medical and marine items; in historic house. First Sun. every month 2–5, and by appt.

Mineral Point

MINERAL POINT HISTORICAL SOCIETY. (Davis St.) Lead and zinc mining tools, mineralogy collections; in historic Gundry Mansion of 1867. Late May–early Sept. daily 1–5.

Neenah

DOTY CABIN. (City Park) Indian collection, family furnishings in house of territorial governor. Daily (except Mon.) 9–11:30, 1:30–5.

JOHN NELSON BERGSTROM ART CENTER AND MUSEUM. (N. 165 Park Ave.) American paintings; European and antique glass. Wed., Thurs., Sat., Sun. 1–6.

Oconto

BEYER HOME, OCONTO COUNTY HISTORICAL MUSEUM. (917 Park Ave.) Indian Burial Grounds, Indian mounds; old logging camp; county history, furnishings, vehicles, tools; building of 1860. June–Sept. daily 2–4.

Oshkosh

OSHKOSH PUBLIC MUSEUM. (1331 Algoma Blvd.) Menominee Indian artifacts; local documents; firearms; pressed glass. Mon.–Sat. 9–12, 1:30–5, Sun. 2–5.
PAINE ART CENTER AND ARBORETUM. (1410 Algoma Blvd.) Barbizon paintings, period rooms. June–Aug. Tues.–Sun. 2–5; Tues., Thurs., Sat. 2–5; first Sun. every month.

Prairie du Chien

VILLA LOUIS. Restored mansion, 1843, of American Fur Co. agent; maintained by State Historical Society.
THE WISCONSIN MUSEUM OF MEDICAL PROGRESS. (S. Beaumont Rd.) Early surgical and dental equipment; history of medicine, medical quackery, early medical education. Daily 9–5, May–Oct.

Racine

RACINE COUNTY HISTORICAL MUSEUM. (County Courthouse) Local history, industry, natural history. Mon.–Fri. 8–12, 1–5.
RACINE ZOOLOGICAL PARK. (2131 N. Main St.) Zoo. Mon.–Sat. 10–6 (winter to 5); Sun. 10–7.
WUSTUM MUSEUM OF FINE ARTS. (2519 Northwestern Ave.) *Exhibitions.* Mon.–Sat. 10–5, Sun. 2–5.

Rhinelander

RHINELANDER LOGGING MUSEUM. (City Hall) Replica of logging camp; logging equipment; photos. June 11–Labor Day daily 9–8.

Sturgeon Bay

DOOR COUNTY HISTORICAL MUSEUM. County history. Tues.–Sat. 1–5.

Superior

DOUGLAS COUNTY HISTORICAL MUSEUM. (1827 John Ave.) Indian artifacts; Chiefs Sitting Bull and Red Cloud memorabilia; county archives. Mon.–Fri. 10–12, 1–5; 2d and 4th Sun. 2–5.

Viroqua

VERNON COUNTY HISTORICAL MUSEUM. (Courthouse basement) Local history; summer exhibitions. Winter: Wed., Thurs. 1–4. Summer: daily 1–4.

Watertown

HISTORICAL SOCIETY OF WATERTOWN. (919 Charles St.) Historic Octagon House of 1854, original furnishings; Civil War relics; also First Kindergarten Building of 1856, first in U.S., with period equipment. May 15–Oct. Mon.–Sat. 1–5, Sun. 10–5.

Waupaca

WAUPACA HISTORICAL SOCIETY. (City Park, 902 S. Main St.) Local history, in restored Hutchinson House of 1854.

Wausau

MARATHON COUNTY HISTORICAL SOCIETY. (403 McIndoe St.) Local history. Mon.–Fri. 9–5, Sun. 2–5.

West Bend

WASHINGTON COUNTY HISTORICAL MUSEUM. (710 4th Ave., High School Bldg.) County history. Wed. during school year.

WYOMING

Buffalo

JOHNSON COUNTY JIM GATCHELL MEMORIAL MUSEUM. (Fort St.) Local history, Indian items; coll. of Jim Gatchell, pioneer and historian. June–Sept. Mon.–Sat. 1–9.

Cheyenne

WYOMING STATE MUSEUM. (State Office Bldg., 23d St. and Central Ave.) State history, archives, ethnology, mineralogy. Mon.–Fri. 9–4:30, Sun. 12–5; summer also Sat. 9–5.

Cody

BUFFALO BILL HISTORICAL CENTER, BUFFALO BILL MUSEUM. (836 Sheridan Ave.) Cowboy, pioneer, Indian items; Buffalo Bill memorabilia; June–Aug. daily 7 A.M.–10 P.M.; May, Sept., Oct. daily 9–5. †*
BUFFALO BILL HISTORICAL CENTER, THE WHITNEY GALLERY OF WESTERN ART. (720 Sheridan Ave.) Indian, western art; Remington studio collection; exhibitions. June–Aug. daily 7 A.M.–10 P.M.; May, Sept., Oct. daily 9–5. †*

Devils Tower

DEVILS TOWER NATIONAL MONUMENT. Park museum. Archaeology, zoology. Summer daily 8–6; winter weekends. *

Douglas

WYOMING PIONEER MUSEUM. Preservation project: Oregon Trail, pioneer items. Daily 10–5.

Fort Bridger

FORT BRIDGER. (U.S. 30S) Park museum. Old bldgs. of 1843 post, later military reservation; Indian, military items; old school, Pony Express stables; barracks. May–mid-Sept. daily 8–7; Apr. and mid-Sept.–Oct.: Tues.–Sun. 9–5; Nov.–mid-Dec.: weekends 9–4.

Fort Laramie

FORT LARAMIE NATIONAL MONUMENT. Park museum. Site of old stockade of 1834, military post of 1849–90; on Oregon Trail. Indian, pioneer, military, transportation items; old bldgs. including adobe Sutler's Store of 1830s, Old Bedlam officers' club of 1851, several officers' quarters and a barracks. Mon.–Sat. 8–4:30, Sun. 8:30–5; July–Aug. to 5:30, Sun. to 6:30.

Laramie

UNIVERSITY OF WYOMING GEOLOGICAL MUSEUM. Paleontology. Mon.–Fri. 8–5, Sat. 1–5, Sun. 2–5.
UNIVERSITY OF WYOMING, ROCKY MOUNTAIN HERBARIUM. (Nelson Bldg.) Teaching coll. During school year, Mon.–Fri. 8–5.

Moose

GRAND TETON NATIONAL PARK. Natural history; geology, zoology. History. Thomas Moran sketches and prints. Historic old cabins and other bldgs. Mid-June–early Sept. 8–5. *

Rawlins

CARBON COUNTY MUSEUM. (Carbon County Courthouse) Indian items; county archives. Fri. 1–4.

Thermopolis

PIONEER ASSOCIATION OF THERMOPOLIS, PIONEER MUSEUM. Local history, costumes, crafts, minerals. Daily 1–5.

Yellowstone Park

YELLOWSTONE NATIONAL PARK, YELLOWSTONE PARK MUSEUMS. Natural history; archaeology, ethnology; exploration of west; trailside displays; firearms; Thomas Moran paintings. June–Aug. daily 8 A.M.–10 P.M.; Sept.–May 8–12, 1–5. Headquarters Museum: Oct.–May, 5 days a week. **

PUERTO RICO

Mayaguez

UNIVERSITY OF PUERTO RICO ZOOLOGICAL GARDEN AND AQUARIUM. Botanical garden; oceanography; research; expeditions.

Ponce

MUSEUM OF ART OF PONCE. *Survey, Kress.* (Under construction.)

Rio Piedras

UNIVERSIDAD DE PUERTO RICO, MUSEO DE ANTROPOLOGIA HISTORIA Y ARTE.

(Campus) Puerto Rican paintings; local history; anthropology; exhibitions. Mon.–Fri. 8 A.M.–10 P.M., Sat. 8–5. *

San Juan

AMIGOS DE CALLE DEL CRISTO 255, LA CASA DEL LIBRO. (Calle del Cristo 255) Art; printing and publishing; rare and historic books. Daily (except Sun.) 11–5. †*

ATENEO PUERTORRIQUEÑO. (Avenida Ponce de León) Puerto Rican paintings; performing arts; physical sciences; civic arts center. Daily (except Sun.) 8–12, 2–4, 7:30–10:30.

MUSEO DE HISTORIA NATURAL DEL DEPARTAMENTO DE AGRICULTURA Y COMERCIO. (Parque Luis Muñoz Rivera) Old Spanish powderhouse; natural history. Tues.–Sun. 8–4:30.

INDEX